OECD Tourism Trends and Policies 2022

OECD
BETTER POLICIES FOR BETTER LIVES

This document, as well as any data and map included herein, are without prejudice to the status of or sovereignty over any territory, to the delimitation of international frontiers and boundaries and to the name of any territory, city or area.

The statistical data for Israel are supplied by and under the responsibility of the relevant Israeli authorities. The use of such data by the OECD is without prejudice to the status of the Golan Heights, East Jerusalem and Israeli settlements in the West Bank under the terms of international law.

Note by the Republic of Türkiye
The information in this document with reference to "Cyprus" relates to the southern part of the Island. There is no single authority representing both Turkish and Greek Cypriot people on the Island. Türkiye recognises the Turkish Republic of Northern Cyprus (TRNC). Until a lasting and equitable solution is found within the context of the United Nations, Türkiye shall preserve its position concerning the "Cyprus issue".

Note by all the European Union Member States of the OECD and the European Union
The Republic of Cyprus is recognised by all members of the United Nations with the exception of Türkiye. The information in this document relates to the area under the effective control of the Government of the Republic of Cyprus.

Please cite this publication as:
OECD (2022), *OECD Tourism Trends and Policies 2022*, OECD Publishing, Paris, https://doi.org/10.1787/a8dd3019-en.

ISBN 978-92-64-37750-9 (print)
ISBN 978-92-64-48095-7 (pdf)
ISBN 978-92-64-45366-1 (HTML)
ISBN 978-92-64-48119-0 (epub)

OECD Tourism Trends and Policies
ISSN 2076-7765 (print)
ISSN 2076-7773 (online)

Photo credits: Cover © vectomart/Shutterstock.com; © saref/Shutterstock.com.

Corrigenda to publications may be found on line at: www.oecd.org/about/publishing/corrigenda.htm.

Foreword

OECD Tourism Trends and Policies is an international reference and benchmark on how countries are supporting sustainable and inclusive tourism growth. The publication highlights good practices and key policy and governance reforms, providing a global perspective with the inclusion of 50 OECD member and partner countries. It is a rich source of data on domestic, inbound and outbound tourism, as well as on the overall size of the tourism economy, and provides comparative knowledge through thematic chapters and country-specific policy and statistical profiles.

The 2022 edition of OECD Tourism Trends and Policies follows nearly three unprecedented and challenging years for the tourism economy and comes at a time of uncertainty for the recovery that had begun to take roots. Tourism was hit hard by the depth and duration of the crisis triggered by the COVID-19 pandemic. The shock has been a reminder of the tourism's vital role as an economic and social force in OECD member and partner countries. Tourism is a key part of a growing services economy, and an important source of job creation, export revenue and domestic value added. Before the pandemic, across OECD countries, on average, tourism directly contributed 4.4% of GDP, 6.9% of employment and 20.5% of service-related exports.

While the rebound seen in tourism in 2022 exceeded expectations in many countries, the economic fallout from Russia's aggression against Ukraine, and the changed economic and geopolitical context brings new challenges and casts a shadow over the recovery outlook. As tourism navigates these challenges, policy makers must not miss the opportunity to learn the lessons from the pandemic and put in place measures to shape a more resilient, sustainable and inclusive tourism economy for the future.

Continued growth in tourism over six decades led to the widely held belief in the inherent resilience of the tourism economy. The crisis has aggravated new and existing structural weaknesses and highlighted the need for tourism to be better prepared to respond, adapt and recover from future shocks. Urgent action is also needed to address the existential threat from climate change. Tourism is reliant, and impacts, on the natural environment, and more needs to be done to accelerate the transition to greener models of tourism.

OECD Tourism Trends and Policies 2022 provides an analysis of tourism performance and policy approaches to support the recovery. It examines key tourism recovery challenges and the outlook, and highlights the need for co-ordinated, forward-looking policy approaches to set tourism on a path to a more resilient, sustainable and inclusive future. Tourism policy priorities, reforms and developments are analysed, and examples of country practices highlighted. Thematic chapters provide insights on building resilience in the tourism ecosystem and promoting a green tourism recovery.

This flagship publication was produced by the Centre for Entrepreneurship, SMEs, Regions and Cities (CFE) of the OECD, with co-financing from the European Union. It was approved by the OECD Tourism Committee through written procedure in October 2022.

Acknowledgements

This report presents the 2022 edition of the OECD Tourism Trends and Policies publication. It was produced by the OECD Centre for Entrepreneurship, SMEs, Regions and Cities (CFE), led by Lamia Kamal-Chaoui, Director, as part of the programme of work of the OECD Tourism Committee. The report was undertaken in co-operation with the European Union*.

The report benefitted from significant contributions, feedback and guidance from policy makers and statisticians from OECD member and partner countries. It also benefitted from consultation and feedback from industry representatives and associations, including Business@OECD, and intergovernmental organisations, including UN Environment, UN World Tourism Organization (UNWTO) and the International Labour Organization (ILO). The report has also been informed by discussions at the Global Forum on Tourism Statistics, Knowledge and Policies hosted by Korea in 2021, on the theme *Reshaping tourism for a more resilient and sustainable tomorrow*,

The report was co-ordinated and edited by Jane Stacey, Head of the Tourism Unit, under the supervision of Celine Kauffmann, Head of the Entrepreneurship, SMEs and Tourism Division (CFE) and Nadim Ahmad, Deputy Director (CFE). She was supported by Kristen Corrie, Policy Analyst (CFE), co-author of chapter 1 and author of chapter 2, as well as James Tops, Junior Policy Analyst (CFE) and Jenna Cunningham, Junior Consultant, who managed the preparation of the country policy profiles and undertook substantial co-ordination, drafting and editing. Sergio Montoya, Statistician (CFE), managed the statistical database and developed country statistical profiles and synthesis tables. Monserrat Fonbonnat, Assistant (CFE), provided administrative support. Pilar Philip and François Iglesias (CFE) served as publication co-ordinators. The statistical component of the report is available via the OECD's statistical online platform – OECD.Stat.

Richard Dickinson (*Tomorrow's Tourism*) provided drafting inputs for Chapter 1 and the country profiles. Chapter 3 was drafted by Susanne Becken and Daniel Scott (University of Surrey), with inputs from the Secretariat. In addition, the report benefitted from contributions and feedback provided by other OECD colleagues in the Centre for Entrepreneurship, SMEs, Regions and Cities (CFE) and the Environment Directorate (ENV).

Co-funded by
the European Union

* This document was produced with the financial assistance of the European Union. The views expressed herein can in no way be taken to reflect the official opinion of the European Union.

Table of contents

Foreword 3

Acknowledgements 4

Reader's Guide 9

Executive Summary 15

Chapter 1. Tourism trends and policies for recovery 17

- Tourism trends in times of crisis and recovery 18
- Strengthening the governance of tourism to respond and support recovery 29
- Tackling policy priorities for the tourism recovery 37
- Reshaping a more sustainable, resilient and inclusive future for tourism 44
- References 51
- Notes 53

Chapter 2. Building resilience in the tourism ecosystem 54

- Setting the scene: tourism resilience, crisis management and sustainability 55
- Learning from previous exogenous shocks to address tourism vulnerabilities 57
- Building a more resilient tourism ecosystem 63
- Policy considerations to set a path forward for tourism policy makers 77
- References 78

Chapter 3. Promoting a green tourism recovery 82

- Accelerating the transition to a green tourism economy 84
- Encouraging greener tourism business models and destinations 87
- Promoting green tourism recovery and transformation 97
- Policy considerations to support the green tourism recovery 104
- References 106

Part I OECD country profiles 109
Australia 110
Austria 115
Belgium 120
Canada 126
Chile 131
Colombia 136
Costa Rica 141
Czech Republic 146
Denmark 151
Estonia 156
Finland 161
France 166
Germany 171
Greece 176
Hungary 181
Iceland 186
Ireland 191
Israel 196
Italy 201
Japan 206
Korea 211
Latvia 216
Lithuania 221
Luxembourg 226

Mexico 231
Netherlands 236
New Zealand 241
Norway 246
Poland 251
Portugal 256
Slovak Republic 261
Slovenia 266
Spain 271
Sweden 276
Switzerland 281
Türkiye 286
United Kingdom 291
United States 296
Part II Partner country profiles **301**
Brazil 302
Bulgaria 307
Croatia 312
Indonesia 317
Malta 322
Montenegro 327
Morocco 332
Peru 337
Romania 342
Saudi Arabia 347

Serbia 352

South Africa 357

Reader's Guide

This reader's guide provides information and methodological notes on the data sources used in this book: International Recommendations for Tourism Statistics 2008, Tourism Satellite Account: Recommended Methodological Framework 2008 and Balance of Payments and International Investment Position Manual.

The statistical data, metadata and sources in this report are accessible online in a single, consolidated source of tourism statistics *http://stats.oecd.org/*. Individual data sets can be accessed through the following links: Domestic tourism, Inbound tourism, Outbound tourism, Enterprises and employment, Internal tourism consumption, Key indicators in percentage.

The data closely align with the main methodological references and international standards used for tourism statistics:

- International Recommendations for Tourism Statistics 2008, UN/UNWTO, *http://unstats.un.org/unsd/publication/SeriesM/seriesm_83rev1e.pdf*.
- Tourism Satellite Account: Recommended Methodological Framework 2008, UN/UNWTO/EUROSTAT/OECD, *http://unstats.un.org/unsd/publication/Seriesf/SeriesF_80rev1e.pdf*.
- Sixth Edition of the IMF's Balance of Payments and International Investment Position Manual 2010, IMF, *http://www.imf.org/external/pubs/ft/bop/2007/bopman6.htm*.

This note provides the reader with a methodological summary. For more detailed information, please refer to the above-mentioned methodological tools.

International Recommendations for Tourism Statistics (IRTS)

The International Recommendations on Tourism Statistics (IRTS) provides a common reference framework for countries to use in the compilation of tourism statistics. It presents an internally consistent system of definitions, concepts, classifications and indicators, and provides general guidance with respect to data sources and data compilation methods.

Tourism can be regarded as a social, cultural and economic phenomenon related to the movement of people outside their usual place of residence. Tourism refers to the activity of visitors.

A **visitor** is a traveller taking a trip to a main destination outside his/her usual environment, for less than a year, for any main purpose (business, leisure or other personal purpose) other than to be employed in the country or place visited.

A visitor is a **tourist** if his/her trip includes an overnight stay; otherwise, a visitor is classified as a **same -day visitor** (or excursionist).

Three basic forms of tourism can be distinguished:

- **Domestic tourism** comprises the activities of a resident visitor within the country of reference.
- **Inbound tourism** comprises the activities of a non-resident visitor within the country of reference.
- **Outbound tourism** comprises the activities of a resident visitor outside the country of reference.

Measuring the flows of visitors: both arrivals and nights are used to assess the flows of visitors. A distinction is made between arrivals at borders and in accommodation, and nights spent in accommodation. As far as overnight tourism is concerned, accommodation statistics are an important statistical source of information on domestic and inbound visitors.

Tourism Satellite Account: Recommended Methodological Framework (TSA:-RMF)

The Tourism Satellite Account (TSA) is a conceptual framework for the economic measurement of tourism in its different components (domestic, inbound and outbound). It also highlights the relationship between consumption by visitors and the supply of goods and services in the economy, principally those from tourism industries. With this instrument, it is possible to estimate tourism GDP, establish the direct contribution of tourism to the economy and develop further analyses using the links between the TSA, the System of National Accounts and the Balance of Payments.

Tourism characteristic products and activities

The TSA reconciles tourism data related with supply and demand. Tourism measurement and analysis therefore require a classification of products, mainly those belonging to tourism expenditure, and productive activities that are the basis for defining tourism industries. Tourism characteristic activities are those that typically produce **tourism characteristic products**. A **tourism industry** represents the grouping of those establishments whose main activity is the same tourism characteristic activity.

The IRTS 2008 and the TSA-RMF 2008 provide the typology of tourism characteristic consumption products and activities (tourism industries):

Tourism characteristic consumption products	Tourism characteristic activities (tourism industries)
Accommodation services for visitors	Accommodation for visitors
Food- and beverage-serving services	Food- and beverage-serving activities
Railway passenger transport services	Railway passenger transport
Road passenger transport services	Road passenger transport
Water passenger transport services	Water passenger transport
Air passenger transport services	Air passenger transport
Transport equipment rental services	Transport equipment rental
Travel agencies and other reservation services	Travel agencies and other reservation services activities
Cultural services	Cultural activities
Sports and recreational services	Sports and recreational activities
Country-specific tourism characteristic goods	Retail trade of country-specific tourism characteristic goods
Country-specific tourism characteristic services	Other country-specific tourism characteristic activities

Note: for detOECD Tourism Trends and Policiesailed information on the coverage, please see annexes 2 and 3 of the IRTS 2008.

Internal tourism consumption

The TSA Framework makes a distinction between tourism expenditure and tourism consumption. Tourism expenditure refers to monetary transactions, whereas tourism consumption also includes other transactions: services associated with vacation accommodation on own account, tourism social transfers in kind and other imputed consumption. However, the latter transactions have to be separately evaluated. Therefore, the data might refer to either consumption or expenditure, depending on the country.

Three forms of consumption are distinguished:

- **Domestic tourism consumption**: the tourism consumption of a resident visitor within the economy of reference.
- **Inbound tourism consumption**: the tourism consumption of a non-resident visitor within the economy of reference.
- **Internal tourism consumption**: the tourism consumption of both resident and non-resident visitors within the economy of reference. It is the sum of domestic tourism consumption and inbound tourism consumption.

Tourism Direct Gross Domestic Product and other aggregates

The Gross Domestic Product (GDP) of an economy is defined as the sum of the gross value added generated by all industries. Tourism GDP corresponds to the part of GDP generated by all industries in response to internal tourism consumption. A further distinction must be made between direct tourism GDP and indirect tourism GDP. Put simply, **tourism direct GDP** reflects the direct value-added generated by industries directly in contact with visitors, while indirect tourism GDP reflects all of the upstream value-added- generated by industries supplying inputs to industries directly in contact with the visitors. The TSA Framework limits its recommendations to the evaluation of direct tourism GDP. The evaluation of indirect tourism GDP would require the use of input-output techniques or adjustments (for imports) of expenditure based measures.

Domestic, inbound and outbound tourism

A variety of different data sources are used to measure flows of visitors. Data can be collected directly from individuals about their tourism trips. These 'demand-side' sources include visitor or border surveys to measure inbound tourism flows, and resident travel or household surveys to measure domestic and outbound tourism flows. These surveys feed into the tourism consumption (i.e. demand) tables of the TSA (Tables 1-4). Data on domestic and inbound visitors can also be collected from accommodation providers ('supply-side').

Data from tourism demand surveys are presented in the country profile statistical tables. In the absence of data from these sources, or where data gaps exist, data from accommodation surveys are published.

For more detailed information on the data sources for individual countries, please refer to relevant datasets and metadata in the online tourism database http://stats.oecd.org/.

Balance of Payments and International Investment Position Manual – Sixth Edition

The following items of the Balance of Payments are used to assess the monetary flows of visitors.

Travel

Travel credits (**international travel receipts**) cover goods and services for own use or to give away acquired from an economy by non-residents during visits to that economy. Travel debits (**international travel expenditure**) cover goods and services for own use or to give away acquired from other economies by residents during visits to these other economies.

The goods and services may be purchased by the persons concerned or by another party on their behalf (e.g. business travel). The standard component breakdown of travel is between business and personal travel. *Business travel* covers goods and services acquired for personal use by persons whose primary purpose of travel is for business. *Personal travel* covers goods and services acquired by persons going abroad for purposes other than business, such as vacations, participation in recreational and cultural activities, visits with friends and relatives, pilgrimage, and education- and health-related purposes. This breakdown allows for closer links with tourism satellite accounts as well as supply and use tables.

Passenger services

Passenger services cover the transport of people. This category covers all services provided in the international transport of non-residents by resident carriers (credit or **international passenger transport**

receipts) and that of residents by non-resident carriers (debit or **international passenger transport expenditure**). Passenger services include fares and other expenditure related to the carriage of passengers, any taxes levied on passenger services, and fares that are a part of package tours, cruise fares, rentals, charters, and leases of vessels, aircraft, coaches, or other commercial vehicles with crews for the carriage of passengers.

Other issues

Enterprises in tourism: An establishment is an enterprise or part of an enterprise that is situated in a single location and in which only a single productive activity is carried out or in which the principal productive activity accounts for most of the value added. For the purposes of comparability across countries, unless otherwise stated, all statistics for enterprises refer to establishments.

Employment in tourism: data on employment refer to people or jobs. In the case of people, the data refer to employees only or to employees and self-employed people (employed people). Full-time equivalent employment is the number of full-time equivalent jobs, defined as total hours worked divided by average annual hours worked in full-time jobs.

Data expressed in US dollar terms: for some tables, national currency data have been converted to US dollar data. Exchanges rates are collected from the OECD database.

Metadata and sources

The vast majority of the data used in this publication are submitted by countries. All the detailed metadata and sources can be found under the right-hand side information panel in the on-line OECD database at http://stats.oecd.org/.

Country coverage

The OECD member countries are: Australia, Austria, Belgium, Canada, Chile, Colombia, Costa Rica, the Czech Republic, Denmark, Estonia, Finland, France, Germany, Greece, Hungary, Iceland, Ireland, Israel, Italy, Japan, Korea, Latvia, Lithuania, Luxembourg, Mexico, the Netherlands, New Zealand, Norway, Poland, Portugal, the Slovak Republic, Slovenia, Spain, Sweden, Switzerland, Türkiye, the United Kingdom and the United States.

Other partner countries covered in this report are: Brazil, Bulgaria, Croatia, Indonesia, Malta, Montenegro, Morocco, Peru, Romania, Saudi Arabia, Serbia and South Africa.

Codes used for currencies

- AUD Australian Dollar
- BGN Bulgarian Lev
- BRL Brazilian Real
- CAD Canadian Dollar
- CHF Swiss Franc
- CLP Chilean Peso
- COP Colombian Peso
- CRC Costa Rican Colon

- CZK Czech Koruna
- DKK Danish Krone
- EUR Euro (Austria, Belgium, Estonia, Finland, France, Germany, Greece, Ireland, Italy, Latvia, Lithuania, Luxembourg, Malta, Montenegro, Netherlands, Portugal, Slovak Republic, Slovenia, Spain)
- GBP United Kingdom Pound Sterling
- HRK Croatia Kuna
- HUF Hungarian Forint
- IDR Indonesian Rupiah
- ILS Israeli Shequel
- ISK Iceland Krona
- JPY Japanese Yen
- KRW Korean Won
- MAD Moroccan Dirham
- MXN Mexican Peso
- NOK Norwegian Krone
- NZD New Zealand Dollar
- PEN Peruvian Sol
- PLN Polish Zloty
- RON Romanian Leu
- RSD Serbian Dinar
- SAR Saudi Riyal
- SEK Swedish Krona
- TRY Turkish Lira
- USD United States Dollar
- ZAR South African Rand

Symbols for missing data and abbreviations

These symbols are used in the country tables:

| Break in series

.. Data is not available

e Estimated data or data based on the use of a limited amount of data

f Forecast value

In some cases, due to rounding and specifics of electronic data processing technologies, slight discrepancies may occur between totals and sums of components in those tables that are based on survey information

Executive Summary

Tourism has been hard hit by the crisis triggered by the COVID-19 pandemic, demonstrating its importance as a driver of economic prosperity, jobs, income and well-being. Just as the sector is starting to bounce back, the economic and social fallout from Russia's war in Ukraine is dealing a fresh blow to recovery prospects. As the sector navigates these challenges amid an uncertain outlook, steady and transformative action is needed to drive recovery, and to set tourism on a path to a more resilient, sustainable and inclusive future.

Tourism trends in times of crisis and recovery

Tourism remains seriously challenged by the unprecedented depth and duration of the COVID-19 shock. Restrictions on the movement of people hit the tourism economy at its core, with severe economic and social consequences for tourism workers and businesses, destinations and the wider ecosystem. With international tourism coming to a near complete halt around the world at the height of the pandemic, and domestic tourism severely constrained in many countries, tourism's direct contribution to GDP fell by 1.9 percentage points (to 2.8%), and the share of service exports fell by 10.6 percentage points (to 9.9%) in OECD countries, on average.

Tourism bounced back strongly in 2022, driven by pent-up demand and the lifting of travel restrictions. The recovery is fragile and uneven across countries however, with new uncertainties from the economic slowdown and geopolitical instability, precipitated by Russia's war in Ukraine. While domestic tourism, which proved to be an important lifeline for many jobs and businesses during the pandemic, is projected to recover to pre-pandemic levels by 2023, the full recovery of international tourism is now expected to take up until 2025, or beyond.

Tourism businesses, already struggling to recover from the pandemic, are now also facing rising energy, food and other input costs, as well as labour shortages and skills gaps. This is compounding a cost-of-living crisis that is putting pressure on household budgets, with discretionary items like tourism on the front line of potential cuts. As governments and businesses look to address these new challenges, there is a risk that the momentum to create a more resilient, sustainable and inclusive tourism will be stalled.

Top policy priorities to reshape tourism for a stronger, more sustainable future

The unprecedented shock to tourism has been a call to action for governments, at all levels, and the private sector, to respond in a co-ordinated way to support and consolidate a sustainable and resilient recovery. While the impact has been profound, threatening the survival of many businesses, the shock has left in its wake several positive legacies. Awareness of tourism's role as an economic and social force has been elevated at the highest levels, with governments taking equally unprecedented steps to help tourism businesses, workers and visitors, supported by the emergence of new collaborations across the public and private sectors. In turn, the pandemic accelerated momentum for more sustainable and resilient tourism. The opportunity now exists to build on these experiences, to tackle current and future tourism challenges.

Restoring safe mobility and consumer confidence continues to be a priority, along with supporting fragile tourism businesses and destinations confronted by labour and skills shortages, and investment needs to diversify the tourism offer. It is also critical that opportunities are not missed to address long-term priorities, rethink the tourism system and prepare for future shocks, while moving to stronger, fairer and more sustainable models of tourism development.

This requires looking back as well as forward. Delivering on a brighter future for the sector involves addressing structural weaknesses that have impeded the sector in the past, not least to avoid a return to unbalanced tourism development and ensure jobs, well-being and other benefits from tourism flow to local communities. Looking forward, accelerated action is needed on greening the recovery and climate change, and the mitigation and adaptation measures required, including financing and investment, for tourism to play its part. At the same time, actions are needed to ensure that the sector is fully able to benefit from opportunities presented by the digital transition, where many tourism businesses and destinations are still lagging despite the accelerated up-take during the pandemic, including access to skills and infrastructure.

Key policy messages

Foster integrated, agile, forward-looking policies to shape a brighter tourism future

- Promote forward-looking tourism strategies to boost recovery, accelerate the green and digital transition, and build capacity across government to prepare, react and adapt to future shocks.
- Build on the innovative approaches to design and deliver COVID-19 response measures, in co--operation with the private sector and civil society, to address the structural transformation needed to build a stronger, more sustainable sector, and tackle future tourism policy issues.

Build resilience in the tourism ecosystem

- Foster a business environment where tourism SMEs can succeed and get stronger, by improving access to finance, building skills and capacity, and promoting greener, digital practices.
- Encourage collaboration between actors across the tourism ecosystem, to respond and adapt to events, share information and experiences, and develop understanding of risks and opportunities.
- Support sustainable and diverse destinations with flexible, tailored and adequately resourced destination management plans, effective monitoring mechanisms and engagement of actors.
- Build robust and comparable data and tools to measure and monitor tourism resilience, fill data gaps, and inform quick response and effective decision making for future crises.

Promote a green tourism recovery

- Develop long term integrated strategies with a sustainable tourism vision, goals and targets, with action plans and mechanisms to leverage resources and co-ordinate across government.
- Implement a mix of evidence-based policies prioritising high impact interventions along the tourism value chain, to raise awareness, regulate and incentivise green practices, and investment.
- Promote carbon literacy and build capacity of tourism actors to develop innovative solutions, empower sustainable travel choices, and help businesses to reduce their environmental impact.
- Leverage the role of government in catalysing the green transition, and organise publicly funded or procured tourism infrastructure to contribute to environmental and climate resilient development.

Chapter 1. Tourism trends and policies for recovery

This chapter covers recent tourism trends, and associated developments in tourism governance and policy, set against the backdrop of the COVID-19 pandemic and Russia's war in Ukraine. It is based on policy and statistical inputs from OECD member and partner countries. The chapter outlines the economic and social consequences of the tourism crisis triggered by the pandemic and examines the key recovery challenges and outlook ahead, including in the context of increasingly uncertain economic and geopolitical context. The role of governments in supporting a sustainable, resilient and inclusive tourism recovery is set out, and tourism policy priorities, reforms and developments are analysed with examples of country practices highlighted.

Tourism trends in times of crisis and recovery

Tourism is being seriously challenged by the depth and duration of the crisis triggered by COVID-19. Restrictions on the movement of people hit the tourism economy at its core, leading to a near-complete cessation of tourism activity around the world at the height of the pandemic. The combined economic and health impacts made this a crisis like no other in terms of the size of its impact and duration. The consequences have been devastating for local communities, regions and tourism businesses, 85% of which are SMEs.

Just as the tourism economy was starting to rebound from the pandemic, Russia's war in Ukraine has dealt a fresh blow to recovery prospects. This is creating new uncertainties for the tourism recovery. With the impacts of the pandemic still lingering, the war is dragging down growth and putting additional upward pressure on prices amid tightening labour markets. Already fragile tourism businesses are faced with rising energy, food and other input costs, and the cost-of-living crisis is putting pressure on consumer spending power, with discretionary items like tourism on the front line of potential cuts.

The strong bounce in tourism seen in many countries in 2022 was built on the back of pent-up demand but shows signs of faltering. The economic and geopolitical climate is putting stress on the sector, creating a very uncertain outlook. As tourism navigates these challenges, existing and new structural weaknesses are being aggravated, while large-scale social, economic, political, environmental and technological trends continue to impact the sector.

As governments address these critical challenges, transformative policies are needed to set tourism on a path to a more resilient, sustainable and inclusive future. Co-ordinated, forward-looking action across all levels of government, and with the private sector, is needed more than ever to support a sustainable recovery of tourism businesses and destinations across the tourism ecosystem. Action is also needed to prepare for future shocks, stay ahead of the digital curve, support the low-carbon transition, and promote the structural transformation needed to build a stronger, more sustainable tourism economy.

COVID-19 crisis highlighted tourism's role as a driver of economic prosperity

Tourism is a driver of economic prosperity, and the crisis has been an important reminder of the vital role tourism plays in global, national and local economies. Before the pandemic, the tourism sector directly contributed 4.4% of GDP and 6.9% of employment, and tourism generated 20.5% of service-related exports in OECD countries, on average. The sector is a key part of a growing services economy, generating income and foreign exchange, creating jobs, stimulating regional development, and supporting local communities. In many countries, tourism was growing at a faster rate than the national economy before the pandemic.

The unprecedented shock from COVID-19 saw the average direct contribution of tourism to GDP fall to 2.8% in 2020 across OECD countries with data available[1]. This equates to an average decline of 1.9 percentage points compared to pre-COVID-19 (Figure 1.1).

The direct economic impact of the tourism sector is far-reaching and has knock-on consequences for the wider economy. Countries with a sizeable tourism sector pre-COVID-19, such as Iceland (8.1% of GDP), Mexico (8.0%) and Portugal (8.1%), have experienced some of the biggest declines in the sector's direct contribution to GDP, and in overall GDP (Figure 1.2). OECD analysis shows that the pre-pandemic size of the tourism sector better explains cross-country differences in GDP impacts in 2020 than exposure to any of the other sectors considered most vulnerable to COVID-19, or the average stringency of wider country lockdown measures during 2020 (Rustelli and Turner, 2021[1]). These impacts are also highly localised. Places where tourism is a large part of the local economy are particularly adversely impacted, such as Corsica in France, the Ionian Islands in Greece and the Balearic and Canary Islands in Spain, as well as the Algarve region in Portugal (OECD, 2022[2]; OECD, 2020[3]).

Figure 1.1. Direct contribution of tourism to selected OECD countries, pre-COVID-19 and 2020

As percentage of GDP, 2019 (or latest available year pre-COVID-19) and 2020

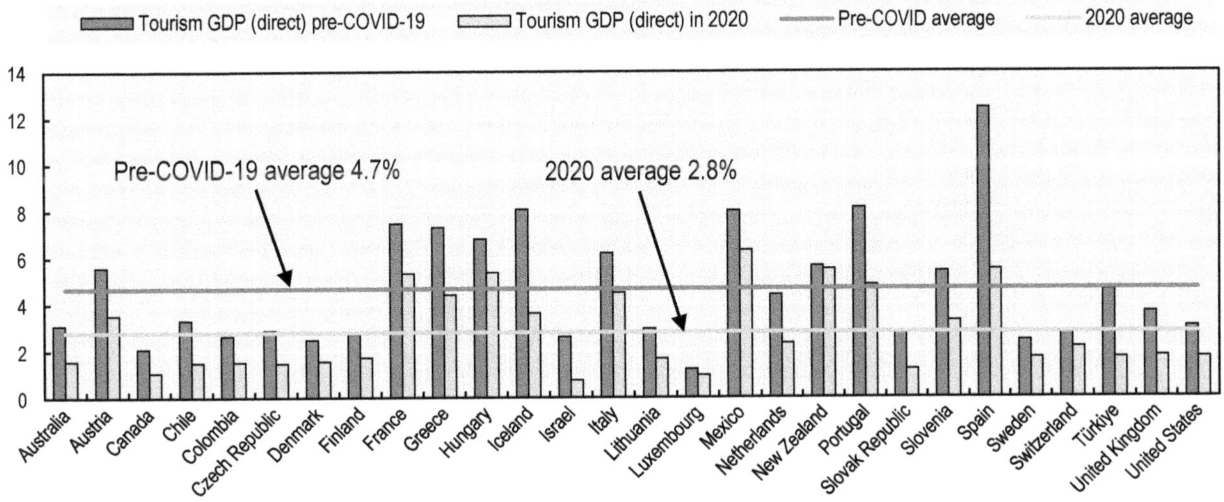

Note: Tourism Direct GDP is the preferred indicator. Pre-COVID-19 is 2019, or latest available pre-pandemic year.
Tourism Direct GVA data is used for Canada, Colombia, Denmark, Finland, Greece, Hungary, Israel, Italy, Lithuania, the Netherlands, New Zealand, Portugal, Switzerland, Türkiye, United Kingdom and United States.
Spain includes direct and indirect effects.
France refers to Internal Tourism Consumption as a percentage of GDP; data is based on constant price shares.
Source: Tourism Statistics (Database)

StatLink https://stat.link/b743av

The indirect impacts of tourism are also significant, owing to linkages to upstream sectors. OECD estimates from before the pandemic indicate that more than one-third of value added generated in the domestic economy through tourism comes from indirect impacts, reflecting the breadth and depth of linkages between tourism and other sectors (e.g. food production, agriculture, transport, business services) (OECD, 2019[4]).

Job retention schemes helped mitigate the impact of the pandemic on tourism employment, but labour shortages and skills gaps risk constraining the recovery. Tourism's share of total employment fell to 4.3% in 2020 across reporting OECD countries[2] that prepared a Tourism Satellite Account, down 0.8 percentage points across this group of countries compared with pre-COVID-19, on average. However, these supports did not reach all workers, including some self-employed workers such as tour guides and informal workers in the sector. The disruption in the sector also led many workers to seek more stable employment opportunities in other sectors. In the first quarter of 2022, employment in accommodation and food services was, on average, 9.0% below its pre-COVID-19 level (OECD, 2022[5]).

Figure 1.2. Correlation between the direct contribution of tourism pre-COVID-19, and GDP growth in 2020, selected OECD countries

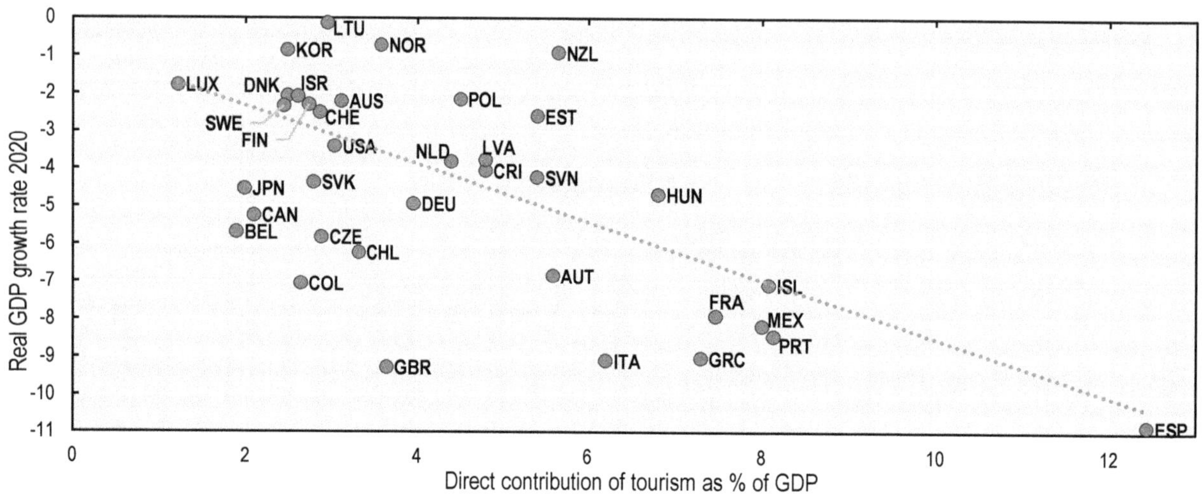

Note: Tourism Direct GDP is the preferred indicator. Pre-COVID-19 is 2019, or latest available pre-pandemic year.
Tourism Direct GVA data is used for Canada, Colombia, Denmark, Finland, Greece, Hungary, Israel, Italy, Lithuania, the Netherlands, New Zealand, Portugal, Switzerland, Türkiye, United Kingdom and United States.
Spain includes direct and indirect effects.
France refers to Internal Tourism Consumption as a percentage of GDP; data is based on constant shares.
Source: OECD Tourism Statistics (Database) and OECD Economic Outlook (Database)

StatLink https://stat.link/wazhtr

Recent rebound in international tourism raised hope of a demand-driven recovery

International tourism was decimated by the crisis, with the recovery in 2022 driven by pent-up demand and the lifting of travel restrictions in most countries. The closure of international borders and introduction of travel restrictions saw international tourist arrivals worldwide plummet by 72% to 409 million in 2020, with only a marginal improvement in 2021 (UNWTO, 2022[6]). This dramatic drop in international tourism flows followed six decades of consistent growth. The latest available data indicates that globally, international tourism flows recovered to almost 60% of pre-pandemic levels by July 2022. International tourist arrivals almost tripled during the period from January to July 2022 compared with the same period in 2021. Europe and the Middle East led the recovery (with arrivals reaching 74% and 76% of 2019 levels, respectively), followed by the Americas and Africa. Arrivals in the Asia Pacific region, however, remained 86% below 2019 levels by July 2022 (UNWTO, 2022[6]).

OECD countries are playing a driving role, but the recovery varies significantly across countries as governments adopt different approaches to reopening. International tourist arrivals to OECD countries fell by 68% in 2020 to 262 million, on average – slightly below the fall globally. The small improvement recorded in 2021 (up 16% to 303 million) outpaced the global average (up 9%), and available evidence indicates this has continued into 2022. OECD countries welcomed two out of every three international tourist arrivals in 2021 (68%, up from 57% in 2019). This reflects the different response measures taken by governments and the earlier reopening of cross-border tourism in Europe in particular. The accelerated roll-out of vaccinations in most OECD countries also played a key role. Countries in the Asia Pacific region adopted tighter cross-border travel policies, and these are still being unwound. For example, Japan reopened fully to international tourists on 11 October 2022.

Table 1.1. International tourist arrivals in OECD and partner countries, 2019-21

	Type of indicator	2021	Growth rate 2019 to 2020	Growth rate 2020 to 2021	Growth rate 2019 to 2021
		Thousand	%		
Australia	Visitors	246	-81%	-87%	-97%
Austria[1]	Tourists	12,728	-53%	-16%	-60%
Belgium[1]	Tourists	2,313	-73%	28%	-66%
Canada	Tourists	3,062	-87%	3%	-86%
Chile	Tourists	190	-75%	-83%	-96%
Colombia	Visitors	2,123	-69%	52%	-53%
Costa Rica	Tourists	1,347	-68%	33%	-57%
Czech Republic	Tourists	3,768	-73%	-4%	-74%
Denmark	Tourists	7,047	-60%	19%	-52%
Estonia	Tourists	801	-69%	-22%	-76%
Finland[1]	Tourists	807	-73%	-10%	-75%
France	Tourists	48,395	-54%	16%	-47%
Germany[1]	Tourists	11,688	-69%	-6%	-70%
Greece	Visitors	15,246	-78%	106%	-55%
Hungary	Tourists	6,973	-58%	5%	-56%
Iceland	Tourists	698	-78%	44%	-68%
Ireland[2]	Tourists	2,700	-78%	29%	-71%
Israel	Tourists	397	-82%	-52%	-91%
Italy	Tourists	26,888	-61%	7%	-58%
Japan	Visitors	246	-87%	-94%	-99%
Korea	Visitors	967	-86%	-62%	-94%
Latvia	Tourists	478	-67%	-25%	-75%
Lithuania	Tourists	948	-67%	1%	-67%
Luxembourg[1]	Tourists	756	-50%	44%	-27%
Mexico	Tourists	31,860	-46%	31%	-29%
Netherlands[1]	Tourists	6,248	-64%	-14%	-69%
New Zealand	Visitors	207	-74%	-79%	-95%
Norway[1]	Tourists	1,435	-76%	3%	-76%
Poland[1]	Tourists	9,722	-60%	15%	-54%
Portugal	Tourists	6,345	-76%	51%	-63%
Slovak Republic[1]	Tourists	576	-65%	-33%	-77%
Slovenia[1]	Tourists	1,832	-74%	51%	-61%
Spain	Tourists	31,181	-77%	65%	-63%
Sweden	Tourists	..	-74%	..	..
Switzerland[1]	Tourists	4,390	-69%	19%	-63%
Türkiye	Tourists	29,925	-69%	88%	-42%
United Kingdom	Visitors	6,194	-73%	-44%	-85%
United States	Tourists	22,100	-76%	15%	-72%
Brazil	Tourists	..	-66%	..	..
Bulgaria	Visitors	7,188	-60%	45%	-43%
Croatia[1]	Tourists	10,641	-68%	92%	-39%
Indonesia	Tourists	1,546	-74%	-61%	-90%
Malta	Tourists	968	-76%	47%	-65%
Montenegro[1]	Tourists	1,554	-86%	343%	-38%
Morocco	Tourists	3,722	-79%	34%	-71%
Peru	Tourists	444	-79%	-50%	-90%
Romania[1]	Tourists	841	-83%	85%	-69%
Saudi Arabia	Tourists	3,477	-76%	-16%	-80%
Serbia[1]	Tourists	871	-76%	95%	-53%

	Type of indicator	2021	Growth rate 2019 to 2020	Growth rate 2020 to 2021	Growth rate 2019 to 2021
		Thousand		%	
South Africa	Tourists	2,256	-73%	-19%	-78%
EU27		218,512	-66%	21%	-59%
OECD members		302,829	-68%	16%	-63%
World[3]		446,000	-72%	9%	-70%

Notes: For more information, please see the country profiles.
Tourists: International tourist arrivals (excluding same-day visitors).
Visitors: International visitor arrivals (including same-day visitors).
[1]Data from supply side surveys.
[2]Data for Ireland is estimated for 2020 and provisional for 2021.
[3]UNWTO data (World Tourism Barometer, Statistical Annex, September 2022).
Source: OECD Tourism Statistics (Database).

The shock has been unprecedented even in countries that saw the smallest falls in international arrivals in 2020, with inbound tourism remaining significantly below 2019 levels through 2021. For example, international tourists to Mexico declined by almost half (46%) in 2020, despite an open border strategy and the third-highest number of arrivals among OECD countries. Australia, Canada, Israel, Japan and Korea saw declines of more than 80% in inbound arrivals in 2020, with Australia, Chile, Japan and New Zealand recording further declines of more than 80% in 2021. Canada saw a slight improvement in arrivals in 2021 (up 3%), while several other countries, including Greece (up 106% in 2021), Spain (65%) and Türkiye (88%), experienced a stronger rebound during 2021, and into 2022. A breakdown of international tourist arrivals to OECD member and selected partner countries is provided in Table 1.1.

Many OECD countries have seen a strong recovery in 2022 driven by demand coming into the northern hemisphere summer, but this recovery is uneven. In January 2022, international tourism remained 54.6% below the same period in 2019 across reporting OECD countries, on average. This improved month-on-month, reaching 19.9% below 2019 levels in July 2022. In Europe, Denmark, Greece, Luxembourg, Portugal, Slovenia and Spain recorded arrivals in excess of 2019 levels in this month. This contrasts strongly with countries bordering Russia and Ukraine, where arrivals remain significantly down, including Estonia (down 30%), Finland (32%), Latvia (33%) and Lithuania (44%). Tourism to countries in the Asia Pacific region was also at least 40% below pre-pandemic levels in July 2022, including Australia (down 44%), Japan (95%) and New Zealand (44%).

The top tourism destinations and markets have shifted around the world, reflecting the uneven impact and recovery across countries. International tourist arrivals to Mexico and Türkiye overtook the United States, and together with France, Italy and Spain, these five destinations received almost 38% of worldwide arrivals in 2021 (UNWTO, 2022[6]). The People's Republic of China also dropped out of the top five destinations, and at the time of writing, remains closed to international tourists. Outbound travel similarly remains restricted from China, previously the world's largest outbound market and a powerhouse of the global tourism economy.

The drop in international tourism spending has been less pronounced than the drop in visitor flows. However, this should be interpreted with caution, as it may be influenced by a range of factors, including exchange rates, purchasing power and long-stay visitors already in market. Tourism was the fifth-largest traded services sector globally in 2019. In 2020, international travel receipts fell by 63.0% to USD 548 billion, down from almost USD 1 483 billion in 2019, and remained 58.1% below pre-COVID-19 levels in 2021 (USD 621 billion) (UNWTO, 2022[6]). OECD countries accounted for two-thirds (67.2%) of global travel receipts in 2020, up from 61% in 2019. Table 1.2 provides a summary of international travel receipts (exports), expenditure (imports) and the travel balance for OECD and partner countries.

Table 1.2. International travel receipts and expenditure in OECD and partner countries, 2019-20

USD, Millions

	Travel receipts		Travel expenditure		Travel balance	
	2019	2020	2019	2020	2019	2020
Australia	45,709	25,822	35,989	6,766	9,720	19,056
Austria	22,941	13,848	11,602	4,483	11,339	9,365
Belgium	8,908	6,608	18,758	13,011	-9,850	-6,403
Canada	29,776	13,506	35,349	12,081	-5,573	1,425
Chile	2,303	413	2,459	540	-157	-128
Colombia	5,682	1,568	4,935	1,358	747	210
Costa Rica	3,989	1,328	1,036	243	2,953	1,085
Czech Republic	7,303	3,628	5,889	3,423	1,414	205
Denmark	8,652	3,965	10,038	5,630	-1,386	-1,665
Estonia	1,744	591	1,546	598	197	-7
Finland	3,726	1,264	5,680	1,677	-1,955	-412
France	63,508	32,564	50,542	27,777	12,966	4,787
Germany	41,806	22,080	93,243	38,868	-51,438	-16,788
Greece	20,351	4,933	3,072	906	17,279	4,027
Hungary	7,305	3,205	2,749	1,157	4,556	2,048
Iceland	2,678	659	1,572	524	1,105	135
Ireland	6,478	1,879	8,256	2,366	-1,778	-487
Israel	7,600	2,500	8,154	1,804	-554	696
Italy	49,595	19,797	30,338	10,939	19,257	8,858
Japan	46,054	10,701	21,265	5,501	24,790	5,200
Korea	20,867	10,276	32,739	16,092	-11,872	-5,816
Latvia	1,015	432	749	303	267	129
Lithuania	1,493	579	1,389	542	104	37
Luxembourg	5,785	4,797	3,631	2,764	2,155	2,033
Mexico	24,573	10,996	9,881	3,475	14,692	7,521
Netherlands	19,729	10,016	23,124	8,175	-3,394	1,841
New Zealand	10,533	5,751	4,300	1,444	6,233	4,307
Norway	5,855	1,564	16,513	3,700	-10,658	-2,135
Poland	14,013	8,199	9,286	5,266	4,727	2,933
Portugal	20,476	8,812	5,736	3,133	14,740	5,679
Slovak Republic	3,203	1,292	2,589	1,269	614	24
Slovenia	3,183	1,370	1,679	820	1,504	551
Spain	79,709	18,506	27,778	8,650	51,931	9,856
Sweden	9,193	4,373	14,366	6,172	-5,173	-1,799
Switzerland	17,950	9,064	18,753	9,557	-803	-494
Türkiye	29,813	10,221	4,108	1,040	25,705	9,181
United Kingdom	52,724	18,822	70,616	21,601	-17,893	-2,780
United States	198,982	72,481	132,271	34,159	66,711	38,322
Brazil	5,995	3,044	17,593	5,394	-11,599	-2,350
Bulgaria	4,287	1,624	1,826	1,039	2,461	585
Croatia	11,773	5,238	1,763	763	10,010	4,475
Indonesia	16,911	3,312	11,308	1,653	5,603	1,658
Malta	1,897	417	530	128	1,367	289
Montenegro	1,224	166	58	30	1,166	136
Morocco	8,187	3,848	2,176	1,113	6,010	2,735
Peru	3,819	794	2,818	744	1,001	50
Romania	3,578	1,431	6,001	3,026	-2,424	-1,595
Saudi Arabia	16,431	4,036	15,140	8,533	1,292	-4,497

	Travel receipts		Travel expenditure		Travel balance	
	2019	2020	2019	2020	2019	2020
Serbia	1,604	1,245	1,806	1,115	-201	130
South Africa	8,390	2,607	3,141	928	5,249	1,679
EU27	424,911	182,135	343,794	153,581		
OECD	905,203	368,408	731,979	267,810		
World[1]	1,483,000	548,000	1,483,000	548,000		

Note: For more information, please see the country profiles.
[1]UNWTO data (World Tourism Barometer, Statistical Annex, September 2022).
Source: OECD Tourism Statistics (Database).

Tourism accounted for 77c of every USD 1 of lost revenue from the decline in service exports in OECD countries in 2020. This increases to 90c in every USD 1 when passenger transport receipts are included. Tourism's share of services exports for OECD countries fell from 20.5% in 2019 to 9.9% in 2020 on average. All OECD countries experienced a decline, but this was more pronounced in countries like Colombia, Greece and Spain. Luxembourg, Belgium, the Netherlands and Ireland have been relatively less impacted, as tourism accounted for less than 10% of services exports pre-pandemic (Figure 1.3).

Figure 1.3. Contribution of tourism to service exports, 2019-20

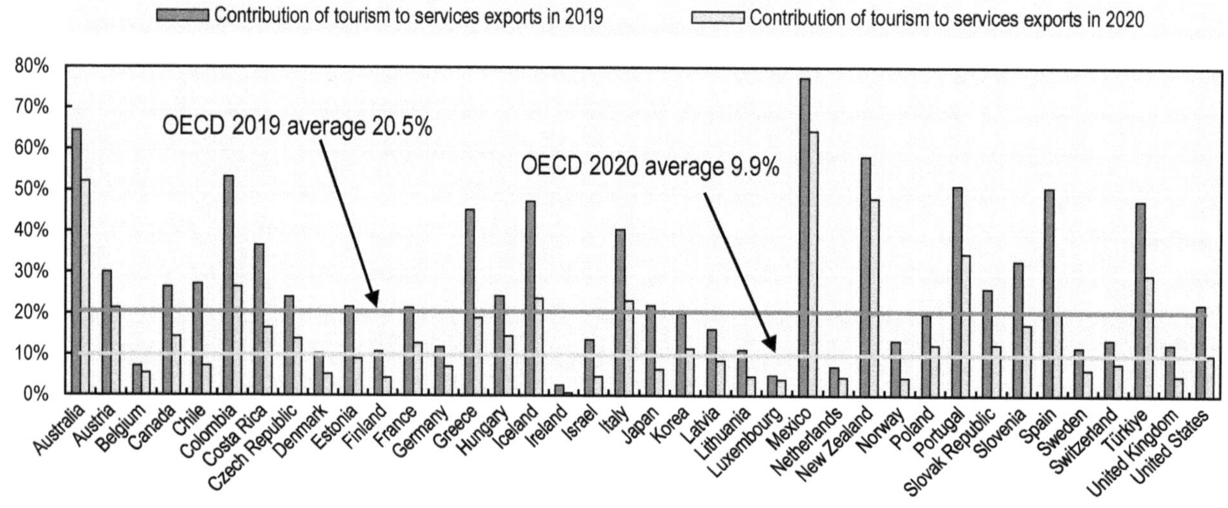

Source: OECD Trade in services by partner country (Database), extracted September 2022.

StatLink https://stat.link/ktr6gc

Tourism exports are economically important, as they generate value added in the economy, directly and indirectly. Analysing tourism from a trade in value added approach shows that tourism expenditure (using non-resident expenditure as a proxy) generates bigger impacts on the domestic economy than overall exports. Data from the OECD Trade in Value Added (TiVA) data base show that on average across OECD countries 89% of tourism exports reflect domestic value added in OECD countries, compared with 81% for overall exports.

Figure 1.4. Domestic value added generated by tourism expenditure in OECD countries

Domestic value added/export ratio for non-resident expenditure and for the total economy

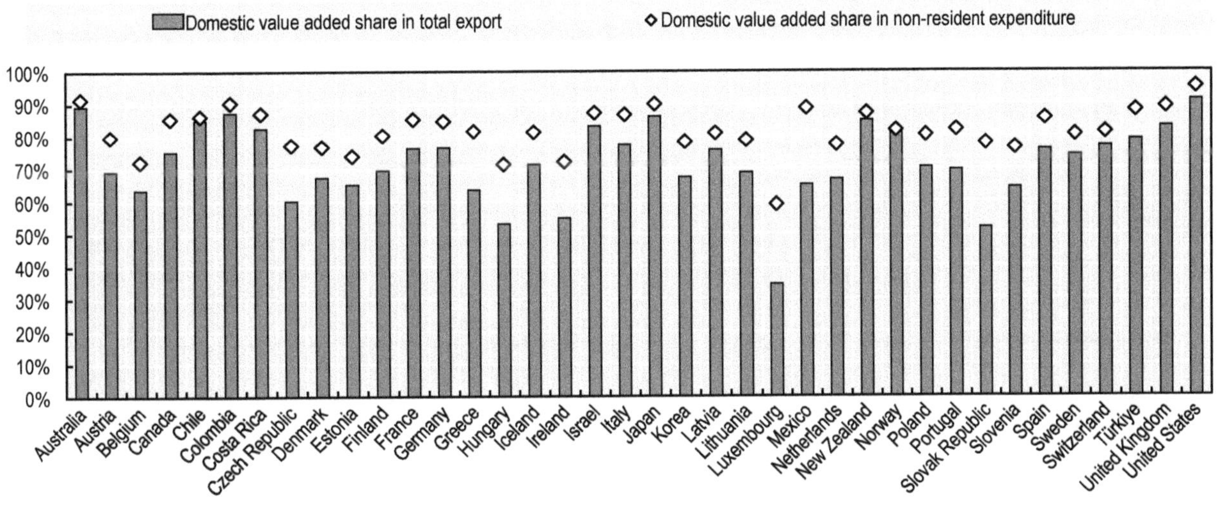

Note: Non-resident expenditure as a proxy for tourism expenditure.
Source: OECD Inter-Country Input-Output, 2019

StatLink https://stat.link/tbcvue

Domestic tourism has helped sustain the sector, but cannot compensate for the loss of international tourism

Domestic tourism was also hard hit by the pandemic but has fared better than international tourism. The easing of localised and domestic restrictions in the middle of 2020 saw domestic tourism activities resume earlier than international tourism in many countries. This led to a pick-up in domestic tourism, in part reflecting restrictions on international travel. It also led to a renewed focus on domestic tourism and recognition of its importance, as destinations and businesses looked to mitigate the loss of international markets. This has been supported by increased domestic marketing, travel vouchers and subsidies to stimulate domestic tourism demand.

Long an important driver of tourism, domestic demand has provided a lifeline to many jobs and businesses since the start of the pandemic but does not compensate for the loss of international markets. Even as recent as 2021, domestic overnight trips were still 19.1% below pre-COVID-19 levels among OECD countries with data[3]. Indeed, only Denmark, Iceland, Luxembourg, Norway, Sweden and Switzerland saw increases in domestic overnight trips in 2020. In 2021, domestic tourist trips exceeded 2019 levels in Belgium, Finland, Lithuania and Slovenia. In all other OECD countries, domestic trips remained below pre-pandemic levels.

The importance of domestic tourism varies considerably by country, and with it the exposure of destinations and businesses to the loss of international visitors. Domestic tourism is the main stay of the sector in most OECD countries. Before the pandemic, residents were responsible for 75% of tourism expenditure, on average. However, this share is significantly lower in countries like Estonia, Hungary, Iceland, Luxembourg and Slovenia, where domestic tourism represented less than 30%, leaving the tourism sector in these countries more exposed to drops in inbound visitor flows. This compares with countries like Australia, Canada, Chile, Germany, Japan, Mexico, the United Kingdom and the United States, where domestic tourism represented over 70% of internal tourism consumption before the pandemic.

The generally lower impact on domestic tourism saw its share of total tourism consumption increasing in most OECD economies (Figure 1.5). In the case of Australia, Canada and the United States, domestic tourism increased to more than 90% of total tourism expenditure during the pandemic.

Figure 1.5. Domestic tourism consumption in selected OECD countries, pre-COVID-19 and in 2020

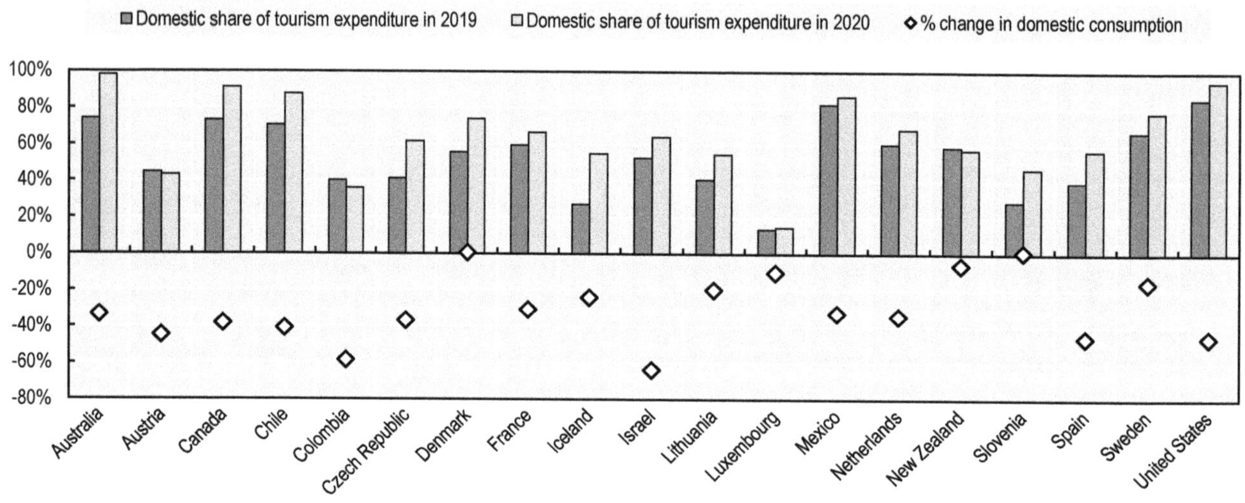

Source: OECD Tourism Statistics (Database).

StatLink https://stat.link/tgxvn3

Uncertain outlook for tourism recovery brings new challenges

The tourism recovery in 2022 has exceeded expectations for many countries. Based on a survey of OECD and partner countries on the latest tourism performance and recovery outlook to inform the preparation of this chapter, almost half of responding countries reported that tourism has performed better than expected in 2022, with many of these countries recording strong domestic results. A rapid return of domestic tourism, pent-up demand, pre-bookings and unused travel vouchers helped to boost recovery prospects for 2022. However, in most of these countries tourism performance remains below (three-fifths of countries) or significantly below (one-fifth) 2019 levels.

The lifting of sanitary restrictions and intra-regional travel boosted the strong tourism performance in Europe, supported by exchange rate fluctuations. The comparatively weaker Euro against the US dollar made European destinations more attractive to visitors from the United States in the lead-up to the peak European summer tourism period, helping to boost demand. In the first six months of 2022, on average across EU countries with data, arrivals at accommodation establishments were 17.5% below the same period in 2019, improving month-on-month as international tourism demand returned (Eurostat, 2022[7]). This contrasts with countries like Australia, Korea and New Zealand, where international tourism remains relatively low.

Expectations for the tourism recovery in many OECD countries have been delayed, with domestic tourism now expected to recover by 2023, and international tourism taking up until 2025 or beyond. While more than half of responding countries reported that domestic tourism has already fully recovered, or is expected to recover by the end of 2022, more than a third do expect a return to 2019 levels until 2023. Two countries expect the full recovery of domestic tourism to take until 2024 or 2025 due to the uncertain economic outlook. International tourism recovery is expected to take longer. Just over one third of countries expect international tourism to fully recover by 2023, while another third do not expect recovery until 2025 or beyond. Of OECD countries, Denmark, France and Türkiye report or anticipate a full recovery in 2022. Croatia also reports a full recovery to 2019 levels in 2022.

The OECD survey of recent tourism performance and outlook for recovery highlights the shift in focus as the tourism sector faces many challenges, beyond the pandemic, with countries in particular highlighting the impact of global inflation and price rises on tourism businesses and tourist spending. Economic insecurity, energy constraints and labour shortages are also barriers to the recovery. While travel restrictions are lifting, geopolitical uncertainty and the absence of key source markets due to COVID-19 and Russia's war in Ukraine is also expected to impede the tourism recovery in some countries. The restart of international tourism also brings unforeseen challenges which risk constraining the recovery, including for example, processing backlogs for visas and travel documentation.

Russia's war in Ukraine has dealt a blow to the economic recovery, as the impacts of the pandemic still linger, with significant consequences for tourism. Recent macroeconomic estimates show that global GDP growth is projected to remain subdued in the second half of 2022, before slowing further in 2023 to 2.2% (OECD, 2022[8]) The war has also triggered a cost-of-living crisis, affecting people worldwide. Inflationary pressures are now broadening beyond food and energy, with businesses throughout the economy passing through higher energy, transport and labour costs to consumers. This is sapping growth and will impact real incomes and curb spending, weighing down on the tourism sector's nascent recovery from the pandemic (OECD, 2022[8]).

Countries neighbouring Russia and Ukraine have seen a slower recovery in 2022 compared with elsewhere in Europe, and the war is casting a shadow over the tourism outlook. Estonia, Finland, Latvia and Lithuania all reported remaining below or significantly below 2019 levels in 2022. Domestic tourism has already recovered in Estonia and Finland, but for international tourism is not expected until 2024 or 2025 for all four countries. Beyond the loss of tourist flows, tourism businesses in these and other countries have been stepping in to provide accommodation and jobs for Ukrainians fleeing the war. Countries such as Poland are also experiencing labour shortages as Ukrainians working in the tourism sector have returned to Ukraine.

Inflationary pressures are likely to further impact the aviation sector. ForwardKeys, which tracks air travel booking patterns, estimated that intra-European flight bookings were 5% lower during the summer of 2022 due to disruption in the aviation sector, including through labour shortages (ForwardKeys, 2022[9]). Total employment in the sector is expected to remain below pre-pandemic levels for some time. Oil and fuel price inflation is exacerbating these challenges, as well as eroding consumer purchasing power.

Governments must continue to closely monitor this situation amid growing concerns of a 'false dawn', as there is a risk that recovery may stall rather than consolidate in the coming months. European countries are expected to be hardest hit by the economic crisis, with greater exposure to the war through energy imports (OECD, 2022[10]). The full impacts are yet to play out as winter approaches. Airline financial performance is expected to improve in all regions in 2022, but North America is the only region expected to return to profitability this year (IATA, 2022[11]). At the same time, the opportunity to optimise the strength and quality of the recovery should not be missed, including to accelerate the green and digital transitions.

Recovery plans bring opportunities for more resilient, sustainable and inclusive tourism

The crisis triggered by COVID-19 presents a unique opportunity to rethink tourism policy and take steps so the measures put in place today can shape a more resilient, sustainable and inclusive tourism economy for the future. This includes tackling the consequences for and of climate change and the depletion of natural capital; the energy crisis could help to accelerate the transition to more sustainable models of energy consumption and rethink tourism infrastructure to ensure it can adapt to climate change and natural disasters. More needs to be done also to enable all tourism stakeholders to benefit fully from digital opportunities and deliver more equitable and inclusive benefits to everyone engaged in and impacted by the sector, including through providing decent work opportunities in the sector.

This calls for the mainstreaming of sustainability into the strategic direction for tourism, supported by effective policies and implementation structures to develop and manage tourism sustainably, across all levels of government. Many sustainability issues are best tackled at the local destination level to address diverse and specific needs, with broad stakeholder engagement and involvement of local tourism communities. Co-ordinated multi-level and multi-stakeholder policy approaches are needed to support this, along with improved capacity of government at all levels, and the private sector.

Securing a robust and stable tourism sector in uncertain times can promote a job-rich recovery, support fragile tourism businesses, particularly SMEs, and benefit local communities. The pandemic has led to a greater focus on the resilience of tourism. This comes at a time when shocks are becoming more frequent, and businesses and governments are required to continually respond. Chapter 2, Building Resilience in the Tourism Ecosystem, analyses policy approaches to support the recovery and enhance the resilience of the tourism economy for the future. It considers actions to boost tourism recovery prospects, tackle the long-term consequences of the crisis, and better prepare for future shocks, while encouraging the shift to more resilient, sustainable and inclusive models of tourism.

Sustained and transformative action is needed to promote a green tourism recovery, if the sector is to play its part in climate action. The halt in tourism at the height of the pandemic has allowed the sector to rethink the tourism offer. Governments, businesses, tourists and communities have been provided with an opportunity to consider the environmental impact of tourism and how it might be mitigated. Chapter 3, Promoting a Green Tourism Recovery, examines policy approaches to support the recovery of the tourism economy in a green and environmentally sustainable way, while delivering benefits to local communities and economies.

Continued progress is needed to improve the evidence base for tourism planning, policy and decision-making, to move to more sustainable, resilient and inclusive models in the future. Governments need to commit to these principles through future-focused and evidence-based policies. Effective policy making, planning and management all rely on the availability of robust evidence, preferably in the form of reliable and timely data that is sufficiently disaggregated and comparable. The pandemic has reinforced the urgency to have new tourism data measures and complementary data sources to react quickly under uncertainty, and this will be more evident as governments look to measure new sustainable policies.

Identifying critical uncertainties to mitigate possible issues and take advantage of opportunities will be important for governments and businesses as tourism recovers. Ongoing changes and external forces will continue to influence travel behaviours. Considering the different critical uncertainties can inform decisions on the supports the sector may require to rebuild stronger, fairer and greener. For example, price impacts could see the trend to *go local* consolidated as people look to reduce transport costs. They could also amplify existing issues, including seasonality and lack of dispersal as the number of trips are reduced, and visitors look to make their limited holidays count in the summer or winter months and at 'bucket list' destinations. Some critical uncertainties for tourism are presented in Box 1.1, including the impacts of long--term trends like the digital and green transitions.

Box 1.1. Critical uncertainties for shaping a resilient and sustainable tourism future

Recent and ongoing crises are significantly impacting consumer preferences and business structures, accelerating existing trends (e.g. digitalisation) and leading to the emergence of new behaviours (e.g. momentum around domestic tourism). Strategic foresight approaches that consider the 'known unknowns' can help policy makers to better understand and better prepare for the future. Key questions to consider include:

- Will Russia's war in Ukraine have long-lasting impacts on tourism?
- Will the energy crisis and higher fuel costs lead to long-lasting changes in travel patterns?
- Will social trends toward sustainability accelerate the greening of tourism businesses and consumer behaviours?
- Will climate action create winners and losers in tourism, and who will they be?
- Will tourism destinations return to a growth-at-all-costs model, or shift to more sustainable models of tourism?
- Will labour shortages and skills gaps continue to hinder the tourism recovery?
- Will business travel return to previous levels, and what will it look like in the future?
- Will city tourism return amid the newfound desire for nature-based experiences?
- Will tourism businesses of all sizes benefit from digital opportunities, or will the gap continue to widen with tourism SMEs left behind?
- How will technological advances shape tourism experiences and behaviours in the future (e.g. long-haul travel, space tourism, virtual tourism)?
- Will access to tourism experiences broaden for a more inclusive and accessible sector?

Strengthening the governance of tourism to respond and support recovery

The COVID-19 crisis has been a call to action to governments, at all levels, and to the private sector, to respond in a co-ordinated way, and has highlighted the importance of integrated tourism policy approaches to support recovery. Governments at all levels, and the private sector, need to be better prepared and have the capacity to react and adapt quickly. This requires more robust risk assessment and crisis response mechanisms, and closer co-ordination across government and with the private sector, to ensure general measures address the needs of the tourism sector (or, at a minimum, do not unnecessarily adversely affect the sector) and that specific measures are well targeted. The pandemic has also brought about a need to co-ordinate with health authorities, a relatively new area of engagement for tourism.

Governments were required to take unprecedented steps to mitigate the impact on the economy, including tourism, while responding to the health crisis. Delivering well-targeted and accessible support as quickly and efficiently as possible to tourism businesses, workers and visitors has been vital for the recovery of the tourism economy. This has required policy makers and the private sector to move quickly and adapt to the changed operating environment. The increased recognition of the importance of tourism at the highest levels of government, as well as the importance of international co-operation, has supported the response.

Specific governance arrangements vary across countries, depending on factors including the system of government. In most OECD countries, responsibility for tourism at the national level is situated within the economic development or trade and industry ministries. Other common partnerships include those with regional development, culture or sport. Responsibility for tourism has recently moved to the Ministry of Labour and Economy in Austria, for example, while in Iceland, the tourism portfolio recently moved to the

Ministry of Culture and Business Affairs. Perhaps recognising the importance of the tourism economy, Italy created a dedicated new Ministry of Tourism in 2021.

In general, the changes in tourism governance arrangements since the start of the pandemic have not been structural but have taken place instead through the development of ad hoc taskforces and other frameworks to increase collaboration and co-ordination across government, levels of government, and with the private sector. Countries should seek to build on these experiences and take forward the approaches successfully used during the pandemic to tackle future challenges facing the tourism sector. This will provide momentum for more innovative and integrated approaches to tourism development in the future and support the sustainable development of tourism and ensure the sector is better prepared for future crises.

Strengthening co-ordination and capacity across government for agile, targeted policies

Tourism presents an interdependent ecosystem of industries. This creates additional complexity in the policy making process requiring strong co-operation between multiple government actors. The wide and varied nature of the tourism ecosystem means the quick and effective provision of sectoral support from the start of the pandemic required strong collaboration across government, both horizontally and vertically. This has been particularly essential to respond to the pandemic, and now in the face of the cost-of-living crisis, to ensure that new policies aligned with existing and planned economy-wide measures, and that targeted support measures were adequate for the needs of the tourism economy.

It also means that tourism policy makers have had to co-ordinate with health colleagues to a far greater extent than in the past, and in many cases for the first time. This has required quick upskilling, creating new networks and building trust. In Italy, for example, tourism policy makers worked closely with health colleagues to promote the tourism recovery, providing information to support the tourism experience and developing "Covid-free tourist corridors". Malta collaborated with the Ministry for Health to understand the COVID-19 situation and the policy initiatives to address it. The Czech Republic worked with the Ministry of Health in the design of enabling conditions for tourism services to operate during the pandemic and will maintain this relationship to promote medical tourism.

Greater recognition of the importance of co-operation has led to many countries to formalise these ad hoc communication structures for horizontal and vertical co-ordination moving forward. The main purpose of these groups is to integrate tourism into broader national strategies and policy frameworks and ensure that tourism issues are addressed more broadly. However, some structures have been developed to address specific longstanding issues within the sector.

Germany created the national platform "Future of Tourism" as a central instrument for further developing a national tourism strategy (Box 2.6). This is to be overseen by a steering committee with high-ranking members of the relevant ministries responsible for developing the key points for the national tourism strategy and agreeing on a working programme for the Federal Government. The platform will expand to include representatives of the sixteen federal states and stakeholders of the tourism sector early in 2023.

The Czech Republic has taken an issues-based approach. The new Tourism Development Strategy 2021-30 supports greater co-ordination of tourism development and integration of tourism issues into other national strategies and policy areas. This includes a range of bilateral meetings and thematic working groups on key issues like visas and transport, economic diplomacy, financial support mechanisms, cultural and heritage tourism and sustainable tourism. The Czech Republic has also introduced a co-ordination platform to aid inter-ministerial and interdisciplinary co-ordination, which also allows for the collection of regional feedback on marketing activities and product development.

Greece has concentrated on preparedness rather than reaction by developing, within the framework of the UNWTO Technical Assistance Programme, a Tourism Crisis Management Plan and a Crisis

Communication Strategy covering a wide range of potential crises that can impact tourism, including health, environmental, economic, and societal crises. These plans aim to increase the effectiveness and agility of the Greek tourism sector in responding to future challenges.

Enhancing engagement with the private sector

The private sector is a key stakeholder in tourism policy making. There was already a growing recognition of this before the pandemic. However, the fragmented nature of the tourism economy, made up of different branches with sometimes competing interests, makes it a challenging sector for policy makers to engage with. Since the beginning of the pandemic there have been many good examples of close co-operation between government and the private sector, and with civil society – at local, national and international levels. The opportunity now exists to bring forward these experiences, to tackle future tourism policy challenges.

Box 1.2. Taking forward public-private sector co-operation – selected country approaches

Estonia: The Tourism Advisory Board consists of the Ministry of Economic Affairs and Communications and Ministry of Culture, the Tourism Board, professional tourism associations, destinations and major gateways, which will meet twice annually. It was developed after the success of a regular roundtable during COVID-19, which has also been continued as an informal meeting style.

Finland: A High-Level Working Group on Tourism was established in September 2021. Chaired by the Ministry of Economic Affairs and Employment, it comprises relevant ministries, regional councils, state administrations, regional tourism organisations, travel companies, research and educational institutions and organisations. The Working Group will serve as an expert advisory body on strategy related to tourism development through 2028. It will also monitor and assess the sector's operating environment and current phenomena and support the preparation of tourism policy measures.

Ireland: The Hospitality and Tourism Forum was created in October 2020 to provide structured engagement between the private sector and relevant government departments. Its purpose is to allow key issues of relevance to the sector to be discussed, with a view to identifying practical (national or local) government and private sector action.

Netherlands: A national taskforce on leisure and tourism was formed to strengthen the co-operation between national government and industry stakeholders. The short-term objective of the task force was to respond to the COVID-19 crisis and restart tourism. Medium and long-term objectives include a robust co-operation for a resilient and sustainable tourism and hospitality sector. The Taskforce is also responsible for progressing the joint action agenda on Perspective 2030, the national tourism strategy.

Poland: The Tourism Experts Council is a continuation of the Council of Experts, developed in 2021. Council tasks are to: identify and provide advice on tourism issues; propose systemic solutions; present proposals and provide advice on legislative initiatives; and initiate activities to enhance sustainable development, competitiveness and innovation. It will also provide inputs for the new medium and long-term programmes related to the transformation and development of tourism.

Switzerland: An advisory group consisting of tourism stakeholders, entrepreneurs, government officials, tourism associations, the cantons and the academic community will oversee the implementation of Switzerland's federal tourism strategy. This will ensure the tourism strategy is implemented in a targeted and group-oriented manner.

Many countries set up tourism taskforces or advisory groups consisting of both public and private sector actors. In Morocco, for example, public and private actors came together at national and regional levels to establish a joint plan to revive the tourism sector for 2020-22. The Tourism and Morocco Post COVID-19 Plan includes 21 measures to adapt to new market realities, anticipate changes in the consumption patterns of tourists and take advantage of new opportunities.

The increased level of constructive co-operation between the public and private sectors may be one of the positive legacies to emerge from this crisis (OECD, 2020[11]). Many countries are now building on the legacy of collaboration during the pandemic by formalising longer-term collaboration structures. These government and private sector groups are being utilised to drive strategic direction, create action plans for national strategies, and provide advice on programmes for long-term development in the sector. Several country-specific examples are set out in Box 1.2.

At the international level, the International Civil Aviation Organisation Council Aviation Recovery Taskforce, for example, brought together public and private representatives, including public health authorities, to provide practical, aligned guidance to governments and industry operators to support a co-ordinated restart of the international air transport sector (ICAO, 2021[13]). Events like the OECD Global Forum on Tourism Statistics, Knowledge and Policies are also providing a platform for the tourism community to work together to support recovery and develop a common transformation agenda for the tourism economy.

The private sector has also taken the lead in this area, with one international example being the World Travel and Tourism Council Tourism Recovery Taskforce created to bring together policy makers and the private sector on a global scale. The recent creation of an Informal Tourism Contact Group by *Business@OECD* is a further example that is feeding into OECD work on tourism.

Trust and collaboration between government, the private sector and civil society are essential to tackle resilience and sustainability challenges (OECD, 2021[14]). It is important to learn from and build on these innovations, to take this forward to respond to future tourism challenges. This will also be key in the shift to a greener, digital tourism economy.

Promoting international and multilateral co-operation to boost recovery

The crisis has highlighted the complexity and interdependence of the global tourism system. Solid multilateral co-operation and institutions have never been more important. Countries need to work together, as the actions taken by one government have implications for travellers and businesses in other countries, and for the global tourism system. Countries need to develop collaborative systems across borders to safely resume travel, restore traveller and business confidence, stimulate demand and accelerate tourism recovery. More efficient international co-ordination systems are also needed to respond to future shocks.

During the pandemic there were many examples of increased bilateral co-ordination, for the establishment of safe travel corridors between countries. Estonia, Latvia and Lithuania introduced the Baltic 'travel bubble' in 2020, allowing free movement without any self-isolation obligations of citizens and residents between the three countries, as infection rates in the three neighbouring countries were similar. Regional co-operation is also playing a role, including through more formalised groups.

Reflecting the increased recognition of the importance of tourism at national level, tourism is high on the global agenda. There has also been increased attention on tourism at the multilateral level, including at the highest levels in the OECD and other international institutions. The OECD, United Nations, World Bank, World Trade Organisation and others issued calls for action to support the tourism recovery and take the opportunity to shift to more sustainable, inclusive and resilient models of tourism for the future (OECD, 2020[11]; UN, 2020[14]; World Bank, 2020[15]; WTO, 2020[16]). The first High -Level Thematic Debate on Tourism at the UN General Assembly took place in May 2022.

There have also been additional efforts to co-ordinate across these international institutions and countries, through for example the OECD Initiative on International Safe Mobility (Box 1.6). The UNWTO-led Global

Tourism Crisis Committee brought together representatives from countries and international institutions, including the World Health Organisation, OECD, ICAO, International Maritime Organisation, the European Commission, as well as private sector representatives from International Air Travel Association (IATA) and Cruise Lines International Association.

The creation of a formal G20 Tourism Working Group under the G20 Saudi Arabia Presidency in 2020 has further spurred co-ordinated action at the international level, and has continued under the Presidencies of Italy in 2021 and Indonesia in 2022 (e.g. G20 Rome Guidelines for the Future of Tourism, G20 Bali Guidelines for Strengthening Communities and MSMEs as Tourism Transformation Agents), with commitments secured in subsequent G20 Leaders Declarations to support tourism recovery. Other international institutions have also expanded their work and collaboration on tourism, including Asia Pacific Economic Cooperation (APEC), Association of South East Asian Nations, the Asian Development Bank and the European Union. The APEC Tourism Ministers, for example, recently endorsed Policy Recommendations for Tourism of the Future: Regenerative Tourism (APEC, 2022[18]).

Ensuring strong collaboration across these groupings and maintaining the momentum of tourism work streams, even in times of 'normality', provides important avenues and momentum to advance work to build a resilient and sustainable global tourism ecosystem. The European Commission is seizing this opportunity through a collaborative co-creation process to develop and secure action commitments to support the Transition Pathway for Tourism - a plan for the tourism ecosystem detailing key actions, targets and conditions to achieve the transition and long-term resilience of the sector (Box 1.3).

Box 1.3. Toward a green and digital transition of tourism in the European Union

The European Commission's Transition Pathway for Tourism, launched in February 2022, was developed through a co-creation process with tourism actors, incorporating workshops, stakeholder meetings and a survey (which included responses from 200 stakeholders from 24 EU Member States plus Norway and the United Kingdom) into the design process. The Transition Pathway for Tourism followed the updated European Commission's Industrial Strategy of 2021.

The tourism transition pathway aims to accelerate the green and digital transition and to increase the long-term resilience of the tourism sector. The transition pathway calls on the whole tourism ecosystem to implement measures, targets and conditions in 27 areas, including to:

- Invest in circularity to reduce energy, waste, water and pollution, and at the same time to better meet the increasing demand for sustainable tourism.
- Enhance data sharing practices to allow for new innovative tourism services and improve the sustainable management of destinations.
- Invest in skills to ensure the availability of a qualified workforce and attractive careers in the ecosystem.

The European Commission has now moved to implementation and invited tourism stakeholders to present their commitments to the transition for tourism. The objective is to encourage all stakeholders in the tourism ecosystem to play their part in the initiative. Collaboration processes are designed for co-implementation and monitoring of measures facilitated by an online stakeholder collaboration platform.

Source: EC Transition Pathway for Tourism (European Commission, 2022[19]).

Developing strategies amid uncertainty to shape a sustainable and resilient recovery

Before the tourism crisis triggered by COVID-19, OECD work highlighted the importance of implementing a long-term and sustainable vision for tourism, supported by forward-looking strategies and action plans. As tourism recovers, governments face the challenge of balancing short-term recovery needs with longer-term strategic objectives. While the pandemic highlighted weaknesses (new and existing) in the tourism ecosystem, the slowdown it precipitated also presented an opportunity to address these in the recovery, and for the longer term. Policy interventions now must already take this into account as the sector navigates the recovery from COVID-19 while addressing new challenges arising from the changed economic and geopolitical environment, if the opportunity is not to be missed.

The development of new tourism strategies in countries provides an important chance to address this. Many OECD countries were in the process of creating or updating their long-term tourism strategies at the beginning of the pandemic. While the pandemic led to some strategies being delayed, countries have also considered it an opportunity to reshape their new and existing strategies to reflect the new operating environment and optimise the strength and quality of the recovery. Some countries, including the Czech Republic, Italy, Japan and Latvia, have responded to the uncertainty by implementing shorter-term recovery strategies or action plans, typically covering two-to-three-year timeframes.

Many countries have also adopted long-term strategies during 2022, typically spanning to 2027 or 2030. In the United States, the National Travel and Tourism Strategy 2022 focuses on promoting the United States as a premier destination grounded in the breadth and diversity of its communities, and fostering a travel and tourism sector that drives economic growth, creates good jobs, and bolsters conservation and sustainability (Box 1.4). Other countries that have recently introduced, or are developing, new long-term tourism strategies include Australia, Croatia, Denmark, Finland, France, Greece, Hungary and Israel.

There is also evidence of countries seeking to incorporate a more flexible approach to strategic tourism planning and development. The United Kingdom, for example, adopted a two-pronged approach, with the first aim to recover back to 2019 levels, while longer-term, strategic aims include objectives to encourage greater regional spread, support the business events sector, build greater sector resilience, and increase accessibility and sustainability. Hungary developed a revised Tourism 2.0 Strategy in 2021, incorporating the impacts of COVID-19 and the lessons learned through the first three years of the National Tourism Development Strategy 2030.

Sustainability remains a strategic pillar and strong focus for tourism policy development. There is evidence of an increased focus on climate change mitigation and adaptation in countries like Italy and the United States. Italy is currently developing a new Strategic Plan for Tourism 2023-27 and is exploring the use of behavioural insights to encourage more sustainable and environmentally friendly behaviours for tourists and businesses, and better match the product offer to tourists. Switzerland, launched a new three-year "Swisstainable" Strategy in 2021, aiming to become the world's most sustainable tourism destination.

Portugal has developed a comprehensive 2020-23 Sustainable Tourism Plan, with a practical focus on encouraging sustainable actions by tourism businesses. These include reducing energy consumption and adopting circular economy solutions, relevant training and skills development, support for sustainable construction techniques and improved water efficiency at golf courses. The Estonian Tourism Strategy 2022-25 includes a vision that 'Estonia is a smart and green destination that offers an integrated visitor journey and a sustainable tourism product.' Sustainability programmes have also been developed in Belgium, with Flanders adopting the Travel to Tomorrow: Recommendations for Tourism Policy 2019-24 plan, and Romania developing a Strategy for Ecotourism Development.

Box 1.4. National Travel and Tourism Strategy 2022 in the United States

The National Travel and Tourism Strategy 2022 aims to support broad-based economic growth in travel and tourism across the United States, drawing on engagement and capabilities from across the Federal Government. The Federal Government will work to implement the Strategy under the leadership of the Tourism Policy Council and in partnership with the private sector, aiming toward an ambitious five-year goal of 90 million international visitors spending approximately USD 279 billion annually by 2027.

The Strategy follows a four-point approach:

- **Promoting the United States as a travel destination:** Leverage existing programmes and assets to promote the United States to international visitors and broaden marketing efforts to encourage visitation to underserved communities.
- **Facilitating travel to and within the United States:** Reduce barriers to trade in travel services and make it safer and more efficient for visitors to enter and travel within the United States.
- **Ensuring diverse, inclusive, and accessible tourism experiences:** Extend the benefits of tourism by supporting the development of diverse products, focusing on under-served communities and populations. Address travel and tourism businesses' financial and workplace needs, supporting destination communities as they grow their tourism economies. Deliver world-class experiences and customer service at federal lands and waters that showcase the nation's assets while protecting them for future generations.
- **Fostering resilient and sustainable travel and tourism:** Reduce travel and tourism's contributions to climate change and build a travel and tourism sector that is resilient to natural disasters, public health threats, and the impacts of climate change. Build a sustainable sector that protects natural resources, supports the tourism economy and ensures equitable development.

Recent strategies also consider the idea of value over volume, digitalisation, and workforce issues. These are key drivers in the implementation of Austria's Plan T - Masterplan for Tourism, which was developed before the pandemic with a focus on quality rather than quantity and a culture of co-operation. Australia's THRIVE 2030 strategy includes an *'industry led, government enabled'* action plan that works towards a resilient, sustainable, innovative, and competitive visitor economy, with a focus on unique and high-quality products and growing a secure and resilient workforce.

As existing recovery strategies expire and countries develop new long-term strategies, these will need to be under-pinned by concrete action plans and resources for implementation.

Resourcing response and recovery efforts

Delivering on the ambition and strategies for tourism requires resources. Tourism both contributes to government revenues and benefits from government expenditure. The complexity of the sector means it is challenging to precisely identify the level of public funding supporting the sector – this has been amplified since the start of the pandemic with the wide-scale introduction of whole-of-economy measures and support for SMEs (OECD, 2020[19]).

Box 1.5. Multifaceted support to respond to the COVID-19 pandemic – selected country approaches

Australia: In addition to economy-wide assistance, targeted visitor economy support included Business Events Grants (AUD 56 million) to reinvigorate the business travel sector, the Consumer Travel Support Programme (AUD 258 million) to assist businesses including travel agents, inbound tour operators and outbound tour operators, and support for nine regions highly reliant on international tourism via the Recovery for Regional Tourism programme (AUD 50 million). The Tourism and Aviation Network Support programme was introduced to support the aviation sector and drive domestic tourism.

Austria: The tourism sector was supported with several measures administered by the Austrian Bank for Tourism Development including guarantees for bridging loans (cap: EUR 1.6 billion), support for event organisers (cap: EUR 300 million), support for package travel organisers (cap: EUR 300 million) and EUR 10 million to incentivise hospitality businesses to invest in open-air seating. Furthermore, there was support for landlords of private accommodations and farms that offered accommodation services, and a tax relief package, including VAT reductions for accommodation food and drink tax reductions (to 5%). A restart bonus supported part-time employment caused by lower occupancy to top-up salaries in the visitor economy.

Canada: Tourism businesses received an estimated CAD 23 billion in emergency support. In addition to broad programmes such as the Canada Emergency Response Benefit and the Canada Emergency Wage Subsidy, multifaceted COVID relief programmes such as the Tourism and Hospitality Recovery Programme, the Hardest Hit Businesses Programme, the Local Lockdown Programme, and the Canada Recovery Hiring Programme were implemented with supports to tourism business extended until May 2022.

Morocco: Support to employees of tourist companies and guides was provided through a monthly flat-rate allowance, tax exemptions on additional remuneration of employees and the establishment of social cover for tourist guides. Morocco also postponed social security contributions and debt repayments for tourism businesses and provided a partnership agreement to accelerate the development of tourism SMEs in the Souss-Massa region.

Slovak Republic: Established a framework through their Tourism Support Act for the creation of state aid schemes and minimum aid for the tourism sector (totalling EUR 100 million). Offering aid to tourism businesses who suffered revenue losses of 40% or more in 2020, the aim was to maintain employment and ensure the competitiveness of tourism businesses.

Slovenia: Ten packages and a special intervention law were implemented to mitigate the effects of the pandemic, preserve jobs and alleviate corporate liquidity problems. The measures included cash transfers, grants, tax relief, payroll support, loan guarantees for SMEs and tourist vouchers for citizens to boost domestic tourism. Approximately 3.7 million vouchers were redeemed across 2020 and 2021, valued at almost EUR 393 million.

The tourism sector has benefited significantly from these wider economic support measures as well as substantial sector-specific support, such as business grants and loans, regional support, support for niche products and programmes to boost consumer demand. Canada estimates that from the onset of the pandemic to April 2022, the tourism and hospitality sector received an estimated CAD 23 billion in support through federal emergency programmes. Examples of other programmes introduced by governments in response to the COVID-19 pandemic are presented in Box 1.5.

During the pandemic, international marketing budgets were frequently cut or diverted to domestic marketing, and operating budgets for some tourism authorities were impacted by the loss of tax revenues (e.g. tourist, bed and passenger tax). In Greece, a "Tourism for All" programme introduced in 2020 aimed to boost domestic tourism demand, through subsidised stays in hotels and other accommodation. In total, EUR 100 million has been allocated to finance the programme between 2020 and 2025.

For the 2020-21 budget cycles, many countries reported an increase in their core tourism operating budgets. In addition to tourism business supports, marketing is a key driver of this increase in the short-term. In 2021, Visit Sweden's budget allocation included an additional SEK 20 million for domestic marketing, while Destination Canada received CAD 100 million for marketing initiatives in 2021. The United States is providing USD 250 million in relief funding to Brand USA for the fiscal year 2022 to fill a gap in the funding stream due to reduced international visitors. The Estonian Tourist Board funding for development activities has increased from EUR 2.0 million in 2021 to EUR 11.5 million in 2022.

Some countries also invested funds to increase internal capacity. In the 2022/23 budget New Zealand provided an additional NZD 8 million for tourism data and policy, for example, while Australia earmarked AUD 4.8 million to improve tourism data and analysis.

In the European Union, countries are also being supported by additional funds, including within the frame of the Recovery Plan for Europe and the Next Generation EU. Poland for example has tourism specific projects funded by EU structural funds, including the EU Green Deal in the period 2021-27. In Slovenia, the tourism sector is also benefitting from NextGen EU and React EU funds. Under the Tourism Flagship projects, the EU Technical Support Instrument 2022 is supporting the recovery and reform agenda in seven countries – Croatia, Greece, Italy, Malta, Portugal, Slovenia and Spain – to build more sustainable, resilient and digital tourism ecosystems. These projects are focusing on reforms and improvements, including to tourism data and statistics with a focus on the tourism satellite accounts, the development sustainable tourism indicators, governance and destination management tools, and SME supports and digitalisation of the tourism ecosystem.

Many budgets, especially those at the regional and destination level, remain uncertain. Amid the uncertain outlook for tourism, the sector is likely to require ongoing support through this period to ensure that it not only survives but can align to the future strategic objectives for the sector.

Tackling policy priorities for the tourism recovery

The recovery of the tourism sector comes with new and existing challenges. The pandemic led to severe declines in tourism, exposing underlying weaknesses in tourism development models and the wider tourism economy. Initial priorities to encourage and facilitate recovery began with restoring consumer confidence and the operating capacity of businesses, together with restoring the safe mobility of people and supporting businesses financially. A further priority is to address severe workforce shortages to meet the return of tourism demand, and the need for renewed investment in the sector to attract visitors. While these are essential for the sector to rebuild, it is important to consider where the sector should be in the future, ensuring that it builds back better. Governments and businesses must act now so that the short-term actions for recovery have long-term strategic benefits for the sector.

Ensuring safe and seamless mobility, to restore traveller confidence and demand

Tourism depends on the mobility of people. Providing the right conditions to facilitate travel is both a short and long-term requirement, involving measures to foster traveller confidence and enable safe and seamless mobility. Providing seamless and safe travel experiences was already an issue high on the tourism policy agenda before the pandemic and is an integral part of a resilient and inclusive tourism recovery, while also addressing the sustainability agenda.

Travel restrictions put in place to prevent the spread of COVID-19 effectively shut down the tourism system. Recent experience has shown the complexity of lifting these restrictions and getting the interdependent parts of this system back up and running smoothly, especially in a complex sector like aviation. Building visitor confidence in these actions has been needed to encourage people that it is safe to travel, and assure recipient countries, communities and workers that it is safe to receive travellers (OECD, 2021[21]).

A key issue has been virus testing and vaccine recognition, through a co-ordinated approach to ensure that measures do not unnecessarily impede or create obstacles for travellers or remain in place longer than strictly necessary. The return to travel through opening borders and lifting restrictions has been facilitated through the administration of health certificates and vaccination monitoring. Countries have implemented this through vaccination passports for travellers, safe tourism certification programmes for businesses and safe travel zones for cities and countries.

For example, Türkiye introduced the Safe Tourism Certification Programme, which defines and advises an extensive series of measures to be taken regarding transport and accommodation. In Morocco, the Welcome Safely label was set up in collaboration with the health authorities. This includes an online platform to assist accommodation operators in Morocco in adhering to compliance measures. Greece introduced the Health First certification label to certify the compliance of tourist accommodation establishments with the mandatory government-issued health protocols against COVID-19.

Indonesia launched the Cleanliness, Health, Safety and Environmental Sustainability protocol which provided training and certification to prepare for the reopening of the tourism sector post-pandemic. The protocol developed into several handbooks ranging from hotel safety protocol to specific destination models that can be applied to tourism businesses. There is also a certification programme which is renewed annually and has certified almost 12 000 tourism businesses.

The EU Digital COVID-19 Certificate is valid in all EU countries and 49 non-EU countries at time of writing (European Commission, 2022[22]). This allows for the safe crossing of borders, as well as the use of hospitality services in many countries, by showing proof of recent vaccination or recovery from COVID-19. Online platforms like the EU Reopen map and UNWTO/IATA dashboard have also provided information to travellers on travel restrictions and health requirements to facilitate mobility. These schemes remain in place as waves of the pandemic continue. It will also be important to take forward the learnings and experiences from the COVID-19 response to prepare for future health events.

Experience during the pandemic has underlined the need for transparency, consistency and clarity in decision-making and communications about travel. This requires close engagement and co-ordination between governments, tourism, health experts and transport bodies, together with the private sector. The multinational dimension of travel also requires co-operation between countries in tackling safe mobility issues (OECD, 2021[21]). Co-ordinated action and collaboration on agreed standards and the interoperability of systems and technology can help to improve the traveller experience whilst enhancing safety and security, which are especially critical in times of crisis (OECD, 2020[23]).

This has been the driving force behind the OECD Initiative for Safe International Mobility, endorsed by OECD Ministers, which has sought to co-ordinate the work across governments at the national level, between international organisations and with the private sector during the pandemic (Box 1.6). A High-Level Meeting on Safe International Travel brought together both health and tourism decision makers to discuss and identify areas where action could be taken to accelerate safe international travel, facilitate and sustain the return of cross-border travel to pre-pandemic levels and improve preparedness against future global crises.

Extending the focus beyond the safe reopening of travel, and the wider tourism system, to consider the importance of seamless mobility is important for the recovery, and for the future, facilitated by digital technologies. Seamless travel provides a smooth, efficient, safe and enjoyable travel experience from a traveller's point of origin to a destination, within the destination, and back again (OECD, 2020[24]). Restoring consumer confidence in the reliability of the system and integrating digital solutions at borders to simplify travel remain key areas of consideration.

Box 1.6. OECD Initiative for Safe International Mobility

OECD Ministers endorsed an initiative to promote safe international travel during the COVID-19 pandemic, including a safe travel blueprint and a temporary international cross-sectoral forum for knowledge sharing. The forum has allowed governments and stakeholders to share information in real-time on plans and approaches to facilitate travel. The blueprint promotes greater certainty, safety and security in travel as re-opening occurs. It builds on existing initiatives and aims to increase interoperability between travel regimes. It is implemented by countries on a voluntary basis.

A High-Level Meeting on Safe International Travel, hosted by Spain and the OECD in July 2022, brought together ministers, deputy ministers, and high-level authorities mainly responsible for the sectors of health, tourism, and foreign affairs. In the context of international travel, participants identified several issues where improved coordination would be required in order to make international travel safer and easier for travellers. Participants committed to recognise a set of common principles and procedures.

The Chair's Statement highlighted: the impact of the crisis on tourism, the interoperability of digital systems for health certificates recognition among different international approaches for demonstrating vaccination and testing status; responding to new variants of concern by ensuring co-ordinated, evidence-informed and risk-based approaches to travel regulations; the development of a co-ordinated set of risk-based criteria for international mobility; and how such criteria might evolve for use in future pandemics to promote appropriate health measures for travel and advance consistency in policies on international travel.

Source: OECD (2022), High-Level Meeting on Safe International Travel (OECD, 2022[25]).

Supporting fragile tourism businesses to navigate the recovery

Tourism is a highly fragmented and diverse sector, composed of many different branches, and dominated by micro, small and medium-sized enterprises, which represent around 85% of businesses in OECD countries. These small tourism businesses co-exist with, and are often heavily dependent on, each other and the large tourism businesses that structure the sector. The crisis exposed the interdependent nature and fragilities of the tourism economy. What happens in one part of the tourism ecosystem, such as aviation and tour operators, can have profound follow-on effects through the tourism value chain.

The complex tourism system was shut down for an extended period of time through the pandemic and is now facing new challenges and ongoing uncertainties stemming from economic slowdown and Russia's war in Ukraine. Through the shutdown period, tourism businesses benefited from extensive and unprecedented government support. This has included a mix of whole-of-economy support measures (e.g. employee support, tax reductions, business grants or loans) and sector-specific support.

This government support has been essential in protecting and enabling many tourism businesses to survive. However, as pandemic restrictions have been lifted, so too have most of these business supports. Many tourism businesses are in a fragile situation and face ongoing challenges, including limited cash reserves, increased debt, labour and skills shortages and operational uncertainty. This is being compounded by significantly higher prices, energy constraints and an expected sharp slowdown in the economic recovery.

A strong demand-driven recovery in 2022 has helped to boost the cash flows of tourism businesses but may not be enough to maintain these businesses moving forward. As pent-up demand dissipates and the rising cost-of-living crisis starts to put pressure on discretionary tourism budgets, the outlook is highly uncertain, and many tourism businesses are already looking ahead to 2023 with caution.

In this context, tourism businesses will likely require continued support through the recovery phase. Temporary fiscal measures are being used to cushion the immediate impact of higher food and energy costs for consumers and businesses, but these should be balanced against the need to lower energy consumption, limit further demand stimulus at a time of high inflation and ensure debt sustainability (OECD, 2022[10]).

Future support needs to shift from survival mechanisms toward support for the recovery and investment for the future, including for the green and digital transition. As visitors return and travel certainty is restored, businesses can move away from support mechanisms and return to unassisted operating. However, there is a risk that recent positive performance in the sector will see mechanisms removed, leaving businesses to face future disruptions without support.

Business support was one of the most common interventions throughout the pandemic. Countries like Italy and Spain have also acknowledged the need to provide ongoing certainty to businesses by extending their support. For example, Italy has created a national tourism fund that provides tapered funding through 2024 (Box 1.7).

Box 1.7. Fund to support tourism under the National Tourism and Resilience Plan in Italy

The Unique National Tourism Fund was created under the Italian Budget Law for 2022, with a budget of EUR 120 million for the period 2022-23 and EUR 40 million for 2024. This Fund looks to rationalise measures aimed at attracting and promoting tourism in the national territory, supporting operators in the sector in the process of mitigating the effects of the crisis and boosting production and employment in synergy with the measures provided for in Italy's National Recovery and Resilience Plan. The purposes of the Fund include: i) the adoption of safeguarding measures for economic operators in the sector to be able to exploit the potential of the sector in the face of the effects of systemic or sectoral crises, ii) concentrating measures in favour of operators for which conditions remain that limit the ordinary possibility of carrying out productive and working activities, and iii) the promotion of tourism development policies capable of producing positive economic and social impacts on the territories concerned and for the productive and social categories involved.

Businesses took action to adapt their operations to remain viable through the pandemic. This included: managing cash flow and accessing government support to protect businesses; promoting COVID-safe business operations; adapting business models and service offerings; pivoting operations to cater to new markets; supporting the pandemic response effort (OECD, 2020[12]).

They must now take action to react to the changing future. Adopting operating models that respond to changing consumer demands, especially digital and sustainable practices, will be imperative. Governments will need to provide support, especially to SMEs, as this transition takes place.

Tackling labour and skills shortages to rebuild the tourism workforce

Tourism is a highly labour-intensive sector and offers strong potential to support a job-rich recovery for people of all ages and skill levels, including young people, women and migrants. At the same time, the sector is highly dependent on quality human resources to develop and deliver a competitive tourism offer, and to adapt and benefit from the green and digital transitions. Tourism trends and wider transitions are changing the nature of work and highlighting the need to upskill and reskill the tourism workforce to adapt to changing consumer and business needs.

However, the disruption caused by COVID-19 led tourism workers to leave the sector for job opportunities elsewhere in the economy. Tourism workers benefited significantly from the general employee/employment support packages introduced by countries, as well as from targeted supports for the tourism sector. However, these supports did not reach all workers in the sector, including some self-employed and informal workers. Despite this, tourism's share of total employment fell in all reporting countries, and recent OECD analysis highlights that labour supply shortages in hospitality and tourism in November 2021 were more severe than before the pandemic in around 60% of OECD countries (OECD, 2022[5]). This has made it a critical and immediate challenge for the tourism economy.

Workforce shortages have also been exacerbated by longstanding issues impacting the ability of the sector to attract and retain workers (e.g. job insecurity, salary levels, career prospects). Increasing labour market tightness is making it difficult for tourism to compete for the required workforce in a competitive global job market (OECD, 2022[5]). This was further amplified by the rapid increase in tourism demand coming into the summer peak season period in the northern hemisphere in 2022, which could not be well anticipated by the sector, given the ongoing uncertainty linked with the pandemic and the geopolitical environment.

The inability of tourism businesses to attract and retain the labour and skills needed for a strong tourism workforce is having a noticeable impact on the sector's recovery. For example, employment in the aviation sector is expected to remain below the pre-pandemic level for some time. Pre-work requirements like recruitment, training and security checks have presented a well-publicised challenge for the aviation industry in 2022 (IATA, 2022[11]). The interconnected nature of the tourism ecosystem means that shortages experienced in the aviation and transport sectors have critical flow-on effects for all tourism businesses.

To attract the necessary workforce, the sector needs to address longstanding issues in terms of wages, working conditions and reputation. This has been acknowledged through the incorporation of workforce pillars in the recovery plans and long-term strategies developed by many OECD and partner countries, including Australia, Austria, Belgium Wallonia, Estonia, France, Germany, Greece, Lithuania, Poland, Slovak Republic, Slovenia, Spain, Sweden and the United States.

It is also a focus of the European Commission's Transition Pathway for Tourism, which aims to increase fairness and equality in tourism jobs while developing and renewing tourism education in partnership with the industry and education providers (European Commission, 2022[19]). Goals include:

- Strengthening the attractiveness of the tourism sector and knowledge of the diversity of jobs and professional opportunities.
- Facilitating recruitment, particularly in jobs with significant needs for the coming seasons and in view of the major events to come.
- Attracting more young people to training courses leading to these professions.

The EU Pact for Skills – Skills partnership for the tourism ecosystem was launched in 2022 as a partnership to promote joint actions to improve existing skills (upskilling), provide new skills (reskilling) and address labour shortages.

Governments are aware of the issues that workforce shortfalls create for the sector, but may find it challenging to alter the dynamics of the wider labour market, particularly after such a systemic shock. Promoting the acquisition of skills, competencies and qualifications for tourism workers throughout their working lives is at the heart of a human-centred approach to crisis recovery and the future of work (International Labour Organisation, 2022[26]). Improving skills levels, enhancing qualifications, supporting training and developing recruitment initiatives are all ways countries are encouraging talent into the sector (Box 1.8). Action on these issues is needed to support recovery in the short term, but also to ensure a pipeline of new workers coming into the sector via education and training routes in the coming years.

The private sector also must play its role in addressing the labour and skills issues in the tourism sector. Businesses need to consider their action to address internal influences. Global hotel chains like Accor, IHG Hotels and Resorts, Marriott International and Hilton have also recognised the issue, acknowledging that low pay and career prospects are likely to have played a role in current shortages. They are taking steps to increase work and recruitment flexibility and career development.

Small tourism businesses are also taking steps, for example, in re-organising shift patterns and raising wages in the hospitality sector to be more attractive to workers. However, tourism SMEs do not have the capacity and resources to replicate the structures of large enterprises. It may be possible to learn from larger players in the sector or to adapt some practices for use in SMEs, either at the enterprise level or through public-private support programmes. Large enterprises also interact with many SMEs in the tourism value chain, and there may be mutual benefits from working closely on human resource issues.

Box 1.8. Initiatives to enhance workforce skills and recruitment – selected country approaches

France: A communications campaign in 2022 targeted young people aged 16-25 years who are looking for a job or undergoing professional retraining, with a budget of EUR 8 million. The campaign looks to strengthen and perpetuate jobs and skills in the sector to improve the attractiveness of tourism employment. An amplification mechanism is also planned by mobilising all the local institutional players, including schools, training institutions, employment centres, prefectures, regions, professional federations, and the private sector.

Hungary: A campaign to promote employment in the tourism sector aims to encourage students facing a career choice or retraining to choose tourism and hospitality, with short films, image videos and a new website.

Ireland: A new recruitment marketing and awareness campaign was launched in early 2022 to attract people to the sector. Additional initiatives include the creation of a Learning Hub to provide free high-quality, self-directed learning courses to upskill staff and build business capability, and a new Employer Excellence Programme is being developed to support businesses to drive employee engagement and build workplace appeal.

Malta: A EUR 5 million online training programme aims to develop the skills of the tourism workforce and the tourism product. It seeks to ensure that tourism employees have the skills necessary to deliver a high-quality experience to Malta's visitors.

Peru: An online educational platform launched in 2021 provides access to training and certification on topics related to business, digital tools, innovation and commercial intelligence. The Virtual Classroom has more than 5 000 users nationwide.

Poland: A special law easing access to the labour market has been introduced, making refugees from Ukraine eligible for employment even if they did not have a work permit or a population registration number.

Portugal: The Programme "Training + Next" was implemented in January 2022 and aims to train 75 000 professionals over three years, free of charge and adapted to the local needs of each municipality throughout the territory. The programme will implement upskilling and reskilling processes that contribute to adding value to the local business fabric and their respective territories and functions as an instrument to attract talent, including qualifying people from other sectors or unemployed people. Content will be adapted to the diversity of tourism companies and the sector's future needs.

Co-operation between governments and the tourism sector opens up opportunities to create better solutions to this long-term issue and should be explored. For example, the Australian Government is investing in "The Hub" – a portal run by the Australia Accommodation Association – to support new and existing travel and tourism workers seeking to connect to education, employment and other information about building a career in the visitor economy.

The strength and resilience of the sector will depend on its ability to transform itself, which will require the sector to recruit and develop the necessary skills for its future workforce. Tourism lags other sectors in the adoption and use of advanced new technologies. Portugal has recognised the change in the levels of qualifications required by tourism businesses, and is investing in innovative equipment and infrastructure to position the teaching of tourism at a higher level and allow training to be adapted to the new needs and demands of consumers through the Tourism Innovation Centre.

The green transition will also require a new set of skills to meet the growing demand from environment-conscious travellers. Examples of 'green skills' include conducting energy audits, measuring the sustainability of tourism activities, and training staff on recycling programmes (European Commission, 2022[27]).

Focusing investment to support recovery and promote sustainable tourism development

Action to support recovery and build a stronger, more resilient and sustainable tourism economy for the future will require ongoing investment and the provision of appropriate, necessary and quality infrastructure to meet the needs of the sector and local communities. Governments will need to ensure the sector can resume and keep innovating and transforming, while tourism businesses and destinations need to adjust their offer to respond to digital and other trends, as well as the need for structural and sustainability transformations.

In recent years, successful tourism destinations have established and maintained programmes to attract internal and external direct investment in tourism products and operations and to maintain a public sector budget to support tourism-related services and destination management. The COVID-19 pandemic has placed significant additional strain on these programmes and created additional risk in the sector for investors and lenders (OECD, 2021[21]). Russia's war in Ukraine brought a further negative shock and disruption to the world economy, which had a profound and immediate impact on Foreign Direct Investment (FDI) and other capital flows (OECD, 2022[28]).

FDI in tourism remained low in 2021 and the first half of 2022. Ongoing geopolitical uncertainty, an inflationary global economy, disruption of international supply chains, increasing workforce shortages and growing pressures on consumers' cost of living has put capital expenditure plans across the tourism sector on hold (UNWTO, 2022[29]). This will impact the longer-term investment that is required to provide accommodation, transport and other tourism-related services and the infrastructure necessary to meet demand while enhancing economic, social and environmental outcomes.

Investment and access to finance are needed at the individual business level. Tourism businesses will need support to update service delivery, pivot to alternative markets and adjust business models, take advantage of new opportunities and integrate digital and low-carbon solutions. However, after two years of limited operations and multiple closures, tourism businesses now have limited cash reserves to relaunch and invest in their business, with SMEs facing particular challenges. Investment programmes will be necessary to incentivise actions amid ongoing uncertainty and an already challenging risk profile for tourism.

Many countries acknowledge the need to update and modernise products and develop destinations to meet tourists changing expectations and are taking action to address this. In Canada, for example, the Tourism Relief Fund provides financing for product and destination development (Box 1.9). Spain has introduced a EUR 720 million package for tourism, with EUR 565 million to finance projects that enhance innovation and competitiveness through the greater use of digital technologies, energy efficiency and sustainable practices. In 2022, Chile committed CLP 18 million to promote participation in international tourism investment events, disseminate sector opportunities in priority markets and improve information for investment decision-making. A commitment of this agreement and the Action Plan for Attracting

Tourism Investment 2020-25 is the creation of an international agenda that will consider international tour development and round tables with investors and sectoral workshops, among other activities.

Creating a more sustainable and competitive tourism offering also requires investment in public infrastructure. Mexico has taken a proactive approach by developing tourist bicycle lanes to connect local communities and allowing visitors to travel to natural and cultural destinations. The *Ciclovía Maya*, the largest tourist bikeway in the world, will connect and integrate economic activities for dozens of local communities in the Yucatan Peninsula. This initiative will promote sustainable mobility and 'zero emissions tourism'.

Successful policy intervention will require significant co-operation and co-ordinated strategies across government, and between different levels of government, as part of a comprehensive national long-term plan, given the length of time needed to realise sustainable development. It also demands the involvement of the private sector and civil society and the sharing of best practices and new ideas between the various actors driving the shift to a new model of sustainable tourism development (OECD, 2021[21]).

Box 1.9. Tourism Relief Fund to support product and destination development in Canada

In Canada, the Tourism Relief Fund provides CAD 500 million to the tourism sector across 2021-23. The Fund comprises CAD 485 million delivered by the Regional Development Agencies and CAD 15 million for a national project component provided by the Department of Innovation, Science and Economic Development. Eligible projects fall under one of two themes:

- **Product Development:** to support projects that enhance tourism experiences, help tourism businesses adapt to the 'new normal,' modernise tourism offerings, and encourage the sector to adopt more environmentally sustainable practices.
- **Destination Development:** to support projects that can help communities take advantage of post-pandemic opportunities through strategic planning for medium to long-term investments and supporting destination development.

The national component of the Fund supports pan-Canadian and national stakeholder associations to help their members address challenges at a national level. These include measures to assist in labour market skills development and recruitment, strategies for digital adoption, and bolstering organisational capacity.

The Tourism Relief Fund also includes CAD 50 million dedicated to Indigenous tourism initiatives to support tourism businesses in adapting their operations to meet public health requirements while investing in products and services for future growth.

Reshaping a more sustainable, resilient and inclusive future for tourism

The crisis is an opportunity to rethink the tourism system, and move toward fairer, more sustainable and resilient models of tourism development. This will require policies that address structural weaknesses that have impeded the sector in the past, and avoid a return to the tourism management and unbalanced development issues facing the sector before the crisis. Policy interventions will also be necessary to advance the digital and low-carbon transitions. Governments need to consider these issues as they design and put in place comprehensive tourism recovery strategies and action plans.

Economic and social factors to be addressed include seasonality of demand, economic leakages, overcrowding and overconsumption, exclusion and inequity, overdependence on tourism, poor remuneration and career prospects and low financial margins. Urgent action is also needed on climate change, and the mitigation and adaptation measures required of the tourism economy. At the same time, it is recognised that these issues and impacts vary considerably between destinations (OECD, 2021[14]). Actions need to be taken to reshape the future of tourism, moving away from a growth-at-all-costs model and towards a competitive, sustainable, digital, inclusive and resilient future.

Promoting the digital transition to benefit all tourism stakeholders

The evolution and application of digital technologies are profoundly changing the way people live, work, travel and do business, and are transforming and reshaping tourism. However, the resulting opportunities also present challenges to the level playing field, including a growing gap between tech-driven and globally connected tourism businesses and traditional micro and small businesses often characterised by low-tech business practices (OECD, 2021[21]).

The pandemic has accelerated many of these trends, and the digitalisation of the tourism sector continues to be a priority for OECD and partner countries. Digital technologies present wide-reaching opportunities to facilitate increased reach to consumers, productivity, and the transition to a more sustainable and inclusive future. Policies are needed to promote equity and inclusiveness, delivering benefits to micro and small businesses and local communities as well as to visitors (OECD, 2021[14]). Policies also need to consider the new challenges that digitalisation presents including increase cyber and data security and technical support, particularly for SMEs.

Many countries are encouraging and facilitating the digital transition for tourism businesses. Initiatives include providing new digital platforms, education, digital services and funding. Bulgaria, for example, sees SME digital enhancements as the key to increasing competitiveness and contributing to a green transition. Cross-government collaboration has enabled Bulgaria to transform SMEs in the tourism sector and digitalise cultural heritage as part of the National Recovery and Resilience Plan. Estonia is running master classes in service design and digitalisation of services for tourism companies for the second consecutive year. Greece is also developing a unique electronic register for tourism enterprises (e-MHTE) to improve the quality of services and enhance interoperability with new applications and systems.

Latvia is implementing programmes to support the digitalisation of processes, training of digital skills and development of new digital products. The Tourism Transitions Programme in New Zealand has a similar focus. In Portugal, only 47% of companies in the accommodation and restaurant sectors currently have websites. A new Upgrade Training Programme, part of Portugal's Reactivate Tourism – Building the Future plan, is focused on ensuring businesses are connected as a priority. Serbia has introduced a central information system that combines data on all accommodation providers and accommodation facilities. Canada launched the Canada Digital Adoption Program to support SMEs, including tourism businesses, to capitalise on digital opportunities.

In Lithuania, the TravelTech Sandbox is an online platform to welcome innovators to its growing TravelTech ecosystem, providing the right conditions for sandboxing ideas that can potentially change the market. Iceland has also mapped the digital needs of its tourism companies and developed a digital 'sandbox' – a platform to support innovation in tourism stimulated by partnerships with technology companies.

Digitalisation also provides opportunities to use technology to provide solutions for wider sectoral issues such as the green transition and sustainable tourism management. Sweden has developed a digital knowledge bank and a national monitoring system to move towards greater sustainability in tourism. Italy is exploring medium to long-term solutions by creating a Digital Tourism Hub to connect and promote the country's tourism offer, better manage tourism flows and promote sustainable tourism. It aims to address the high fragmentation of the Italian tourism ecosystem, particularly the regional differences and the gap across different tourism destinations and businesses. Outside of tourism management, Korea is harnessing innovative digital technology to market and provide unique experiences through a metaverse platform (Box 1.10).

Box 1.10. Developing a metaverse platform for tourism in Korea

To entice the digitally sensitive future generation who are potential tourists to Korea and to raise awareness of Korea as a safe destination, Korea has been exploring the use of new and innovative technology in tourism promotion: the metaverse platform. The metaverse is a virtual space within the digital environment where users can work, play, socialise, and travel. This targets the Gen Z consumer, the generation referred to as 'digital natives' who grew up with smartphones and tablets.

Korea has re-created the Han river park on 'Zepeto,' an Augmented Reality avatar game platform with over 200 million players worldwide, to provide various digital travel experiences. Players can enjoy water activities that are available on the Han river, such as riding on a yacht, water taxi, tubester (a tube-boat for up to six people), and kayak. Other popular Han river experiences for international tourists are also available, including visiting the night market and enjoying Korean-style fried chicken and ramen on the riverside.

Beyond the 3D virtual experiences within the game, Korea collaborated with the K-pop idol ITZY to better promote Korea as a tourist destination to K-pop fans, hosted multiple cultural events and competitions on the platform, and collaborated with digital influencers to build the interest of future visitors. Korea plans to expand its digital landscape further and re-create more popular tourist attractions, international meetings, incentives, conference and events platforms and online travel agency markets on metaverse platforms.

Diversifying the tourism offer and markets to build resilience

The impacts of the crisis on tourism have been asymmetrical, with some countries, destinations, businesses and people more exposed than others. Better planning and more community engagement are required (OECD, 2021[21]). Too many destinations have been over-dependent on tourism, which might have been avoided by seeking tourism growth within the context of broader economic and regional development planning. Tourism value chains become less vulnerable if the businesses involved have access to a range of sources of income. Destinations and businesses with a diversified market base are also generally less exposed to potential market failure.

Diversifying the tourism ecosystem needs a strategic approach, considering all facets of the tourism offer, including:

- **A varied visitor mix that is not overly reliant on a single source market.** During the pandemic, most countries shifted marketing efforts to increase domestic tourism demand. This was an essential strategy to fill the gap from the loss of the international market due to cross-border travel restrictions. As tourism recovered, countries have embraced the importance of domestic tourism but are also reconsidering the (over) reliance on specific international markets.
- **The dispersal of visitors geographically and seasonally.** Heavy visitation volumes in popular destinations have a negative impact on both tourists and the community. An over-reliance on a single location or season makes the entire tourism ecosystem susceptible to shocks. Countries are looking to create a more even spread of visitors by dispersing visitors to regional destinations or providing new off-peak experiences.
- **A unique and varied product offering is essential for sustainable and resilient tourism.** For example, venue-based activities (e.g. theatre, cinema, museums) were heavily affected by social distancing measures during the pandemic, with immediate impacts on revenues and livelihoods and wider value chains, like tourism (OECD, 2022[30]). Inversely, some of these culture-based

products also rely on tourism revenues. By diversifying the product offering to include both indoor and outdoor activities and attractions, destinations would be less impacted by shocks.

Encouraging innovation in the development of visitor experiences and diversifying all areas of the tourism ecosystem will build resilience, better protecting it against future shocks. The tourism offer and product base may need to be adapted to meet new markets. Structural shifts in the market, notably for business tourism, need to be addressed and are evoking new and innovative responses. This is explored further in Chapter 2 on Building Resilience in the Tourism Ecosystem [CFE/TOU(2021)2/PART2].

Countries are adopting several approaches to build a more diversified tourism economy. Slovenia has implemented strategies to increase visitation to popular national parks outside of peak summer periods. The Czech Republic launched a spa voucher scheme to discount stays in spa locations. Croatia plans to build tourism destinations beyond Dubrovnik to reduce reliance on the city.

Innovation stemming from a co-ordinated approach with related sectors could help to create a more diverse offering in destinations. For example, by leveraging the potential synergies between the tourism, cultural and creative sectors, including the ability to leverage the benefits of cultural and creative tourism to address sustainability and to disperse tourists across different cities, towns and places (OECD, 2022[31]).

Strengthening the capacity of destinations to manage tourism sustainably

Before the pandemic, there was already a growing recognition of the need for tourism to be better managed, to deliver development that is economically, socially and environmentally balanced. This has intensified since the crisis, as the return of tourism also brings pressures on destinations. Many resilience and sustainability issues are best tackled at the local destination level, to address diverse and specific needs, with broad stakeholder engagement and involvement of local tourism communities. Co-ordinated policy approaches are needed to support this, along with improved capacity of government at all levels, and the private sector. Many places are placing a new priority on destination management planning, addressing issues such as the geographic and temporal spread of visitation, and involving close consultation with local communities.

A key part of this process involves feeding impacts and experiences from the sub-national level into the development of national tourism plans and strategies, and then developing local and regional plans that align with and support the delivery of desired outcomes (OECD, 2021[32]). For example, Colombia's integrated destination management strategy relies on the systemic planning and management of activities, resources and stakeholders involved in the development of tourism in the territory. It includes the definition, execution and follow-up of policies aimed at facilitating the consolidation of the destination. Colombia works with destinations within their territorial context, development needs and individual challenges to develop synergies between local governments, stakeholders, the private sector and communities to achieve sustainability.

Consistent destination management requires adequate funding. However, evidence from countries suggests that destination management also requires:

- **Strong working connections:** robust connections between national, regional and local interests increase the opportunities for long-term success.
- **A clear understanding of roles and responsibilities at each level:** activities such as the delivery of marketing and management measures must be defined with exact roles clearly agreed upon.
- **A jointly agreed plan in place:** this should be a practical, actions-based plan related to the national strategy. It typically has a common vision and clear goals and is focused on a relatively small number of core priorities which are regularly evaluated.

Box 1.11. New approaches to regional and destination management - selected country initiatives

Bulgaria: Nine Regional Tourism Management Organisations' were established in 2018-19. New projects were launched for 2019-22 to support the organisations' functioning and capacity building for effective tourism management at the destination level. These focused on providing support for the creation and functioning of the management organisations and improving the quality of services of SMEs in tourism through the use of ICT and web-based marketing.

Greece: New legislation has been introduced to facilitate the establishment of Destination Management and Marketing Organisations (DMMOs) as a critical factor for sustainable management and growth of tourism destinations. The task of the DMMOs is to create a stable and effective co-operation framework between the public and private sectors, thus ensuring continuity in the promotion of tourism products and the quality of services provided. Funded under the Recovery and Resilience Plan, each DMMO will have a Sustainable Tourism Development Observatory to access and monitor data for the integrated planning of tourism strategies.

Hungary: A new destination management services network will implement unified management and support the co-operation of local stakeholders to achieve a shared vision for the destination. The aim is for the destination management services to ensure effective communication between local and central levels and within the destination to promote a destination-based approach to product development and successful market entry.

Netherlands: The Centre of Expertise Leisure, Tourism and Hospitality (CELTH) has a multi-year "Conscious Destination" knowledge agenda for the hospitality domain based on five urgent themes: living environment, human capital, organisational capacity, smartness and leisure offer. The Conscious Destination strives for an outcome in which tourism has the most positive possible social, ecological and economic impact and leads to the highest possible quality of life, experience and work. The destination level is expressly chosen because that is where all the different sub-sectors and actors come together.

New Zealand: Regional Tourism Organisations (RTOs) have traditionally been responsible for promoting their destinations and recently assumed leadership in bringing together local stakeholders to develop destination management plans. The RTOs' destination management work has been accelerated through COVID-19 funding packages and with the support of their membership organisation, Regional Tourism New Zealand.

Norway: Regional reforms were initiated in 2020 to give counties renewed roles and wider responsibilities. This is expected to provide a more efficient framework to solve cross-sectoral challenges for the tourism industry's benefit.

The sustainable management of tourism involves the strengthening of local governance structures and giving a strong voice to local communities (OECD, 2021[14]). Destination management organisations (DMO) can mobilise stakeholders to work together, creating co-ordinated action in destinations and producing better outcomes for the tourism sector. This includes engaging directly with the local community. Visit Berlin has recently taken a new approach to community engagement by implementing the Citizen Advisory Council for Tourism, which will be made up of two volunteer members from each of the 12 districts to help develop ideas for sustainable and city-compatible tourism (Berlin City, 2022[33]).

Actions have been taken by many OECD and partner countries to support destination management by implementing new DMO structures, reviewing existing operating models and providing capacity-building activities for the regions, a strategic focus for many countries (Box 1.11). The United Kingdom undertook an independent review of their destination management systems and have committed to a number of responses, including a new accreditation system and a new tiered funding model (Box 2.10).

The need to enhance destination management is also acknowledged at the international level. For example, Pacific Asia Travel Association's Tourism Destination Resilience programme combines risk assessment, risk management and adaptive capacity building through 10 online modules which cover steps required for destination resilience and long-term sustainability (PATA, 2022[34]).

Improving the evidence base for data-driven decision making

Improving the evidence base to inform policy and business decisions is a key policy priority. Effective policy making, planning and management all rely on the availability of robust evidence, preferably in the form of reliable and timely data that is sufficiently disaggregated and comparable across destinations and territorial levels. More progress is also needed to better measure the economic, environmental and social dimensions of tourism, and develop timely and robust indicators and tools to monitor the effectiveness of tourism policies and the resilience and sustainability of tourism development.

The pandemic highlighted shortcomings in the existing tourism data and information systems, further strengthening the need for more integrated, timely, comparable and granular data. The lack of robust, comparable and timely data to quantify the impact of the crisis on tourism inhibited evidence-based decision-making for policy makers and businesses. Countries responded by looking beyond traditional survey approaches to capture information in a more timely manner using alternate and complementary data sources. This includes a better use of administrative data sources, anonymised real-time data from mobile phones, transaction data from banks and credit card providers and bookings data (Box 1.12). The European Commission (Eurostat) is also compiling data from four major booking platforms – Airbnb, Booking.com, TripAdvisor and Expedia Group.

The shortcomings in the availability of timely, comparable, granular data in quickly evolving situations mean reliable and consistent indicators are needed to evaluate the effectiveness of programmes and initiatives and monitor progress on tourism recovery and resilience (OECD, 2020[12]). This extends beyond the current crisis period, with the measurement of sustainability and resilience through indicators a key priority for countries and international organisations alike. Better data is needed to inform the design and implementation of tourism policies and programmes, and influence the behaviour of consumers and practices of businesses, including for greener outcomes.

Alternate and complementary data sources provide an opportunity for the development of more diverse and timely indicators for decision-making. However, understanding the challenges and balancing the trade-offs of potential data sources is essential, and the best long-term solution is likely a combination of new and official data. Alternate data sources can be expensive, and the lack of targeted information may have relatively low utility compared with survey data, especially for the compilation of official economic statistics like the Tourism Satellite Account. Access is a further challenge.

The renewed interest in data and data sharing has been one of the opportunities presented through COVID-19. This has created a closer collaboration between government ministries, tourism bodies and national statistical organisations. Brazil has made a wide range of tourism data available through the General Co-ordination of Data and Information. This includes official data produced by the tourism and labour ministries, the federal police, and the Institute of Geography and Statistics, as well as information provided by the tourism associations.

Norway is working on a national monitor, which uses big data and analytical tools to give a more comprehensive view of the tourism sector. Hungary has initiated partnerships with the private sector to exploit similar opportunities, focusing on labour market data for hospitality. At a European level, data and data sharing is an important pillar of the EC Transition Pathway for Tourism.

Maintaining this momentum will be important to not miss this opportunity and continue to build on the current foundations. More timely and comprehensive data is important not only to mitigate future crises, but also to ensure the continued sustainable development of the sector. Linked to this, the development of data and indicators measuring the sustainability of tourism is a focus of much attention at national and sub-national levels, and at the international level. Work is underway to develop and pilot a core set of sustainable tourism indicators at the sub-national level, under Spain's Recovery and Resilience Programme, for example. Eurostat is working to prepare a common set of sustainable tourism indicators, while the EU Tourism Dashboard brings together existing data to understand the country and regional tourism performance under the pillars of digitalisation, environmental impacts and socio-economic vulnerability. The UNWTO, in partnership with UN Statistical Division and leading countries, is developing an international statistical framework for Measuring the Sustainability of Tourism, to guide the production of reliable and comparable data on the social, economic and environmental aspects of tourism.

Significant improvements and innovative data approaches are needed to adapt to the new data environment, meet changing user needs, and enable more effective data-driven policy decisions, including integrating non-conventional data sources and methods into the tourism data ecosystem. Meanwhile, digitalisation has opened up new opportunities to support data-driven policy decisions and meet the policy demand for new, more granular and more timely data in a rapidly changing world.

Box 1.12. Data-driven policy development and monitoring

To address ongoing information gaps at a time when traditional visitor surveys have become more difficult to maintain, countries have resorted to new data sources to track the performance of tourism (including recovery prospects) and develop policy. A survey of OECD and partner countries in 2022 found that more than half of respondents were utilising new data or experimental methods to measure the performance of tourism. The most common data types included:

- **Bank or credit card transactions data:** being utilised or initiated by Austria, Denmark, Estonia, Greece, Hungary, Italy, Korea, New Zealand, Portugal, Spain and Sweden.
- **Tracking aviation bookings or performance:** being utilised by Austria, Canada, Czech Republic, Denmark, Estonia, Finland, Hungary, Italy, Malta and Portugal.
- **Tracking hotel bookings or performance:** being utilised by Austria, Denmark, Estonia, Finland, Hungary, Italy, Malta and Spain.
- **Administrative data:** monthly survey (Serbia), border crossing and visa information (Canada, Costa Rica, Spain and the United States) and pension services data to measure employment (Croatia, Estonia).
- **Mobile positioning data:** being utilised or piloted by Austria, Denmark, Estonia, Hungary, Indonesia, Portugal and Spain.

Canada has developed a composite index to track a more holistic measure of tourism activity against previous levels. Italy is looking to utilise behavioural insights to understand and influence sustainable behaviours for tourists and tourism businesses.

To understand future performance, nine countries were considering forecasts (either internally developed or purchased). The majority of these expect tourism to return to 2019 levels in 2024 or later.

References

APEC (2022), *Policy Recommendations for Tourism of the Future: Regenerative Tourism*, https://www.apec.org/meeting-papers/sectoral-ministerial-meetings/tourism/11th-apec-tourism-ministerial-meeting/policy-recommendations-for-tourism-of-the-future-regenerative-tourism. [18]

Berlin City (2022), *Berlin gets a citizen advisory council for tourism*, https://www.berlin.de/en/news/7711047-5559700-berlin-gets-new-citizens-council-tourism.en.html. [33]

European Commission (2022), *EU Digital COVID Certificate*, https://ec.europa.eu/info/live-work-travel-eu/coronavirus-response/safe-covid-19-vaccines-europeans/eu-digital-covid-certificate_en. [22]

European Commission (2022), *New taxonomy of skills for the green transition*, https://ec.europa.eu/newsroom/empl/items/741088/en. [27]

European Commission (2022), *Transition pathway for tourism*, https://data.europa.eu/doi/10.2873/344425. [19]

Eurostat (2022), *Tourism data database*, https://ec.europa.eu/eurostat/web/tourism/data/database. [7]

ForwardKeys (2022), *2022 summer travel trends: record breaking summer for flights to Greece and Turkey*, https://forwardkeys.com/2022-summer-travel-trends/. [9]

IATA (2022), *Global outlook for air transport - June 2022*, https://www.iata.org/en/iata-repository/publications/economic-reports/airline-industry-economic-performance---june-2022---report/. [11]

ICAO (2021), *Council Aviation Recovery Taskforce (CART)*, https://www.icao.int/covid/cart/Pages/default.aspx. [13]

International Labour Organisation (2022), *Technical meeting on COVID-19 and sustainable recovery in the tourism sector*, https://www.ilo.org/sector/activities/sectoral-meetings/WCMS_824066/lang--en/index.htm. [26]

OECD (2022), *Economic Outlook, Interim Report September 2022: Paying the price of war.*, https://www.oecd.org/economic-outlook/september-2022/. [10]

OECD (2022), *Economic Outlook, November 2022: Confronting the crisis*, https://doi.org/10.1787/f6da2159-en. [8]

OECD (2022), *Employment Outlook 2022*, https://www.oecd.org/employment-outlook/2022/. [5]

OECD (2022), *G20 TWG Discussion Paper on tourism and cultural and creative sectors*. [31]

OECD (2022), *High-Level Meeting on Safe International Travel*, https://www.oecd.org/health/safe-international-travel/. [25]

OECD (2022), *International investment implications of Russia's war against Ukraine*, https://www.oecd-ilibrary.org/finance-and-investment/international-investment-implications-of-russia-s-war-against-ukraine_a24af3d7-en;jsessionid=0YTWIB_hhafMMhdPJK42ytgtHUuZbexF8SB86uHV.ip-10-240-5-110. [28]

OECD (2022), *Regions and cities at a glance 2022*, https://www.oecd.org/regional/oecd-regions-and-cities-at-a-glance-26173212.htm. [2]

OECD (2022), *The Culture Fix: Creative people, places and industries*, https://www.oecd.org/cfe/the-culture-fix-991bb520-en.htm. [30]

OECD (2021), *G20 Rome guidellines for the future of tourism*, https://www.oecd-ilibrary.org/industry-and-services/g20-rome-guidelines-for-the-future-of-tourism_d11080db-en. [21]

OECD (2021), *Managing tourism development for sustainable and inclusive recovery*, https://www.oecd-ilibrary.org/industry-and-services/managing-tourism-development-for-sustainable-and-inclusive-recovery_b062f603-en. [32]

OECD (2021), *OECD global forum on touirsm statisitics, knowledge and policies: Reshaping touirsm for a more resilient and sustainable tomorrow*, https://www.oecd.org/industry/tourism/Highlights-Global-Forum-on-Tourism-%20Statistics-Knowledge-and-Policies.pdf. [14]

OECD (2020), *Coronavirus (COVID-19): SME Policy responses*, https://www.oecd.org/coronavirus/policy-responses/coronavirus-covid-19-sme-policy-responses-04440101/#section-d1e3087. [20]

OECD (2020), *Mitigating the impact of COVID-19 on tourism and supporting the recovery.*, https://www.oecd-ilibrary.org/industry-and-services/mitigating-the-impact-of-covid-19-on-tourism-and-supporting-recovery_47045bae-en. [12]

OECD (2020), *Policy Responses to Coronavirus (COVID-19), From pandemic to recovery: Local employment and economic development*, https://read.oecd-ilibrary.org/view/?ref=130_130810-m60ml0s4wf&title=From-pandemic-to-recovery-Local-employment-and-economic-development. [3]

OECD (2020), *Safe and seamless travel and improved traveller experience*, https://www.oecd-ilibrary.org/industry-and-services/safe-and-seamless-travel-and-improved-traveller-experience_d717feea-en. [23]

OECD (2020), *Safe and seamless travel and improved traveller experience: OECD report to G20 Tourism Working Group*, https://www.oecd.org/cfe/tourism/Safe-and-seamless-travel-and-improved-traveller-experience-OECDReport-for-the-G20-TWG_merged.pdf. [24]

OECD (2019), *Providing new OECD evidence on tourism trade in value added*, https://www.oecd-ilibrary.org/industry-and-services/providing-new-oecd-evidence-on-tourism-trade-in-value-added_d6072d28-en. [4]

PATA (2022), *Tourism Destination Resilience*, https://crc.pata.org/tourism-destination-resilience/. [34]

Rustelli, E. and D. Turner (2021), *The economic costs of restricting international mobility*, https://www.oecd-ilibrary.org/docserver/dcad4c73-en.pdf?expires=1664197374&id=id&accname=ocid84004878&checksum=7A0CC933A8EE0639A7276CF4044E911E. [1]

UN (2020), *Policy Brief: COVID-19 and transforming tourism*, https://unsdg.un.org/resources/policy-brief-covid-19-and-transforming-tourism. [15]

UNWTO (2022), *Tourism Investment Report 2022*, https://www.unwto.org/investment/tourism-investment-report-2022. [29]

UNWTO (2022), *World Tourism Barometer, September 2022*, https://www.unwto.org/taxonomy/term/347. [6]

World Bank (2020), *Rebuilding Tourism Competitiveness: Tourism response, recovery and resilience to the COVID-19 crisis*, https://openknowledge.worldbank.org/handle/10986/34348. [16]

WTO (2020), *International trade in travel and tourism services: economic impact and policy responses during the COVID-19 crisis*, https://www.wto.org/english/res_e/reser_e/ersd202011_e.htm. [17]

Notes

[1] Reporting countries: Australia, Austria, Canada, Chile, Colombia, Czech Republic, Denmark, Finland, France, Greece, Hungary, Iceland, Israel, Italy, Lithuania, Luxembourg, Mexico, Netherlands, New Zealand, Portugal, Slovak Republic, Slovenia, Spain, Sweden, Switzerland, Türkiye, United Kingdom, United States.

[2] Reporting countries: Australia, Austria, Canada, the Czech Republic, Denmark, Finland, Israel, Lithuania, Luxembourg, Mexico, Netherlands, New Zealand, Sweden, Switzerland and the United States.

[3] Reporting countries: Australia, Austria, Belgium, Canada, Chile, Colombia, Czech Republic, Denmark, Estonia, Finland, France, Germany, Greece, Hungary, Iceland, Ireland, Israel, Italy, Japan, Latvia, Lithuania, Luxembourg, Netherlands, Norway, Poland, Portugal, Slovak Republic, Slovenia, Spain, Sweden, Türkiye and United States.

Chapter 2. Building resilience in the tourism ecosystem

Continued growth in tourism over six decades led to the widely held belief in the inherent resilience of the tourism economy. However, consecutive global shocks have demonstrated the importance of building systemic resilience across the tourism ecosystem. This chapter provides analyses policy approaches to support the recovery and enhance the resilience of the tourism economy for the future, with a focus on the COVID-19 pandemic. It considers actions to boost tourism recovery prospects, tackle the long-term consequences of the crisis, and better prepare for future shocks, while encouraging the shift to more resilient, sustainable and inclusive models of tourism. Key policy considerations are identified to set a path forward for policy makers to address structural weaknesses and to build resilience in the tourism ecosystem.

As the tourism economy recovers from the devastating impacts of the COVID-19 pandemic, it faces new uncertainties from Russia's war of aggression in Ukraine. In addressing these immediate and pressing priorities, governments must take action to optimise the strength and quality of the tourism recovery. The crisis triggered by the pandemic is an opportunity to build back greener and more inclusive. There is also a need to enhance the resilience of the sector, undertake structural reform and ensure tourism is better placed to adapt and respond to the impacts of future shocks, natural or man-made. Action is needed now to build on this momentum, or risk being forgotten once the recovery comes.

Resilience is an underdeveloped topic in tourism. Continued growth in tourism over six decades led to the widely held belief in the inherent resilience of the tourism economy. Further work is needed to understand tourism resilience and the implications for tourism planning and development, including capacity building. This is true for policy makers and businesses alike. Current resilience actions in tourism are generally aligned with crisis management and sustainability concepts, and measurement is focused on recovery. Individually, these components help to build resilience in the tourism ecosystem – and enable the sector to adapt and respond in the face of a crisis – but they lack the forward-looking systemic focus needed to drive resilience.

The length and depth of the pandemic and the consequences of Russia's war in Ukraine mean the tourism sector remains in 'recovery mode'. While many countries have experienced a rapid return of tourism demand in 2022, rising inflation and the slowdown in economic recovery are likely to have flow-on effects into next year as discretionary spending tightens. Therefore, it might yet take some time to understand the impacts, both direct and indirect, of the pandemic and the tourism response strategies that were effective. As governments and businesses shift focus towards the longer term, it is important to already consider how to minimise or avoid disruptive impacts from future shocks and strengthen the tourism economy more generally.

Tourism has been proven vulnerable to exogenous shocks, but the crisis has also highlighted underlying endogenous weaknesses. It is these endogenous weaknesses that policy makers and businesses must look to proactively address, to build systemic resilience while creating opportunities for future growth. This chapter seeks to better understand the concept of resilience as it relates to tourism. Endogenous vulnerabilities in the tourism ecosystem are explored, with a strong focus on the COVID-19 pandemic. This is considered through the lens of institutional intervention and support measures. Strategies and frameworks to address these vulnerabilities are presented, drawing on examples of recent actions within the tourism sector, and from resilience work in other sectors. Finally, the chapter sets out a path forward for policy makers to integrate resilience thinking into tourism strategies and decision-making.

Setting the scene: tourism resilience, crisis management and sustainability

Resilience refers to the capacity to absorb disturbance, recover from disruption and adapt to changing conditions while retaining essentially the same function as prior to the shock. It goes beyond risk management and concerns the performance of the economic system once a threat has materialised (Hynes et al., 2020[1]) It is characterised by the speed and strength of recovery, in particular through adaptation and transformation.

Resilience relates to action both before and after an event occurs:

- **Prior to a shock:** Actions to mitigate the risk and limit the size of the impact by detecting endogenous vulnerabilities and reducing the future impact.
- **After a shock:** Actions to promote recovery through adaptation and transformation, particularly through learning from previous crises and adapting to better deal with future threats of a similar nature (OECD, 2021[2]).

Box 2.1. Adapting to changing business tourism trends

There has been a strong shift in business tourism trends since the start of the pandemic, and this is being further impacted by the acceleration of digitalisation and remote working. Pre-pandemic, business travel represented approximately 12% of global international tourism arrivals, or 175 million visitors in 2018 (UNWTO, 2021[3]). The advances in information and communication technology required to sustain economies through prolonged global shutdowns have significantly decreased, at least in the short term, the perceived need for business travel, with in-person meetings and conferences being replaced by virtual and hybrid options.

Some parts of the sector are adapting to the new virtual workspace by promoting 'digital nomadism' rather than relying on a complete recovery of business travel. Accommodation provider Accor has recognised that international business travel is unlikely to return to previous patterns, replaced by virtual and hybrid meetings. Instead, Accor is looking to the rise of digital nomadism, especially among younger generations, and its potential to fill some of this gap. Accor is adapting to provide co-living spaces that include hotel services and combine a place to live with a place to work and focus on the local use of hotels (Accor, 2020[4]).

Countries such as Costa Rica, Estonia, Greece and Iceland also looking to build on this trend. Costa Rica has introduced legislation to attract 'digital nomads', Iceland has introduced a long-term visa for remote workers, and Estonia introduced a visa for teleworking which allows remote workers to live in Estonia and legally work for their employer or own company registered abroad for up to a year. A new law has been established in Greece to introduce a series of incentives and visas for digital nomads.

The tourism sector has already shown signs of adaptation, shifting to take advantage of new business tourism trends (Box 2.1). However, tourism policies and strategies need to take into account all dimensions of resilience to prepare for future shocks. This includes a particular focus on impact absorption and recovery through adaptation and transformation, which may require different but complementary policy actions.

Crisis management relates to the actions during a crisis to reduce the initial negative impacts. Previous OECD Tourism Committee work has called on policy makers to develop crisis management strategies to better prepare for and respond to largely unpredictable events, such as security incidents, political instabilities, pandemics and natural disasters (OECD, 2018[5]). While strong risk management and crisis management plans are imperative for tourism, the current crisis has highlighted the need to consider also the recovery phase and take action to prepare for future shocks. Resilience builds beyond the initial shock and considers the actions to recover and adapt once the crisis has subsided.

Resilience and sustainability are interdependent but distinct concepts. Sustainable development meets the needs of the present without compromising the ability of future generations to meet their own needs. It requires the harmonisation of economic growth, social inclusion and environmental protection (United Nations, 2022[6]), and can be addressed through initiatives like building a circular economy. Strategies for sustainable tourism development typically take into account existing trends and forecasts, and consider the actions required to shape economic activity for future prosperity. This differs from resilience, which is focused on the ability to endure and recover from a shock.

A tourism business or destination that is economically viable, has minimal negative environmental impact and has positive community outcomes is more likely to be resilient in the face of adversity. There can also be compounding positive effects for resilience, as a more stable and sustainable environment leads to fewer shocks in the future. This is a two-way relationship, as without resilience, a destination would never be able to maintain its sustainability efforts (PATA, 2022[7]).

Tourism is a global sector that relies on the efficient movement and interaction of people and global value chains. This comes with risks that are beyond the control of the tourism sector, and creates vulnerabilities within the tourism ecosystem. Tourism is also a complex, integrated system of actors, each of which is reliant on the actions of another. It is highly fragmented, composed of many small businesses that interact with large global players that structure the global tourism economy. This heightens the need for resilience within the sector, as disruption to any part of the value chain has ramifications for other parts of the sector.

Building resilience through a systemic approach would support the tourism sector to endure the shocks and build back by adapting to the new normal, which is often unknown. Policy approaches based on systems thinking recognise that although it is not possible to know what will trigger the next crisis, there are certain factors that will make it more likely and more damaging, and that there are better policy options than waiting for it to happen (OECD, 2020[8]). The processes of systemic resilience also provide the means to pursue multiple policy objectives at the same time (Hynes et al., 2022[9]).

Anticipating the future needs of tourism is challenging while the sector is still in recovery mode, and faces medium and long-term uncertainties (Box 1.1). However, the opportunity exists to use the crises as a catalyst to drive the (often-difficult) structural reforms and transformation widely recognised as necessary in the sector. This requires that resilience is embedded into the ongoing tourism policy response and future planning, without which the sector runs the risk of letting resilience planning fall by the wayside until the next crisis, meaning future impacts are deeper than necessary.

Learning from previous exogenous shocks to address tourism vulnerabilities

The widespread nature of the COVID-19 pandemic impacted all parts of the tourism ecosystem. Rapid, multi-faceted responses were needed to restore tourism demand, support tourism workers, businesses and destinations, and improve institutional capacity for decision-making.

The policies implemented to support the tourism sector in response to the COVID-19 crisis varied widely across countries but can generally be categorised into 11 key themes. Matching these measures to the intended recipient provides a framework to understand the vulnerabilities within the tourism ecosystem, and the areas that need strengthening for the future (Figure 2.1). This framework is used to analyse the vulnerabilities of the sector in this section and build on pillars adopted by previous OECD resilience work – economy, environment, society and government (or institutions) (Box 2.2).

Figure 2.1. Using COVID-19 support mechanisms to assess tourism vulnerabilities

BUSINESSES
- Employee payment guarantees
- Business grants or subsidies
- Labour supply, skills and training
- Government backed loans or liquidity

DESTINATIONS
- Regional or destination specific funding
- Investment funds
- Health and safety protocols

INSTITUTIONS
- New formal communication channels between Government and Industry
- New data collections

CONSUMERS
- Domestic demand stimulation (travel vouchers/ marketing)
- Consumer guarantees

Box 2.2. Assessing tourism vulnerabilities based on COVID-19 support mechanisms

Effective policy design generally starts with accurately diagnosing the issue or vulnerability it aims to address. Taking the opposite approach following a shock can also help to understand who or what the mechanism was specifically designed to support. Mapping the key COVID-19 policy responses against the intended beneficiary, a number of vulnerabilities across multiple elements of the ecosystem are identified:

- **Businesses:** Emergency response and mitigation initiatives mainly focused on providing income continuity for workers and ensuring tourism businesses, and in particular SMEs, were in a position to restart operations when containment measures ended (OECD, 2020[10]). Income support measures were used widely by countries to ensure business-employee ties were maintained through periods of shutdown. Business support mechanisms such as liquidity support measures and tax incentives were implemented to help businesses meet or reduce ongoing fixed costs through periods when operations were restricted or closed. To promote recovery after the pandemic and prepare for future shocks, Denmark provided compensation to tourism businesses, totalling DKK 15 billion. This compensation kept many businesses operational and allowed for the promotion and recovery of tourism once restrictions were lifted.
- **Destinations:** New protocols were put in place to increase tourist and worker safety. Luxembourg's "Safe to serve" campaign combined a series of initiatives aimed at preserving the health and safety of staff and customers. The campaign included a charter where professionals guarantee their customers a high level of health and safety, designed as a reassurance mechanism and underpinned by legal obligations. Location-specific programmes provided support for tourism-reliant destinations at risk of economic failure without additional support. For example, the Australian Recovery for Regional Tourism Programme provided targeted support for nine regions that were economically reliant on international visitors.
- **Consumers:** Programmes to stimulate demand for travel as restrictions were lifted included travel vouchers or subsidies, marketing and new consumer guarantees particularly related to refunds. Bulgaria provided compensation grants to tour operators to reimburse customers, and Austria provided guarantees for package travel providers to secure down-payments of tourists in 2021 and 2022. In 2020, an additional ISK 3 billion was added to Iceland's tourism services budget for marketing and promotion, including a domestic travel voucher campaign and international marketing campaign.
- **Institutions:** New procedures have been introduced to enhance timely and evidence-based decision-making for institutions. For example, new formal communication channels were established between the private sector and institutions to help information gathering and ensure targeted support measures would be successful. Brazil made a broad range of official data available through the General Co-ordination of Data and Information mechanism to support private sector decision-making. Countries also purchased new data sets or signed data sharing agreements, with accommodation and bookings data among the most popular sources.

While this framework is designed based on COVID-19 support mechanisms, analysis of previous crisis support reveals similar vulnerabilities:

- 9/11 terrorist attacks in the United States (2001), with wider impacts on the perception of safety for travellers globally. The attacks led to the introduction of global aviation safety measures, many of which remain in place today, including increased airport scanning and co-operation between the aviation industry and institutions (IATA, 2021[11]).

- Global economic and financial crisis (2009), which impacted businesses and consumer spending capacity. The main response was through fiscal stimulus packages, which included tax cuts and spending boosts for businesses and consumers (OECD, 2009[12]).
- Previous health crises and pandemics (e.g. SARS, 2002, Swine Flu, 2009), which impacted the movement and interaction of people. Response mechanisms to reduce the spread of the virus included localised lockdowns, then returning consumer sentiment and demand once safe to do so.
- Natural disasters (e.g. bushfires, tsunamis, earthquakes and severe weather events) negatively impact tourism, but generally remain isolated. Responses include crisis management, with fiscal packages to restore business and consumer demand at the destination level when safe to do so.

During the COVID-19 pandemic (and previous crises), governments have implemented programmes for consumers to encourage tourism, drive demand and reduce booking hesitancy. Government guarantees and refunds were used to counteract booking hesitancy due to cancellation or business failure. Travel vouchers and subsidies were introduced to drive demand, creating an urgency amongst travellers to book and travel in the short term.

Crises in tourism are underpinned by a need to enable a demand-led recovery driven by consumers travelling again and contributing to each part of the ecosystem organically. This is not necessarily a structural weakness that can be addressed prior to a crisis, but a fundamental requirement to restart the tourism ecosystem to ensure other resilience measures can take effect.

Box 2.3. Exogenous variables impacting the tourism recovery

Exogenous variables are inherently hard to plan for as they cannot be controlled from within the (tourism) system. Recognising these variables and understanding the possible impacts is necessary to respond to the challenges and build system resilience. Exogenous variables that will likely impact tourism in the short to medium term include:

Inflation: Inflationary pressures have intensified since Russia's invasion of Ukraine and have broadened beyond food and energy, with businesses now passing through higher energy, transport and labour costs (OECD, 2022[13]). Discretionary spending like tourism will be the first to be cut.

Oil prices: Spurred by oil uncertainty, prices surged in early 2022 – crude oil and jet fuel prices were almost double pre-pandemic prices in April 2022 (IATA, 2022[14]). While oil prices are expected to trend downwards until at least 2023 (IATA, 2022[15]), tourism is reliant on the transport of people and goods and will remain exposed to oil price volatility.

Supply-chain shortages: Global disruption is impacting international supply chains and contributing to inflationary pressures. Shortages and supply delays for raw materials in the construction industry could slow infrastructure investment. This can have wider implications for the growth and competitiveness of the tourism sector, but also the sustainable and digital transitions.

Societal shifts: In many OECD countries, middle-income growth has remained stagnant. Technology is automating semi-skilled jobs that used to be carried out by middle-class workers, reducing the ability of the middle-class to save (OECD, 2019[16]). Coupled with an aging population, especially in the middle to upper-class brackets, this could reduce the pool of travellers.

Climate change: Accelerating climate impacts have negative consequences for tourism, especially in low-lying coastal areas and mountain areas. It also leads to the increased risk of natural disasters, which are expected to become more prevalent. Adaptation measures are required for a resilient tourism sector. Tourism also needs to play its role in mitigation efforts and achieving net zero targets.

Taking stock of the fragilities that have been presented through the COVID-19 pandemic and previous crises provides insights into the areas of focus for the future and when these vulnerabilities may occur. Coupled with strategic foresight exercises, this can help tourism policy makers anticipate alternative futures and inform the development of forward-looking policies (OECD, 2018[5]). While this chapter focuses on the endogenous structural vulnerabilities of the tourism sector, strategic foresight activities seek to scan the horizon to respond to possible scenarios and consider also the impact of exogenous variables on tourism (Box 2.3).

Diversifying destinations to build resilience to shocks

The extent of the economic impact of a shock depends on several broad but interlinked factors. Beyond the nature of the shock itself, these can include the nature of the tourism offer, the impact of travel restrictions on visitor flows, the extent to which the event coincides with peak tourism periods, the extent of damage to the physical tourism infrastructure, the scale and complexity of business operations, the return of main source markets, the size of the domestic tourism market and exposure to international source markets. Additionally, places where there is a lack of economic diversity and a heavy reliance on tourism to support local jobs and businesses are more vulnerable (OECD, 2020[17]).

The impact of shocks on employment and economic activities can be asymmetric and highly localised between and within countries. Countries where tourism makes a large contribution to GDP (e.g. France and Spain) have been more exposed to the negative impacts of the COVID-19 pandemic (Rusticelli and Turner, 2021[18]). The prolonged halt in tourism activity has impacted the wider economy and required public spending to support the sector. This is also reflected at the destination level, as places where there is a lack of economic diversity and a heavy reliance on tourism to support local jobs and businesses were more vulnerable (OECD, 2020[17]).

In many destinations, an increased economic reliance on tourism, lack of diversity in the visitor mix and product offering, and lack of integration of tourism into wider economic development has increased the risk profile for tourism and the wider economy. This is true for countries, but it is even more evident at the level of regional and local destinations, as consistent tourism growth in the past has created growth-oriented expectations and a focus on targeting high-growth international visitor markets.

In places where tourism accounted for a significant share of economic activity, the loss of tourism presented a devastating situation for the wider local economy. During the pandemic, this saw countries including Australia and Mexico implement regional tourism support packages. The reliance on tourism also led to a strong push and introduction of measures to support the safe reopening of the sector as soon as sanitary conditions allowed and support the sector to pivot to new markets.

In addition to strong economic reliance, these destinations often portrayed other well-documented and often overlapping vulnerabilities including:

- Seasonality, with a concentration of visitors during peak periods, as often seen in coastal areas.
- Market dependence, with an (over) reliance on specific visitors, either a country source market or a specific visitor type, like business visitors.
- Product dependence, based on a single iconic attraction or product offering, like winter sports.

As the tourism economy recovers, these overlapping vulnerabilities need to be addressed, so destinations are stronger and better prepared to adapt in the future. As decision-making competencies vary across national, regional and local levels, and tourism is predominantly made up of small businesses with limited capacity beyond running the day-to-day operations, destination management organisations can play a role to support this (OECD, 2020[19]).

Safety and security remain an important concern for tourists around the world, with perception often as important as reality. These issues can affect the image of the destination, visitor arrivals and tourism growth, and are also an important part of building a more robust and sustainable tourism economy. Tourists who believe they can safely and easily travel to, from and around the destination are more likely to explore secondary attractions.

The pandemic created a new threat and uncertainty for travellers. It put health and safety at the centre of the discretionary travel decision. Portugal's Clean & Safe label provides a good example of an ongoing initiative to support safe mobility. It not only considers the ongoing health threats caused by COVID-19, but also extends to consider the impacts of future crises (Box 2.4).

Box 2.4. Reinforcing consumer confidence in Portugal

To reinforce confidence in Portugal as a safe destination for tourists, employees in the sector and the population in general, a new version of the Clean & Safe label was launched in June 2022. This was extended to support companies through crisis management. The Clean & Safe label promotes excellence in company hygienic-sanitary performance, but also act as a tool for future public health crises (e.g. pandemics, heat waves). It now incorporates a new dimension of security for tourist activities, covering risk situations arising from extreme natural events (e.g. rural fires, floods, earthquakes, tsunamis) and international events (e.g. cybercrime, repatriations, refugees). The label was initially developed in close co-operation with the Ministry of Health. Partnerships with NOVA Medical School, AGIF Management of Rural Fires Agency, the National Emergency and Civil Protection Authority, the High Commissioner for Migration and the National Cybersecurity Centre have also been established. Technical support, including models of Clean & Safe Action Plans and Technical Support Guides, is available on the portugalcleanandsafe.com platform. The Clean & Safe Seal remains optional, free and valid until June 2024.

Strengthening businesses' preparedness for future shocks, particularly tourism SMEs

Building a more resilient tourism sector requires that businesses of all sizes and types are better prepared to face future shocks. Tourism businesses sustained extended periods from the start of the pandemic where revenues were slashed due to restricted or closed operations and ongoing capacity constraints. This has caused significant disruption to existing business models. Large tourism businesses have seen dramatic losses and have required government support, particularly airlines. Small tourism businesses have faced particular challenges.

SMEs are a key part of the tourism supply chain, making up approximately 85% of tourism businesses, and their survival is essential for the recovery. However, SMEs lack the capacity and resources to cope with the changes and costs that such shocks entail (OECD, 2020[17]) and face unique challenges that create vulnerabilities and inhibit resilience (OECD, 2009[20]). This includes an inability to downsize due to their already small size, less diversified economic activities, and weaker financial structures with fewer financing options. In response, support programmes were introduced to help reduce financial burdens or enhance business cash flow. This included but was not limited to: business cash grants; government-backed loans; tax incentives; and deferrals for rental and/or utility payments.

Many support mechanisms for SMEs and entrepreneurs came in the form of debt which, if unwound too rapidly, could precipitate a wave of bankruptcies that jeopardise the recovery (OECD, 2021[21]). High levels of debt and delayed recovery of the tourism economy have further raised the already high-risk profile of tourism businesses, making access to finance more difficult and creating new barriers to entry or scaling up.

Tourism SMEs face additional challenges linked with the structure and nature of the tourism economy, which are exacerbated in times of crisis. The tourism sector is highly fragmented and heterogeneous and covers a wide range of industries, with many demonstrating a dual structure characterised by a very small group of large businesses combined with many SMEs (OECD, 2021[22]). The sector is globally interconnected and depends on the availability of workers with a mix of skills to deliver quality tourism services, while temporal and spatial concentration is a frequent feature. This is acknowledged, for example, in the G20 Rome Guidelines for the Future of Tourism and the G20 Bali Guidelines for Strengthening Communities and MSMEs as Tourism Transformation Agents, which note that resilience in the tourism sector relates in particular to the needs of SMEs. Recognising these challenges, Greece developed a roadmap to better support tourism SMEs through the recovery, with a particular focus on micro-enterprises and job retention.

Many tourism workers and businesses benefited significantly from whole-of-economy job retention measures, but the sector is still experiencing widespread labour and skills shortages in the wake of the crisis due to:

- Loss of workers to more stable and higher paying opportunities in other sectors, when faced with ongoing disruption and uncertainty for tourism businesses.
- Reduced mobility of workers within and between countries during the pandemic, compounded by the return of many temporary workers to their home country (OECD, 2021[23]).
- Competition from other sectors, as tourism businesses sought to rapidly scale up operations in response to the rebound in demand in a tight labour market.

The struggle to attract and maintain an adequate workforce is presenting significant issues for the tourism sector as it looks to recover. Workforce shortages are constraining the ability of tourism businesses to reopen, leading them to reduce operating hours or capacity.

While the successive shocks caused by COVID-19 and Russia's war in Ukraine have been unprecedented and were generally unforeseen, tourism businesses need to be supported to develop and implement comprehensive and iterative risk management plans to better prepare for future crises. Japan has adopted a forward-looking approach, creating and publishing a guidebook for the introduction of tourism crisis management in local governments and tourism-related operators. This was developed by collecting and analysing examples of good practices related to tourism crisis management in Japan and other countries. It is anticipated that each region and tourism operator will create a tourism crisis management plan with reference to these materials, thereby assisting to build crisis resilience in tourism across the country.

Active government responses to reduce the impact of shocks and promote a quick recovery

A resilient society is driven by people, but individual resilience can and should be supported by institutions. This requires institutional resilience, which comprises capacity to deliver and enhance results over time credibly, legitimately and adaptively, as well as the ability to manage shocks and change (OECD, 2020[24]). To support resilience in the tourism sector, institutions need to be prepared, quick to act and agile. More granular and timely data is required to understand the impacts of crises on the tourism sector and enable agile and responsive policy-making that is fit for purpose.

Strategic and adaptive institutional processes can expedite response and transformation measures. However, policy design frameworks are often structured and rigid. Institutions have processes that require proven impacts, multiple levels of approval, and specific implementation methods. In a crisis, these features of good governance can slow the response and increase the length of exposure of businesses and consumers to the shock, resulting in deeper impacts and greater scarring in the recovery phase. The lack of agile and flexible policy design processes limits the quick implementation of targeted policy responses which can be easily adapted, if needed, to meet the intended purpose.

Resilience is built from experiences through learning and adapting to address previous shocks. During the pandemic, countries that had learnt from similar experiences in the past had existing mechanisms in place and were better prepared to respond. Germany, for example, was able to mobilise a labour support programme introduced during the global financial crisis. This, combined with the National Pandemic Preparedness Plan, allowed Germany to react quickly and reduce the financial burden on businesses and employees by supplementing wages.

Quick, targeted, and effective action in a crisis is dependent on reliable data for evidence-based decision-making. Insufficient data and information have inhibited the development of targeted, evidence-based policy since the start of the pandemic. The uptake of alternative and complementary data sources such as administrative and 'big data' accelerated through the pandemic. Some countries used existing non-tourism data to infer new tourism performance insights (Box 1.12).

While this data provided more timely insights than traditional data, it is not targeted at tourism, which presents limitations. These data sets are not a complete solution to the existing data and information issues; more needs to be done to explore new and improve existing methods.

Building a more resilient tourism ecosystem

Exogenous shocks, like COVID-19 and Russia's war in Ukraine, are hard to predict and even more difficult to control. This can inhibit the response, particularly in systemic environments like tourism. Working towards greater resilience will support the tourism sector to adapt and transform in the face of acute shocks in the future and continue to adjust to the megatrends of evolving visitor demand, sustainable tourism growth, enabling technologies and digitalisation and changing traveller mobility (OECD, 2018[5]).

Strengthening the resilience of the tourism economy is the focus of much attention, and action is needed if the new and long-standing weaknesses in the tourism economy are to be addressed, or they risk being forgotten after this crisis has passed. Since the pandemic, resilience has been a key theme appearing in tourism recovery guidelines, plans and strategies, at national (e.g. US Travel and Tourism Strategy 2022) and international levels (e.g. European Commission's Transition Pathway for Tourism, G20 Rome Guidelines for the Future of Tourism). Implementation and action is now key, to build on the platform of change and collaboration from the crisis, better manage tourism development and transition to a stronger, fairer and more sustainable tourism system (Box 2.5).

Adopting integrated, agile and flexible governance systems for tourism

Agile, flexible and well-co-ordinated tourism policy approaches are a key part of responding and adapting to change and building a more resilient tourism system. The cross-cutting nature of tourism means tourism impacts and is impacted by many policy areas. Co-ordination across policy areas and levels of government is important to ensure that tourism is integrated into broader crisis response and risk management strategies. Once in place, it is also important that policies and programmes can be adapted to meet changing needs, while measures that impede tourism activities do not continue longer than necessary.

The first step in sound policy making is to identify and properly understand a problem, and then develop the appropriate responses to address it (OECD, 2018[25]). This often requires three key steps:

- Identifying a specific problem or issue negatively affecting the tourism economy.
- Collecting evidence to understand the problem and evaluate its impacts.
- Designing a policy that is not only right for the problem but also meets legal and constitutional requirements, aligns with broader government agendas, and meets the expectations of industry stakeholders, who often have competing issues.

Box 2.5. COVID-19 crisis: an opportunity for sustainable and digital action

Crises present serious negative consequences, but they also provide opportunities for adaptation and sustainable development. To analyse resilience without considering the potential opportunities that arise from disruption would be remiss. Taking stock of these opportunities and their potential long-term benefits is necessary. Evidence from business surveys worldwide shows that up to 70% of SMEs intensified their use of digital technologies due to COVID-19 (OECD, 2021[26]). In tourism, this could include the introduction of digital payment methods, updated ordering and ticketing systems and new contact tracing technology. While born from necessity, this surge in innovation will continue to drive productivity in the sector moving forward. Advancement of digital technologies and development of digital service models offer small businesses enhanced accessibility to business tools, which enable the quick adaptation of activities during crises with limited upfront investment (OECD, 2021[27]).

The reduction in tourists provided an opportunity for governments, destinations, businesses and consumers to rethink the future of tourism, creating a renewed focus on sustainability, green development and community inclusion in destination and community planning. Immediate action is critical to ensure these issues are engrained in future planning, and that the tourism sector does not just revert to previous operations when visitors return. Importantly, these opportunities can co-exist as digital technologies can be a key enabler of the green transition, suggesting that these and ongoing innovations need to be addressed jointly in the recovery phase and beyond. There are synergies and opportunities for double dividends in policy implementation (OECD, 2021[28]).

Selected country approaches:

- **Finland:** In 2020, a call for funding applications was organised for regional tourism organisations to support the recovery of the tourism industry and the regions. The projects responded to local development needs, benefited multiple operators in the regions and brought long-term positive effects for the tourism sector. EUR 4 million was allocated across 28 projects that focused on developing digital capabilities and solutions, increasing year-round tourism, creating new tourism products and reaching target groups.
- **Canada:** Announced in 2021, the Canada Digital Adoption Program was established to help SMEs, including in the tourism sector, realise their full potential by adopting digital technologies. The CAD 4 billion programme comprises two separate funding components, including *Grow Your Business Online* grants for smaller, consumer-facing businesses, including those in service industries like tourism.
- **Greece:** As part of the National Recovery and Resilience Plan, a key area of focus is on the digital transformation of SMEs, including in tourism. This includes support for investments in digital technologies and services, including electronic payments, digital advertising tools, business analytics, upgrading of digital skills, artificial intelligence, integrated solutions for seamless service, cyber security systems, and POS ecosystem upgrade.

In times of crisis, these steps have to be taken more rapidly and in quicker succession than under normal circumstances. Implementation takes time and often requires wide stakeholder engagement and multiple levels of approval.

During the pandemic, countries moved quickly to introduce unprecedented, economy-wide measures to cushion people, businesses and communities from the full impact. While tourism has benefited from these supports, experience has also highlighted how whole-of-economy approaches to policy making can lead to gaps in support mechanisms, particularly when introduced quickly. The highly fragmented and heterogeneous nature of tourism meant that businesses often 'fell through the cracks' when they did not meet the criteria for support, particularly when non-employing and subject to strong seasonal incomes.

When asked about the key lessons learned through the crisis (in September 2021), Canada and New Zealand acknowledged issues in creating targeted support to the tourism sector, particularly SMEs, while Estonia added that addressing issues was a process of 'learning by doing'.

Reflecting on the lessons from the pandemic response and adapting future processes will create better preparedness in the face of future crises. Learning from the pandemic response is a core part of the EC Transition Pathway for Tourism, in order to put in place the right structures, procedures and rules to be able to deal quickly with future exceptional circumstances with minimal disruption to travel and tourism (European Commission, 2022[29]).

Both horizontal and vertical policy co-ordination are essential for tourism resilience (OECD, 2018[5]). Policy decisions are made across all levels of government, but a unified approach, with common goals, underpinned by strong co-operation and planning is required to create a resilient sector. National governments might hold budgetary decisions, but local governments are often better placed to administer programmes and ensure the implementation meets the needs of tourism businesses. Local governments can be more closely connected with businesses, and this can help to better design and implement programmes, evaluate the outcomes, and respond if changes are required. Germany has implemented a new central instrument to help develop the next national tourism strategy in a co-ordinated way (Box 2.6).

Box 2.6. Integrated tourism policy development in Germany

In May 2022, Germany established a steering committee consisting of high-ranking members across all relevant ministries to tourism in Germany. The main task of this steering committee is to develop key points for the National Tourism Strategy and to agree upon a working programme for the Federal Government. Germany is now creating the national platform "Future of Tourism" as the central instrument for co-operation and integration for the development of a National Tourism Strategy. The platform will be expanded to include representatives of the sixteen federal states and stakeholders of the tourism sector early in 2023. Within this platform, all actors will work together to evaluate, adjust and amend the measures of the working programme. This will utilise different working groups to ensure the right people are addressing the right issues.

Effective multi-level governance also requires clarification on how responsibilities are assigned to different government levels, and that this process is explicit, mutually understood and clear for all actors. A periodic review of jurisdictional responsibilities should be made to ensure flexibility in the system (OECD, 2021[30]).

Building resilience also requires co-operation and action by both the public and private sectors. Close collaboration between government and the private sector allows for a faster and more targeted response in a crisis, reducing the impact of crises and increasing the effectiveness of response and recovery measures. Throughout the COVID-19 pandemic, many countries implemented communication and collaboration strategies between government and industry bodies, including partnerships, frequent bilateral meetings and information and data sharing. This created a platform to develop trust-based relationships and enhance evidence-based decision-making. Maintaining these relationships beyond the crisis would provide support for a quicker, more holistic response to future shocks, and well-targeted policy design more broadly, with institutional actions based on industry needs.

This is being addressed through the establishment of formal advisory groups and taskforces for the ongoing development of tourism (explored further in Chapter 1 – Box 1.2), but also through the establishment of new communication channels for information sharing. In the Slovak Republic, unifying all stakeholders that participate in tourism is a priority. The Slovak Republic is setting up new information channels on a national level through regional tourism offices, the national tourism board, municipalities and private entities. With great ambition for collaboration, the Slovak Republic will also seek to set new communication channels between national and overseas stakeholders, especially in EU countries, under the 2030 National Sustainable Tourism Strategy.

Strategic foresight and futures-oriented institutional planning approaches can support countries to foresee and prepare for possible scenarios and be ready to react quickly to events when they do happen. Similar to resilience, strategic futures and foresight methods embrace uncertainty, and encourage the analysis and consideration of a range of future possibilities to inform decision-making and public policy (OECD, 2020[31]). Strategic foresight exercises can help tourism policymakers anticipate alternative futures and inform the development of forward-looking policies (OECD, 2018[5]). The principles for strategic foresight in tourism are set out in Box 2.7.

Collaborative governance frameworks help to align initiatives and processes, allowing for quicker design and implementation of policies when required. Such frameworks also provide mechanisms for greater peer learning and an integrated approach to future policy challenges, rather than just responding to shocks. In exploring potential policy measures to support the tourism sector, Australia considered key developments and initiatives being introduced internationally to help streamline the policy making process by learning and understanding various approaches to support measures internationally. This provided an opportunity to identify gaps and establish an evidence base on the broad range of tourism support programmes introduced globally and their impact in addressing challenges. Drawing insights from various demand-driving incentive measures (e.g. voucher schemes, travel discounts) was useful for the development and implementation of the Tourism Aviation Network Support programme, designed to boost travel and increase confidence.

Box 2.7. Principles for effective use of strategic foresight in tourism policy making

Strategic foresight can assist policymakers to anticipate possibilities for the future and design forward-looking policies. Various strategic foresight methods can be used to analyse trends, envision various plausible futures and prepare effectively for the challenges and opportunities the future holds. Some broad principles can provide guidance to tourism policymakers to maximise the value of strategic foresight as a policy tool. These include:

- **Agility:** Utilise existing evidence and projections, while being agile enough to adapt to emerging realities, acknowledging that they will be faced with unanticipated opportunities and challenges.
- **Multiplicity:** Prepare for and think about alternative futures when designing policies and programmes – the future cannot be predicted with certainty and there are many possible futures.
- **Proactivity**: Take proactive steps to work towards the desired future. Current action or inaction are both going to influence the future.
- **Long-term sustainability:** Consider the impact of policies on future generations and take responsible actions in the present. Policy decisions should not just be geared towards short-term or medium-term goals.
- **Engagement and inclusion**: Engage with diverse stakeholders that represent a range of perspectives and interests. This will help to avoid narrow visions of the future.
- **International collaboration:** Policies and decisions need to be globally sustainable. The world is becoming increasingly globalised. Policymakers cannot operate in silos and must collaborate internationally to ensure tourism gains are inclusive, equitable and globally sustainable.

Source: OECD (2018), Analysing megatrends to better shape the future of tourism (OECD, 2018[5]).

Promoting diversified, robust and stable tourism destinations

Steady growth in tourism over many years led to a widely held belief in the inherent resilience of tourism, and at times fostered a focus on 'growth above all else'. This contributed to the tourism management and unbalanced development issues that were already facing the sector before the pandemic. This includes, for example, an over-reliance on tourism as a driver of economic development and job creation, as well as an (over) dependence on key source markets and service offerings, and a high spatial and temporal concentration of tourism activities. This lack of diversification makes the sector more susceptible to shocks and inhibits recovery, thus making it less resilient, and less competitive.

The pandemic revealed the vulnerabilities of an over-reliance on international visitors in many countries, with governments introducing support to help destinations and businesses shift the focus to the domestic market early in the pandemic. Many destinations have become more aware of the international visitor mix and the negative impacts of an (over) reliance on individual source markets. A recent survey of OECD member and partner countries identified that closed borders in key markets remains a significant barrier for the tourism recovery, identified by almost half of responding countries.

Destinations and tourism businesses alike need to ensure that the product offering has broad appeal to be able to maintain a base operation through disruption. This includes the spatial spread of tourists and attractions to ensure tourism can continue in the case of localised crises. Achieving a more geographically and temporally diverse tourism sector is also a policy priority in most countries. This has led to a wider discussion around destination management and the approaches required to ensure tourism is more sustainable, inclusive and resilient for the future (Box 2.8).

Box 2.8. Managing tourism development for a more resilient, sustainable and inclusive future

An integrated approach to tourism policy is key to achieving a sustainable and inclusive future, with input and support from industry and civil society. Particular emphasis is needed on environmental sustainability, inclusiveness, diversification, and innovation, prioritising visitor management over visitor attraction. There is no one-size-fits-all solution. Destinations are adopting a multiplicity of approaches to place sustainability at the centre of their tourism development. However, common to all is the overarching objective to evolve, sometimes radically, current tourism business models. It will be critical for all destinations to establish effective and representative multi-level governance mechanisms. Key policy considerations to help avoid potential pitfalls of the pre-COVID-19 era, and implement a sustainable vision for the future include:

- Reconsidering perceptions of tourism success.
- Adopting an integrated policy-industry-community approach.
- Mainstreaming sustainable policies and practices.
- Developing more sustainable tourism business models.
- Implementing better measurement for better management.

Source: OECD (2021) Managing tourism development for sustainable and inclusive recovery (OECD, 2021[30]).

Diversification can involve adapting the tourism offering to reduce seasonality. Mountain, national parks and coastal tourism activities and destinations are examples of tourism offerings where the annual economic activity can be condensed into a short period of time, sometimes just a few months or even weeks. Seasonal tourism can put substantial strain on local infrastructure and exacerbate environmental damage caused by the sector. For instance, marine litter in the Mediterranean region has been found to increase by up to 40% during peak tourist season (One Planet, 2022[32]). Diversifying the product offering to increase visitors in the shoulder and off-peak periods can help to lessen the impact of disruption in peak periods and help lead to sustainable year-round jobs and businesses.

Slovenia, supported by React EU funding, committed EUR 69 million across 20 projects to transform mountain destinations into year-round resorts for active holidays outside of the traditional ski season. This will help to restructure the facilities and invest in new and existing accommodation. Similarly, in France the Mountain Futures Plan (Plan Avenir Montagnes) launched in 2021 aims to support mountain areas to implement a tourism development strategy to promote the diversification of the tourism economy, and adaptation to the challenges of ecological transition. Ensuring that destinations have access to infrastructure and resources to provide diversified products and reduce seasonal reliance is a key part of the plan.

A strong destination management framework is key to enhance destination resilience. This emphasises the broader functional view for destination management organisations (DMOs) that goes beyond being solely a marketing entity. This contemporary and more managerial view suggests that a DMO should be concerned with tourism development in its widest sense (OECD, 2020[19]). The understanding of the need to transition away from destination marketing towards destination management and stewardship is also reflected in the Pacific Asia Tourism Association's Tourism Destination Resilience Programme (Box 2.9).

Box 2.9. Enabling resilience at the tourism destination level

The Pacific Asia Travel Association's Tourism Destination Resilience programme was developed to help destinations recover from the COVID-19 crisis and, at the same time, prepare them for future crises that will come. The end goal is to help build a more resilient tourism industry.

The programme enables destinations to 'withstand adversity and bounce forward from crises'. To help destinations build capacity around risk assessment, risk management and adaptive capacity, PATA built a course which covers the steps towards destinations' resilience and long-term sustainability. Potential outcomes from the course include:

- Understanding the need to transition away from destination marketing towards destination management and stewardship.
- Identifying the key capacities that need to be strengthened in the destination in order to build resilience.
- Reframing the destination's values and business models to be more holistic, thus including diverse stakeholders in a destination's journey towards resilience.
- Recognising the long-term benefits of resilience for the community, the environment and the economy.
- Understanding how to secure investments for resilience programmes and projects.

Source: Tourism Destination Resilience (PATA, 2022[7]).

Many countries are still transitioning their governance structures to represent a contemporary destination management style. In the United Kingdom, an independent review of the destination management structures in 2021 found that DMOs in England were underutilised and required better funding structures to move beyond business-centric marketing and support the implementation of policies to ensure destination competitiveness and sustainability. The UK Government has committed to a number of key actions to address these findings (Box 2.10).

Box 2.10. Independent review of destination management structures in the United Kingdom

In 2021, an independent review of destination management structures in England was commissioned in recognition of the important role DMOs can play in driving growth in regional visitor economies, and involved a significant amount of stakeholder engagement conducted over a short time span. The review identified a number of recommendations to improve the functioning and structure of DMOs. In response, the UK Government has committed to a number of key actions, including:

- Changing the name of DMOs to Local Visitor Economy Partnerships (LVEPs) to capture the wider strategic focus on the visitor economy and the breadth of activity and relationships they will establish to support the local visitor economy.
- Introducing a new accreditation system in 2022-23, with new funding allocated to VisitEngland to develop and administer the scheme. The new national portfolio of accredited, high-performing LVEPs aims to reduce fragmentation and bring coherence to the destination management landscape, helping actors across the private and public sectors.
- Piloting a tiered approach for LVEPs and providing multi-year core funding in a region of England. This will give one top tier LVEP, or collection of LVEPs (a Destination Development Partnership), the space and firm foundation to engage in a wide range of destination management activities as well as prompt increased private sector investment.

Source: UK Government (2021) The de Bois Review: an independent review of Destination Management Organisations in England (UK Government, 2021[33]).

Greece elaborated a governance framework to strengthen destination management with the enactment of their Destination Management and Marketing Organisation Law, while Iceland formalised new DMOs and updated regional destination management plans. Governance frameworks with strong links between national and destination decision-making provide opportunities to ensure recovery and future growth align with national policy agendas.

There is a substantial overlap in policies that make economies resilient and regions economically prosperous, including policies to support a dynamic business environment, diversified industrial base and local skills development (OECD, 2022[34]). Resilient destinations also promote sustainable development, well-being and inclusive growth. There is growing recognition of the importance of social inclusion and community sentiment in destination management, as seen for example through New Zealand's Mood of a Nation survey, measuring residents' perceptions of tourism. Place-based approaches are another way to enhance the incorporation of the wants and needs of the local community. Decision-makers need to understand the destination and invest in planning and development that can both improve resilience and enhance human connectivity to places (Chand, 2018[35]).

Place-based tourism policies are gaining traction in a number of countries. In Sweden, a place-based approach is a key pillar of the National Strategy for Sustainable Tourism and a Growing Tourism Industry, acknowledging that sustainable development and resilience requires strong local roots, which is facilitated if the local community is considered and treated as a key stakeholder. The Netherlands Centre of Expertise on Leisure, Tourism and Hospitality (CELTH) has put together a multi-year knowledge agenda under the "Conscious Destination". CELTH specifically opts for the destination level because that is where all the different sub-sectors and actors come together. In a conscious destination, parties strive for an outcome which has the most positive possible social, ecological and economic impact and in which it leads to the highest possible quality of life, experience and work.

Addressing supply-side fragilities, with a focus on tourism SMEs

The large number of SMEs in the tourism sector brings opportunities for entrepreneurship, employment and economic benefits to local economies. However, it also brings inherent vulnerabilities. Since the start of the pandemic, the capacity of many tourism SMEs to adapt has been limited by operational constraints, skills deficiencies and lags in the adoption of digital technologies (OECD, 2021[27]).

Building SME resilience, individually and collectively, is vital for sector-wide resilience in tourism, and the economy more broadly. Firstly, there needs to be a better understanding of what it takes for a tourism business to be resilient. However, it needs to be positioned as an iterative process which is updated as the business or environment changes. From the private sector perspective, resilience can be enhanced through strengthened risk management and due diligence strategies that emphasise awareness, transparency, accountability and agility (OECD, 2021[2]).

Encouraging tourism businesses of all sizes to adopt proactive risk identification approaches that consider the possible impacts of wider economic and societal events will better prepare these businesses to react in future crises. Initiatives like the Wharf Hotel's 'living manual' provide a concrete, practical example of how tourism businesses can be more proactive. The living manual refers to crisis management system and risk register that is updated as the operating environment changes. This requires ongoing scanning of the economic, environmental and political climate to ensure the responses are up to date. This idea of continued adaptation and transparent communication presents a starting point for the evolution of resilient businesses. Such an approach can be scaled and adapted to tourism businesses of all sizes.

Even with the implementation of 'future-proof' strategies, SMEs will maintain fundamental vulnerabilities, particularly in relation to cash flow. Decision-makers need to take stock of the pain points for tourism businesses and be better prepared to address these in the future. In July 2022, Chile launched a new reactivation plan, which targets the reactivation of MSMEs. The Chile Supports Tourism 2022 Programme is designed to finance training, business planning, consultancy, technical assistance, working capital and/or investment projects. It will run in all 16 regions of the country and will finance 100% of the costs of tourism-related projects, up to CLP 4 million. Continued evaluation of the support measures introduced throughout the pandemic is needed to understand their effectiveness and gaps to underpin the preparation of future responses.

SMEs also require targeted support to access finance, including green finance, which they often struggle to obtain due to knowledge, financial, policy and size barriers. It is important to expand structures, strategies, incentives, and policies that are tailored to the needs of smaller players, as well as to raise their awareness of existing mechanisms (UNEP, 2021[36]). Without targeted assistance, SMEs will often find it financially unfeasible to implement measures to become more sustainable, and therefore more resilient.

Not all tourism businesses will survive a crisis, with resilience built on the ability to adapt and transform. Unprecedented support for tourism SMEs limited business bankruptcies through the pandemic. However, this can reduce business dynamism, causing a slowdown in sector innovation, reduced competition and decreased efficiency, highlighting the importance of ensuring that support measures are targeted and temporary. In addition, governments can remove unnecessary regulatory barriers to competition, reduce entry barriers into the sector like increased scrutiny and risk profiling from financial institutions, improve judicial efficiency and bankruptcy regulations, and ensure the vigorous enforcement of competition laws (OECD, 2021[2]). Credit risk appetite frameworks have had some observed adjustments for vulnerable sectors, with most banks adjusting their underwriting standards, with an evident tightening for sectors like energy, tourism, arts and recreation (BIS, 2022[37]).

Embracing digitalisation can help tourism businesses exploit the opportunities new technologies open up for marketing, product and destination development, as well as investing in human capital and skills to retain and develop a skilled workforce (OECD, 2021[22]). Korea is supporting the digital transformation of tourism by providing vouchers to enhance the digital competency of tourism SMEs. This includes knowledge sharing with MSMEs and traditional travel operators to harness the digital transformation through new business model development, undertake professional training on new trends, and create digital capacity-building programmes to understand systems, processes, digital content creation and planning.

Finland's DataHub aims to support the digitalisation of tourism SMEs, which typically lag behind in the adoption of digital technologies. It is a national database for the tourism sector, providing all tourism businesses the opportunity to have a digital presence for free, with ongoing marketing opportunities through the Visit Finland digital channels (Box 2.11). Policy responses and initiatives for digital transformation have been enhanced in some countries to help the sector build resilience and respond to the accelerated pace of digitalisation, but still remain substantially underdeveloped more generally.

However, these initiatives have had challenges in engaging tourism SMEs, and smaller businesses in particular. This may stem from systemic challenges to helping those firms most likely to benefit from digital transformation. Some countries are looking to the natural links of DMOs to SMEs to demonstrate and promote those benefits (OECD, 2021[22]). The "Tourist Office 3.0" initiative in Switzerland is an action to support digitalisation by bringing together technology partners, tourist offices and other stakeholders locally to analyse the future significance and function of the tourist office against the background of digitalisation and the changing needs and expectations of guests and service providers in a priority sector for the Swiss national tourism strategy. The Swiss strategy recognises that the wider DMO sector has the potential to promote digitalisation by example and through its natural links to connect with local SMEs.

The EC Transition Pathway for Tourism acknowledges that SMEs face several challenges in engaging with the digital transition, including a lack of knowledge of existing good practices and access to tools to implement them. It recommends establishing a collaboration platform for tourism SMEs and destinations that supports their access to information, specific tools, best practices and knowledge-sharing opportunities to support their engagement in the twin transition (European Commission, 2022[29]).

Box 2.11. Building a national database of tourism businesses and services in Finland

The DataHub is a national database which allows tourism businesses in Finland to store and showcase information about the business and the products and services offered. Visit Finland aims to grow the most comprehensive database of Finland's tourism offer, both regionally and by product category. International and domestic tourism operators can search for and publish product information on DataHub's interface, for example in marketplaces and product catalogues. The DataHub information is available via the DataHub web interface, and can be easily integrated into third-party apps. The product information will also be utilised for marketing purposes in Visit Finland's digital channels, including the new visitfinland.com website. The service is free for users and Visit Finland is committed to the development and maintenance of DataHub. Since its launch in August 2021, the DataHub had gained almost 1500 registered companies and organisations as well as close to 5 000 tourism products by October 2022.

Improving conditions to promote a skilled and inclusive workforce

Tourism is highly labour-intensive and offers strong potential to support a job-rich recovery. The sector is also dependent on quality human resources to develop and deliver a competitive tourism offering. However, workforce issues have been a long-standing vulnerability for the tourism sector. Many countries faced labour and skills shortages in tourism before the pandemic, generated from a complex web of underlying drivers including: a lack of skilled workers; a high reliance on international labour; low wages; high levels of informal and casual work; seasonal work; and the perception of tourism being a short-term job, not a long-term career option.

The pandemic exacerbated long-standing issues impacting the ability of the sector to attract and retain workers (e.g. job insecurity, salary levels, career prospects, competition from other sectors). The interconnected nature of the sector means that shortages in one part of the tourism ecosystem has knock on impacts during the sector. For example, labour shortages in the aviation sector are preventing people from reaching their destination, hotel and other tourism activities. A recent survey of OECD member and partner countries found that labour shortages remain one of the key barriers for the recovery of the tourism sector, behind economic and energy insecurity and inflation. However, there is evidence from some countries, such as Ireland, that businesses are increasing wage levels and changing shift patterns to attract workers (Box 2.12).

Countries and businesses need to implement long-term plans to address these fundamental issues and ensure the ability to rebound after crises is not impeded. New Zealand is pursuing an immigration rebalance policy, which, over time, will limit the flow of lower-paid temporary migrants, with the aim to raise wages and conditions, and create more career pathways for New Zealanders. They are also utilising the government-funded Go with Tourism organisation to undertake activities to change New Zealander's perceptions of tourism as a career and attract New Zealanders to the sector. Accor have recognised the need for change and have introduced 'work your way' and 'same day hire' programmes in the Pacific regions. This looks to increase flexibility for workers and fast-track recruitment processes. They have also improved career development opportunities through the Accor Academy and cross-country opportunities.

Box 2.12. Improving working conditions to address workforce shortages in Ireland

In the wake of the pandemic, workforce shortages were viewed as a key inhibitor for the recovery of the tourism sector in Ireland. Some reports estimated a shortage of up to 40 000 workers in the sector at the beginning of 2022. A survey of tourism businesses found that 30% of those surveyed were facing closure if recruitment challenges were not resolved. Key barriers for employees were noted as the rate of pay and the working conditions, but they would be willing to return to the sector if these issues were resolved. In October 2022, workforce shortages remain a key challenge for Ireland's tourism sector, but pressure has started to ease as employers increase pay rates, introduce more flexibility in shift patterns and introduce penalty rates. This saw vacancies reduce from 40 000 to 22 000 in tourism and hospitality jobs. This was facilitated by a campaign by state tourism officials and industry leaders to address the foundational issues behind the sector staffing crisis and capability-building initiatives to support businesses to leverage this campaign and stand out in a competitive labour market. A Learning Hub has been created to provide free high-quality and self-directed learning courses to help upskill staff and build capability within businesses.

Increased digitalisation, green technology and an aging population will all impact skills requirements for the future. The digital transition will require developing knowledge on the supply and demand of digital skills in the tourism sector, improving incentives to develop digital skills and ensuring they are easily accessible to both workers and managers (OECD, 2021[22]). Ensuring that the workforce is equipped with the right skills to meet future needs will require working closely with the industry and education providers (OECD, 2018[5]). Portugal is investing in innovative equipment and infrastructure to position the teaching of tourism at a higher level and allow training to be adapted to the new needs and demands of consumers. Greece implemented a programme working with Google to enhance digital skills for the tourism workforce.

The green transition will require new skills to meet the growing demand from environment-conscious travellers. 'Green skills' can include how to conduct energy audits, measure the sustainability of tourism activities, as well as training staff on recycling programmes (European Commission, 2022[38]).

Tourism has the potential to promote a job-rich recovery, in particular for young people still reeling from some of the shocks of the pandemic, as well as women and migrants who face persistent challenges to labour-market integration. The tourism workforce has strong female participation, but from an inclusion perspective, increased participation of minority groups could help to address labour shortages. Greater participation of women and minority groups in senior leadership positions is also vital. This is not an easy problem to address, nor is there a one size fits all solution. More work needs to be done to understand both the needs and the barriers for employees and employers alike to create a stronger, more resilient workforce. Egypt has taken stock of their tourism workforce, both formal and informal, as a first step to setting up an emergency fund to support them during future crises. Chile's updated Strategic Plan for Human Capital for the period 2023-26, which will be implemented through a public-private commission, will bring together different actors from the tourism sector to develop and strengthen human capital.

Strengthening data, insights and indicators to measure and monitor tourism resilience

Improving the evidence base to inform policy and business decisions through information gathering, research and data analysis is imperative for resilience. Reliable and consistent data, insights and indicators are needed to evaluate the effectiveness of programmes and initiatives introduced to respond and adapt to a crisis and monitor progress on tourism recovery and resilience in the longer-term (OECD, 2020[39]). Developing methods to quantify resilience are pivotal so that trade-offs between a system's efficiency and resilience can be made explicit (OECD, 2020[8]). Policymakers also need adequate tools to detect the vulnerabilities that can result in severe crises, while taking timely actions before it is too late (OECD, 2021[2]).

In an ideal environment, this would involve the development of real-time data tools that integrate data and automate a selection of management alternatives, based on explicit policy trade-offs in real-time (OECD, 2020[8]). However, the tourism data environment is currently not capable of this. The pandemic has highlighted shortcomings in the availability of timely, comparable, granular data in quickly evolving situations (OECD, 2020[39]). While many institutions and businesses adapted their existing capabilities, this was often not adequate to meet the data requirements for effective decision-making in a timely manner.

Governments and the private sector should consider the data deficiencies that hindered decision-making and explore solutions while it is still fresh. Greece is one country that is taking steps in this direction, through work to assess and evaluate the data gaps and needs exposed by the pandemic, to improve data gathering to measure the impact of the pandemic and to better cope with future shocks. This includes the recent launch of a web platform to share timely tourism data and information, which is intended to be expanded to include new data sources.

The EC Transition Pathway for Tourism, meanwhile, acknowledges the need to improve the coverage of tourism statistics, which will most likely require revisiting the legal basis for harmonised data collection, including to develop Tourism Satellite Accounts, and innovative approaches to statistical sources (European Commission, 2022[29]). With significant advances in data capability through the crisis, international co-operation and learning across institutions and industry will be vital to understand tourism data capability moving forward.

The complex nature of tourism has led to a reliance on traditional survey methods for measurement. These are often costly and time-consuming and require aggregation for reporting. These methods provide reliable, robust and comparable statistics, but may not be granular or responsive enough for decision-making. Reliably harnessing new data that becomes available through digital transformation to improve timeliness and granularity, and continuing to adapt as new sources become available, opens up opportunities for more responsive evidence-based decision-making.

Box 2.13. Use of new data sources to inform policy making: selected country examples

Australia: reviewed the data landscape in 2017 to determine how well official data met the needs of tourism data consumers and the suitability of alternative data sources for tourism statistics. The review identified gaps related to visitor pathways, visitor sentiment, experience quality and data granularity. Australia has further increased their knowledge of alternative data sources through multiple proof-of-concept projects. The combined learnings have led to priority work on mobility and bookings data. Testing of mobility data has demonstrated the capacity of the data to define and measure a range of insights for domestic tourism at more granular geographic levels.

Japan: enables accelerated evidence-based policy making for local governments through the Regional Economy and Society Analysing System (RESAS). It provides insights on industrial structures, demographic movements and population flows, and creates easy-to-understand visualisations of economic and social data compiled from government and private sector sources. RESAS analyses tourist behaviour and search rankings for tourist destinations. Local governments can identify popular stopping places by RESAS and design sightseeing routes which connect these sites for tourists. V - RESAS analyses and visualises the economic impact of COVID-19 in Japan in real-time, using data such as location information for cellular phones, accommodation and food and goods consumption. The data is used to formulate policies in relation to COVID-19 for local government.

Indonesia: uses mobile positioning data to supplement its official surveys to fill data gaps for international arrivals, domestic tourism, and outbound travel. Statistics Indonesia entered a commercial relationship with Positium, an Estonian company that specialises in mobile positioning data for official statistics. Utilising mobile positioning data was challenging, but it has provided more accurate, detailed and frequent data, which has had a positive impact on business performance.

New Zealand: utilises aggregated electronic card transaction data to develop regional tourism indicators. This provides granular and reliable estimates that were not possible with the International Visitor Survey and the Domestic Travel Survey. Beyond tracking long-term growth and changes in tourism spending, the regional tourism indicators assess the impact of marketing efforts and other factors affecting tourism spending. As the data is published with less than one month delay, the indicators provide policymakers and tourism operators with regular and timely updates of tourism spending and growth at a pace and depth never before achievable.

Singapore: the Singapore Tourism Analytics Network (STAN) platform provides deeper insights from administrative and industry 'big data' through 15 data-sharing agreements with some of the largest data providers in the world, including Expedia, Grab and Tencent. STAN has been used by the Singapore Tourism Board to analyse key source markets, help retailers make campaign and product adjustments and analyse hotel habits allowing hoteliers to design more targeted packages and enhance cross-selling.

Thailand: the "Tourism Smart Data, The Time Is Now" initiative was launched in late 2018 to support strategic planning and data-based decision-making. Nationally, a live dashboard is available for public use, with dynamic tourism statistics by province. To effectively manage tourist volumes and safety Phuket has installed over 1 000 free WiFi hotspots, a CCTV vehicle license plate recognition system and smart sensors for beach and ocean safety. The goal is to integrate these with other big data sources in a centralised database to allow greater data visualisation and analysis.

Source: OECD Survey responses and Asia Development Bank (2022) Big data for better tourism policy, management and sustainable recovery from COVID-19 (Asian Development Bank, 2021[40]).

Work to understand the reliability of alternate and complementary data sources for tourism has mainly focused on telecommunications, transactions and bookings data (Box 2.13). Many countries are also looking to administrative and industry-specific data, including almost real-time flights and accommodation data. Norway initiated a pre-study on the possibility of establishing a national monitor, a big data analysis tool for the tourism sector intended to provide a comprehensive view of tourism as a sector. Korea established the 'Korea Tourism Data Lab' in 2021. The Korea Tourism Data Lab is a platform that provides several tourism big data and convergence analysis services. This platform supports the operation of tourism companies, local governments, and the sector more broadly.

Slovenia has adopted a different approach, based on two reliable administrative sources - the Register of Accommodation Establishments and eTurizem mandatory electronic reporting system for tourism accommodation providers. Using these sources, Slovenia is able to collect data on tourism flows (e.g. arrivals, overnight stays) and tourist accommodation establishment capacities (e.g. number of units, permanent bed places, all bed places) in almost real-time. This method assures very detailed, granular, reliable, comparable and timely data on tourist arrivals and overnight stays in accommodation establishments in Slovenia.

Measuring and monitoring resilience for tourism remains undiscovered, limited to a few studies aiming to create a rigorous and holistic measurement framework in order to manage and develop the destination from a resilience perspective (Della Corte et al., 2021[41]). However, work has begun to establish sets of indicators and develop measures for tourism resilience, including at an international level. This includes:

- European Commission: Bottom-up approach using available data to develop an EU Tourism Dashboard measuring environmental, digital and socio-economic pillars, to monitor tourism resilience.
- World Bank: Tourism Resilience Risk Model or vulnerability score, using the World Economic Forum's Travel and Tourism Competitiveness Index (World Bank, 2020[42]). It considers resilience risk factors, including policy environment for business, health and hygiene, ICT readiness, government prioritisation of tourism, air transport and the quality of tourist infrastructure.
- UNWTO: The Tourism Recovery Tracker considers the tourism recovery in relation to international visitors, aviation capacity and travel sentiment bringing together data from existing sources at a national level, including ICAO, ForwardKeys, Google, STR, AirDNA, Sojern and TCI Research.
- World Economic Forum Travel and Tourism Development Index: Redeveloped in 2022 to focus on sustainability and resilience, the Index measures a set of 112 indicators across 17 pillars (WEF, 2022[43]). This includes a pillar of socio-economic resilience and conditions which considers workers' rights, gender equality and social protection. Other key pillars include environmental sustainability, safety and security and human resources and the labour market.
- More needs to be done to understand the right indicators for resilience and how to measure them. These indicators need to be actionable, robust and comparable. While new or complementary data measures could be more insightful, it could mean that the data is not consistent or timely across countries. Instead, initial indicators could rely on existing national data or international data sets that could be manipulated (OECD, 2021[44]). Pooling and sharing knowledge and results from ongoing work on resilience and on other tourism indicators (e.g. sustainability, competitiveness, digitalisation) will help to establish comparable data and evidence-gathering programmes.
- Resilience indicator sets outside of tourism can provide a framework to inform preliminary thinking. Resilience indicators can be mapped across four pillars that are pertinent and provide a starting point also for work on tourism resilience indicators – Social, Economic, Environment and Institutional (OECD, 2018[45]).

Table 2.1. Initial ideas for tourism resilience indicators

Social	Tourism wage compared to national average
	Level of tourism job security - full-time employee share of the tourism workforce
	Community sentiment in regard to tourism and tourists
	Measure of visitor satisfaction and intention for repeat visits
	Travel openness and facilitation – visas and border closures
	Workforce inclusiveness - gender ratio and inclusion of disability and indigenous workers
Economic	Tourism's direct share of economic activity (GVA/ GDP)
	Tourism's direct share of total employment
	Visitor diversification - the reliance on individual markets
	Dispersal of visitors across destinations - share of visitors in key destinations
	Sectoral reliance on SMEs - the SME share of tourism businesses and revenue
	Employee retention and workforce shortages
	Tourism business insolvency or mortality rates
	Availability of insurance for tourism businesses and insurance uptake rates
	Tourism transport mix - the share of visitors using specific transport methods (e.g. plane, train)
	Tourist yield - average spend per tourist
Environment	Existence of sustainable tourism policies
	Level of CO_2 emissions
	Share of businesses with sustainable status, where sustainable certification is in place
	Likelihood of shocks - average occurrence of significant natural disasters (e.g. earth quakes, cyclones, flooding)
	Number of recognised natural heritage sites and preserved areas
	Share of food that is produced locally
	Share of total annual energy consumed which is from renewable sources
Institutional	Existence of a disaster action plan
	Tourism's proportion of government spending
	Existence of a tourism communications plan (Government and Industry)
	Level of trust in government
	Provision of data sources in open fora for decision making
	Digital infrastructure - internet coverage and average connection speeds

Building on wider OECD work on resilience indicators, Table 2.1 provides some initial ideas for indicators that could be adopted or adapted to measure and monitor tourism resilience in future work. The indicators presented are first proposals to stimulate and inform reflection. The list has been informed by the OECD COVID-19 Recovery Dashboard and work on resilient cities, as well as previous work on tourism indicators. It has also been informed by the EU Tourism Dashboard, and work of other institutions, including the World Bank and World Economic Forum. Further work is needed to review and develop a limited set of meaningful and robust indicators useful for decision-makers to evaluate and measure tourism resilience, and to guide policy choices. This also requires that decision makers have the capacity to understand, analyse and use the indicators, to take informed decisions that support the long-term success and resilience of tourism destinations.

Resilience indicators also need to provide evidence to allow both policy makers and industry to minimise the impact of crisis and provide a strong understanding of the environment for recovery to ensure institutional programmes and future business decisions are targeted and evidence based. This means that, similar to sustainability, a framework for measuring the resilience of the sector will require new measurement methodologies with indicators empowered by up-to-date data and technology (Asian Development Bank, 2021[40]). Considerable research is required to identify the right indicators for tourism resilience and how these are measured reliably across the globe.

Policy considerations to set a path forward for tourism policy makers

Governments and policy makers have an important role to ensure a more resilient tourism ecosystem for the future. Addressing the structural vulnerabilities that have presented under recent pressures and preparing for the multitude of scenarios that could present in an adapting, uncertain and crisis-prevalent future will lay the foundations for a more resilient framework. As the sector focuses on the short-term recovery and looks to adapt to the new normal, governments must take a strategic approach to be better prepared for future shocks.

- **Establish integrated, proactive and forward-looking governance systems for tourism.** Resilience is a key pillar for future tourism development, and resilience thinking needs to be integrated into tourism strategies and decision-making processes. Crisis management for tourism should also be built into national crisis management plans. Policy makers can utilise foresight activities for proactive and preventative policy development through understanding potential future disruptions and the key vulnerabilities of the sector. Linked with strategic foresight, stress-testing of the sector and future legislation could be incorporated into policy making to understand and assess sustainability and resilience for tourism. This process can enable the creation of pre-emptive and innovative responses that can be implemented rapidly and effectively. High-quality policy-driven foresight is underutilised by governments due to a dominant culture of forecast-based policy planning.
- **Provide a business environment where SMEs can succeed, become stronger and benefit from the digital and green transition.** SMEs are a crucial part of the tourism supply chain, but they are also the most vulnerable. Policy makers should take actions to ensure that the business environment can support the resilience of SMEs and foster the transition to sustainable and digital operations. Initiatives could consider: enhancing digital uptake; shifting to greener and more sustainable business practices; improving access to finance, including for SMEs with a greater risk profile; and building the skills and capacity of businesses and business owners.
- **Facilitate sustainable and diverse destinations with tailored destination management plans.** Actions need to be taken to create more sustainable and resilient destinations. Many of these issues are best tackled at the local level to address diverse and specific needs, with broad stakeholder engagement and involvement of local communities. This requires the implementation of crisis management plans that respond to the specific needs of the destination, which should address potential risks and be flexible to change. The requirements of resilience underline the importance of monitoring the delivery and impact of strategies and action plans, enabling more capacity and resources to be allocated where and when necessary. Significant work has been done to address sustainable destination management and can act as a foundation to build destination resilience.
- **Encourage greater collaboration across the tourism ecosystem at all levels.** Building on the strong collaboration initiatives formed through the pandemic can provide a more integrated approach for the tourism ecosystem. This should be supplemented with increased international collaboration across governments, international organisations and across the private sector to ensure actions are effective and complementary, responding and adapting to disruptive events. Creating diverse collaboration structures can help to support information sharing, develop an understanding of emerging risks and opportunities, and learn from previous experiences. This should be supported by opportunities for informal knowledge exchange, including by leveraging digital platforms.
- **Build data to monitor resilience.** There is a need to better understand robust and comparable data sources that could be used to indicate resilience, while also considering the gaps in current data sets. Countries can build experience from developing recovery monitoring tools, but also need to maintain long-term and aspirational goals to measure and monitor tourism resilience. Resources

will be required to understand the impacts of disruptive events, and the measures that might prevail as indicators. While utilising existing data might be a quick fix, it is important to fully understand the issues to ensure both quick response and effective decision-making for future crises.

References

Accor (2020), *2020 Integrated report*, https://www.google.com/url?sa=t&rct=j&q=&esrc=s&source=web&cd=&ved=2ahUKEwih7Yvy48X2AhVS1xoKHelcA3oQFnoECAYQAQ&url=https%3A%2F%2Fgroup.accor.com%2F-%2Fmedia%2FCorporate%2FInvestors%2FDocuments-de-reference%2F2020_Integrated_report_def.pdf&usg=AOvVaw31kuRr. [4]

Asian Development Bank (2021), *Big data for better tourism policy, management and sustainable recovery from COVID-19*, https://www.adb.org/publications/big-data-tourism-policy-management-recovery-covid-19. [40]

BIS (2022), *Newsletter on Covid-19 related credit risk issues*, https://www.bis.org/publ/bcbs_nl26.htm. [37]

Chand, A. (2018), "Place Based Approach to plan for Resilient Cities: a local government perspective", *Procedia Engineering*, Vol. 212, pp. 157-164, https://www.sciencedirect.com/science/article/pii/S1877705818300304. [35]

Della Corte, V. et al. (2021), "Destination resilience and innovation for sdvanced sustainable tourism management: A bibliometric analysis", *Sustainability*, Vol. 13/22, pp. 1-19. [41]

European Commission (2022), *New taxonomy of skills for the green transition*, https://ec.europa.eu/newsroom/empl/items/741088/en. [38]

European Commission (2022), *Transition pathway for tourism*, https://op.europa.eu/s/xaRs. [29]

Hynes, W. et al. (2022), "Systemic resilience in economics", *Nature Physics*, Vol. 18, pp. 381-384, https://www.nature.com/articles/s41567-022-01581-4.pdf?origin=ppub. [9]

Hynes, W. et al. (2020), *Bouncing forward: a resilience approach to dealing with COVID-19 and future systemic shocks*, Springer. [1]

IATA (2022), *Jet fuel price monitor*, https://www.iata.org/en/publications/economics/fuel-monitor/. [14]

IATA (2022), *Soaring jet fuel prices now trending downward*, https://www.iata.org/en/iata-repository/publications/economic-reports/soaring-jet-fuel-prices-now-trending-downward/. [15]

IATA (2021), *How the industry learned the lessons from 9/11*, https://airlines.iata.org/analysis/how-the-industry-learned-the-lessons-from-911. [11]

OECD (2022), *Economic Outlook, Interim Report September 2022: Paying the price of war*, https://www.oecd-ilibrary.org/sites/ae8c39ec-en/index.html?itemId=/content/publication/ae8c39ec-en. [13]

OECD (2022), *Policies for resilient local economies*, https://www.oecd-ilibrary.org/industry-and-services/policies-for-resilient-local-economies_872d431b-en. [34]

OECD (2021), *Economic resilience during crisis: Opportunities and challenges from Covid-19*, https://www.oecd.org/digital/strengthening-economic-resilience-following-the-covid-19-crisis-2a7081d8-en.htm. [28]

OECD (2021), *Enhancing SMEs' resilience through digitalisation: The case of Korea*, https://www.oecd.org/economy/enhancing-smes-resilience-through-digitalisation-23bd7a26-en.htm. [27]

OECD (2021), *Fostering economic resilience in a world of open and integrated markets*, https://www.oecd.org/newsroom/OECD-G7-Report-Fostering-Economic-Resilience-in-a-World-of-Open-and-Integrated-Markets.pdf. [2]

OECD (2021), *High-level dashboard of indicators to guide a strong, resilient, green and inclusive recovery*, https://www.oecd.org/mcm/The-OECD-Dashboard-to-Monitor-a-Strong,-Resilient,-Green-and-Inclusive-Post-Covid-19-Recovery.pdf. [44]

OECD (2021), *International Migration Outlook 2021*, https://www.oecd.org/migration/international-migration-outlook-1999124x.htm#:~:text=3.7%20million%20people,level%20of%20migration%20since%202003. [23]

OECD (2021), *Managing tourism development for sustainable and inclusive recovery*, https://www.oecd-ilibrary.org/industry-and-services/managing-tourism-development-for-sustainable-and-inclusive-recovery_b062f603-en. [30]

OECD (2021), *Preparing the tourism workforce for the digital future*, https://www.oecd.org/publications/preparing-the-tourism-workforce-for-the-digital-future-9258d999-en.htm. [22]

OECD (2021), *SME and Entrepreneurship Outlook 2021*, https://www.oecd-ilibrary.org/sites/97a5bbfe-en/index.html?itemId=/content/publication/97a5bbfe-en. [21]

OECD (2021), *The digital transformation of SMEs*, https://www.oecd.org/industry/smes/PH-SME-Digitalisation-final.pdf. [26]

OECD (2020), *A systemic resilience approach to dealing with Covid-19 and future shocks*, https://www.oecd.org/coronavirus/policy-responses/a-systemic-resilience-approach-to-dealing-with-covid-19-and-future-shocks-36a5bdfb/. [8]

OECD (2020), *Development co-operation report 2020: Learning from crises, building resilience*, OECD, https://www.oecd-ilibrary.org/sites/f6d42aa5-en/index.html?itemId=/content/publication/f6d42aa5-en. [24]

OECD (2020), *Mitigating the impact of COVID-19 on tourism and supporting recovery*, https://www.oecd-ilibrary.org/industry-and-services/mitigating-the-impact-of-covid-19-on-tourism-and-supporting-recovery_47045bae-en. [17]

OECD (2020), *Observatory of Public Sector Innovation: Futures & Foresight*, https://oecd-opsi.org/guide/futures-and-foresight/. [31]

OECD (2020), *Operationalisation of destination management organisations in Romania*, https://www.oecd-ilibrary.org/industry-and-services/operationalisation-of-destination-management-organisations-in-romania_9074fc18-en. [19]

OECD (2020), *Rebuilding tourism for the future: Covid-19 policy responses and recovery*, https://www.oecd.org/coronavirus/policy-responses/rebuilding-tourism-for-the-future-covid-19-policy-responses-and-recovery-bced9859/. [39]

OECD (2020), *Tourism policy responses to the coronavirus (COVID-19)*, https://www.oecd.org/coronavirus/policy-responses/tourism-policy-responses-to-the-coronavirus-covid-19-6466aa20/. [10]

OECD (2019), *Under pressure: The squeezed middle class*, https://www.oecd.org/social/under-pressure-the-squeezed-middle-class-689afed1-en.htm. [16]

OECD (2018), *Analysing megatrends to better shape the future of tourism*, https://www.oecd-ilibrary.org/docserver/d465eb68-en.pdf?expires=1647266234&id=id&accname=ocid84004878&checksum=E3A1491AB3752E8C14E720487FE12AAE. [5]

OECD (2018), *Draft policy framework on sound public governance*, https://www.oecd.org/governance/policy-framework-on-sound-public-governance/. [25]

OECD (2018), *Indicators for resilient cities*, https://www.oecd-ilibrary.org/development/indicators-for-resilient-cities_6f1f6065-en. [45]

OECD (2009), *Policy Responses to Economic Crisis: Investing in innovation for Long-term growth*, https://www.oecd.org/sti/42983414.pdf. [12]

OECD (2009), *The impact of the Global Crisis on SME and entrepreneurship financing and policy responses*, https://www.oecd.org/cfe/smes/theimpactoftheglobalcrisisonsmeandentrepreneurshipfinancingandpolicyresponses.htm. [20]

One Planet (2022), *Tourisms plastic pollution problem*, https://www.oneplanetnetwork.org/programmes/sustainable-tourism/global-tourism-plastics-initiative/tourisms-plastic-pollution-problem. [32]

PATA (2022), *Tourism Destination Resilience*, https://crc.pata.org/tourism-destination-resilience/. [7]

Rusticelli, E. and D. Turner (2021), *OECD working paper: The economic costs of restricting international mobility*, https://www.oecd-ilibrary.org/docserver/dcad4c73-en.pdf?expires=1647524633&id=id&accname=guest&checksum=D627A429C0984FEF572E929667DE75DD. [18]

UK Government (2021), *The de Bois Review: An independent review of destination management organisations in England*, https://assets.publishing.service.gov.uk/government/uploads/system/uploads/attachment_data/file/1011664/2585-C_The_de_Bois_Review_ACCESSIBLE__for_publication_.pdf. [33]

UNEP (2021), *Greening the SMEs: Improving SME access to green finance in Mauritius*, https://www.unepfi.org/wordpress/wp-content/uploads/2021/11/Greening-the-SMEs-Improving-SME-Access-to-Green-Finance-in-Mauritius.pdf. [36]

United Nations (2022), *The Sustainable Development Agenda*, https://www.un.org/sustainabledevelopment/development-agenda/. [6]

UNWTO (2021), *Global and regional tourism performance*, https://www.unwto.org/global-and-regional-tourism-performance. [3]

WEF (2022), *Travel & Tourism Development Index 2021: Rebuilding for a sustainable and resilient future*, https://www.weforum.org/reports/travel-and-tourism-development-index-2021/. [43]

World Bank (2020), *Rebuilding tourism competitiveness: Tourism response, recovery and resilience in the Covid-19 crisis*, https://openknowledge.worldbank.org/handle/10986/34348. [42]

Chapter 3. Promoting a green tourism recovery

Significant progress has been made to better understand tourism's impacts on the natural environment, and to mainstream the concept of sustainability in tourism policy. However, more needs to be done, and with a greater sense of urgency, to accelerate the transition to a greener tourism economy, to translate commitments into real actions and outcomes, and to embed environmental objectives into tourism policies. This chapter examines policy approaches to support the tourism recovery in a green and environmentally sustainable way, while delivering benefits to local communities and economies. It highlights key policy considerations to promote the transition to greener business models and destinations needed to transform the tourism system, and to deliver sustainable outcomes for the long-term.

Tourism has a complex relationship with the environment as, more than many other sectors, it both impacts and is highly dependent on the quality of the environment. Significant progress has been made in recent decades to better understand the impacts of tourism on the natural environment and host societies, and to mainstream the concept of sustainability in tourism policy. This requires adaptation to climate and other changes to be addressed alongside actions to mitigate and reduce the environmental impacts from tourism, while supporting the well-being of communities. However, more needs to be done, and with a greater sense of urgency, to accelerate the transition to a greener tourism economy, to translate commitments into real actions and outcomes, and to embed environmental objectives into tourism policies.

The COVID-19 pandemic has led to a greater awareness of these issues, providing an enhanced incentive and opportunity to tackle them, throughout the tourism ecosystem. The disruption creates significant opportunities to reimagine the tourism sector, fast track the move to greener, more sustainable models of tourism development through innovative policies, and ensure recovery plans are aligned with the Paris Agreement and the Sustainable Development Goals (SDGs). With Russia's war in Ukraine putting additional upward pressure on prices, this may provide a further boost to accelerate transitions to net-zero, as economies reprioritise energy security and businesses shift to more resource-efficient practices.

The window of opportunity is closing to integrate green measures in tourism recovery plans, and ensure the green transition does not get side-tracked by a demand-driven tourism rebound. Urgent action is needed to address the existential threat of climate change, target reduced carbon emissions and pollution, enhance energy and resource efficiency, and prevent the loss of biodiversity and ecosystems from tourism activities. This requires active tourism policies and recovery measures to drive the transition to greener tourism business models and value chains, and improve the environmental outcomes for destinations, while delivering benefits to local economies and communities. Key areas of focus should include:

- **Decarbonisation**: advance sustainable production and consumption by increasing energy efficiency, promoting circular economy models, and reducing tourism's greenhouse gas emissions (GHG), to reach net-zero by 2050.
- **Climate change adaptation**: build tourism resilience to respond to and prepare for climatic hazards and related environmental and socio-economic impacts.
- **Ecosystem restoration**: halt and reverse, where possible, the decline in biodiversity and destruction of fragile habitats, and actively contribute to improving the health of ecological systems.
- **Inclusiveness**: improve equality, and empowerment of individuals, communities, and cultures in line with the SDGs.

Prior to the pandemic, tourism development was economically, socially and environmentally unbalanced in many countries and destinations, often due to rapid and unplanned growth in visitor numbers. Tourism now has an opportunity to build a wider policy momentum to drive the transition to greener tourism business models, as well as promote greening along the tourism value chain involving a wide range of up and downstream processes and actors. Major shifts are necessary for businesses of all sizes in all parts of the tourism ecosystem, such as the shift from a linear to a circular economy which aims to generate a sustainable economic system by fundamentally reducing resource consumption and waste, and decoupling natural resource extraction from the growth of economic activity and well-being (OECD, 2021[1]) (UNEP and World Bank, 2021[2]).

The chapter begins by outlining the urgent need for accelerated action towards green recovery, followed by an assessment of how governments can support greener business models and destinations. Innovative policy approaches are discussed, focusing on several key levers, as well as policy options to assist those involved in the tourism value chain to make a meaningful and lasting contribution to the green transition. The chapter closes by emphasising that the green transition, including building resilience to multiple crises, needs to be embedded across all aspects of tourism recovery and in strategies for the future.

Accelerating the transition to a green tourism economy

The next ten years will be pivotal for addressing both the existential threat of climate change and the ecosystem crisis, as any further delay in taking climate action will sharply increase the risks of irreversible changes of planetary systems. Momentum for a green tourism transformation was building before the pandemic, and has been given new impetus given the urgency and heightened awareness of governments for action.

Restarting tourism whilst redesigning the system is complex and hampered by a wide range of factors that further test the resilience of tourism, and is made more challenging by the relatively narrow window of opportunity to act. Labour shortages coupled with strong pent-up demand have led to travel chaos at major transport hubs, and are constraining recovery overall as businesses struggle to attract skilled and unskilled workers. Russia's war in Ukraine is undermining geopolitical stability and denting travel confidence. It is also adding additional flight hours from rerouted flight paths. Rising energy costs and the cost-of-living crisis are reducing people's ability to afford travel, and increasing the cost of doing business.

Box 3.1. Opportunities to promote a green tourism recovery

Recent events, including the crisis triggered by the COVID-19 pandemic and the changed economic and geopolitical context, have resulted in a changed environment for tourists, businesses and destinations. These changes also bring opportunities to promote the green transition within the sector through:

- Sustainable local products and destination development: catering to tourists with a greater appreciation of the environment and desire to connect with nature
- Shifts toward local tourism: driven by increasing costs, uncertainty and sustainable choices. This can reduce GHG emissions and encourage diversification from local visitor opportunities.
- Longer-stay visitors (including digital nomads): building on new opportunities from increased remote work and work flexibility to increase the value, both for the destination and the traveller.
- Better destination management: understanding tourist volumes and investing in the required infrastructure and mechanisms to manage these sustainably.
- Innovative business models: businesses have an opportunity to restructure, upskill and invest in new technology as part of the recovery to be more digital, sustainable, resilient and inclusive.
- More government and private sector co-operation: the pandemic triggered a whole-of-government response that could present countries with an opportunity to evaluate the positive cross-sectoral interactions and integration, and apply these governance innovations to future policy challenges.

Governments across the OECD and in partner economies have rolled out targeted measures to support households and firms. The energy crisis highlights synergies between the green transition and energy security, and the need for government to support energy efficiency improvements and invest in the capacity of firms to adapt their energy consumption and shift away from fossil fuels (OECD, 2022[3]). The combination of these factors creates a volatile mix, but reinforces the need to pivot towards a greener, more resilient tourism model.

Redefining prosperity, wealth and what tourism success looks like is at the heart of a successful and green recovery. Tourism can help drive the sustainable transition, building on principles that were reinforced through the pandemic including improved management of visitor volumes and flows, and a desire for tourists to be in nature (Box 3.1)

However, progress will be limited if tourism returns to 'business as usual', based on a volume over value business model. Progress also depends on changes in other sectors and parts of the economy, given the highly interconnected nature of the tourism economy (e.g. transport, agriculture). As tourism recovers, and governments look to rethink and reshape a greener, more sustainable tourism economy, these efforts can benefit from initiatives such as reflecting on a new economic narrative and new ways of measuring progress, as proposed in OECD work on the Elements for a New Growth Narrative (OECD, 2018[4]).

Mitigating and adapting tourism to climate change

Climate risk is a key concern, both in terms of tourism's substantial contribution to greenhouse gas emissions, and its exposure to multiple and often cumulative climate impacts (Scott et al., 2019). Reliably estimating tourism's carbon footprint is challenging, but recent estimates range from 8% to 11% of global emissions (WTTC and UNEP, 2021[5]). Global temperatures increased by 1.1°C between the periods 1850-1900 and 2010-19 (IPCC, 2021[6]). Warming of 1.5ºC is likely to be reached by 2030, with wide ranging consequences for tourism destinations. Catastrophic flooding events such as those experienced in Germany and Belgium, or bushfires that threatened tourists and locals in Australia, France, Greece, Portugal and the United States in recent years are pertinent examples. The 2022 heatwaves in the northern hemisphere are another reminder of changing climate conditions.

Tourism policies to address greenhouse gas (GHG) emissions (mitigation) and prepare for climatic changes (adaptation) remain limited, and policy integration across tourism and climate change also needs to be strengthened. Policy is particularly lacking in the area of transport, which is a core element of the tourism value chain and a key contributor to carbon emissions. UN World Tourism Organization /International Transport Forum analysis found that tourism CO_2 emissions grew by at least 60% during the period 2005-16, with transport-related emissions from tourism representing 5% of global emissions in 2016, and could rise by a further 25% or more in CO_2 emissions by 2030 (UNWTO and ITF, 2019[7]). According to the ITF, current decarbonisation policies are considered insufficient to pivot passenger air transport onto a sustainable path (ITF, 2021[8]). In this context, the ambitious target recently adopted by the International Civil Aviation Organisation (ICAO) Air Transport Action Group to achieve net-zero carbon emissions by 2050, through accelerated efficiency measures, energy transition and innovation across the aviation sector and in partnership with governments, is welcome.

There is a growing recognition in the tourism sector of the urgency of climate risks and need to accelerate action. Signatories to the Glasgow Declaration on Climate Action in Tourism adopted at COP26 in 2021 commit to taking action to reduce emissions by 50% by 2030, and to reach net zero as soon as possible before 2050. In 2021, the World Travel and Tourism Council (WTTC), together with the UN Environment Programme (UNEP) put forward a net zero roadmap for travel and tourism businesses, while the World Economic Forum's Clean Skies for Tomorrow coalition has set the target of powering global aviation with 10% sustainable aviation fuel by 2030.

Programmes like the One Planet Sustainable Tourism Programme and 10-Year Framework of Programmes on Sustainable Consumption and Production Patterns are also helping to drive action on this important agenda. Under the G20 Italy Presidency in 2021, G20 Leaders endorsed the Rome Guidelines for the Future of Tourism, with green transformation one of seven pillars to rethink and reshape tourism (OECD, 2021[9]). Linked with the EU Green Deal, the European Commission Transition Pathway for Tourism includes a focus on the transition to greener business models, including through sustainable mobility and integrated circularity for tourism services (European Commission, 2022[10]).

Promoting efficient resource use and reducing ecosystem decline through tourism

The linkages between climate change and ecosystem degradation are widely recognised. Climate change has led to or accelerated irreversible losses of species in all environmental ecosystems – on land, sea and in fresh water. It also compromises ecosystem structure and function, and undermines resilience. It is estimated that around 1 million species are now threatened with extinction, and 75% of terrestrial and 66% of marine environments are "severely altered" by human actions (IPBES, 2019[11])). The UN Decade on Ecosystem Restoration 2021-30 aims to prevent, halt and reverse the degradation of ecosystems worldwide. Restoring the health of ecosystems is essential to re-establish planetary health; a new concept that connects human health and civilisation with ecosystem health (IPCC, 2022[12]).

Tourism, like many sectors, contributes to ecological decline in multiple ways, while natural landscapes and biodiversity are also drivers and assets for tourism. One major issue is plastics pollution, as reflected in the agreement to develop a global treaty on plastics pollution. Global plastics production soared from 234 million tonnes in 2000 to 460 million tonnes in 2019 (OECD, 2022[13]). While the decline in economic activity caused by COVID-19 temporarily curtailed this growth, certain plastics applications such as personal protective equipment grew significantly. Plastic pollution poses substantial risks to tourism livelihoods, especially those that depend on the integrity of marine and terrestrial ecosystems.

Addressing the negative impacts of tourism's resource consumption requires a transition towards the circular economy, in which economic activities regenerate human and natural capital (UNEP and World Bank, 2021[2]).This involves identifying, fostering and investing in sustainable processes focused on reducing, reusing, repairing, refurbishing, recycling, and repurposing (business to business). These changes can help to minimise wastage, reduce emissions, and diminish economic leakages in tourism whilst creating new business opportunities and promoting shorter, local supply chains. As a service sector there is also considerable potential to decouple economic tourism activity from environmental impacts through the development of low consumption activities (e.g. guided walking tours).

Addressing social dimensions of environmental challenges linked with tourism

Climate resilient development brings together governments, civil society and the private sector through multi-dimensional governance that focuses on risk reduction, equity and justice (IPCC, 2022[12]). A green tourism transition involves reconsideration of governance arrangements and collaboration across the tourism value chain. Increased multi-stakeholder governance in tourism has continued to develop through the pandemic, including through multi-lateral and global agreements and frameworks that provide guidance for national policy-making. Networked governance arrangements connect national opportunities with the local level context and help to optimise decision making. Fostering the networks developed through the pandemic and building more integrated governance systems has the potential to increase tourism's ability to transition, as stakeholders at all levels are actively involved in the design process. Participative approaches that involve all actors with an inherent stake in achieving sustainable outcomes in a destination can increase the chances of long-term success.

Increasing consumer awareness can also support both private and public sector actions for a more sustainable tourism model. A recent Eurobarometer survey on attitudes of Europeans towards tourism highlighted that 82% of EU citizens expressed interest in supporting more sustainable tourism, for example, by consuming locally (55%), choosing environmentally friendly transport (36%), paying more to protect nature (35%) or to benefit the local community (33%) (European Commission, 2021[14]). These findings are echoed by 2021 surveys from Booking.com and Skyscanner and the growing trend of 'flight shaming' which is representative of this shifting consumer sentiment.

Toward a greener, more sustainable future for tourism

Momentum is gathering in the sector for the green tourism transition. However, decision makers need to navigate several systemic and acute challenges to convert this momentum into actions with impact:

- Financial constraints: Tight budgets demand that the transition is cost-effective and value-generating.
- Labour shortages and skills gaps: Ongoing labour shortages and gaps in knowledge or skills, including those related to green service delivery, could hinder the tourism recovery.
- Inefficient infrastructure and assets: Green and sustainable tourism need new and more efficient infrastructure (e.g. charging stations for electric vehicles, cycle paths, renewed building stock).
- Limited tourism policy integration: Key policy areas like transportation, environment, infrastructure, regional economic development, and emergency services are pivotal to the green transition and the lack of integration poses barriers to coherent strategies to facilitate green tourism.

The unprecedented support measures introduced in response to the pandemic have been an opportunity to strategically support those parts of the tourism system that are more likely to form part of the green transition. However, analysis shows that only one-third of pandemic support and recovery packages were classified as environmentally positive and supporting sustainability and transformation (OECD, 2022[15]). For example, only 2% of total funding support during 2020-21 to the aviation sector was assessed to be environmentally positive. Governments should not miss the opportunity to make support measures conditional on making progress on environmental challenges, and catalyse conditions that foster a greener tourism transformation.

Encouraging greener tourism business models and destinations

Governments have a key role to play to support greener businesses and destinations, and ensure that sustainability principles are firmly embedded in recovery plans. This means taking steps to incorporate decarbonisation, climate resilience, ecosystem restoration and inclusion into policies, programmes and future-oriented strategies that are also aligned with the Paris Agreement and SDGs. It involves having a strategic view across the tourism system, and creating favourable framework conditions at the national level, to provide an effective compass to guide policy and decision making.

Coherent and co-ordinated action across policy areas is important to work toward common goals, maximise the positive outcomes for tourism, and wider greening measures, and avoid unintended consequences. Facilitating the collaboration of key actors is another important role for government at all levels, and one where regional and local governments are increasingly active. Managing system change can only be successful if all relevant actors are involved. In Ireland, for example, a guiding principle of the Sustainable Tourism Working Group is all of government working together with industry towards achieving a sustainable tourism sector (Box 3.2).

Businesses are at the forefront of the green transition, with the many small and medium sized businesses (SMEs) that connect the visitor with the place through creating experiences having a particularly critical role to play. Delivering on the SDGs and carbon reduction targets requires much greater engagement with SMEs, which make up around 85% of tourism businesses in OECD countries, on average. This requires support in the form of targeted financial assistance, alongside capacity building to encourage sustainability innovation and new business opportunities (OECD, 2021[1]).

The business case for sustainability action has never been more prominent, as is the opportunity to capitalise on wider societal shifts to more sustainable consumption patterns. Rapidly increasing operational costs are putting pressure on many tourism businesses, but also create significant interest in energy savings and resource programmes, and provide a strong inventive to consider energy efficiency investments and make changes to conserve resources. The growing awareness of customers and opportunities for green branding support such changes.

Destination decision makers and businesses often face similar challenges but can also join forces to maximise opportunities. Government can advance, in turn, the business and destination transition by reducing barriers (e.g. information, resources) by promoting awareness around changing legislation and technology (e.g. renewable energy solutions, smart metres, zero waste solutions), providing better access to skills (e.g. long-term planning, digital skills, practical skills for repair and repurpose) and implementing financing and funding to undertake green action (OECD, 2021[1]).

Box 3.2. Actions to promote sustainable tourism practices in Ireland

The Sustainable Tourism Working Group was established under Ireland's Tourism Action Plan 2019-21 and sets the ambition for Ireland to be amongst the world-leaders in sustainable tourism practices. The Group has identified a range of actions to promote sustainable tourism practices, through an interim action plan from 2021-23. This involves building greater sustainability awareness among tourism stakeholders and the general public, and take sustainability into account in policy development, business planning, destination management and promotional activity. Some of the key recommendations include:

- Ensuring greater community involvement in destination planning to maximise the potential of nature-based solutions in local tourism.
- Providing better access to information and tools for visitors to practice responsible tourism through the development of carbon calculators which will allow visitors to evaluate the impact of their carbon footprint on the environment.
- Stimulating change in the tourism sector by identifying and delivering incentive schemes to address key change barriers and drivers.
- Developing a sustainability pledge for visitors to support Ireland's efforts to help preserve the environment and act in a responsible and sustainable manner.
- Assigning responsibilities within the tourism agencies to provide strategic direction and increased profile for sustainable tourism development.
- Assigning a senior industry representative to act as a sustainability champion.
- Identifying and developing destinations that have the potential to be promoted as best in class in terms of sustainability.

Work to develop a new national tourism policy will be informed by the Sustainable Tourism Working Group. In particular, the actions which aim to build an evidence base and measurement mechanisms across social and community considerations will help shape policy.

OECD work on SMEs highlights that the share of green spending targeted at SMEs in general is modest, representing 2.9% of green recovery packages (OECD, 2022[16]). Additional measures are needed to ensure that SMEs are equipped to finance actions to reduce their carbon footprint and contribute to sustainability objectives. Countries are looking to implement both financial (e.g. grants, loans, subsidies, tax breaks) and non-financial (e.g. advice, consultancy, tools) supports for businesses. To benefit, tourism SMEs will need to be able to access these supports. Businesses providing different types of tourism services (e.g. business, holiday, events) in different destinations (e.g. mountain, beach, city) and types of tourism have specific needs and profiles. This may require some flexibility and adaptability to ensure the supports cater to tourism businesses in all parts of the tourism ecosystem. In South Africa, for example, the Green Tourism Incentive Programme aims to encourage and support tourism businesses to adopt more sustainable business practices (Box 3.3).

Box 3.3. Incentivising greener tourism business practices in South Africa

Launched in 2017, South Africa's Green Tourism Incentive Programme is a resource efficiency incentive programme that assists small and micro-tourism businesses to adopt sustainable tourism practices. The programme is linked to South Africa's policy for pursuing responsible, sustainable tourism, as set out in the National Tourism Sector Strategy, and the White Paper on the Development and Promotion of Tourism.

Through grant funding, the programme focuses on promoting energy-efficient operations for the tourism sector. It funds water and energy efficiency assessments, which establish the most optimal green solutions for each audited establishment. The solutions are then funded on a sliding scale from 50% to 90% capped at ZAR 1 million (USD 54 553). Participants in the programme benefit from a reduction of their overall operational costs over time with the associated advantages in respect of competitiveness. Beneficiaries include guest houses and lodges reflecting the focus on small and micro enterprises.

Prior to the full roll out, a pilot was implemented, focusing on retrofitting tourism facilities with solar photovoltaic energy generating systems at eight major sites. One such project was implemented at the UNESCO World Heritage Site, Robben Island Museum. The island had a ZAR 25 million (USD 1.4 million) solar powered mini-grid plant installed under the project. At the time, the island was operating entirely on diesel generation as it has never been connected to the country's electricity grid. The intervention was projected to reduce the use of diesel generators by over 40% and generate a saving of ZAR 5 million (USD 274 492) per annum whilst also saving tons of carbon emissions. The "payback period" for the project was therefore five years.

Reducing tourism's carbon footprint to support better environmental management

Reducing carbon intensity contributes significantly to the wider goal of a green tourism transition. Reductions in energy use in particular often bring positive flow-on effects for additional resource efficiencies (especially in relation to the energy-water nexus) and dematerialisation of products. Also, companies that invest in future-proof technologies, processes and markets tend to deliver better business performance, higher staff retention, customer loyalty and community support (Whelan and Fink, 2016[17]).

Carbon literacy and low-carbon innovation

Greater carbon literacy is needed across the tourism ecosystem and among all tourism actors, to encourage action and identify new solutions. Building carbon literacy improves awareness of climate change and impacts in everyday practices and behaviour. It can be enhanced through formal education and training, online resources, business networks and clusters, and bespoke outreach and tools for tourism decision makers, such as decision making frameworks and templates to build the business case. Understanding the GHG emissions profile of tourism also helps governments decide where and how to invest into innovation to maximise the decarbonisation impact.

Helping businesses and destinations measure their carbon and wider environmental footprints (e.g. water) is one approach that can help raise awareness. Tangible evidence of the carbon implications of different market segments or tourism activities supports businesses to design low carbon portfolios and invest in energy management (Box 3.4). Measurement also helps destination management organisations develop low carbon strategies and attract preferred consumers. The approach of measuring tourists' carbon footprint is complemented by private sector initiatives which inform travellers about the carbon emissions associated with different travel options, to inform more sustainable choices (e.g. Skyscanner, Google, Bookdifferent.com).

Destination foot-printing is in its early stages but can benefit from initiatives to reduce GHG emissions – an opportunity for policy integration between national and urban/local government agencies. Examples of destination actions are set out in (Box 3.5).

Norway has developed a strategic planning tool to measure emissions and promote climate friendly tourism. The CO2rism calculator estimates the amount of transport-related CO_2 emissions associated with visitors travelling to and within Norway (Box 3.6). Similarly, Visit Finland is creating sustainable route suggestions and a digital trip planner targeting responsible visitors.

Box 3.4. Building carbon literacy in the tourism sector: selected country approaches

Colombia: An online training platform with practical interactive content aims to build skills for tourism businesses related to best practices in sustainable tourism. A complementary online course on sustainable gastronomy was launched in October 2020 in partnership with World Wildlife Fund Colombia and the UN Environment Programme.

Malta: The Ministry of Tourism, in partnership with SUNx (Strong Universal Network), is working to accelerate climate action through the development of a capacity building diploma in climate-friendly travel for the next generation of tourism-climate ambassadors.

New Zealand: The Tourism Industry Aotearoa Association carbon challenge urges tourism businesses to measure their carbon footprint, take action to significantly reduce carbon emissions by 2030, and contribute to a tourism sector that is net zero carbon ahead of New Zealand's 2050 goal. The carbon challenge is complementary to the Tourism Sustainability Commitment and Qualmark – two quality and sustainability assurance programmes available to businesses.

Peru: The Ministry of Foreign Trade and Tourism developed an eco-efficiency manual for the hotel sector to improve energy management, in co-ordination with The Ministry of Energy and Mines. The Ministry of Foreign Trade and Tourism is in the process of harmonising the Good Practice System, aimed at promoting practices on circular economy, use of clean technologies, and reduction of greenhouse gas emissions for tourism service providers. It has also worked with the Ministry of the Environment to develop the Carbon Footprint Tool of Peru for tourism businesses.

Saudi Arabia: Climate action is being addressed through the Saudi Green Initiative and new Sustainable Tourism Global Centre, which is a collaboration between the Ministry of Tourism and Ministry of Energy. The new Centre supports the Tourism Panel on Climate Change, an independent science-based collaboration of global experts to deliver a tourism-specific assessment of climate knowledge and action.

Box 3.5. Destination-specific actions to reduce carbon emissions: selected country approaches

Austria: The two destinations, Nassfeld-Pressegger See/Lesachtal/Weißensee and Zell am See-Kaprun, are designated as Climate and Energy Model Regions. Since 2021, they are being supported with EUR 1 million each by the Climate and Energy Fund to increase the use of local energy resources, improve energy efficiency, and decarbonise mobility. The Clean Alpine Region project in Tyrol is also supporting tourism regions to implement measures in the areas of climate protection, sustainability and energy and in developing further as climate-friendly regions.

Canada: The mountain resort community of Whistler has had a Community Energy and Climate Action Plan in place for nearly a decade. Updated in 2020, the Action Plan commits to reducing GHG emissions by 50% below 2007 levels by 2030. It focuses on a Climate Action Big Moves Strategy to enable Whistler demonstrate leadership in redefining tourism in a low carbon world. These big moves occur in transport (e.g. 50% of all trips are by transit and active transportation), buildings (e.g. new buildings by 2030 are zero carbon, reduce emissions from residential buildings by 20% and commercial buildings by 40%), and waste (e.g. reduce waste emissions by 95%).

Greece: A pioneering project aims to make Astypalea the first smart and sustainable island with energy autonomy in the Mediterranean, and achieve zero-emissions mobility by 2030. It involves the gradual replacement of conventional private and public vehicles on the island with electric vehicles, and the introduction of an innovative transportation system based on shared mobility. It also promotes the production of electricity from renewable energy sources. The project is being implemented over six years, in partnership with the Volkswagen Group.

Spain: Visit Valencia is taking action to become a carbon neutral destination by 2025 by using the SDG compass to monitor and improve performance. The decarbonisation roadmap involves: i) baseline footprint calculations, ii) implementation of a digital management system, and iii) development of compensation projects at the destination. The climate strategy also addresses improving quality of life of residents and enhancement of cultural and natural heritage.

Regulating and incentivising good practice

Policy instruments, such as carbon taxes, emission standards for vehicles, fuel mandates, and building standards often play a part in wider economic decarbonisation strategies, including in the tourism sector. Tourism-specific regulation is less common, with governments opting for support programmes and incentives to build a greener tourism production model. In Germany, for example, the ClimaHost programme aims to support accommodation establishments that have implemented innovative climate action measures and contribute to sustainable tourism in the Alps region.

The pandemic provided motivation for countries to reconsider how to improve and encourage uptake of sustainability programmes for tourism businesses and destinations. Evaluating the impact of existing programmes should be a priority, alongside consolidation as multiple programmes could confuse and undermine the purpose of initiatives targeting tourists and businesses.

The private sector is also taking a more proactive role in putting in place initiatives or levers that foster a green transition (e.g. new award schemes). Analysis by TUI, verified by UNEP, shows that hotels with sustainability certifications achieve 10% lower CO_2 emissions, 24% lower waste volume per guest night, and used 23% more green energy. Hotels with sustainability certifications also received higher customer satisfaction scores, compared to non-certified hotels (One Planet, 2021[18])

Box 3.6. Measuring tourism-related transport emissions in Norway

Norway has developed a tool, CO2rism, for estimating the amount of transport-related CO_2 emissions associated with visitors travelling to and within Norway. It is one of several operational tools to support destinations shift to more sustainable tourism planning and development under the National Tourism Strategy 2030. It takes a passenger-based approach and was developed by Innovation Norway, in collaboration with the Norwegian Institute for Air Research. The CO2rism tool is used by destinations to gain insights into the emissions profile of different tourists. By combining emissions data with data on tourist arrivals, the main transport mode from different source markets, and tourist travel patterns, the calculator estimates CO_2 emissions connected to each of the markets. Length of stay is also calculated, with information on emissions per day.

Users of the tool have multiple choices to adjust the input data according to tourist numbers, length of stay, and origin markets. The emissions of each transport mode (air, ferry, train, car, bus and camper) are distributed to the tourist based on the number of passengers that share the emissions. The resulting output is a measure of tourist emissions travelling to, from and at a destination, based on the place of origin, destination region and length of stay of the tourist. The highest CO_2 emissions from tourism transport to and in Norway are from aviation (71% of total CO_2 travel emissions), followed by ferries and cruises (21%). More than 50 destinations in Norway use the tool to report on tourism transport emissions. The tool is also helping to raise awareness, highlight the consequences of shifting markets, and stimulate actions for longer stays and the change to low-emission transport, where possible.

Most OECD countries have some form of quality standard or green certification programme in place for tourism; however, participation is often voluntary and 'hard measures' or targets are lacking, including for the measurement and reduction of GHG emissions. France, for example, in 2022 implemented a new classification system for tourism accommodations based on sustainability standards. For hotels, the number of sustainability criteria has doubled, while the number of mandatory criteria has increased fourfold. New standards include waste management, energy and water consumption, integration into local supply chains, and the use of organic, fair-trade and ecological products. Importantly, one criterion concerns the information given to guests on low carbon transport, highlighting how decarbonisation involves hosts and tourists alike.

There is an increasing interest in measuring and auditing destination performance, linked with the shift in focus from destination marketing to destination management. Austria has created a new ecolabel for destinations, to accelerate the green transition, improve regional value chains and respond to the increased demand for sustainable holidays (Box 3.7). The comprehensive criteria include innovative measures such as the requirement that at least 30% of promoted tourism products must be considered sustainable, and the recommendation that finance destination activities are financed using certified green finance products.

Norway has expanded and adjusted its Sustainable Destination Certification scheme, which enhances destination management, and a new regulatory framework for more sustainable fishing tourism has been implemented. The sustainable tourism policy of Norway has also included measures on marking a growing number of National Hiking Trails to make them more robust, accessible and attractive for visitors.

Box 3.7. Ecolabel for tourism destinations in Austria

In 2022, Austria created a new ecolabel for tourism destinations to accelerate the green transition, improve regional value chains and respond to the increased demand for sustainable holidays. The ecolabel is targeted at tourism destinations at the regional level and not at the operational level (e.g. locations such as resorts, amusement parks). A key requirement is the co-operation of tourism management with political actors and tourism businesses of the destination as well as sufficient financial, personnel and time resources for implementation.

The ecolabel criteria were developed in a comprehensive discussion process with relevant stakeholders and experts from the tourism sector, including 19 pilot destinations, and is based on the European Tourism Indicator System and the internationally recognised criteria of the Global Sustainable Tourism Council. The label comprises a comprehensive set of 63 mandatory and 56 optional criteria, the latter based on a scoring system with a minimum number of points to be achieved at the time the application is submitted. The criteria cover the following areas:

- Management: sustainability strategy and mission statement, planning and development, offers and advertising, partner commitment.
- Socio-economic impact: regional economy and infrastructure, education and work, diversity and accessibility, fair trade.
- Environmental protection: climate protection and climate change adaptation; nature conservation and biodiversity, landscape protection; energy; water, waste, air, noise, light.
- Mobility: connectivity arrival/departure, mobility on site, co-operation and offers.
- Culture: cultural assets and intangible heritage, traditional and contemporary culture, visitor management.

Incentivising better practice in tourism could benefit from alignment with other, non-tourism programmes. In Colombia, the Ministry of Tourism has aligned with the National Circular Economy Strategy to launch a competition to finance innovative waste management or eco-design projects that advance circular economy models in tourism. A circular economy connections programme for the tourism value chain and its suppliers is specifically designed to encourage SME participation. Thailand is taking a similar approach, by aligning tourism recovery with the national Bio-Circular Green Economy Plan, opening support for new approaches and products, including agritourism and community-based tourism initiatives.

Adapting to climate change and building tourism resilience

Climate and other risks demand more attention from businesses and destinations to identify threats and devise strategies to manage them. Many larger companies are already required to undertake climate risk assessments and disclose them to their stakeholders, with implications for tourism (Box 3.8).

However, businesses of all sizes frequently lack the knowledge and resources to undertake such assessments. Facilitating knowledge transfer and data access (e.g. sea level rise, flood maps), creating business tools (e.g. calculating financial implications of climate risks), and implementing preventive actions are all areas where government can play a role. In Mexico, the ADAPTUR project aims to support the tourism sector in climate adaptation, and strengthen business capacity to undertake concrete actions, such as economic risk assessments for the hotel sector and real estate projects, and tourism involvement in restoring and protecting mangroves and coral reefs.

Box 3.8. Implications of mandatory climate risk disclosure for tourism businesses

Mandatory disclosure of climate risk for publicly traded companies was supported by the G7 countries in the Carbis Bay G7 Summit Communiqué in June 2021, in line with the recommendations of the Task Force on Climate-related Financial Disclosures. Mandatory disclosure requirements were also a key part of the financial sector response at COP 26 in Glasgow the same year.

Guidance has also been developed by the European Bank for Reconstruction and Development and the Global Centre for Excellence on Climate Adaptation. The recommendations most important to tourism operators include:

- Assess exposure to all first-order physical climate impacts.
- Assess physical climate risks over the duration of an asset's lifetime.
- Provide detailed information on the financial impacts of recent extreme weather events.
- Disclose the impacts of weather variability on value chains.
- Perform forward-looking assessments of physical climate risks.
- Identify opportunities based on managing physical climate risks and related market shifts.
- Consider current and desired GHG concentration pathways and related warming projections as a basis for scenario analysis of physical climate risks and opportunities.

Source: European Bank for Reconstruction and Development and the Global Centre of Excellence, 2018[13]

Several destinations are proactively investing in climate change adaptation. In Iceland, the Varða/Sites of Merit programme aims to integrate climate adaptation into a wider destination management framework at popular tourist sites. Australia is investing in the resilience of coral reefs through the AUD 150 million Reef Restoration and Adaptation Program, which is looking at new initiatives to help coral reefs adapt to climate change, and the AUD 100 million Oceans Leadership Package. The Oceans Leadership package will invest to protect oceans, support blue carbon habitats and ecosystems and contribute to emissions reduction through the restoration of mangroves and tidal marshes to store carbon and reduce methane and nitrous oxide emissions.

Climate resilience needs to consider the whole value chain, with the links between tourism and primary industries such as agriculture and forestry particularly important. Fostering links between tourism and agriculture, for example, can build resilience for both sectors. Local and traditional food and agricultural products have been highlighted as an important opportunity. For example, Hungary's Traditions Flavours Regions Programme protects the designations of origin for wine products and food specialities. In Costa Rica, the Tourism Local Development Engine created in 2021 aims to improve the life of agricultural communities through the identification of market opportunities in the tourism sector for sustainable agriculture value chains adapted to climate change.

Building resilience in destinations that are particularly exposed to risks is an important strategy, especially when political or economic goals such as regional development depend on a healthy tourism sector. In France, for example, the Mountain Futures Plan launched in 2021 aims to promote sustainable and resilient mountain tourism through three priorities, namely diversification of both products and customers, improvement of ecological performance of activities, and revitalising recreational real estate. The plan represents a commitment of over EUR 640 million of public funds for the mountains, generating nearly EUR 1.8 billion of investment in these areas. This is explored further in Chapter 2, Building Resilience in the Tourism Ecosystem.

Promoting ecosystem restoration through tourism

Improving the responsible use of natural capital is a core aspect of more sustainable tourism models. Governments can support the alliance between tourism and conservation by implementing mechanisms targeted at different parts of the value chain simultaneously, variously targeting tourism businesses, workers, infrastructure and natural assets (Box 3.9). Awareness raising is one important instrument – the Global Tourism Plastics Initiative, for example, unites the tourism businesses, governments and other tourism stakeholders behind a common vision to take concerted action, leading by example in the shift towards circularity in the use of plastics (One Planet, 2022[19]).

Other instruments include initiatives to better integrate environmental considerations into tourism curricula and training, introduce visitor management systems, temporary closures of national parks and protected areas, and deployments of smart technology to optimise visitor flows. The Emilia-Romagna region of Italy launched a digital platform in 2022 to support local administrations and operators to better organise activities, prevent overcrowding and guarantee quality and sustainability of the activities related to nature and culture. There is also a trend to encourage visitors to 'give back' through programmes such as the Trees that Count initiative in New Zealand.

Financial incentives are another option. In Colombia, the Together with Nature Sustainable Tourism Policy rewards land acquisition for projects that serve both tourism and conservation outcomes through a 25% discount on income tax.

Box 3.9. Strengthening the tourism-nature relationship: selected country approaches

Businesses/organisations:

- **Peru:** A compensation mechanism for Ecosystem Services encourages tourism businesses to make a contribution to conservation, recovery, and sustainable use of ecosystems.
- **United Kingdom:** The Green Recovery Challenge Fund (GBP 80 million) supports projects that restore nature, address climate change and connect people to nature, while supporting jobs.

Workforce:

- **Colombia:** A preservation-oriented handbook for nature tourism guides called "Contemplation, Comprehension, Conservation" is designed to ensure the quality of nature tourism experiences.
- **Lithuania:** 12-month nature guide training courses have been launched under the wider project of Nature Guides Network with Germany and Poland as partner countries.

Infrastructure and natural assets:

- **Australia:** A fund was launched (AUD 33.5 million) for conservation work and infrastructure upgrades across 23 national and world heritage sites.
- **Canada:** Investment of CAD 2.3 billion over five years to conserve up to 1 million square kilometres of land and inland waters. In addition, Canada is investing CAD 200 million over three years to support natural and hybrid infrastructure projects, such as parks, green spaces, ravines, waterfronts and wetlands.
- **Latvia:** New investments for smart solutions to monitor tourism flows in protected areas and assess environmental impacts have been implemented.

Nature-based solutions are a great way to align disaster mitigation, conservation, and sustainable tourism. Restoring and protecting wetlands, for example, can improve water quality, support biodiversity, reduce flood risk, sequester carbon, and provide opportunities for ecotourism. The 2022 USA National Travel Tourism Strategy embraces nature-based solutions as a key strategy, supported by three actions based around collaboration, investment and information for communities and stakeholders.

Empowering local communities to promote a green tourism transition

Environmental challenges are intricately linked with social issues. A more inclusive tourism requires the empowerment of local residents to participate in and drive decision making for tourism, including to support the green transition. Participative, community-led destination management and experience development approaches can help to achieve this in a way that benefits local actors. Promoting local entrepreneurship opportunities also helps integrate tourism into the community, with economic diversification through tourism entrepreneurship – including in rural areas – part of a green recovery.

Costa Rica, for example, ran an initiative in 2020 to identify key challenges and solutions for a green tourism recovery. A total of 13 projects out of 195 proposals were selected and funded. Similarly, the Swiss innovation programme, Innotour, has been extended to 2023 at the level of CHF 30 million, and a Competence Centre has been set up to connect Swiss tourism more purposefully to the SDGs. In Mexico, the FORESSTUR project is an example of using tourism as a social welfare tool with complementary economic benefits in forest communities, whilst contributing to the preservation and health of the ecosystems It is aimed at social enterprises, which can make important contributions to economic and inclusive growth, community members and land holders.

Inclusion and empowerment can be fostered through greater access to knowledge for those who lack resources or capability. Internet connectivity is a key facilitator in this process, particularly in rural areas. Vulnerable and marginalised groups require particular supports, also to ensure that they are not unfairly and negatively impacted by measures to promote the green tourism transition. Governments can also help to address inclusion through programmes tailored for women young people, migrants and indigenous populations which may require particular supports (OECD, 2020[20]; OECD, 2020[21]). Non-governmental organisations are also providing online support platforms for training, capacity building and networking (OECD, 2022[22]), for example Tourism Cares' Meaningful Travel Platform.

Indigenous culture remains a key part of many communities, and can play a central role in an inclusive and sustainable tourism ecosystem. Indigenous knowledge and participation can also benefit the green transition through their traditional knowledge systems (MBIE, 2022[23]). In Australia, the Camping with Custodians programme builds community-operated campgrounds on Aboriginal and Torres Strait Islander land where visitors have the chance to stay with traditional owners to experience Aboriginal culture. The programme provides job security for Indigenous communities through seed funding and developing small-scale resilient and sustainable tourism enterprises that are then transitioned back to Traditional Owners. In Canada, the Indigenous Tourism Association of Canada has facilitated the COVID-19 Development Stimulus Grant to support indigenous tourism SMEs, through non-repayable grants, to develop or maintain business activity.

New Zealand has developed a values-based approach to regenerative tourism. A Tourism Adaptation Roadmap is being developed, through voluntary initiatives bringing together leaders from the public and private sectors to investigate the state of natural resources, and to commit to priority actions that will halt and reverse declines (Box 3.10).

Box 3.10. Shift to a values-based regenerative and climate resilient tourism in New Zealand

In New Zealand, financial support is available to support destination management in the form of grants to the 31 Regional Tourism Organisations as part of the 2020 'Tourism Recovery Package' and the 2021 'Tourism Communities: Support, Recovery and Re-Set Plan'. The investment aligns with growing momentum towards regenerative tourism – set out in the 2021 Industry Transformation Plan – that is reflected in a wellbeing approach and explicit recognition of the values that underpin tourism.

New Zealand has developed a values-based approach to regenerative tourism. The Department of Conservation has developed a 'tourism tree' to visualise the importance of values, multiple outcomes from tourism, and the importance of 'giving back' to nature and people (Becken and Kaur, 2021[24]). It connects directly to the Heritage and Visitor strategy's key pillars of Protect, Connect and Thrive. More work will be required to connect with Māori values and associated knowledge systems.

Aligned with the 2021 Industry Transformation Plan, a Tourism Adaptation Roadmap is also developed for local communities to respond to climate impacts. The roadmap is initiated by the Aotearoa Circle, an initiative that brings together leaders from the public and private sectors to investigate the state of natural resources, and to commit to priority actions. The development of the Roadmap aims to identify the risks of a changing climate for New Zealand's tourism sector, and to increase climate resilience.

Promoting green tourism recovery and transformation

The disruption caused by COVID-19 provided an opportunity to reflect and redesign the tourism system through new policies and governance arrangements. While governments have stepped up efforts to build sustainability capacity, foster innovation, and measure tourism's performance through enhanced multi-impact frameworks, more needs to be done to embed this into future tourism frameworks.

Embedding green principles in strategic tourism planning and policy

National tourism strategies are central to providing strategic direction and maximising the positive contribution of tourism to a country's prosperity and well-being. Strategies often reflect core values and provide an overall framework for more specific policy development, investment and stakeholder collaboration. Many countries are preparing tourism recovery plans and strategies which provide opportunities to embed targets and actions to promote the green transition.

In the new National Travel and Tourism Strategy 2022, the United States has put measures to reduce tourism's contribution to climate change at the centre of fostering a resilience and sustainable tourism economy that also protects natural resources, and supports the tourism economy and equitable development. Sustainability is positioned as the backbone of Peru's Reactivation of the Tourism Sector Strategy 2021-23, with the sustainable management of the unique experiences based on its natural and cultural wealth also central to competitiveness. Actions planned include the introduction of environmental regulations and streamlining of environment procedures for tourism, as well as tools to advance the circular economy, use clean technologies, and improve service quality. Korea launched a '2050 Carbon Neutral Promotion Strategy' in 2020 and conducted a study on tourism policies to respond to achieve carbon neutrality.

Box 3.11. Estonia's National Tourism Strategy 2022-25

Estonia's National Tourism Strategy 2022-25 has a goal to become a sustainable tourism destination that offers visitors diverse and unique travel experience in all seasons. Estonia's cross-cutting approach on sustainability is defined by three principles: valorisation of the local culture, the environment and the community; co-operation; and contribution to fulfilling the UN SDGs. Activities already set out by the Estonian Tourist Board for the period 2022-25 to enhance the sustainability and resilience of Estonian tourism sector include:

- Participating in international Green Destinations programme, running annual GreenEST summit and circular economy programmes.
- Recognising sustainable tourism operators and enhancing application of eco-labels.
- Sharing information and best practices about green investment and resource saving support options and the best sharing practices.
- Providing financial support for sustainable and inclusive tourism sector product development (EUR 14.1 million from REACT EU measures).
- Supporting new business models.
- Developing thematic networks and routes.

The Strategy also sets out several measurable goals for the tourism sector to be achieved by 2025. These goals include increasing the average length of stay of international tourists to at least four nights, increase participation in the network of sustainable tourism businesses to include at least 150 firms, and at least six Estonian destinations have received the Green Destinations Award.

The successful implementation of tourism strategies requires financial support and dedication of other resources. In Estonia, for example, the green transformation is an underlying principle of the Tourism Strategy 2022-25, and is supported by an overall investment of EUR 126.3 million in tourism development and marketing. This includes EUR 21 million for development of sustainable products and destinations, with a further EUR 17 million of REACT EU funding to directly support businesses to develop sustainable products and digital solutions for the tourism sector Box 3.11). Tourism strategies anchored in sustainability, and supported through robust performance measurements, may also help countries tap into international green finance, for example the Green Climate Fund established by the UNFCCC.

Connecting tourism strategies to wider government priorities reduces policy conflict, and provides an opportunity to leverage existing investment and programmes designed at a larger scale than tourism alone. A greener tourism model needs to improve the integration of tourism with other sectors; politically, economically and socially. Egypt leveraged the Government's Sustainable Development Strategy to undertake a tourism gap analysis, for example, resulting in the development of 18 strategic goals for a green and digital transition in line with the UN SDGs.

Tourism is also often affected by broader government decisions or regulation in other policy areas. In environmental regulation, tourism organisations are required to comply with standards or rules typically created by non-tourism departments. Transport is another example of a policy area where decisions have a direct impact on tourism, such as recent announcements in the Netherlands on limiting the number into Schiphol Airport, and plans to halve the number of domestic flights in France. This highlights the importance co-operation across government to manage change related to the green transition.

The interdependences and linkages between tourism and other key value chains make the sector a strategic entry point to accelerate sustainability and circularity across the wider economy. For example, the food and beverage sector has strong supply linkages with tourism and is integral to tourism operations, contributing 9% of tourism's global carbon footprint, rising to 17% if including agriculture. Building resilience and sustainability of the tourism sector therefore inevitably requires a holistic, cross-sectoral approach which considers related value chains and leverages potential synergies when designing policy interventions.

Collaborative tourism policy and programmes to support green action

Strong governance is a key enabler of the green tourism transition, requiring greater levels of efficiency, transparency, collaboration and stakeholder support (Becken and Loehr, 2022[25]). Fostering multi-level governance is appropriate for tourism, which is characterised by its global-local public-private sector elements of the value chain. Fit-for-purpose governance helps optimise decision-making and allocation of resources (e.g. financial, knowledge, data, networks).

Suitable governance arrangements should be designed for the intended purpose. In Mexico, the Tlatocan or Great Council for Tourism Sustainability, brought together more than 130 participants, including government agencies, international organisations, civil society, indigenous communities, social enterprises, private companies, and academia. The initiative sat under the framework of the Mexico is Reborn Sustainable initiative which was developed collaboratively to transform the pandemic crisis into an opportunity to generate a radical change in tourism.

Partnerships are central to pandemic recovery responses designed to deliver sustainable outcomes in new ways that tourism agencies could not deliver by themselves (Table 3.1). These partnerships often include NGOs or private sector actors. In Greece, the Rhodes Co-Lab is a 'futures lab' for sustainable tourism established jointly by the TUI Group, TUI Care Foundation and the Government of the Region of the Southern Aegean. The Co-Lab will work with the local tourism sector and international partners to find innovative solutions to improve energy, water or waste management, and implement them on Rhodes. A think tank with international experts will further develop the sustainability transformation of the tourism sector. In Denmark, a partnership is set up to develop tourism initiatives to support the national reduction target on greenhouse gas emissions by 2030 (Box 3.12).

Box 3.12. Partnerships for green and sustainable tourism in Denmark

The National Strategy for Sustainable Growth in Danish Tourism incorporates many green and sustainable initiatives, to reduce greenhouse gas emissions, a 'comply or explain' model for sustainability standards, and legislation promoting electric car charging stations in popular tourism regions. A partnership consisting of VisitDenmark, Danish Coastal and Nature Tourism, Danish City Tourism (Wonderful Copenhagen) and Danish Business and Conferencing Tourism is working together to co-ordinate and disseminate initiatives to meet the national target of a 70% reduction in greenhouse gas emissions by 2030. Destination companies, relevant business and interest groups, ministries and experts are involved via established co-operation forums. It is intended to develop a method for measuring tourism's greenhouse gas emissions and the individual tourist's climate footprint. This will form the basis for identifying and organising initiatives that can reduce climate footprints in the long run. The partnership is also promoting the spread of certification schemes, highlight business opportunities to work sustainably and contribute to the green transition of accommodation capacity.

Table 3.1. Cross-government green tourism initiatives: selected country approaches

Country	Lead organisation	Partnership institution(s)	Initiative and purpose
Austria	Federal Ministries of Labour and Economy and of Climate Action	Several European countries: Ministries of tourism, climate action and transport	UNECE 'THE PEP Partnership on Sustainable Tourism Mobility' with the aim of bringing together national authorities, experts and stakeholders from all over Europe and raising awareness about the benefits of making sustainable mobility an integral part of tourism.
Costa Rica	Costa Rican Tourism Board	National Forest Financing Fund	Programme for visitors to plant trees and assist natural regeneration and agroforestry systems in the areas selected between both partners.
Denmark	Ministry of Industry, Business and Financial Affairs	VisitDenmark, Danish Coastal and Nature Tourism, Danish City Tourism (Wonderful Copenhagen), Danish Business and Conferencing Tourism	Co-ordinate and disseminate initiatives to meet the national target of a 70% reduction in greenhouse gas emissions by 2030. Develop a method for measuring tourism's emissions and the tourist's climate footprint. The partnership will also promote certification schemes, highlight business opportunities for the green transition of accommodation.
France	Ministry for The Economy - Directorate General for Enterprise	Caisse des Dépôts in conjunction with the Ministry of Economy, Finance and Recovery	Over EUR 3 billion in loans and repayable advances, amongst others, for the renovation of tourism real estate (hotels, tourist residences, holiday villages, open-air hotels, youth hostels, in all types of destinations) and for stakeholders in social and solidarity tourism.
Latvia	Ministry of Environment and Regional Development	Ministry of Economy, local authorities, non-governmental organisations, and others	Several projects, co-financed by the EU, focus on Latvia's coastline, for example "Vidzeme coastal cultural and natural heritage inclusion in the development and development of tourism services".
New Zealand	Department of Conservation	Ministry of the Environment	Jobs for Nature programme helps revitalise communities through nature-based employment, often partnering with tourism companies and stimulating the economy post COVID-19.
Peru	Ministry of Foreign Trade and Tourism	Ministry of the Environment	Promote climate change mitigation through the Carbon Footprint Tool, achieving 27 tourism companies registered, with 14 completing their carbon footprint measurement.
Romania	Ministry of Tourism	Ministry of Environment, Waters and Forests, the National Institute for Research and Development in Tourism, Ecotourism Association of Romania	Developed the system for evaluating ecotourism destinations in Romania, system based on the Global Criteria for Sustainable Tourism and the European Ecotourism Standard. So far, five tourism destinations have received this recognition.

Measuring and monitoring green tourism transition progress

Good governance involves monitoring and evaluation, and this goes hand in hand with improving tourism data and impact measurement via a range of sustainability indicators. Measurement is important to generate baselines, assess progress towards defined goals, and evaluate the effectiveness of specific interventions. It is also important to inform the development of evidence-based policy and programmes to promote the green transition. More progress is needed to better measure the economic, environmental and social dimensions of tourism, and develop timely and robust indicators and tools to monitor the effectiveness of tourism policies and the resilience and sustainability of tourism development.

In Germany, work by the German Federal Agency for the Environment (2021) to develop a Tourism Sustainability Satellite Account (TSSA) found that tourism's carbon intensity was higher than the average of the economy. Similarly, tourism's working conditions were on average poorer compared with other industries in the country. Innovatively, the German TSSA measures the raw material required worldwide throughout the entire value chain for the domestic provision of touristic products, alongside tourism-related expenditure on environmental protection services. Insights derived from these diverse sustainability dimensions inform the design of tourism support programmes in priority areas. Croatia is implementing a project to establish a Tourism Sustainability Satellite Account as part of the National Recovery and

Resilience Plan 2021-26.Statistics Canada, with the support of Destination Canada, is also examining opportunities to provide GHG emissions data generated by Canadian economic activity associated with tourism.

Systematic measurement of tourism impacts is essential for target setting and interim progress on longer term commitments like net zero by 2050. Norway's National Tourism Strategy 2030 sets a target of a 50% reduction of tourism's greenhouse gas emissions by 2030 (based on 2019 levels). To help achieve this, the aim is to reduce annual transport emissions by 10%. Target setting is also an important part of Portugal's Sustainable Tourism Plan and Finland's Sustainable Travel Finland Programme (Box 3.13). In 2022, Flanders in Belgium launched a new sustainability plan with 20 indicators to monitor destination management and the business operations of VisitFlanders, with a time horizon of 2030.

The private sector is also active in these issues – in Iceland, a new recovery dashboard by the Icelandic Travel Industry Association monitors performance against policy goals set out in the Tourism Future Vision until 2030, using indicators such as the share of companies with measurable sustainability goals, and the condition of tourist attractions within protected areas. Greece is also developing indicators to inform the adoption of climate change mitigation and adaptation measures in the tourism sector, as part of the National Strategy to Adapt to Climate Change.

Box 3.13. Measuring sustainable tourism progress: selected country approaches

Portugal: A Tourism Strategy 2027 was launched in 2017 with the vision to affirm tourism as a hub for economic, social and environmental development, and to position Portugal as a key competitive and sustainable tourism destination. In line with the Strategy, and the UN SDGs, Portugal has since developed a Sustainable Tourism Plan 2020-23 which follows on from the recovery plan Reactivate Tourism - Building the Future. Under the Plan, a set of 43 sustainability indicators are used to benchmark and assess progress for tourism businesses and the sector as a whole. Regular surveys are carried out on environmental practices and social responsibility in hotels and golf courses. The Plan stipulates the following targets for 2023: 75% of tourism companies with energy efficiency, water and waste management systems, and not using Single-Use Plastics; Clean & Safe Seal: 25 000 members, 30 000 graduates and 1 000 audited; and 50 000 professionals trained in the areas of sustainability. The set of initiatives covered by the Plan contribute to promoting an increasingly distinctive offer and to accelerating sustainability of tourism companies.

Finland: Visit Finland has developed sustainable tourism indicators as part of the national Sustainable Travel Finland Programme, which aims to support tourism companies and destinations in their sustainable development efforts. The indicators are based on extensive research and benchmarking against international criteria, standards and certification systems, and have been developed in close co-operation with the private sector. Helsinki, Lapland and other regions are committed to measuring their carbon footprint and integrating it into the national carbon footprint monitoring system to be developed. The set of indicators takes into account the requirements of Finland's northern location and the diversity of the tourism sector. It provides information about environmental impacts and destination management, as well as economic and sociocultural sustainability. Data captured is at national and regional, as well as company and destination level. Information comes from various sources, including official statistics, data provided by the companies and destinations taking part in the Sustainable Travel Finland Programme, as well as data from a pilot survey for visitors and local citizens. The first phase of reporting on the indicators began in the spring 2022, and the overall results of this round will be available in 2023.

Focusing on monitoring a particular tourist activity, the New Zealand Ministry of Business, Innovation and Employment provided NZD 800 000 to support the installation of approximately 100 visitor counters across the Ngā Haerenga Cycle Trails network. Bicycle tourism is a low-carbon form of travel that is also positively associated with positive economic activity in remote regions, particularly through supporting a diverse range of tourism SMEs. Data are used to evaluate the visitor experience, identify areas for improvement (e.g. congestion, infrastructure) and estimate economic impact of the cycle trail investment. Elsewhere, Austria is also measuring satisfaction of the local population regarding tourism in their region, alongside the share of renewable energy sources of total energy consumption of the hotel and gastronomy sector.

The European Union is piloting the EU Tourism Dashboard, an online tool that assembles and visualises tourism indicators to monitor progress on the green and digital transitions of the tourism ecosystem. The aim is to have the full dashboard available on the EU country level, and with selected indicators available at the regional and local level depending on data availability. The environmental policy pillar includes data on air travel emission intensity, tourism GHG intensity, tourism energy intensity, share of trips by train, bathing water, and dependence on long-distance tourists. Several countries are also piloting the Statistical Framework for Measuring the Sustainability of Tourism (SF-MST) advanced by the UNWTO to measure tourism sustainability in a coherent accounting system compatible with the statistical frameworks of national accounts.

Greening tourism infrastructure and services

Directing economic stimulus packages towards greener infrastructure and service is a tangible example of how to achieve policy integration between economic and sustainability goals. Tourism-targeted recovery programmes have mainly focused on economic aspects. Making recovery supports conditional on sustainability criteria, or even more importantly, directly support core elements of the green transition (e.g. investments into renewable energy and circular economy infrastructure), will help to promote a green recovery. As an important procurer of goods and services, the impact of public sector leadership on markets and norms should also not be underestimated. Ensuring that public sector funded or procured tourism infrastructure adheres to the highest environmental standards and contributes to both climate mitigation and adaptation is therefore important.

Decarbonising tourism transport infrastructure is a core dimension of the green transition. Several countries have used the pandemic to accelerate the uptake of electric vehicles in tourism. Iceland made funding available to accelerate the electrification of harbours and the rental car fleet. Similarly, the United Kingdom announced an investment of GBP 950 million in 2020 to extend the electric vehicle charging station network. This includes a sub-programme that could be used by small accommodation providers to install charging stations. Encouraging an electric charging network and vehicle fleet that is also suitable for longer distance holiday travel is an important step towards lower carbon tourism.

Encouraging a modal shift towards low emissions and human powered transport options is another element of the green tourism transition. Several countries are investing in rail networks, including the re-establishment of night trains. The EU Rail Baltica transport infrastructure project aims to integrate Estonia, Latvia and Lithuania into the European rail network. Rail Baltica will be fully electrified using the most up to date technology to minimise emissions.

Public sector investments into rail infrastructure can also support private sector initiatives such as the GreenCityTrip sleeper trains that now connect travellers from the Netherlands with 15 European city destinations. In Germany, the aviation sector and the national railways have joined forces to replace short domestic flights with train connections in a new joint action plan. In Morocco, the national tourist office and the national railway office signed a partnership agreement in 2021 for marketing and development of attractive travel solutions in sustainable mobility to stimulate domestic tourist flows.

Some new tourism products require a combination of public sector infrastructure investment and private sector entrepreneurship. Walking and cycling tracks are a pertinent example as their availability allows businesses to start up with different types of tours and value-add activities, such as linking to local food production and other cultural experiences. In Türkiye, for example, the Ministry of Culture and Tourism in partnership with the Turkish Tourism Promotion and Development Agency developed an online platform with cycling routes across Türkiye leading to regional spread and 'slower' forms of tourism. The Ministry also issues a Certificate of Bicycle-Friendly Accommodation Facility for bicycle-friendly providers.

Slovenia's investment in sustainable gastronomy is a further example of greening the tourism offer. The Slovenia Green Gourmet Route and the Slovenia Green Cuisine label for restaurants are innovative extensions of the Green Scheme of Slovenian Tourism standard that credibly connect the unique place (nature, culture, food) with the visitor experience.

In Greece, the new Investment Incentives Law supports green investment, focusing on technologies that contribute to environmental protection and energy upgrade of tourism accommodation, through a simple framework that allows the business community to plan, develop and implement their initiatives. Tourism investments related to the promotion of special forms of tourism, considering the specific geographical, social and cultural characteristics of the different regions of the country are widely promoted.

Targeting and encouraging responsible tourist behaviour

Building on consumer changes and reinforcing positive actions can enable a smoother green transition. Some governments have proactively invested into marketing campaigns that encourage a shift towards more sustainable segments and behaviours. Switzerland's 'Swisstainable' programme for example aims to create an effective movement toward broader change in tourism practices, together with the Swiss tourism sector. The Japan National Tourism Office is integrating aspects of 'responsible travel' into its promotional campaigns, with the aim of spreading tourism regionally, fostering nature activities and increasing environmental awareness.

Several countries demonstrate a major shift and innovation in how they position themselves with sustainability and a future-focus as the core of the message. This responds to evidence from the pandemic where people were looking for nature-based experiences and more sustainable (and safe) forms of travel. Visit Portugal for example launched a tourism campaign Can't Skip Tomorrow, with the sub-slogan "Tomorrow is Today. Act Today, change Tomorrow. For a better Planet, a better tourism. Travel better". Similarly, Visit Scotland promotes tourism through "Scotland: yours to enjoy. Responsibly." This message is further supported by: "Let's keep Scotland special now and for generations to come." The Faroe Islands have gone one step further to promote 'giving back' by visitors and encourage visitors (at certain times of the year) who will actively engage in connecting to nature and making a contribution. The campaign is "Closed for maintenance, open for voluntourism".

There is growing recognition among governments and business of the benefits of better understanding tourists' motivations, beliefs and attitudes. A promising approach is promoting green behaviours through behavioural insights (Box 3.14).

To change tourist behaviour, countries are also developing visitor pledges and codes of conduct. The Icelandic Pledge encourages people to take a more active role in managing impacts (and safety); as such it sets norms or expectations and is likely to increase environmental awareness. To be effective, pledges need to be accompanied by rules and regulations, for example those implemented in Rome to prevent littering or climbing monuments, or those in Amsterdam, to stop unruly behaviour. Other examples of pledges are New Zealand's Tiaki Promise, the Sustainable Travel Finland Pledge, and the Aspen Pledge in the United States. The 'pledge' is supported by infrastructure and systems that allow the visitor to adhere to the code of conduct (e.g. toilets, rubbish bins). This requires collaboration between national and local governments, as well as the private sector.

Box 3.14. Promoting green behaviours through behavioural insights

Behavioural science provides an innovative solution to reinforcing sustainable tourism by providing key empirical data on travel behaviour. Achieving ambitious sustainable tourism policy objectives can be challenging since they rely overwhelmingly on individuals' behaviours and preferences. Behavioural science provides an innovative solution to reinforcing sustainable tourism by providing key empirical data on travel behaviour, leveraging knowledge about human behaviour simplifying the pursuit of sustainable tourism decision-making, and generating human-centred services and polices tailored and targeted to their intended audience.

Inspiring small changes among individuals can optimise both commercial practices and sustainable tourism habits. These can be as simple as ensuring the green options are the default choice for consumers. For example, reducing meat consumption at events by making vegetarian the default or making lower-emission transport the default option in tour packages. Programmes to promote and encourage greener consumer behaviours are starting to be introduced across countries. The Philippines are utilising behavioural gamification methods which uses challenges, competition and reward-based incentives to inspire individuals to complete eco-friendly missions. The city of Helsinki leveraged choice architecture to develop a centralised digital platform to help residents, businesses and tourists make more responsible and eco-friendly decisions every day.

Adapting to shifts like local travel closer to home or longer stays for long distance travel, several countries have developed new visa policies. Countries are also looking to the growing market of 'digital nomads', as people adapt to the flexibility of remote working arrangements being adopted post pandemic. More than twenty countries have introduced new 'digital nomad' or remote worker visas to attract these new markets to come and stay for extended periods. In Costa Rica, the legislation provides legal security and incentives to workers who choose Costa Rica as their temporary home through the total exemption from income tax. Indonesia has extended a new visa for a period of five years and visitors are not required to pay taxes on income earned in other countries.

Policy considerations to support the green tourism recovery

The disruption caused by the COVID-19 pandemic has created the conditions for new future models of tourism where recovery measures play a central role in greening the tourism sector. This includes a people-centred green recovery focused on businesses, local communities and travellers. For this, it is critical to understand the tourism value chain, its dependence on the environment and physical resources, and socio-political levers for systemic change.

Tourism has its part to play in accelerating the transition to a low carbon, resource efficient and socially inclusive economy. Cleaner air quality, healthier water, effective waste management, and enhanced biodiversity protection not only reduce the vulnerability of communities and destinations, but also have the potential to boost economic activity, generate income, create quality jobs, and reduce inequalities. To achieve these goals, active policies will be needed to target reduced carbon emissions and pollution, enhance energy and resource efficiency, and prevent the loss of biodiversity and ecosystems. Building resilience and empowering communities and other voices in tourism provide a foundation for these changes.

A green recovery and transition necessitate a whole-of-system approach that understands not only the tourism value chain, but also wider economic and socio-cultural systems in which tourism is embedded. The symbiotic relationship between tourism and ecosystem conservation and restoration must be integral as well; also because healthy ecosystems play a key role in building resilience and responding to climate change. This chapter has presented a wide range of policies, enabling factors and specific initiatives to facilitate progress for businesses, destinations and the sector as a whole. These pathways and instruments are often interdependent, and policies can be targeted at different levels and scales (e.g. national versus business or destination-focused). Innovative governance mechanisms are need to foster policy coherence and integration, while implementation depends on fit-for-purpose governance arrangements and financial support.

Enablers that are common to all pathways include the need to build capacity and literacy and to create a learning environment that provides evidence (e.g. robust and meaningful tourism data; critical review of interventions and unintended side effects) for future policy decisions. The increasingly uncertain operating environment requires agility in the policy and governance approach. For tourism to resolve the challenges outlined in this chapter, further research and innovation and investment in future technologies and practices is needed.

Based on the analysis discussed in this chapter, key policy considerations to further promote a green recovery and accelerate the transition to a green tourism economy include:

- **Develop long-term strategies that set out a vision for a sustainable future for tourism**, including the desired contribution to economic, environmental, and social wellbeing. This should be supported by action plans with clearly defined responsibilities, interim goals and measurable targets which can drive the green recovery.
- **Leverage government's role in catalysing the green tourism transition**, including through leading by example (e.g. decarbonisation of agencies) and ensuring all public sector funded or procured tourism infrastructure adhere to highest environmental standards and contribute to climate resilient development (e.g. nature-based solutions).
- **Improve co-ordination of tourism policy with relevant policy areas to support the green transition**, and in particular conservation and environmental management, climate action, sustainable transport, and social development (including health and regional economic development). Policy integration is not only important for improved policy coherence and effectiveness, but also to leverage resources across portfolios.
- **Establish tourism governance mechanisms that connect and align action on greening across all levels of government**, and promote transparency and accountability. In complex and uncertain times, it is important to ensure that governance structures are sufficiently flexible, responsive, and resilient at local destination level with national and international level, to deliver the desired outcomes.
- **Implement a mix of evidence-based policies and interventions to promote greener tourism practices.** Prioritise actions targeting high impact areas along the tourism value chain, on the supply and demand side. Apply a combination of direct interventions (e.g. investment), regulations, incentives and awareness raising to accelerate progress towards a greener tourism model.
- **Develop and improve monitoring frameworks to measure progress**, through the provision of robust and meaningful data and indicators. This is important to build understanding among visitors, businesses and destinations the environmental impact of their actions, and to inform the development of effective policies, strategies and programmes.
- **Promote the integration of tourism into the wider economy,** including with primary industries such as agriculture and forestry and at the destination level. Leverage linkages to strengthen the sustainability and resilience of tourism and other key supply and value chains (e.g. food, transport), maximise local benefits and advance principles of the circular economy (closing resource loops).
- **Build capacity and literacy to support action on greening across the tourism system** (consumer to operator to investors). Promote understanding of sustainability and related concepts, such as sustainable procurement, resource efficiency and circular innovation. Empower people to create their own solutions and make sustainable travel choices by promoting consumer information

tools. Support tourism businesses to take action and to measure progress to reduce their GHG emissions and environmental impact, including though skills development and access to finance. Governments can foster learning and exchange and support alternative products or business models, including via mechanisms that transfer or scale up cutting edge innovations.

- **Encourage the development of sustainable tourism experiences that generate positive outcomes for the environment, and visitors.** Innovate in the area of experience design to give visitors the opportunity to contribute positively to the destination through greener travel decisions, including by leveraging digital solutions.

References

Becken, S. and J. Kaur (2021), "Anchoring "tourism value" within a regenerative tourism paradigm–a government perspective.", *Journal of Sustainable Tourism* 30(1), pp. 52-68. [24]

Becken, S. and J. Loehr (2022), "Tourism governance and enabling drivers for intensifying climate action", *Journal of Sustainable Tourism*, pp. 1-19. [25]

Becken, S. et al. (2020), "Tourism and climate change: evaluating the extent of policy integration", *Journal of Sustainable Tourism*, Vol. 28/10, pp. 1603-1624. [26]

European Bank for Reconstruction and Development and the Global Centre of Excellence (2018), *Advancing TCFD guidance on physical climate risks and opportunities*, https://www.tcfdhub.org/resource/advancing-tcfd-guidance-on-physical-climate-risks-and-opportunities/. [27]

European Commission (2022), *Transition Pathway for Tourism*, https://ec.europa.eu/docsroom/documents/49498.org. [10]

European Commission (2021), *Attitudes of Europeans towards tourism*, https://europa.eu/eurobarometer/surveys/detail/2283. [14]

IPBES (2019), *Global assessment report on biodiversity and ecosystem services of the Intergovernmental Science-Policy Platform on Biodiversity and Ecosystem Services*, https://ipbes.net/global-assessment. [11]

IPCC (2022), *Climate change 2022: Impacts, adaptation, and vulnerability*, https://www.ipcc.ch/report/ar6/wg2/. [12]

IPCC (2021), *Summary for Policymakers. In: Climate Change 2021: The Physical Science Basis*, https://www.ipcc.ch/report/ar6/wg1/downloads/report/IPCC_AR6_WGI_SPM_final.pdf. [6]

ITF (2021), *Decarbonising air transport: Acting now for the future*, https://www.itf-oecd.org/decarbonising-air-transport. [8]

MBIE (2022), *The Tourism Futures Taskforce interim report – We are Aotearoa*, https://www.mbie.govt.nz/immigration-and-tourism/tourism/tourism-recovery/tourism-futures-taskforce/tourism-futures-taskforce-interim-report/. [23]

OECD (2022), *Carbon pricing and COVID-19: Policy changes, challenges and design options in OECD and G20 countries*, https://www.oecd.org/environment/carbon-pricing-and-covid-19-8f030bcc-en.htm. [15]

OECD (2022), *Environment at a glance*, https://www.oecd.org/environment/environment-at-a-glance/. [28]

OECD (2022), *Financing SMEs and Entrepreneurs 2022: An OECD scoreboard*, https://www.oecd.org/cfe/smes/financing-smes-and-entrepreneurs-23065265.htm. [16]

OECD (2022), *Global Plastics Outlook: Economic drivers, environmental impacts and policy options*, https://www.oecd-ilibrary.org/environment/global-plastics-outlook_de747aef-en. [13]

OECD (2022), *Policy brief on making the most of the social economy's contribution to the circular economy*, https://www.oecd-ilibrary.org/industry-and-services/policy-brief-on-making-the-most-of-the-social-economy-s-contribution-to-the-circular-economy_e9eea313-en. [22]

OECD (2022), *Why governments should target support amidst high energy prices*, https://www.oecd.org/ukraine-hub/policy-responses/why-governments-should-target-support-amidst-high-energy-prices-40f44f78/. [3]

OECD (2021), *G20 Rome guidelines for the future of tourism*, https://www.oecd.org/cfe/g20-rome-guidelines-for-the-future-of-tourism-d11080db-en.htm. [9]

OECD (2021), *Managing tourism development for sustainable and inclusive recovery*, https://www.oecd.org/publications/managing-tourism-development-for-sustainable-and-inclusive-recovery-b062f603-en.htm. [29]

OECD (2021), *No net zero without SMEs. Exploring the key issues for SMEs and green entrepreneurship*, https://www.oecd-ilibrary.org/energy/no-net-zero-without-smes_bab63915-en. [1]

OECD (2020), *Linking Indigenous Communities with Regional Development in Australia*, https://www.oecd-ilibrary.org/urban-rural-and-regional-development/linking-indigenous-communities-with-regional-development-in-australia_ab4d8d52-en. [20]

OECD (2020), *Linking Indigenous Communities with Regional Development in Canada*, https://www.oecd-ilibrary.org/urban-rural-and-regional-development/linking-indigenous-communities-with-regional-development-in-canada_fa0f60c6-en;jsessionid=Zc5O7zT-STKGaXO0IO_jwewyJLegy6mhPOmTNmwF.ip-10-240-5-71. [21]

OECD (2018), *Elements for a new growth narrative*, https://www.oecd.org/naec/SG_NAEC(2018)1_Elements%20for%20a%20new%20growth%20narrative.pdf. [4]

One Planet (2022), *Global tourism plastics initiative*, https://www.oneplanetnetwork.org/programmes/sustainable-tourism/global-tourism-plastics-initiative. [19]

One Planet (2021), *Encouraging sustainable procurement practices through the use of third-party certification schemes*, https://www.oneplanetnetwork.org/knowledge-centre/resources/encouraging-sustainable-procurement-practices-through-use-third-party?page=2. [18]

UNEP and World Bank (2021), *Towards a Circular Tourism Economy: Drivers and strategies for a green transition*, https://www.oneplanetnetwork.org/knowledge-centre/resources/towards-circular-tourism-economy-drivers-and-strategies-green-transition. [2]

UNWTO (2021), *World tourism barometer: Volume 19, no 5*, https://www.e-unwto.org/toc/wtobarometereng/19/5. [30]

UNWTO and ITF (2019), *Transport-related CO2 Emissions of the Tourism Sector*, https://www.e-unwto.org/doi/book/10.18111/9789284416660. [7]

Whelan, T. and C. Fink (2016), "The comprehensive business case for sustainability", *Harvard Business Review* 21. [17]

WTTC and UNEP (2021), *A Net Zero Roadmap for Travel & Tourism: Proposing a New Target Framework for the Travel & Tourism Sector*, https://wedocs.unep.org/20.500.11822/37355. [5]

Part I OECD country profiles

Australia

Tourism in the economy and outlook for recovery

Tourism plays a significant part in Australia's economy, contributing to both GDP and employment. In 2020-21, tourism directly contributed AUD 32.4 billion to GDP, representing 1.6% of total GDP. This was a decline of almost 50% compared with 2018-19, when tourism represented 3.1% of total GDP. The tourism sector comprised 507 000 jobs at the end of 2020-21, down 167 400 jobs compared to 2018-19. In the same time period, tourism exports fell 96% to AUD 1.7 billion in 2020-21.

The number of international visitors declined by over 97%, from 9.5 million in 2019 to 246 200 in 2021. Border closures led to declines across all international markets. Stringent travel restrictions saw China fall out of the top two markets in 2021 for the first time since 2011.

The number of domestic overnight trips declined by 30% to 82.1 million between 2019 and 2021. This relatively smaller decline in domestic trips saw domestic tourism consumption increase from 74% of total consumption in 2018-19 to 98% in 2020-21.

Domestic tourism is forecast to return to the average pre-pandemic level in 2022-23 and to surpass its 2018-19 peak the following year. A more moderate growth trajectory is forecast for the period through to 2025-26. The international tourism recovery is expected to take some time.

Tourism governance and funding

The Australian Trade and Investment Commission (Austrade), Tourism Australia, the Department of Foreign Affairs and Trade, and state and territory governments work closely to co-ordinate the delivery of whole-of-government tourism objectives. Austrade is the federal government agency responsible for tourism policy, programmes and research. Within Austrade, Tourism Research Australia provides international and domestic tourism data, statistics and analysis.

Tourism Australia is the government agency responsible for attracting international visitors to the country. While international border measures were closed, Tourism Australia's focus shifted to stimulating domestic demand, working closely with the sector, state and territory tourism organisations and key partners to roll out targeted domestic campaign activity. Tourism Australia was allocated AUD 155.3 million in 2021-22.

The Department of Foreign Affairs and Trade works to strengthen bilateral tourism relationships and leverage key multilateral tourism bodies. All state and territory governments in Australia incorporate tourism into their portfolios to ensure effective international and domestic tourism promotion and sector development.

The Tourism Ministers' Meetings (TMM) bring together tourism ministers from the Federal state and territory governments to discuss tourism policy matters of mutual interest. This work is supported by the Australian Standing Committee on Tourism (ASCOT), which is chaired by Austrade and includes representatives from Tourism Australia, state and territory tourism organisations, and relevant state departments with responsibility for tourism policy. Representatives from the tourism sector and other relevant federal and state departments can be invited to attend ASCOT and TMM meetings as necessary.

Australia: Organisational chart of tourism bodies

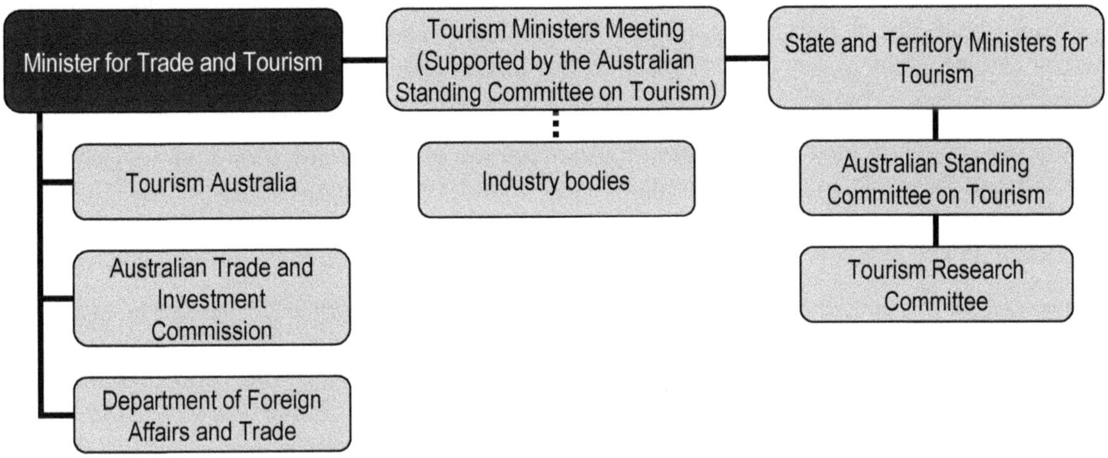

Source: OECD, adapted from the Australian Government, 2022.

Tourism policies and programmes

Australia's long-term national visitor economy strategy, THRIVE 2030, was released in March 2022. Industry-led and government-enabled, THRIVE 2030 aims to help the visitor economy rebuild and return to long-term sustainable growth. It sets a target to return to pre-pandemic visitor expenditure of AUD 166 billion by 2024 and to grow it to AUD 230 billion by 2030. Regional destinations comprise approximately 40% of this goal. The strategy's action plan is focused on the initial recovery phase to 2024. It has seven priority areas with 66 actions for governments and the tourism sector. There are 21 federal government agencies involved in the delivery of THRIVE 2030.

In May 2022, the Federal Government committed AUD 48 million to tourism-related measures. This package will provide support for quality tourism products, infrastructure upgrades, training and upskilling of workers and assistance for businesses in attracting international visitors.

Australia's immediate focus during the COVID-19 pandemic was to provide support to heavily impacted areas of tourism. Since March 2020, the Australian Government has provided more than AUD 20 billion in assistance to the tourism and hospitality sector through targeted and non-targeted support, including wage subsidies (e.g. JobKeeper) and sectoral assistance programmes. This included partnering with states and territories to deliver business support programmes.

As part of this assistance, short-term measures funded by the AUD 1 billion COVID-19 Relief and Recovery Fund included: Regional Airlines Funding Assistance (AUD 100 million), Regional Air Network Assistance (AUD 198 million), the COVID-19 Consumer Travel Support (AUD 258 million), Regional Recovery Partnerships (AUD 100 million), the Business Events Grant programme (AUD 56 million) and the Supporting Australia's Zoos and Aquariums programme (AUD 139.6 million) (see box below).

Medium-term measures to support a return to growth for the sector include an AUD 1.2 billion tourism and aviation package as part of the National Economic Recovery Plan, the Tourism Aviation Network Support programme (AUD 204 million), the Recovery for Regional Tourism programme (AUD 50 million), and the expansion of the SME Loan Guarantee Scheme. Associated funding was also provided through

AUD 233 million for tourism and other infrastructure in Commonwealth National Parks and additional support to strengthen Australia's cultural and creative sector (approximately AUD 800 million).

While Australia's international borders were closed, recovery was driven by Australians holidaying at home. Tourism Australia implemented a domestic recovery campaign, "Holiday Here This Year," urging Australians to support the tourism sector by taking a domestic holiday. Elements included the "Epic Journeys" and "the gift of travel" campaigns. In addition, Tourism Australia launched its National Experience Content Initiative, an AUD 12 million programme which subsidises new marketing materials and assets that tourism experience operators can use to better market and promote themselves.

Tourism Australia continued to focus on keeping Australia top of mind in international markets, generating long-term demand for travel and priming audiences to book travel to Australia as soon as it was practical to do so. As international borders reopened, Tourism Australia launched a global consumer campaign to drive conversion in key markets that offer the best potential to build Australia's tourism recovery.

To promote long-term recovery and prepare for future shocks, in April 2021 Austrade announced the appointment of the Reimagining the Visitor Economy Expert Panel to advise the government on how to chart a course for sustainable long-term growth over the next ten years. The report developed by this Expert Panel, Reimagining the Visitor Economy, informed the development of *THRIVE 2030*.

Supporting exhibiting zoos and aquariums in Australia

Zoos and aquariums are one of Australia's top tourism attractions, hosting over 22 million visitors annually, employing more than 7 000 people, and supported by 10 000 volunteers. COVID-19 severely impacted these attractions' ability to maintain their animal populations and retain essential capabilities.

This programme provided a total of AUD 139.6 million to eligible zoos and aquariums to cover the costs of maintaining animal populations whilst COVID-19 restrictions and international border closures were in place. It was designed in consultation with key stakeholders, including the Zoo and Aquarium Association, the Department of Agriculture, Water and the Environment and state and territory tourism organisations. The intended outcome was to help these businesses remain viable and ensure readiness to welcome visitors when travel restrictions were lifted.

Eligible applicants were unique attractions that met relevant animal welfare standards, contributed to the conservation and presentation of animals and drove interstate and international visitation. Applicants had to demonstrate that their business usually derived income from tourism and had experienced a reduction in revenue of at least 30% due to COVID-19 restrictions.

When the programme closed on 30 June 2022, over AUD 127.7 million had been paid to 145 eligible zoos and aquariums in nine payment rounds. The programme received an overwhelmingly positive response from the sector, which had struggled due to prolonged COVID-19 restrictions.

Statistical Profile

Australia: Domestic, inbound and outbound tourism

	2017	2018	2019	2020	2021
TOURISM FLOWS, THOUSAND					
Domestic tourism					
Total domestic trips	291 797	310 166	365 797	236 706	242 543
Overnight visitors (tourists)	98 484	104 822	117 448	72 514	82 074
Same-day visitors (excursionists)	193 313	205 344	248 349	164 192	160 469
Nights in all types of accommodation	352 085	371 528	417 907	275 404	321 109
Hotels and similar establishments	87 519	95 298	101 047	51 589	67 162
Other collective establishments	94 045	94 416	111 905	79 557	90 006
Private accommodation	170 521	181 814	204 955	144 258	163 940
Inbound tourism					
Total international arrivals	8 815	9 246	9 466	1 828	246
Overnight visitors (tourists)	..	..	..	..	..
Same-day visitors (excursionists)	..	..	..	..	..
Top markets					
New Zealand	1 360	1 385	1 434	243	97
United Kingdom	733	733	716	201	22
United States	781	789	818	189	17
Singapore	433	448	479	58	16
India	303	358	399	84	13
Nights in all types of accommodation	263 797	273 793	274 477	68 973 e	16 779 e
Hotels and similar establishments	28 805	29 232	28 840	..	..
Other collective establishments	126 744	135 269	138 774	..	..
Private accommodation	108 247	109 293	106 863	..	..
Outbound tourism					
Total international departures	10 535	11 061	11 309	2 832	301
Overnight visitors (tourists)	..	..	..	..	..
Same-day visitors (excursionists)	..	..	..	..	..
Top destinations					
New Zealand	1 436	1 437	1 463	439	160
United States	1 075	1 096	1 056	236	17
United Kingdom	629	663	663	147	15
Singapore	403	415	417	88	6
China (People's Republic of)	541	594	608	122	5
TOURISM RECEIPTS AND EXPENDITURE, MILLION AUD					
Inbound tourism					
Total international receipts	57 376	63 253	68 949	38 382	..
International travel receipts	54 470	60 276	65 752	37 521	..
International passenger transport receipts	2 906	2 977	3 197	861	..
Outbound tourism					
Total international expenditure	51 727	56 853	59 507	11 573	..
International travel expenditure	44 896	49 514	51 770	9 831	..
International passenger transport expenditure	6 831	7 339	7 737	1 742	..

.. Not available; e Estimated value
Source: OECD Tourism Statistics (Database).

StatLink https://stat.link/oefvlu

Australia: Enterprises and employment in tourism

	Number of establishments[1]	Number of persons employed				
	2020	2017	2018	2019	2020	2021
Total	..	**651 800**	**674 400**	**636 200**	**507 000**	..
Tourism industries	**334 511**	**631 000**	**653 600**	**615 500**	**486 000**	..
Accommodation services for visitors	13 303	85 600	83 400	74 700	62 700	..
Hotels and similar establishments	..	..	..	..	..	..
Food and beverage serving industry	91 533	212 700	216 100	205 800	198 400	..
Passenger transport	42 201	69 100	73 200	71 100	56 000	..
Air passenger transport	5 377	41 600	43 900	43 500	27 900	..
Railways passenger transport	97	2 800	3 300	3 100	2 800	..
Road passenger transport	36 727	24 700	26 000	24 500	25 300	..
Water passenger transport	..	..	..	..	..	..
Passenger transport supporting services	..	..	..	..	..	..
Transport equipment rental	..	..	..	..	..	..
Travel agencies and other reservation services industry	8 872	43 700	45 000	42 600	31 300	..
Cultural industry	17 390	16 600	19 600	19 400	17 000	..
Sports and recreation industry	16 106	29 900	32 500	27 500	27 900	..
Retail trade of country-specific tourism characteristic goods	145 106	109 400	113 700	110 900	92 100	..
Other country-specific tourism industries	..	63 800	69 900	63 600	500	..
Other industries	..	**20 800**	**20 800**	**20 700**	**21 000**	..

.. Not available

1. Data refer to number of enterprises.

Source: OECD Tourism Statistics (Database).

StatLink https://stat.link/igk6po

Australia: Internal tourism consumption

Million AUD

	2020		
	Domestic tourism expenditure	Inbound tourism expenditure	Internal tourism consumption
Total	..	..	..
Consumption products	**81 707**	**1 692**	..
Tourism characteristic products	45 897	1 300	..
Accommodation services for visitors	12 715	1 002	..
Food and beverage serving services	15 283	104	..
Passenger transport services	6 512	78	..
Air passenger transport services	..	..	..
Railways passenger transport services	..	..	..
Road passenger transport services	..	..	..
Water passenger transport services	..	..	..
Passenger transport supporting services	..	..	..
Transport equipment rental services	1 077	12	..
Travel agencies and other reservation services industry	5 422	71	..
Cultural services	..	..	..
Sports and recreation services	4 889	34	..
Country-specific tourism characteristic goods	..	..	..
Country-specific tourism characteristic services	..	..	..
Other consumption products	35 809	391	..
Tourism connected products	34 705	359	..
Non-tourism related consumption products	1 104	32	..
Non-consumption products	..	..	..

.. Not available

Source: OECD Tourism Statistics (Database).

StatLink https://stat.link/4nvm7k

Austria

Tourism in the economy and outlook for recovery

Tourism is an important driver of the Austrian economy. In 2019, tourism directly contributed EUR 22 billion to the Austrian economy, equating to 5.6% of GDP, according to the Austrian Tourism Satellite Account. This resulted in 205 700 full-time equivalent jobs directly attributed to tourism, contributing to 5.2% of total employment in Austria. Travel exports represented 30% of total service exports in 2019.

The impacts of the COVID-19 pandemic saw the direct contribution of tourism to the economy fall to 3.5% of both GDP and employment. The pandemic resulted in a significant decline in tourists. In 2020, there were 15.1 million international arrivals, down 53% compared to 2019, which declined an additional 15.7% in 2021. This decline in international tourists had a significant impact on international travel receipts, which remained 56.3% below 2019 levels in 2021, at EUR 10.1 billion.

The Austrian tourism sector has traditionally been international-dominant, with international tourists accounting for almost three-quarters of nights prior to the pandemic. In 2021, domestic tourists were 34.2% below pre-pandemic levels, with 9.4 million tourists recorded, but their share of nights increased to 37%.

While in January 2022 overnight stays were still 32.6% behind figures of the same month in 2019, the tourism sector has recovered well throughout the year with 112.8 million overnights recorded between January and September (down 11 % compared to 2019), in particular due to a strong summer season (May-September, down 1.4% to 2019). The outlook for the winter season 2022/2023 is considered widely positive.

Tourism governance and funding

According to the Austrian Federal Constitution, the nine federal provinces (Länder) have legislative and executive responsibility for tourism affairs. However, as tourism is a cross-cutting sector, federal and European laws apply.

At the national level, the Federal Ministry of Labour and Economy (the State Secretary for Tourism) is responsible for tourism policy. A Parliamentary Committee for Tourism within the Austrian Parliament oversees policy. Synergies between the national and regional levels continue to be strengthened via a Steering Group for Tourism. Co-operation with other ministries, departments, institutions and the tourism sector is organised on specific topics either via permanent groups or round tables (e.g. communication, sustainable mobility, visas, tourism ethics, cycle tourism) or on a case-by-case basis (e.g. new funding schemes, new legislation affecting tourism).

The Austrian National Tourist Office (ANTO) is the national tourism marketing organisation. ANTO is responsible for market research, brand management, marketing, tourism networking and information provision. The Ministry and the Austrian Federal Economic Chamber jointly fund ANTO. It co-operates closely with the Austrian tourism trade (e.g. Länder tourist boards, destinations, tourism businesses).

In 2021, the national tourism administration had a total budget of EUR 57.3 million. Of this, EUR 28.4 million was dedicated to financial support for SMEs, administered by the Austrian Bank for Tourism Development, a specialised bank acting in a public-private partnership. ANTO received over EUR 24 million for their annual budget (whereas in 2020, ANTO received an additional EUR 40 million for specific marketing measures to support the recovery). The Ministry disbursed EUR 5 million through individual subsidies for co-financed tourism projects and service contracts.

SMEs in the tourism sector received EUR 70 million from the European Recovery Programme for loans. In addition to the national budget, all nine Länder have their own tourism budgets to support their specific tourism development programmes.

In order to support tourism during the COVID-19 pandemic, the national tourism administration spent EUR 201 million on direct grants and provided guarantees on loans (cap: EUR 1.6 billion). In addition to above mentioned sector-specific measures, undertakings in tourism were eligible for most horizontal measures (including mainly direct grants) administered by the Ministry of Finance.

Austria: Organisational chart of tourism bodies

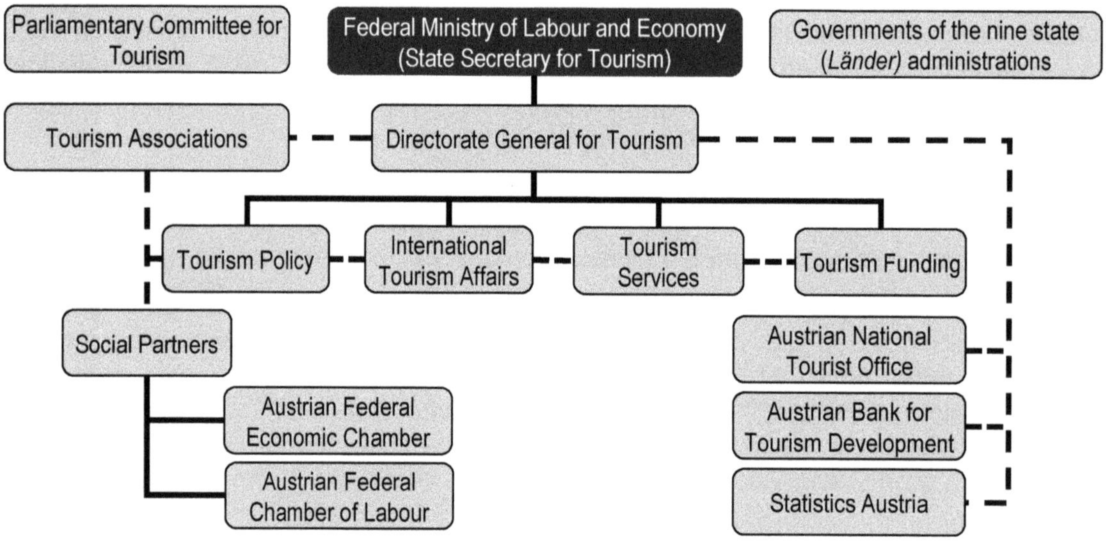

Source: OECD, adapted from the Federal Ministry of Labour and the Economy, 2022

Tourism policies and programmes

Austria's national tourism strategy Plan T - Masterplan for Tourism continues to be the base of national tourism policy. However, there are a number of updates in key focus areas for the medium and long term across the demand, supply and governance of tourism, and a maintained focus on quality rather than on quantity, as well as consumer safety and security.

Following the COVID-19 pandemic, Austria implemented comprehensive public support to help the tourism sector survive, through both whole-of-economy and sector-specific measures. Targeted support was necessary, especially for accommodation, hospitality and travel organisation industries, including:

- Free and comprehensive COVID-19 testing in 2020-22 for the tourism workforce and guests, reinforcing trust and confidence in Austria as a safe tourism destination (see box below).
- Tax relief package, including the reduction of VAT to 5% on accommodation and food (previously 10%) as well as drinks (previously 20%) for the period 1 July 2020 to 31 December 2021.

- Investment bonuses consisting of grants of 7% of the investment value as an incentive for enterprises to invest in their business and strengthen their competitiveness. Grants were doubled for investments in greening, digitalisation or health (total volume of EUR 7.8 billion).
- Guarantees of up to 100% for bridging loans used to cover temporary liquidity shortages caused by decreases in turnover due to COVID-19 (until the end of 2021) and grants to cover fixed costs and losses for enterprises affected by closures (until September 2021).
- Support for event organisers with financial compensation in case the event is cancelled or restricted due to COVID-19 (March 2021 - December 2022); total volume of EUR 300 million (administered by the Austrian Bank for Tourism Development). Maximum support per event organiser amounts to EUR 10 million.
- Support for package travel organisers where the Austrian Bank for Tourism Development guaranteed down payments by travellers in case of insolvency of the package travel organiser in 2021-22 (total package limit of EUR 300 million).
- Support for private accommodation landlords and farms that offer accommodation services through "Agrarmarkt Austria GmbH" - which ended in March 2022.

In the longer term, enterprises need continued support with new financing arrangements, particularly given many businesses' difficult liquidity and equity positions, while also addressing labour force shortages and skills requirements. In addition, a stronger focus is put on the green and digital transition in tourism and the development of regions and cities. In 2022, Austria created a new ecolabel for tourism destinations to accelerate the green transition, improve regional value chains and respond to the increased demand for sustainable holidays (see Box 3.7).

Strong governance, co-ordination and information are key for the tourism sector in Austria, with co-ordination between tourism and regional policy to strengthen local and regional value chains a necessity.

Changes in consumer trends present new challenges and opportunities. The recent strategic reorientation of the Austrian National Tourist Office (ÖW2026) will facilitate addressing promising markets with enhanced communication, co-operation and innovation.

Free COVID-19 testing for visitors and tourism employees in Austria

During the COVID-19 pandemic, Austria offered unlimited, free-of-charge testing for visitors. As of April 2022, the limit was set to five self-tests and five PCR tests per person/month. This was supported by a nationwide testing infrastructure, including PCR tests, antigen tests and self-tests offered in various settings, and a dedicated testing website that contained the entire testing offer and allowed online registration.

In addition to the general testing infrastructure, in July 2020 the Ministry of Tourism introduced a testing programme named "Safe Hospitality" (Testangebot Sichere Gastfreundschaft) for the tourism industry that ran until April 2022. The initiative offered up to one free COVID-19 PCR test per week for employees in the accommodation, gastronomy, travel agency, skiing, snowboarding and tour guide sectors.

The process was fully digital and started with voluntary online registration. The Ministry of Tourism provided a list of approximately 40 participating laboratories from which employees could choose. The laboratories offered a mobile service, visiting establishments for employee convenience.

By April 2022, 2.5 million tests were conducted in over 10 000 establishments - compared to 630 000 tests in 6 700 establishments in 2020.

Statistical Profile

Austria: Domestic, inbound and outbound tourism

	2017	2018	2019	2020	2021
TOURISM FLOWS, THOUSAND					
Domestic tourism					
Total domestic trips	..	..	..	..	..
Overnight visitors (tourists)	13 619	14 033	14 312	9 939	9 416
Same-day visitors (excursionists)	..	..	..	..	..
Nights in all types of accommodation	38 523	39 390	39 944	31 596	29 599
Hotels and similar establishments	33 539	34 201	34 767	25 724	24 577
Other collective establishments	1 543	1 734	1 737	2 267	2 098
Private accommodation	3 441	3 454	3 440	3 605	2 924
Inbound tourism					
Total international arrivals	..	..	..	..	..
Overnight visitors (tourists)	29 460	30 816	31 884	15 091	12 728
Same-day visitors (excursionists)	..	..	..	..	..
Top markets					
Germany	13 443	14 092	14 383	8 550	7 810
Netherlands	1 935	2 001	2 074	1 361	934
Switzerland and Liechtenstein	1 454	1 445	1 451	805	573
Italy	1 102	1 099	1 108	331	335
United Kingdom	942	996	966	304	86
Nights in all types of accommodation	105 977	110 430	112 765	66 280	49 964
Hotels and similar establishments	81 179	84 078	85 982	47 408	35 753
Other collective establishments	4 865	5 216	5 404	3 735	4 282
Private accommodation	19 933	21 136	21 379	15 137	9 930
Outbound tourism					
Total international departures	14 068	13 646	14 388	5 072	8 628
Overnight visitors (tourists)	11 491	11 043	11 902	3 965	7 522
Same-day visitors (excursionists)	2 577	2 604	2 486	1 108	1 106
Top destinations					
Italy	2 221	2 058	2 269	749	1 994
Germany	2 189	2 044	2 559	1 154	1 633
Croatia	1 413	1 375	1 000	237	845
Greece	375	322	577	93	469
Spain	620	504	629	129	351
TOURISM RECEIPTS AND EXPENDITURE, MILLION EUR					
Inbound tourism					
Total international receipts	19 952	21 404	23 127	13 436	10 094
International travel receipts	18 112	19 559	20 493	12 124	8 762
International passenger transport receipts	1 840	1 845	2 634	1 312	1 332
Outbound tourism					
Total international expenditure	11 300	11 967	12 491	4 526	7 463
International travel expenditure	9 454	10 019	10 364	3 925	6 810
International passenger transport expenditure	1 846	1 948	2 127	601	653

.. Not available
Source: OECD Tourism Statistics (Database).

StatLink https://stat.link/420s5l

Austria: Enterprises and employment in tourism

	Number of establishments[1]	Number of persons employed				
	2018	2017	2018	2019	2020	2021
Total	..	..	..	..	..	..
Tourism industries	**89 544**	**191 466**	**199 293**	**205 674**	**137 756**	..
Accommodation services for visitors	..	..	130 563	134 686	102 465	..
Hotels and similar establishments	16 577	..	..	..	..	..
Food and beverage serving industry	31 597	..	..	..	..	..
Passenger transport	12 489	..	34 536	35 750	12 124	..
Air passenger transport	169	..	6 668	..	..	..
Railways passenger transport	32	..	3 490	..	..	..
Road passenger transport	12 199	..	20 869	..	..	..
Water passenger transport	89	..	244	..	..	..
Passenger transport supporting services	..	..	..	..	..	..
Transport equipment rental	2 675	..	33	34	32	..
Travel agencies and other reservation services industry	2 488	..	11 480	11 868	10 836	..
Cultural industry	21 980	..	22 681	23 337	12 300	..
Sports and recreation industry	1 738	..	6 036	..	..	..
Retail trade of country-specific tourism characteristic goods	..	..	..	..	..	..
Other country-specific tourism industries	..	..	..	..	..	..
Other industries	..	..	..	..	..	..

.. Not available
1. Data refer to number of enterprises.
Source: OECD Tourism Statistics (Database).

StatLink https://stat.link/tzcpwk

Austria: Internal tourism consumption

Million EUR

	2020		
	Domestic tourism expenditure	Inbound tourism expenditure	Internal tourism consumption
Total	**9 148**	**11 760**	**21 265**
Consumption products	..	..	..
Tourism characteristic products	..	..	..
Accommodation services for visitors	..	..	7 512
Food and beverage serving services	..	..	4 319
Passenger transport services	..	..	2 575
Air passenger transport services	..	..	708
Railways passenger transport services	..	..	413
Road passenger transport services	..	..	1 444
Water passenger transport services	..	..	10
Passenger transport supporting services	..	..	..
Transport equipment rental services	..	..	39
Travel agencies and other reservation services industry	..	..	660
Cultural services	..	..	1 380
Sports and recreation services	..	..	..
Country-specific tourism characteristic goods	..	..	..
Country-specific tourism characteristic services	..	..	..
Other consumption products	..	..	4 780
Tourism connected products	..	..	..
Non-tourism related consumption products	..	..	..
Non-consumption products	..	..	..

.. Not available
Source: OECD Tourism Statistics (Database).

StatLink https://stat.link/u6edq9

Belgium

Tourism in the economy and outlook for recovery

In Belgium, tourism is under the respective authority of three regions: Flanders, Wallonia, and Brussels. This section provides a national overview of the impact of tourism in the country, followed by detail of the respective governance and policy initiatives of the Flanders and Wallonia regions.

Tourism remains a strong contributor to Belgium's economy. The most recent Tourism Satellite Account shows that in 2016 tourism's direct contribution to GVA was 4.3% in Flanders, 5.3% in the Brussels Capital region, and 4.1% in Wallonia.

Belgium's tourism sector was hit hard by the pandemic. International tourists at hotels and similar establishments fell 73%, to 1.8 million. A small recovery in 2021 saw international tourists return to 2.3 million (up 28% from 2020).

Domestic tourism has grown in important in Belgium. Before the COVID 19 pandemic, the domestic market made up 42% of all tourists in hotels, which increased to 63% in 2021.

Overall, there were 11.0 million domestic and international arrivals in all types commercial accommodation (including camping grounds) in Belgium during 2021. Of these 6.8 million visited Flanders, 1.3 million visited Brussels, and 2.8 million visited Wallonia. The top market sources were France, the Netherlands and Germany, with a total market share of 71% in 2021, up from 51% from 2019. A recovery in international tourism is expected in 2025.

Flanders Region

Tourism governance and funding

In Flanders, tourism is the responsibility of the Flemish Minister for Justice and Enforcement, Environment and Spatial Development, Energy and Tourism. The Tourism Unit of the Flanders Department of Chancellery and Foreign Affairs is responsible for international tourism policy and relations.

The overall public sector budget allocated to tourism has remained the same, with the exception of the extra support given to the sector during the COVID-19 pandemic. In 2021, EUR 28.5 million was allocated to the social tourism sector, with an additional EUR 40 million for subsidies to the whole tourism sector. Besides this budget, the tourism sector also benefits from more general support for enterprises, such as financial support, temporary unemployment support and loans.

Flanders: Organisational chart of tourism bodies

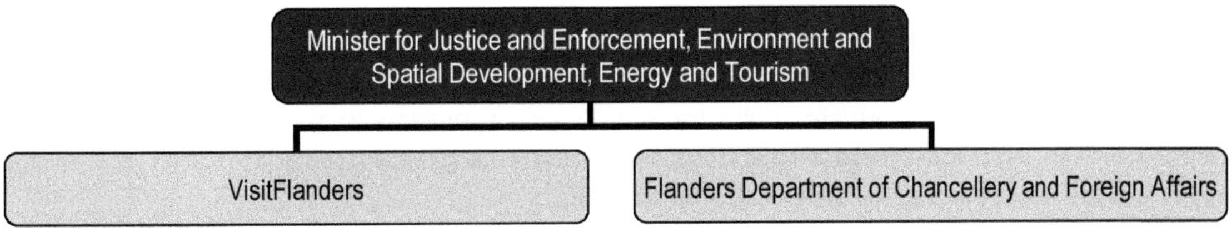

Source: OECD, adapted from the Flanders Department of Chancellery and Foreign Affairs, 2022.

Tourism policies and programmes

Flanders has defined a regional recovery plan, "Flemish Resilience" (Vlaamse Veerkracht), for the period of 2022-26. This plan aims to help all economic sectors, including tourism, to 'stand up' from the crisis, with a total budget of approximately EUR 4.3 billion. Within this plan, EUR 150 million has been reserved for tourism. These investments will mainly focus on larger-scale infrastructure and supra-local visitor experiences to support:

- The meetings, conferences and events sector with investment in multiple state-of-the-art MICE infrastructure projects. This investment will help increase the sector's competitiveness and aid the transition to digital and hybrid events.
- Landmark tourism projects, which will be targeted on themes that the Flemish Minister for Tourism has set out and will be financed through a mix of direct financing and theme-based open project subsidy calls. The theme focus is on heritage, cycling, culinary, nature and social tourism.

In 2021, Flanders implemented a programme to help individual tourism entrepreneurs make strategic investments, with 100% pre-financing given for investments in sustainability, health, digitalisation and professionalisation, to be partially repaid after five years. This reimbursement period was chosen to coincide with the expected recovery of international tourism. The Flemish Government allocated a budget of EUR 30 million for this programme, supplemented by additional funds from provincial and local authorities.

The longer-term strategy for tourism in Flanders is based upon the principles of "Travel to Tomorrow" (see box below). Travel to Tomorrow is a value-driven vision built on balance and sustainable tourism principles, but also considers quality, creativity and co-operation. This vision has been created in conjunction with the private sector, and aims to achieve flourishing communities and vibrant destinations.

Travel to Tomorrow Strategy in Flanders, Belgium

Travel to Tomorrow, based on sustainability and the principle that all stakeholders in the tourism ecosystem can benefit from tourism, calls for a different approach to measuring, developing, and promoting travel in response to recent shocks. To achieve a needed paradigm shift in tourism, the strategy is guided by principles to steer action into 2030:

- Searching for the right balance: Flanders wants to create broad social value through tourism for locals and visitors, by offering them a qualitative and inspiring travel experience and connections. Understanding the full value equation by factoring in the 'loss of value', such as the environmental cost, is equally important.
- Responding to the effects of COVID-19 pandemic: Staying home has made people value travel more than ever. At the same time, people are more aware of the vulnerability and the consequences of our travel behaviour on the ecosystem. Tourism must reinvent itself and take advantage of this opportunity for a hard reset.
- Connecting people, places and activities in a unique story: A flourishing destination offers impactful experiences that inspire people, enhance well-being and enrich visitors, locals, entrepreneurs and service providers. Tomorrow's tourism is a tailor-made welcome 'for everyone' - because a destination can only flourish if nobody is excluded.

Wallonia Region

Tourism governance and funding

In Wallonia, tourism is the responsibility of the Minister for Public Service, Tourism, Heritage and Road Safety. The German-speaking community in Wallonia has made an agreement with Wallonia to manage tourism in its territory.

Two main bodies support the Wallonia tourism sector:

- The General Tourism Commission (CGT) is the main tourism administration in Wallonia and focuses on developing quality tourism. It provides support to the sector through advice, recognition, labelling and financial aid.
- Wallonia Belgium Tourism (WBT) is responsible for promoting Walloon tourism in Belgium and foreign markets.

The 2020 Walloon budget allocated to tourism was EUR 67 million, of which EUR 11.4 million was for measures to support tourism operators due to the COVID-19 crisis. The 2021 Walloon tourism budget was EUR 54 million, of which EUR 10 million supported tourism operators affected by the pandemic. A variety of European funds have additionally been used for dedicated tourism projects.

Wallonia: Organisational chart of tourism bodies

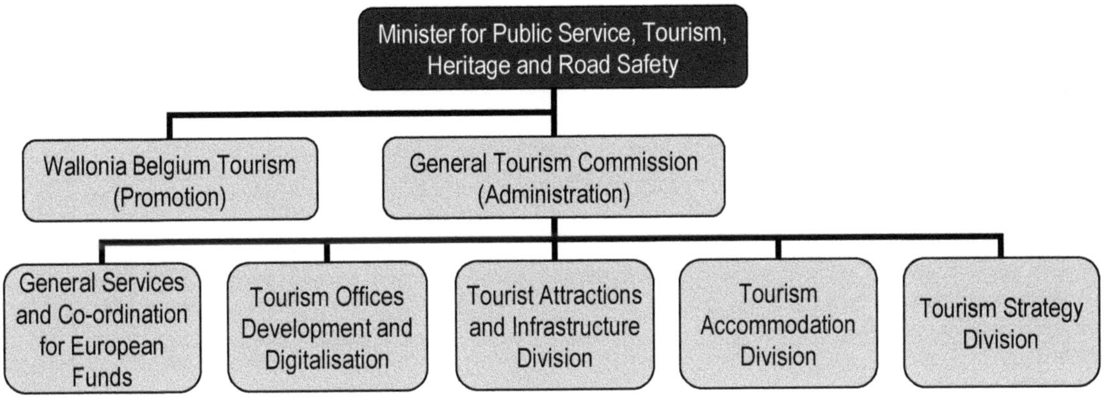

Source: OECD, adapted from the General Tourism Commission of Wallonia, 2022.

Tourism policies and programmes

The COVID-19 crisis confirmed, and at times accentuated, a series of emerging trends for tourism in Wallonia. These included: a shift towards local and domestic tourism; an increase in nature-based tourism, including outdoor activities like walking and cycling; a greater awareness of local culture; and a greater focus on sustainability, digitalisation and well-being. A continuation of macro-trends will also impact tourism, such as an ageing population and urbanisation. This has created a shift in the needs of the tourism sector moving forward.

In the short term, the Walloon tourism sector benefitted from economy-wide and tourism-targeted initiatives by the Walloon Government. Targeted support plans, valued at EUR 24.4 million, were primarily established under the "Get up Wallonia" plan. This Walloon recovery plan will receive both Walloon and European funding. The plan includes the development of a COVID-19 recovery plan and action plan with innovative actions for tourism focused on:

- Stepping up the digitalisation of the sector.
- Developing the image of "Destination Wallonia" using tourism as a vector.
- Developing sustainable infrastructure dedicated to cycle tourists.
- Redeveloping the major Eau d'Heure lake complex.
- Developing river tourism.
- Creating national parks to highlight Wallonia's natural assets.

Focusing on the medium and long-term needs of the sector, the Walloon Minister of Tourism asked for an examination of the digital strategy and the creation of a new tourism strategy in 2021. The new Tourism Strategy 2030 has objectives to:

- Increase the economic benefits of the sector by increasing average spend.
- Develop a strategic positioning relating to two themes that characterise Walloon tourism: Nature and Escape; and Culture, Heritage and Agritourism.
- Increase the development of skills and the attractiveness of the sector.
- Attract more Belgian, French, Dutch and German tourists and business tourism.
- Implement innovative tools to develop an understanding of the expectations and needs of visitors.

Statistical Profile

Belgium: Domestic, inbound and outbound tourism

	2017	2018	2019	2020	2021
TOURISM FLOWS, THOUSAND					
Domestic tourism					
Total domestic trips	..	..	..	..	..
Overnight visitors (tourists)	3 997	4 872	5 362	4 284	6 911
Same-day visitors (excursionists)	..	18 480	..	..	19 013
Nights in all types of accommodation	13 701	19 925	18 627	17 407	26 169
Hotels and similar establishments	8 849	11 092	10 376	9 458	16 048
Other collective establishments	1 386	1 666	1 301	1 901	2 742
Private accommodation	3 446	7 166	6 950	6 049	7 379
Inbound tourism					
Total international arrivals	..	..	..	..	..
Overnight visitors (tourists)	6 313	6 700	6 800	1 804	2 313
Same-day visitors (excursionists)	..	..	..	..	..
Top markets					
Netherlands	1 032	1 037	1 038	361	611
France	963	1 010	1 036	391	571
Germany	701	726	756	234	268
Spain	348	345	346	66	88
Italy	228	250	263	64	79
Nights in all types of accommodation	..	..	..	..	..
Hotels and similar establishments	11 632	12 424	12 669	3 480	4 341
Other collective establishments	..	..	..	..	..
Private accommodation	..	..	..	..	..
Outbound tourism					
Total international departures	..	..	..	..	..
Overnight visitors (tourists)	14 638	15 626	17 322	7 109	8 593
Same-day visitors (excursionists)	4 742	5 458	6 396	3 080	2 280
Top destinations					
France	4 370	4 919	4 780	2 712	3 267
Spain	1 755	1 797	1 813	550	964
Netherlands	1 724	1 594	2 112	796	844
Italy	1 075	933	1 289	504	636
Germany	946	945	1 375	465	515
TOURISM RECEIPTS AND EXPENDITURE, MILLION EUR					
Inbound tourism					
Total international receipts	8 518	8 748	9 460	6 530	..
International travel receipts	7 419	7 530	7 957	5 785	..
International passenger transport receipts	1 099	1 218	1 503	745	..
Outbound tourism					
Total international expenditure	15 721	17 638	18 773	12 180	..
International travel expenditure	13 738	15 655	16 756	11 391	..
International passenger transport expenditure	1 983	1 983	2 017	789	..

.. Not available
Source: OECD Tourism Statistics (Database).

StatLink https://stat.link/cwpalm

Belgium: Enterprises and employment in tourism

	Number of establishments	Number of persons employed				
	2021	2017	2018	2019	2020	2021
Total	..	..	..	..	..	..
Tourism industries	..	..	..	..	..	..
Accommodation services for visitors	9 516	..	..	..	..	..
Hotels and similar establishments	..	..	..	..	..	..
Food and beverage serving industry	..	..	..	..	..	..
Passenger transport	..	..	..	..	..	..
Air passenger transport	..	..	..	..	..	..
Railways passenger transport	..	..	..	..	..	..
Road passenger transport	..	..	..	..	..	..
Water passenger transport	..	..	..	..	..	..
Passenger transport supporting services	..	..	..	..	..	..
Transport equipment rental	..	..	..	..	..	..
Travel agencies and other reservation services industry	..	..	..	..	..	..
Cultural industry	..	..	..	..	..	..
Sports and recreation industry	..	..	..	..	..	..
Retail trade of country-specific tourism characteristic goods	..	..	..	..	..	..
Other country-specific tourism industries	..	..	..	..	..	..
Other industries	..	..	..	..	..	..

.. Not available
Source: OECD Tourism Statistics (Database).

StatLink https://stat.link/dzteix

Canada

Tourism in the economy and outlook for recovery

Tourism is an important sector of Canada's economy and is a large source of jobs and growth. In 2019, the sector directly represented 2.1% of GVA and 3.6% of all jobs across Canada. The COVID-19 pandemic has had a significant impact on the sector. In 2021, tourism provided 498 900 jobs, down 197 500 jobs from 2019, and tourism GVA was CAD 24.2 billion, 1.0% of the Canadian economy.

After a record high of 22.1 million international tourists in 2019, visitation fell to 3.0 million in 2020. International tourist arrivals remained low in 2021, at 3.1 million tourists. Domestic tourism fell from 93.7 million overnight stays to 68.2 million in 2020. Domestic tourism trips recovered slightly in 2021 but remained 26% below pre-pandemic levels.

Total tourism expenditure fell from CAD 105.1 billion in 2019 to CAD 52.8 billion in 2020. This was held up by the relatively stronger performance of domestic tourism, which increased from 73.2% of total expenditure in 2019 to 91.8% in 2021.

Domestic tourism is expected to return faster than international tourism, with a return to pre-pandemic levels forecast in 2024. Recovery of international arrivals is expected in 2026. During the period January to July 2022, international tourists remained 48.6% lower than in the same time period in 2019.

Tourism governance and funding

In Canada the Federal Government, ten provincial governments, three territorial governments and the municipalities all play a role in supporting the tourism sector. The Federal Government holds exclusive responsibility in key policy areas, including border, air and visa policies.

The Minister of Tourism and Associate Minister of Finance (supported by the Department of Innovation, Science and Economic Development) is responsible for tourism at the federal level.

Other key federal players include Destination Canada, the national destination marketing organisation. Destination Canada works with partners in both the public and private sectors to promote Canada abroad as a premier tourism destination. As a Crown corporation, it reports to Parliament through the Minister responsible for tourism.

The seven Regional Economic Development Agencies play a critical role in providing direct support to tourism businesses and communities throughout the country. Provincial and territorial governments are responsible for domestic (and some international) tourism promotion, destination and product development, accommodation regulation, and hospitality and tourism education.

Canada has various mechanisms to ensure horizontal and vertical co-ordination and collaboration. Chief among these is the Canadian Council of Tourism Ministers, which annually brings together federal, provincial and territorial tourism ministers to discuss trends and issues facing Canada's tourism sector and to identify opportunities for collaboration.

Canada continued to make investments specifically tailored to the tourism sector in the 2021 Budget, totalling CAD 1 billion over three years. Measures included a CAD 500 million Tourism Relief Fund (Box 1.9), CAD 200 million to support internationally renowned festivals, and CAD 200 million to support smaller events in communities throughout the country. Budget 2021 also sought to drive demand for Canadian tourism by investing CAD 100 million in marketing initiatives through Destination Canada. In total, from the onset of the pandemic to April 2022, Canada's tourism and hospitality sector received an estimated CAD 23 billion in support through federal emergency programmes.

Canada: Organisational chart of tourism bodies

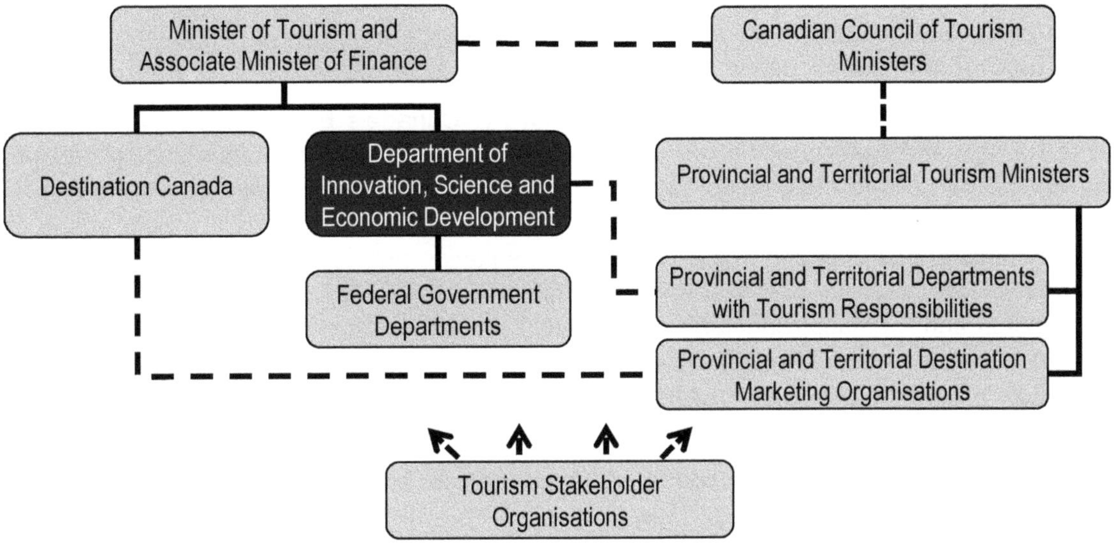

Source: OECD, adapted from Department of Innovation, Science and Economic Development, 2022.

Tourism policies and programmes

In 2019, the Federal Tourism Growth Strategy was announced, an overarching national strategy to support long-term sustainable growth in the sector. The strategy was built on three pillars: building tourism in communities, attracting investment, and promoting public-private collaboration. As part of the 2019 Strategy, the Government launched a CAD 58.5 million Canadian Experiences Fund (CEF) to enable communities to create, improve or enhance tourism products, facilities and experiences. The CEF investments were disbursed over two years (2019-20 and 2020-21) for tourism development projects in five priority areas: winter and shoulder-seasons; indigenous; inclusiveness (LGBTQ2); rural and remote; and culinary.

With the onset of the pandemic, the Federal Government recognised the critical need for an economy-wide suite of core measures to support businesses, families, and individuals. Canada made resources available through the COVID-19 emergency economic response to help businesses survive the pandemic. These liquidity measures ensured that businesses could access credit, keep employees on the payroll, and pay their rent.

In response to the duration of the crisis and the specific needs of tourism businesses, Canada brought in the Highly Affected Sectors Credit Availability Programme to provide government-backed loans of up to CAD 1 million per business to the hardest-hit sectors, including tourism. Furthermore, 25% of the CAD 2 billion Regional Relief and Recovery Fund was earmarked for tourism businesses.

As an example of the sector's increasing significance, tourism is steadily becoming an important economic contributor and job creator for Indigenous communities across the country. Cultural experiences that Indigenous Peoples share with visitors are important attractions for Canadian tourism, especially within international markets.

With the devastating impact of COVID-19 on the tourism sector, Indigenous communities that rely heavily on tourism have been disproportionately affected. The Tourism Relief Fund will continue to invest in Indigenous tourism by setting a national target of CAD 50 million for Indigenous tourism projects. In addition, through Budget 2022, Canada provided CAD 20 million for new Indigenous tourism funding to help the Indigenous tourism sector recover from the pandemic and position itself for long-term, sustainable growth. The Federal Government also proposes to provide CAD 4.8 million to the Indigenous Tourism Association of Canada to support its operations, which continue to help the Indigenous tourism sector rebuild and recover from the pandemic.

As the sector looks forward to a post-pandemic recovery, Canada's Budget 2022 announced that the Minister of Tourism and Associate Minister of Finance would work with the tourism sector, provincial and territorial counterparts, and Indigenous tourism operators to develop a new, post-pandemic Federal Tourism Growth Strategy to plot a course for growth, investment, and stability. To help shape the new Strategy, the Minister has engaged in an extensive consultation process with domestic and international tourism stakeholders, totalling over 400 engagements since May 2022. The engagement process has included regional and thematic roundtables on tourism investment, workforce, rural, sport, Indigenous, cultural, and culinary tourism. Regional roundtables provided a platform for tourism businesses and industry leaders across the country to highlight their needs, challenges, and interests.

The Minister of Tourism is also committed to developing a national strategy to promote trails tourism in Canada. This strategy will provide direction for the enhancement and maintenance of Canada's extensive trails network, such as the Trans Canada Trail.

Statistical Profile

Canada: Domestic, inbound and outbound tourism

	2017	2018	2019	2020	2021
TOURISM FLOWS, THOUSAND					
Domestic tourism					
Total domestic trips	328 454	278 060 |	275 418	198 032	202 267
Overnight visitors (tourists)	117 368	95 445 |	93 665	68 247	69 318
Same-day visitors (excursionists)	211 086	182 615 |	181 753	129 784	132 949
Nights in all types of accommodation	356 977	268 258 |	262 950	206 351	236 875
Hotels and similar establishments	..	..	..	..	..
Other collective establishments	..	..	..	..	..
Private accommodation	..	..	..	..	..
Inbound tourism					
Total international arrivals	31 081	31 274	32 430	5 068	4 282
Overnight visitors (tourists)	20 652	21 134	22 145	2 960	3 062
Same-day visitors (excursionists)	10 429	10 140	10 285	2 108	1 220
Top markets					
United States	14 238	14 650	14 977	1 929	2 093
France	547	593	658	96	121
United Kingdom	794	762	883	96	112
Germany	385	386	394	40	54
China (People's Republic of)	674	719	717	94	40
Nights in all types of accommodation	..	..	..	..	..
Hotels and similar establishments	..	..	..	..	..
Other collective establishments	..	..	..	..	..
Private accommodation	..	..	..	..	..
Outbound tourism					
Total international departures	..	..	..	..	..
Overnight visitors (tourists)	32 730	33 440	33 064	8 971	4 954
Same-day visitors (excursionists)	..	..	..	..	..
Top destinations					
..	..	..	..	..	..
..	..	..	..	..	..
..	..	..	..	..	..
..	..	..	..	..	..
..	..	..	..	..	..
TOURISM RECEIPTS AND EXPENDITURE, MILLION CAD					
Inbound tourism					
Total international receipts	36 938	39 959	44 323	18 894	17 847
International travel receipts	32 446	35 391	39 507	18 114	16 459
International passenger transport receipts	4 492	4 568	4 816	780	694
Outbound tourism					
Total international expenditure	54 368	54 830	57 383	18 739	12 824
International travel expenditure	45 010	44 740	46 901	16 203	9 637
International passenger transport expenditure	9 358	10 090	10 482	2 536	1 593

.. Not available; | Break in series
Source: OECD Tourism Statistics (Database).

StatLink https://stat.link/q42bvz

Canada: Enterprises and employment in tourism

	Number of establishments	Number of persons employed[1]				
	2021	2017	2018	2019	2020	2021
Total	..	**677 500**	**684 600**	**696 400**	**491 300**	**498 900**
Tourism industries	**207 139**	**551 200**	**556 900**	**567 900**	**393 800**	**396 200**
Accommodation services for visitors	20 925	136 100	138 800	142 900	93 000	95 900
Hotels and similar establishments	..	..	..	..	..	..
Food and beverage serving industry	86 025	223 500	226 400	230 100	154 400	167 000
Passenger transport	44 099	80 100	80 600	83 300	67 900	57 000
Air passenger transport	..	..	..	..	..	..
Railways passenger transport	..	..	..	..	..	..
Road passenger transport	..	..	..	..	..	..
Water passenger transport	..	..	..	..	..	..
Passenger transport supporting services	..	..	..	..	..	..
Transport equipment rental	..	..	..	..	..	..
Travel agencies and other reservation services industry	7 315	40 800	39 800	40 100	29 800	24 500
Cultural industry	..	..	..	..	..	..
Sports and recreation industry	48 775	70 700	71 400	71 600	48 800	51 800
Retail trade of country-specific tourism characteristic goods	..	..	..	..	..	..
Other country-specific tourism industries	..	..	..	..	..	..
Other industries	..	**126 300**	**127 700**	**128 600**	**97 500**	**102 800**

.. Not available
1. Data refer to number of jobs.
Source: OECD Tourism Statistics (Database).

StatLink https://stat.link/lf826d

Table 3. Canada: Internal tourism consumption

Million CAD

	2021		
	Domestic tourism expenditure	Inbound tourism expenditure	Internal tourism consumption
Total	..	..	..
Consumption products	**53 640**	**4 792**	**58 432**
Tourism characteristic products	28 814	3 576	32 390
Accommodation services for visitors	8 425	1 287	9 712
Food and beverage serving services	10 151	712	10 863
Passenger transport services	5 442	1 144	6 586
Air passenger transport services	..	..	..
Railways passenger transport services	..	..	..
Road passenger transport services	..	..	..
Water passenger transport services	..	..	..
Passenger transport supporting services	..	..	..
Transport equipment rental services	..	..	..
Travel agencies and other reservation services industry	1 328	108	1 436
Cultural services	3 468	325	3 793
Sports and recreation services	..	..	..
Country-specific tourism characteristic goods	..	..	..
Country-specific tourism characteristic services	..	..	..
Other consumption products	24 826	1 216	26 042
Tourism connected products	..	..	..
Non-tourism related consumption products	..	..	..
Non-consumption products	..	..	..

.. Not available
Source: OECD Tourism Statistics (Database).

StatLink https://stat.link/37megc

Chile

Tourism in the economy and outlook for recovery

Tourism has been a growth sector of the Chilean economy. Provisional estimates suggest that tourism accounted for 3.3% of Chile's GDP in 2019, contributing CLP 6.5 trillion to the economy. Tourism-related industries employed 645 773 people, contributing to 7.2% of total employment in 2019. This fell to 504 000 people in 2021, representing 6.1% of total employment.

International tourists fell by 75.2% in 2020 to 1.1 million. The decline was further exacerbated in 2021, with 190 000 international tourists. While inbound tourism represented 34.8% of services exports in 2019, this declined to 10.5% in 2020 and represented 1.7% in 2021.

Domestic overnight tourists decreased by 26.8% to 39.3 million in 2020. In 2021 domestic tourists rebounded to 49.1 million but remained 8.7% below pre-pandemic levels.

Chile expects tourism to return to pre-pandemic levels in mid-2023 or early 2024.

Tourism governance and funding

Tourism in Chile comes under the responsibility of the Undersecretary for Tourism within the Ministry of Economy, Development and Tourism, which oversees the design and implementation of national tourism policies and strategies.

The Undersecretary of Tourism oversees the National Tourism Service, SERNATUR, responsible for executing tourism policies and strategies. SERNATUR has regional offices in each of Chile's 16 administrative regions, headed by a Regional Director. It also has provincial offices in certain territories, including Easter Island, San Pedro de Atacama, Chiloé and Puerto Natales.

Through this regional network, SERNATUR co-ordinates activities with regional governments. The regional governments also work with other central government services, including the Chilean Economic Development Agency (CORFO), which supports entrepreneurship, innovation and competitiveness, and the Technical Co-operation Service (SERCOTEC). Most local administrations have tourism offices that support the sector, and SERNATUR has also established a network of 309 municipalities with local tourism offices.

In terms of governance, there is a new Tourism Law in progress, where the Undersecretary of Tourism and SERNATUR are exploring the possibility of merging into one institution towards a decentralisation policy. The co-ordination between the two institutions has improved as they are now located in the same facility.

In 2021, the Undersecretary of Tourism received a budget of CLP 3.6 billion, while SERNATUR had a budget of CLP 22.5 billion, drawn from the Ministry of Economy. The National Fund for Regional Development also offers funding to support tourism projects.

Chile: Organisational chart of tourism bodies

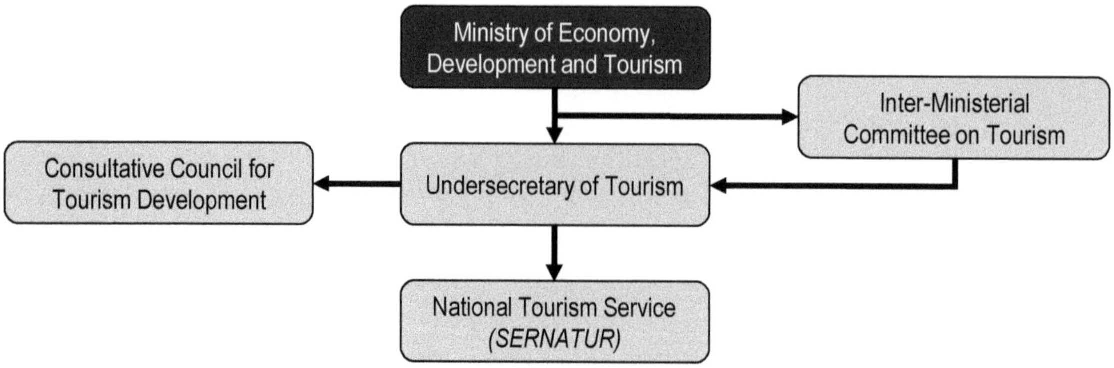

Source: OECD, adapted from the Ministry of Economy, Development and Tourism, 2022.

Tourism policies and programmes

In 2020, the Ministry of Economy, Development and Tourism and SERNATUR started developing the National Tourism Plan, which covers the period to 2030. This includes finance, health and hygiene protocols and joint work with the tourism sector to reactivate tourism SMEs that have been hit hard by the global health crisis. The plan is founded on four main strategic pillars: sustainability, digitalisation, local development and the tourist experience. In addition, reactivation and gender equality are fundamentals of all institutional work.

A reactivation plan focusing on three areas is being developed to deliver assistance to the tourism sector in the short and medium term:

- Reactivate the tourism sector within the health and safety protocols.
- Provide subsidies of CLP 7 billion to the tourism sector, which will be allocated through the Technical Co-operation Service, SERCOTEC.
- Promote domestic travel within Chile and its regions through funding of CLP 3 billion.

Commercialising diverse, high-quality tourism experiences is a key area of focus in the recovery plan, with action being taken in a number of priority areas, including:

- **Rural and indigenous tourism:** in order to stimulate local economic growth, work has been focused on the improvement of the quality, attractiveness, and diversity of the tourism offer while ensuring coherence with cultural heritage. The adaptation of health regulations to the rural reality and the implementation of sustainable sanitary solutions for rural entrepreneurs are also undertaken as part of the social improvement led by tourism. The Undersecretary of Tourism co-ordinates initiatives together with the National Association of Indigenous Tourism (ANTI), National Corporation for the Indigenous Development (CONADI) and the National Agricultural Development Institute (INDAP).
- **Wine and gastronomy tourism:** work has been focused on improving the quality, attractiveness and diversity of the wine and gastronomy tourism offer and the role suppliers play in the gastronomy tourism value chain. The Multi-regional Strategic Programme of Sustainable Wine Tourism is a public-private initiative which brings together big and small wine producers from several regions with the tourism industry. Gastronomy tourism is being co-ordinated in a public-private commission led by the Undersecretary of Tourism and the Transform Tourism (Transforma Turismo) programme.

- **Cultural and heritage tourism:** a national Culture Tourism Plan is now underway, co-ordinated by the Ministry of Cultures, Arts and Heritage and the Undersecretary of Tourism.
- **Adventure tourism:** initiatives in the adventure tourism sector include strengthening host communities' capacities around national parks, modification of adventure tourism regulations, approval of international certifications and the interaction of the adventure tourism segment. Transform Tourism (Transforma Turismo) programme leads the Mountain Adventure and Nature Tourism National Promotion Plan, which co-ordinates a public-private commission for the development of adventure tourism.

Domestic travel demand has been driven by the Social Tourism Programme, which subsidises tourism packages for seniors, students and families to travel around Chile, worth CLP 8.7 billion in 2021. This programme benefits a yearly average of 67 tourism destinations and 750 tourism services providers, mostly micro, small and medium-sized companies.

A Tourism Infrastructure Masterplan co-ordinated with the Ministry of Public Works has recently been implemented for the 2021-25 period. This CLP 1.4 billion plan is focused on infrastructure for national parks, scenic routes development, coastline recovery and renovation, provision of tourism attractions and road connectivity.

An Executive Committee for the Attraction of Tourism Investments was established in 2020, formed by 11 public institutions, with the strategic role of strengthening a pro-investment ecosystem in tourism. The Committee developed a 2020-25 Action Plan to facilitate the delivery of the investments system, the definition of investment portfolios and its diffusion. The Invest Tourism initiative (Invierte Turismo), developed together with Invest Chile, the Chilean agency for foreign investment attraction, maps tourism investment opportunities at the regional level and highlights investment opportunities throughout the country.

The Strategic Plan for Human Capital is being updated for the period 2023-26. Its implementation relies on a public-private commission that brings together different actors from the tourism, hotel and gastronomy industry who work together for the development and strengthening of the human capital of the sector.

Tourism Reactivation Plans 2021-22 in Chile

In 2021 Chile implemented a reactivation plan for tourism which utilised a Community Reactivation Index. This index identified and ranked the effects of the COVID-19 crisis in Chilean communities. The index considered a number of variables, including the days each territory spent in strict quarantine and the relevance of tourism in local economies.

From this, 33 destinations were prioritised throughout the country, and regional interviews took place to identify triggering initiatives for each prioritised territory. In the long term, connectivity and formalisation were among the most important identified initiatives, while the diversification of high-quality touristic products was identified in the short term. Once internal travelling limitations were lifted, the Reactivation Plan shifted to a new set of breaches.

In July 2022, a new Reactivation Plan was launched, which targets the reactivation of MSMEs. Aligned with the "Chile Apoya" (Chile Supports) inclusive recovery programme, the Plan is designed to finance training, business planning, consultancy, technical assistance, working capital and/or investment projects. The Chile Supports 2022 Programme will run in all 16 regions of the country and will finance 100% of the costs of tourism-related projects, up to a limit of CLP 4 million.

Statistical Profile

Chile: Domestic, inbound and outbound tourism

	2017	2018	2019	2020	2021
TOURISM FLOWS, THOUSAND					
Domestic tourism[1]					
Total domestic trips	63 773	73 344	74 459	54 425	68 377
Overnight visitors (tourists)	46 016 e	52 974 e	53 749	39 323	49 062
Same-day visitors (excursionists)	17 756 e	20 370 e	20 711 e	15 102 e	19 315 e
Nights in all types of accommodation	15 325 |	15 742	15 150	..	..
Hotels and similar establishments	..	..	..	..	..
Other collective establishments	..	..	..	..	..
Private accommodation	..	..	..	..	..
Inbound tourism					
Total international arrivals	7 621	6 603	5 431	1 310	192
Overnight visitors (tourists)	6 450	5 723	4 518	1 119	190
Same-day visitors (excursionists)	1 171	880	913	191	2
Top markets					
Peru	394	389	411	98	27
Argentina	3 324	2 422	1 435	414	21
United States	212	222	225	62	18
Brazil	545	589	542	78	14
Bolivia	480	541	468	133	4
Nights in all types of accommodation	..	..	..	..	..
Hotels and similar establishments	..	..	..	..	..
Other collective establishments	..	..	..	..	..
Private accommodation	..	..	..	..	..
Outbound tourism					
Total international departures	4 367	4 605	4 091 |	1 162	519
Overnight visitors (tourists)	3 620	3 825	3 346 |	963	514
Same-day visitors (excursionists)	747	780	745	198	6
Top destinations					
Peru	1 100	1 055	1 018 |	..	..
Argentina	1 014	1 123	996 |	..	..
United States	292	306	295 |	..	..
Brazil	248	301	284 |	..	..
Europe	..	..	193 |	..	..
TOURISM RECEIPTS AND EXPENDITURE, MILLION USD					
Inbound tourism					
Total international receipts	4 115	3 911	3 278	1 033	633
International travel receipts	3 152	2 897	2 303	413	113
International passenger transport receipts	984	1 040	1 000	628	520
Outbound tourism					
Total international expenditure	3 094	3 124	3 142	720	580
International travel expenditure	2 329	2 394	2 459	540	301
International passenger transport expenditure	789	761	714	190	279

.. Not available; e Estimated value; | Break in series

1. Trips from demand side surveys; Nights from supply side surveys.

Source: OECD Tourism Statistics (Database).

StatLink https://stat.link/6hamq0

Chile: Enterprises and employment in tourism

	Number of establishments[1]	Number of persons employed[2]				
	2020	2017	2018	2019	2020	2021
Total	**170 268**	..	**636 477**	**645 773**	**456 513**	**504 000**
Tourism industries	**126 738**	..	**395 517**	**400 185**	**266 811**	**306 471**
Accommodation services for visitors	12 666	..	..	..	..	..
Hotels and similar establishments	5 040	..	..	..	..	..
Food and beverage serving industry	54 123	..	..	..	..	..
Passenger transport	34 000	..	107 244	104 056	87 176	92 388
Air passenger transport	166	..	..	..	..	..
Railways passenger transport	8	..	..	..	..	..
Road passenger transport	33 443	..	..	..	..	..
Water passenger transport	383	..	..	..	..	..
Passenger transport supporting services	..	..	133 716	141 533	102 526	105 141
Transport equipment rental	5 473	..	..	..	..	..
Travel agencies and other reservation services industry	2 685	..	..	..	..	..
Cultural industry	4 223	..	..	..	..	..
Sports and recreation industry	7 888	..	..	..	..	..
Retail trade of country-specific tourism characteristic goods	5 680	..	..	..	..	..
Other country-specific tourism industries	..	..	..	..	..	..
Other industries	**43 530**	..	..	..	..	..

.. Not available
1. Data refer to number of enterprises.
2. Data refer to number of employees.
Source: OECD Tourism Statistics (Database).

StatLink https://stat.link/9xi5um

Chile: Internal tourism consumption

Million USD

	2021		
	Domestic tourism expenditure	Inbound tourism expenditure	Internal tourism consumption
Total	**5 846 e**	**99**	..
Consumption products	..	..	..
Tourism characteristic products	..	..	..
Accommodation services for visitors	..	..	..
Food and beverage serving services	..	..	..
Passenger transport services	..	..	..
Air passenger transport services	..	..	..
Railways passenger transport services	..	..	..
Road passenger transport services	..	..	..
Water passenger transport services	..	..	..
Passenger transport supporting services	..	..	..
Transport equipment rental services	..	..	..
Travel agencies and other reservation services industry	..	..	..
Cultural services	..	..	..
Sports and recreation services	..	..	..
Country-specific tourism characteristic goods	..	..	..
Country-specific tourism characteristic services	..	..	..
Other consumption products	..	..	..
Tourism connected products	..	..	..
Non-tourism related consumption products	..	..	..
Non-consumption products	..	..	..

.. Not available; e Estimated value
Source: OECD Tourism Statistics (Database).

StatLink https://stat.link/mx9t7u

Colombia

Tourism in the economy and outlook for recovery

The tourism sector is an important contributor to Colombia's economy. In 2019, tourism directly contributed 2.6% to Colombia's GVA, or COP 25.3 billion. This fell to just 1.6% in 2021 as the tourism GVA fell to COP 16.7 billion. Tourism industries employed 489 588 people in 2021, a decline of 300 794 jobs compared to 2019 according with the Tourism Satellite Account.

Tourism has become the primary services export in Colombia and the second-highest overall export behind the oil industry. In 2021, export services in tourism amounted to USD 3 239 million, a 47.7% decrease with respect to 2019 (USD 6 784 million). However, the first semester of 2022 saw a total recovery with tourism exports at USD 3 207 million (compared to USD 3 170 million in the same period of 2019).

The country received 2.1 million international visitors in 2021, a 56% increase with respect to 2020. Between January and September 2022, with 3.2 million visitors, there was a 97% recovery compared to the same period of 2019. During that period, visitors increased from the United States (up 23.7%), Mexico (up 17.1%), Peru (up 3.9%) and Ecuador (up 36.0%).

In terms of recovery, tourism is expected to be at 2019 levels by the end of 2022.

Tourism governance and funding

The guidelines for tourism are based on the National Development Plan (NDP), which changes every four years with the President. Under the NDP, the Ministry of Commerce, Industry and Tourism (MINCIT) creates the Sectoral Plan for Tourism. An Integrated Destination Management Strategy allows for cross governmental co-ordination in the planning and management of activities, resources and stakeholders involved in tourism development.

At the national level, MINCIT works with three main organisations:

- FONTUR: the National Tourism Fund affiliated with the Ministry.
- PROCOLOMBIA: the agency charged with international promotion; expansion of Colombian companies; attraction of foreign direct investment; positioning of the country as a tourism destination; and the country's brand.
- Colombia Productiva: helps industry and companies produce better quality services and greater added value to increase productivity and competitiveness.

MINCIT works with other ministries (e.g. Ministry of Environment and Sustainable Development, Ministry of Culture, National Planning Department) and consults stakeholders and representatives from the private sector on all policies and strategies. At the regional level, activities are decentralised, and implementation is co-ordinated with regional authorities and local communities. Local authorities for tourism promote the tourism industry in each territory.

Funding for the tourism sector comes from the general budget, compulsory contributions from tourism service providers, income from tourism properties and brands owned by the government, and a USD 15 tourism tax on international arrivals by air. The tourism sector had a total budget of COP 288.3 million in 2021, 25% more than in 2020. The Vice-Ministry of Tourism received over COP 169 million (60% of the general budget) in 2021, 28% more than in 2020 and 124% more than in 2019.

Colombia: Organisational chart of tourism bodies

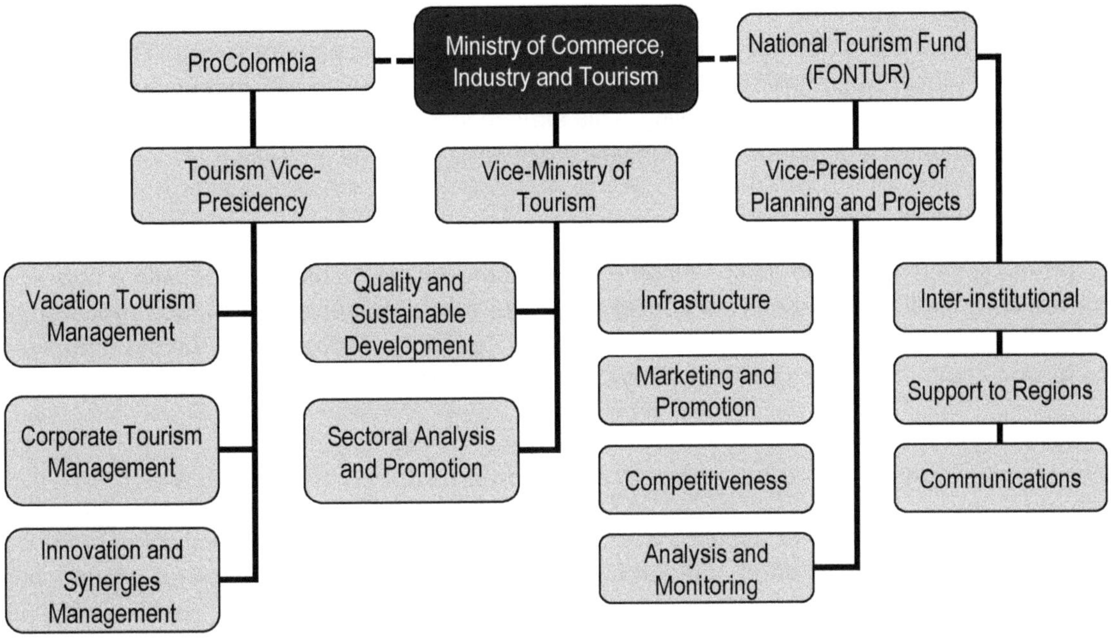

Source: OECD, adapted from the Ministry of Commerce, Industry and Tourism, 2022.

Tourism policies and programmes

In recent years, and more so during the pandemic, Colombia considers sustainable tourism a responsibility and an opportunity. It has developed the Sustainable Tourism Policy "Together with Nature" as a long-term strategic vision for the sector. The Policy seeks to unite all industry stakeholders towards the goal of developing sustainable tourism and consists of a strategic plan for 2030 comprised of six strategies consistent with the global Agenda for Sustainable Development.

Under the Policy, Colombia developed the strategy "Colombia Sustainable Tourism: Training for Tourism Entrepreneurs and Businesses". The Strategy has three fundamental activities:

- An e-learning platform, with practical, digital and interactive content to acquire knowledge and skills and learn from successful sustainability case studies. More than 2 000 entrepreneurs have registered on the platform and are undertaking the modules.
- A manual of good practices in sustainability for tourism entrepreneurs has also been developed with tools to identify the environmental impacts of tourism and the actions to take for mitigation and compensation.
- 50 virtual and in-person workshops are being run in the 32 departments of the country to disseminate the main components of the strategy.

Colombia's main federal policy priorities for tourism are sustainability, reactivation of the economy, and developing a long-term integrated strategy. Due to COVID-19, Colombia prioritised supporting the recovery and strengthening the resilience of the tourism economy. The new General Law of Tourism, created in 2020, aims to help economic recovery through short, medium and long-term measures (see box below).

The COVID-19 crisis highlighted the gap between formal and informal workers in the sector and the government's capacity to react and adapt when different support mechanisms are required to support vulnerable communities. Colombia aims to increase the percentage of workers in the formal sector to advance programmes that can benefit them.

Colombia has begun a transition to reduce the negative impacts of tourism and protect its ecosystems, communities and diversity to develop a sustainable, responsible and peaceful sector. This policy is being guided by the many local communities in the country. This includes worked with indigenous representatives to develop the first Indigenous Tourism Policy. This aims to increase participation and improve social and economic development of indigenous communities, while enhancing the protection of their heritage, culture and traditions.

Colombia is also working with the United Nations Environment Programme and the World Wildlife Fund to design a practical training course on sustainable gastronomy for the tourism sector, with a corresponding guide for restaurants and lodgings. This course promotes the sustainable use of food procurement and production, the continuous monitoring of food waste and its proper disposal, and the strengthening if the local production chain of organic products. There are over 1 710 participants on the platform.

General Law of Tourism to mitigate impacts and support recovery in Colombia

In 2020, the new General Law of Tourism was created to help the economic reactivation of the sector. It includes a combination of short, medium and long-term measures developed around building confidence, resilience, and sustainability. The Law is focused on four main points: sustainability, quality, training, and reactivation.

Within the Law, there are several financial measures designed to help the reactivation of the sector. This includes tax exemptions or reductions for hotels and tourism services, the sale of food and beverages, and passenger air tickets. The Law temporarily suspended energy surcharge payments for certain tourism service providers and provided subsidies to air transportation providers to promote air travel services in regions with low accessibility and connectivity.

On sustainability, the law provides rent discounts for investments made in environmental control, conservation, improvement, and measures to counteract coastal erosion. To attract investment to boost tourism and encourage projects focused on senior citizens, the Law also provides a ten-year preferential rate on income for assistance centres for elderly tourists.

Statistical Profile

Colombia: Domestic, inbound and outbound tourism

	2017	2018	2019	2020	2021
TOURISM FLOWS, THOUSAND					
Domestic tourism					
Total domestic trips	78 334	81 084	83 856	32 436 p	42 974 p
Overnight visitors (tourists)	43 846	45 280	46 279	19 419 p	25 660 p
Same-day visitors (excursionists)	34 488	35 804	37 577	13 017 p	17 314 p
Nights in all types of accommodation	212 355	219 303	219 816	123 614 p	138 843 p
Hotels and similar establishments	..	..	..	..	..
Other collective establishments	..	..	..	..	..
Private accommodation	..	..	..	..	..
Inbound tourism					
Total international arrivals	4 056	4 398	4 531	1 396	2 179 p
Overnight visitors (tourists)	..	..	..	..	..
Same-day visitors (excursionists)	..	..	..	..	..
Top markets					
United States	529	648	705	230	517 p
Venezuela	371	399	400	112	182 p
Mexico	172	182	198	52	81 p
Peru	141	151	181	48	67 p
Ecuador	169	164	159	38	58 p
Nights in all types of accommodation	..	..	..	..	..
Hotels and similar establishments	..	..	..	..	..
Other collective establishments	..	..	..	..	..
Private accommodation	..	..	..	..	..
Outbound tourism					
Total international departures	4 017	4 368	4 479	1 275	2 276 p
Overnight visitors (tourists)	..	..	..	..	..
Same-day visitors (excursionists)	..	..	..	..	..
Top destinations					
United States	1 242	1 383	1 410	485	1 252 p
Mexico	396	461	499	139	300 p
Spain	362	427	489	105	143 p
Panama	424	404	396	103	107 p
Ecuador	301	300	285	78	39 p
TOURISM RECEIPTS AND EXPENDITURE, MILLION USD					
Inbound tourism					
Total international receipts	5 899	6 655	6 784	1 945	..
International travel receipts	4 921	5 621	5 682	1 581	..
International passenger transport receipts	978	1 034	1 102	364	..
Outbound tourism					
Total international expenditure	5 135	5 531	5 658	1 540	..
International travel expenditure	4 475	4 784	4 935	1 358	..
International passenger transport expenditure	661	747	723	182	..

.. Not available; p Provisional data
Source: OECD Tourism Statistics (Database).

StatLink https://stat.link/pes902

Colombia: Enterprises and employment in tourism

	Number of establishments	Number of persons employed				
	2021	2017	2018	2019	2020	2021
Total	..	..	..	..	..	..
Tourism industries	**47 099 p**	**708 121**	**686 192**	**790 382**	**411 253 p**	**489 588 p**
Accommodation services for visitors	..	323 057	308 307	349 466	189 156 p	220 985 p
Hotels and similar establishments	30 457 p	..	..	..	..	..
Food and beverage serving industry	1 272 p	..	..	..	..	..
Passenger transport	..	232 869	229 857	271 634	100 982 p	131 882 p
Air passenger transport	..	..	..	..	..	..
Railways passenger transport	..	..	..	..	..	..
Road passenger transport	828 p	..	..	..	..	..
Water passenger transport	..	..	..	..	..	..
Passenger transport supporting services	..	..	..	..	..	..
Transport equipment rental	325 p	..	..	..	..	..
Travel agencies and other reservation services industry	9 831 p	33 605	29 340	29 976	22 895 p	18 859 p
Cultural industry	..	..	..	..	..	..
Sports and recreation industry	..	93 687	91 204	113 681	90 094 p	108 103 p
Retail trade of country-specific tourism characteristic goods	..	..	..	..	..	..
Other country-specific tourism industries	4 386 p	24 903	27 485	25 626	8 126 p	9 758 p
Other industries	..	..	..	..	..	..

.. Not available; p Provisional data
Source: OECD Tourism Statistics (Database).

StatLink https://stat.link/v9fplo

Colombia: Internal tourism consumption

Million COP

	2021		
	Domestic tourism expenditure	Inbound tourism expenditure	Internal tourism consumption
Total	..	..	..
Consumption products	..	..	..
Tourism characteristic products	9 162 183 p	16 169 208 p	25 331 391 p
Accommodation services for visitors	1 031 613 p	2 098 500 p	3 130 113 p
Food and beverage serving services	2 701 510 p	4 949 010 p	7 650 520 p
Passenger transport services	..	..	..
Air passenger transport services	1 061 948 p	1 675 596 p	2 737 543 p
Railways passenger transport services	..	..	..
Road passenger transport services	1 133 829 p	2 494 577 p	3 628 406 p
Water passenger transport services	..	..	..
Passenger transport supporting services	..	..	..
Transport equipment rental services	21 166 p	.. p	21 166 p
Travel agencies and other reservation services industry	84 664 p	70 913 p	155 577 p
Cultural services	431 554 p	1 260 707 p	1 692 261 p
Sports and recreation services	..	..	..
Country-specific tourism characteristic goods	1 254 143 p	3 238 283 p	4 492 426 p
Country-specific tourism characteristic services	1 441 758 p	381 621 p	1 823 379 p
Other consumption products	..	..	..
Tourism connected products	..	..	..
Non-tourism related consumption products	..	..	..
Non-consumption products	..	..	..

.. Not available; p Provisional data
Source: OECD Tourism Statistics (Database).

StatLink https://stat.link/drq4bk

Costa Rica

Tourism in the economy and outlook for recovery

Tourism is an important sector for the Costa Rican economy and directly accounted for 4.8% of total GDP in 2019, according to the Tourism Satellite Account. In 2021, tourism employed 150 483 people, an increase compared to 2020, but still 20 387 people below 2019 levels. Tourism enterprises in the hospitality sector remained stable at 3 700 enterprises in 2020 due to ongoing support through the pandemic, and increased by an additional 4% in 2021.

International tourism receipts declined 66.6% to USD 1.5 billion in 2020. This was driven by a 67.8% decline in international tourists to 1.0 million in 2020. International tourist arrivals in Costa Rica recovered to 1.3 million in 2021 but remained 57.1% below pre-pandemic levels.

The United States remained the largest market in 2021 with 868 986 arrivals, followed by Europe with 229 813 arrivals, coming mainly from Germany, Spain, France and Switzerland. Costa Rica expects international visitors to return to pre-pandemic levels by 2024.

Tourism governance and funding

The Minister of Tourism chairs the Tourism Sector, which is made up of the Costa Rican Tourism Institute (ICT), Ministry of Culture and Youth, Ministry of Public Security, Government and Police and the Costa Rican Institute of Pacific Ports.

The Costa Rican Tourism Institute is an autonomous state institution whose main purpose is to increase tourism in Costa Rica, promote spending and a pleasant stay by international visitors, promote the construction and maintenance of tourist accommodation and attractions, brand and promote the country overseas, and attract national and foreign investments through the Investment Attraction Unit. As a public institution, the ICT is responsible for the formulation of public policy, as well as the design and execution of technical and legal instruments to carry out these policies. The ICT is also in charge of drawing up and managing the National Tourism Plan.

The Regional Tourism Offices collaborate with the tourism sector by processing the country's quality programmes, such as the Tourism Declaration and the Certificate for Sustainable Tourism, tourist transportation certificates and tourist guide credentials, and the Safe Travels seal developed in response to COVID-19. In addition, they collaborate in the promotion of their regions in the development of international press tours.

The Costa Rican Tourism Institute leads the country's tourism sector with collaboration from a number of bodies, such as the Ministries of Foreign Relations, Economy and Trade, Transport, Environment and Energy, Health, and Foreign Trade. In particular, there is a strategic alliance between the Costa Rican Tourism Institute and the Costa Rican Investment Promotion Agency through a co-operation agreement for the promotion and attraction of foreign investment projects for tourism infrastructure.

The Costa Rican Tourism Institute is financed mainly by revenue from entry and departure taxes and non-tax revenues from rents and leases. In 2021, 84.4% of the ICT budget came from tax revenues, and 2.6% came from non-tax revenues. The remaining 13% came from a CRC 3 billion transfer from the central government. Prior to the COVID-19 pandemic, the income received was CRC 32.9 billion, representing a 37% year-on-year increase between 2015 and 2019 associated with an increase in international arrivals and the departure of nationals.

In 2022, the ICT`s budget was CRC 16.7 billion, mostly funded through taxes (99.5%), with the remainder funded through non-tax revenues. Revenues are recovering, and projections expect a return to 2019 levels by the end of 2023.

Costa Rica: Organisational chart of tourism bodies

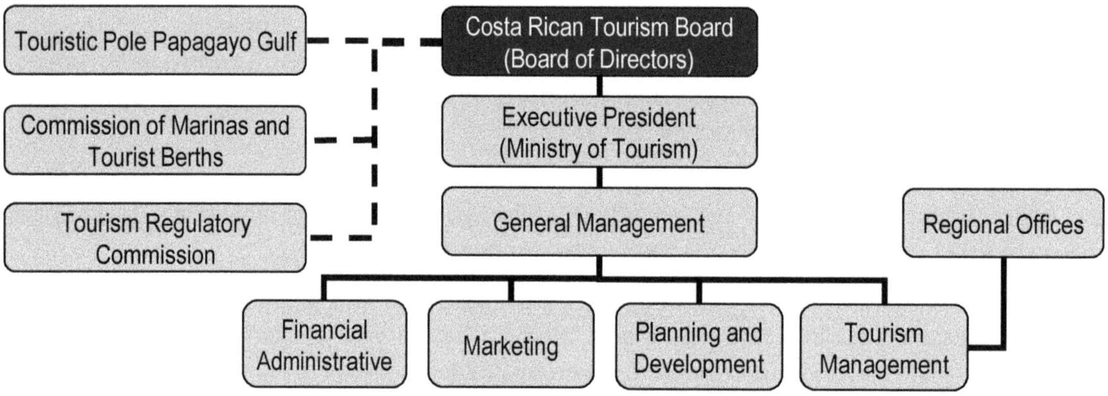

Source: OECD, adapted from the Costa Rican Tourism Board, 2022.

Tourism policies and programmes

The National Tourism Plan 2022-27 is being updated to include new strategic proposals for the next five years, with a special focus on five strategic axes:

- Promoting the efficient use of the tourist space and maintaining natural sites. This involves the responsibility for acquiring land and managing construction.
- Developing and diversifying the tourism product, including for digital nomads.
- Differentiating Costa Rica's positioning, focusing on high-quality products, experience, and well-being.
- Generating productive value chains across different subsectors.
- Enhancing the tourist experience with a commitment to health and safety.

Each of these axes contains grouped objectives, goals and specific actions to develop. Tourism is also included in the sectoral strategic proposal of the National Development Plan 2018-21.

In 2021, Costa Rica launched the Tourism Local Development Engine (Tu-MoDeLo) initiative aimed at improving the livelihoods of agricultural communities through the identification of market opportunities in the tourism sector for sustainable agriculture value chains adapted to climate change. Costa Rica's sustainability values are based on a commitment to the principles of decarbonisation and respect for the environment. Costa Rica prioritises the reuse of materials, use of sustainable elements, energy savings, and hiring local personnel to achieve its sustainability principles. Other values include culture, sustainable gastronomy and the application of health protocols against COVID-19. Costa Rica's focus is promoting the country as a year-round destination, with multiple outdoor activities that can be visited safely and sustainably.

Since the beginning of the pandemic, Costa Rica has worked on the reactivation of tourism, including the development of 17 health protocols for each tourism sub-sector against COVID-19, in conjunction with the private sector.

Following the recovery from the pandemic, a key target sector for Costa Rica is longer-term visitors who will make more local purchases and redistribute money along the tourism value chain, including a focus on digital nomads. Additionally, Costa Rica is now positioning itself as a filming destination in recognition of the growing television on-demand industry. Costa Rica is pursuing new airline routes and frequencies to align with these objectives.

Certificate of Tourism Sustainability 2.0 in Costa Rica

The Costa Rican Tourism Institute launched the original Certification for Sustainable Tourism in 1997. This programme awards companies that follow sustainable practices. In 2018, Costa Rica restructured and updated the programme to adapt to new international standards, including the Sustainable Development Goals and the criteria of the Global Sustainable Tourism Council. The updated tool also adapts to the size of different companies and eliminates the need for face-to-face evaluation in some cases.

The objectives of Certificate for Sustainable Tourism 2.0 are:

- Differentiate Costa Rica as a sustainable tourist destination.
- Provide reliable information to tourists on certified companies and organisations.
- Use sustainability as a competitive element within the tourism sector.
- Incorporate technological advances to remain innovative and updated.
- Strengthen the social, cultural, environmental and economic development of tourist destinations.

As of 2022, more than 400 tourism companies are CST-certified, including hotels, restaurants, travel agencies and tourism attractions.

Statistical Profile

Costa Rica: Domestic, inbound and outbound tourism

	2017	2018	2019	2020	2021
TOURISM FLOWS, THOUSAND					
Domestic tourism					
Total domestic trips	..	..	..	..	..
Overnight visitors (tourists)	..	..	..	..	..
Same-day visitors (excursionists)	..	..	..	..	..
Nights in all types of accommodation	..	..	..	..	..
Hotels and similar establishments	..	..	..	..	..
Other collective establishments	..	..	..	..	..
Private accommodation	..	..	..	..	..
Inbound tourism					
Total international arrivals	3 230	3 313	3 378	1 147	1 376
Overnight visitors (tourists)	2 960	3 017	3 139	1 012	1 347
Same-day visitors (excursionists)	271	296	239	135	29
Top markets					
United States	1 199	1 265	1 335	435	869
Europe	462	480	501	170	230
Central America	735	691	699	202	78
South America	181	190	196	50	60
Canada	202	217	235	116	53
Nights in all types of accommodation	35 222 e	35 295 e	39 552 e	13 054 e	18 320 e
Hotels and similar establishments	..	..	..	..	..
Other collective establishments	..	..	..	..	..
Private accommodation	..	..	..	..	..
Outbound tourism					
Total international departures	..	..	..	..	..
Overnight visitors (tourists)	1 150	1 079	1 153	324	588
Same-day visitors (excursionists)	..	..	..	..	..
Top destinations					
North America	371	376	418	131	333
United States	254	251	280	94	245
Central America	588	583	604	167	222
Panama	241	301	310	89	128
Nicaragua	220	141	151	47	44
TOURISM RECEIPTS AND EXPENDITURE, MILLION USD					
Inbound tourism					
Total international receipts	3 758	4 072	4 340	1 450	..
International travel receipts	3 656	3 769	3 989	1 328	..
International passenger transport receipts	102	304	351	122	..
Outbound tourism					
Total international expenditure	1 322	1 198	1 451	678	..
International travel expenditure	1 044	838	1 036	243	..
International passenger transport expenditure	278	360	415	434	..

.. Not available; e Estimated value
Source: OECD Tourism Statistics (Database).

StatLink https://stat.link/3ztvrm

Costa Rica: Enterprises and employment in tourism

	Number of establishments	Number of persons employed				
	2021	2017	2018	2019	2020	2021
Total	..	..	..	..	..	..
Tourism industries	**5 004**	**155 296**	**160 976**	**170 870**	**127 570**	**150 483**
Accommodation services for visitors	..	..	..	..	..	..
Hotels and similar establishments	3 765 e	28 677	27 622	31 743	17 938	24 293
Food and beverage serving industry	421	98 844	99 402	103 099	89 448	100 963
Passenger transport	..	4 074	8 353	6 993	2 744	6 131
Air passenger transport	17	..	..	..	..	..
Railways passenger transport	..	..	..	..	..	..
Road passenger transport	..	..	..	..	..	..
Water passenger transport	31	..	..	..	..	..
Passenger transport supporting services	..	..	..	..	..	..
Transport equipment rental	55	3 835	6 585	6 843	7 052	5 070
Travel agencies and other reservation services industry	527	5 852	6 178	5 025	3 014	2 295
Cultural industry	..	7 823	5 777	8 122	3 746	6 685
Sports and recreation industry	125	6 191	7 059	9 045	3 628	5 046
Retail trade of country-specific tourism characteristic goods	..	..	..	..	..	..
Other country-specific tourism industries	63	..	..	..	..	..
Other industries	..	..	..	..	..	..

.. Not available; e Estimated value
Source: OECD Tourism Statistics (Database).

StatLink https://stat.link/r9jyl3

Czech Republic

Tourism in the economy and outlook for recovery

Tourism in the Czech Republic experienced stable growth for almost a decade prior to COVID-19. In 2019, tourism directly accounted for 2.9% of GDP and employed 239 506 people (4.4% of total employment). The impacts of the COVID-19 pandemic saw tourism GDP almost halve in 2020 (down CZK 82 billion), with tourism's share of GDP falling to 1.5%. Tourism employment was less impacted, declining by 17 494 people (or 7.3%).

The country welcomed 3.9 million international tourists in 2020, a decline of 73.2% compared to the previous year. International nights in tourism-related accommodation were 7.4 million, a significant decline from 27.2 million in 2019. International tourist nights fell further in 2021 to 6.5 million nights.

The impacts of the pandemic were less severe for domestic tourism, which returned to 8.8 million tourists in commercial accommodation in 2021, 20.7% below 2019 levels. The relative strength in domestic tourism saw the domestic share of tourism expenditure increase to 61.1% in 2020 despite an absolute decline of 36.1% (to CZK 79.1 billion).

The Czech Republic expects international tourism to return to 2019 levels by 2024 or 2025.

Tourism governance and funding

The Ministry of Regional Development is the central administrative tourism body and includes two main departments dealing with competitiveness and legislation in the area of tourism. The Ministry develops strategic documents and supports tourism via subsidies for public tourism infrastructure, marketing activities and support to NGOs.

Close co-operation between national and regional tourism organisations is subject to the agreed CzechTourism marketing strategy, which follows the balanced scorecard model and includes the perspectives of both stakeholders and residents. The National Collegium of Tourism is the consultative and advisory body of the Ministry. It facilitates co-operation between state departments and agencies, professional associations, the academic sector, unions and other stakeholders. The Ministry has also established a co-ordination platform to aid inter-ministerial and interdisciplinary co-ordination and co-operation in tourism which includes negotiation, information and feedback from regions regarding marketing activities and product development.

Each region has a co-ordinator whose role is to synchronise marketing activities across all public tourism bodies in that region and provide two-way communication between regional public tourism bodies and CzechTourism at the national level. Twice a year, there is a meeting of these co-ordinators with CzechTourism and the delegates of the Ministry. Once a year, the territorial destination management organisations are invited to share knowledge, needs and information.

The overall 2021 budget for tourism is approximately CZK 1.2 billion, with the main source of funding being the state budget. There is a specific local tourism tax at the municipality level, but the purpose for which income is spent in that municipality is decided locally. EU Funds will remain an important mechanism for supporting tourism in the years 2021-27, including investment in tourism infrastructure.

Czech Republic: Organisational chart of tourism bodies

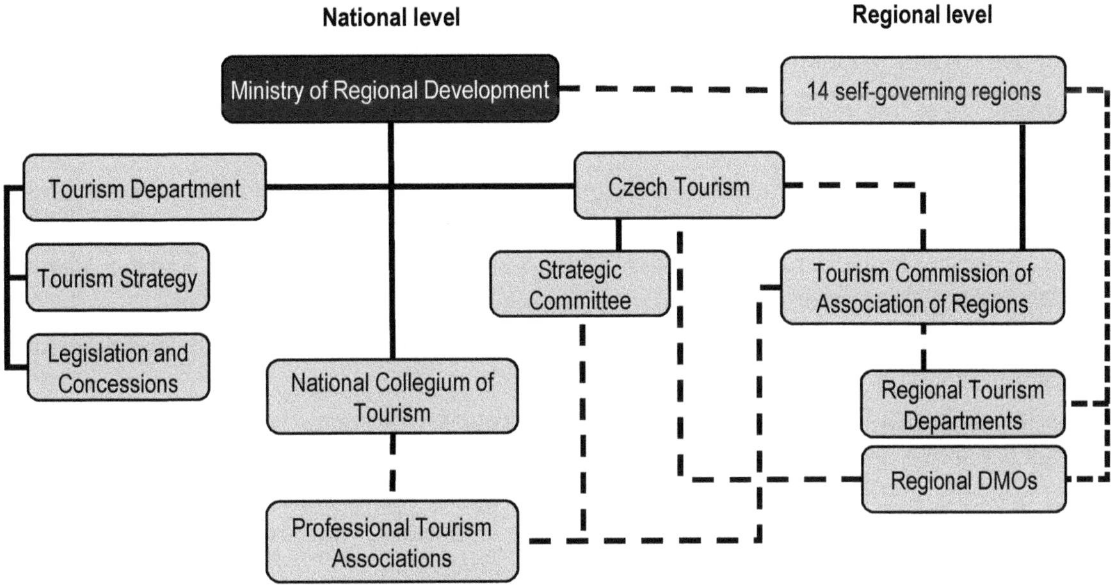

Source: OECD, adapted from the Ministry of Regional Development, 2022.

Tourism policies and programmes

The Tourism Development Strategy of the Czech Republic 2021-30, agreed in 2021, is the framework that underpins tourism policy. An Action Plan for the period 2022-23 focuses on the restart of tourism and enabling the provision of tourism services. Priorities include improving tourism management and financing systems, developing innovative offers and experiences, stimulating demand, building understanding through research and monitoring, and focusing on people as a key determinant of a quality tourism experience.

A consequence of the domestic tourism trend has been a preference for active holidays in rural areas, putting pressure on protected natural areas due to increased visitor numbers. Consumers also have higher expectations in regard to hygiene and safety protocols, along with a preference for online communications.

The Strategy aims to move the Czech Republic to t30th place in the WEF Travel and Tourism Competitiveness index by 2029 (up from 38th in 2019). This target will be set in the context of structural reforms, changing the perceptions of tourism both within government and the wider public and focusing on a number of priorities including:

- Ensuring safe and sustainable tourism.
- Using tourism as a tool for regional development, including support for the construction, modernisation and renewal of public and business infrastructure.
- Spreading tourists among destinations effectively.
- Developing the targeting and integration of marketing communication.
- Improving the availability and sharing of tourism data and supporting the wholesale digitalisation of the tourism sector, including further development of the TSA and its regionalisation.

- Ensuring the availability and quality of employees in tourism.
- Supporting the improvement of the quality of tourism services.

Due to the fragmented nature of tourism in the Czech Republic, activities related to tourism development also fall within the competencies of other central government bodies. The Tourism Strategy supports greater co-ordination of tourism development and integration of tourism issues into other national strategies and policy areas. This includes a range of bilateral meetings and thematic working groups. Typical priorities include co-operation with:

- The Ministry of the Interior and the Ministry of Foreign Affairs about visa issues in third countries, especially concerning the enabling conditions for travel and transport during the pandemic.
- The Ministry of Foreign Affairs on economic diplomacy and the development of inbound tourism through interdisciplinary co-operation.
- The Ministry of Industry and Trade on matters relating to entrepreneurship and the establishment of financial support schemes for tourism entrepreneurs and small businesses.
- The Ministry of Health to promote medical tourism and the design of enabling conditions for tourism services during the pandemic.
- The Ministry of Culture in regard to cultural tourism development, the protection of heritage sites and sustainable tourism.
- The Ministry of Environment in regard to active and cultural tourism, nature conservation and sustainable tourism development, as well as monitoring the impacts of tourism and the attractiveness of regions for residents, investors and visitors.

Support scheme for health spas in the Czech Republic

To compensate for the lack of tourism demand during the COVID-19 pandemic, particularly the decrease in international inbound tourism, the Czech Republic developed a spa voucher scheme in June 2020 that lasted until December 2021. The scheme provided a discount for a week's stay at a Czech spa with treatments provided to citizens of the Czech Republic, EU or EEC. The European Commission supported the scheme, which was underpinned by approximately EUR 39 million.

The initial results of the scheme were encouraging. In Q3 2020, 246 800 guests stayed in spa collective accommodation establishments (a year-over-year increase of 2.6%). Of these, 199 500 were residents (up 43.8%) and 47 300 were non-residents (down 57.2%). Guests made a total of 1.7 million overnight stays (down 18.2%). 1.5 million overnight stays were made by residents (up 6%), and 227 000 overnight stays were made by non-residents (down 67.5%).

The support provided for spas successfully sheltered them from the worst impacts of the pandemic – more spa visitors were recorded in Q3 2021 than compared to the same quarters of 2019-20.

Statistical Profile

Czech Republic: Domestic, inbound and outbound tourism

	2017	2018	2019	2020	2021
TOURISM FLOWS, THOUSAND					
Domestic tourism					
Total domestic trips	..	..	..	..	..
Overnight visitors (tourists)	9 840	10 636	11 108	8 052	8 814
Same-day visitors (excursionists)	..	..	..	..	..
Nights in all types of accommodation	26 962	28 754	29 844	23 994	25 377
Hotels and similar establishments	15 897	16 974	17 552	13 931	15 935
Other collective establishments	11 066	11 780	12 293	10 064	9 442
Private accommodation	..	..	..	..	..
Inbound tourism					
Total international arrivals	34 701	36 268	37 202	10 267 p	10 014 p
Overnight visitors (tourists)	13 665	14 283	14 651	3 919 p	3 768 p
Same-day visitors (excursionists)	21 036	21 986	22 551	6 347 p	6 246 p
Top markets					
..	..	..	..	..	..
..	..	..	..	..	..
..	..	..	..	..	..
..	..	..	..	..	..
..	..	..	..	..	..
Nights in all types of accommodation	44 893	46 077	46 617	13 785 p	12 894 p
Hotels and similar establishments	24 136	24 427	24 916	6 699 p	6 067 p
Other collective establishments	2 692	2 931	2 860	1 035 p	750 p
Private accommodation	18 064	18 720	18 842	6 051 p	6 077 p
Outbound tourism					
Total international departures	11 431	12 839	12 974	5 398 p	..
Overnight visitors (tourists)	8 893	9 686	9 655	4 489 p	..
Same-day visitors (excursionists)	2 538	3 153	3 319	909 p	..
Top destinations					
Slovak Republic	1 271	1 504	1 357	670 p	..
Austria	657	676	692	465 p	..
Croatia	850	813	740	412 p	..
Italy	636	607	605	..	..
Greece	371	472	407	..	..
TOURISM RECEIPTS AND EXPENDITURE, MILLION CZK					
Inbound tourism					
Total international receipts	178 956	179 957	182 740	90 198	..
International travel receipts	162 071	161 717	167 476	84 204	..
International passenger transport receipts	16 886	18 240	15 263	5 995	..
Outbound tourism					
Total international expenditure	128 782	131 879	138 372	80 958	..
International travel expenditure	127 210	129 653	135 042	79 436	..
International passenger transport expenditure	1 572	2 226	3 329	1 521	..

.. Not available; p Provisional data
Source: OECD Tourism Statistics (Database).

StatLink https://stat.link/l98h4m

Czech Republic: Enterprises and employment in tourism

	Number of establishments	Number of persons employed				
	2020	2017	2018	2019	2020	2021
Total	..	**235 178**	**238 337**	**239 506**	**222 013 p**	..
Tourism industries	..	**231 699**	**234 812**	**235 969**	**218 529 p**	..
Accommodation services for visitors	11 330	..	..	..	..	..
Hotels and similar establishments	..	41 814	42 560	43 135	36 757 p	..
Food and beverage serving industry	48 131	67 733	68 881	68 692	60 365 p	..
Passenger transport	..	..	..	..	..	..
Air passenger transport	..	2 274	2 216	2 342	1 782 p	..
Railways passenger transport	..	12 486	12 787	12 701	12 596 p	..
Road passenger transport	..	12 130	12 381	12 481	12 576 p	..
Water passenger transport	..	50	52	52	48 p	..
Passenger transport supporting services	..	4 067	4 291	4 318	4 287 p	..
Transport equipment rental	..	136	140	143	145 p	..
Travel agencies and other reservation services industry	..	14 159	13 861	14 041	12 622 p	..
Cultural industry	..	12 471	12 492	12 511	11 970 p	..
Sports and recreation industry	..	2 840	2 836	2 831	2 717 p	..
Retail trade of country-specific tourism characteristic goods	..	..	..	..	..	..
Other country-specific tourism industries	..	61 539	62 316	62 723	62 664 p	..
Other industries	..	**3 479**	**3 525**	**3 537**	**3 483 p**	..

.. Not available; p Provisional data
Source: OECD Tourism Statistics (Database).

StatLink https://stat.link/e7rd6s

Czech Republic: Internal tourism consumption

Million CZK

	2020		
	Domestic tourism expenditure	Inbound tourism expenditure	Internal tourism consumption
Total	..	..	..
Consumption products	**79 117 p**	**48 957 p**	**135 812 p**
Tourism characteristic products	51 469 p	32 250 p	91 458 p
Accommodation services for visitors	13 786 p	9 803 p	31 328 p
Food and beverage serving services	17 068 p	9 814 p	26 882 p
Passenger transport services	8 901 p	8 952 p	17 854 p
Air passenger transport services	5 236 p	8 244 p	13 480 p
Railways passenger transport services	598 p	168 p	766 p
Road passenger transport services	2 992 p	541 p	3 533 p
Water passenger transport services	75 p	.. p	75 p
Passenger transport supporting services	2 169 p	1 697 p	3 866 p
Transport equipment rental services	150 p	68 p	217 p
Travel agencies and other reservation services industry	2 352 p	306 p	2 658 p
Cultural services	4 401 p	1 295 p	5 696 p
Sports and recreation services	1 981 p	316 p	2 296 p
Country-specific tourism characteristic goods	..	..	..
Country-specific tourism characteristic services	660 p	.. p	660 p
Other consumption products	27 648 p	16 707 p	44 355 p
Tourism connected products	27 648 p	16 707 p	44 355 p
Non-tourism related consumption products	..	..	..
Non-consumption products	..	..	..

.. Not available; p Provisional data
Source: OECD Tourism Statistics (Database).

StatLink https://stat.link/kn70l5

Denmark

Tourism in the economy and outlook for recovery

Tourism is a significant contributor to the Danish economy. The direct contribution of tourism was 2.5% of GVA and 4.1% of employment in 2019. Tourism GVA fell by 37.2% to DKK 31.5 billion in 2020, representing 1.6% of total GVA.

In 2019, tourists spent DKK 139.2 billion in Denmark. Inbound tourists spent DKK 61.5 billion, representing 44% of total tourism expenditure, and 4.4% of all Danish exports. Total tourism spending fell to DKK 103.7 billion in 2020, driven by a 59.8% decline in international tourists, falling to 5.9 million international overnight visitors.

Preliminary estimates suggest that tourism began to recover in 2021, with tourism expenditure increasing to DKK 115.8 billion. Domestic tourism, which continued to grow through the pandemic, contributed DKK 86.9 billion or 75% of total tourist spending in 2021. Compared to pre-pandemic levels, domestic nights increased by 4.7% in 2020, and 20.5% in 2021 to reach 34.3 million nights in tourism-related accommodation.

Denmark is projecting a return of inbound tourism to pre-pandemic levels already by 2022, primarily driven by the German and Dutch tourist markets. Other important tourist markets are still below 2019 levels.

Tourism governance and funding

The Danish Tourism Law, which came into effect in 2015, regulates the structure, governance and responsibilities of public agencies at the national and local levels. The Ministry of Industry, Business and Financial Affairs is responsible for tourism, but also co-operates with several other ministries on issues relating to tourism, including those with responsibilities for foreign affairs, culture, environment and transport. VisitDenmark manages international branding and marketing and is also responsible for market research and monitoring trends and activity.

The national tourism administration consists of the Danish National Tourism Forum, the Danish Tourism Advisory Board and four national tourism development organisations: VisitDenmark; Danish Coastal and Nature Tourism; Wonderful Copenhagen (including the tourism development organisation Danish City Tourism); and Danish Business and Conferencing Tourism.

Between 2018 and 2020, as part of an agreement with Local Government Denmark, the number of regional destination management organisations (DMOs) was reduced from 80 to 19 to ensure more consistency between organisations. The role of the 19 decentralised DMOs is to organise, co-ordinate and operate strategic local business-supporting activities, developing geographic areas in Denmark into strong and coherent tourist destinations. The tasks range from developing international marketing activities in collaboration with VisitDenmark to facilitating strategic tourism development projects, which bolster the existing local product and tourist experiences.

The Danish National Tourism Forum was established to strengthen and co-ordinate collaboration within the tourism sector in Denmark. The Forum is chaired by the State Secretary of the Ministry of Industry, Business and Financial Affairs and has representatives from VisitDenmark, Danish Coastal and Nature Tourism and Wonderful Copenhagen, Local Government Denmark, the tourism industry and academia. The Forum is also responsible for drafting national tourism strategies and reporting on the national state of Danish tourism.

The Danish Tourism Advisory Board advises the Danish National Tourism Forum on opportunities and challenges to Danish tourism. It is chaired by the Deputy Permanent Secretary of the Ministry of Industry, Business and Financial Affairs and has additional members from other ministries, industry representatives and civil society.

Denmark: Organisational chart of tourism bodies

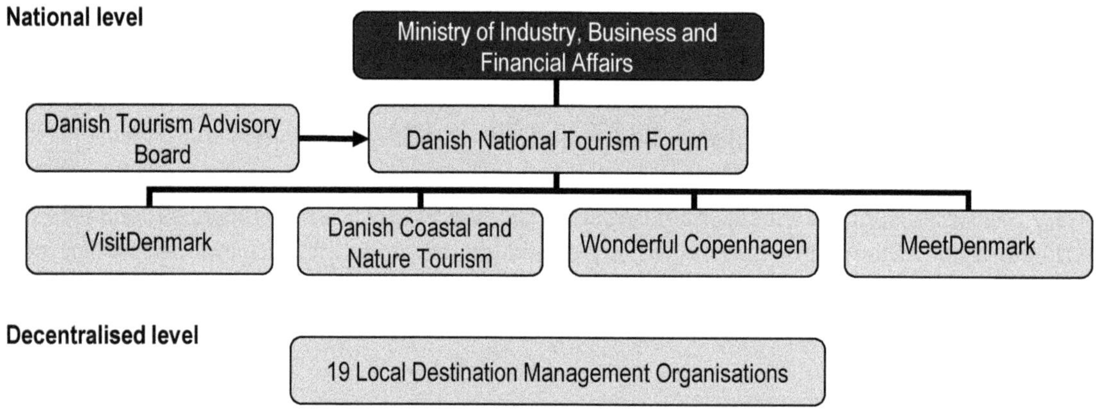

Source: OECD, adapted from the Ministry of Industry, Business and Financial Affairs, 2022.

Tourism policies and programmes

To promote recovery after the COVID-19 pandemic and prepare for future shocks, Denmark has provided compensation to tourism businesses, totalling more than DKK 19.8 billion. Additional measures were introduced to prevent the bankruptcy of tourism businesses. These included a special focus on hotels, restaurants and conference centres to initiate sustainable initiatives or necessary renovations. Denmark also promoted summer packages in 2020-21 to help hard-hit sectors while creating great holiday experiences for tourists.

In 2022, Denmark launched its new National Strategy for Sustainable Growth in Danish Tourism. It is the guiding strategic framework for the development of Danish tourism towards 2030. The Strategy sets out a common direction for the work of the national tourism organisations and relevant stakeholders by highlighting opportunities and challenges for sustainable tourism, digitalisation trends, international competition and a resilient recovery from the COVID-19 pandemic. The Strategy also incorporates many green and sustainable initiatives, including a partnership to reduce greenhouse gas emissions (Box 3.12).

Starting from a common vision, the strategy sets out three goals that balance environmental, economic and social sustainability towards 2030:

- Pursuing green and sustainable solutions with low environmental and climate footprints.
- Attracting more tourists and larger tourism consumption in Denmark.
- Ensuring that tourists, citizens and employees are satisfied.

These goals are measured with nine indicators. Based on the goals and indicators, the strategy puts forward a set of initiatives to strengthen Danish tourism within five development tracks towards 2030:

- Returning international tourism to Denmark as soon as possible.
- Ensuring the recovery of urban tourism is sustainable.
- Establishing Denmark as an attractive destination for business and conferencing tourism.
- Taking advantage of new potentials and opportunities.
- Following and adapting to the changing preferences of tourists.

With regards to urban tourism, Comeback Copenhagen 2023, a recovery plan for the capital's tourism and cultural life, was launched as part of a collaboration between Wonderful Copenhagen, Copenhagen Municipality and the Ministry of Industry, Business and Financial Affairs. The plan contains several initiatives to prepare the tourism industry in Copenhagen for international competition and to strengthen sustainability initiatives.

Statistical Profile

Denmark: Domestic, inbound and outbound tourism

	2017	2018	2019	2020	2021
TOURISM FLOWS, THOUSAND					
Domestic tourism					
Total domestic trips	64 888 e	63 160	67 901	64 215	65 643 p
Overnight visitors (tourists)	16 333 |	16 619	17 794	19 341	23 414
Same-day visitors (excursionists)	48 555 e	46 541	50 107	44 874	42 229
Nights in all types of accommodation	66 222 |	67 017	68 025 |	89 266 e	108 032 p
Hotels and similar establishments	19 654	20 334	21 816 |	23 288	28 990
Other collective establishments	9 674 |	9 789	9 314 |	9 484	10 455
Private accommodation	36 894	36 894	36 894 |	56 494 e	68 587
Inbound tourism					
Total international arrivals	29 766 e	30 089 e	30 089 e	15 594 e	15 883 p
Overnight visitors (tourists)	12 426 e	12 749 e	14 763 e	5 935 e	7 047
Same-day visitors (excursionists)	17 340 e	17 340 e	17 340 e	9 660 e	8 835
Top markets					
Germany	3 312 e	3 452 e	4 009 e	2 463 e	2 669 e
United States	746 e	780 e	1 063 e	247 e	563 e
Sweden	1 560 e	1 572 e	1 490 e	403 e	557 e
Norway	1 892 e	1 886 e	1 532 e	488 e	412 e
United Kingdom	937 e	942 e	944 e	275 e	240 e
Nights in all types of accommodation	54 914 |	55 931	57 847 |	31 464 e	34 813 p
Hotels and similar establishments	28 744 |	29 306	31 599 |	16 893	17 832
Other collective establishments	4 129	4 584	3 224 |	2 531	2 835
Private accommodation	22 041 e	22 041 e	23 024 |	12 039 e	14 146
Outbound tourism					
Total international departures	..	..	..	..	..
Overnight visitors (tourists)	8 087	7 475 |	9 088	4 230	3 182
Same-day visitors (excursionists)	..	..	..	..	..
Top destinations					
..	..	..	..	..	..
..	..	..	..	..	..
..	..	..	..	..	..
..	..	..	..	..	..
..	..	..	..	..	..
TOURISM RECEIPTS AND EXPENDITURE, MILLION DKK					
Inbound tourism					
Total international receipts	74 889	73 702	74 074	31 651	34 798
International travel receipts	56 114	57 533	57 704	25 939	28 357
International passenger transport receipts	18 775	16 169	16 370	5 711	6 441
Outbound tourism					
Total international expenditure	76 294	79 016	80 279	41 158	..
International travel expenditure	64 659	66 574	66 948	36 830	..
International passenger transport expenditure	11 635	12 442	13 331	4 328	..

.. Not available; e Estimated value; p Provisional data; | Break in series
Source: OECD Tourism Statistics (Database).

StatLink https://stat.link/oxph9v

Denmark: Enterprises and employment in tourism

	Number of establishments[1]	Number of persons employed				
	2020	2017	2018	2019	2020	2021
Total	..	..	..	..	..	..
Tourism industries	**23 764**	**259 419**	**267 140**	**273 199 f**	..	..
Accommodation services for visitors	1 915	20 791	21 370	21 940	..	..
Hotels and similar establishments	919	..	..	..	..	..
Food and beverage serving industry	14 277	115 668	119 601	123 092	..	..
Passenger transport	3 719	55 266	55 723	56 169	..	..
Air passenger transport	90	4 545	4 320	3 757	..	..
Railways passenger transport	119	6 096	6 074	6 058	..	..
Road passenger transport	3 397	24 997	25 439	25 855	..	..
Water passenger transport	113	19 717	19 893	20 499	..	..
Passenger transport supporting services	10	..	..	..	..	..
Transport equipment rental	264	..	..	..	..	..
Travel agencies and other reservation services industry	555	6 661	6 746	6 824	..	..
Cultural industry	1 032	28 363	29 419	29 850	..	..
Sports and recreation industry	1 992	32 670	34 281	35 324	..	..
Retail trade of country-specific tourism characteristic goods	..	..	..	..	..	..
Other country-specific tourism industries	..	..	..	..	..	..
Other industries	..	..	..	..	..	..

.. Not available; f Forecast value

1. Data refer to number of enterprises.

Source: OECD Tourism Statistics (Database).

StatLink https://stat.link/4fct1b

Denmark: Internal tourism consumption

Million DKK

	2020		
	Domestic tourism expenditure	Inbound tourism expenditure	Internal tourism consumption
Total	..	..	..
Consumption products	**76 734**	**27 001**	**103 735**
Tourism characteristic products	40 098	9 967	50 064
Accommodation services for visitors	7 534	3 714	11 248
Food and beverage serving services	11 081	3 640	14 721
Passenger transport services	13 497	1 706	15 202
Air passenger transport services	..	..	..
Railways passenger transport services	..	..	..
Road passenger transport services	..	..	..
Water passenger transport services	..	..	..
Passenger transport supporting services	..	..	..
Transport equipment rental services	..	..	..
Travel agencies and other reservation services industry	2 798	223	3 021
Cultural services	5 093	625	5 718
Sports and recreation services	..	..	..
Country-specific tourism characteristic goods	..	..	..
Country-specific tourism characteristic services	96	59	155
Other consumption products	36 637	17 034	53 671
Tourism connected products	26 403	9 900	36 303
Non-tourism related consumption products	10 234	7 134	17 368
Non-consumption products	..	..	..

.. Not available

Source: OECD Tourism Statistics (Database).

StatLink https://stat.link/9pqxu3

Estonia

Tourism in the economy and outlook for recovery

Tourism is an important contributor to the Estonian economy, directly providing 5.4% of GDP and 4.4% of employment before the COVID-19 crisis. In 2019, tourism services accounted for one-third of all services exports totalling EUR 2.1 billion, of which international tourist expenditure accounted for EUR 1.6 billion. The impacts of the COVID-19 crisis meant tourism's direct share of employment fell to 3.3% in 2021.

International tourists declined 69.3% to 1.0 million in 2020, down from 3.3 million in 2019. Arrivals declined further in 2021, to 801 200. The majority of international tourists came from neighbouring countries, with 69% of travel services exports coming from Finland, Latvia, Russia or Sweden in 2020.

The COVID-19 pandemic led to a shift towards domestic tourism. In 2019, domestic visitors accounted for one-third of nights in commercial accommodation. By 2021, the share of domestic nights in accommodation increased to 68%. Domestic tourism helped Estonian businesses maintain jobs and services, but has not been enough to cover the losses incurred by the reduction in inbound tourism, which made up 86% of total expenditure in 2017.

The tourism recovery in Estonia is expected to be relatively slow, with inbound tourism projected to reach 2019 levels by 2025.

Tourism governance and funding

The Ministry of Economic Affairs and Communications co-ordinates national tourism policy in close co-operation with the Estonian Tourist Board at the joint organisation of KredEx and Enterprise Estonia, a state foundation. Other bodies regularly involved in tourism policy development and implementation include the Estonian Travel and Tourism Association, Estonian Hotel and Restaurant Association, Estonian Rural Tourism, Estonian Spa Association and the Estonian Convention Bureau.

The Estonian Tourist Board is responsible for tourism policy implementation and has a key role in strengthening the destination management organisation (DMO) network and co-ordinating tourism product development and customer journey experience activities. In 2021 the Estonian Tourist Board began a phased reform of the country's DMO structure, consolidating the 40 currently in operation to a maximum of eight to allow for more specialisation, greater strategic vision and co-operation for destinations.

Regional county development centres located in all 15 Estonian counties offer free advisory services to enterprises, local government, non-profit associations and foundations. The Estonian Tourist Board has specialist partners that offer data management services in every county. These are either county development centres, local government-related, unions of local governments or foundations. In larger cities, local government has devoted structures to tourism development.

Government and EU funding for the tourism sector was approximately EUR 11-13 million a year from 2020-21. Funding has increased to EUR 46 million in 2020-23 but will stabilise to EUR 16-18 million in 2024-25. Additional COVID-19 support has been paid to tourism enterprises as part of general support to all sectors to protect jobs. Financing from the state budget for Estonian Tourism Board tourism development activities in 2021 was just under EUR 2 million but increased to EUR 11.5 million in 2022. The allocation of EU structural funds to the national tourism board was EUR 7 million in 2021 and EUR 14 million in 2022.

Estonia: Organisational chart of tourism bodies

Source: OECD, adapted from the Ministry of Economic Affairs and Communications, 2022.

Tourism policies and programmes

Estonia approved a new Tourism Strategy for 2022-25 in March 2022, with the vision that in 2025 the Estonian tourism sector will be resilient and adaptable. To implement this vision, Estonia has set strategic goals in three priority areas:

- Product and destination development: become a sustainable tourism destination that offers visitors a diverse and unique travel experience in all seasons (Box 3.11).
- Restoration of demand: exceed pre-crisis levels in the number of tourists and the export of tourism services.
- Ensuring connectivity: be well-connected to the main markets and have easily accessible tourism products and services, both physically and virtually.

Estonia aims to achieve these goals by increasing the length of stay and spending, aiming for tourism to become more sustainable and create greater added value. Every year a supporting action plan will be developed in line with the 2022-25 Tourism Strategy. Safety, innovation, and customer orientation are cross-cutting priorities in the strategy, as is sustainability. Estonia's approach to sustainability is defined by three principles:

- We are proud of Estonia: we value the local culture, the environment and the community.
- We co-operate closely to develop, market and promote the sector, and we prefer solutions based on Estonia's tourism as a whole and its long-term development objectives.
- We contribute to the fulfilment of the UN Sustainable Development Goals (SDGs).

To best implement the goals set out in the strategy, a national tourism advisory council has been established to facilitate collaboration between the Ministry of Economics and Communication, the Estonian Tourist Board and related actors. In particular, the council aims to encourage partnerships with business associations, carriers, ports of arrival, destinations, other ministries (e.g. ministries covering culture, rural affairs, foreign affairs and labour) and state agencies (e.g. the Consumer Protection and Technical Regulatory Authority).

Several initiatives have been launched to tackle tourism labour and skills challenges. In 2021-22, the Estonian Unemployment Insurance Fund together with the Estonian Hotel and Restaurants Association organised a free seminar series with the aim to swiftly train people for the restaurant and accommodation sector. Over 1 200 people attended the series which included four webinars. In December 2022, the Ministry of Economics and Communication issued a study and policy recommendations for tourism sector stakeholders to address labour and skills challenges. The study included comparative case studies, inquiries among tourism students and entrepreneurs, and interviews with all sector and related governmental stakeholders.

The tourism sector and policymakers have learned to be more flexible and reactive to the urgent policy changes needed to tackle the spread of COVID-19 and the consequences of Russia's aggression against Ukraine. Co-operation between the public and private sectors has advanced as a result, with more frequent and open communication.

The main priority for inbound tourism is restoring demand in neighbouring and nearby markets as soon as possible. This will be followed by more distant European countries with a historical interest in Estonia (e.g. Germany and the United Kingdom) and new potential markets that are discovering Estonia (e.g. Switzerland, Austria, the Netherlands, Belgium and Italy). More distant markets will be focused on in co-operation with neighbouring countries (e.g. the Baltic States and Finland). At an international level, Estonia works with other Baltic and Nordic countries in common marketing activities and undertakes many initiatives as part of the EU Baltic Sea Region Strategy.

Statistical Profile

Estonia: Domestic, inbound and outbound tourism

	2017	2018	2019	2020	2021
TOURISM FLOWS, THOUSAND					
Domestic tourism[1]					
Total domestic trips	..	12 616	..	..	7 466
Overnight visitors (tourists)	3 277	4 399	3 486	2 136	2 267
Same-day visitors (excursionists)	..	8 217	..	..	5 200
Nights in all types of accommodation	2 359	2 456	2 591	2 270	2 716
Hotels and similar establishments	2 359	2 455	2 590	2 268	2 715
Other collective establishments	..	1	2	2	1
Private accommodation	..	..	..	..	..
Inbound tourism[2]					
Total international arrivals	6 145	6 033	6 103	1 695	1 302
Overnight visitors (tourists)	3 244	3 226	3 336	1 023	801
Same-day visitors (excursionists)	2 901	2 807	2 766	673	500
Top markets					
Finland	1 223	1 145	1 130	419	215
Latvia	292	298	320	178	138
Germany	219	245	269	56	67
Russia	460	464	463	112	44
Sweden	121	119	129	19	30
Nights in all types of accommodation	4 150	4 175	4 376	1 404	1 283
Hotels and similar establishments	4 150	4 164	4 362	1 399	1 280
Other collective establishments	..	11	13	5	3
Private accommodation	..	..	..	..	..
Outbound tourism					
Total international departures	3 605	3 607	3 641	1 335	1 226
Overnight visitors (tourists)	3 137	3 088	3 116	1 151	1 050
Same-day visitors (excursionists)	469	520	525	184	176
Top destinations					
Finland	561	520	513	273	214
Latvia	351	301	288	200	81
Sweden	240	219	215	74	75
Germany	230	213	213	87	74
Russia	220	255	268	56	54
TOURISM RECEIPTS AND EXPENDITURE, MILLION EUR					
Inbound tourism					
Total international receipts	1 872	1 974	2 065	761	..
International travel receipts	1 463	1 510	1 558	517	..
International passenger transport receipts	409	464	508	244	..
Outbound tourism					
Total international expenditure	1 232	1 397	1 616	596	..
International travel expenditure	1 101	1 241	1 381	523	..
International passenger transport expenditure	131	156	235	73	..

.. Not available

1. Trips from demand side surveys; Nights from supply side surveys.
2. Arrivals from demand side surveys; Nights from supply side surveys.

Source: OECD Tourism Statistics (Database).

StatLink https://stat.link/pm730c

Estonia: Enterprises and employment in tourism

	Number of establishments[2]	Number of persons employed				
	2020	2017	2018	2019	2020	2021
Total	..	..	..	..	..	..
Tourism industries	..	..	..	..	..	..
Accommodation services for visitors[1]	1 327	7 300	7 100	7 000	5 600	..
Hotels and similar establishments	..	..	..	..	..	..
Food and beverage serving industry	..	19 100	17 900	19 600	16 804	..
Passenger transport	..	..	..	..	..	..
Air passenger transport	..	..	..	..	..	..
Railways passenger transport	..	..	..	..	..	..
Road passenger transport	..	..	..	..	..	..
Water passenger transport	..	..	..	..	..	..
Passenger transport supporting services	..	..	..	..	..	..
Transport equipment rental	..	..	..	..	..	..
Travel agencies and other reservation services industry	..	1 800	1 800	1 900	1 600	..
Cultural industry	..	..	..	..	..	..
Sports and recreation industry	..	..	..	..	..	..
Retail trade of country-specific tourism characteristic goods	..	..	..	..	..	..
Other country-specific tourism industries	..	..	..	..	..	..
Other industries	..	..	..	..	..	..

.. Not available

1. Data for accommodation service for visitors refer to number of establishments.
2. Data refer to number of enterprises.

Source: OECD Tourism Statistics (Database).

StatLink https://stat.link/rjyx05

Estonia: Internal tourism consumption

Million EUR

	2017		
	Domestic tourism expenditure	Inbound tourism expenditure	Internal tourism consumption
Total	..	..	..
Consumption products	**269**	**1 721**	**2 359**
Tourism characteristic products	236	1 130	1 706
Accommodation services for visitors	72	298	511
Food and beverage serving services	49	370	419
Passenger transport services	54	306	534
Air passenger transport services	29	97	178
Railways passenger transport services	2	1	7
Road passenger transport services	9	28	66
Water passenger transport services	13	166	239
Passenger transport supporting services	..	9	9
Transport equipment rental services	0	4	34
Travel agencies and other reservation services industry	51	71	140
Cultural services	4	65	69
Sports and recreation services	2	11	13
Country-specific tourism characteristic goods	..	..	..
Country-specific tourism characteristic services	5	10	21
Other consumption products	33	591	654
Tourism connected products	18	47	85
Non-tourism related consumption products	15	544	569
Non-consumption products	..	..	..

.. Not available

Source: OECD Tourism Statistics (Database).

StatLink https://stat.link/kfpwti

Finland

Tourism in the economy and outlook for recovery

Before the pandemic, tourism was an important sector of the Finnish economy. In 2017-19, international tourism demand increased faster than other sectors at an annual rate of approximately 8%. In 2019, the sector directly provided 133 200 jobs (5.8% of total employment), and supported 28 500 businesses.

In 2019 tourism directly contributed 2.7% of GDP, which decreased to 1.7% in 2020. The number of people employed in tourism decreased by 29 000 people in 2020, with tourism's direct share of employment falling to 4.9%. At the same time, the number of hours worked decreased by 22%.

In 2020, international tourists arrivals fell 72.8% to 895 577 tourists. This contributed to a 41% decline in total tourism expenditure to EUR 9.7 billion. According to 2021 estimates, total tourism expenditure recovered to EUR 11.2 billion due to the growth of domestic tourism. The share of domestic spending increased from 63% in 2019 to almost 84% in 2021. This occurred as domestic tourists returned to pre-pandemic levels, and international tourism declined further in 2021.

Russia's war in Ukraine, along with the uncertainty related to COVID-19, has created new concerns over the recovery and growth of the Finnish tourism sector. According to the latest forecast, the 2019 level of international arrivals is predicted to be reached in 2024.

Tourism governance and funding

The Ministry of Economic Affairs and Employment is responsible for tourism policy development and support. It participates in drafting legislation on tourism and maintains international relations regarding tourism. In developing the sector, the Ministry collaborates closely with other ministries.

To focus on recovery and resilience, the Ministry of Economic Affairs and Employment established a High-Level Working Group on Tourism in 2021. It is composed of ministries that are of key importance to the tourism sector, including regional councils, state administrations, regional tourism organisations, travel companies, and research and educational institutions and organisations.

Business Finland gathers together all the services related to the promotion of innovation funding, exports, investments and tourism. The Team Finland network brings together all state-funded internationalisation services, from advice to funding. Business Finland is part of this network. Visit Finland is a unit of Business Finland and receives its funding from the state budget. Visit Finland is the national expert organisation responsible for promoting Finland as a destination, supporting Finnish travel companies to internationalise and develop and sell and market high-quality travel products. Visit Finland and the tourism industry conduct joint product campaigns and arrange familiarisation trips for foreign tour operators and the media.

Regional Councils provide support for tourism development projects, general marketing, advisory services, training and research in Finland's 19 regions. Finland has a total of 15 Centres for Economic Development, Transport and the Environment (ELY Centres), which are tasked with promoting regional competitiveness, well-being and sustainable development and curbing climate change. They offer financial, advisory, consulting and training services to tourism businesses and grant investment support. They also manage matters related to the local infrastructure in their areas.

Finland has allocated funding for developing tourism as part of ministries' own budgets. The budget allocated for Visit Finland's tourism development actions was EUR 9.8 million in 2021-22. In addition to this, EUR 4.7 million was allocated from the Government Programme for 2021. During the years 2021-24, Business Finland (and, as a part of it, Visit Finland) will be allocated funding of approximately EUR 12 million from Finland´s national Recovery and Resilience Plan, as the organisation has been given responsibility for implementing the tourism-specific investment included in this Plan.

In 2020-21, the Ministry of Education and Culture awarded a total of EUR 3.95 million in discretionary government grants to cultural tourism development projects through a one-time appropriation from the Government Programme.

A total of EUR 38.1 million was directed to Metsähallitus by the Ministry of the Environment and Ministry of Agriculture and Forestry in 2021. Metsähallitus is a state-owned enterprise that plays a key role in the management of Finland's physical environment and related outdoor and nature-based tourism.

Finland: Organisational chart of tourism bodies

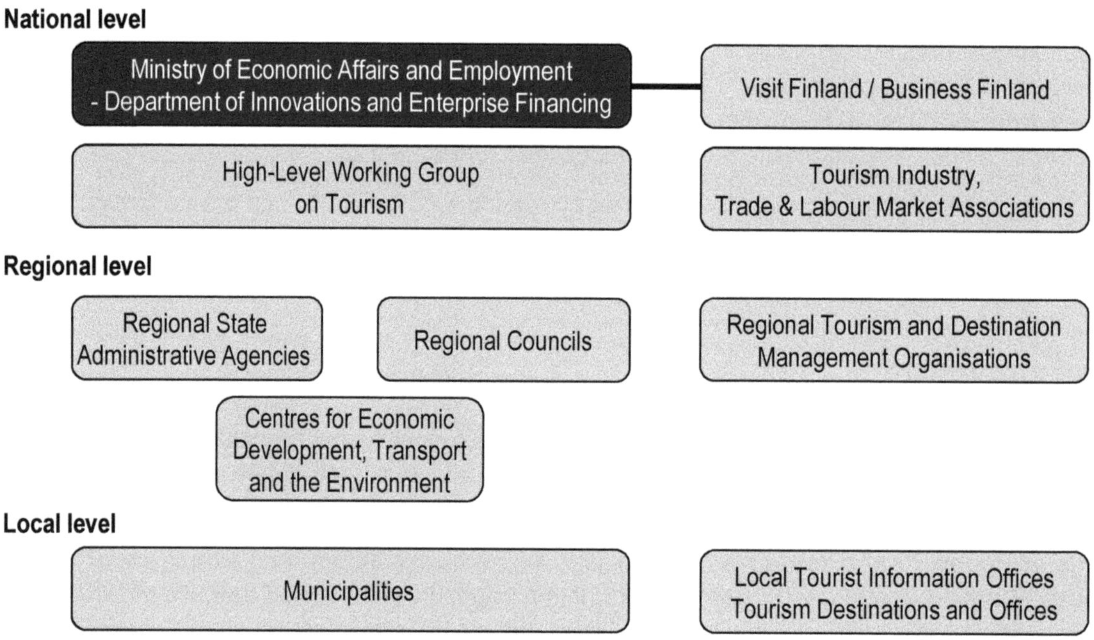

Source: OECD, adapted from the Ministry of Economic Affairs and Employment, 2022.

Tourism policies and programmes

Finland's national tourism policy is implemented under the Achieving More Together - Sustainable Growth and Renewal in Finnish Tourism Strategy for the period 2022-28. This Strategy includes an Action Plan for the years 2022-23. In 2022, Finland updated the Strategy and Action Plan drawn up in 2019, to better reflect the changing operational environment, including the COVID-19 pandemic and Russia's aggression against Ukraine. The focus of the update was on the future outlook and measures to be taken in accordance with the new situation.

The key mission of Finland's national tourism policy is to ensure that tourism is developed as a responsible and growing sector that generates well-being and employment throughout the year. The Strategy's main objective is to make Finland the most sustainable tourism destination in the Nordic countries. The strategy identifies four priorities to facilitate the sustainable growth and renewal of the tourism sector: i) supporting sustainable development; ii) responding to the digital transformation; iii) improving accessibility; and iv) ensuring an operating environment that supports competitiveness.

During the COVID-19 pandemic, a variety of government organisations provided financing through direct support for the companies and industries most affected. In 2020, EUR 263 million was granted to the tourism sector as COVID-19 funding. A significant part of the financing was allocated to hotels and other accommodation services, as well as the activities of tour operators and reservation services. Finland also granted a state guarantee of approximately EUR 600 million to support the national airline, Finnair.

Other priorities aimed at tackling the consequences of the crisis include raising the resilience and competitiveness of the tourism sector, utilising knowledge-based decision making and ensuring that up-to-date data and information on global trends are available. Overarching these aims is the encouragement and support for the tourism sector to shift towards a more sustainable way of operating.

Russia's war in Ukraine brought up new insecurities for the tourism sector and is slowing down its recovery from the pandemic. The absence of Finland's biggest tourism export market, Russia, along with severely weakened accessibility from Asian markets due to the flight ban over Russia, is creating annual losses of more than EUR 1 billion for Finland. In Q3 2022, as part of its goal to increase the vitality of eastern Finland due to the economic effects of Russia's aggression against Ukraine, the Finnish government proposed that tourism be promoted by EUR 7.5 million by strengthening tourism marketing and improving the conditions and services for nature tourism, for example.

Finland is supporting the recovery and ensuring the prerequisites for the sector's long-term development by paying attention to all dimensions of sustainability – economic, ecological, social and cultural – along with supporting digitalisation initiatives and management by data (Box 2.11).

Visit Finland has been developing national sustainable tourism indicators as part of the national Sustainable Travel Finland Programme, targeted at tourism companies and destinations to support their efforts in sustainable development (Box 3.13). The development of indicators is done in close co-operation with the Finnish tourism sector.

Statistical Profile

Finland: Domestic, inbound and outbound tourism

	2017	2018	2019	2020	2021
TOURISM FLOWS, THOUSAND					
Domestic tourism					
Total domestic trips	..	45 280	..	..	61 300
Overnight visitors (tourists)	30 160	29 130	29 320	23 340	29 380
Same-day visitors (excursionists)	..	16 160	..	..	31 920
Nights in all types of accommodation	80 460	78 360	81 760	90 240	102 260
Hotels and similar establishments	13 510	13 360	12 920	8 370	9 930
Other collective establishments	9 900	10 940	10 720	13 230	14 210
Private accommodation	57 050	54 060	58 120	68 640	78 120
Inbound tourism					
Total international arrivals	..	..	..	..	..
Overnight visitors (tourists)	3 180	3 224	3 290	896	807
Same-day visitors (excursionists)	..	..	..	..	..
Top markets					
Russia	297	304	313	96	106
Germany	229	230	220	52	89
Sweden	341	323	320	56	85
Estonia	94	95	96	56	53
United Kingdom	126	139	143	41	43
Nights in all types of accommodation	6 743	6 843	7 056	2 291	2 085
Hotels and similar establishments	6 421	6 505	6 695	2 155	1 968
Other collective establishments	322	337	361	136	117
Private accommodation	..	..	..	..	..
Outbound tourism					
Total international departures	10 480	10 480	10 440	2 690	2 260
Overnight visitors (tourists)	9 330	9 450	9 410	2 330	1 800
Same-day visitors (excursionists)	1 160	1 030	1 030	360	460
Top destinations					
Sweden	1 670	1 790	1 780	350	420
Estonia	2 060	1 670	1 600	620	390
Spain	820	880	790	270	230
Germany	310	330	310	150	100
Norway	..	..	..	..	..
TOURISM RECEIPTS AND EXPENDITURE, MILLION EUR					
Inbound tourism					
Total international receipts	4 593	4 883	5 000	1 562	..
International travel receipts	3 002	3 103	3 328	1 107	926
International passenger transport receipts	1 591	1 780	1 672	455	..
Outbound tourism					
Total international expenditure	5 940	6 127	5 074	1 730	..
International travel expenditure	4 945	5 152	5 074	1 468	1 181
International passenger transport expenditure	995	975	..	262	..

.. Not available
Source: OECD Tourism Statistics (Database).

StatLink https://stat.link/tcaz5i

Finland: Enterprises and employment in tourism

	Number of establishments	Number of persons employed				
	2020	2017	2018	2019	2020	2021
Total	..	..	..	..	..	..
Tourism industries	**33 723**	**123 300**	**129 600**	**133 200**	**104 200 p**	..
Accommodation services for visitors	2 448	13 300	14 000	14 300	10 000 p	..
Hotels and similar establishments	1 030	..	..	..	..	..
Food and beverage serving industry	13 225	63 200	65 900	68 300	54 100 p	..
Passenger transport	8 270	31 800	34 300	34 500	26 100 p	..
Air passenger transport	75	3 800	4 100	3 900	2 100 p	..
Railways passenger transport	43	2 300	4 400	4 600	4 300 p	..
Road passenger transport	7 953	20 700	20 700	20 800	16 100 p	..
Water passenger transport	199	5 000	5 100	5 200	3 600 p	..
Passenger transport supporting services	..	..	..	..	..	..
Transport equipment rental	362	1 300	1 500	1 600	1 400 p	..
Travel agencies and other reservation services industry	1 462	1 800	1 900	2 000	1 500 p	..
Cultural industry	3 935	5 200	5 200	5 800	5 200 p	..
Sports and recreation industry	4 021	6 700	6 800	6 700	5 900 p	..
Retail trade of country-specific tourism characteristic goods	..	..	..	..	..	..
Other country-specific tourism industries	..	..	..	..	..	..
Other industries	..	..	..	..	..	..

.. Not available; p Provisional data
Source: OECD Tourism Statistics (Database).

StatLink https://stat.link/aziqeb

Finland: Internal tourism consumption

Million EUR

	2019		
	Domestic tourism expenditure	Inbound tourism expenditure	Internal tourism consumption
Total	**8 851**	**5 288**	**16 261**
Consumption products	**8 593**	**5 228**	**15 942**
Tourism characteristic products	5 490	4 023	11 363
Accommodation services for visitors	860	586	2 243
Food and beverage serving services	1 635	988	2 623
Passenger transport services	1 830	2 067	4 822
Air passenger transport services	685	1 672	2 987
Railways passenger transport services	206	27	297
Road passenger transport services	572	194	995
Water passenger transport services	367	174	543
Passenger transport supporting services	..	..	..
Transport equipment rental services	94	77	182
Travel agencies and other reservation services industry	425	15	558
Cultural services	308	81	389
Sports and recreation services	337	210	547
Country-specific tourism characteristic goods	..	..	..
Country-specific tourism characteristic services	..	..	..
Other consumption products	3 103	1 203	4 577
Tourism connected products	1 272	149	1 692
Non-tourism related consumption products	1 831	1 054	2 885
Non-consumption products	**259**	**60**	**319**

.. Not available
Source: OECD Tourism Statistics (Database).

StatLink https://stat.link/r8lx4k

France

Tourism in the economy and outlook for recovery

Tourism is a major sector in France. As measured by combining tourism-related spending by both French residents and non-residents, the sector accounted for 7.5% of GDP in 2019. Tourism directly employed 1.5 million people, approximately 7.5% of the national workforce. The impacts of COVID-19 saw tourism GDP fall by 34% to EUR 114.5 billion, or 5.3% of the economy in 2020. Employment was less impacted, but there was still a loss of 155 764 jobs. Three-quarters of the jobs lost were in the accommodation and food services sectors.

In 2019, almost 91 million international tourists visited France. At that time, international revenues exceeded EUR 56 billion, accounting for 21% of French service exports. In 2020, France recorded 41.7 million international tourists, a decline of 54.2%. This translated to a 49.7% decline in international travel receipts. In 2021, there was a slight recovery, with international tourists increasing to 48.4 million.

The domestic market was an important backbone for tourism in 2020, declining just 26.7% to 152 million tourists. This saw the domestic share of tourism expenditure increase from 59.7% in 2019 to 66.7% in 2020. In 2021, domestic tourists recovered to 187.3 million, remaining only 9.8% below 2019 numbers.

Tourism governance and funding

Since 2022, the Ministry in charge of Economy is mainly responsible for tourism policy (previously responsibility was shared with the Ministry for European and Foreign Affairs). Other ministries involved in monitoring tourism issues include the ministries of Foreign Affairs, Ecological Transition, Sport, Culture, Territorial Cohesion, and the Ministry of France Overseas.

All territorial levels of public governance have tourism responsibility. The Regional Council, with the support of the Regional Tourism Committee, co-ordinates public and private initiatives in tourism development, information and promotion, including initiatives in foreign markets. It also ensures the collection of local data and the processing and dissemination of data relating to tourism activity in its territory. The Departmental Council can create a Departmental Tourism Committee, whose actions are focused on structuring the offer and supporting tourism actors. Municipalities also formulate local tourism policies.

Until 2022, an Inter-Ministerial Council for Tourism met regularly under the chair of the Prime Minister, bringing together ministers, elected representatives and sector professionals to present France's roadmap for tourism in the context of key issues for discussion. To better co-ordinate public and private tourism governance, in 2020 the Inter-Ministerial Council for Tourism set up a Committee for the Tourism Sector to enable stakeholders to consult each other and allow for the co-construction of tourism policies by professionals (nearly 300 members) and public authorities. This committee was useful in raising the concerns of professionals and improving support measures for the sector during the COVID-19 crisis.

The total state's tourism budget (including spending by various ministries, such as culture) is estimated to be EUR 7.5 billion. The cumulative budget of the Regional Tourism Committee exceeds EUR 120 million, and the Departmental Tourism Committee receives EUR 230 million.

France: Organisational chart of tourism bodies

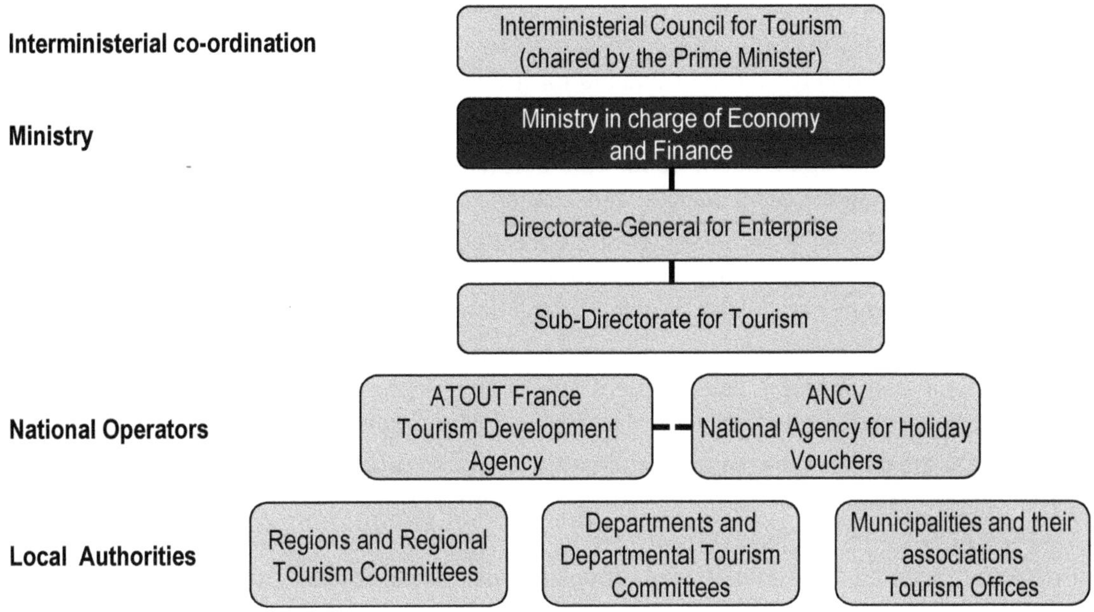

Source: OECD, adapted from the Directorate-General for Enterprise, 2022.

Tourism policies and programmes

Following the COVID-19 pandemic, France increased support measures for all sectors, with a particular focus on tourism. These included solidarity funds, fixed cost schemes, partial activity (where the Government covers some of employees' salaries), and state-guaranteed loans. The measures, totalling EUR 36 billion, made it possible to preserve employment and avoid losing knowledge and long-acquired assets.

In addition to the support measures to overcome the crisis, France has also announced recovery measures.

Firstly, in May 2020, stimulus measures to support investment (totalling EUR 1.3 billion) with a focus on the hotel and restaurant sector and events and business tourism (EUR 100 million) were introduced. Some measures related to standardisation, for example, the modernisation and greening of accommodation classifications. The themes of sustainability and digital technology are very present in the plan.

Priority lines of action for France include the quality and structuring of the tourist offer, state support for investments, training and employment, support for digitalisation and information sharing, and providing access to holidays for as many people as possible.

Secondly, in May 2021, France launched the Future of Mountains plan *(Avenir Montagnes)* to enhance sustainable and resilient mountain tourism which addresses its objective through three priorities:

- Encouraging the diversification of the tourism offer and the development of new customers.
- Stepping up the pace of the ecological transition of tourism activities in the mountains.
- Revitalising recreational real estate and stopping the development of empty beds.

In total, Avenir Montagnes represents a commitment of over EUR 640 million of public funds for mountain regions, generating nearly EUR 1.8 billion of investment in these areas. France is launching the Avenir Montagnes fund with a budget of EUR 331 million, including EUR 300 million for investment support (with six regions committing the same amounts) and EUR 31 million allocated to providing engineering support to regions.

Thirdly, at the end of 2021, the Destination France plan was launched for the revival and transformation of the tourism sector. The plan lays the foundations for tourism policy in France over the next ten years. It allocates almost EUR 2 billion, and the main lines of action include:

- Win over and win back talent (see box below) through a major communication campaign particularly targeted at young people, aimed at showing the rich diversity of jobs in tourism.
- Strengthen the resilience of the sector and encourage quality upgrades of product. Support will be targeted towards major events, trade fairs, exhibitions and congresses with an international dimension who were particularly affected by the health crisis.
- Promote and develop French tourism assets by creating a Destination France fund. EUR 51 million is earmarked to support the development of French tourism assets, and another EUR 55 million is allocated to promote and strengthen a tourism engineering support offer for regions.
- Respond to the challenges of transforming the sector by promoting sustainable tourism, a reduced eco-footprint, investment in sustainable tourism infrastructure, digital transformation and supporting the development and scale-up of start-ups in the tourism sector.
- Promote France as a destination and consolidate its market share by strengthening communication aimed at tourists and investors.

Campaign to win over and win back tourism workers in France

In September 2022, France launched a large-scale communication campaign to tackle tourism workforce challenges and to enhance the attractiveness of the sector following the pandemic (*Conquérir et Reconquérir les Talents*). The campaign is a key component under the Destination France plan, and aims to strengthen and to sustain tourism jobs and skills. Three major objectives are formulated:

- Strengthen attractiveness of the tourism sector and raise awareness on the rich diversity in professional tourism opportunities.
- Facilitate recruitment, particularly in areas where there is a great need for the upcoming tourism seasons, and in the view of major events in 2023 (e.g. the Rugby World Cup and the Olympic Games).
- Attract more young people to tourism training and courses leading to these professions.

The campaign targets people between 16-25 years old who are looking for a job or career in tourism, as well as people who consider to change careers. A co-ordination mechanism is also planned to mobilise all the local institutional players including schools, training institutes, job centers, regions, professional federations, as well as private tourism actors.

France's tourism communication campaign is of unprecedented scope, and mobilises EUR 8 million. It will include the broadcasting of three spots on most TV channels and on digital channels (social networks, YouTube, etc.), digital billboards in high-traffic areas. Continuous development and support will be made to sustain reoccurring tourism workforce needs in 2022-23.

Statistical Profile

France: Domestic, inbound and outbound tourism

	2017	2018	2019	2020	2021
TOURISM FLOWS, THOUSAND					
Domestic tourism					
Total domestic trips	276 537	268 152	299 315 |	212 547	252 240
Overnight visitors (tourists)	191 636	189 755	207 624 |	152 119	187 321
Same-day visitors (excursionists)	84 901	78 397	91 691 |	60 428	64 919
Nights in all types of accommodation	895 659	897 591	921 767 |	768 138	865 396
Hotels and similar establishments	..	..	306 077 |	235 128	277 539
Other collective establishments	..	..	87 991 |	64 311	77 925
Private accommodation	..	..	527 698 |	468 699	509 932
Inbound tourism					
Total international arrivals	207 274	211 998	217 877	117 109	141 297
Overnight visitors (tourists)	86 758	89 322	90 914	41 684	48 395
Same-day visitors (excursionists)	120 516	122 676	126 963	75 424	92 902
Top markets					
Belgium	10 448	10 507	11 854	7 203	8 314
Germany	12 256	12 272	13 606	6 447	7 515
Switzerland	7 013	6 772	6 506	3 657	4 750
Spain	6 753	6 734	6 730	3 242	4 735
Netherlands	4 307	4 730	5 599	3 799	3 935
Nights in all types of accommodation	582 100	596 784	619 887	298 289	375 456
Hotels and similar establishments	..	..	..	..	..
Other collective establishments	..	..	..	..	..
Private accommodation	..	..	..	..	..
Outbound tourism					
Total international departures	44 265 |	48 069	52 542 |	20 803	21 366
Overnight visitors (tourists)	29 055	30 509	38 301 |	11 461	13 108
Same-day visitors (excursionists)	15 209 |	17 560	14 241 |	9 342	8 258
Top destinations					
Spain	4 429	4 526	6 175 |	1 652	2 990
Italy	3 192	3 311	3 847 |	1 149	1 556
Belgium	1 660	1 727	2 012 |	998	931
Portugal	1 555	1 627	1 906 |	642	876
Germany	1 372	1 472	1 509 |	532	686
TOURISM RECEIPTS AND EXPENDITURE, MILLION EUR					
Inbound tourism					
Total international receipts	59 612	61 555	63 304	31 444	..
International travel receipts	52 097	55 490	56 730	28 510	..
International passenger transport receipts	7 515	6 065	6 574	2 934	..
Outbound tourism					
Total international expenditure	47 443	50 164	53 405	27 367	..
International travel expenditure	38 949	41 978	45 148	24 319	..
International passenger transport expenditure	8 494	8 186	8 257	3 048	..

.. Not available; | Break in series
Source: OECD Tourism Statistics (Database).

StatLink https://stat.link/2np4d6

France: Enterprises and employment in tourism

	Number of establishments[1]	Number of persons employed[2]				
	2020	2017	2018	2019	2020	2021
Total	..	**1 361 019**	**1 382 831**	**1 495 842 |**	**1 340 078 p**	..
Tourism industries	**333 350 p**	**1 344 350**	**1 367 134**	**1 495 842 |**	**1 340 078 p**	..
Accommodation services for visitors	55 287 p	214 866	216 623	233 270 |	194 278 p	..
Hotels and similar establishments	20 671 p	173 445	176 046	178 728 |	147 310 p	..
Food and beverage serving industry	200 397 p	691 794	710 313	860 291 |	782 305 p	..
Passenger transport	3 902 p	271 747	274 683	200 638 |	183 894 p	..
Air passenger transport	632 p	60 867	60 809	61 189 |	57 439 p	..
Railways passenger transport	13 p	165 708	167 493	94 533 |	84 476 p	..
Road passenger transport	2 229 p	35 461	36 202	34 208 |	31 386 p	..
Water passenger transport	1 028 p	9 711	10 179	10 708 |	10 593 p	..
Passenger transport supporting services	.. p	..	..	..	..	..
Transport equipment rental	4 541 p	14 197	14 518	14 408 |	12 970 p	..
Travel agencies and other reservation services industry	9 361 p	45 210	45 549	46 101 |	39 563 p	..
Cultural industry	908 p	12 904	13 000	14 371 |	13 342 p	..
Sports and recreation industry	58 954 p	93 632	92 448	126 763 |	113 726 p	..
Retail trade of country-specific tourism characteristic goods	..	..	..	..	..	..
Other country-specific tourism industries	..	..	..	..	..	..
Other industries	..	**16 669**	**15 697**	..	..	..

.. Not available; p Provisional data; | Break in series
1. Data refer to number of enterprises.
2. Data refer to number of employees.
Source: OECD Tourism Statistics (Database).

StatLink https://stat.link/7df45g

France: Internal tourism consumption

Million EUR

	2020		
	Domestic tourism expenditure	Inbound tourism expenditure	Internal tourism consumption
Total	..	..	**114 500**
Consumption products	**62 100**	**31 000**	**107 200**
Tourism characteristic products	38 400	22 900	82 700
Accommodation services for visitors	12 100	10 500	44 000
Food and beverage serving services	7 100	3 700	10 800
Passenger transport services	12 700	6 200	18 900
Air passenger transport services	3 400	2 800	6 200
Railways passenger transport services	3 600	600	4 200
Road passenger transport services	900	800	1 700
Water passenger transport services	300	200	500
Passenger transport supporting services	..	..	..
Transport equipment rental services	3 900	1 500	5 400
Travel agencies and other reservation services industry	2 900	300	3 200
Cultural services	500	700	1 200
Sports and recreation services	3 100	1 500	4 600
Country-specific tourism characteristic goods	..	..	..
Country-specific tourism characteristic services	..	..	..
Other consumption products	23 700	8 100	31 800
Tourism connected products	..	..	..
Non-tourism related consumption products	..	..	..
Non-consumption products	**5 900**	**1 400**	**7 300**

.. Not available
Source: OECD Tourism Statistics (Database).

StatLink https://stat.link/qy1uzc

Germany

Tourism in the economy and outlook for recovery

Prior to the COVID-19 pandemic, tourism in Germany generated over EUR 123.8 billion for the economy. The sector directly contributed 4.0% to total GVA and provided over 2.1 million tourism jobs, or 4.7% of total employment in 2019. The impact of COVID-19 saw tourism employment fall to 1.5 million in 2020, or 3.5% of the national workforce. Economic losses for the tourism sector resulting from the COVID-19 crisis are estimated to be EUR 68.7 billion in 2020 and EUR 58.9 billion in 2021.

The recovery of tourism in Germany has been moderate. In 2021 there were 96.8 million tourists (domestic and international), 1.3% lower than in 2020. Of these, 11.7 million were international tourists, and 85.1 million were domestic tourists. International tourists remained 70.5% below 2019 levels, and domestic tourists remained 43.8% down.

In 2021, 266.1 million nights were registered in accommodation establishments. This was an increase of 2.0% compared to 2020. Expectations for the recovery of the German tourism sector to pre-pandemic levels range from 2022 to 2024.

Tourism governance and funding

The Federal Minister for Economic Affairs and Climate Action has lead responsibility for tourism policy development. The Minister is supported by the Advisory Council on Tourism Issues which brings together the interests of government, commerce, academia and others. The Commissioner for SMEs and Tourism is responsible for co-ordinating tourism policy within the Federal Government and with the German Parliament, in particular with the Parliamentary Tourism Committee.

The 16 Federal States (Länder) are responsible for developing, shaping and promoting tourism policy. Their ministries are charged with designing, implementing and funding policies to promote local tourism development. Each federal state has a Destination Management Organisation that represents the interests of regional and municipal organisations. Local tourism offices co-ordinate the work of tourism SMEs, promote product design and undertake relevant marketing activities. The Joint Federal/Länder Scheme for the Improvement of Regional Economic Structures (GRW) is the central instrument of the Federal Government's regional policy. GRW project funding is provided in the form of investments in trade and industry, including the tourism economy, as well as municipal investments in economic infrastructure, including basic infrastructure for tourism (e.g. developing land for tourism and public tourist facilities).

The budgetary funds available to the Federal Ministry for Economic Affairs and Climate Action for tourism are concentrated on institutional support for the German National Tourist Board (DZT) with a 2022 budget of EUR 39 million. Support for tourism remains a focal point of the Federal Government's regional policy. The GRW budget set aside for tourism was EUR 1.3 billion for 2016-20, divided evenly between federal and Länder contributions. This funding is invested in both the tourism sector and tourism infrastructure. Compared to 2015-19, this constitutes an average increase of 13%. Financing for tourism in Germany at municipal, regional, and Länder levels comes from various sources; in addition to public funds, revenue is also generated from spa and tourism taxes and bed taxes.

Germany: Organisational chart of tourism bodies

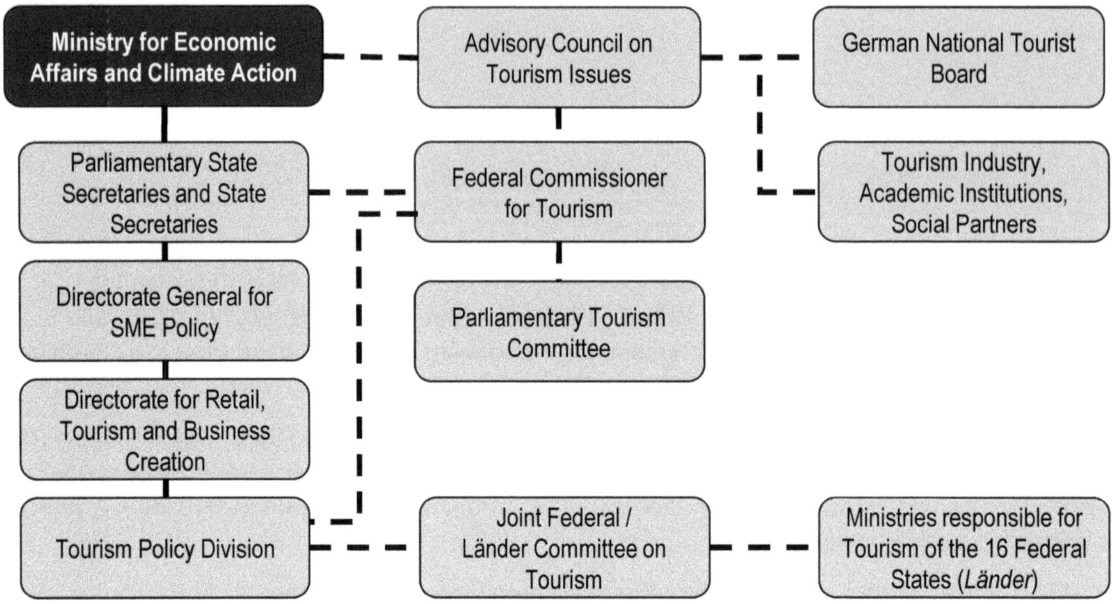

Source: OECD, adapted from the Federal Ministry for Economic Affairs and Energy, 2022.

Tourism policies and programmes

In 2019, Germany adopted principles for a new National Tourism Strategy. This strategy aims to strengthen tourism as a part of the economy and prepare the entire sector for the future. This also answers to the needs of the post-crisis recovery. The principles of the Strategy fed into the development of six goals:

- Exploit the many different areas of economic potential in tourism, including creating additional employment opportunities in rural areas.
- Strengthen Germany's competitiveness as a tourism destination and bolster the tourism sector with a focus on SME development.
- Create modern, accessible, reliable and sustainable mobility and digital infrastructure that takes account of tourists' needs and challenges associated with an expected post-crisis tourism increase.
- Develop quality tourism that flourishes and preserves valuable natural and cultural habitats, providing quality of life for all - whether visitors or residents.
- Utilise the potential of tourism to boost economic development in other parts of the world and foster peace, tolerance and international understanding.
- Support tourism development that is environmentally and climate friendly.

The National Tourism Strategy also considers the impact of outbound tourism on developing countries. The Federal Ministry for Co-operation and Development supports over 90 projects in developing countries that contribute to achieving the Sustainable Development Goals and Agenda 2030. COVID-19 has created a need for further robust policy responses that go beyond the principles of the National Tourism Strategy. This has been necessary to strengthen the sector's resilience, particularly in terms of increasing the competitiveness of SMEs in the sector and supporting future structural changes that are now necessary.

Policy responses include:

- Promoting projects for digitalisation and sustainability in tourism (e.g. guidance of visitors, avoiding queues at airports or simplified and compliant booking processes).
- Safeguarding qualified employment by promoting professional training, particularly in the travel and catering sectors.
- Creating the national platform "Future of Tourism" as the central instrument for the further development of a National Tourism Strategy. The platform will include representatives of the sixteen federal states and stakeholders of the tourism sector early in 2023 (Box 2.6).
- Continuing further development of online tools offering businesses and others guidance on the funding opportunities relating to tourism promotion and development.
- Promoting the development of scientific knowledge and know-how with the help of the LIFT Wissen programme initiated by the Federal Ministry for Economic Affairs and Climate Action (see box).

The crisis showed that the safeguarding of tourism jobs is a fundamental requirement. Despite measures like offering short-time work to secure jobs, many qualified employees left for jobs in other sectors and are now being sought to return to help the relaunch of the sector. As a result, Germany provided a package of measures to combat the impact of COVID-19 on companies.

The trend toward nature and outdoor tourism has helped stimulate the development of sustainable offers, which are increasingly in demand by German travellers. Germany is also focusing on further advancements in digitalisation with smart services. Online offers are frequently the first source of information in areas such as art and culture. Destinations also benefit from digital applications in management terms, for example, by guiding visitors to avoid peak times. Additionally, COVID-19 has increased the demand for reliable, digitally delivered information about regulations, hygiene, security and the state of infections in destination areas.

To show economic and environmental issues related to tourism, the Federal Statistical Office of Germany (Destatis) compiled the Tourism Satellite Accounts (TSA) for the reporting period 2015-19. The methodological approach of the TSA is making economic and environmental issues associated with tourism visible in the statistical systems of national accounts and environmental-economic accounts.

Promoting innovation for the revitalisation of tourism in Germany

The tourism sector is facing a changed market as the pandemic created profound changes in society, consumer needs and demands, as well as a renewed set of framework conditions. In order to tackle the challenges created by COVID-19 and enable a fact-based, sustainable tourism restart, the German Federal Ministry for Economic Affairs and Climate Action introduced the LIFT-Wissen funding programme for Performance improvement and innovation funding in tourism – knowledge. (Leistungssteigerung und Innovationsförderung im Tourismus – Wissen). LIFT Wissen aims to promote tourism-specific, scientifically substantiated know-how. It supports innovative projects to gain greater insight into upcoming trends and future economic challenges for the tourism sector (e.g. through studies or the development of concepts). LIFT Wissen addresses SMEs, institutions and associations and welcomes joint projects between those interests. It supports the exchange between economics, science and politics, advancing the science and practice of tourism. The knowledge generated will inform policy and advisory expertise. The programme will also assist associations and companies by providing blueprints through the publication of project results. This knowledge also aims to strengthen the performance and competitiveness of SMEs in tourism for the short- and medium-term and support evidence-based policy.

Statistical Profile

Germany: Domestic, inbound and outbound tourism

	2017	2018	2019	2020	2021
TOURISM FLOWS, THOUSAND					
Domestic tourism					
Total domestic trips	..	..	..	..	..
Overnight visitors (tourists)	135 005	140 494	151 381	85 696	85 146
Same-day visitors (excursionists)	..	..	..	..	..
Nights in all types of accommodation	318 052	332 594	347 694	229 025	235 371
Hotels and similar establishments	291 279	302 831	316 631	197 243	204 071
Other collective establishments	26 773	29 763	31 063	31 783	31 300
Private accommodation	..	..	..	..	..
Inbound tourism					
Total international arrivals	..	..	..	..	..
Overnight visitors (tourists)	37 307	38 748	39 563	12 449	11 688
Same-day visitors (excursionists)	..	..	..	..	..
Top markets					
Netherlands	4 588	4 717	4 820	2 282	2 038
Switzerland	3 185	3 311	3 399	1 404	1 208
Austria	1 976	2 064	2 116	820	842
Denmark	..	..	..	692	704
United States	2 808	2 969	3 057	594	701
Nights in all types of accommodation	83 111	86 962	89 261	31 733	30 732
Hotels and similar establishments	78 833	82 167	84 568	29 562	29 094
Other collective establishments	4 278	4 794	4 693	2 171	1 638
Private accommodation	..	..	..	..	..
Outbound tourism					
Total international departures	194 276	208 172	212 143	103 117	100 720
Overnight visitors (tourists)	92 402	108 542	99 533	36 867	48 667
Same-day visitors (excursionists)	101 874	99 630	112 610	66 250	52 053
Top destinations					
Austria	11 275	14 396	11 718	7 494	7 252
Italy	10 973	13 573	11 633	4 151	7 552
Netherlands	5 673	7 413	7 091	4 082	3 459
Spain	11 093	11 672	10 985	2 716	5 414
France	6 231	6 143	6 468	2 653	3 383
TOURISM RECEIPTS AND EXPENDITURE, MILLION EUR					
Inbound tourism					
Total international receipts	35 493	50 642	37 344	19 331	..
International travel receipts	35 282	36 391	37 344	19 331	..
International passenger transport receipts	14 471	14 251	..	..	..
Outbound tourism					
Total international expenditure	78 865	88 141	83 292	34 029	..
International travel expenditure	78 839	80 934	83 292	34 029	..
International passenger transport expenditure	26	7 207	..	..	..

.. Not available
Source: OECD Tourism Statistics (Database).

StatLink https://stat.link/4r1hsb

Germany: Enterprises and employment in tourism

	Number of establishments[2]	Number of persons employed				
	2021	2017	2018	2019	2020	2021
Total	..	..	..	..	..	..
Tourism industries	**29 410**	**2 122 014**	**2 179 830**	**2 145 026**	**1 546 927**	..
Accommodation services for visitors	..	1 760	1 806	1 752	1 335	..
Hotels and similar establishments[1]	29 410	..	..	..	..	..
Food and beverage serving industry	..	1 482 155	1 517 082	1 493 927	999 938	..
Passenger transport	..	..	..	..	..	..
Air passenger transport	..	55 786	58 380	59 568	59 167	..
Railways passenger transport	..	..	..	..	..	..
Road passenger transport	..	465 354	482 486	469 768	399 433	..
Water passenger transport	..	9 732	10 007	9 742	.. c	..
Passenger transport supporting services	..	..	..	..	..	..
Transport equipment rental	..	..	..	..	..	..
Travel agencies and other reservation services industry	..	107 227	110 069	110 269	87 054	..
Cultural industry	..	..	..	..	..	..
Sports and recreation industry	..	..	..	..	..	..
Retail trade of country-specific tourism characteristic goods	..	..	..	..	..	..
Other country-specific tourism industries	..	..	..	..	..	..
Other industries	..	..	..	..	..	..

.. Not available; c Confidential data
1. Data for hotels and similar establishments refer to number of establishments.
2. Data refer to number of enterprises.
Source: OECD Tourism Statistics (Database).

StatLink https://stat.link/xyghkt

Germany: Internal tourism consumption

Million EUR

	2019		
	Domestic tourism expenditure	Inbound tourism expenditure	Internal tourism consumption
Total	..	..	..
Consumption products	**246 985**	**46 884**	**329 558**
Tourism characteristic products	148 793	35 855	199 768
Accommodation services for visitors	36 735	13 551	54 365
Food and beverage serving services	46 547	10 801	57 348
Passenger transport services	34 594	10 257	44 851
Air passenger transport services	14 558	7 880	22 438
Railways passenger transport services	3 831	373	4 204
Road passenger transport services	14 326	814	15 140
Water passenger transport services	1 880	1 190	3 070
Passenger transport supporting services	..	..	..
Transport equipment rental services	2 644	242	2 886
Travel agencies and other reservation services industry	9 764	848	10 612
Cultural services	..	..	..
Sports and recreation services	18 508	157	29 706
Country-specific tourism characteristic goods	..	..	..
Country-specific tourism characteristic services	..	..	..
Other consumption products	98 192	11 029	129 790
Tourism connected products	36 302	2 203	38 505
Non-tourism related consumption products	61 891	8 826	91 285
Non-consumption products	..	..	..

.. Not available
Source: OECD Tourism Statistics (Database).

StatLink https://stat.link/vuy923

Greece

Tourism in the economy and outlook for recovery

Tourism is one of the key drivers in the Greek economy. The impact of COVID-19 saw tourism GVA decline 44.8% to EUR 6.4 billion in 2020 to directly contribute 4.4% to the national economy. Employment has been less impacted, with the tourism-related share of the workforce falling to 13.0% in 2021, down 1.4 percentage points from 2019.

International arrivals decreased from 34 million in 2019 to 7.4 million in 2020, down 78%. This caused a decline in travel receipts of EUR 13.9 billion (down 76% compared to 2019). A strong recovery in 2021 saw arrivals return to 15.2 million, but this remained 55.2% below 2019 levels. Domestic tourists declined to 4.5 million in 2020 (down 14.1% compared to 2019), before increasing to 4.8 million in 2021.

Domestic and international tourists spent 73.9 million nights in registered accommodation in 2021. Despite signs of recovery, this was still 48.5% below 2019 levels. International tourism remains vital to the Greek tourism economy, accounting for 80% of nights in 2021.

Tourism governance and funding

The Ministry of Tourism shapes Greece's tourism policy and international marketing strategy, introduces legislation on tourism, undertakes tourism planning and ensures co-operation with other ministries and local administration. Another part of its mission is the implementation of tourism education and training programmes to improve the quality and competitiveness of Greek tourism.

The Ministry of Tourism operates 14 Regional Tourism Offices, which aim to ensure a high-quality tourism product. The Regional Tourism Offices are responsible for: licensing, conducting quality control regarding the services provided by tourism businesses, monitoring the official classification of tourist accommodation, and imposing administrative sanctions on tourism businesses.

The Executive Structure for the Tourism Sector is responsible for the National Strategic Reference Framework for the Tourism Sector. The Special Service for the Promotion and Licensing of Tourism Investments acts as a "one-stop-shop" aimed at boosting and facilitating major tourism investments by providing full and personalised support to investors at all stages of the planned investment.

The Department of Tourism Policy Planning is responsible for developing adequate short- and long-term marketing strategies to promote Greece as a tourist destination. It also participates in co-operation schemes with the Ministry of Foreign Affairs. The Department of International Relations and EU Affairs is responsible for EU affairs, bilateral and multilateral co-operation in tourism, and the representation of Greece in tourism-related international organisations. The Department of Special Forms of Tourism is responsible for planning, promoting and regulating matters related to thematic and special forms of tourism. It works together with other ministries (e.g. Health, Culture and Sports, Maritime Affairs and Insular Policy and Rural Development and Food) and co-operates with thematic tourism stakeholders).

For the development of smooth processes to facilitate both safe and seamless travel during the pandemic, intense co-operation was developed with the Ministries of Foreign Affairs, Health and Digital Governance, the former General Secretariat for Civil Protection and the National Civil Aviation Authority.

Local administrations (regions and municipalities) draw up and implement programmes and activities for tourism development and promotion in the areas under their jurisdiction. All promotional activity is aligned with the national tourism promotion strategy.

The total budget for tourism in Greece was EUR 55.1 million in 2019 and EUR 68.3 million in 2020.

Greece: Organisational chart of tourism bodies

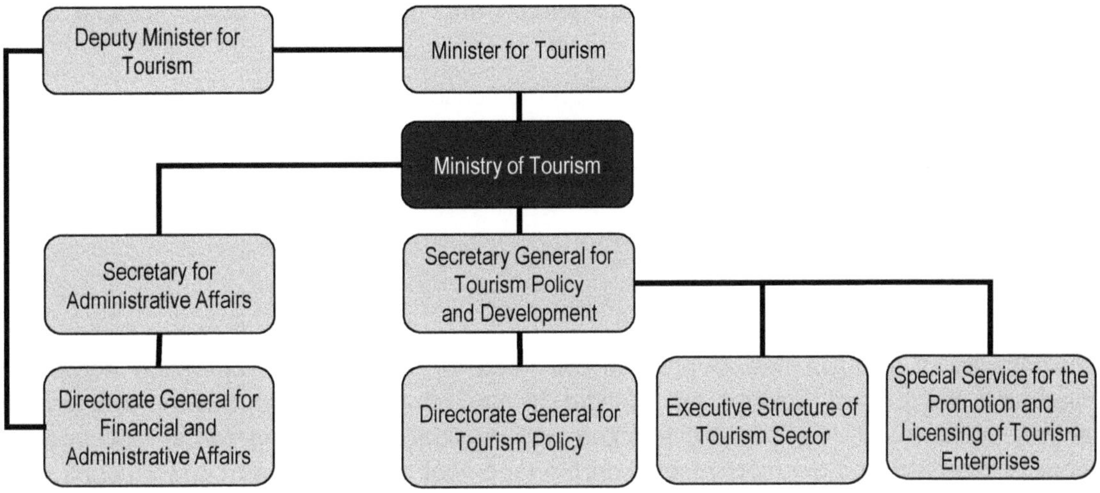

Source: OECD, adapted from the Ministry of Tourism, 2022.

Tourism policies and programmes

Greece pursues sustainable tourism development within the context of broader economic and regional development planning. Strategic planning to fulfil the aims of the national tourism policy involves extending the tourism season, dispersing tourism demand throughout the country, focusing on quality tourism, developing synergies with the private sector and boosting tourism investments. Measures focus on greater integration of tourism into national strategic planning, policies to strengthen tourism governance, support for tourism investment, promotion of skills development, encouragement of the sector's digitalisation and fostering of sustainable destination management.

The National Recovery and Resilience Plan (Greece 2.0) funds individual projects for tourism development. These projects include developing mountain, health and wellness tourism and agrotourism and gastronomy, improving marine and coastal infrastructure, implementing accessibility improvements, and promoting upskilling and reskilling in tourism through programmes to upgrade existing and acquire new skills.

The Ministry's Annual Action Plan 2022 includes projects aimed at establishing and implementing the national strategy for sustainable tourism development and the optimal management of the individual tourism destinations of the country. There is also a focus on measuring and monitoring sustainable tourism development through the establishment of a National Sustainable Tourism Observatory, local Sustainable Tourism Observatories and Tourism Satellite Accounts.

The following projects are also being implemented:

- Digital Transformation of the Greek National Tourism Organisation (GNTO), with four sub-projects: the creation of a digital tourist map; the creation of a digital repository of the country's cultural assets; the development of an innovative information system for tourists and citizens based on second-generation artificial intelligence technology; and the digitisation of GNTO's historical archive.
- Creation of a unique electronic register for tourism enterprises (e-MHTE) to improve the quality of services and enhance interoperability with new applications and systems.

At the same time, the National Strategic Plan for Tourism Development (NSSTA) is under elaboration, i.e. the development of a ten-year integrated national strategic plan for tourism development entitled the National Pact for Sustainable Tourism 2021-30. Key axes are product development and visibility, accessibility and connectivity, sustainable management and development, quality private and public infrastructure, and funding opportunities.

A Tourism Crisis Management Plan and a Crisis Communication Strategy in Greece covers a wide range of potential crises that can impact tourism, including health, environmental, economic, and societal crises. Both plans aim to increase the effectiveness and agility of the Greek tourism sector in responding to eventual future challenges.

A gew governance framework for destination management in Greece

Greece's Ministry of Tourism has recognised the need for enhanced co-operation between local authorities and the central government in light of the complex development challenges of its destinations. As a result, the Ministry enacted new legislation providing for a new governance framework to establish and operate Destination Management and Marketing Organisations (DMMO) and Tourism Sustainable Development Observatories.

The DMMOs aim to improve the governance of individual tourism destinations, facilitate co-operation among various authorities at the local and regional levels, and form a quality, competitive, and sustainable tourism product. Furthermore, a Sustainable Tourism Development Observatory within each DMMO will make available and monitor the necessary data for the integrated planning of tourism strategies. This approach helps identify destination management gaps and avoids overlapping functions regarding destination promotion. The establishment of a Sustainable Tourism Development Observatory in each above DMMO is funded by the Recovery and Resilience Facility.

Statistical Profile

Greece: Domestic, inbound and outbound tourism

	2017	2018	2019	2020	2021
TOURISM FLOWS, THOUSAND					
Domestic tourism[1]					
Total domestic trips	24 650	26 301	27 879	23 507	21 899
Overnight visitors (tourists)	5 492	5 691	5 180	4 448	4 831
Same-day visitors (excursionists)	19 158	20 610	22 699	19 059	17 069
Nights in all types of accommodation	21 975	24 064	23 623	12 277	14 963
Hotels and similar establishments	21 189	23 209 |	22 682	11 685	14 360
Other collective establishments	785	855 |	941	593	603
Private accommodation	..	..	..	..	..
Inbound tourism					
Total international arrivals	30 161	33 072	34 005	7 406	15 246
Overnight visitors (tourists)	..	..	..	..	..
Same-day visitors (excursionists)	..	..	..	..	..
Top markets					
Germany	3 706	4 381	4 026	1 526	3 001
United Kingdom	3 002	2 943	3 499	1 069	1 591
France	1 420	1 524	1 542	469	1 175
Italy	1 441	1 667	1 553	373	806
Bulgaria	2 546	3 135	3 883	663	762
Nights in all types of accommodation	213 516	230 727	236 547	64 172	133 735
Hotels and similar establishments	..	..	..	..	..
Other collective establishments	..	..	..	..	..
Private accommodation	..	..	..	..	..
Outbound tourism					
Total international departures	7 685	7 961	7 848	2 324	2 026
Overnight visitors (tourists)	..	..	..	..	..
Same-day visitors (excursionists)	..	..	..	..	..
Top destinations					
Germany	421	500	584	227	225
Bulgaria	2 186	2 371	1 916	617	212
Italy	351	405	438	146	184
North Macedonia	1 787	1 352	1 138	343	174
Cyprus	214	255	239	134	171
TOURISM RECEIPTS AND EXPENDITURE, MILLION EUR					
Inbound tourism					
Total international receipts	16 621	18 444	20 618	5 353	11 621
International travel receipts	14 630	16 086	18 179	4 319	10 503
International passenger transport receipts	1 991	2 359	2 439	1 034	1 119
Outbound tourism					
Total international expenditure	2 920	3 314	3 764	1 321	1 891
International travel expenditure	1 905	2 191	2 744	793	1 113
International passenger transport expenditure	1 015	1 123	1 021	528	778

.. Not available; | Break in series
1. Trips from demand side surveys; Nights from supply side surveys.
Source: OECD Tourism Statistics (Database).

StatLink https://stat.link/qehykj

Greece: Enterprises and employment in tourism

	Number of establishments	Number of persons employed				
	2021	2017	2018	2019	2020	2021
Total	..	..	..	..	..	..
Tourism industries	**77 543**	**537 886**	**541 285**	**564 003**	**535 801**	**509 037**
Accommodation services for visitors	52 053	91 333	100 442	99 494	75 312	92 395
Hotels and similar establishments	9 745	86 532	94 700	93 635	69 635	84 689
Food and beverage serving industry	..	263 222	266 227	287 398	273 443	239 031
Passenger transport	..	105 355	99 643	99 748	105 346	104 301
Air passenger transport	..	7 539	4 712	3 804	5 840	8 592
Railways passenger transport	..	78 450	87 027	87 404	59 153	73 534
Road passenger transport	9 097	2 665	2 000	2 322	3 943	2 756
Water passenger transport	..	65 310	63 740	62 783	65 912	55 033
Passenger transport supporting services	..	..	..	..	..	..
Transport equipment rental	..	3 762	6 094	7 224	5 244	4 186
Travel agencies and other reservation services industry	6 554	20 138	14 136	15 251	17 483	16 456
Cultural industry	..	19 093	17 638	19 444	17 985	17 062
Sports and recreation industry	..	34 982	37 106	35 444	40 990	35 606
Retail trade of country-specific tourism characteristic goods	..	..	..	..	..	..
Other country-specific tourism industries	94	..	..	..	..	..
Other industries	..	..	..	..	..	..

.. Not available
Source: OECD Tourism Statistics (Database).

StatLink https://stat.link/7bzsmg

Note by the Republic of Türkiye

The information in this document with reference to "Cyprus" relates to the southern part of the Island. There is no single authority representing both Turkish and Greek Cypriot people on the Island. Türkiye recognises the Turkish Republic of Northern Cyprus (TRNC). Until a lasting and equitable solution is found within the context of the United Nations, Türkiye shall preserve its position concerning the "Cyprus issue".

Note by all the European Union Member States of the OECD and the European Union

The Republic of Cyprus is recognised by all members of the United Nations with the exception of Türkiye. The information in this document relates to the area under the effective control of the Government of the Republic of Cyprus.

Hungary

Tourism in the economy and outlook for recovery

Tourism has been a driver of the Hungarian economy. In 2019, tourism directly contributed 6.8% to total GVA and 9.5% of the national workforce (421 036 jobs). The impact of COVID-19 has had a significant impact on the tourism sector, with preliminary estimates suggesting tourism GVA fell to HUF 2 194 billion or 5.4% of the national economy in 2020.

In 2019, there were 15.9 million international tourists in Hungary, and international expenditure accounted for 75% of total tourism expenditure. As a result of the pandemic, international tourists fell to 6.6 million (down 58.5%) in 2020 before rebounding to 6.9 million in 2021. The decline in tourists saw international receipts fall to HUF 1 738 billion in 2021 (down 41.6% compared to 2019).

Domestic tourism began to rebound in 2021. Domestic overnight tourists increased by 14.2% in 2021 but remained 28.5% under pre-pandemic levels.

Tourism governance and funding

Overall responsibility for tourism is with the Minister leading the Cabinet Office of the Prime Minister. The Deputy Prime Minister is responsible for religious tourism, while the Minister for Agricultural Policy, in co-operation with the Minister for Tourism, is responsible for the development of rural tourism.

The Hungarian Tourism Agency carries out the management of the Hungarian tourism sector on the basis of a mandate from the government. The responsibilities for destination management are divided into local, regional and central activities. The Agency and its subsidiaries carry out central tasks at the national and regional levels. Roles include the management of the tourism sector, strategy development, development and management of tourism products, central marketing, international sales, communication campaigns and the co-ordination of specific tourism developments.

The Agency co-ordinates and manages professional and other tasks related to destination management and plays a role in the professional co-ordination of Tourinform and the destination management organisation network. The role of Tourinform is to support local marketing and ensure the bilateral flow of information. Clear identification of tourist areas allows for planning, implementation, co-ordination and communication tasks for each destination.

The Agency is creating a new destination management services network. The new model will implement unified management and support the co-operation of local stakeholders to achieve a shared vision for the destination. The aim is for the destination management services, as key players in the tourism ecosystem, to ensure effective communication between local and central levels and within the destination to promote a destination-based approach to product development and successful market entry.

The central budget available to the Hungarian Tourism Agency for the period 2021-30 is HUF 90 billion in 2021, decreasing to HUF 45.9 billion by 2024 and staying at HUF 45.9 billion until 2030.

Hungary: Organisational chart of tourism bodies

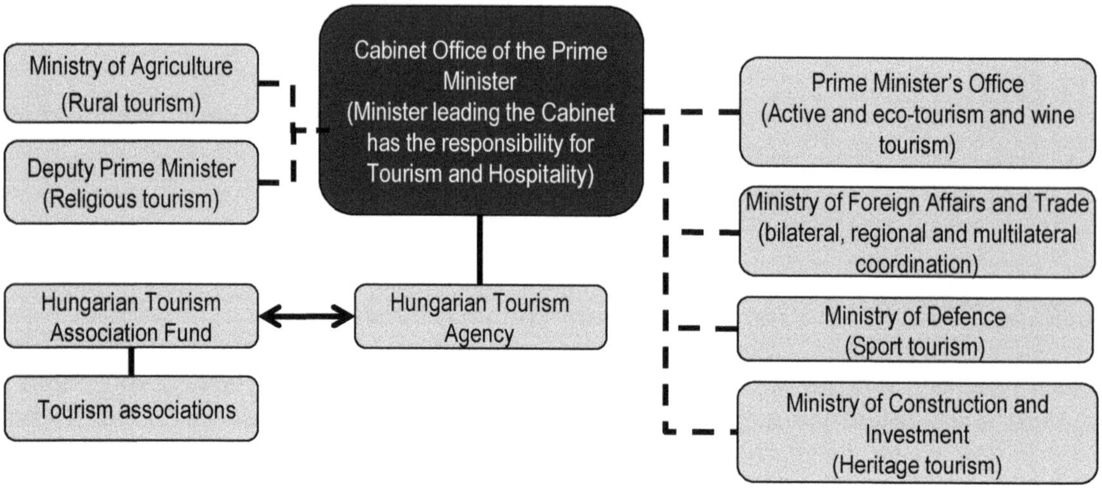

Source: OECD, adapted from the Hungarian Tourism Agency, 2022.

Tourism policies and programmes

In 2021, Hungary developed a revised Tourism 2.0 Strategy which incorporates the impacts of COVID-19 and the lessons learned through the first three years of the National Tourism Development Strategy 2030. COVID-19 created a new context for tourism, with new objectives being set and related activities defined:

- Complement the previous supply and product-based approach with a strong demand and needs-based approach. The focus of the Strategy is shifting from development to marketing, with a well-developed understanding of international and domestic market segment needs, used for marketing, sales and future development.
- Define a new model of governance whereby sectoral governance is complemented at the destination level. The new network of destination management organisations links central management with the tourism regions.
- Strengthen the role of the Hungarian Tourism Agency in education and career-path shaping to help improve the quality of the workforce.
- Utilise digital solutions to accompany and support the travel process. In addition to the Agency's role, sectoral interests also need to play an active role in developing and connecting digital solutions to improve the guest experience and understanding the opportunities of big data by looking in detail at sub-sectors, such as hospitality and the labour market.
- Promote sustainability as a strategic objective, channelled through sector-based interests to involve actors across all sectors. Sustainability considerations are reflected in product development at the destination level through the introduction of a sustainability trademark and priority development for sustainable and ecotourism attractions (e.g. national park visitor centres and water recreation sites). This will help lay the foundations for a sustainable profile for tourism in Hungary.

The timeframe of the updated Strategy remains unchanged and sets out the direction and priorities until 2030. Tourism 2.0 aims for a 20% increase in guest nights by 2030 compared to 2019. The goal is to increase the number of nights to 50 million per year. These 50 million nights will be generated by 20 million tourists, with an equal distribution of domestic and international tourists. For sustainable growth, it is aimed to share increases between Budapest and rural destinations.

The Strategy identifies areas for development to attract international visitors, especially in the realms of nature, culture and active tourism. Health tourism is also attractive at the regional level from neighbouring source markets. For example, Hungary features 12 internationally important spa towns that account for one-fifth of overnight stays. Consequently, cultural and active tourism attractions, complementary services and the upgrading of spas to an internationally attractive level could be the most important breakthrough for Hungary and individual destinations.

Hungary's Strategy identifies a range of other issues that will complement the structural changes. These include unified destination branding, the use of targeted and personalised marketing channels and quality improvement. Relatively small-scale improvements to quality can strengthen the wider offer. Education and training remain a core theme, as does sector financing. Tailored funding solutions and familiarisation with the needs and performance of the sector are necessary to ensure the continued availability of capital. It is also proposed to alleviate the administrative burden of complex regulation through the interconnection and re-regulation of data services and improved co-operation between sectoral interests, ensuring a clear division of roles and responsibilities between public and other stakeholders.

In terms of the recovery from COVID-19, domestic tourism is expected to be a significant driver of demand. Hungary expects that car-friendly and nature destinations will be popular with visitors, especially those from neighbouring countries.

Statistical Profile

Hungary: Domestic, inbound and outbound tourism

	2017	2018	2019	2020	2021
TOURISM FLOWS, THOUSAND					
Domestic tourism[1]					
Total domestic trips	46 816	48 310	47 923	29 932	38 810
Overnight visitors (tourists)	14 374	14 386	14 249	8 919	10 183
Same-day visitors (excursionists)	32 442	33 924	33 674	21 013	28 628
Nights in all types of accommodation	20 790	22 053	22 445	15 736	17 996
Hotels and similar establishments	11 553	12 302	12 394	7 877	8 701
Other collective establishments	5 114	5 188	5 054	2 948	3 599
Private accommodation	4 123	4 563	4 997	4 911	5 696
Inbound tourism[2]					
Total international arrivals	22 371	55 462 |	58 619	29 057	33 050
Overnight visitors (tourists)	14 102	16 766 |	15 949	6 624	6 973
Same-day visitors (excursionists)	8 270	38 696 |	42 670	22 433	26 077
Top markets					
Romania	2 076	11 898 |	13 249	6 733	8 026
Slovak Republic	1 562	10 000 |	10 072	5 606	5 216
Austria	1 254	8 523 |	9 053	5 167	5 140
Germany	1 865	3 202 |	3 075	1 371	2 269
Poland	427	2 425 |	2 435	1 193	1 438
Nights in all types of accommodation	19 077	20 162	20 794	5 035	7 200
Hotels and similar establishments	12 754	13 094	13 413	3 126	4 139
Other collective establishments	2 188	2 246	2 339	648	932
Private accommodation	4 135	4 822	5 042	1 261	2 129
Outbound tourism					
Total international departures	10 874	19 248 |	20 722	8 782	8 753
Overnight visitors (tourists)	6 707	7 771 |	8 318	2 762	3 101
Same-day visitors (excursionists)	4 167	11 477 |	12 404	6 019	5 653
Top destinations					
Germany	1 007	943 |	938	356	394
Austria	897	840 |	701	356	364
Croatia	344	523 |	470	216	268
Romania	705	788 |	941	272	244
Slovak Republic	769	883 |	841	416	213
TOURISM RECEIPTS AND EXPENDITURE, MILLION HUF					
Inbound tourism					
Total international receipts	2 299 013	2 608 871	2 979 032	1 291 019	1 738 388
International travel receipts	1 694 330	1 870 832	2 123 363	987 013	1 243 701
International passenger transport receipts	604 683	738 039	855 669	304 007	494 687
Outbound tourism					
Total international expenditure	831 196	877 872	976 583	410 014	519 438
International travel expenditure	672 179	715 494	799 100	356 203	440 144
International passenger transport expenditure	159 016	162 379	177 484	53 812	79 294

| Break in series
1. Trips from demand side surveys; Nights from supply side surveys.
2. Arrivals from demand side surveys; Nights from supply side surveys.
Source: OECD Tourism Statistics (Database).

StatLink https://stat.link/jlu47e

Hungary: Enterprises and employment in tourism

	Number of establishments[1]	Number of persons employed				
	2021	2017	2018	2019	2020	2021
Total	..	..	..	..	..	..
Tourism industries	**194 333**	**418 017**	**412 674**	**421 036**	..	..
Accommodation services for visitors	39 741	35 838	41 486	44 305	..	..
Hotels and similar establishments	1 968	30 588	35 201	..	..	..
Food and beverage serving industry	33 806	146 097	131 214	134 382	..	..
Passenger transport	10 828	98 840	91 674	104 111	..	..
Air passenger transport	124	..	..	..	..	..
Railways passenger transport	4	33 138	29 386	37 236	..	..
Road passenger transport	10 519	60 186	55 229	55 980	..	..
Water passenger transport	181	..	..	..	..	..
Passenger transport supporting services	5 480	25 163	30 772	24 753	..	..
Transport equipment rental	4 986	..	..	..	..	..
Travel agencies and other reservation services industry	3 293	8 087	6 298	6 683	..	..
Cultural industry	46 386	39 466	43 468	41 673	..	..
Sports and recreation industry	21 051	27 339	33 598	36 361	..	..
Retail trade of country-specific tourism characteristic goods	..	..	..	..	..	..
Other country-specific tourism industries	28 762	29 546	31 837	26 778	..	..
Other industries	..	..	..	..	..	..

.. Not available
1. Data refer to number of enterprises.
Source: OECD Tourism Statistics (Database).

StatLink https://stat.link/3yh20r

Hungary: Internal tourism consumption

Million HUF

	2019		
	Domestic tourism expenditure	Inbound tourism expenditure	Internal tourism consumption
Total	..	..	..
Consumption products	**723 466**	**2 247 976**	**2 971 441**
Tourism characteristic products	426 434	1 339 993	1 766 427
Accommodation services for visitors	146 771	359 885	506 656
Food and beverage serving services	142 551	287 457	430 008
Passenger transport services	61 016	273 349	334 366
Air passenger transport services	48 796	227 696	276 492
Railways passenger transport services	6 180	4 458	10 638
Road passenger transport services	6 035	38 998	45 032
Water passenger transport services	6	2 197	2 203
Passenger transport supporting services	6 653	30 372	37 025
Transport equipment rental services	89	5 363	5 452
Travel agencies and other reservation services industry	26 162	7 759	33 921
Cultural services	8 375	77 484	85 859
Sports and recreation services	28 057	150 531	178 588
Country-specific tourism characteristic goods	..	..	..
Country-specific tourism characteristic services	6 760	147 792	154 552
Other consumption products	297 031	907 982	1 205 014
Tourism connected products	279 775	791 420	1 071 195
Non-tourism related consumption products	17 257	116 563	133 819
Non-consumption products	..	..	..

.. Not available
Source: OECD Tourism Statistics (Database).

StatLink https://stat.link/2d8if0

Iceland

Tourism in the economy and outlook for recovery

Prior to the COVID-19 pandemic, tourism was the major export earner in Iceland. In 2019, the sector accounted for ISK 470 billion in exports, equivalent to 35% of total export revenue and 67% of total service exports. The sector also directly contributed 8.1% to total GDP and employed 28 813 people, representing 15.9% of the workforce. In 2020, tourism's contribution to total GDP fell to 3.6%, and the sector employment fell to 20 426 people.

International tourists have been the driver of Iceland's tourism economy, accounting for 73% of total tourism expenditure in 2019. Following the COVID-19 pandemic, tourism came to a halt, with 486 000 international tourists in 2020, a 78% decline from the previous year. International tourism receipts fell to ISK 89.2 billion. This rebounded in 2021, but international tourists remained 68% below 2019 levels.

Domestic tourism has traditionally been stable but increased considerably during the pandemic due to border restrictions. Domestic tourists increased to 1.2 million in 2021, 70% higher than in 2019.

The recovery of the sector has been stronger than expected. In 2022, Iceland expects to receive 1.7 million international arrivals and a significant rise in tourism's contribution to GDP.

Tourism governance and funding

The Ministry of Culture and Business Affairs is responsible for developing tourism policy and co-ordinating governmental bodies' work. The Department of Business Affairs and Tourism is the lead department and oversees the operation and performance of the Icelandic Tourist Board. The Icelandic Tourist Board's responsibilities include implementing government tourism policy, planning and support for regional development, licensing and monitoring licensed activities, data collection, processing and presentation, safety, quality and consumer protection in tourism, and administration of the Tourist Site Protection Fund.

Visit Iceland is the official destination marketing organisation charged with attracting visitors to the country. It is part of Business Iceland, a public-private partnership overseen by the Ministry for Foreign Affairs. Business Iceland was established to promote Icelandic exports, foreign direct investments and Iceland as a tourism destination. A revised Tourism Council will partially take over the role of the Tourism Task Force, which co-ordinated implementing the actions in Iceland's Road Map for Tourism during the period 2015-20. The Tourism Council includes representatives from the ministries of tourism, finance, environment and infrastructure, the Icelandic Association of Local Authorities and the Icelandic Travel Industry Association.

Local municipalities are responsible for the planning and management of many visitor attractions. With the support of the Icelandic Regional Development Institute, associations of municipalities operate Development Agencies which deliver tourism projects. Destination management organisations established in each region as public-private entities are responsible for developing and implementing regional destination management plans and co-ordinating tourism priorities in collaboration with stakeholders, including Business Iceland and the Icelandic Tourist Board, which provides financial support.

The general overall budget allocated to tourism in 2020 was ISK 2 billion. In 2021 this was increased to ISK 2.6 billion, allocated as follows: ISK 679.6 million to the Icelandic Tourist Board, ISK 823 million to the Tourist Site Protection Fund and ISK 1 billion for tourism services, of which ISK 300 million was for marketing and promotion. An additional ISK 750 million was added to the tourism services budget for one year.

In 2020 an additional ISK 3 billion was added to the tourism services budget for one year for marketing and promotion, including domestic travel vouchers and international marketing campaigns.

Iceland: Organisational chart of tourism bodies

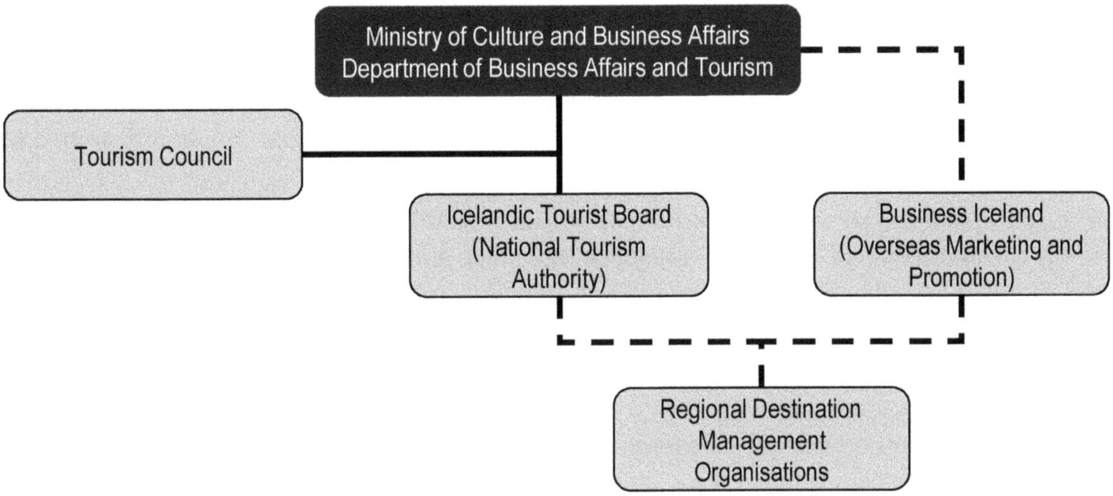

Source: OECD, adapted from the Ministry of Culture and Business Affairs, 2022.

Tourism policies and programmes

The Tourism Policy Framework 2020-30, published in 2019, sets out the future vision for tourism in Iceland. The framework has an overarching focus on sustainable development and is Iceland's policy document for tourism development. It emphasises value creation, innovation, quality of life for locals, a unique visitor experience, environmental conservation and a reduced carbon footprint. Work on a new action-oriented tourism strategy for 2020-25 was underway until the pandemic hit.

Iceland's main policy priority is to devise a new action-oriented strategy, considering new circumstances post-COVID-19, to support its Tourism Policy Framework to 2030. Another priority is implementing the Tourism Balance Axis, a measurement tool for the carrying capacity of the environment, infrastructure, society and economy. Until a new tourism strategy is in place, the following initiatives continue:

- Development of the Varða/Sites of Merit programme launched in 2021. The programme aims to lay a foundation for exemplary holistic destination management at popular tourist sites. Þingvellir National Park was the first destination awarded the Sites of Merit label in June 2022.
- Investment in infrastructure at tourist sites through the Tourist Site Protection Fund and the National Infrastructure Plan.
- Formalisation of regional destination management organisations and updates to regional destination management plans.
- Improvements to the regulatory framework of the tourism sector, following an OECD Competition Assessment Review of Laws and Regulations published in 2020.

- Implementation of a new law on the utilisation of state-owned land for commercial purposes, enabling a concessions regime for tour operations.
- Digitalisation projects, including a digital toolbox mapping the digital needs of tourism companies and a digital sandbox, a platform promoting collaboration between tourism and technology companies.
- Tourism-specific policy actions to reduce carbon emissions, including plans to increase the proportion of rental cars running on alternative fuels and the electrification of harbours.
- A renewed research plan by the Icelandic Tourist Board, including a study on the adaptability and resilience of the tourism industry and the development of macroeconomic and tourism forecasting models.
- Continued marketing support in 2022, including an ISK 550 million addition to the international marketing campaign for Iceland as a destination and marketing support for the airports at Egilsstaðir and Akureyri in East and North Iceland to encourage tourist distribution around Iceland.

Iceland's main lesson from the COVID-19 crisis is how important it is to diversify its economy, having become very dependent on tourism. Regarding specific COVID-19 measures, the reduced work-hour scheme effectively sustained employer-employee relations and prevented high unemployment. Other successful measures included loans for SMEs, simpler rules on financial restructuring and the establishment of a Package Travel Guarantee fund (see box below).

Throughout the pandemic, steps have been taken to support a competitive and sustainable tourism recovery. These steps include increased funding for infrastructure at tourist sites, airport extensions and improvements, road and harbour improvements, infrastructure to speed up the electrification of harbours and rental car fleet, additional funding for innovation, the launch of domestic travel vouchers and an international marketing campaign. Statistical indicators show that international visitors stay longer and spend more than pre-COVID-19. There are also opportunities to continue to focus more on the domestic market in the future.

Package Travel Guarantee Fund in Iceland

Package travel organisers in Iceland suffered heavily during the COVID-19 crisis. The insolvency protection system for package travel proved to be burdensome for package travel organisers following cancellations, reimbursements and issuing vouchers due to COVID-19.

To support the recovery of the sector and to make the insolvency system competitive with other systems in the EU area, Iceland supported the establishment of a Package Travel Guarantee Fund in June 2021. The Fund is mandated by law for all package travel providers. The establishment of the Fund reduces the heavy financial commitments of the previous system and provides better protection for consumers.

The Fund is a self-owned private institution financed by companies active in the sector. Package travel organisers pay an annual fee to the Fund, which becomes part of the Fund´s equity and helps it grow and provide secure protection for consumers. Although established during the pandemic, the Fund is not a temporary but a permanent measure.

Statistical Profile

Iceland: Domestic, inbound and outbound tourism

	2017	2018	2019	2020	2021
TOURISM FLOWS, THOUSAND					
Domestic tourism					
Total domestic trips	..	..	..	..	..
Overnight visitors (tourists)	686	701	699	890	1 191
Same-day visitors (excursionists)	..	..	..	..	..
Nights in all types of accommodation	1 098	1 105	1 090	1 468	1 939
Hotels and similar establishments	599	661	581	745	1 097
Other collective establishments	451	402	450	586	726
Private accommodation	49	42	59	137	116
Inbound tourism[1]					
Total international arrivals	2 690	..	2 598	489	717
Overnight visitors (tourists)	2 225	2 316	2 202	486	698
Same-day visitors (excursionists)	466 e	..	189	2	19
Top markets					
United States	576	695	464	53	227
Germany	156	139	132	44	64
United Kingdom	323	298	262	102	54
Nordic Countries	182	165	149	39	41
France	100	97	98	28	37
Nights in all types of accommodation	7 277	7 444	7 317	1 828	3 072
Hotels and similar establishments	4 974	5 200	5 211	1 275	2 142
Other collective establishments	1 527	1 519	1 389	367	702
Private accommodation	776	724	716	186	228
Outbound tourism					
Total international departures	..	..	..	..	..
Overnight visitors (tourists)	638	668	631	133	219
Same-day visitors (excursionists)	..	..	..	..	..
Top destinations					
..	..	..	..	..	..
..	..	..	..	..	..
..	..	..	..	..	..
..	..	..	..	..	..
..	..	..	..	..	..
TOURISM RECEIPTS AND EXPENDITURE, MILLION ISK					
Inbound tourism					
Total international receipts	501 446	519 374	467 864	89 198	..
International travel receipts	321 721	337 272	328 278	89 198 p	..
International passenger transport receipts	179 725	182 103	139 586	..	..
Outbound tourism					
Total international expenditure	184 233	206 964	211 109	70 957	..
International travel expenditure	177 049	198 178	192 782	70 957 p	..
International passenger transport expenditure	7 184	8 786	18 327	..	..

.. Not available; e Estimated value; p Provisional data

1. Arrivals from demand side surveys; Nights from supply side surveys.

Source: OECD Tourism Statistics (Database).

StatLink https://stat.link/wi1ay7

Iceland: Enterprises and employment in tourism

	Number of establishments[1]	Number of persons employed[2]				
	2021	2017	2018	2019	2020	2021
Total	**2 147**	..	..	..	..	..
Tourism industries	**2 147**	**28 854**	**30 474**	**28 813**	**20 426**	**20 258**
Accommodation services for visitors	562	6 646	6 768	6 663	4 051	4 076
Hotels and similar establishments	401	6 133	6 228	6 147	3 722	3 713
Food and beverage serving industry	672	10 023	9 815	9 269	7 286	8 163
Passenger transport	163	6 008	7 438	6 484	4 637	3 780
Air passenger transport	16	..	..	..	..	..
Railways passenger transport	0	0	0	0	0	0
Road passenger transport	126	..	..	..	..	..
Water passenger transport	21	..	..	..	..	..
Passenger transport supporting services	..	2 709	1 931	1 609	1 231	1 167
Transport equipment rental	52	1 201	1 210	1 131	793	774
Travel agencies and other reservation services industry	463	2 978	2 948	2 830	1 679	1 608
Cultural industry	55	532	559	550	532	522
Sports and recreation industry	143	735	791	839	720	737
Retail trade of country-specific tourism characteristic goods	..	..	..	..	..	..
Other country-specific tourism industries	37	732	946	1 047	730	598
Other industries	..	..	..	..	..	..

.. Not available
1. Data refer to number of enterprises.
2. Data refer to number of employees.
Source: OECD Tourism Statistics (Database).

StatLink https://stat.link/hkcd9z

Iceland: Internal tourism consumption

Million ISK

	2021		
	Domestic tourism expenditure	Inbound tourism expenditure	Internal tourism consumption
Total	**148 654 p**	**188 762 p**	**348 656 p**
Consumption products	**.. p**	**.. p**	**.. p**
Tourism characteristic products	113 271 p	154 418 p	278 890 p
Accommodation services for visitors	43 174 p	40 138 p	83 553 p
Food and beverage serving services	12 137 p	20 447 p	32 760 p
Passenger transport services	12 745 p	33 883 p	50 234 p
Air passenger transport services	11 130 p	28 020 p	41 999 p
Railways passenger transport services	.. p	.. p	.. p
Road passenger transport services	1 520 p	4 255 p	6 388 p
Water passenger transport services	94 p	1 608 p	1 847 p
Passenger transport supporting services	.. p	.. p	.. p
Transport equipment rental services	7 013 p	21 997 p	29 278 p
Travel agencies and other reservation services industry	16 846 p	30 587 p	47 699 p
Cultural services	6 336 p	1 855 p	8 191 p
Sports and recreation services	15 021 p	5 511 p	20 532 p
Country-specific tourism characteristic goods	.. p	.. p	.. p
Country-specific tourism characteristic services	.. p	.. p	6 643 p
Other consumption products	35 383 p	34 344 p	69 766 p
Tourism connected products	.. p	.. p	.. p
Non-tourism related consumption products	35 383 p	34 344 p	69 766 p
Non-consumption products	**.. p**	**.. p**	**.. p**

.. Not available; p Provisional data
Source: OECD Tourism Statistics (Database).

StatLink https://stat.link/3tmk0o

Ireland

Tourism in the economy and outlook for recovery

Tourism is one of Ireland's most important sectors for revenue and jobs. The total value of tourism expenditure to the economy in 2019 (including domestic receipts and fares to Irish carriers) was EUR 9.5 billion, equivalent to 2.7% of GDP. In 2019, tourism-related sectors employed 284 838 people directly, 12.3% of national employment. The impacts of the COVID-19 pandemic saw the tourism share of employment fall to 10.3% in 2020.

In 2020, international tourists decreased by almost 80% compared to a record high of 9.4 million in 2019. This represented a significant reduction in tourism revenue, as inbound tourism generally accounts for 70% of total tourism revenue.

Despite declines, domestic tourism has become the main source of tourism revenue, generating over EUR 1.5 billion in 2020 and EUR 1.3 billion in 2021. There were an estimated 7.7 million domestic trips in 2020 and 5.7 million domestic overnight trips in 2021 (down 51.3% compared to 2019). Ireland estimates that domestic visitors represented over 85% of the country's total tourism economy in 2021.

Domestic tourism is expected to account for between 50% and 60% of the tourism economy in 2022, with international tourism expected to track at approximately 75% of 2019 levels. The medium to long-term outlook indicates that tourism in Ireland will return to 2019 levels by 2025 or 2026.

Tourism governance and funding

The Tourism Division of the Department of Tourism, Culture, Arts, Gaeltacht, Sport and Media sets the national tourism policy and provides strategic direction to support the growth of a competitive and sustainable tourism sector. Fáilte Ireland and Tourism Ireland operate under the responsibility of the Department to administer the national tourism policy.

Fáilte Ireland is the National Tourism Development Authority. Its role is to support the tourism sector and work to sustain Ireland as a high-quality and competitive tourism destination. It provides a range of practical business supports to help tourism businesses better manage and market their products and services and develop experiences in line with Fáilte Ireland's experience brands.

Tourism Ireland promotes tourism to the island of Ireland and is responsible for marketing the island of Ireland overseas as a holiday and business tourism destination. Tourism Ireland is accountable to the North South Ministerial Council, with funding being provided by the Department for the Economy in Northern Ireland and by the Department of Tourism, Culture, Arts, Gaeltacht, Sport and Media in Ireland.

Local Authorities (city and county councils) are active in many aspects of tourism, such as the organisation and funding of events and the development of public tourism infrastructure. All local authorities have an officer with responsibility for tourism to co-ordinate tourism development in each authority area.

The Hospitality and Tourism Forum was established by the Minister for Tourism and the Minister for Enterprise, Trade and Employment to engage with a wide spectrum of industry stakeholders to assess the continuing impact of the COVID-19 pandemic and to help improve understanding and responses to the crisis. It provides a platform for structured engagement between the Hospitality and Tourism sector, the tourism agencies and relevant Government Departments.

The overall central budget allocated to tourism amounted to EUR 184 million in 2020 and increased to EUR 221 million in 2021. Of the 2021 figure, EUR 2.4 million is allocated to the Department, EUR 154.8 million to Fáilte Ireland and EUR 63.8 million to Tourism Ireland. Local authorities may provide additional funds.

Ireland: Organisational chart of tourism bodies

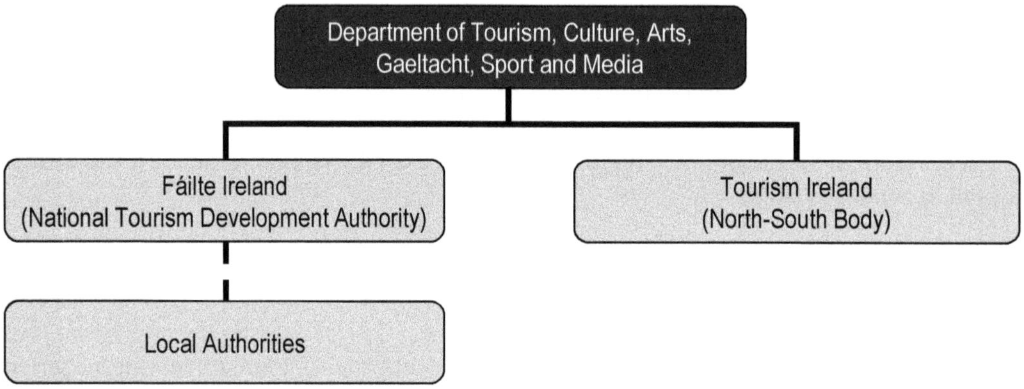

Source: OECD, adapted from the Department of Tourism, Culture, Arts, Gaeltacht, Sport and Media, 2022.

Tourism policies and programmes

The COVID-19 pandemic left Ireland's tourism sector in a weakened state but has provided an opportunity to address sustainable tourism development in a more meaningful way. Ireland is working towards developing a new national tourism policy that will mainstream sustainability. The Sustainable Tourism Working Group (see Box 3.2) will inform the development of this new policy and be consistent with sectoral climate change targets and commitments. The new national tourism policy will be published in 2023 and will cover 2023-30.

In the initial response to the pandemic, Ireland's Tourism Recovery Taskforce prepared a Tourism Recovery Plan 2020-23, which includes a set of recommendations on how the Irish Tourism sector can adapt and recover. A Recovery Oversight Group was established in December 2020 to monitor the implementation of the recommendations of the Tourism Recovery Plan and monitor the sector's recovery. The Group submitted its fourth report to the Minister for Tourism in September 2022. The report evaluated the progress made to date and made a number of further recommendations, particularly in relation to business supports. The Minister and the Tourism Agencies will continue to use the reports from the Recovery Oversight Group as important policy considerations in supporting the sector's recovery.

Ireland's Programme for Government, "Our Shared Future," includes a commitment to develop a new tourism initiative to aid recovery in the sector following the pandemic. This initiative will seek to build on the enduring strengths of Ireland's unique artistic and cultural tourism offering. Similarly, the Tourism Recovery Plan 2020-23, includes a recommendation to develop a Global Invitation programme to stimulate international demand. A global tourism marketing campaign has been proposed to assist with the delivery of these objectives. This project will provide an opportunity to aid the recovery in multiple sectors that have been particularly affected by the COVID-19 pandemic and the restrictions imposed to contain it.

Recruitment continues to be a significant challenge for the tourism sector, with up to two-thirds of businesses reporting reduced capacity due to staff shortages. A new recruitment marketing and awareness campaign was launched in early 2022 to help attract new staff to the sector. Several capability-building initiatives were also created to support businesses to leverage this campaign and stand out in a competitive labour market. A Learning Hub has been created to provide free high-quality, self-directed learning courses to help upskill staff and build business capability. These focus on upskilling new staff in core and basic skills, building employees' capability at the management level, and driving continuous professional development (see Box 2.12).

A new Employer Excellence Programme is also being developed to support businesses to drive great employee engagement and build their workplace's appeal. The programme aims to reposition the sector's employer brand so businesses can recruit and retain the talent and skills it needs to recover and grow.

Statistical Profile

Ireland: Domestic, inbound and outbound tourism

	2017	2018	2019	2020	2021
TOURISM FLOWS, THOUSAND					
Domestic tourism					
Total domestic trips	..	..	..	..	..
Overnight visitors (tourists)	9 626	10 919	11 621	7 721	5 663
Same-day visitors (excursionists)	..	..	..	..	..
Nights in all types of accommodation	25 539	28 393	29 469	23 518	17 886
Hotels and similar establishments	..	..	..	..	..
Other collective establishments	..	..	..	..	..
Private accommodation	..	..	..	..	..
Inbound tourism					
Total international arrivals	..	..	..	..	..
Overnight visitors (tourists)	8 722	9 273	9 353	..	..
Same-day visitors (excursionists)	..	..	..	..	..
Top markets					
United Kingdom	3 239	3 253	3 269	..	..
Other Europe	2 081	2 203	2 321	..	..
États-Unis et Canada	1 682	1 924	1 863	..	..
Germany	637	755	723	..	..
France	508	521	529	..	..
Nights in all types of accommodation	..	..	..	..	..
Hotels and similar establishments	..	..	..	..	..
Other collective establishments	..	..	..	..	..
Private accommodation	..	..	..	..	..
Outbound tourism					
Total international departures	7 939	8 276	8 814	2 417 e	2 314
Overnight visitors (tourists)	7 728	8 085	8 620	2 365 e	2 276
Same-day visitors (excursionists)	211	191	194	52 e	38
Top destinations					
..	..	..	..	..	..
..	..	..	..	..	..
..	..	..	..	..	..
..	..	..	..	..	..
..	..	..	..	..	..
TOURISM RECEIPTS AND EXPENDITURE, MILLION EUR					
Inbound tourism					
Total international receipts	12 541	13 015	13 297	3 674	..
International travel receipts	4 972	5 796	5 787	1 645	..
International passenger transport receipts	7 569	7 219	7 510	2 029	..
Outbound tourism					
Total international expenditure	5 897	6 557	7 459	2 148	..
International travel expenditure	5 814	6 474	7 375	2 071	..
International passenger transport expenditure	83	83	84	77	..

.. Not available; e Estimated value
Source: OECD Tourism Statistics (Database).

StatLink https://stat.link/7j096z

Ireland: Enterprises and employment in tourism

	Number of establishments[1]	Number of persons employed				
	2020	2017	2018	2019	2020	2021
Total	..	..	..	..	..	..
Tourism industries	**45 472**	**225 542**	**233 524**	**284 838**	..	..
Accommodation services for visitors	18 397	169 926	175 591	210 697	..	..
Hotels and similar establishments	..	..	..	..	..	..
Food and beverage serving industry	..	..	..	..	..	..
Passenger transport	14 282	21 841	22 684	25 792	..	..
Air passenger transport	..	..	..	..	..	..
Railways passenger transport	..	..	..	..	..	..
Road passenger transport	..	..	..	..	..	..
Water passenger transport	..	..	..	..	..	..
Passenger transport supporting services	..	..	..	..	..	..
Transport equipment rental	..	..	..	..	..	..
Travel agencies and other reservation services industry	1 484	8 172	8 632	10 070	..	..
Cultural industry	11 309	25 603	26 617	38 279	..	..
Sports and recreation industry	..	..	..	..	..	..
Retail trade of country-specific tourism characteristic goods	..	..	..	..	..	..
Other country-specific tourism industries	..	..	..	..	..	..
Other industries	..	..	..	..	..	..

.. Not available
1. Data refer to number of enterprises.
Source: OECD Tourism Statistics (Database).

StatLink https://stat.link/oa7wth

Ireland: Internal tourism consumption

Million EUR

	2007		
	Domestic tourism expenditure	Inbound tourism expenditure	Internal tourism consumption
Total	..	..	..
Consumption products	**3 142**	**3 637**	**6 779**
Tourism characteristic products	2 337	2 875	5 212
Accommodation services for visitors	228	672	900
Food and beverage serving services	983	932	1 915
Passenger transport services	762	1 062	1 824
Air passenger transport services	..	..	..
Railways passenger transport services	..	..	..
Road passenger transport services	..	..	..
Water passenger transport services	..	..	..
Passenger transport supporting services	..	..	..
Transport equipment rental services	..	..	..
Travel agencies and other reservation services industry	155	12	167
Cultural services	209	197	406
Sports and recreation services	..	..	..
Country-specific tourism characteristic goods	..	..	..
Country-specific tourism characteristic services	..	..	..
Other consumption products	805	762	1 567
Tourism connected products	..	..	..
Non-tourism related consumption products	..	..	..
Non-consumption products	..	..	..

.. Not available
Source: OECD Tourism Statistics (Database).

StatLink https://stat.link/ba17ty

Israel

Tourism in the economy and outlook for recovery

Tourism maintained a steady share of Israel's economy prior to COVID-19, and in 2019 directly accounted for 2.6% of GDP In 2019, a peak year for inbound tourism, direct tourism employment was estimated at approximately 149 900 jobs, or 3.8% of total employment. It is estimated that direct tourism jobs fell to 108 174 in 2021, while tourism's share of GDP fell to 1.1%.

International tourist arrivals fell 81.7% to 832 000 tourists in 2020. In 2021, this fell further to 397 000 arrivals, 91.3% below pre-pandemic levels. In 2021, the top source markets were the United States (37.5% of inbound travellers), France (10.6%) and the United Kingdom (8.1%).

Domestic tourism generally accounts for just over half of total tourism expenditure. Domestic tourists declined 52.2% to 3.9 million tourists in 2020 but fully recovered in 2021, with a record 8.6 million domestic tourists and 18.4 million domestic nights. Domestic tourism expenditure was ILS 20.4 million in 2021, 83% of total tourism expenditure in 2021.

Despite the recovery in domestic tourism, overall pre-COVID travel levels are not expected to return until 2023-24 after Israel fully opened its borders in May 2022.

Tourism governance and funding

The Ministry of Tourism is the national government entity responsible for steering tourism policy and the sector. The Ministry continuously engages with all parts of the tourism sector, putting particular emphasis on emergency support programmes for hotels and inbound tour operators and preparing SMEs for the recovery of domestic and inbound tourism. The Ministry co-operates with other relevant ministries, authorities and agencies on an ad-hoc basis and within the framework of joint steering committees.

Large local authorities usually have tourism policies co-ordinated with national policy, particularly in relation to domestic and inbound marketing activities. Smaller, mainly rural authorities, tend to cluster into regional tourism destination management organisations (DMOs) to develop more coherent products and enable more effective branding and marketing policies. The Ministry has a continuous working relationship with regional DMOs and tourism departments and co-ordinates marketing, product development and regional branding. The Ministry also assists local authorities in tourism development research and feasibility studies, especially for infrastructure development and zoning. The Ministry organises professional coaching and training programmes in product development and marketing for SMEs, with the active participation of regional DMOs.

The total tourism budget for 2022 is ILS 825 million, up from ILS 380 million in 2020 but still down from ILS 1.2 billion in 2018. The tourism budget is split into three areas of activity:

- Development of accommodation through grants to hotels (investment amounting to ILS 100 million in 2020-21, expected to increase to ILS 175 million in 2022).
- Development of public tourism infrastructure (ILS 180 million in 2020 and ILS 350 million in 2022).

Marketing (ILS 100 million in 2020-21 and expected to be ILS 200 million in 2022) In addition, ILS 90 million is used by the Ministry for various needs such as planning strategy, administration of the Ministry's employees, and industry training.

Israel: Organisational chart of tourism bodies

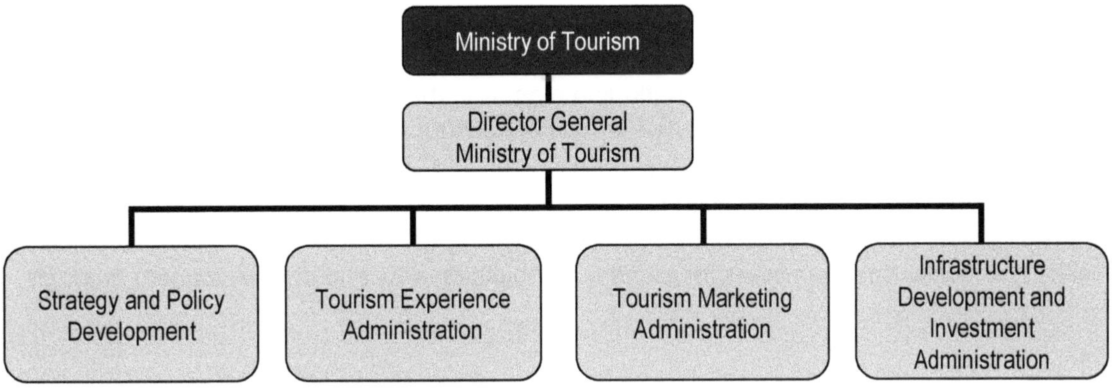

Source: OECD, adapted from the Ministry of Tourism, 2022.

Tourism policies and programmes

The Ministry of Tourism is in the process of updating its 2030 strategy in light of COVID-19. An updated set of 2030 targets and intermediate objectives for 2022-25 are being formulated.

The Ministry is developing new sub-products in rural areas, alongside Wine Tourism and Adventure Tourism, focusing on programmes that will bring a more diverse and customised product. Current activities are based on the understanding that tourists are looking for more sustainable products in the open air and outside cities.

The Ministries of Tourism, Health, Foreign Affairs and Transportation helped co-ordinate tourism-related policy and action during the pandemic. Upon the outbreak of COVID-19, the Ministry of Tourism liaised with the Ministry of Health to maximise the potential for resuming and expanding tourism activities.

In 2021, a pilot for inbound tourist groups was initiated in co-ordination with the Airport Authorities and the Ministries of Health and Transportation. This allowed a small number of fully vaccinated tourist groups to enter Israel and tour the country. This programme was cancelled after all limitations were lifted in March 2022.

The Ministry is in continued contact with other relevant Ministries and the tourism sector for contingency planning, should COVID-19 or other sources of danger require the reintroduction of limitations. The Ministry is also part of the Israeli Governmental preparedness planning for future health and safety threats, including earthquake and other emergency mitigation and response planning.

The Ministry of Tourism has now redefined its goals for crisis management, recovery, and activity to include:

- **Preservation of infrastructure and human capital:** the Ministry has invested in developing public tourism infrastructure and increasing the supply of accommodation in Israel, aided by additional investment from other public bodies and the private sector. To minimise the damage to infrastructure and protect the tourism workforce throughout the pandemic, the Ministry allocated funding for assistance to hotels, guided tours, increasing domestic tourism, assisting inbound tour operators, marketing activities abroad, business support and working to open up international routes for tourists.

- **Preparation for recovery from the crisis and return of inbound tourism:** the Ministry is executing its action plans for a speedy recovery of inbound tourism traffic. The plan includes action on three levels: 1) increasing demand among potential target audiences abroad by planning online and digital campaigns and strengthening PR operations, 2) developing marketing channels with agents and wholesalers abroad and with online travel agencies, and 3) restoring collaborations with airlines and encouraging them to open new routes. The Ministry has also introduced a joint recruitment platform, backed by a marketing plan, with the hotel sector and Israel Airport Authority. The objective is to alleviate the acute human capital shortages at airports and hotels.
- **Development and improvement of tourist products for the well-being of the tourist:** activities include the development of public tourism infrastructure to generate tourism traffic, encouraging new and diversified tourist accommodation, promoting the improvement of maintenance at tourist sites, promoting strategic plans for tourism and building new and diverse tourism products.

Statistical Profile

Israel: Domestic, inbound and outbound tourism

	2017	2018	2019	2020	2021
TOURISM FLOWS, THOUSAND					
Domestic tourism					
Total domestic trips	..	..	..	..	..
Overnight visitors (tourists)	8 043	8 071	8 243	3 941	8 575
Same-day visitors (excursionists)	..	..	..	..	..
Nights in all types of accommodation	17 264	17 105	17 341	8 943	18 422
Hotels and similar establishments	14 531	14 482	14 589	7 474	15 585
Other collective establishments	2 038	2 005	2 142	999	2 138
Private accommodation	695	618	609	470	700
Inbound tourism					
Total international arrivals	3 863	4 390	4 905	887	402
Overnight visitors (tourists)	3 613	4 121	4 552	832	397
Same-day visitors (excursionists)	250	269	353	56	6
Top markets					
United States	806	898	1 008	206	149
France	312	346	377	59	42
United Kingdom	212	218	260	47	32
Germany	229	263	306	52	17
Russia	398	316	394	60	14
Nights in all types of accommodation	12 940	13 862	14 420	2 609	1 059
Hotels and similar establishments	12 177	13 018	13 621	2 191	866
Other collective establishments	698	770	735	403	178
Private accommodation	65	75	64	16	15
Outbound tourism					
Total international departures	7 597	8 473	9 179	1 544	3 022
Overnight visitors (tourists)	..	..	..	..	..
Same-day visitors (excursionists)	..	..	..	..	..
Top destinations					
..	..	..	..	..	..
..	..	..	..	..	..
..	..	..	..	..	..
..	..	..	..	..	..
..	..	..	..	..	..
TOURISM RECEIPTS AND EXPENDITURE, MILLION USD					
Inbound tourism					
Total international receipts	7 602	8 048	8 439	2 661	2 517
International travel receipts	6 834	7 225	7 600	2 500	2 301
International passenger transport receipts	768	823	839	161	216
Outbound tourism					
Total international expenditure	8 986	9 975	10 390	..	..
International travel expenditure	7 057	7 878	8 154	1 804	3 213
International passenger transport expenditure	1 929	2 097	2 236	371	656

.. Not available
Source: OECD Tourism Statistics (Database).

StatLink https://stat.link/wv3hjg

Israel: Enterprises and employment in tourism

	Number of establishments	Number of persons employed				
	2021	2017	2018	2019	2020	2021
Total	..	**142 300**	**141 140**	**149 900**	**117 670**	**108 174**
Tourism industries	..	**138 400**	**137 550**	**146 100**	**113 610**	**104 274**
Accommodation services for visitors	1 673	45 000	45 000	46 500	24 400	27 500
Hotels and similar establishments	437	..	..	..	..	..
Food and beverage serving industry	11 606	15 400	15 790	16 200	12 690	13 000
Passenger transport	..	17 300	18 080	20 760	18 920	14 300
Air passenger transport	..	11 900	12 900	15 130	13 660	9 630
Railways passenger transport	..	..	..	..	..	..
Road passenger transport	..	5 400	5 180	5 630	5 260	4 670
Water passenger transport	..	..	..	..	..	..
Passenger transport supporting services	..	..	..	..	..	..
Transport equipment rental	..	5 100	5 490	5 950	6 290	5 160
Travel agencies and other reservation services industry	1 226	22 100	20 330	19 610	16 650	11 530
Cultural industry	..	..	..	..	..	..
Sports and recreation industry	..	11 900	12 250	16 220	14 950	12 872
Retail trade of country-specific tourism characteristic goods	..	21 600	20 610	20 860	19 710	19 912
Other country-specific tourism industries	..	..	..	..	..	..
Other industries	..	**3 900**	**3 590**	**3 840**	**4 010**	**3 900**

.. Not available
Source: OECD Tourism Statistics (Database).

StatLink https://stat.link/3kiyc0

Israel: Internal tourism consumption

Million ILS

	2021		
	Domestic tourism expenditure	Inbound tourism expenditure	Internal tourism consumption
Total	..	..	..
Consumption products	**20 419**	**4 233**	**24 652**
Tourism characteristic products	..	..	..
Accommodation services for visitors	..	..	..
Food and beverage serving services	..	..	..
Passenger transport services	..	..	..
Air passenger transport services	..	..	..
Railways passenger transport services	..	..	..
Road passenger transport services	..	..	..
Water passenger transport services	..	..	..
Passenger transport supporting services	..	..	..
Transport equipment rental services	..	..	..
Travel agencies and other reservation services industry	..	..	..
Cultural services	..	..	..
Sports and recreation services	..	..	..
Country-specific tourism characteristic goods	..	..	..
Country-specific tourism characteristic services	..	..	..
Other consumption products	..	..	..
Tourism connected products	..	..	..
Non-tourism related consumption products	..	..	..
Non-consumption products	..	..	..

.. Not available
Source: OECD Tourism Statistics (Database).

StatLink https://stat.link/rzhmue

The statistical data for Israel are supplied by and under the responsibility of the relevant Israeli authorities. The use of such data by the OECD is without prejudice to the status of the Golan Heights, East Jerusalem and Israeli settlements in the West Bank under the terms of international law.

Italy

Tourism in the economy and outlook for recovery

Tourism is a key sector of the Italian economy. In 2019, tourism directly accounted for 6.2% of total GVA, or EUR 99.9 billion. Tourism directly employed 2.1 million people, contributing 8.8% of total employment and supported over 218 000 enterprises in 2019. The impacts of COVID-19 saw the direct contribution of tourism to Italy's GVA fall to 4.5% in 2020.

In 2020, international arrivals decreased by 61.0% to 25.2 million, while domestic tourism decreased by 37.1% to 34.1 million. An estimated EUR 27.0 billion was lost in tourism expenditure from international visitors. In 2021, international arrivals remained 58.3% below 2019 levels, totalling 26.9 million tourists. The top source markets in 2021 were Germany (17.1%), France (14.5%) and Austria (9.3%). Tourism expenditure from international tourism was EUR 21.2 billion in 2021, 52% below 2019.

Domestic tourism is an important part of the Italian tourism sector, accounting for 56.4% of total tourism expenditure in 2019. Domestic tourism has rebounded more strongly recording, 37.2 million tourists in 2021, 31.5% below pre-pandemic levels.

Tourism governance and funding

A new Ministry dedicated to tourism was created in 2021. The Ministry of Tourism is responsible for national strategic co-ordination, implementation of development plans, promotion of initiatives to enhance the tourism offer, planning assistance mechanisms for tourists, and playing a leading role in innovation. The Ministry supports and supervises the National Agency for Tourism (ENIT, which oversees the promotion and marketing of the national image and brand) and Club Alpino Italiano (responsible for promoting knowledge of the mountains and safeguarding their natural environment).

Each Italian region has legislative powers and adopts triennial plans. These are organised around annual programmes that define responsibilities, objectives and guidelines for tourism management. Regions and autonomous provinces gather in the "Unified Conference", a public body which ensures strategic and united collaboration between central authorities and local institutions. The main responsibilities of regions include:

- Organisation and distribution of functions between the region, provinces, and municipalities.
- Regulation of tour operators and accommodation facilities, including their standardisation at the regional level.
- Promotion of the image of the region at national and international levels.
- Promotion of projects of regional interest directed at different levels of the supply chain.
- Collection and management of regional tourism statistics and visitor satisfaction surveys.

The Italian Budget Law for 2022 created the Unique National Tourism Fund (FUNT), with a budget of EUR 120 million for 2022-23 and EUR 40 million for 2024 (see Box 1.7).

Italy: Organisational chart of tourism bodies

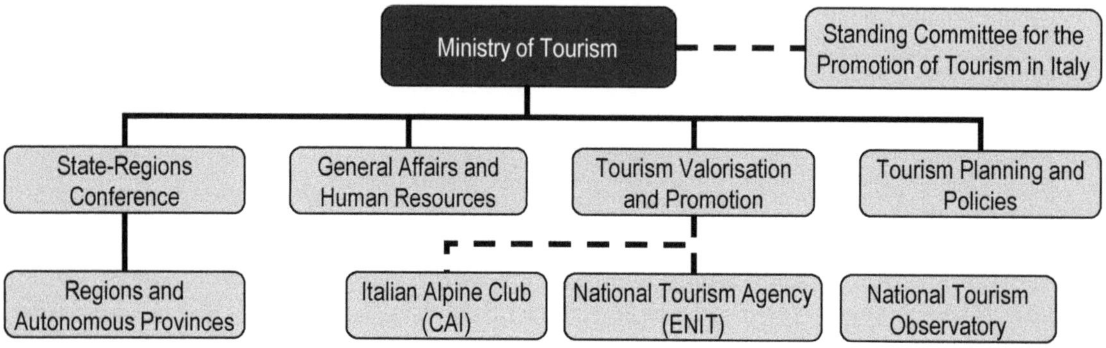

Source: OECD, adapted from the Ministry of Tourism, 2022.

Tourism policies and programmes

The Ministry of Tourism has implemented various measures to respond to the COVID-19 crisis. Short-term measures focused on public health issues and initiatives to mitigate the economic and social impact of the crisis on businesses and workers (over EUR 2.3 billion). These included economic stimulus packages to provide financial liquidity, fiscal and tax relief measures to companies along the tourism supply chain and income continuity for tourism workers.

Italy's National Recovery and Resilience Plan (NRRP) was developed in line with the Strategic Tourism Plan 2017-22 and presents a strategic framework to face the structural challenges of the sector while adapting national tourism strategies to the policy context emerging after the COVID-19 crisis. In this context, the NRRP is the main medium to long-term strategic document guiding the development of the tourism sector during the period 2021-26.

The Strategic Tourism Plan 2017-22 is receiving an update in 2022. While digital transformation was included in the 2017-22 plan, the COVID-19 crisis highlighted that low levels of digitalisation are a key limiting factor for the competitiveness and resilience of operators.

The crisis also highlighted the necessity to address the fragmentation of the Italian tourism ecosystem, particularly the regional differences, including the gap between large and small attractions and operators of the supply chain. There is a need to invest in training programmes directed at SMEs, support them in the digitalisation of their offer, increase competitiveness and productivity, and provide tools that address inclusion and sustainability in the provision of services.

For these reasons, a revision and updating of strategies became necessary. Priority pillars for the New Strategic Plan 2023-27 are:

- **A shared governance and monitoring model:** as tourism is constitutionally a subject of residual competence for regions, there is a need for an increased focus on a shared model of governance and monitoring. This aims to create and consolidate a participatory and effective decision-making process, ensuring continuity of action even in emergencies due to outside factors.
- **Digital tourism:** this pillar concerns the digitalisation and innovation of the tourism ecosystem and the implementation of projects such as the Tourism Digital Hub. Digitalisation affects the entire supply and value chains of the tourism product. It must arise through a process of sharing better transition experiences from a 'classic' type of tourism to an 'innovative' tourism. This is also made available through SME incubation tools at the community level.
- **A sustainable and integrated tourism system:** this pillar involves promoting culturally and environmentally sustainable growth. The tourism model should incorporate circularity, protection

of biodiversity, and access to sustainable transport and contribute to the Green Deal's decarbonisation objectives and a more sustainable global economy.

This pillar includes 'proximity tourism', the promotion of sustainable tourist transportation, intermodality and facilitating local public transport access for tourists, the exchange of experiences between different localities and territories on sustainable tourism models and support for the adoption of circular economy models and sustainable waste management systems in tourist destinations.

- **Tourism for all, in terms of safety, accessibility and quality:** this pillar requires encouraging the recovery and growth of the individual and the community. Tourism is a powerful tool for developing communities and enhancing heritage and territorial specificities. It is an important driving force for retaining and attracting jobs and businesses.

  Quality must be sought in the product offered at any level, with a particular focus on the high-end range, to enhance - from a tourist perspective - manufacturing excellence and the traditions of making. The main tourist products (e.g. MICE tourism, wellness tourism, health tourism, ecotourism, school tourism, cultural and religious tourism, and tourism for shopping) are covered in this strategic category.
- **Offering a high-level education:** offering training through an in-depth study of existing courses and new thematic specialisation schools (e.g. mountain, marine and cultural offers). This includes training in the fields of hospitality, attraction and tourism organisation at a high level. Training paths from vocational schools to technical high schools, universities and postgraduate programmes must be clearly traced.

To draft the new Strategic Plan, thematic working tables involving different stakeholders will be established to examine each of the five strategic lines of the Plan.

Statistical Profile

Italy: Domestic, inbound and outbound tourism

	2017	2018	2019	2020	2021
TOURISM FLOWS, THOUSAND					
Domestic tourism[1]					
Total domestic trips	121 851	145 307	132 858	74 654	73 000
Overnight visitors (tourists)	53 647	62 861	54 253	34 130	37 183
Same-day visitors (excursionists)	68 203	82 446	78 604	40 524	35 817
Nights in all types of accommodation	209 970	212 334	216 077	143 003	183 055
Hotels and similar establishments	176 666	179 432	188 592	122 346	158 150
Other collective establishments	33 305	32 903	27 485	20 658	24 905
Private accommodation	..	..	..	..	..
Inbound tourism					
Total international arrivals	89 931	93 229	95 399	38 419	40 186
Overnight visitors (tourists)	58 253	61 567	64 513	25 190	26 888
Same-day visitors (excursionists)	31 678	31 661	30 886	13 229	13 298
Top markets					
Germany	12 451	13 518	13 951	5 161	4 604
France	7 202	7 641	7 978	3 687	3 910
Austria	3 690	4 020	4 309	2 034	2 488
Switzerland	3 309	3 216	..	1 561	1 415
United Kingdom	4 932	5 659	6 006	1 756	909
Nights in all types of accommodation	365 939	384 426	398 963	182 214	208 525
Hotels and similar establishments	170 412	177 738	175 649	54 228	53 537
Other collective establishments	56 659	66 547	73 335	25 543	32 700
Private accommodation	138 868	140 141	149 980	102 444	122 288
Outbound tourism					
Total international departures	60 042	61 195	62 207	21 448	17 588
Overnight visitors (tourists)	31 805	33 347	34 703	11 960	12 354
Same-day visitors (excursionists)	28 237	27 848	27 505	9 489	5 234
Top destinations					
France	5 525	5 787	5 631	2 522	2 667
Spain	3 120	3 567	3 694	943	1 648
Germany	2 769	3 048	3 517	1 396	1 155
Austria	2 219	2 191	2 327	1 025	709
Switzerland	1 565	1 182	1 193	596	526
TOURISM RECEIPTS AND EXPENDITURE, MILLION EUR					
Inbound tourism					
Total international receipts	41 038	43 860	46 440	17 708	..
International travel receipts	39 155	41 712	44 302	17 332	..
International passenger transport receipts	1 884	2 148	2 138	376	..
Outbound tourism					
Total international expenditure	30 649	31 972	33 896	11 455	..
International travel expenditure	24 557	25 485	27 100	9 577	..
International passenger transport expenditure	6 091	6 487	6 796	1 878	..

.. Not available

1. Trips from demand side surveys; Nights from supply side surveys.

Source: OECD Tourism Statistics (Database).

StatLink https://stat.link/9qda6y

Italy: Enterprises and employment in tourism

	Number of establishments	Number of persons employed				
	2021	2017	2018	2019	2020	2021
Total	..	..	..	..	..	..
Tourism industries	..	**2 099 565**	..	**2 136 578**	..	..
Accommodation services for visitors	220 457	504 030	..	524 528	..	..
Hotels and similar establishments	217 889	302 488	..	315 698	..	..
Food and beverage serving industry	..	1 075 932	..	1 080 934	..	..
Passenger transport	..	182 534	..	184 591	..	..
Air passenger transport	..	14 033	..	15 172	..	..
Railways passenger transport	..	31 194	..	31 001	..	..
Road passenger transport	..	99 196	..	96 887	..	..
Water passenger transport	..	38 111	..	41 531	..	..
Passenger transport supporting services	..	..	..	..	..	..
Transport equipment rental	..	10 931	..	12 948	..	..
Travel agencies and other reservation services industry	..	48 607	..	52 051	..	..
Cultural industry	..	128 322	..	135 758	..	..
Sports and recreation industry	..	149 209	..	145 768	..	..
Retail trade of country-specific tourism characteristic goods	..	..	..	..	..	..
Other country-specific tourism industries	..	..	..	..	..	..
Other industries	..	..	..	..	..	..

.. Not available
Source: OECD Tourism Statistics (Database).

StatLink https://stat.link/omei6s

Italy: Internal tourism consumption
Million EUR

	2019		
	Domestic tourism expenditure	Inbound tourism expenditure	Internal tourism consumption
Total	..	..	..
Consumption products	**71 589**	**55 437**	**164 012**
Tourism characteristic products	55 313	42 195	134 328
Accommodation services for visitors	16 438	16 951	59 863
Food and beverage serving services	12 169	10 683	23 913
Passenger transport services	9 665	3 404	17 440
Air passenger transport services	3 543	1 810	8 381
Railways passenger transport services	2 038	360	3 295
Road passenger transport services	2 020	790	3 256
Water passenger transport services	2 064	444	2 508
Passenger transport supporting services	..	..	..
Transport equipment rental services	432	616	1 455
Travel agencies and other reservation services industry	3 528	515	6 673
Cultural services	411	585	1 744
Sports and recreation services	1 319	1 878	4 325
Country-specific tourism characteristic goods	11 351	7 564	18 915
Country-specific tourism characteristic services	..	..	..
Other consumption products	16 277	13 242	29 684
Tourism connected products	..	..	..
Non-tourism related consumption products	..	..	..
Non-consumption products	..	..	..

.. Not available
Source: OECD Tourism Statistics (Database).

StatLink https://stat.link/jgdr5k

Japan

Tourism in the economy and outlook for recovery

In 2019, tourism accounted for 2.0% of Japan's GDP. Following the COVID-19 pandemic, international visitors fell to 4.1 million in 2020, down by 87% from 2019. The inbound tourism expenditure in 2020 was JPY 1.2 trillion, a 77.1% decrease from the previous year. In 2021, international arrivals decreased to 246 000, a 99% decrease compared to pre-pandemic levels.

Asian markets remain the key source of inbound visitors for Japan, accounting for 3.4 million international tourists in 2020, or 83%.

The domestic market was relatively less impacted. In 2021, the total number of domestic overnight trips was 141.8 million, down 54.5% compared to 2019. According to the National Tourism Survey, this contributed to JPY 7 trillion, or 76.1% of total tourism expenditure.

Japan is working on the recovery of domestic demand as a first step in the recovery of the tourism economy.

Tourism governance and funding

The Japan Tourism Agency, an external body of the Ministry of Land, Infrastructure, Transport and Tourism, takes a leading role in tourism policy and its co-ordination. The Agency represents Japan on issues relating to tourism and the promotion of Japan as a tourist destination. It executes the Visit Japan campaign and other marketing activities through Japan National Tourism Organization (JNTO).

A Ministerial Council for the Promotion of Japan as a tourism-oriented country attended by all ministers unifies government efforts on tourism. A cross-ministerial budget has enabled numerous projects to be delivered. This budget has been maintained and now includes a subsidy to support historic landscapes, cultural tourism centres and national parks. The private sector is invited to regular Tourism Strategy Promotion Council meetings as experts in the field to give their opinion on relevant topics.

Local government's role is to improve the attractiveness of local destinations. The national government supports regional initiatives by providing statistical data, initiating area-wide co-operation and supporting regional development. Destination management organisations, in co-operation with stakeholders, including national and local governments, formulate and co-ordinate the implementation of strategies for destinations.

The Japan Tourism Agency's budget for 2022 was JPY 142.6 billion (twice the 2019 budget of JPY 71.1 billion). This includes JPY 8 billion from a new international tourist tax established in January 2019. The budget is broken down as follows:

- JPY 10 billion is allocated to create signature products and services which are profitable and contribute to the local economy.
- JPY 13 billion is allocated to preparing the receiving environment for inbound tourists (e.g. multi-language signboards, cashless systems, automation of immigration processes).

- JPY 100 billion is allocated towards revitalisation and adding higher value to existing tourist destinations.

In addition, the Japan National Tourism Organization receives an operating expenses subsidy of JPY 6.5 billion from the central government to implement projects, including promoting travel to Japan.

Japan: Organisational chart of tourism bodies

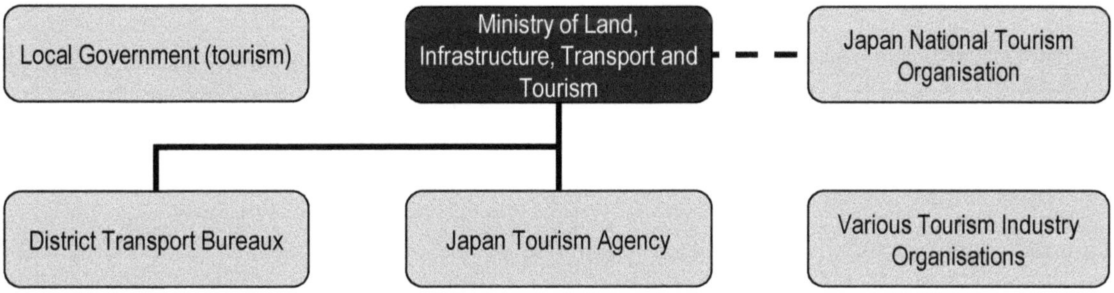

Source: OECD, adapted from the Ministry of Land, Infrastructure, Transport and Tourism, 2022.

Tourism policies and programmes

In December 2020, Japan formulated the Policy Plan to Prevent the Spread of Infection and Restore Demand for Tourism, focusing on the post-pandemic period. The plan includes improvements to productivity and the diversification of demand, both of which have been areas of concern for some time.

The main short-term focus is on stimulating demand for domestic travel (see box below). Key areas set out in the Policy Plan include:

- **The revival of hotels, traditional inns and tourist areas:** a subsidy and expanded financing system, specifically for restoring tourist facilities and creating high-quality environments based on regions' regeneration plans.
- **Product development:** provision of a richer product to attract domestic and international tourists, enriching tourism resources using digital technology, creating tourist sites that are profitable and attractive and enabling visitors to gain a deeper experience in local areas. This involves collaboration with tourism operators and destination management organisations, together with a wide range of stakeholders such as transport businesses, the fishing industry, agriculture, and local suppliers.
- **Popularisation of 'workcations':** creating travel opportunities and equalising travel demand by promoting workcations (work and vacation), bleisure (business and leisure), and the use of satellite offices by implementing model projects that improve the environment for both companies and the community.

While the number of tourism business closures increased significantly, the number of bankruptcies in the accommodation and travel sectors was fewer than during the global financial crisis (2008-09) and the Great East Japan Earthquake (2011) due to government support measures.

Additional measures for the revival of international business tourism include introducing new technology and knowledge necessary for hosting hybrid meetings, incentive, conference and events (MICE) events that combine face-to-face and online participation and the acquisition of international accreditation for infectious disease control at MICE-related facilities.

To address the issue of low productivity in the tourism sector (relative to other sectors), recovery plans involve initiatives to increase revenue through value-added services and introduce new demand while reducing the costs of digital transformation technologies. The aim is to have a stronger tourism sector with improved labour productivity and wages.

Various initiatives will be promoted in anticipation of the post-COVID era to reconstruct a tourism sector that supports local economies. Such initiatives include increasing repeat visitors and length of stay and creating a more profitable product.

Go To TRAVEL campaign in Japan

The Go To TRAVEL campaign was launched in July 2020 to stimulate the recovery of domestic travel demand during the pandemic by offering discounts on travel prices and issuing coupons for use in travel destinations. The scheme subsidised 35% of accommodation and day trip expenses for domestic travel. In addition, visitors received a regional coupon for 15% of the cost of accommodation or day trips, which could be used in the travel destination.

The campaign led to at least 88 million guest nights in accommodation facilities, with financial support totalling at least JPY 540 billion. The economic effects of the campaign impacted widely throughout Japan, with many tourist facilities reporting that the coupons led to an increase in sales and customers.

Due to the dynamic health situation, Japan introduced various support measures designed to create an environment in which it is easy for visitors to cancel their plans. Operators who do not charge cancellation fees are compensated financially in lieu of cancellation fees. The compensation is calculated at 35% of travel costs, or 50% for travel around the New Year period.

The Go To TRAVEL campaign was suspended at the end of 2020. However, the Government is implementing a regional tourism business financial support scheme and a discount programme for districts where the pandemic has subsided. Moreover, the Nationwide Travel Support programme started in October 2022 as a measure to continue to stimulate domestic travel demand.

Statistical Profile

Japan: Domestic, inbound and outbound tourism

	2017	2018	2019	2020	2021
TOURISM FLOWS, THOUSAND					
Domestic tourism[1]					
Total domestic trips	647 510	561 779	587 103	293 408	268 208
Overnight visitors (tourists)	323 328	291 052	311 624	160 703	141 768
Same-day visitors (excursionists)	324 182	270 727	275 478	132 705	126 440
Nights in all types of accommodation	429 906	443 726	480 265	311 309	313 457
Hotels and similar establishments	421 781	435 959	472 615	307 462	310 784
Other collective establishments	8 126	7 767	7 650	3 847	2 673
Private accommodation	..	..	..	..	..
Inbound tourism[2]					
Total international arrivals	28 691	31 192	31 882	4 116	246 p
Overnight visitors (tourists)	..	..	..	..	..
Same-day visitors (excursionists)	..	..	..	..	..
Top markets					
China (People's Republic of)	7 356	8 380	9 594	1 069	42 p
Viet Nam	..	..	..	..	27 p
United States	1 375	1 526	1 724	219	20 p
Korea	7 140	7 539	5 585	488	19 p
Nepal	..	..	..	..	12 p
Nights in all types of accommodation	79 691	94 275	115 656	20 345	4 317
Hotels and similar establishments	79 401	93 892	115 297	20 100	4 276
Other collective establishments	289	383	359	245	41
Private accommodation	..	..	..	..	..
Outbound tourism					
Total international departures	17 889	18 954	20 081	3 174	512
Overnight visitors (tourists)	..	..	..	..	..
Same-day visitors (excursionists)	..	..	..	..	..
Top destinations					
..	..	..	..	..	..
..	..	..	..	..	..
..	..	..	..	..	..
..	..	..	..	..	..
..	..	..	..	..	..
TOURISM RECEIPTS AND EXPENDITURE, MILLION JPY					
Inbound tourism					
Total international receipts	4 146 454	4 999 529	5 364 344	1 228 714	..
International travel receipts	3 819 713	4 648 362	5 020 374	1 142 541	..
International passenger transport receipts	326 741	351 168	343 970	86 174	..
Outbound tourism					
Total international expenditure	2 890 814	3 104 607	3 175 483	727 647	..
International travel expenditure	2 040 138	2 232 381	2 318 068	587 350	..
International passenger transport expenditure	850 677	872 226	857 416	140 298	..

.. Not available; p Provisional data

1. Trips from demand side surveys; Nights from supply side surveys.
2. Arrivals from demand side surveys; Nights from supply side surveys.

Source: OECD Tourism Statistics (Database).

StatLink https://stat.link/kd3pwy

Japan: Enterprises and employment in tourism

	Number of establishments[1]	Number of persons employed				
	2016	2017	2018	2019	2020	2021
Total	**796 440**	..	..	..	..	..
Tourism industries	**796 440**	**6 192 000**	**6 450 840**	**6 568 380**	..	..
Accommodation services for visitors	..	..	..	..	..	..
Hotels and similar establishments	48 963	586 380	638 330	658 050	..	..
Food and beverage serving industry	590 847	3 366 620	3 586 800	3 604 080	..	..
Passenger transport	33 571	937 560	910 530	924 260	..	..
Air passenger transport	922	45 040	56 670	56 170	..	..
Railways passenger transport	4 277	262 030	241 810	261 490	..	..
Road passenger transport	23 028	562 940	555 380	539 200	..	..
Water passenger transport	5 344	67 550	56 670	67 400	..	..
Passenger transport supporting services	66 772	630 490	646 060	651 540	..	..
Transport equipment rental	..	..	..	..	..	..
Travel agencies and other reservation services industry	..	..	..	..	..	..
Cultural industry	..	..	..	..	..	..
Sports and recreation industry	56 287	670 940	669 120	730 450	..	..
Retail trade of country-specific tourism characteristic goods	..	..	..	..	..	..
Other country-specific tourism industries	..	..	..	..	..	..
Other industries	**4 544 343**	**60 640 000**	**61 555 160**	**62 046 620**	..	..

.. Not available

1. Data refer to number of enterprises.

Source: OECD Tourism Statistics (Database).

StatLink https://stat.link/ug7f2w

Japan: Internal tourism consumption

Million JPY

	2019		
	Domestic tourism expenditure	Inbound tourism expenditure	Internal tourism consumption
Total	..	..	..
Consumption products	**23 369 164**	**5 343 761**	**29 145 212**
Tourism characteristic products	14 456 661	3 629 621	18 518 568
Accommodation services for visitors	4 003 348	1 498 966	5 934 601
Food and beverage serving services	3 002 180	1 100 095	4 102 275
Passenger transport services	5 636 276	810 257	6 446 532
Air passenger transport services	2 412 756	360 706	2 773 462
Railways passenger transport services	2 490 048	365 337	2 855 384
Road passenger transport services	626 887	81 795	708 682
Water passenger transport services	106 585	2 419	109 004
Passenger transport supporting services	..	..	..
Transport equipment rental services	353 414	66 721	420 135
Travel agencies and other reservation services industry	352 212	24 352	376 563
Cultural services	394 119	64 758	458 877
Sports and recreation services	715 112	64 473	779 585
Country-specific tourism characteristic goods	..	..	..
Country-specific tourism characteristic services	..	..	..
Other consumption products	8 912 503	1 714 140	10 626 643
Tourism connected products	8 061 075	1 690 802	9 751 877
Non-tourism related consumption products	851 428	23 338	874 767
Non-consumption products	..	..	..

.. Not available

Source: OECD Tourism Statistics (Database).

StatLink https://stat.link/vslpbx

Korea

Tourism in the economy and outlook for recovery

Tourism is considered a sector for economic growth in Korea. In 2019 tourism directly contributed to 2.5% of total GDP. Tourism-related businesses employed 275 619 people in 2019, which fell to 191 005 people in 2020, representing 0.7% of total employment. Travel exports represented 11.5% of total service exports in 2020, down from 20.1% in 2019.

Following a record high of 17.5 million international arrivals in 2019, tourism was hit hard from the very start of the pandemic. In 2020, arrivals to Korea fell by 86% to 2.5 million and decreased further in 2021 to less than 1 million. The decrease in visitor volumes was reflected in a sharp decline in international expenditure, down 50.9% to USD 10.2 billion in 2020 and USD 10.3 billion in 2021.

Domestic tourism is generally an important sector for Korea, contributing approximately two-thirds of total tourism expenditure pre-pandemic. In 2020, domestic tourists fell 45% to 88.5 million. Domestic tourism recovered slightly in 2021, returning to 43.8% of pre-pandemic levels.

Tourism governance and funding

Since August 2018, tourism has been the responsibility of the Ministry of Culture, Sports and Tourism (MCST) with two main directorates:

- Tourism Policy Bureau, encompassing the Tourism Policy Division, Domestic Tourism Promotion Division, International Tourism Division and Tourism Service Enhancement Division.
- Tourism Industry Policy Bureau, comprised of the Tourism Industry Policy Division, Convergence Tourism Industry Division and Tourism Development Division.

The Ministry works closely with the Korea Tourism Organisation, a publicly funded national tourism organisation. The Council for National Tourism Strategy, chaired by the Prime Minister, was established to co-ordinate matters between 13 relevant Ministries, including Foreign Affairs, Maritime Affairs, and the Forestry Agency, regarding the strategic planning and promotion of tourism.

Korea has maintained a whole-of-government approach to tackling COVID-19. The Prime Minister heads the Central Disaster and Safety Countermeasures Headquarters Meeting, which comprises MCST, other relevant ministries, the seventeen provinces and major cities. In addition, the Ministry of Culture, Sports and Tourism is in close co-operation with the Ministry of Health and Welfare, Korea Disease Control and Prevention Agency, Ministry of Foreign Affairs, and relevant authorities under the Korea Disease Control and Prevention Agency Task Force to monitor the influx of COVID-19 confirmed cases from overseas.

In 2021, the Tourism Promotion and Development Fund had a total expenditure of approximately KRW 1 500 billion, including subsidies for tourism industry promotion, tourism infrastructure and other projects to attract foreign tourists. In addition, KRW 1 350 billion in 2020 and KRW 1 400 billion in 2021 were allocated to support the tourism sector, including:

- Provision of loans and redemption grace periods (KRW 2.8 billion).

- COVID-19 emergency relief funds (KRW 124 billion).
- Job retention support for tourism businesses and capacity building of tourism workers (KRW 710 billion).
- Tax reductions (KRW 70.1 billion).
- COVID-19 response supplies and travel facilitation campaigns (KRW 153 billion).

In February 2022, a supplementary budget of around USD 3 million supported the salaries of 33 000 tourism employees.

Korea: Organisational chart of tourism bodies

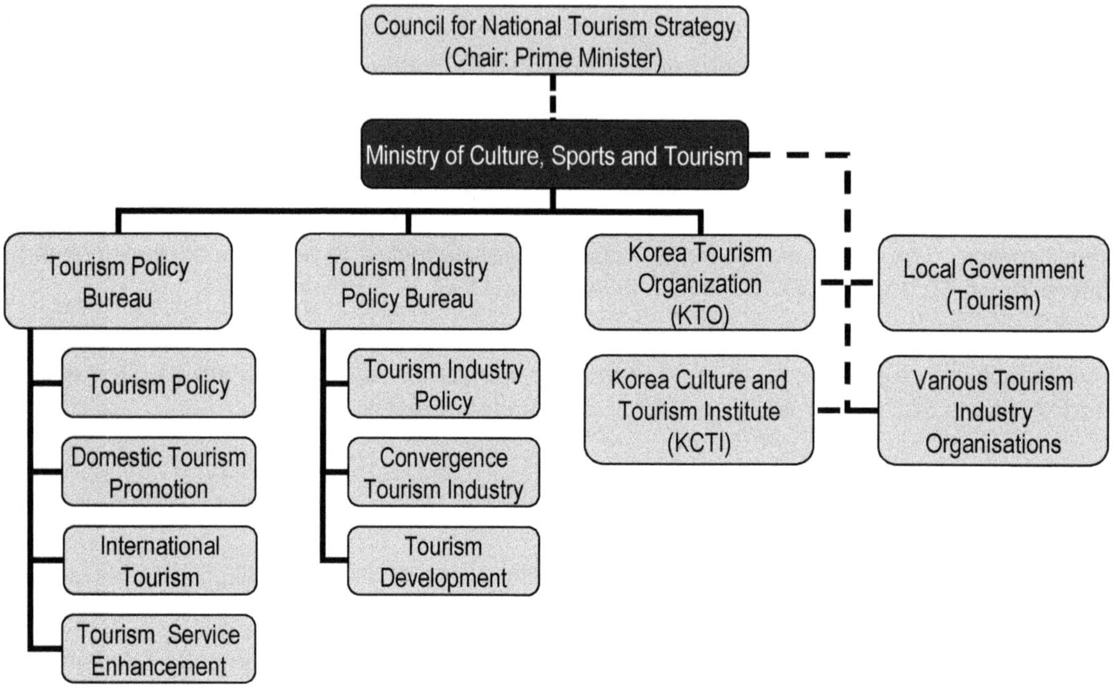

Source: OECD, adapted from the Ministry of Culture, Sports and Tourism, 2022.

Tourism policies and programmes

In light of the pandemic, the tourism sector in Korea continues to face a wide range of issues and challenges. Key challenges include: supporting the survival of tourism businesses and their workforce, strengthening the competitiveness of tourism SMEs and their workers in response to future tourism trends, increasing traveller confidence and managing the return of tourism safely.

The halt of international tourism presented an opportunity for the tourism sector to evaluate and identify how to use better and integrate new and innovative technologies and move towards a safe recovery. Korea announced its policy vision for 2022 in the Annual Plan titled "Preparing for the fast recovery of the tourism sector through safe travel", which identifies strategies to support the safe resumption of tourism, increase the attractiveness of Korea as a global tourist destination, and establish the infrastructure for future tourism.

To respond to key challenges, the Plan includes initiatives to assist tourism businesses and the workforce through financial aid, job retention, support for tourism businesses, capacity building for tourism workers, tax reductions, and health and hygiene support.

Korea has launched measures to support innovation in the travel sector's digital transformation by providing financial support in the form of vouchers to enhance the digital competency of tourism SMEs. This includes knowledge sharing with MSMEs and traditional travel operators to:

- Harness the digital transformation through new business model development.
- Undertake professional training on new trends.
- Provide ICT support and develop management skills, including human resources, tax, accounting, legal, and marketing.
- Create digital capacity-building programmes to understand systems, processes, digital content creation and planning.
- Provide practical application through theory and training practice.

To disperse pent-up demand for travel safely, Korea has harnessed a big data service platform that forecasts the degree of congestion of domestic tourist destinations to provide guidance on destination selection and reinforce safety protocols. Korea has also leveraged new and innovative technology to boost traveller confidence post-pandemic, maintain the interest of future travellers, and spur future demand for international tourism (see Box 1.10). Digital technology, such as the 'metaverse' platform and digital influencers, are being used to promote Korea as a safe destination.

Statistical Profile

Korea: Domestic, inbound and outbound tourism

	2017	2018	2019	2020	2021
TOURISM FLOWS, THOUSAND					
Domestic tourism					
Total domestic trips	284 966	311 153 |	344 750	225 199	..
Overnight visitors (tourists)	112 784	163 204 |	162 376	88 450	..
Same-day visitors (excursionists)	172 182	147 949 |	182 374	136 749	..
Nights in all types of accommodation	307 492	408 941 |	403 336	211 127	..
Hotels and similar establishments	..	..	..	..	..
Other collective establishments	..	..	..	..	..
Private accommodation	..	..	..	..	..
Inbound tourism					
Total international arrivals	13 336	15 347	17 503	2 519	967
Overnight visitors (tourists)	..	..	..	..	..
Same-day visitors (excursionists)	..	..	..	..	..
Top markets					
United States	869	968	1 044	220	204
China (People's Republic of)	4 169	4 790	6 023	686	170
Japan	2 311	2 949	3 272	431	15
Chinese Taipei	926	1 115	1 260	167	4
Hong Kong, China	658	684	695	89	1
Nights in all types of accommodation	..	..	..	..	..
Hotels and similar establishments	..	..	..	..	..
Other collective establishments	..	..	..	..	..
Private accommodation	..	..	..	..	..
Outbound tourism					
Total international departures	26 496	28 696	28 714	4 276	1 223
Overnight visitors (tourists)	..	..	..	..	..
Same-day visitors (excursionists)	..	..	..	..	..
Top destinations					
..	..	..	..	..	..
..	..	..	..	..	..
..	..	..	..	..	..
..	..	..	..	..	..
..	..	..	..	..	..
TOURISM RECEIPTS AND EXPENDITURE, MILLION USD					
Inbound tourism					
Total international receipts	17 173	23 104	25 457	11 775	..
International travel receipts	13 368	18 567	20 867	10 276	10 282
International passenger transport receipts	3 805	4 537	4 589	1 248	627
Outbound tourism					
Total international expenditure	34 453	38 022	35 340	16 705	..
International travel expenditure	31 691	35 133	32 739	16 092	13 851
International passenger transport expenditure	2 762	2 889	2 600	548	494

.. Not available; | Break in series
Source: OECD Tourism Statistics (Database).

StatLink https://stat.link/0c1ypm

Korea: Enterprises and employment in tourism

	Number of establishments	Number of persons employed[1]				
	2020	2017	2018	2019	2020	2021
Total	..	..	..	..	..	..
Tourism industries	**32 015 p**	**280 270**	**267 561**	**275 619**	**191 005 p**	..
Accommodation services for visitors	2 223 p	71 769	69 926	70 658	49 930 p	..
Hotels and similar establishments	..	..	..	..	..	..
Food and beverage serving industry	3 237 p	28 998	32 785	35 644	26 446 p	..
Passenger transport	..	..	..	..	..	..
Air passenger transport	..	..	..	..	..	..
Railways passenger transport	..	..	..	..	..	..
Road passenger transport	..	..	..	..	..	..
Water passenger transport	..	..	..	..	..	..
Passenger transport supporting services	..	..	..	..	..	..
Transport equipment rental	..	..	..	..	..	..
Travel agencies and other reservation services industry	16 660 p	107 209	99 077	103 311	61 784 p	..
Cultural industry	..	..	..	..	..	..
Sports and recreation industry	8 785 p	60 129	56 673	55 771	44 462 p	..
Retail trade of country-specific tourism characteristic goods	..	..	..	..	..	..
Other country-specific tourism industries	1 110 p	12 166	9 100	10 235	8 383 p	..
Other industries	..	..	..	..	..	..

.. Not available; p Provisional data
1. Data refer to number of employees.
Source: OECD Tourism Statistics (Database).

StatLink https://stat.link/p16c0f

Korea: Internal tourism consumption

Million KRW

	2019		
	Domestic tourism expenditure	Inbound tourism expenditure	Internal tourism consumption
Total	**57 088 564 p**	**30 467 398 p**	**96 139 553 p**
Consumption products	**56 611 040 p**	**30 369 552 p**	**95 564 182 p**
Tourism characteristic products	55 129 470 p	26 652 595 p	89 138 991 p
Accommodation services for visitors	6 152 958 p	4 917 722 p	11 100 697 p
Food and beverage serving services	17 047 188 p	3 909 557 p	20 956 745 p
Passenger transport services	7 846 449 p	7 070 601 p	14 917 050 p
Air passenger transport services	5 785 402 p	5 320 402 p	11 105 804 p
Railways passenger transport services	795 512 p	697 066 p	1 492 578 p
Road passenger transport services	1 069 258 p	1 025 983 p	2 095 241 p
Water passenger transport services	196 277 p	27 150 p	223 427 p
Passenger transport supporting services	0	0	0
Transport equipment rental services	9 857 849 p	624 362 p	10 482 211 p
Travel agencies and other reservation services industry	1 269 650 p	6 336 p	1 275 986 p
Cultural services	1 503 970 p	226 659 p	1 730 629 p
Sports and recreation services	995 422 p	1 842 295 p	2 843 333 p
Country-specific tourism characteristic goods	10 455 985 p	7 649 733 p	25 427 011 p
Country-specific tourism characteristic services	0	405 331 p	405 331 p
Other consumption products	1 481 570 p	3 716 957 p	6 425 191 p
Tourism connected products	327 000 p	2 503 795 p	4 057 459 p
Non-tourism related consumption products	1 154 570 p	1 213 162 p	2 367 732 p
Non-consumption products	**477 524 p**	**97 846 p**	**575 370 p**

p Provisional data
Source: OECD Tourism Statistics (Database).

StatLink https://stat.link/tysb7d

Latvia

Tourism in the economy and outlook for recovery

Tourism is an important sector in Latvia, directly contributing to 4.8% of Latvian GDP in 2019. Following the pandemic, total tourism expenditure in 2020 was down 73% from 2019 to EUR 145.4 million, and held steady in 2021 at EUR 145.5 million. In 2021, employment in tourism-related sectors represented 7.1% of the total workforce, down from 8.3% in 2019.

Inbound tourism recovery has been limited: the total number of international tourists in 2021 was 24.9% less than in 2020, totalling 478 000 tourists – 75.3% below 2019 levels. Latvia's top source markets are the neighbouring countries of Lithuania, Estonia and Russia, which contributed to 60% of 2020 international arrivals, up 18% from 2019.

Domestic tourism is an important pillar of Latvian tourism. Domestic tourists totalled 2.5 million in 2019. In 2021, 2.4 million domestic tourists were recorded, with a total expenditure of EUR 163.3 million.

Latvia aims to bring tourism back to pre-pandemic levels by 2024. However, the impacts of Russia's war in Ukraine and energy crisis in Europe risk further delays to the full return of tourism.

Tourism governance and funding

The Ministry of Economics is responsible for developing national tourism policy and organising and co-ordinating its implementation. The Ministry supervises the Investment and Development Agency of Latvia, which is responsible for implementing tourism policy and promoting Latvia at national and international levels.

The Ministry (along with the Investment and Development Agency) co-operates actively with the regions of Latvia via four regional tourism associations. It co-operates with local municipalities and tourism information centres as required. Regional and local authorities take part in creating the Latvian Tourism marketing strategy, marketing campaigns and printed and digital informative materials.

The Ministry of Economics works closely with the Latvian Hotel and Restaurant Association, the Association of Latvian Travel Agents and Operators, the Country Tourism Association and other trade bodies. In the case of nationally important issues, the Latvian Tourism Advisory Council is brought together with a variety of ministries and association members.

The Ministry of Economics co-operates with other ministries in development policy concerning tourism and reviews and comments on policy guidelines developed by the ministries of Culture, Environmental Protection and Regional Development, and Transport. When the competence and opinion of tourism sector professionals are required, Latvia creates working groups, including local authorities, associations, other governmental organisations and non-governmental organisations.

In 2021, the total budget for tourism marketing was EUR 2.7 million, including state funding of roughly EUR 700 000 and funding of EUR 2.0 million from the European Regional Development Fund. Tourism marketing activities are implemented by the Tourism Department of the Latvian Investment and

Development Agency. The Agency is also responsible for implementing the "Promotion of international competitiveness" programme, co-financed by the European Regional Development Fund (ERDF), which supports tourism entrepreneurs in various marketing activities.

Latvia: Organisational chart of tourism bodies

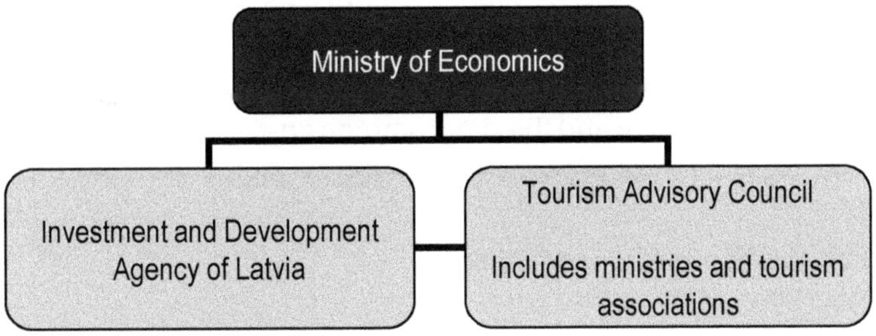

Source: OECD, adapted from the Ministry of Economics, 2022.

Tourism policies and programmes

The Tourism Development Plan for 2021-29 was created before the COVID-19 pandemic. Due to the difficulties in long-term planning during the pandemic, the Ministry of Economics decided to shift to a short-term Tourism Recovery plan for a period of 1-2 years. A new plan is being developed to account of the geopolitical situation and the ongoing recovery of the tourism sector in 2022. This plan will include additional activities to stimulate the sector. Budget limitations are still being identified.

The Investment and Development Agency of Latvia has developed the Latvian Tourism Marketing Strategy, which determines priority tourism markets and activities for promoting inbound tourism and addressing future tourism challenges. The marketing strategy aims to improve the image of Latvia, develop sustainable tourism and foster investment. In addition, the Agency co-operated with regional tourism associations and local authorities to organise domestic promotional campaigns to partially compensate for the decrease in international tourists and to support local businesses (see box below).

Latvia had several support programmes in place for the tourism sector to deal with the effects of the COVID-19 crisis, including:

- Salary compensation programme for tourism enterprises (EUR 19.4 million).
- Special support for cultural and entertainment venues.
- Tax payment extensions: the possibility to split tax payments or defer them for up to three years.
- Loans for current assets: funding with reduced collateral requirements (EUR 210 million).
- Self-isolation programme: indirect support to hotels (EUR 141 000).
- Guarantees for loan holidays (EUR 47.5 million).
- Aid for business rental costs.

The positive effect of the pandemic was new knowledge and skills gained, such as the ability to organise online and hybrid events, making it possible to invite speakers and participants who would not previously have been able to attend.

Latvia has set longer-term priorities to increase the competitiveness and export capacity of the tourism sector. The main priorities are:

- Building value through a focused cluster system: development of new, innovative and creative tourism products through a tourism cluster system with high added value and return on investment. The programme will support eight tourism clusters: four thematic clusters (MICE, health tourism, cultural tourism and nature tourism) and four regional clusters. The programme is co-financed with ERDF funding of EUR 6.5 million.
- Digitalisation of the tourism sector: enterprises will have the opportunity to participate in the EU Recovery and Resilience Facility and the programmes co-financed by the EU's multiannual budget, which support the digitisation of processes, training of digital skills and the development of new digital products.
- Improving data acquisition and dissemination.

Domestic tourism promotion campaigns in Latvia

In response to the dramatic decline in inbound tourism and growing demand for domestic tourism, the Investment and Development Agency of Latvia, in co-operation with regional tourism associations and local authorities, organised several domestic promotional campaigns aiming to partially compensate for the decrease in international tourists and to support local businesses. In 2021, the number of nights spent by domestic tourists was 1.5 million, an increase of 9.5 % compared to the previous year. The campaign included:

- "Open Days in the Countryside", which attracted 26 000 visitors to 240 rural guest houses, restaurants and other rural tourism businesses.
- "Home Café Days", which involved 448 pop-up cafes, attracted more than 40 000 visitors and was repeated in 2022 due to its success.
- "Zoom Latvia Closer", a campaign game organised from July to October 2021, which included 33 destinations all over the country. The campaign was repeated in 2022 with new routes and destinations.
- "Let's visit Latvian castles and manors!", a travel campaign organised from May to September 2022 for domestic cultural tourists to experience the cultural heritage of various castles, manors, and parks.

Statistical Profile

Latvia: Domestic, inbound and outbound tourism

	2017	2018	2019	2020	2021
TOURISM FLOWS, THOUSAND					
Domestic tourism					
Total domestic trips	12 532	10 948	10 416	6 153	8 282
Overnight visitors (tourists)	2 942	2 584	2 501	1 367	2 392
Same-day visitors (excursionists)	9 590	8 365	7 915	4 786	5 890
Nights in all types of accommodation	7 068	5 514	5 792	4 083	6 604
Hotels and similar establishments	562	478	538	477	759
Other collective establishments	906	508	676	542	856
Private accommodation	5 601	4 528	4 577	3 065	4 989
Inbound tourism					
Total international arrivals	7 726	7 775	8 342	3 204	1 937
Overnight visitors (tourists)	1 949	1 946	1 935	636	478
Same-day visitors (excursionists)	5 776	5 829	6 408	2 568	1 459
Top markets					
Russia	243	244	298	85	76
Lithuania	300	275	309	205	66
Germany	255	260	245	44	48
Estonia	192	176	210	90	45
Finland	102	81	83	36	18
Nights in all types of accommodation	8 865	7 864	8 266	2 872	2 847
Hotels and similar establishments	3 125	3 049	3 549	757	390
Other collective establishments	276	395	320	424	596
Private accommodation	5 464	4 419	4 397	1 691	1 861
Outbound tourism					
Total international departures	2 056	2 176	2 384	689	629
Overnight visitors (tourists)	1 265	1 368	1 480	432	512
Same-day visitors (excursionists)	790	807	904	258	117
Top destinations					
Estonia	173	206	161	90	83
Lithuania	154	157	166	54	31
Sweden	80	100	100	..	30
Germany	148	80	98	48	27
	..	..	..	..	..
TOURISM RECEIPTS AND EXPENDITURE, MILLION EUR					
Inbound tourism					
Total international receipts	1 248	1 376	1 398	478	..
International travel receipts	838	896	907	378	..
International passenger transport receipts	410	480	491	100	..
Outbound tourism					
Total international expenditure	815	857	871	318	..
International travel expenditure	642	660	669	265	..
International passenger transport expenditure	173	197	202	53	..

.. Not available

Source: OECD Tourism Statistics (Database).

StatLink https://stat.link/ynzcea

Latvia: Enterprises and employment in tourism

	Number of establishments	Number of persons employed				
	2020	2017	2018	2019	2020	2021
Total	..	..	..	..	..	..
Tourism industries	**16 857**	**75 400**	**77 100**	**75 600**	**68 300**	**61 200**
Accommodation services for visitors	1 483	4 900	5 600	6 600	6 300	4 600
Hotels and similar establishments	513	3 700	4 500	5 400	5 000	3 000
Food and beverage serving industry	4 950	24 800	26 700	25 500	23 300	21 200
Passenger transport	1 523	17 800	16 800	13 600	11 300	12 000
Air passenger transport	18	2 100	2 200 e	..	..	..
Railways passenger transport	59	3 800	2 700	2 100	..	..
Road passenger transport	1 416	11 000	10 900	9 500	8 000	8 200
Water passenger transport	30	..	..	..	..	..
Passenger transport supporting services	..	..	..	..	..	..
Transport equipment rental	922	..	..	..	..	..
Travel agencies and other reservation services industry	940	2 800	2 500	2 000	2 100	..
Cultural industry	2 408	12 900	11 500	12 600	13 000	11 600
Sports and recreation industry	4 631	11 500	13 700	15 000	11 600	9 900
Retail trade of country-specific tourism characteristic goods	..	..	..	..	..	..
Other country-specific tourism industries	..	..	..	..	..	..
Other industries	..	..	..	..	..	..

.. Not available; e Estimated value
Source: OECD Tourism Statistics (Database).

StatLink https://stat.link/rd0kft

Lithuania

Tourism in the economy and outlook for recovery

Tourism is an important sector in Lithuania. In 2020, tourism directly contributed to 1.7% of total GVA in Lithuania, down from 2.9% in 2019. The tourism sector accounted for 45 769 jobs in 2020, representing 4.7% of total employment in the country. This represented 5 619 fewer jobs than in 2019.

In 2021, 948 000 international tourists visited Lithuania, an increase of 1.2% compared to 2020, but 67% below pre-pandemic levels. International tourism accounted for 1.2 million nights and EUR 494 million in expenditure - amounting to 3.9% of service exports in 2021.

Lithuania's top market source in 2021 was Latvia, with 180 000 overnight visitors. The next top market sources were Poland, Germany, Belarus, and Russia. Russia's war in Ukraine has created uncertainty for Lithuania's tourism recovery.

Increasing domestic tourism and a shift towards neighbouring markets had a positive impact on overall numbers. Domestic tourism became the main market in 2020-21, contributing to 54.6% of tourism expenditure in 2020, up from 40.5% in 2019. In 2021, 3.1 million overnight domestic tourist trips were recorded, a 26.7% increase compared to 2020 and 9.3% above pre-pandemic levels.

Tourism governance and funding

The Ministry of Economy and Innovation has lead responsibility for tourism, with the Tourism Policy Division responsible for shaping national tourism policy, destination development and international relations. The Ministry of the Economy and Innovation works closely with other ministries, including Health, Culture, Transport and Communications, Foreign Affairs, Agriculture, and Environment, as well as municipalities and the private sector. Particular attention has been paid to health and safety protocols, with significant investments made to support tourism businesses.

Lithuania Travel is the national tourism organisation responsible for raising awareness of Lithuania as a tourism destination through marketing and tourism promotion and developing inbound and domestic tourism. Lithuania Travel is a public institution and reports to the Ministry of the Economy and Innovation. The State Consumer Rights Protection Authority is responsible for the supervision of tour operators, travel agencies and accommodation providers and represents consumer interests in the event of tour operator insolvency.

Municipalities are involved in tourism at the local level, including through the operation of Tourism Information Centres. The Ministry actively communicates with all sector representatives, and a monthly format for presenting issues and answering questions has been created to aid communication. The Working Group on the Co-ordination of the Application of Emergency Measures to Business at the State Level holds meetings to discuss the most important issues with representatives from various business areas, including tourism.

Lithuania's tourism budget is approximately EUR 3 million, with a further EUR 1 million allocated from EU funding. Because of COVID-19, in the last three years, Lithuania dedicated additional sums to the recovery of tourism - EUR 17 million in 2020, EUR 6 million in 2021 and EUR 4 million in 2022. All Lithuanian health resorts and main cities introduced a tourist tax of EUR 1 per person per night, levied on visitors using accommodation services. The tax revenues fund international marketing activities and improve the cities' infrastructure and quality of life for residents. A similar tax was initially applied in five other towns and resorts and the capital Vilnius.

Lithuania: Organisational chart of tourism bodies

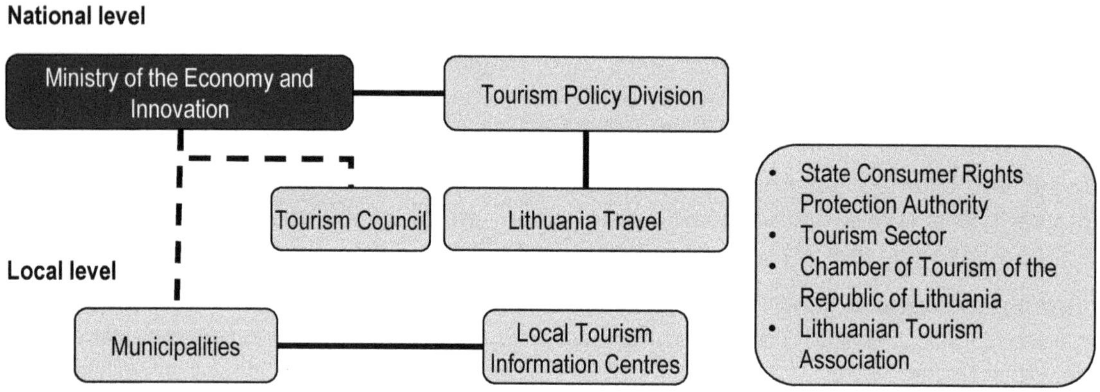

Source: OECD, adapted from the Ministry of the Economy and Innovation, 2022.

Tourism policies and programmes

The main challenges for Lithuanian tourism are recovery from COVID-19 and the sector's resilience to Russia's war in Ukraine. The impacts of COVID-19 have driven the short-term priorities for the tourism sector. Programmes implemented to respond to the pandemic include:

- 'Tourism Innovation' measures intended to create, improve, and represent tourism services and digital training for the sector.
- Loans for tour operators, accommodation, and catering providers to enable settlements with tourists who refuse travel vouchers.
- Holiday vouchers worth EUR 200 for medical workers in Lithuania. Vouchers pay for a package of services provided by local tour operators, accommodation providers, transport, catering, spas, and entertainment.
- Investment in skills development, including languages, sales and marketing skills, professionalism, and intercultural competence.

To manage and mitigate the impact of COVID-19 on the tourism sector, Lithuania initiated a tourism sector promotion plan, which included measures to promote recovery and transform the tourism ecosystem. The COVID-19 pandemic also necessitated a change in the legal framework for the tourism sector. Amendments were made to the Civil Code of the Republic of Lithuania and the Law on Tourism, allowing tourist coupons valid for 12 months for trips that did not occur due to an emergency.

Medium and long-term priorities have previously been set out in a tourism-specific strategy. As of 2021, sectoral strategies are no longer prepared in Lithuania. The tourism strategy is now part of the Economic Transformation and Competitiveness Development Programme. This programme underpins the development of the Lithuanian economy for the period to 2030 and will pursue the objectives set out in the

National Progress Plan. Overall, the Tourism Promotion section of the Programme aims to increase the competitiveness of the Lithuanian tourism sector. Implementation measures address relevant issues, including those related to the areas of regulation of other ministries, such as accessibility; improving the image of Lithuania as an attractive country for tourism; improving human resources competencies; investing in infrastructure; adaptations for people with disabilities and using innovation to improve the quality of tourism services.

Lithuania is currently reviewing two progress measures and implementing actions dedicated to tourism:

- Transformation of the tourism sector: aimed at making structural reforms to the tourism data collected, disseminated, and used in the decision-making process.
- Progressive tourism infrastructure and marketing: seeks to implement model destination management organisations in the country and invest in infrastructure and create new means to promote Lithuanian tourism products and communicate abroad.

As part of efforts to identify the most effective ways to increase the competitiveness of the tourism sector and prepare sustainable tourism development guidelines, Lithuania is working with neighbouring countries in the Baltic Sea Region to achieve the UN Sustainable Development Goals as they apply to tourism. In this context, the 1st Youth Sustainable Tourism Forum and Competition of Sustainable Tourism Ideas has been organised.

Statistical Profile

Lithuania: Domestic, inbound and outbound tourism

	2017	2018	2019	2020	2021
TOURISM FLOWS, THOUSAND					
Domestic tourism[1]					
Total domestic trips	14 247	14 678	14 785	11 389	11 593
Overnight visitors (tourists)	2 528	2 641	2 827	2 438	3 090
Same-day visitors (excursionists)	11 719	12 037	11 958	8 951	8 503
Nights in all types of accommodation	3 934	4 355	4 804	3 812	4 360
Hotels and similar establishments	3 901	4 285	4 717	3 758	4 239
Other collective establishments	32	70	87	55	121
Private accommodation	..	..	..	..	..
Inbound tourism[2]					
Total international arrivals	5 590	6 115	6 150	2 284	2 096
Overnight visitors (tourists)	2 523	2 825	2 875	937	948
Same-day visitors (excursionists)	3 067	3 291	3 275	1 348	1 148
Top markets					
Latvia	308	362	357	86	180
Poland	218	250	248	89	108
Germany	214	242	243	113	81
Belarus	432	443	424	103	67
Russia	257	286	273	70	34
Nights in all types of accommodation	3 431	3 737	4 143	1 120	1 183
Hotels and similar establishments	3 397	3 695	4 091	1 104	1 167
Other collective establishments	34	42	51	16	15
Private accommodation	..	..	..	..	..
Outbound tourism					
Total international departures	4 294	4 703	4 882	1 643	1 743
Overnight visitors (tourists)	2 032	2 244	2 347	682	830
Same-day visitors (excursionists)	2 262	2 458	2 534	961	913
Top destinations					
Latvia	233	250	260	118	111
Poland	160	169	178	61	89
Germany	123	132	146	58	54
United Kingdom	213	215	217	57	45
Norway	88	94	101	47	36
TOURISM RECEIPTS AND EXPENDITURE, MILLION EUR					
Inbound tourism					
Total international receipts	1 381	1 503	1 442	581	..
International travel receipts	1 169	1 274	1 333	507	..
International passenger transport receipts	212	229	109	74	..
Outbound tourism					
Total international expenditure	1 158	1 361	1 420	523	..
International travel expenditure	984	1 186	1 241	475	..
International passenger transport expenditure	174	175	180	48	..

.. Not available

1. Trips from demand side surveys; Nights from supply side surveys.

2. Arrivals from demand side surveys; Nights from supply side surveys.

Source: OECD Tourism Statistics (Database).

StatLink https://stat.link/zqu9n2

Lithuania: Enterprises and employment in tourism

	Number of establishments[2]	Number of persons employed				
	2020	2017	2018	2019	2020	2021
Total	..	..	..	..	..	..
Tourism industries	**23 273 p**	**47 168**	**49 090**	**51 388**	**45 769 p**	..
Accommodation services for visitors[1]	3 943	14 457	14 856	14 889	12 535 p	..
Hotels and similar establishments	486	14 457	14 856	14 889	12 535 p	..
Food and beverage serving industry	3 947	13 065	14 785	15 660	15 130 p	..
Passenger transport	10 393	9 124	8 548	7 883	7 291 p	..
Air passenger transport	139	824	943	1 042	793 p	..
Railways passenger transport	1	385	185	96	15 p	..
Road passenger transport	10 211	7 908	7 405	6 738	6 478 p	..
Water passenger transport	42	7	15	7	5 p	..
Passenger transport supporting services	..	730	638	840	351 p	..
Transport equipment rental	1 049	459	525	673	615 p	..
Travel agencies and other reservation services industry	1 071	3 377	3 212	4 628	2 770 p	..
Cultural industry	954	2 875	3 709	4 255	4 954 p	..
Sports and recreation industry	1 916	3 081	2 816	2 560	2 123 p	..
Retail trade of country-specific tourism characteristic goods	..	..	..	..	..	..
Other country-specific tourism industries	..	..	..	..	..	..
Other industries	..	..	..	..	..	..

.. Not available; p Provisional data
1. Data for accommodation service for visitors refer to number of establishments.
2. Data refer to number of enterprises.
Source: OECD Tourism Statistics (Database).

StatLink https://stat.link/b4xpz2

Lithuania: Internal tourism consumption

Million EUR

	2020		
	Domestic tourism expenditure	Inbound tourism expenditure	Internal tourism consumption
Total	..	..	..
Consumption products	**804 p**	**668 p**	**1 472 p**
Tourism characteristic products	457 p	317 p	773 p
Accommodation services for visitors	130 p	57 p	186 p
Food and beverage serving services	106 p	154 p	260 p
Passenger transport services	87 p	31 p	118 p
Air passenger transport services	50 p	23 p	73 p
Railways passenger transport services	8 p	1 p	9 p
Road passenger transport services	27 p	6 p	33 p
Water passenger transport services	2 p	1 p	3 p
Passenger transport supporting services	20 p	13 p	33 p
Transport equipment rental services	66 p	39 p	105 p
Travel agencies and other reservation services industry	33 p	2 p	35 p
Cultural services	8 p	13 p	22 p
Sports and recreation services	7 p	8 p	15 p
Country-specific tourism characteristic goods	..	..	..
Country-specific tourism characteristic services	..	..	..
Other consumption products	347 p	351 p	698 p
Tourism connected products	..	..	..
Non-tourism related consumption products	..	..	..
Non-consumption products	..	..	..

.. Not available; p Provisional data
Source: OECD Tourism Statistics (Database).

StatLink https://stat.link/chz48a

Luxembourg

Tourism in the economy and outlook for recovery

Tourism directly contributed to 1.2% of Luxembourg's GDP and provided 38 617 direct jobs in 2019, 8.3% of total employment. Travel exports represented 5.0% of total service exports in 2019. In 2020, tourism jobs remained relatively stable at 38 336 jobs, but declined to 7.6% of total employment. The share of services exports fell to 4.0%.

In 2021, 853 000 tourists (international and domestic) were recorded in registered tourism accommodation. International visitors usually comprise 90% of total visitors. There was a rebound in international tourists in 2021 to 756 000, but they still remained 27.3% below 2019 levels. Luxembourg's main source markets in 2021 were its neighbouring countries: Belgium (20.0% of nights), the Netherlands (16.0%), Germany (16.2%) and France (12.6%).

A total of 2.1 million visitor nights were recorded in 2021. This was a 40% increase in nights compared to 2020, however, still 24% below pre-pandemic levels. International nights hit 1.8 million (up 51% from 2020), and domestic tourism was 303 000 overnights (down 1% from 2020).

Luxembourg expects tourism to return to 2019 levels in 2023 or 2024.

Tourism governance and funding

Tourism is part of the Ministry of Economy, within a General Directorate for Tourism (DGT). In addition to regulating the sector, it grants aid to accommodation businesses, associations, local authorities and other interests. The main objectives are to increase the quality of the tourism offer and the quality of life.

In addition, the DGT pursues a policy to promote and optimise the national tourism offer. It works on developing tourism in various ways by creating standards, professionalising marketing and maintaining close relations with international partners.

Luxembourg for Tourism (LfT) is an Economic Interest Group created in December 2015, with the primary task of marketing and promoting Luxembourg as a destination. Along with the government, Regional Offices for Tourism (ORT), professional associations and the private sector co-finance LfT. Regional offices are tasked with co-ordinating local interests in developing the regional tourism offer. The capital, Luxembourg City, has its own structure, the Luxembourg City Tourist Office, while the Luxembourg Convention Bureau (LCB) is the designated body for developing the business events sector.

The budget voted by the General Directorate for Tourism of the Ministry of Economy was EUR 23.0 million in 2020, EUR 22.2 million in 2021, and EUR 30.9 million in 2022. The following financial contributions are an integral part of the DGT budget:

- Contribution to large-scale tourism projects and initiatives organised by tourist boards and other interests: EUR 2.9 million in 2020, EUR 3.1 million in 2021, and EUR 3.0 million in 2022.
- Contribution to the costs of the Luxembourg for Tourism Economic Interest Group (GIE) of EUR 4 million in 2020, EUR 4.4 million in 2021, and EUR 5.1 million in 2022.

Luxembourg: Organisational chart of tourism bodies

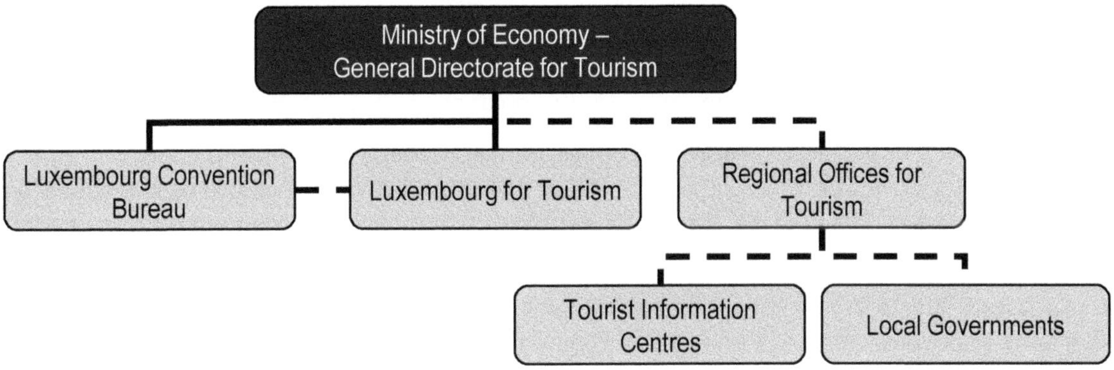

Source: OECD, adapted from the Ministry of Economy, 2022.

Tourism policies and programmes

Due to the COVID-19 pandemic, the General Directorate for Tourism, in close consultation with the sector, drew up a detailed recovery plan to support leisure tourism and the business events sector. Plans included the "Lëtzebuerg - Dat ass Vakanz!" (Luxembourg - That's a holiday) promotional strategy and the creation of a label to promote health and safety measures implemented across the events sector.

Actions to tackle the consequences of the crisis included:

- **Aid for businesses:** Multiple aid measures totalling over EUR 500 million were implemented to support SMEs. These aid packages were extended into 2022 for tourism, events, culture, entertainment and hospitality businesses.
- **Enhancement and support of domestic tourism:** Charters were put in place to promote the implementation of quality and health and safety protocols that both slowed down the spread of the virus and provided businesses with visibility among the general public.
- **The "Lëtzebuerg, dat ass Vakanz" campaign (2022):** Multiple innovative projects were brought together under the campaign, aimed at residents, cross-border commuters and foreign tourists to make them more aware of Luxembourg's tourist attractions. Outputs included: the "Guide for one day" initiative (172 guided tours and 1 081 participants); the "Vëlosummer" (see box below); the Movewecarry.lu initiative (1 018 pieces of luggage transported free of charge); the new culinary project "Vakanz genéissen" and the VisitLuxembourg application that is continuously expanded.
- **The "Safe to serve" campaign:** A series of initiatives aimed at preserving the health and safety of staff and customers in the hospitality sector while respecting hospitality and conviviality, supported by the Chamber of Commerce. Adherence to this charter guarantees customers a high level of health and safety, designed to create reassurance when visiting restaurants or cafés.

The challenges to supporting recovery and development include digitalisation, sustainability, innovative tourism products, transparency of the offer (particularly in the sale of accommodation), rural tourism accommodation, professionalisation of tourism structures, and reliable statistics.

In 2021 discussions were conducted on the positioning of Luxembourg as a destination. These discussions also considered the potential effects of the pandemic on tourist activities in the medium and long term. A strategic process was initiated to refine, reframe and develop the major priorities of the tourism policy. In order to involve the various stakeholders, the General Directorate for Tourism organised theme-based work groups with selected stakeholders, residents and municipal representatives.

The General Directorate for Tourism is developing a new strategy for the business events sector. The impact of the health crisis has intensified and accelerated existing trends, such as digitalisation and hybrid and virtual events. The aim is to map the state of the sector at the national level and to take stock of the initial effects of the measures already implemented while identifying major emerging trends at the international level to draw up a long-term policy for the business events sector.

In this context, a new tourism strategy with the central theme "Humans, regions and economy: value-driven tourism as an active driver for more quality of life and residence" was developed. It focuses on three objectives: improving the quality of life, the visitor experience and the reinforcement of the economy.

Therefore, six fields of action have been defined. First, the General Directorate for Tourism intends to provide a modern offer rich in experiences predominantly in active, cultural and gastronomic tourism. Second, it aims to develop attractive and resilient tourist businesses. Third, it aims to ensure that the stay in Luxembourg is sustainable and accessible for everyone. Fourth, inclusive and consumer-oriented digitalisation will be further developed. Fifth, trusting collaborations and strong networks between the different actors in the tourism industry are encouraged. Lastly, the General Directorate for Tourism aims for a targeted implementation of its objectives and a continuous collection of data.

Expanding Scenic bike tourism in Luxembourg

"Vëlosummer" was first launched in the summer of 2020 and has since become a regular fixture. Each year, municipalities, Regional Offices for Tourism, and other interested parties submit proposals for scenic bike tours that highlight Luxembourg's tourist assets. Co-operation with visitor attractions and hospitality establishments along bike routes is also recommended.

Luxembourg analyses the feasibility of the various proposed routes submitted in close co-operation with the Regional Offices for Tourism and the Road Administration to develop a coherent cycle route concept for Vëlosummer. During the summer, road sections throughout the country are reserved for cyclists, providing a unique opportunity. Some routes are reserved for cyclists at weekends, while others are reserved for the whole month of August. To help residents and tourists prepare their route, a map highlighting closed roads and illustrating cycle routes is produced in co-operation with the association ProVelo. For stays of at least two nights in two different accommodation establishments, a luggage service allowed cyclists to have their luggage delivered free of charge from one accommodation to the next.

Statistical Profile

Luxembourg: Domestic, inbound and outbound tourism

	2017	2018	2019	2020	2021
TOURISM FLOWS, THOUSAND					
Domestic tourism					
Total domestic trips	..	..	..	..	..
Overnight visitors (tourists)	110	121	124	130	97
Same-day visitors (excursionists)	..	..	..	..	..
Nights in all types of accommodation	318	346	348	307	303
Hotels and similar establishments	232	254	256	236	189
Other collective establishments	86	92	91	71	114
Private accommodation	..	..	..	..	..
Inbound tourism					
Total international arrivals	..	..	..	..	..
Overnight visitors (tourists)	1 046	1 018	1 041	525	756
Same-day visitors (excursionists)	..	..	..	..	..
Top markets					
Belgium	211	208	207	116	151
Netherlands	182	170	188	105	128
Germany	147	148	149	74	123
France	139	136	134	71	95
United Kingdom	68	66	66	32	41
Nights in all types of accommodation	2 573	2 575	2 505	1 210	1 829
Hotels and similar establishments	1 720	1 715	1 652	752	1 214
Other collective establishments	853	860	853	458	615
Private accommodation	..	..	..	..	..
Outbound tourism					
Total international departures	3 817	4 063	4 063	2 452	2 759
Overnight visitors (tourists)	2 355 |	2 510	2 548	1 460	1 814
Same-day visitors (excursionists)	1 462	1 554	1 515	992	944
Top destinations					
France	466 |	490	494	379	464
Germany	326 |	330	373	201	218
Belgium	181 |	208	218	177	194
Spain	177 |	175	181	91	143
Italy	175 |	232	212	100	139
TOURISM RECEIPTS AND EXPENDITURE, MILLION EUR					
Inbound tourism					
Total international receipts	5 462	5 632	5 636	4 465	..
International travel receipts	5 076	5 166	5 168	4 200	..
International passenger transport receipts	386	466	468	265	..
Outbound tourism					
Total international expenditure	2 607	2 872	3 287	2 458	..
International travel expenditure	2 560	2 813	3 243	2 420	..
International passenger transport expenditure	47	59	44	38	..

.. Not available; | Break in series
Source: OECD Tourism Statistics (Database).

StatLink https://stat.link/1ad5cv

Luxembourg: Enterprises and employment in tourism

	Number of establishments	Number of persons employed				
	2019	2017	2018	2019	2020	2021
Total	..	..	..	..	..	..
Tourism industries	**494**	**35 583**	**36 872**	**38 617**	**38 336**	..
Accommodation services for visitors	422	3 635	3 584	3 634	3 474	..
Hotels and similar establishments	227	3 177	3 087	3 110	2 928	..
Food and beverage serving industry	..	16 554	17 141	18 300	18 135	..
Passenger transport	..	10 574	11 235	11 582	11 711	..
Air passenger transport	..	3 131	3 325	3 346	3 311	..
Railways passenger transport	..	3 256	3 366	3 452	3 630	..
Road passenger transport	..	4 149	4 502	4 721	4 720	..
Water passenger transport	..	38	42	63	50	..
Passenger transport supporting services	..	..	..	..	..	..
Transport equipment rental	..	467	417	474	484	..
Travel agencies and other reservation services industry	72	590	608	697	668	..
Cultural industry	..	1 833	1 907	2 441	2 401	..
Sports and recreation industry	..	1 930	1 980	1 487	1 465	..
Retail trade of country-specific tourism characteristic goods	..	..	..	..	..	..
Other country-specific tourism industries	..	..	..	..	..	..
Other industries	..	..	..	..	..	..

.. Not available
Source: OECD Tourism Statistics (Database).

StatLink https://stat.link/zrihkb

Luxembourg: Internal tourism consumption

Million EUR

	2020		
	Domestic tourism expenditure	Inbound tourism expenditure	Internal tourism consumption
Total	..	..	..
Consumption products	**423**	**2 496**	**2 965**
Tourism characteristic products	340	618	997
Accommodation services for visitors	48	242	305
Food and beverage serving services	130	201	332
Passenger transport services	83	125	208
Air passenger transport services	37	81	118
Railways passenger transport services	0	37	37
Road passenger transport services	44	5	49
Water passenger transport services	1	2	3
Passenger transport supporting services	..	..	..
Transport equipment rental services	11	5	16
Travel agencies and other reservation services industry	42	0	67
Cultural services	26	45	71
Sports and recreation services	..	..	..
Country-specific tourism characteristic goods	..	..	..
Country-specific tourism characteristic services	..	..	..
Other consumption products	83	1 878	1 968
Tourism connected products	..	..	..
Non-tourism related consumption products	..	..	..
Non-consumption products	..	..	..

.. Not available
Source: OECD Tourism Statistics (Database).

StatLink https://stat.link/exrypd

Mexico

Tourism in the economy and outlook for recovery

Tourism is a significant component of the Mexican economy, directly accounting for 8.0% of national GDP and 5.8% of the total workforce in 2019. The impacts of the pandemic saw tourism's contribution to GDP fall to 6.3% in 2020 or MXN 1.5 billion. Tourism employment fell by 12.3% to 2.0 million employees, or 5.3% of the workforce. Travel exports represented 77.5% of total service exports in 2019, which fell to 64.5% in 2020.

International tourism expenditure accounted for 17.9% of total tourism expenditure in 2019. This fell to 13.4% in 2020, driven by a 46.1% decline in international overnight visitors (down to 24.3 million). A rebound was recorded in 2021 but remained 29.2% below 2019 numbers despite Mexico's top market, the United States (32% of the total market), almost returning to pre-pandemic levels.

Domestic tourism was significantly impacted by the COVID-19 pandemic, with domestic overnight visitors falling 52.7% to 48.0 million in 2020, down from a record high of 101.7 million visitors in 2019. Nights in hotels and similar establishments fell 52.4% to 83.1 million.

Mexico expects international tourism expenditure to return to 2019 levels in 2022.

Tourism governance and funding

The Ministry of Tourism is responsible for leading the design and implementation of public policies to strengthen tourism development. This includes promoting innovation in the sector, improving the quality of tourism services and the competitiveness of national tourism, and promoting strategies that articulate governmental priorities and contribute to the sustainable and inclusive growth of tourism. FONATUR is Mexico's agency for the development of tourism investment.

Three co-ordination mechanisms contribute to formulating strategies and actions to achieve a comprehensive development of national tourism activity. These mechanisms are:

- The Executive Tourism Commission, an inter-ministerial body whose purpose is to fully understand and resolve tourism-related matters.
- The Tourism Advisory Council, whose purpose is to suggest strategic responses and co-ordinate actions with the agencies of the Federal Government, with the full participation of the public and private sectors, to achieve comprehensive development of tourism activity.
- The National Tourism Conference, a co-ordinating body between the three levels of government, is in charge of establishing the policy, planning and programming of tourist activity throughout Mexico.

In the Ministry of Tourism, the Tlatocan, or 'Great Council', for tourism sustainability has been established, which brings together more than 130 participants. Among these are dependencies of the Mexican government, international organisations, civil society, indigenous communities, social enterprises, private companies and academia.

Mexico: Organisational chart of tourism bodies

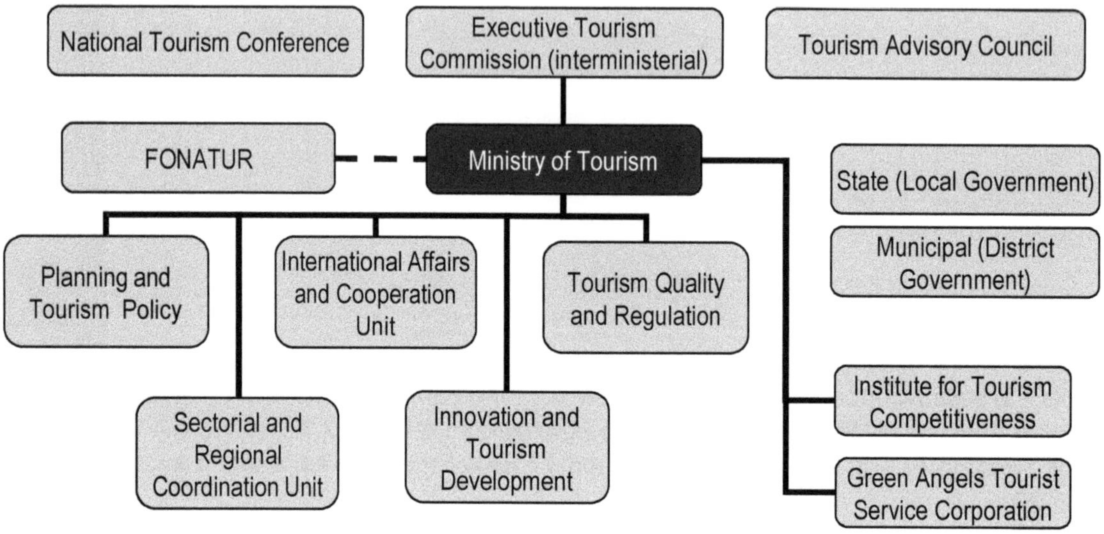

Source: OECD, adapted from the Ministry of Tourism, 2022.

Tourism policies and programmes

The Tourism Sectorial Programme 2020-24 (PROSECTUR) is the framework that governs National Tourism Policy in Mexico. It derives from and relates to the National Development Plan 2019-24. PROSECTUR contains four priority objectives:

- Guarantee a social approach and respect for human rights in tourism.
- Promote the balanced development of tourism destinations in Mexico.
- Strengthen the diversification of tourism markets at national and international levels.
- Promote sustainable tourism in the national territory.

PROSECTUR involves social, ethical and economic redevelopment aimed at promoting tourism as a right that includes all population sectors, especially the most vulnerable. The goal is for tourism activity to permeate all regions, destinations and communities as a tool for social integration and reconciliation to create well-being for all. A report has been undertaken on the progress and results obtained during the fiscal year 2020 in regard to the fulfilment of the priority objectives and well-being goals contained in the PROSECTUR framework.

In 2020, the Ministry of Tourism launched the Sustainable Tourism Strategy 2030 in close co-ordination with different government actors, civil society, international organisations, academia, the private sector, and local communities. The Strategy's objective is to transform the COVID-19 crisis into an opportunity to generate a radical change in tourism. The Strategy aims to make Mexico's destinations benchmarks for sustainable, resilient tourism, encouraging sustainable consumption and production value chains, local communities' engagement, and biodiversity preservation. It will prioritise the achievement of the Sustainable Development Goals in the tourism economy, with the long-term aim being that future generations will continue to benefit from natural resources that attract tourists. Lines of action include:

- **Promoting sustainable mobility and the concept of 'zero emissions tourism':** Under this action, tourist bicycle lanes are developed to connect local communities where visitors can travel to natural and cultural destinations. For example, Ciclovía Maya, the largest tourist bikeway in the world, will connect and integrate economic activities for dozens of local communities in the Yucatan Peninsula.

- **Creating solutions for the integrated management of solid waste focused on the goal of zero waste:** This includes implementing local models for integrated solid waste management, seeking to generate zero waste and creating destinations free of single-use plastics.
- **Investing in and promoting the sustainable tourism offer**: this will be done on multi-channels and new innovative marketing platforms, seeking virtual and physical presence in national and international spaces and events.

Statistical Profile

Mexico: Domestic, inbound and outbound tourism

	2017	2018	2019	2020	2021
TOURISM FLOWS, THOUSAND					
Domestic tourism					
Total domestic trips	..	..	..	..	..
Overnight visitors (tourists)	95 600	100 445	101 749	48 042	..
Same-day visitors (excursionists)	..	..	..	..	..
Nights in all types of accommodation	..	..	..	..	..
Hotels and similar establishments	156 765	166 707	174 610 p	83 122	..
Other collective establishments	..	..	..	..	..
Private accommodation	..	..	..	..	..
Inbound tourism					
Total international arrivals	99 349	96 497	97 406	51 128	55 301
Overnight visitors (tourists)	39 291	41 313	45 024	24 284	31 860
Same-day visitors (excursionists)	60 058	55 184	52 382	26 845	23 441
Top markets					
United States	10 340	10 496	10 511	5 151	10 240
Canada	1 985	2 155	2 310	976	504
Spain	377	386	392	100	221
France	261	287	305	116	157
United Kingdom	563	591	581	104	125
Nights in all types of accommodation	..	..	..	..	..
Hotels and similar establishments	90 778	93 323	97 151	43 614	..
Other collective establishments	..	..	..	..	..
Private accommodation	..	..	..	..	..
Outbound tourism					
Total international departures	94 274	86 280	82 752	36 056	32 836
Overnight visitors (tourists)	19 067	19 748	19 810	7 345	11 544
Same-day visitors (excursionists)	75 208	66 531	62 942	28 710	21 292
Top destinations					
..	..	..	..	..	..
..	..	..	..	..	..
..	..	..	..	..	..
..	..	..	..	..	..
..	..	..	..	..	..
TOURISM RECEIPTS AND EXPENDITURE, MILLION USD					
Inbound tourism					
Total international receipts	22 467	23 803	25 848	11 448	..
International travel receipts	21 336	22 526	24 573	10 996	..
International passenger transport receipts	1 131	1 276	1 274	453	..
Outbound tourism					
Total international expenditure	13 647	14 074	12 300	4 286	..
International travel expenditure	10 840	11 230	9 881	3 475	..
International passenger transport expenditure	2 807	2 844	2 419	811	..

.. Not available; p Provisional data
Source: OECD Tourism Statistics (Database).

StatLink https://stat.link/8d46gc

Mexico: Enterprises and employment in tourism

	Number of establishments	Number of persons employed				
	2020	2017	2018	2019	2020	2021
Total	..	**2 278 723**	**2 284 551**	**2 285 690 p**	**2 005 652 p**	..
Tourism industries	**113 038**	**1 584 886**	**1 616 908**	**1 643 684 p**	**1 424 998 p**	..
Accommodation services for visitors	..	194 909	198 977	200 230 p	204 693 p	..
Hotels and similar establishments	24 692	..	..	..	..	..
Food and beverage serving industry	81 149	633 464	651 624	665 757 p	549 719 p	..
Passenger transport	..	566 861	575 996	581 457 p	511 631 p	..
Air passenger transport	..	29 550	30 801	30 980 p	27 842 p	..
Railways passenger transport	..	1 018	990	991 p	961 p	..
Road passenger transport	..	534 569	542 367	547 619 p	481 977 p	..
Water passenger transport	..	1 724	1 838	1 867 p	851 p	..
Passenger transport supporting services	..	3 510	3 456	3 321 p	2 951 p	..
Transport equipment rental	..	4 468	5 185	5 411 p	4 946 p	..
Travel agencies and other reservation services industry	7 197	16 040	14 976	14 557 p	12 323 p	..
Cultural industry	..	37 287	37 554	37 691 p	25 297 p	..
Sports and recreation industry	..	56 825	56 218	54 440 p	42 031 p	..
Retail trade of country-specific tourism characteristic goods	..	71 522	72 922	80 820 p	71 407 p	..
Other country-specific tourism industries	..	..	..	..	..	..
Other industries	..	**693 837**	**667 643**	**642 006 p**	**580 654 p**	..

.. Not available; p Provisional data
Source: OECD Tourism Statistics (Database).

StatLink https://stat.link/0lw287

Mexico: Internal tourism consumption

Million MXN

	2020		
	Domestic tourism expenditure	Inbound tourism expenditure	Internal tourism consumption
Total	..	..	..
Consumption products	**2 043 757 p**	**317 250 p**	**2 361 007 p**
Tourism characteristic products	1 862 848 p	316 455 p	2 179 304 p
Accommodation services for visitors	490 782 p	122 859 p	613 641 p
Food and beverage serving services	397 045 p	71 337 p	468 382 p
Passenger transport services	409 879 p	37 185 p	447 064 p
Air passenger transport services	113 354 p	16 662 p	130 016 p
Railways passenger transport services	5 718 p	..	5 718 p
Road passenger transport services	287 661 p	20 523 p	308 184 p
Water passenger transport services	3 147 p	..	3 147 p
Passenger transport supporting services	19 576 p	65 p	19 641 p
Transport equipment rental services	10 213 p	..	10 213 p
Travel agencies and other reservation services industry	13 120 p	509 p	13 628 p
Cultural services	8 893 p	8 623 p	17 516 p
Sports and recreation services	7 847 p	15 877 p	23 724 p
Country-specific tourism characteristic goods	505 494 p	60 001 p	565 495 p
Country-specific tourism characteristic services	..	..	..
Other consumption products	180 909 p	794 p	181 703 p
Tourism connected products	..	..	..
Non-tourism related consumption products	..	..	..
Non-consumption products	..	..	..

.. Not available; p Provisional data
Source: OECD Tourism Statistics (Database).

StatLink https://stat.link/bxd7vu

Netherlands

Tourism in the economy and outlook for recovery

International and domestic tourism are of substantial importance to the Dutch economy. The sector's value directly comprised 4.4% of the total GVA and provided 496 000 jobs in 2019, accounting for 6.4% of total employment. The impacts of the pandemic saw tourism GVA remain 40.1% lower in 2021 at EUR 19.1 billion, or 2.5% of total GVA. Employment was less impacted, but there were 95 000 fewer tourism jobs in 2021.

In 2020, international tourists fell 63.9% compared to 2019, with a further decline of 13.5% in 2021 to 6.3 million overnight visitors. Typically, more than half of international visitors come from the top three markets of Germany, Belgium and France. In 2021, there were 2.5 million overnight visitors from Germany (39.5% of visitors).

The impacts on domestic tourism were limited, with domestic overnight visitors in tourism-related accommodation establishments falling 22.3% in 2020 and recovering to 25.5 million in 2021, just 1.2% lower than 2019. Domestic expenditure accounts for approximately three-fifths of total tourism expenditure.

Tourism governance and funding

The Ministry of Economic Affairs and Climate Policy is responsible for tourism at the national level. Different provinces and municipalities either have their own tourism strategy or combine it as part of spatial or economic strategies. In addition, regional and local authorities deal with tourism matters such as funding regional and local destination marketing organisations and are responsible for domestic and international marketing and product development.

The Netherlands Board of Tourism and Conventions (NBTC) is the national destination management organisation. NBTC works on the country's positioning, development and marketing for and with partners in different industries. The NBTC is subsidised by the Ministry of Economic Affairs, receiving EUR 9.2 million in 2021 (up from EUR 8.9 million in 2019) and funding from various third parties for specific projects.

The Centre of Expertise Leisure, Tourism and Hospitality (CELTH) is a collaboration between Dutch universities of applied sciences in tourism. The aim is to stimulate public-private partnerships in the field of knowledge and research in order to encourage collaboration between education, industry and government. Recently CELTH developed the Agenda Conscious Destinations (see box below).

During the COVID-19 crisis, the Netherlands worked with stakeholders in the sector to create a national Taskforce on Leisure and Tourism. The purpose of the Taskforce is to strengthen co-operation between the various parties. The Taskforce aims to restart the sector in the short term and form strong co-operation for a resilient and sustainable tourism and hospitality sector in the medium and long term.

Netherlands: Organisational chart of tourism bodies

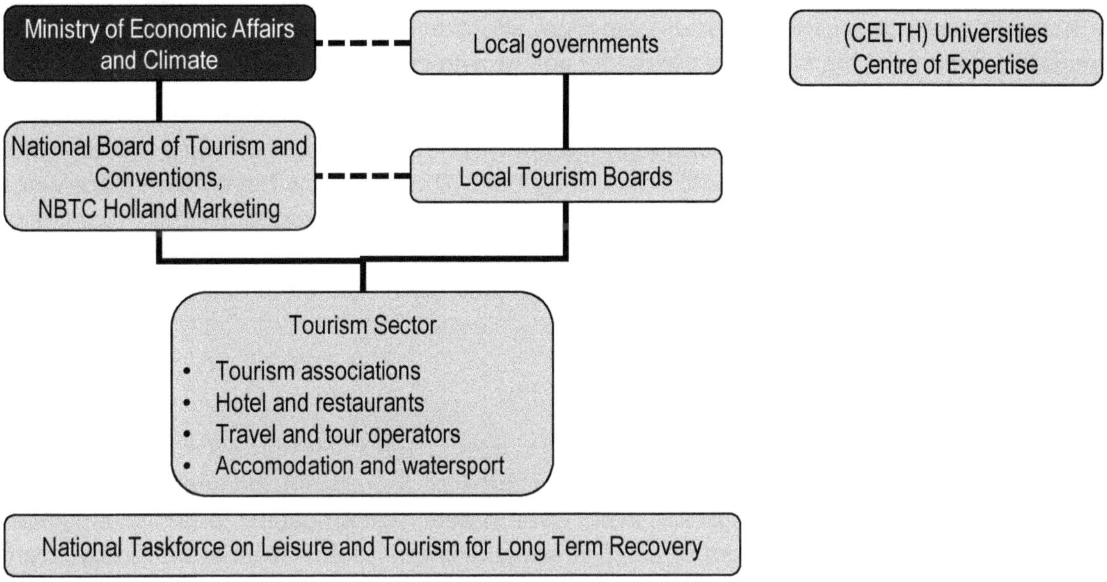

Source: OECD, adapted from Ministry of Economic Affairs and Climate, 2022.

Tourism policies and programmes

In 2019, the Netherlands developed a national tourism vision, Perspective 2030, with the objective that everyone in the country must benefit from tourism. Perspective 2030 is used by the Ministry of Economic Affairs and Climate Policy as a guideline for future policy development and policy objectives. Achieving the ambition of Perspective 2030 requires a switch from promoting destinations to developing destinations and making visitor flows more manageable while capitalising on ambitions and opportunities. The vision centres on the shared interest of residents, visitors and businesses. It is based on five strategic pillars:

- Creating more benefits than burdens from tourism.
- Making the Netherlands attractive everywhere by positioning different destinations.
- Promoting accessibility and reachable tourist destinations.
- Enhancing sustainable tourism with less waste and pollution.
- Building a hospitable experience for visitors.

The NBTC, the Ministry and the provinces adopted a related action programme, used as a living document in which the strategic pillars are worked out. Despite the enormous effect of COVID-19 on the tourism sector, the three main policy goals remain:

- Sustainable growth of tourism.
- Increased co-operation between different layers of government.
- Support for the tourism sector, focusing on opportunities for sustainability, entrepreneurship, innovation and digitisation.

The NBTC, together with stakeholders within the Taskforce, aims to align the Dutch tourism sector in accelerating climate action by developing a Roadmap for Climate Neutral Tourism in the Netherlands. This roadmap, which will be based upon the main pillars of the Glasgow Declaration, will bring together knowledge on the state of the destination regarding climate action.

Tourism is an integral part of the Netherlands' enterprise policy, which focuses on stimulating innovation, entrepreneurship, digitalisation and sustainability, and access to financing and public services for business owners. In recent years the Netherlands has paid more attention to the sustainable development of tourism as the negative impacts of the country's popularity and growth in tourism have become clear.

The Ministry is also responsible for encouraging innovation, digitalisation and sustainability for entrepreneurs, specifically SMEs. To encourage nationwide co-operation, the Ministry, together with NBTC and the provinces, organises the National Tourism Summit. Three editions have taken place since 2018. This involved a broad group of representatives of the business community, tourist organisations and government bodies from all parts of the country. The objective was to work on a joint approach to enable cities, towns and regions to benefit from growing tourism and learn from each other.

Conscious Destinations Agenda in the Netherlands

The Centre of Expertise on Leisure, Tourism and Hospitality (CELTH) has put together a multi-year knowledge agenda for the hospitality domain. Knowledge on five urgent themes is being developed around the Conscious Destination Agenda: living environment, human capital, organisational capacity, smartness, and leisure offer. Partners of CELTH are challenged to co-invest and thereby strengthen the much-needed knowledge foundation in the hospitality domain.

CELTH specifically opts for the destination level because that is where all the different sub-sectors and actors come together. At the destination, hospitality and value are created for tourists, residents and companies. In a conscious destination, parties strive for an outcome in which the hospitality domain has the most positive possible social, ecological and economic impact and in which it leads to the highest possible quality of life, experience and work. In a conscious destination, the social value of the hospitality domain is put first. All actors work on the most positive possible economic, social and ecological impacts for residents (quality of life), visitors (quality of experiences) and professionals within the domain (quality of work).

The approach to integrally optimising a destination is gaining more and more support, and CELTH expects that this will become dominant in the (near) future, not only in the Netherlands but worldwide. Social and political pressure is mounting to reconsider the usual approach that only leads to growth or that sees the hospitality domain as a mere threat. The conscious choices underlying the optimisation approach are in line with the vision of conscious destinations.

Statistical Profile

Netherlands: Domestic, inbound and outbound tourism

	2017	2018	2019	2020	2021
TOURISM FLOWS, THOUSAND					
Domestic tourism					
Total domestic trips	..	..	..	..	..
Overnight visitors (tourists)	24 311	25 132	25 787	20 035	25 472
Same-day visitors (excursionists)	..	..	..	..	..
Nights in all types of accommodation	67 529	69 080	71 692	64 042	82 479
Hotels and similar establishments	52 628	53 614	55 720	46 777	60 027
Other collective establishments	14 901	15 466	15 972	17 266	22 452
Private accommodation	..	..	..	..	..
Inbound tourism					
Total international arrivals	..	..	..	..	..
Overnight visitors (tourists)	17 924	18 780	20 129	7 265	6 248
Same-day visitors (excursionists)	..	..	..	..	..
Top markets					
Germany	5 243	5 689	6 175	3 283	2 471
Belgium	2 224	2 398	2 507	1 102	1 100
France	842	893	963	386	413
America (Continent)	2 013	2 072	2 181	384	350
Asia	1 373	1 360	1 473	253	240
Nights in all types of accommodation	44 169	47 002	51 750	21 372	18 615
Hotels and similar establishments	39 272	41 721	45 848	17 990	15 657
Other collective establishments	4 897	5 282	5 902	3 383	2 958
Private accommodation	..	..	..	..	..
Outbound tourism					
Total international departures	..	..	..	..	..
Overnight visitors (tourists)	22 084 |	22 277	22 925	11 719	10 670 p
Same-day visitors (excursionists)	21 403 |	13 791 |	12 709	5 038	3 940 p
Top destinations					
France	2 807 |	2 876	2 692	1 517	2 032 p
Germany	3 785 |	3 789	3 734	2 570	1 574 p
Belgium	1 628 |	1 579	1 787	1 030	1 113 p
Spain	2 695 |	2 621	2 583	993	1 096 p
Italy	1 462 |	1 440	1 322	533	970 p
TOURISM RECEIPTS AND EXPENDITURE, MILLION EUR					
Inbound tourism					
Total international receipts	21 141	22 529	23 962	10 909	10 554
International travel receipts	15 167	16 236	17 624	8 769	8 183
International passenger transport receipts	5 974	6 293	6 339	2 139	2 371
Outbound tourism					
Total international expenditure	22 319	22 188	23 553	8 083	10 122
International travel expenditure	19 454	19 287	20 656	7 157	9 400
International passenger transport expenditure	2 865	2 901	2 898	925	722

.. Not available; p Provisional data; | Break in series
Source: OECD Tourism Statistics (Database).

StatLink https://stat.link/ut49ai

Netherlands: Enterprises and employment in tourism

	Number of establishments	Number of persons employed				
	2021	2017	2018	2019	2020	2021
Total	..	**459 000**	**479 000**	**496 000**	**419 000 p**	**401 000 p**
Tourism industries	**208 365 p**	..	..	..	..	..
Accommodation services for visitors	10 115 p	..	..	..	..	..
Hotels and similar establishments	5 445 p	..	..	..	..	..
Food and beverage serving industry	54 910 p	..	..	..	..	..
Passenger transport	13 905 p	..	..	..	..	..
Air passenger transport	325 p	..	..	..	..	..
Railways passenger transport	25 p	..	..	..	..	..
Road passenger transport	12 335 p	..	..	..	..	..
Water passenger transport	1 220 p	..	..	..	..	..
Passenger transport supporting services	5 860 p	..	..	..	..	..
Transport equipment rental	1 120 p	..	..	..	..	..
Travel agencies and other reservation services industry	6 055 p	..	..	..	..	..
Cultural industry	93 545 p	..	..	..	..	..
Sports and recreation industry	22 855 p	..	..	..	..	..
Retail trade of country-specific tourism characteristic goods	..	..	..	..	..	..
Other country-specific tourism industries	..	..	..	..	..	..
Other industries	..	..	..	..	..	..

.. Not available; p Provisional data
Source: OECD Tourism Statistics (Database).

StatLink https://stat.link/dzo9ec

Netherlands: Internal tourism consumption

Million EUR

	2021		
	Domestic tourism expenditure	Inbound tourism expenditure	Internal tourism consumption
Total	**37 764 p**	**17 819 p**	**58 928 p**
Consumption products	..	..	..
Tourism characteristic products	..	..	..
Accommodation services for visitors	..	..	..
Food and beverage serving services	..	..	..
Passenger transport services	..	..	..
Air passenger transport services	..	..	..
Railways passenger transport services	..	..	..
Road passenger transport services	..	..	..
Water passenger transport services	..	..	..
Passenger transport supporting services	..	..	..
Transport equipment rental services	..	..	..
Travel agencies and other reservation services industry	..	..	..
Cultural services	..	..	..
Sports and recreation services	..	..	..
Country-specific tourism characteristic goods	..	..	..
Country-specific tourism characteristic services	..	..	..
Other consumption products	..	..	..
Tourism connected products	..	..	..
Non-tourism related consumption products	..	..	..
Non-consumption products	..	..	..

.. Not available; p Provisional data
Source: OECD Tourism Statistics (Database).

StatLink https://stat.link/rntd01

New Zealand

Tourism in the economy and outlook for recovery

New Zealand's international borders have reopened in stages to visitors following closure for most of 2020-21. In the year ending March 2020, tourism directly contributed NZD 16.3 billion, or 5.5% of GDP. The impacts of the pandemic saw this fall to NZD 8.5 billion, or 2.9% of GDP, in the year ending March 2021. Tourism directly employed 218 580 people in 2020, representing 7.9% of total employment. This fell to 146 295 people (5.2% of total employment) in the year ending March 2021, a 33% reduction in the tourism workforce from pre-pandemic levels.

Strict border closures saw international visitors fall to 996 000 in 2020 and to 207 000 in 2021, remaining 94.7% below 2019 levels. This caused a 91% decline in international tourism expenditure, which fell to NZD 1.5 billion in the year ending March 2021. International visitors accounted for 43% of total tourism expenditure prior to the pandemic. Prior to COVID-19, 39% of international arrivals to New Zealand were from Australia. Some of New Zealand's largest international visitor markets are the United States, the United Kingdom, and Japan.

Domestic tourism expenditure increased to NZD 24.6 billion in the year ending March 2021, 2.6% above pre-pandemic levels.

Tourism governance and funding

The Ministry of Business, Innovation and Employment (MBIE) advises the government on creating productive, sustainable and inclusive growth in the tourism sector. MBIE works closely with other government agencies whose portfolios intersect with the tourism sector. These include the Department of Conservation, Department of Internal Affairs, Ministry of Culture and Heritage, and Ministry of Transport. Tourism New Zealand (TNZ), a public body, markets the country as a visitor destination internationally.

Local and regional authorities provide tourism-related infrastructure and local planning frameworks to help communities grow and manage local tourism challenges. Regional Tourism Organisations (RTOs) have traditionally been responsible for promoting their destinations. In recent years, RTOs have also assumed leadership in bringing together local stakeholders to develop destination management plans to ensure their destinations are well-managed and sustainable.

RTOs are largely funded and governed by local or regional councils, with some RTOs receiving additional funding from other sources, including central government, annual membership fees from local industry and industry partnership funding. The RTOs' destination management work has been accelerated through COVID-19 funding packages provided by the central government and with the support of their membership organisation, Regional Tourism New Zealand. By the end of 2022, every RTO in New Zealand is expected to have a published destination management plan for their region.

The New Zealand Government Budget directly related to tourism for the 2022/23 financial year is NZD 296 million. This includes NZD 3 million for tourism data. Budget 2022 reflects the shift away from time-bound COVID-19 funding back towards 'business as usual' levels as borders reopened. The main areas of the tourism-related budget include:

- NZD 112 million allocated to TNZ for the promotion of New Zealand to key markets as a visitor and business destination.
- NZD 54 million for the development of a Tourism Innovation Programme.
- NZD 32 million for the funding of New Zealand's tourism infrastructure, including cycle trails.
- Additional funding to meet COVID-19 response programme commitments.

A feature of the New Zealand tourism funding landscape is revenue from the International Visitor (Tourism and Conservation) Levy. Revenue is tied to the volume of international visitors. Most visitors are required to pay the levy, with some exceptions. In 2022/23, NZD 5 million was allocated from the International Visitor (Tourism and Conservation) Levy for additional tourism data funding.

New Zealand: Organisational chart of tourism bodies

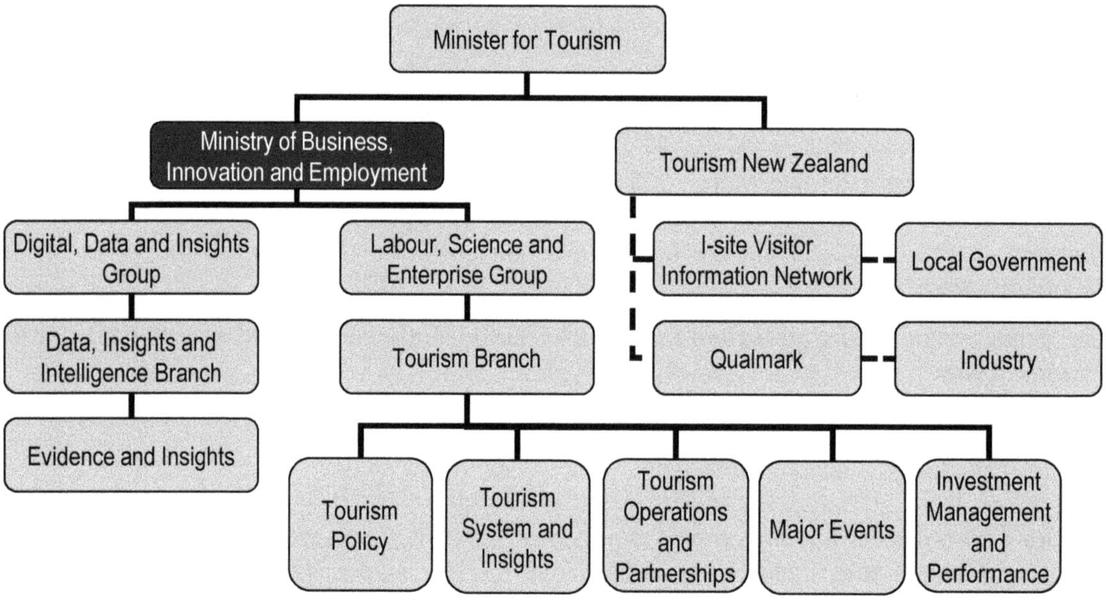

Source: OECD, adapted from the Ministry of Business, Innovation and Employment, 2022.

Tourism policies and programmes

In 2019, the New Zealand-Aotearoa Government Tourism Strategy was released. The Strategy sets out a stewardship role for the government in tourism to ensure tourism enriches New Zealand through more productive, sustainable and inclusive growth. Priority actions for delivering this include co-ordination across the tourism system, developing long-term sustainable funding mechanisms, facilitating destination management and planning, and better data and insight.

In 2020-21, New Zealand provided a range of support to the tourism sector to enable its eventual recovery from the pandemic. In 2020, immediate support came from economy-wide support measures, including NZD 1.8 billion through a Wage Subsidy scheme and NZD 285 million through a Small Business Cash Flow scheme. An NZD 400 million Tourism Recovery Package was also provided, which funded initiatives including a Strategic Tourism Assets Protection programme.

In 2021, an NZD 200 million Tourism Communities: Support, Recovery and Reset Plan invested in new programmes such as psycho-social support and wellbeing services, small business support, tourism infrastructure, the conservation estate, and Māori development. The plan focused on five communities with a high dependence on international tourism in their local economies while advancing a nationwide re-set.

New Zealand has taken the COVID-19 pandemic as an opportunity to accelerate work streams that focus on transforming the tourism industry into a regenerative model. The focus is shifting from survival and recovery to supporting the tourism industry to reflect the new model. The Minister of Tourism has announced four key principles that will guide the recovery and transformation of New Zealand's tourism sector. These are: i) elevate 'Brand New Zealand' so international travellers see New Zealand as a leading aspirational destination, ii) rebuild tourism on a sustainable and regenerative model (see Box 3.10), iii) ensure that tourism's costs and negative impacts are mitigated or priced into the visitor experience, and iv) establish partnerships between the government and industry.

In 2021, the Minister of Tourism announced reforms to freedom camping laws to improve the sustainability of freedom camping, protect the environment, and ensure local communities support the hosting of freedom campers. Increasing numbers of freedom campers have placed burdens on the natural environment and some communities in New Zealand. A Freedom Camping Bill is currently being considered by the House of Representatives.

In 2022, the Minister of Tourism announced an NZD 54 million Innovation Programme for Tourism Recovery. As New Zealand welcomes international visitors, there is a need to look to the future and innovate. The programme is designed to help stimulate a shift towards a regenerative, low-carbon, productive, and innovative tourism sector. The programme is targeted at transformative initiatives that deliver on climate, environmental sustainability and technology outcomes, improve the sector's resilience, or promote and protect things of social and cultural value to Māori across the visitor journey. A Tourism Data Co-Governance Group was appointed in 2022. The group is to provide leadership on the collection, dissemination and understanding of tourism data and recommend needs for future investment in tourism data. Representatives from industry and government previously agreed that a co-governed data system would create value for users of tourism data.

Work on the Tourism Industry Transformation Plan (ITP), which has the overarching objective of establishing a regenerative tourism model, is underway (see box below). The ITP is created in a partnership between the government, tourism industry, Māori, unions and workers. The first phase focuses on Better Work, addressing some of the workforce challenges in tourism. The second phase will focus on the environment.

Tourism Industry Transformation Plan in New Zealand

In 2021, the New Zealand Minister of tourism announced that work would begin on a Tourism Industry Transformation Plan (ITP). The ITP has an overarching objective of establishing a regenerative model of tourism, to create a sector that adds more than only economic value and gives back to the community and the environment in which it operates. The ITP is designed and delivered through a partnership of government, Māori, industry, and workers.

The first phase of the Tourism ITP, Better Work, will identify a series of practical actions that can be taken by actors in the tourism system to address workforce challenges. Several systemic challenges exist in the tourism workforce, including negative perceptions of working in the sector; difficulty attracting and retaining talent; reliance on low-paid, temporary and migrant labour; and seasonality.

The second phase of the Tourism ITP will identify practical actions for the tourism industry to adapt to and mitigate climate change and promote positive ecological outcomes. Ensuring the tourism industry has a positive impact on the environment is critical to achieving a regenerative tourism model.

Statistical Profile

New Zealand: Domestic, inbound and outbound tourism

	2017	2018	2019	2020	2021
TOURISM FLOWS, THOUSAND					
Domestic tourism					
Total domestic trips	..	..	..	..	..
Overnight visitors (tourists)	..	..	..	..	..
Same-day visitors (excursionists)	..	..	..	..	..
Nights in all types of accommodation	22 225	22 778	..	..	23 648
Hotels and similar establishments	16 963	17 279	..	..	15 343
Other collective establishments	5 262	5 499	..	..	8 305
Private accommodation	..	..	..	..	..
Inbound tourism[1]					
Total international arrivals	3 723	3 858	3 888	996	207
Overnight visitors (tourists)	3 555	3 686	3 702	949	205
Same-day visitors (excursionists)	168	172	186	48	2
Top markets					
Australia	1 393	1 411	1 445	360	160
United Kingdom	244	232	225	94	6
United States	315	338	348	125	5
China (People's Republic of)	412	441	395	59	2
Japan	98	96	94	26	1
Nights in all types of accommodation	17 239	17 589	..	..	1 372
Hotels and similar establishments	14 539	14 723	..	..	1 216
Other collective establishments	2 700	2 867	..	..	156
Private accommodation	..	..	..	..	..
Outbound tourism					
Total international departures	2 860	3 045	3 225	511	234
Overnight visitors (tourists)	2 814	2 989	3 072	..	..
Same-day visitors (excursionists)	29	29	29	..	..
Top destinations					
Australia	1 222	1 205	1 250	..	..
United States	204	215	206	..	..
Fiji	176	192	191	..	..
China (People's Republic of)	121	132	142	..	..
United Kingdom	123	125	129	..	..
TOURISM RECEIPTS AND EXPENDITURE, MILLION NZD					
Inbound tourism					
Total international receipts	16 560	17 504	17 920	10 809	..
International travel receipts	14 924	15 717	15 988	8 869	..
International passenger transport receipts	1 636 e	1 787 e	1 932 e	1 940 e	..
Outbound tourism					
Total international expenditure	7 645	8 232	8 280	4 004	..
International travel expenditure	6 272	6 670	6 527	2 227	..
International passenger transport expenditure	1 373 e	1 562 e	1 753 e	1 777 e	..

.. Not available; e Estimated value

1. Arrivals from demand side surveys; Nights from supply side surveys.

Source: OECD Tourism Statistics (Database).

StatLink https://stat.link/be9k17

New Zealand: Enterprises and employment in tourism

	Number of establishments	Number of persons employed				
	2021	2017	2018	2019	2020	2021
Total	..	**208 251**	**221 046**	**219 867**	**218 580**	**146 295**
Tourism industries	..	**170 937**	**181 593**	**180 975**	**179 427**	**113 922**
Accommodation services for visitors	5 763	26 847	28 920	28 761	27 318	12 529
Hotels and similar establishments	..	..	..	..	..	..
Food and beverage serving industry	17 583	59 919	63 525	62 202	62 085	47 078
Passenger transport	..	10 155	10 224	14 907	15 156	9 234
Air passenger transport	369	10 155	10 224	10 677	10 818	5 128
Railways passenger transport	6	..	..	..	..	..
Road passenger transport	8 067	..	..	..	..	..
Water passenger transport	174	..	..	..	..	..
Passenger transport supporting services	..	15 333	16 731	12 669	13 080	2 596
Transport equipment rental	1 500	4 296	4 500	4 488	4 455	3 831
Travel agencies and other reservation services industry	1 965	..	..	..	..	..
Cultural industry	3 621	8 064	8 307	8 598	8 433	6 918
Sports and recreation industry	6 201	..	..	..	..	..
Retail trade of country-specific tourism characteristic goods	..	32 637	34 479	33 480	32 751	23 874
Other country-specific tourism industries	..	13 686	14 907	15 870	16 149	7 863
Other industries	..	**37 314**	**39 453**	**38 895**	**39 153**	**32 373**

.. Not available
Source: OECD Tourism Statistics (Database).

StatLink https://stat.link/wlyxn8

New Zealand: Internal tourism consumption
Million NZD

	2021		
	Domestic tourism expenditure	Inbound tourism expenditure	Internal tourism consumption
Total	..	..	..
Consumption products	**22 390 p**	**1 331 p**	**23 722 p**
Tourism characteristic products	9 287 p	752 p	10 042 p
Accommodation services for visitors	1 492 p	283 p	1 776 p
Food and beverage serving services	2 371 p	249 p	2 621 p
Passenger transport services	4 553 p	220 p	4 774 p
Air passenger transport services	2 306 p	147 p	2 454 p
Railways passenger transport services	..	..	..
Road passenger transport services	..	..	..
Water passenger transport services	..	..	..
Passenger transport supporting services	..	..	..
Transport equipment rental services	..	..	..
Travel agencies and other reservation services industry	..	..	..
Cultural services	..	..	..
Sports and recreation services	..	..	..
Country-specific tourism characteristic goods	871 p	0 p	871 p
Country-specific tourism characteristic services	..	..	..
Other consumption products	12 012 p	496 p	12 504 p
Tourism connected products	..	..	..
Non-tourism related consumption products	..	..	..
Non-consumption products	..	..	..

.. Not available; p Provisional data
Source: OECD Tourism Statistics (Database).

StatLink https://stat.link/veftqm

Norway

Tourism in the economy and outlook for recovery

In the last decade, the economic contribution of the tourism sector in Norway has increased considerably, reaching NOK 127.4 billion in 2019 and representing 3.6% of total GDP. Tourism has also become a significant employer, particularly in rural areas. In 2019, the sector sustained over 182 800 full-time jobs, accounting for 7.4% of total employment.

Total tourism expenditure amounted to NOK 194 billion in 2019, with approximately 30% being spent by international tourists. In 2020, international overnight visitors declined by 76.4% to 1.4 million. There was a limited recovery in 2021 when international arrivals were slightly above 2020 levels. The top source markets in 2021 were Germany, Sweden, the Netherlands and the United States.

Domestic tourism, both for leisure and business purposes, has always dominated the sector, with Norwegians accounting for 70% of all commercial nights in 2019. The impacts of COVID-19 saw the share of domestic tourism increase to 86% of commercial accommodation nights in 2020. This was even higher in 2021, as domestic tourism recovered to 85% of 2019 levels.

Norway projects a recovery of inbound tourism to pre-pandemic years in 2023 or 2024.

Tourism governance and funding

The Ministry of Trade, Industry and Fisheries is responsible for developing and regulating tourism. The Ministry co-operates closely with other principal ministries relevant to tourism, including those dealing with local government, regional development, agriculture, food, transportation, climate and environment.

Through the Ministry of Local Government and Modernisation, regional and local authorities have a key role in promoting tourism development. They establish conditions of key importance to tourism, with responsibility for planning and regulating infrastructure, utilities, national parks and natural and cultural heritage attractions. The Ministry of Local Government and Modernisation owns half of Innovation Norway.

Several regions (and some municipalities) have their own strategies for tourism and give financial support to their regional and local Destination Management Organisations. Regional reform initiated in 2020 gave the counties renewed roles and wider responsibilities and is expected to provide a more efficient framework to solve cross-sectoral challenges to benefit the tourism industry, which interacts with many sectors and stakeholders within and across regional borders.

The Ministry of Climate and Environment and Ministry of Transport are key partners, given their roles in developing policies in favour of a more sustainable tourism sector. In addition, The Ministry of Agriculture and Food is contributing to realising the potential for increased value creation resulting from co-operation between farmers and food producers, restaurants and other parts of the tourism industry.

Innovation Norway, a state-owned company, delivers the national tourism organisation function. Innovation Norway's main goal is to increase overall economic growth and value creation for the Norwegian economy, considering sustainability goals. To reach this target in tourism, Innovation Norway focuses on stimulating product development and promoting Norway as a brand and tourist destination internationally. Innovation Norway is funded mainly by the Ministry of Trade, Industry and Fisheries but also receives funding from other ministries and counties. For its NTO role, Innovation Norway receives approximately NOK 180 million annually.

Innovation Norway allocates travel and tourism companies loans, grants, and guarantees. In 2020/21, these sums increased substantially due to extraordinary measures and transfers to compensate businesses for COVID-19 impacts. In 2020, Innovation Norway allocated NOK 724 million in loans and grants to travel and tourism companies, an increase of 137% from the previous year. Of this amount, NOK 249 million was extraordinary funding. The remaining NOK 475 million was allocated as industry-neutral business support. The funds have largely been used for restructuring activities.

Norway: Organisational chart of tourism bodies

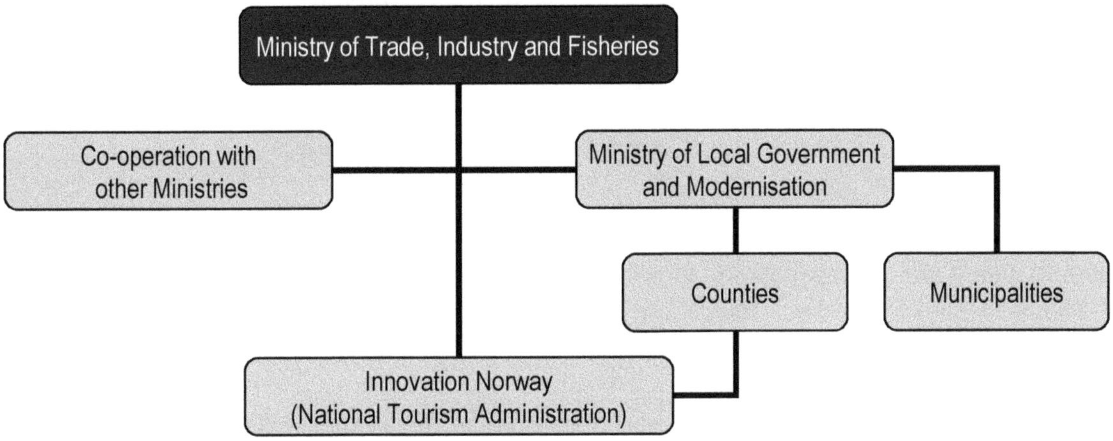

Source: OECD, adapted from the Ministry of Trade, Industry and Fisheries, 2022.

Tourism policies and programmes

In 2020, Norway developed a National Tourism Strategy 2030 - Big impact, small footprint. The Strategy process was completed in co-operation with a wide range of stakeholders. The Strategy aims to set out a series of measures to ensure the development of a more sustainable and profitable tourism sector by 2030. The Strategy was published in May 2021 and outlines 23 policy measures being taken into account in the post-pandemic recovery and possible changes in future travel trends.

Examples of recommended policy measures include:

- Funding to stimulate the recruitment of qualified staff in the recovery phase, focusing on the service sector.
- Initiating Reis21 – a national strategic instrument for creating a long-term platform for knowledge-based innovation and restructuring in the Norwegian tourist industry.
- Creating the Official Norwegian Report (NOU) on framework conditions for the tourism sector.

Furthermore, to improve the evidence base for tourism, Norway has:

- Initiated a pre-study on the possibility of establishing a national monitor, a big data analysis tool for the tourism sector intended to provide a comprehensive view of tourism as a sector.
- Funded the development of a climate-smart digital calculator that links data on CO2 emissions from transportation (see Box. 3.6), and tourism expenditure from the various tourist markets. The

goal is to permit informed strategic choices by tourism stakeholders so that the industry can more easily meet the target of a 10% annual reduction in total greenhouse gas emissions from commercial tourism activity.

A key long-term challenge of the Norwegian tourism sector is its relatively low profitability due to a low share of high value-added tourism products, seasonality and a lack of co-operation in and between destinations. Sustainability is also key and a prerequisite to developing Norway as a tourism destination. In 2021, Norway committed to several new policy measures for sustainable tourism development (see Box below). In addition, the Sustainable Destination Certification scheme, which enhances destination management, has been expanded and adjusted, and a new regulatory framework for more sustainable fishing tourism has been implemented. The sustainable tourism policy has also included measures such as selecting and marking a growing number of National Hiking Trails to make them more robust, accessible and attractive for the visitor.

In recent years, certain places have faced challenges such as overcrowding, with negative effects also reported on local communities and their surroundings. There is a need to increase efforts to spread tourism, both geographically and seasonally, improve interactions between the tourism sector and local communities, and increase the local economic gains from tourism.

Tourism policy measures for sustainable tourism development in Norway

Building on the Strategy 'Big Impact, Small Footprint', Norway is emphasising sustainability at the destination and company levels. The goal is to reduce the negative long-term effects of the pandemic and create more year-round jobs within tourism. Specific measures the government has committed to include:

- Launching a pilot programme for sustainable tourism, supporting local nature and environmental management and emission-free travel to and from Norwegian destinations.
- Developing a national certification system for local and regional guides in co-operation with the relevant organisations.
- Ensuring value creation and adequate facilities locally by enabling municipalities to introduce visitor contributions (a variant of a tourist tax).
- Reviewing the framework conditions for regional Destination Management Organisations in co-operation with the industry.
- Assisting Norwegian tourism companies in their contact with international online travel agencies.
- Developing further the scheme of National Tourist Roads.

Statistical Profile

Norway: Domestic, inbound and outbound tourism

	2017	2018	2019	2020	2021
TOURISM FLOWS, THOUSAND					
Domestic tourism					
Total domestic trips	..	..	..	..	..
Overnight visitors (tourists)	15 080	18 970	14 710	16 580	20 450
Same-day visitors (excursionists)	..	..	..	..	..
Nights in all types of accommodation	52 550	63 280	48 030	66 650	80 100
Hotels and similar establishments	10 880	11 480	10 810	8 850	10 200
Other collective establishments	15 490	15 220	5 480	10 480	11 060
Private accommodation	26 180	36 580	31 740	47 320	58 840
Inbound tourism					
Total international arrivals	..	..	..	..	..
Overnight visitors (tourists)	5 845	5 688	5 879	1 387	1 435
Same-day visitors (excursionists)	..	..	..	..	..
Top markets					
Germany	894 e	1 150 e	1 041 e	258 e	362 e
Sweden	678 e	623 e	574 e	158 e	166 e
Netherlands	438 e	435 e	429 e	83 e	112 e
United States	..	487 e	555 e	105 e	112 e
Denmark	406 e	371 e	319 e	219 e	109 e
Nights in all types of accommodation	9 949	10 138	10 701	3 318	3 310
Hotels and similar establishments	8 001	8 065	8 472	2 689	2 500
Other collective establishments	1 948	2 073	2 230	629	809
Private accommodation	..	..	..	..	..
Outbound tourism					
Total international departures	16 800	16 530	18 624	3 203	3 699
Overnight visitors (tourists)	8 170	8 120	9 070	1 745	2 027
Same-day visitors (excursionists)	8 630	8 410	9 554	1 458	1 672
Top destinations					
Sweden	1 363	1 361	1 918	239	587
Denmark	742	882	1 017	224	284
Spain	1 359	1 170	1 225	216	266
Germany	415	563	548	112	188
United Kingdom	573	638	661	166	79
TOURISM RECEIPTS AND EXPENDITURE, MILLION NOK					
Inbound tourism					
Total international receipts	45 974	59 235	61 891	14 729	..
International travel receipts	45 974	48 214	51 520	14 729 p	..
International passenger transport receipts	..	..	..	..	..
Outbound tourism					
Total international expenditure	134 099	149 039	155 626	34 835	..
International travel expenditure	134 099	138 842	145 315	34 835 p	..
International passenger transport expenditure	..	10 196	10 311	..	..

.. Not available; e Estimated value; p Provisional data
Source: OECD Tourism Statistics (Database).

StatLink https://stat.link/hsv4k3

Norway: Enterprises and employment in tourism

	Number of establishments	Number of persons employed				
	2020	2017	2018	2019	2020	2021
Total	..	..	..	..	..	..
Tourism industries	**26 287**	**165 000**	**179 000**	**182 800**	..	..
Accommodation services for visitors	3 481	22 500	24 500	24 900	..	..
Hotels and similar establishments	1 456	..	..	..	..	..
Food and beverage serving industry	12 251	47 100	56 500	57 200	..	..
Passenger transport	7 217	50 000	51 100	51 700	..	..
Air passenger transport	125	5 900	6 200	6 300	..	..
Railways passenger transport	74	3 700	3 800	3 800	..	..
Road passenger transport	6 593	29 200	29 800	30 100	..	..
Water passenger transport	425	11 200	11 300	11 500	..	..
Passenger transport supporting services	..	..	..	..	..	..
Transport equipment rental	695	7 000	7 400	7 700	..	..
Travel agencies and other reservation services industry	2 643	5 200	5 700	5 800	..	..
Cultural industry	..	24 600	23 400	25 000	..	..
Sports and recreation industry	..	8 600	10 400	10 500	..	..
Retail trade of country-specific tourism characteristic goods	..	..	..	..	..	..
Other country-specific tourism industries	..	..	..	..	..	..
Other industries	..	..	..	..	..	..

.. Not available
Source: OECD Tourism Statistics (Database).

StatLink https://stat.link/45vnmp

Norway: Internal tourism consumption

Million NOK

	2019		
	Domestic tourism expenditure	Inbound tourism expenditure	Internal tourism consumption
Total	..	..	..
Consumption products	**134 905**	**59 425**	**194 330 p**
Tourism characteristic products	92 755	33 535	126 290 p
Accommodation services for visitors	10 961	9 334	20 295 p
Food and beverage serving services	16 365	9 502	25 867 p
Passenger transport services	42 199	12 049	54 248 p
Air passenger transport services	27 104	7 034	34 138 p
Railways passenger transport services	2 837	838	3 675 p
Road passenger transport services	4 516	762	5 278 p
Water passenger transport services	7 742	3 415	11 157 p
Passenger transport supporting services	..	..	..
Transport equipment rental services	400	355	755 p
Travel agencies and other reservation services industry	19 303	477	19 780 p
Cultural services	1 562	757	2 319 p
Sports and recreation services	1 965	1 061	3 026 p
Country-specific tourism characteristic goods	..	..	..
Country-specific tourism characteristic services	..	..	..
Other consumption products	42 150	25 890	68 040 p
Tourism connected products	..	..	..
Non-tourism related consumption products	..	..	..
Non-consumption products	..	..	..

.. Not available; p Provisional data
Source: OECD Tourism Statistics (Database).

StatLink https://stat.link/tby2wx

Poland

Tourism in the economy and outlook for recovery

In 2020, the total value of the tourism economy in Poland was estimated at PLN 104.3 billion – a decrease of 26.4% since 2019. This equates to an estimated 4.5% of Poland's GDP (accounting for direct and indirect impacts). In 2020, 195 539 people were employed in the accommodation and catering sector, a decrease of 6.1% compared to 2019.

After hitting a record high of 21.2 million international tourist arrivals in 2019, Poland recorded just 8.4 million arrivals in 2020, a decrease of 60.2%. Germany remains the largest source market, accounting for 40.7% of inbound tourism. The second largest source market was Ukraine (12.1%). In 2020, international tourism receipts decreased by 60.7% to PLN 28.1 billion, accounting for 2.1% of total export earnings.

In 2021, international arrivals increased to 9.7 million, but remained 54% below pre-pandemic levels. Poland recorded a faster recovery for domestic tourism, with 46.3 million domestic tourists in 2021, only 7.4% below the 2019 level.

At the beginning of the war in Ukraine, Poland experienced a decline in bookings across the country. Due to the persisting uncertainty of the multiple crises, the pace of the tourism rebound in Poland is difficult to forecast. It is projected that in 2024 international arrivals will come close to the pre-pandemic levels, and in 2025 it may exceed this level.

Tourism governance and funding

In 2021, the Minister of Sport and Tourism took over responsibility for tourism from the Minister of Economic Development. The Ministry of Sport and Tourism is responsible for all tourism-related matters, including the sector's management, legislation and regulation.

The Ministry also supervises the Polish Tourism Organisation responsible for marketing and promoting Poland as a tourist destination and ensuring the development and operation of the Polish tourist information system. The organisation has 14 international offices located in established and emerging source markets and co-operates with regional and local tourist organisations and others involved in promoting and developing tourism at the regional level.

At the county and municipal levels, tourism development is the responsibility of regional and local governments. Local or regional-level tasks fall into two groups: tasks not allocated to other bodies under relevant legislation and tasks commissioned by the National Government. Regional Tourism Organisations (RTOs) are organisations within which co-operation is conducted between the local government (particularly at the provincial level) and tourism sector representatives. Joint activities focus on product and tourist information system development, consumer marketing, and promotion in Poland and abroad. As well as promotion, its role typically includes initiating, assessing and supporting tourism infrastructure development and modernisation plans and co-operation with the Polish Tourism Organisation. At the local level, there are about 130 local tourist organisations. Assigned tasks include tourism promotion of designated areas and supporting and developing tourist information systems.

The Minister of Sport and Tourism established the Tourism Experts Council for tourism development in Poland. The Council, made up of experts and practitioners, is designed to support initiatives in favour of a sector that has been hit hard by the COVID-19 pandemic. 2022-23 will be a period of formulating new medium- and long-term programmes related to the transformation and development of tourism at the EU and national levels.

In 2021, the tourism budget was PLN 66.5 million, an increase of PLN 4.7 million compared to 2020, including PLN 56.1 million for the Polish Tourism Organisation. In addition, in 2021-27, specific tourism sector projects are being supported by EU structural funds, such as EU Green Deal.

Poland: Organisational chart of tourism bodies

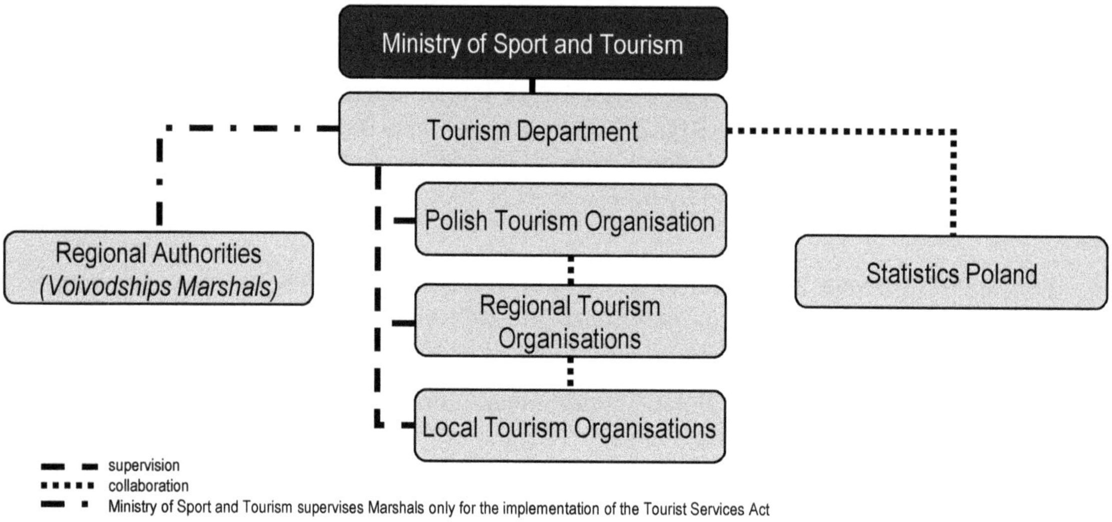

Source: OECD, adapted from the Ministry of Sport and Tourism, 2022.

Tourism policies and programmes

The Programme for Tourism Development defined goals until 2020. The Ministry of Economic Development and Technology has initiated work on developing a new policy document for tourism. Work is currently underway to develop a forecast diagnosis for the strategy document. The most important challenges for the tourism sector are mitigating the impact of the pandemic and Russia's war in Ukraine and the related price and demand shocks.

The Programme aims to define the direction of the development and transformation of tourism, boost resilience in any future crises and enable the sector's continued development. The principles of sustainable development are an important element in all planned actions. The activities will include research and analysis, education and training, tourism product development and promotion support. Work is also underway on ensuring appropriate legislative solutions to assist these aims.

Poland is using the COVID-19 crisis as an opportunity to introduce innovations in tourism, accelerate the green transformation and make necessary regulatory changes. Financial support for the tourism sector has helped it to survive (see box below). In the short-term, substantive support and assistance in reconstruction helped the sector transition from a state of stagnation to full operational activity. Assistance in processing funds, training and strengthening competitiveness are priorities for the immediate future. Due to rising prices, Poland has introduced solutions such as the so-called 'anti-inflation shield'. Moreover, Poland conducts activities to reassure all tourists that it is a safe destination.

The recovery of tourism is based on:

- Sustainable development.
- Improving the competitiveness of SMEs, which are the foundation of the tourism sector.
- Research and transfer of knowledge, particularly using Big Data.
- Development and application of modern digital tools in tourism, in the spirit of green transformation.
- Using tourism as a tool for social and professional development, thereby offering opportunities to more marginal communities.

The pandemic required shifting priorities from long-term planning towards immediate actions supporting the sector. In the long term, the main objective of Poland's national tourism policy is to strengthen the development of a competitive and innovative tourism sector by supporting organisations and initiatives while respecting the principles of sustainable development. The approach focuses on a modern tourism management system, the process of digitalisation and training in tourism-related occupations.

Funding to support tourism businesses survive COVID-19 in Poland

Poland implemented a variety of support funds to help tourism businesses survive the COVID-19 pandemic. These included the following:

- Tourism Reimbursement Fund: a fund of roughly PLN 300 million in grants to more than 100 000 recipients, preventing many bankruptcies and stabilising the sector's financial situation.
- Polish Tourism Voucher: a voucher which covered a single payment of PLN 500 for each child under 18 and a supplementary payment of PLN 500 for children with disabilities, to spend on hotels or tourist events services.
- Tourism Assistance Fund: a fund that provided tour operators loans in case of future cancellation of specific tour events in extraordinary and unavoidable circumstances.
- Support Programme for Local Government Units in Mountain Areas: a programme implemented to support local self-government units in mountain areas. Funds can be used for investments in the construction, extension, reconstruction and modernisation of tourist and municipal tourist infrastructure.
- Polish Health Resorts Programme: allocates funds of approximately PLN 250 million to support health resort municipalities. Government support will cover up to 98% of investment costs.

Statistical Profile

Poland: Domestic, inbound and outbound tourism

	2017	2018	2019	2020	2021
TOURISM FLOWS, THOUSAND					
Domestic tourism					
Total domestic trips	..	95 973	..	..	80 671
Overnight visitors (tourists)	45 952	47 736	50 018	38 570	46 278
Same-day visitors (excursionists)	..	48 237	..	..	34 393
Nights in all types of accommodation	214 207	224 767	233 660	182 815	220 111
Hotels and similar establishments	44 595	47 324	51 912	35 922	42 969
Other collective establishments	66 841	71 902	76 020	52 508	70 937
Private accommodation	102 772	105 541	105 728	94 385	106 206
Inbound tourism					
Total international arrivals	83 804	85 947	88 515	51 076	51 026
Overnight visitors (tourists)	18 258	19 623	21 158	8 418	9 722
Same-day visitors (excursionists)	65 546	66 324	67 356	42 658	41 304
Top markets					
Russia	875	919	955	238	..
Germany	6 504	6 704	7 067	3 426	3 630
Ukraine	1 360	2 038	2 596	1 021	1 496
Belarus	763	793	807	391	490
United Kingdom	851	919	1 002	360	389
Nights in all types of accommodation	113 202	122 065	131 988	57 306	64 531
Hotels and similar establishments	41 390	47 195	52 979	20 637	21 467
Other collective establishments	8 569	13 781	15 849	4 946	4 920
Private accommodation	63 243	61 089	63 160	31 723	38 144
Outbound tourism					
Total international departures	46 681	48 615	50 558	26 893	24 220
Overnight visitors (tourists)	11 958	12 747	13 545	6 187	6 813
Same-day visitors (excursionists)	34 723	35 868	37 013	20 706	17 407
Top destinations					
Germany	2 357	2 438	2 523	1 603	1 797
Croatia	684	703	..	432	492
Greece	..	752	857	..	451
Italy	1 000	1 055	1 114	393	383
Czech Republic	725	762	790	410	383
TOURISM RECEIPTS AND EXPENDITURE, MILLION PLN					
Inbound tourism					
Total international receipts	52 917	56 775	61 514	34 333	..
International travel receipts	47 983	50 613	53 802	31 975	..
International passenger transport receipts	4 934	6 162	7 712	2 358	..
Outbound tourism					
Total international expenditure	35 766	37 970	39 279	21 884	..
International travel expenditure	33 166	34 759	35 653	20 536	..
International passenger transport expenditure	2 600	3 211	3 626	1 348	..

.. Not available

Source: OECD Tourism Statistics (Database).

StatLink https://stat.link/n1d9py

Poland: Enterprises and employment in tourism

	Number of establishments	Number of persons employed[1]				
	2021	2017	2018	2019	2020	2021
Total	..	..	..	..	..	..
Tourism industries	**21 223**	..	..	..	..	..
Accommodation services for visitors	9 942	193 663	195 675	208 257	195 539	..
Hotels and similar establishments	3 949	..	..	..	..	..
Food and beverage serving industry	7 332	..	..	..	..	..
Passenger transport	..	..	..	..	..	..
Air passenger transport	..	..	..	..	..	..
Railways passenger transport	..	..	..	..	..	..
Road passenger transport	..	..	..	..	..	..
Water passenger transport	..	..	..	..	..	..
Passenger transport supporting services	..	..	..	..	..	..
Transport equipment rental	..	..	..	..	..	..
Travel agencies and other reservation services industry	..	..	..	..	..	..
Cultural industry	..	..	..	..	..	..
Sports and recreation industry	..	..	..	..	..	..
Retail trade of country-specific tourism characteristic goods	..	..	..	..	..	..
Other country-specific tourism industries	..	..	..	..	..	..
Other industries	..	..	..	..	..	..

.. Not available

1. Data refer to number of employees.

Source: OECD Tourism Statistics (Database).

StatLink https://stat.link/ld5qan

Poland: Internal tourism consumption

Million PLN

	2015		
	Domestic tourism expenditure	Inbound tourism expenditure	Internal tourism consumption
Total	..	..	..
Consumption products	**21 420**	**36 750**	**65 099**
Tourism characteristic products	15 411	12 854	31 500
Accommodation services for visitors	4 853	3 320	10 244
Food and beverage serving services	4 874	4 328	9 202
Passenger transport services	3 066	2 825	6 599
Air passenger transport services	2 058	1 897	4 121
Railways passenger transport services	219	113	697
Road passenger transport services	783	724	1 685
Water passenger transport services	6	91	97
Passenger transport supporting services	..	..	..
Transport equipment rental services	167	0	547
Travel agencies and other reservation services industry	2 031	458	2 566
Cultural services	419	1 923	2 342
Sports and recreation services	..	..	..
Country-specific tourism characteristic goods	..	..	..
Country-specific tourism characteristic services	..	..	..
Other consumption products	6 009	23 896	33 600
Tourism connected products	..	..	..
Non-tourism related consumption products	..	..	..
Non-consumption products	..	..	..

.. Not available

Source: OECD Tourism Statistics (Database).

StatLink https://stat.link/b1pxfe

Portugal

Tourism in the economy and outlook for recovery

Tourism is a significant part of Portugal's economy, directly accounting for 8.1% of GVA in 2019. This fell sharply to 4.8% in 2020, with preliminary estimates from the Tourism Satellite Account for 2021 pointing to an increase to 5.8% of national GVA (up 27.3% on 2020). Tourism accounted for 20% of exports in 2019, falling to 10% in 2020 driven by a EUR 7.7 billion (58%) decline in tourism receipts. Activities related to accommodation, restaurants and similar services employed 283 700 people in 2020, 12% fewer than in 2019. This represents 6% of total employment in the country.

The Portuguese tourism sector experienced some recovery in 2021. Tourist accommodation data in 2021 showed growth, with total nights increasing 41% compared to 2020 (to 42.6 million nights), but remained 45.2% below 2019 levels. This was driven by a strong rebound in international nights. International tourists increased to 6.3 million, after a 75.6% decline (to 4.2 million) in 2020. International tourism receipts totalled EUR 9.9 billion, 46% below pre-pandemic levels.

The domestic market boosted recovery with a 33.9% growth in nights, to 22.5 million in 2021. This remained just 13.9% below pre-pandemic levels. Domestic tourists accounted for 53% of nights in all accommodation in 2021, up from just 33.6% in 2019.

Portugal recorded a strong 2022 summer season. Between June and August, the number of nights in accommodation was 3% above pre-pandemic levels. The Portuguese Central Bank expects tourism receipts to exceed 2019 levels in 2022. Inbound tourism is expected to return to pre-pandemic levels in 2023.

Tourism governance and funding

The Secretary of State for Tourism is integrated into the Ministry of Economy and Maritime Affairs. Turismo de Portugal, the national tourist authority, reports to the Secretary of State for Tourism, Trade and Services and is the only body with direct responsibility for tourism policy at the national level. The body also covers the promotion, training, investment and sustainability of tourism activities. Turismo de Portugal has tourism promotion offices covering priority tourism markets. Turismo de Portugal's mission is to:

- Develop and qualify tourist infrastructure.
- Encourage and promote training.
- Support investment in the tourism sector.
- Coordinate the internal and external promotion of Portugal as a tourism destination.
- Regulate and inspect gambling activity.
- Plan and organise tourism.
- Organise and link to the provinces and regions.
- Organise and link to industry associations, stakeholders and customers.

At the regional level, there are five Regional Tourism Boards. These are corporate bodies under public law with a specific territorial scope. They act as destination management organisations with financial and administrative autonomy and are responsible for promotion in the domestic market and product development. Additionally, there are two Regional Directorates for Tourism with political and administrative autonomy covering the autonomous regions of Madeira and the Azores.

Turismo de Portugal develops and implements international promotion initiatives in co-ordination with seven Regional Tourism Promotion Agencies. These are non-profit, private law associations composed of private companies and Regional Tourism Boards. They have a formal contractual relationship with Turismo de Portugal for developing promotional activities in international markets.

The total budget of Turismo de Portugal in 2021 was EUR 343 million, of which half came from dedicated taxes (such as the gambling tax) and the remainder from EU Structural Funds and other public funding sources.

Portugal: Organisational chart of tourism bodies

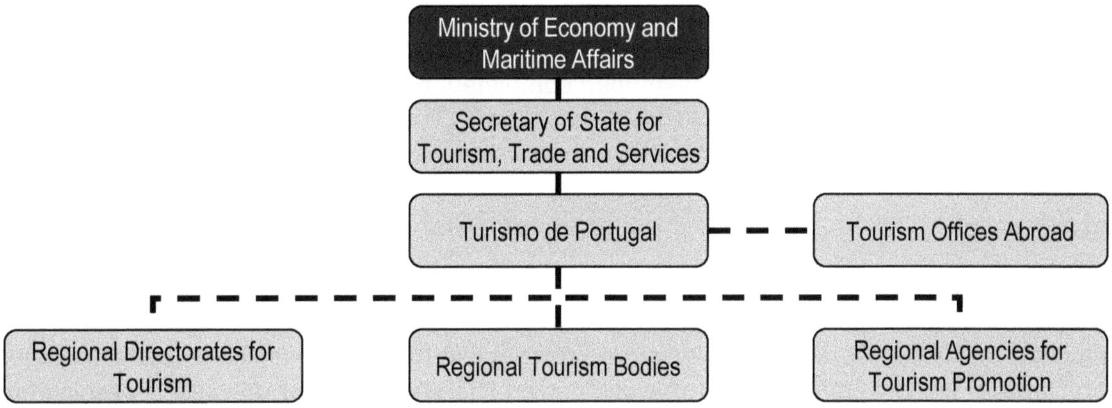

Source: OECD, adapted from Turismo de Portugal, 2022.

Tourism policies and programmes

In 2021, Portugal launched the action plan "Reactivate Tourism - Building the Future, which aims to encourage the recovery of the national tourism sector and includes a EUR 6 billion investment plan.

The Plan is intended to guide both public and private tourism sectors, whose actions are fully integrated with the objectives of the Recovery and Resilience Plan and the Portugal 2030 Strategy. The Plan is composed of specific actions that aim to transform the sector in the short, medium and long term, significantly contributing to GDP growth and a fairer distribution of wealth. There are four axes of action: supporting companies, promoting safety, generating business and building a future. This Plan sets the target of exceeding EUR 27 billion in tourist receipts by 2027.

Policy responses covered by the priorities of the Reactivate Tourism - Building the Future Plan include:

- business support
- the "Clean and Safe" label (see Box 2.4)
- qualifications
- digitisation
- mobility
- climate transition and sustainability.

Business support includes employment, operational strategy, and addressing debt (see box below). EUR 3 million is expected to be directed to this element, out of a total of EUR 6 million for the entire plan. In terms of qualifications, for many years, the tourism sector has been based on a model of low qualifications and low wages.

Portugal developed new programmes in 2022 to support businesses and the tourism workforce. The Empresas Turismo 360º Program formalises a commitment to monitoring, aimed at supporting businesses in their journey of integrating Environmental, Social and Governance (ESG) factors into organisational culture and business strategy. The Programme Formação +Próxima aims to train employees on a large scale in the sector with digital and face-to-face training, with content adapted to the needs of the future throughout the national territory and adapted to the diversity of tourism companies. The programme aims to train 75 000 professionals.

Portugal's Sustainable Tourism Plan 2020-23 was created as a result of the recovery plan Reactivate Tourism - Building the Future, and is in line with the objectives of the UN SDGs and Portugal's 2027 Tourism Strategy. This strategy was launched in 2017 with the vision to affirm tourism as a hub for economic, social and environmental development throughout the country, positioning Portugal as a key competitive and sustainable tourism destination. The set of initiatives covered by the Plan contribute to promoting an increasingly distinctive offer and to accelerating the sustainable growth of tourism companies. There are 18 actions which have been completed, and 77 are currently underway. The other actions will begin later in 2022-23.

COVID-19 Support fund for tourism microenterprises in Portugal

The economic impact of COVID-19 on the tourism sector in Portugal, and the unpredictability of its duration, led to the creation of a financial support fund for micro-enterprises. Financed by Turismo de Portugal, the main purpose of the fund was a swift response to the impact of the sudden decrease in travel on smaller tourism companies. These companies often have greater difficulty accessing finance and in meeting their most urgent needs.

Available to SMEs in the tourism sector and other economic activities related to tourism, the fund provides interest-free loans of EUR 750 per month for each job in the company for three months, up to a maximum of EUR 20 000 for micro companies and EUR 30 000 for small companies. 20% of the value of the support can be converted into grants, provided the company has not terminated employment contracts during the loan period. An additional 20% of the value can be added upon obtaining the Clean & Safe label and completing related training.

Due to the persistence of the pandemic, the fund was increased from EUR 60 million in April 2020 to EUR 170 million in October 2021. There has been very high demand for the fund, reaching a 99% commitment rate with 17 291 allocations approved.

Statistical Profile

Portugal: Domestic, inbound and outbound tourism

	2017	2018	2019	2020	2021
TOURISM FLOWS, THOUSAND					
Domestic tourism[1]					
Total domestic trips	..	..	..	..	..
Overnight visitors (tourists)	18 993	19 593	21 363	13 730	16 506
Same-day visitors (excursionists)	..	..	..	..	..
Nights in all types of accommodation	23 303	24 719	26 115	16 875	22 486
Hotels and similar establishments	15 000	16 048	16 815	10 751	14 867
Other collective establishments	5 595	5 741	6 047	4 293	5 140
Private accommodation	2 707	2 930	3 252	1 831	2 479
Inbound tourism					
Total international arrivals	..	..	..	..	..
Overnight visitors (tourists)	15 432	16 186	17 283	4 208	6 345
Same-day visitors (excursionists)	..	..	..	..	..
Top markets					
Spain	2 122	2 238	2 463	878	1 259
France	1 818	1 851	1 816	518	841
United Kingdom	2 177	2 127	2 220	492	720
Germany	1 704	1 756	1 704	497	655
Netherlands	703	692	672	205	356
Nights in all types of accommodation	49 355	50 480	51 708	13 409	20 122
Hotels and similar establishments	40 734	40 514	41 178	10 178	15 320
Other collective establishments	3 377	3 586	3 581	1 486	1 974
Private accommodation	5 244	6 380	6 948	1 744	2 828
Outbound tourism					
Total international departures	..	..	..	..	..
Overnight visitors (tourists)	2 195	2 486	3 100	680	1 012
Same-day visitors (excursionists)	..	..	..	..	..
Top destinations					
..	..	..	..	..	..
..	..	..	..	..	..
..	..	..	..	..	..
..	..	..	..	..	..
..	..	..	..	..	..
TOURISM RECEIPTS AND EXPENDITURE, MILLION EUR					
Inbound tourism					
Total international receipts	18 941	20 699	21 997	9 210	11 651
International travel receipts	15 550	17 054	18 291	7 715	9 943
International passenger transport receipts	3 391	3 645	3 706	1 495	1 708
Outbound tourism					
Total international expenditure	4 852	5 458	6 101	3 094	3 994
International travel expenditure	4 050	4 584	5 124	2 743	3 574
International passenger transport expenditure	802	874	977	351	420

.. Not available

1. Trips from demand side surveys; Nights from supply side surveys.

Source: OECD Tourism Statistics (Database).

StatLink https://stat.link/ht13o7

Portugal: Enterprises and employment in tourism

	Number of establishments[1]	Number of persons employed				
	2020	2017	2018	2019	2020	2021
Total	..	..	..	..	..	..
Tourism industries	**135 506**	..	..	..	..	..
Accommodation services for visitors	38 374	92 963	107 590	115 803	103 555	..
Hotels and similar establishments	..	..	..	..	..	..
Food and beverage serving industry	73 973	253 523	267 477	283 438	262 340	..
Passenger transport	18 858	50 367	54 617	..	..	..
Air passenger transport	90	..	..	..	..	..
Railways passenger transport	1	..	..	..	..	..
Road passenger transport	18 556	34 596	54 617	..	..	..
Water passenger transport	211	..	..	..	..	..
Passenger transport supporting services	..	..	..	..	..	..
Transport equipment rental	..	..	..	..	..	..
Travel agencies and other reservation services industry	4 301	13 245	14 254	15 022	13 439	..
Cultural industry	..	..	..	..	..	..
Sports and recreation industry	..	..	..	..	..	..
Retail trade of country-specific tourism characteristic goods	..	..	..	..	..	..
Other country-specific tourism industries	..	..	..	..	..	..
Other industries	..	..	..	..	..	..

.. Not available

1. Data refer to number of enterprises.

Source: OECD Tourism Statistics (Database).

StatLink https://stat.link/4idw60

Portugal: Internal tourism consumption

Million EUR

	2019		
	Domestic tourism expenditure	Inbound tourism expenditure	Internal tourism consumption
Total	..	..	..
Consumption products	**10 056**	**21 187**	**32 906**
Tourism characteristic products	7 854	15 981	25 398
Accommodation services for visitors	2 068	5 374	8 605
Food and beverage serving services	2 248	5 762	8 010
Passenger transport services	1 078	3 407	4 646
Air passenger transport services	461	2 981	3 533
Railways passenger transport services	95	36	178
Road passenger transport services	428	366	800
Water passenger transport services	94	24	135
Passenger transport supporting services	..	..	..
Transport equipment rental services	271	898	1 169
Travel agencies and other reservation services industry	751	82	833
Cultural services	67	184	396
Sports and recreation services	694	246	952
Country-specific tourism characteristic goods	..	..	..
Country-specific tourism characteristic services	676	29	787
Other consumption products	2 202	5 206	7 508
Tourism connected products	458	1 568	2 053
Non-tourism related consumption products	1 744	3 638	5 454
Non-consumption products	..	..	..

.. Not available

Source: OECD Tourism Statistics (Database).

StatLink https://stat.link/r7snhq

Slovak Republic

Tourism in the economy and outlook for recovery

Tourism has been of growing importance to the Slovak Republic's economy. Following record numbers in 2019, international tourism receipts fell to EUR 1.1 billion in 2020, 62% lower than in 2019. This decline saw tourism's direct economic contribution fall to 1.2% of GDP (down from 2.8% in 2019), with tourism exports falling to 12.5% of services exports (down from 26.1%). The number of employees in accommodation and catering establishments was 92 600, representing 3.7% of the total workforce in 2020.

In 2020, the Slovak Republic recorded 3.2 million tourists in accommodation establishments, the lowest level in twenty years. The number of international tourists decreased by 65.5% to 854 000 tourists in 2020, before declining further to 576 000 tourists in 2021.

The sector has mainly been supported by domestic tourists, with accommodation providers registering 2.1 million domestic tourists in 2021, down from almost 2.4 million in 2020 and still 45% below pre-pandemic levels.

In total, tourists spent 9.8 million nights in all means of accommodation in 2020, representing a year-on-year decrease of 45%. This declined further in 2021 to 8.2 million nights, 53.9% below 2019 levels.

Tourism governance and funding

The Ministry of Transport and Construction has responsibility for tourism in the Slovak Republic. The Tourism Section of the Ministry is divided into departments covering national tourism policy, regional and international co-operation and tourism state aid.

The Ministry co-operates with other ministries through participation in various committees dealing with issues affecting tourism, including the Working Group to Co-ordinate the Presentation of Slovakia Abroad, the Interdepartmental Commission of the Geo-parks Network, the Impact and Adaptation Steering group, and the Working Group of the Government Council for Vocational Education and Training.

At the regional level, the Slovak Republic delegates tourism responsibilities to self-governing bodies in eight regions and municipalities. Local and regional destination management organisations (DMOs) are responsible for developing tourism products and promotion. Local DMOs are formed by municipalities, tourism business entities, non-profit organisations, foundations and associations. Regional DMOs are formed by the regional self-governing authorities and at least one local DMO. There are 49 local and eight regional DMOs in the Slovak Republic, funded by subsidies provided by the Ministry, membership fees and other sources.

The Ministry established Slovakia Travel in 2021 as the national tourism organisation responsible for tourism marketing and promotion. It also serves as a tourism data centre. The Slovak Tourism Association, made up of representatives of the main tourism organisations, promotes co-operation in the sector and advises on legislative changes. At local and regional levels, tourism associations contribute to quality improvement, professional training and the sharing of best practices.

The ministerial budget for tourism was EUR 9.8 million in 2021, down from EUR 12 million in 2018. Of the 2021 budget, EUR 1.2 million was dedicated to marketing and promotional activities, and EUR 8.1 million was for subsidies to local and regional DMOs, mainly for marketing, product development and tourist infrastructure. There was an additional EUR 257.5 million for state aid in tourism.

Slovak Republic: Organisational chart of tourism bodies

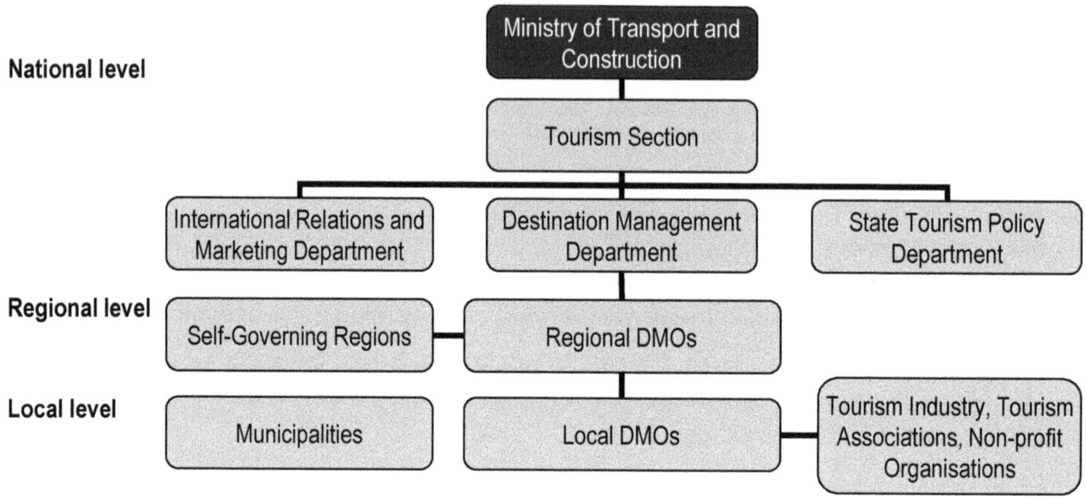

Source: OECD, adapted from the Ministry of Transport and Construction, 2022.

Tourism policies and programmes

To tackle the COVID-19 and geopolitical crises, the National Council of the Slovak Republic approved the Tourism Support Act, which established a framework for the creation of state aid schemes (see box below).

In response to the humanitarian crisis from Russia's war in Ukraine, Slovakia launched the Help for Ukraine website run by the Ministry of Transport and Construction to provide more information on the available accommodation for Ukrainian refugees in state and private facilities. The website includes a reservation system to bring together these public facilities and hotel accommodation capacities. Moreover, the country approved a law called the Lex Ukraine, which will make it easier for refugees to stay in the Slovak Republic.

In 2022, the Slovak Republic worked on redesigning the National Sustainable Tourism Strategy and action plans for 2030. Due to the pandemic, the war in Ukraine and a newly set up national tourism board, a redesign of the existing strategy was needed. A revised Strategy of Sustainable Tourism Development 2030 will aim to increase the competitiveness of tourism, better use its potential, balance regional disparities and create new jobs.

Redesign and state support for employment strategies in hospitality and food services is a key priority in the Slovak Republic as the country is facing a tourism employment crisis. Some workers have refused to return to tourism due to uncertainty and instability and instead stay in the automotive or other sectors.

Further, the sustainability of tourism is a priority. The strategy should set priorities and goals for the intensive and sustainable use of the potential of the tourism sector in the Slovak Republic. The Strategy will reflect the results of a co-creation process of the European Commission´s Transition Pathway for Tourism.

In addition, unifying all stakeholders that participate in tourism is a priority. The Slovak Republic is to set new information channels on a national level through regional tourism offices, the national tourism board, municipalities and private entities. In the 2030 strategy, the Slovak Republic will also set new communication channels between national and overseas stakeholders, especially in EU countries.

Tourism Support Act in the Slovak Republic

In an effort to mitigate the consequences of COVID-19 on the tourism sector in the Slovak Republic, the National Council approved an amendment to the Tourism Support Act in November 2020, which established a framework for the creation of state aid schemes and minimum aid for the tourism sector totalling EUR 100 million. The aim was to maintain employment and ensure the competitiveness of tourism businesses through the compensation of fixed costs.

All domestic tourism entities whose sales fell by more than 40% in 2020 compared to the same period in the previous year were able to apply for this aid. This financial support was available for up to 10% of 2019 revenues, depending on the decrease in revenues suffered. In April 2021, the Slovak Republic released an additional EUR 120 million to help the gastronomy and tourism sectors, with a limit of EUR 200 000 per applicant.

The European Commission approved the state aid scheme under the Temporary Framework, allowing for aid of up to EUR 1 million per undertaking. Its purpose was to support enterprises in the tourism sector, providing a financial contribution to cover an element of fixed costs. The total budget for this state aid scheme was EUR 37 million.

It is important to support it within the framework of a common European co-ordination. Accelerating the green and digital transition and improving the resilience of the tourism ecosystem are priorities in today's work. In addition, entrepreneurs in tourism were able to apply for general support for employment provided by the Ministry of Labour, Social Affairs and Family, and support for rent provided by the Ministry of Economy.

Statistical Profile

Slovak Republic: Domestic, inbound and outbound tourism

	2017	2018	2019	2020	2021
TOURISM FLOWS, THOUSAND					
Domestic tourism					
Total domestic trips	3 213	3 340	3 958	2 356	2 149
Overnight visitors (tourists)	3 213	3 340	3 958	2 356	2 149
Same-day visitors (excursionists)	..	..	..	..	..
Nights in all types of accommodation	9 507	9 819	11 453	7 443	6 704
Hotels and similar establishments	9 233	9 501	11 047	7 054	6 340
Other collective establishments	118	128	131	140	151
Private accommodation	156	189	275	249	213
Inbound tourism					
Total international arrivals	2 162	2 256	2 475	854	576
Overnight visitors (tourists)	2 162	2 256	2 475	854	576
Same-day visitors (excursionists)	..	..	..	..	..
Top markets					
Czech Republic	645	702	777	378	230
Poland	210	226	240	116	59
Germany	192	178	182	63	53
Hungary	101	112	124	43	28
Austria	97	100	97	31	26
Nights in all types of accommodation	5 429	5 696	6 251	2 348	1 465
Hotels and similar establishments	5 124	5 345	5 855	2 121	1 358
Other collective establishments	193	214	193	123	67
Private accommodation	112	138	203	104	41
Outbound tourism					
Total international departures	6 649	8 321	9 669	..	..
Overnight visitors (tourists)	4 244	5 313	5 971	..	..
Same-day visitors (excursionists)	2 405	3 008	3 699	..	..
Top destinations					
Czech Republic	..	1 060	1 281	323	384
Croatia	..	440	423	122	309
Hungary	..	308	240	52	101
Austria	..	309	351	82	99
Italy	..	257	295	.. c	46
TOURISM RECEIPTS AND EXPENDITURE, MILLION EUR					
Inbound tourism					
Total international receipts	2 665	2 817	2 996	1 162	1 001
International travel receipts	2 588	2 710	2 861	1 132	941
International passenger transport receipts	77	107	134	31	59
Outbound tourism					
Total international expenditure	2 296	2 403	2 501	1 171	1 313
International travel expenditure	2 125	2 225	2 313	1 111	1 257
International passenger transport expenditure	171	178	188	61	56

.. Not available; c Confidential data
Source: OECD Tourism Statistics (Database).

StatLink https://stat.link/w9xhgc

Slovak Republic: Enterprises and employment in tourism

	Number of establishments[1]	Number of persons employed				
	2019	2017	2018	2019	2020	2021
Total	..	..	..	..	..	..
Tourism industries	**44 477**	**174 505**	**177 638**	**184 891**	..	..
Accommodation services for visitors	3 393	17 819	17 998	18 384	..	..
Hotels and similar establishments	..	..	..	..	..	..
Food and beverage serving industry	14 482	68 653	70 032	74 540	..	..
Passenger transport	3 454	26 335	26 476	26 635	..	..
Air passenger transport	..	..	..	..	..	..
Railways passenger transport	..	..	..	..	..	..
Road passenger transport	..	..	..	..	..	..
Water passenger transport	..	..	..	..	..	..
Passenger transport supporting services	..	..	..	..	..	..
Transport equipment rental	522	1 187	1 402	1 501	..	..
Travel agencies and other reservation services industry	1 333	3 066	3 327	3 386	..	..
Cultural industry	2 064	9 871	10 152	10 475	..	..
Sports and recreation industry	4 508	18 762	18 932	19 844	..	..
Retail trade of country-specific tourism characteristic goods	..	..	..	..	..	..
Other country-specific tourism industries	14 721	28 812	29 319	30 126	..	..
Other industries	..	..	..	..	..	..

.. Not available
1. Data refer to number of enterprises.
Source: OECD Tourism Statistics (Database).

StatLink https://stat.link/3fz2r4

Slovak Republic: Internal tourism consumption

Million EUR

	2019		
	Domestic tourism expenditure	Inbound tourism expenditure	Internal tourism consumption
Total	..	..	..
Consumption products	**3 049**	**1 645**	**5 875**
Tourism characteristic products	2 290	1 083	4 554
Accommodation services for visitors	515	392	1 020
Food and beverage serving services	582	366	952
Passenger transport services	600	61	1 266
Air passenger transport services	..	..	..
Railways passenger transport services	..	..	..
Road passenger transport services	..	..	..
Water passenger transport services	..	..	..
Passenger transport supporting services	..	..	..
Transport equipment rental services	42	43	85
Travel agencies and other reservation services industry	208	10	219
Cultural services	72	20	331
Sports and recreation services	148	79	307
Country-specific tourism characteristic goods	40	53	94
Country-specific tourism characteristic services	82	60	280
Other consumption products	759	562	1 321
Tourism connected products	..	..	..
Non-tourism related consumption products	..	..	..
Non-consumption products	..	..	..

.. Not available
Source: OECD Tourism Statistics (Database).

StatLink https://stat.link/xtdyo5

Slovenia

Tourism in the economy and outlook for recovery

Tourism has grown steadily in the last decade in Slovenia, with international arrivals more than doubling from 2010 to 2019. Tourism directly contributed 5.4% of total GDP in 2019, which increases to 8.5% with indirect effects included. Tourism-related sectors employed 7.7% of total workforce in 2019. As a result of COVID-19, tourism's direct contribution fell to 3.3% of GDP in 2020, or EUR 1.5 billion, and tourism employment fell to 7.0% of the national workforce. Tourism exports decreased by almost 60% to EUR 1.2 billion.

In 2019, Slovenia recorded 4.7 million international tourists in accommodation establishments. The impacts of COVID-19 saw this fall 74.1% to 1.2 million in 2020. This increased to 1.8 million in 2021, but still remained 61.0% below 2019 levels. There was a decrease of 51% in total arrivals and a 42% decrease in nights in 2020. The number of international arrivals in 2020 decreased by 74.1%.

The large decline in international tourists was partially compensated by domestic tourists, which increased by 21% in 2020 and a further 17.4% to 3.2 million tourists in 2021. This increase in domestic tourists saw the domestic share of tourism expenditure in Slovenia increase to 47% in 2020, up from 28% in 2019. Slovenia expects tourism to return to pre-pandemic levels in 2024.

Tourism governance and funding

At the parliamentary level, the Committee for the Economy is responsible for tourism-related legislation. The Ministry of Economic Development and Technology (MEDT) is the main government department responsible for providing and implementing national tourism policy. MEDT co-operates and consults with the tourism sector and social partners to reflect the close partnership between the public and private sectors and non-governmental organisations (NGOs) dealing with tourism issues.

The Slovenian Tourist Board (STB) oversees the promotion of Slovenia as a tourism destination and related marketing activities. The STB is also responsible for tourist information and data, product development, stakeholder networking, and market research and development. The STB programme of work is adopted on an annual basis and is financed by the national budget.

Twelve Regional Development Agencies (RDAs) undertake tourism development at the regional level. RDAs report to the Regional Councils comprised of the mayors of the local communities in each region. Regional tourism development is governed according to national legislation and strategic development objectives, but specific regional development objectives are included in the overall regional plans. At the local level, each mayor and Community Council is responsible for tourism development according to national legislation and strategic objectives, but with specific local tourism development goals.

In 2020, Slovenia established a Tourism Advisory Council as a special working group comprised of industry representatives, tourism policymakers, the STB and NGOs related to tourism. The Council monitors the current situation in tourism and the impact of the pandemic and the war in Ukraine on the Slovenian tourism sector.

The overall national budget for tourism in 2022 is EUR 63.3 million (EUR 25 million in national funds and EUR 38 million in EU funds). The national budget allocated for tourism development at the local and municipal level and for the operating programme of the Slovene Tourism Board (STB) comes primarily from tourist taxes for overnight stays and concession fees for gambling. The budget has been significantly reduced due to the decrease in the number of visitors due to travel restrictions in 2020-21. The 2021 budget was EUR 14.4 million, up from EUR 12.3 million in 2020 but still below the 2019 budget of EUR 17.4 million. For 2022, the budget allocation for the STB programme was EUR 16 million.

EU Funds, including NextGenEU and React EU, provide investments of EUR 80 million in green, digital and sustainable infrastructure for industry and destinations, for example, investing EUR 50 million in the transformation of mountain destinations.

Slovenia: Organisational chart of tourism bodies

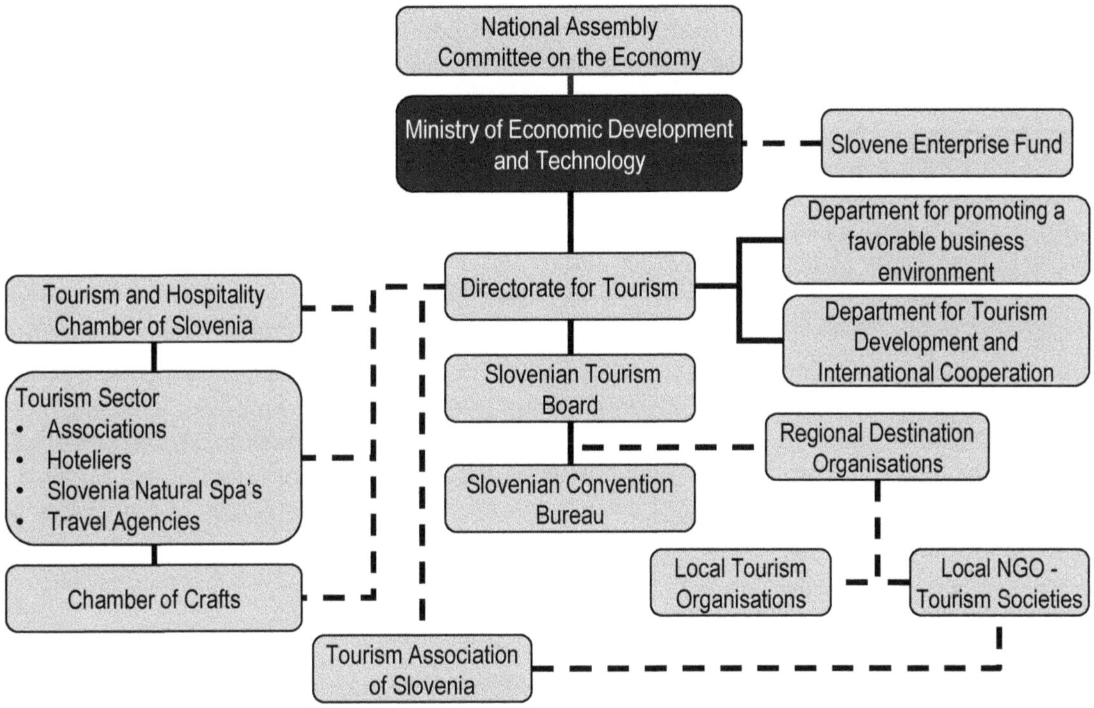

Source: OECD, adapted by the Ministry of Economic Development and Technology, 2022.

Tourism policies and programmes

The Recovery and Resilience Plan of Slovenian Tourism 2020-23, the new Strategy for Slovene Tourism 2022-28, and the recently adopted Strategy for Digital Transformation of Slovenian Tourism 2022-26 define the tourism policy and programmes for Slovenian tourism until 2028. Tourism also features in the Slovenian Industrial Strategy 2030.

The Slovenian Tourism Strategy 2022-28 represents the basic framework for developing Slovenian tourism. The Strategy responds to the new circumstances and challenges and develops and promotes the key advantages of Slovenian tourism (see box below).

The green transition remains the priority in all plans for the recovery and resilience of Slovenian tourism and is a basic principle for the strategic development of tourism in the future. The main tourism development objectives are the green and digital breakthrough of Slovenian tourism with a co-ordinated strategic approach required by the changed consumer behaviour due to the COVID-19 crisis and Russia's the war in Ukraine. Slovenia committed itself to sustainable and green tourism long before the COVID-19 pandemic, aiming to balance the needs of tourists with those of the destination and local population. This remains the priority in all plans for recovery and resilience and will continue as a basic principle for the future strategic development of Slovenian tourism.

One of the main tools for promoting green and sustainable tourism is the Green Scheme of Slovenian Tourism (GSST), a certification programme and tool developed at the national level under the Slovenia Green brand. This programme requires strict national and international standards for responsible tourism to be followed. The growing number of members of the GSST further helps promote Slovenia as a destination committed to green and sustainable tourism.

Slovenia has taken numerous measures to enable the survival and active operation of the Slovenian tourism sector in light of the COVID-19 pandemic and war in Ukraine. Slovenia provided more than EUR 1 billion in aid to the tourism sector within the ten COVID-19 packages and a special intervention law that helped the hospitality and tourism sector mitigate the pandemic's effects, preserve jobs, and alleviate corporate liquidity problems. Among them is a special measure for a one-time supplement of EUR 10 million for the most affected segments of the tourism sector. It aims to help the most affected companies restart their activities after lifting the restrictions related to COVID-19. Companies will be able to obtain up to EUR 6 000 in aid per employee.

Slovenian Tourism Strategy 2022-28

The Tourism Strategy 2022-28 defines Slovenia as "*a role model for smart destinations that strengthens and encourages the development of sustainable, boutique, personalised and innovative experiences*".

The Strategy is aimed at a balanced growth scenario, which envisages a moderate increase in capacity and quantitative indicators. The goal of Slovenia's smart destinations is to empower all stakeholders for data-supported decision-making, an increase in added value, competitiveness and resilience of tourism, promote a sustainable transformation of the whole ecosystem for a smaller footprint, personalise guest experiences (greater value for all), improve knowledge and digital competencies of employees and to ensure a higher quality of life for locals.

The Strategy sets five strategic goals:

- Increase the quality, value and all-year-round tourist offer.
- Increase the satisfaction of locals, employees and guests.
- Position tourism as a generator of value and sustainable development.
- Decarbonise and balance Slovenian tourism.
- Ensure a competent and efficient management structure.

It is expected that the implementation of the Strategy will result in an increase in added value generated in basic tourism activities of 43%, from EUR 0.9 billion in 2019 to EUR 1.3 billion per year until 2028. It is estimated that together with other activities indirectly related to tourism, the total tourist demand will generate EUR 2.1 billion of added value in 2028 (an increase of 59% compared to 2019). The Ministry of Economic Development and Technology, responsible for tourism policy, is preparing an Action Plan for the implementation of the strategy. The Action Plan will be evaluated every two years.

Statistical Profile

Slovenia: Domestic, inbound and outbound tourism

	2017	2018	2019	2020	2021
TOURISM FLOWS, THOUSAND					
Domestic tourism[1]					
Total domestic trips	..	..	..	..	..
Overnight visitors (tourists)	1 513	1 508	1 528	1 849	2 171
Same-day visitors (excursionists)	..	..	..	..	..
Nights in all types of accommodation	4 523	4 519	4 405	5 850	6 457
Hotels and similar establishments	3 926	3 934	3 815	4 983	5 630
Other collective establishments	597	584	589	867	826
Private accommodation	..	..	..	..	..
Inbound tourism					
Total international arrivals	..	..	..	..	..
Overnight visitors (tourists)	3 991	4 425	4 702	1 216	1 832
Same-day visitors (excursionists)	..	..	..	..	..
Top markets					
Germany	437	506	585	289	414
Austria	373	382	396	143	171
Italy	608	599	597	159	162
Netherlands	151	185	187	45	108
Croatia	195	219	235	82	63
Nights in all types of accommodation	9 685	11 176	11 371	3 354	4 794
Hotels and similar establishments	8 452	9 826	9 923	2 802	3 844
Other collective establishments	1 233	1 350	1 448	552	950
Private accommodation	..	..	..	..	..
Outbound tourism					
Total international departures	5 410	5 409	6 049	1 892	3 032
Overnight visitors (tourists)	3 013	3 188	3 170	1 138	2 125
Same-day visitors (excursionists)	2 397	2 221	2 879	754	907
Top destinations					
Croatia	1 680	1 732	1 572	817	1 270
Bosnia and Herzegovina	142	142	200	..	183
Italy	208	236	289	87 e	120
Austria	171	204	189	50 e	79
Germany	168	191	140	..	60 e
TOURISM RECEIPTS AND EXPENDITURE, MILLION EUR					
Inbound tourism					
Total international receipts	2 688	2 870	2 998	1 241	..
International travel receipts	2 523	2 704	2 843	1 200	1 513
International passenger transport receipts	164	166	155	41	..
Outbound tourism					
Total international expenditure	1 443	1 585	1 583	750	..
International travel expenditure	1 322	1 483	1 500	718	877
International passenger transport expenditure	120	103	83	33	..

.. Not available; e Estimated value

1. Trips from demand side surveys; Nights from supply side surveys.

Source: OECD Tourism Statistics (Database).

StatLink https://stat.link/7bft9c

Slovenia: Enterprises and employment in tourism

	Number of establishments[1]	Number of persons employed				
	2021	2017	2018	2019	2020	2021
Total	..	..	..	..	..	..
Tourism industries	**13 801 p**	**65 848**	**68 150**	**69 253**	**62 058**	**66 354**
Accommodation services for visitors	848 p	16 987	17 570	17 796	14 251	16 396
Hotels and similar establishments	751 p	9 818	10 235	10 378	8 870	10 871
Food and beverage serving industry	7 341 p	24 495	25 322	26 106	22 588	24 693
Passenger transport	1 068 p	5 438	5 826	5 420	4 778	4 696
Air passenger transport	113 p	610	736	302	291	312
Railways passenger transport	1 p	.. c	.. c	.. c	.. c	.. c
Road passenger transport	889 p	4 133	4 430	4 449	3 846	3 767
Water passenger transport	65 p	.. c	.. c	.. c	.. c	.. c
Passenger transport supporting services	423 p	3 097	3 126	3 191	5 078	4 965
Transport equipment rental	307 p	435	469	489	457	474
Travel agencies and other reservation services industry	848 p	2 060	2 257	2 368	1 683	1 791
Cultural industry	2 383 p	8 073	8 197	8 372	8 263	8 278
Sports and recreation industry	583 p	5 263	5 383	5 511	4 960	5 061
Retail trade of country-specific tourism characteristic goods	..	..	..	..	..	..
Other country-specific tourism industries	..	..	..	..	..	..
Other industries	..	..	..	..	..	..

.. Not available; c Confidential data; p Provisional data
1. Data refer to number of enterprises.
Source: OECD Tourism Statistics (Database).

StatLink https://stat.link/92xobc

Slovenia: Internal tourism consumption

Million EUR

	2020		
	Domestic tourism expenditure	Inbound tourism expenditure	Internal tourism consumption
Total	..	..	..
Consumption products	**1 326**	**1 506**	**2 908**
Tourism characteristic products	928	627	1 632
Accommodation services for visitors	263	246	555
Food and beverage serving services	295	190	486
Passenger transport services	189	55	244
Air passenger transport services	..	..	..
Railways passenger transport services	..	..	..
Road passenger transport services	..	..	..
Water passenger transport services	..	..	..
Passenger transport supporting services	..	..	..
Transport equipment rental services	..	..	..
Travel agencies and other reservation services industry	27	12	39
Cultural services	70	11	112
Sports and recreation services	84	112	197
Country-specific tourism characteristic goods	..	..	..
Country-specific tourism characteristic services	..	..	..
Other consumption products	398	879	1 277
Tourism connected products	..	..	..
Non-tourism related consumption products	..	..	..
Non-consumption products	..	..	..

.. Not available
Source: OECD Tourism Statistics (Database).

StatLink https://stat.link/ag9whn

Spain

Tourism in the economy and outlook for recovery

Tourism is one of the main sectors of Spain's economy and is an outstanding driver of socio-economic development. In 2019, the total effects of tourism (direct and indirect) contributed EUR 155 billion or 12.4% of total GDP. The sector provided 13.5% of total employment. Following the COVID-19 pandemic, tourism's total contribution to GDP more than halved to 5.5%. Tourism remained an important employment contributor, providing 12% of Spain's total employment.

In 2019, international tourists reached 83.5 million, and tourist expenditure was EUR 84.5 billion. The impacts of the COVID-19 pandemic saw international tourists fall 77.3% to 18.9 million in 2020, while expenditure hit EUR 22.1 billion, down 73.9%. There was a slight recovery in 2021, but international tourists still remained 62.7% below 2019 levels at 31.2 million tourists.

Domestic tourists were also significantly impacted, falling 45.5% to 74.8 million tourists in 2020. Similar to international tourism, domestic tourism rebounded in 2021, increasing 40% to 107.7 million tourists but remaining 21% below pre-pandemic levels.

Spain is projecting a tourism recovery back to pre-pandemic levels in 2023.

Tourism governance and funding

The Ministry of Industry, Trade and Tourism has been responsible for tourism since 2018. The State Secretariat for Tourism continues to be responsible for defining, developing, co-ordinating and implementing tourism policy within the remit of the central government´s responsibility and related institutions at national and international levels. The State Secretariat co-ordinates three organisations at the national level: Turespaña, Paradores de Turismo and SEGITTUR.

Turespaña is an autonomous body attached to the Ministry and is responsible for carrying out the international tourism marketing and promotion of Spain abroad. It undertakes this role using an international network of 33 tourism offices that support the implementation of the agreed marketing plan. Paradores de Turismo is a public company that runs the state-owned hotel network. Most establishments are located in historic sites, national parks or protected areas. There are now 97 establishments employing over 4 000 people. The Organisation for Innovation and Management of Tourism Technology (SEGITTUR) is a public sector body responsible for developing new tourism technologies in the public and private sectors. It researches and manages technology, knowledge and innovation to enhance the competitiveness, quality and sustainability of all aspects of tourism.

Co-ordinating mechanisms between the central and regional administrations and the private sector are key. Entities that play an important role in Spanish tourism policy include:

- The Sectoral Tourism Conference: an advisory and executive co-ordination body bringing together high-level public sector tourism representatives from central government and the autonomous regions. It is chaired by the Minister for Tourism and analyses and debates the key policy issues and regulations affecting tourism.

- The Spanish Tourism Council (CONESTUR): an advisory body which brings together tourism administrations (state, regions and provinces/cities) and the private sector, such as chambers of trade, the National Employers' Association, professional associations, trade unions and a wide spectrum of tourism professionals.
- The Inter-Ministerial Committee for Tourism: represents national ministries responsible for tourism-related matters.
- The Advisory Council of Turespaña: comprises 11 members, five of which come from the private sector, and assists Turespaña in defining and implementing actions and strategies to market Spain abroad.

The State Secretariat for Tourism had an overall budget of EUR 1.3 billion for 2021. A large portion of the budget (81%) is financed by Next Generation EU and the European Recovery Fund, with the rest coming from the general public budget. The current budget for 2022 is EUR 1.7 billion. Of this, EUR 1.56 billion is allocated to implementing the Recovery, Transformation and Resilience Plan for Tourism.

Spain: Organisational chart of tourism bodies

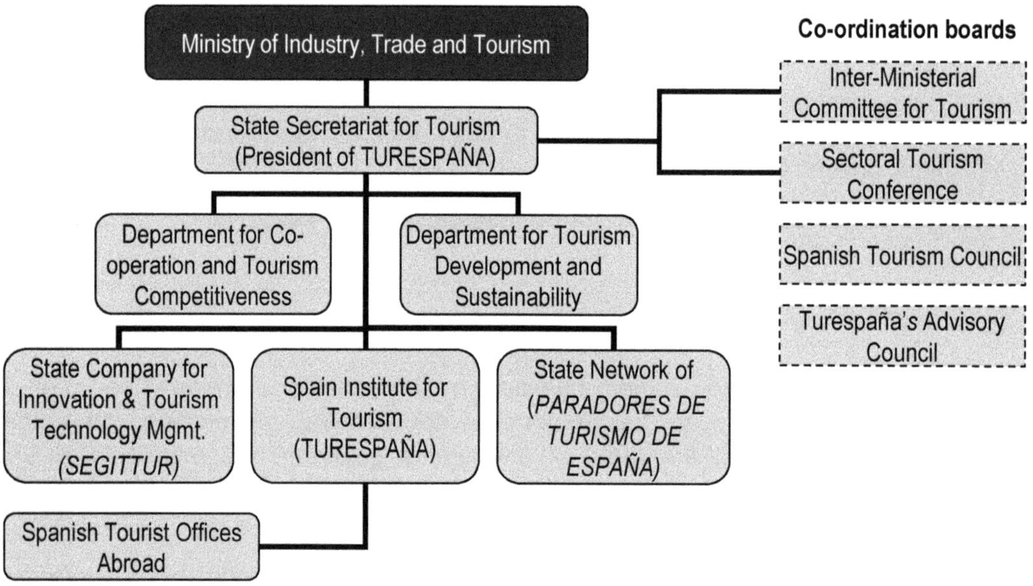

Source: OECD, adapted from Ministry of Industry, Trade & Tourism, 2022.

Tourism policies and programmes

As a lesson learned from the pandemic, Spain has a core objective to transform and modernise the tourism sector by increasing its competitiveness and resilience. The aim is to recover to pre-COVID-19 levels and build a more sustainable, diversified and profitable tourism model.

Spain has defined a range of strategic action areas encouraging investments in innovation, energy efficiency and the green transition, as well as enhancing the effectiveness of policies supporting research. Further actions include sustaining the economy, supporting employment and skills development, improving access to digital learning and broader digitalisation.

The Tourism Sustainability Strategy aims to strengthen the environmental, socio-economic and regional sustainability of tourism and targets tourist destinations, social partners and private operators in the sector to stimulate:

- **Green transition:** including actions concerning environmental restoration, management and public use of protected natural areas, the implementation of tourism certification systems and circular economy measures and investment in cycling and walking paths.
- **Energy efficiency:** including actions to reduce CO2 emissions in buildings, public infrastructure and services, implement environmental technologies and improve urban environments.
- **Digital transformation:** including actions to digitise services for tourists at destinations, develop the digital footprint of the destination and improve tourism demand management (see box below).
- **Competitiveness transformation:** improving local tourism infrastructures and fostering job creation through developing new tourism products relating to culture, nature, gastronomy, traditional crafts and industrial tourism services.

The Tourism Resilience Strategy for the extra-peninsular territories (Canary and Balearic Islands and Ceuta and Melilla) aims to improve the competitiveness and capacity of these territories to adapt to changes in international markets. Investments have been made in public infrastructure, environmental management, waste treatment, public services, training, and the development of alternative tourism products. The Strategy also creates incentives to facilitate the connectivity of these territories and for tourism companies to operate outside the peak seasons. There are also special actions to boost competitiveness by developing new tourism products aligned with the Sustainable Tourism Strategy, such as energy efficiency and circular economy projects.

The National Food and Wine Tourism Plan, which falls within the plan for the modernisation and competitiveness of the tourism sector, will have an investment of EUR 68.6 million which includes tourism sustainability plans in food and wine destinations (EUR 51.4 million), the Spain Tourism Experiences Programme (EUR 10 million), and the International Promotion Programme (EUR 2.2 million). The Plan aims to promote food and wine destinations by financing destination sustainability plans, generating sustainable and diverse gastronomic tourism experiences, and improving worker training and skills.

In 2022, Spain started a multiannual programme to rehabilitate historical heritage buildings in the frame of the Recovery, Transformation and Resilience Plan for Tourism. The budget of this project is EUR 109 million.

Tourism digitisation and intelligence programme in Spain

The aim of Spain's Digitisation and Intelligence Programme is for destinations and the sector to develop smart destination platforms making interoperable public and private services available to tourists. This will be complemented by developing a Tourist Intelligence System and a set of initiatives to boost the Spanish Smart Destinations Network. The actions will also support digital solutions based on artificial intelligence and provide financing for the development of industrial data spaces and the promotion of digital innovation in the tourism sector.

To implement the Recovery, Transformation and Resilience Plan for Tourism, Spain is co-funding different projects to foster digitalisation for tourism destinations within the Spanish Smart Destinations Network and tourism companies. In 2022, EUR 45 million will be spent on implementing Artificial Intelligence in companies in the tourism sector. EUR 115 million will be spent on fostering the digital development of tourism destinations. Projects will be co-funded for the next three years.

Statistical Profile

Spain: Domestic, inbound and outbound tourism

	2017	2018	2019	2020	2021
TOURISM FLOWS, THOUSAND					
Domestic tourism					
Total domestic trips	418 689	425 452	394 810	235 089	320 698
Overnight visitors (tourists)	138 357	139 931	137 191	74 750	107 727
Same-day visitors (excursionists)	280 332	285 521	257 619	160 340	212 971
Nights in all types of accommodation	517 502	507 739	510 938	353 020	441 404
Hotels and similar establishments	90 650	90 648	93 696	38 001	67 638
Other collective establishments	38 664	35 713	33 081	23 661	32 199
Private accommodation	388 187	381 378	384 161	291 358	341 567
Inbound tourism					
Total international arrivals	121 717	124 456	126 170	36 410	51 631
Overnight visitors (tourists)	81 869	82 808	83 509	18 933	31 181
Same-day visitors (excursionists)	39 849	41 647	42 661	17 477	20 451
Top markets					
France	18 807	18 524	18 012	3 150	5 823
Germany	11 897	11 415	11 158	2 391	5 209
United Kingdom	11 267	11 293	11 147	3 888	4 303
Netherlands	5 827	5 804	5 530	1 175	2 049
Nordic Countries	4 223	4 389	4 535	947	1 840
Nights in all types of accommodation	633 697	616 715	594 018	147 986	253 985
Hotels and similar establishments	291 692	287 884	287 764	57 065	108 424
Other collective establishments	32 412	35 599	34 093	7 942	14 832
Private accommodation	309 593	293 233	272 161	82 979	130 729
Outbound tourism					
Total international departures	17 594	19 750	20 097	5 610	7 557
Overnight visitors (tourists)	14 351	16 424	17 126	4 314	6 032
Same-day visitors (excursionists)	3 243	3 326	2 971	1 296	1 525
Top destinations					
France	2 462	2 410	2 560	691	1 102
Portugal	2 086	2 282	2 355	796	1 066
Italy	1 292	1 860	1 895	328	761
Germany	803	948	1 039	217	289
United Kingdom	1 388	1 465	1 487	332	218
TOURISM RECEIPTS AND EXPENDITURE, MILLION EUR					
Inbound tourism					
Total international receipts	66 682	69 168	71 202	16 202	..
International travel receipts	66 682	69 168	71 202	16 202	..
International passenger transport receipts	..	..	..	..	..
Outbound tourism					
Total international expenditure	19 611	22 395	24 813	7 573	..
International travel expenditure	19 611	22 395	24 813	7 573	..
International passenger transport expenditure	..	..	..	..	..

.. Not available
Source: OECD Tourism Statistics (Database).

StatLink https://stat.link/o9aujt

Spain: Enterprises and employment in tourism

	Number of establishments	Number of persons employed				
	2021	2017	2018	2019	2020	2021
Total	..	..	..	..	..	..
Tourism industries	**739 232**	**2 510 795**	**2 604 899**	**2 673 520**	**2 333 736**	**2 367 560**
Accommodation services for visitors	254 433	402 530	409 208	407 804	318 697	317 858
Hotels and similar establishments	17 133	354 740	361 444	360 134	276 236	271 613
Food and beverage serving industry	261 373	1 234 568	1 298 528	1 307 576	1 113 390	1 144 229
Passenger transport	64 491	278 882	281 328	317 596	288 436	265 383
Air passenger transport	240	41 068	43 196	52 334	44 275	46 061
Railways passenger transport	86	28 705	26 791	24 794	21 709	27 098
Road passenger transport	63 363	200 806	199 190	231 537	213 837	185 815
Water passenger transport	802	8 303	12 151	8 932	8 613	6 410
Passenger transport supporting services	24 727	..	..	..	..	..
Transport equipment rental	8 701	212 381	215 580	232 442	242 114	255 530
Travel agencies and other reservation services industry	17 125	65 512	78 698	70 119	63 124	66 315
Cultural industry	49 409	110 266	112 674	115 887	105 101	102 125
Sports and recreation industry	58 973	206 656	208 884	222 096	202 875	216 121
Retail trade of country-specific tourism characteristic goods	..	..	..	..	..	..
Other country-specific tourism industries	..	..	..	..	..	..
Other industries	..	..	..	..	..	..

.. Not available
Source: OECD Tourism Statistics (Database).

StatLink https://stat.link/byzshq

Spain: Internal tourism consumption

Million EUR

	2020		
	Domestic tourism expenditure	Inbound tourism expenditure	Internal tourism consumption
Total	..	..	..
Consumption products	**29 022**	**22 050**	**59 795**
Tourism characteristic products	23 022	14 268	46 013
Accommodation services for visitors	5 384	6 004	17 548
Food and beverage serving services	9 930	2 332	12 336
Passenger transport services	2 511	2 417	6 125
Air passenger transport services	1 365	1 739	3 808
Railways passenger transport services	352	169	685
Road passenger transport services	534	447	1 149
Water passenger transport services	259	63	483
Passenger transport supporting services	..	..	..
Transport equipment rental services	107	150	259
Travel agencies and other reservation services industry	3 571	304	4 036
Cultural services	296	1 370	2 066
Sports and recreation services	1 223	1 693	3 644
Country-specific tourism characteristic goods	..	..	..
Country-specific tourism characteristic services	..	..	..
Other consumption products	6 000	7 782	13 782
Tourism connected products	..	..	..
Non-tourism related consumption products	6 000	7 782	13 782
Non-consumption products	..	..	..

.. Not available
Source: OECD Tourism Statistics (Database).

StatLink https://stat.link/v3kuna

Sweden

Tourism in the economy and outlook for recovery

Tourism grew steadily prior to the COVID-19 pandemic and is an important contributor to the Swedish economy and labour market. Tourism's direct share of the Swedish economy had been relatively stable at around 2.6% of GDP, but dropped to 1.7% in 2020, with a small increase in 2021 to 1.9%. On average,101 000 people were employed in tourism in 2021, equating to 94 303 full-time jobs. This was 1 590 people fewer than in 2019.

Sweden registered 43.3 million tourist nights in 2020, a decline of 36% from 2019. International nights fell by 70% to 5.2 million nights, while domestic nights decreased by 24% to 38.1 million nights. In 2021, international nights increased to 7.3 million, a 40% increase compared to 2020.

Domestic nights increased by 23% to 46.9 million nights in 2021, only 5.8% below 2019. During the pandemic, domestic tourism in Sweden increased, especially in rural areas. In 2021, 86% of total tourist nights were domestic, up from 74% in 2019.

Total tourism expenditure in 2021 was SEK 249 billion, an increase of 18% compared to 2020. International tourism had a turnover of SEK 57 billion in 2021, representing 23% of total expenditure. Germany became the largest international market, overtaking Norway, with almost 1.7 million nights in 2021.

Tourism governance and funding

The Swedish Agency for Economic and Regional Growth, Tillväxtverket, is responsible for developing tourism at the national level. Visit Sweden, fully owned by the government, markets Sweden as a tourist destination internationally. Both organisations report to the Ministry of Enterprise and Innovation.

Tillväxtverket develops, implements, and supports knowledge-based initiatives and activities to promote tourism sector development and entrepreneurship. The Agency is also responsible for official tourism statistics and the production and dissemination of knowledge on tourism and its effects on the Swedish economy. It collaborates with other government agencies related to tourism.

Tillväxtverket is based in Stockholm but has a regional structure. During the pandemic, the agency focused on activities related to COVID-19, supporting stakeholders with statistics, knowledge and activities, including financing for projects and business development. Visit Sweden's task was extended during the pandemic to include domestic marketing focusing on sustainable nature tourism.

Sweden has set up a regional tourism network in regions which do not have a destination management organisation. The network is an important tool for communication and collaboration with industry organisations and national stakeholders. Recently, the work has been developed to include knowledge development activities within a few prioritised areas. The Swedish Association of Local Authorities and Regions (SALAR) is an umbrella organisation for local and regional authorities. An increasing number of municipalities, county councils and regions work actively to support tourism. SALAR offers them support and services through networking platforms, knowledge reports, and conferences, among other activities.

The Council for the Promotion of Sweden works on promoting Sweden abroad. Council members are comprised of the Ministry for Foreign Affairs, the Ministry of Enterprise and Innovation, the Ministry of Culture, the Swedish Institute, Business Sweden and Visit Sweden. Sweden is also part of the Nordic tourism collaboration under the auspices of The Nordic Council of Ministers, which is in a phase of active policy, strategy, and implementation work.

In 2021, Tillväxtverket's budget allocation for tourism was approximately SEK 100 million. The 2022 budget is on the same level. Visit Sweden's budget allocation is SEK 105 million per year, with an additional SEK 20 million in 2021 for domestic marketing. There are also relatively large resources for tourism projects allocated through regional and EU funds.

Sweden: Organisational chart of tourism bodies

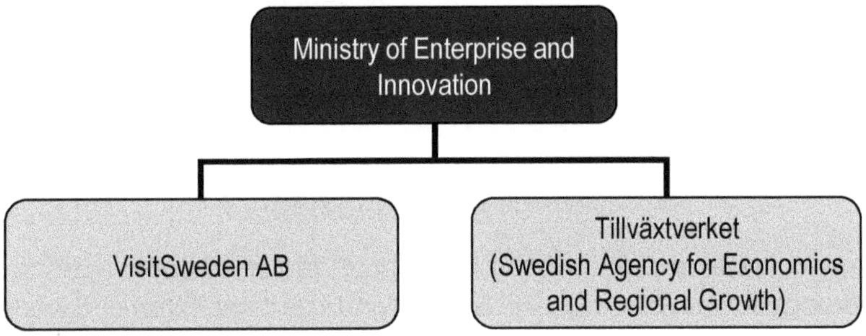

Source: OECD, adapted from the Ministry of Enterprise and Innovation, 2022.

Tourism policies and programmes

Work on developing a ten-year National Tourism Strategy, and the strategies for sustainable tourism and a growing tourism industry, has included co-operation between the Ministries of Enterprise and Innovation, Environment, Infrastructure, Culture, Education, Labour, Foreign Affairs and Finance, and co-operation with industry stakeholders.

The Strategy, launched in 2021, is based upon a national tourism policy review from 2017 and the results of extensive consultation open to all stakeholders. It covers the following strategic areas: easier entrepreneurship, jobs and skills, knowledge and innovation, accessibility, and marketing and communication. The strategy also includes horizontal perspectives of sustainability, digitalisation, place-based development and collaboration.

The multi-policy area approach is key in the Strategy, and there is a strong focus on sustainable development. The Strategy supports the national tourism policy goal: to have sustainable tourism, with a sustainable and competitive tourism sector that grows and contributes to employment and attractive locations for visitors, residents, companies and investments nationwide.

The Strategy sums up the desired situation for Swedish tourism in ten years' time in each of the above-listed areas. It is also designed to support Agenda 2030, the UN's Sustainable Development Goals, and climate policy objectives. Since the tourism industry comprises several different sectors and is so closely connected to many different public and non-profit stakeholders, a transformation into a competitive, fossil-free, and circular economy needs to involve a broad range of actors within different policy areas and in different parts of the system.

Sweden also developed a methodology for tourism development of UNESCO World Heritage Sites, which resulted in a manual for sustainable tourism development in World Heritages and cultural environments published in 2021 (see box below).

Several areas in the strategy have arisen as a high priority by the sector in the aftermath of the COVID-19 pandemic. One is skills and the supply of competencies. There is an increasing challenge in finding staff, particularly in the hospitality sector. Another area is transportation and accessibility, which is a challenge not least due to Sweden's geographical location and the fact that many tourist resorts are located in rural areas, but also given the green transition of the transport sector.

To strengthen its long-term focus, Tillväxtverket is developing a five-year strategic plan anchored in the national strategy and other steering documents, which includes initiatives for enterprises and direct business support.

The strategic plan also includes developing long-term national knowledge support for the tourism sector, such as a digital knowledge bank; quality assurance and delivery of statistics and analysis; follow-up of the pandemic's short- and long-term effects; and advanced knowledge on sustainable tourism. Place-based development is another element, focusing on synergies between policy areas and different parts of the local planning system.

Tourism development guidelines for UNESCO World Heritage sites in Sweden

In 2018, an initiative was taken in collaboration between Swedish national agencies related to tourism to develop a methodology for developing UNESCO World Heritage Sites in Sweden and the Nordics. The initiative was built upon earlier work using UNESCO's guidelines for World Heritage Site development and implemented as a pilot project in the World Heritage Site of Falun. The main partners were the Swedish National Heritage Board, the Swedish Agency for Economic and Regional Growth and the Region of Dalarna.

The project, running from 2019-21, included two parallel processes: one aiming at adapting the UNESCO site development guidelines to Nordic conditions, and one focused on the hands-on development of the site of Falun, testing the methodology in practice. Falun is located on the site of a former copper mine which was operative for around a millennium and is an important part of the Swedish cultural heritage. As a result of the project, a manual for sustainable tourism development in World Heritages and cultural environments was published in 2021.

The work and manual are now being implemented in many of Sweden's World Heritage Sites and UNESCO Biosphere Reserves, where projects are co-funded by the Swedish Agency for Economic and Regional Growth. This is part of a broader initiative on sustainable site development running from 2022-23.

Statistical Profile

Sweden: Domestic, inbound and outbound tourism

	2017	2018	2019	2020	2021
TOURISM FLOWS, THOUSAND					
Domestic tourism[1]					
Total domestic trips	54 216	55 880	56 171	128 792 |	122 669
Overnight visitors (tourists)	37 316	35 686	36 891	49 831 |	51 185
Same-day visitors (excursionists)	16 900	20 194	19 280	78 961 |	71 484
Nights in all types of accommodation	47 017	47 852	49 849	38 122	46 946
Hotels and similar establishments	31 916	33 075	34 712	23 135	29 742
Other collective establishments	15 101	14 777	15 137	14 988	17 204
Private accommodation	..	..	..	..	..
Inbound tourism[2]					
Total international arrivals	..	..	..	..	..
Overnight visitors (tourists)	..	..	..	..	..
Same-day visitors (excursionists)	..	..	..	..	..
Top markets					
..	..	..	..	..	..
..	..	..	..	..	..
..	..	..	..	..	..
..	..	..	..	..	..
..	..	..	..	..	..
Nights in all types of accommodation	16 191	17 327	17 522	5 180	7 274
Hotels and similar establishments	11 000	11 720	11 716	3 851	4 846
Other collective establishments	5 191	5 608	5 806	1 329	2 428
Private accommodation	..	..	..	..	..
Outbound tourism					
Total international departures	22 121	19 939	19 061	6 081 |	7 615
Overnight visitors (tourists)	20 361	18 855	18 000	4 225 |	5 767
Same-day visitors (excursionists)	1 760	1 084	1 061	1 856 |	1 848
Top destinations					
..	..	..	..	..	..
..	..	..	..	..	..
..	..	..	..	..	..
..	..	..	..	..	..
..	..	..	..	..	..
TOURISM RECEIPTS AND EXPENDITURE, MILLION SEK					
Inbound tourism					
Total international receipts	139 226	102 581	104 222	44 966	..
International travel receipts	120 587	87 027	86 948	40 276	..
International passenger transport receipts	18 639	15 554	17 274	4 690	..
Outbound tourism					
Total international expenditure	165 911	159 621	162 002	62 579	..
International travel expenditure	145 184	136 477	135 876	56 847	..
International passenger transport expenditure	20 727	23 144	26 125	5 732	..

.. Not available; | Break in series

1. Trips from demand side surveys; Nights from supply side surveys.
2. Arrivals from demand side surveys; Nights from supply side surveys.

Source: OECD Tourism Statistics (Database).

StatLink https://stat.link/rwe7v8

Sweden: Enterprises and employment in tourism

	Number of establishments[1]	Number of persons employed				
	2021	2017	2018	2019	2020	2021
Total	..	**113 082**	**116 286**	**116 278**	**97 650**	**94 303**
Tourism industries	..	**70 953**	**73 590**	**73 076**	**65 183**	**61 882**
Accommodation services for visitors	..	29 076	30 592	28 987	23 657	25 201
Hotels and similar establishments	2 160	..	..	..	..	..
Food and beverage serving industry	..	17 767	18 411	17 809	15 003	15 489
Passenger transport	..	11 576	12 400	12 894	13 123	8 932
Air passenger transport	..	4 217	4 341	4 719	7 594	3 757
Railways passenger transport	..	2 487	2 779	1 958	2 101	2 169
Road passenger transport	..	3 273	3 486	3 491	2 720	2 273
Water passenger transport	..	1 599	1 794	2 726	708	733
Passenger transport supporting services	..	0	0	0	0	0
Transport equipment rental	..	727	818	987	1 013	924
Travel agencies and other reservation services industry	..	7 273	6 922	7 796	7 625	7 058
Cultural industry	..	2 380	2 439	2 508	2 891	2 550
Sports and recreation industry	..	2 154	2 008	2 095	1 871	1 728
Retail trade of country-specific tourism characteristic goods	..	0	0	0	0	0
Other country-specific tourism industries	..	0	0	0	0	0
Other industries	..	**42 129**	**42 696**	**43 202**	**32 467**	**32 421**

.. Not available
1. Data refer to number of enterprises.
Source: OECD Tourism Statistics (Database).

StatLink https://stat.link/mivzqn

Sweden: Internal tourism consumption

Million SEK

	2021		
	Domestic tourism expenditure	Inbound tourism expenditure	Internal tourism consumption
Total	..	..	..
Consumption products	**191 746**	**57 093**	**248 838**
Tourism characteristic products	131 005	27 108	158 113
Accommodation services for visitors	56 511	7 819	64 330
Food and beverage serving services	20 567	6 630	27 197
Passenger transport services	24 534	7 788	32 322
Air passenger transport services	9 173	3 770	12 943
Railways passenger transport services	1 800	779	2 579
Road passenger transport services	11 648	1 292	12 940
Water passenger transport services	1 912	1 947	3 859
Passenger transport supporting services	..	..	..
Transport equipment rental services	5 649	1 840	7 489
Travel agencies and other reservation services industry	10 564	1 331	11 895
Cultural services	10 188	519	10 707
Sports and recreation services	2 992	1 181	4 173
Country-specific tourism characteristic goods	0	0	0
Country-specific tourism characteristic services	0	0	0
Other consumption products	60 740	29 985	90 725
Tourism connected products	..	..	..
Non-tourism related consumption products	..	..	..
Non-consumption products	..	..	..

.. Not available
Source: OECD Tourism Statistics (Database).

StatLink https://stat.link/6vctou

Switzerland

Tourism in the economy and outlook for recovery

In 2019, Switzerland recorded a historic high in tourism. At that time, the sector directly contributed 2.9% to the GVA and directly employed 173 703 people, with full-time equivalents corresponding to 4.2% of total employment. In 2020, tourism's contribution to GVA dropped to 2.2%, and direct employment fell to 162 766 (full-time equivalents), a 6.3% decrease.

In 2019, there were 11.8 million international tourists, which fell to 3.7 million in 2020. In 2021, there was a slight increase in demand, but international tourists still remained 63.0% below pre-pandemic levels at 4.4 million. The top source markets shifted to neighbouring countries. In 2021, Germany represented 33.1% of international overnight stays in Switzerland (compared to 18.8% in 2019), followed by France with 14.2% (7.0% in 2019).

The number of hotel nights fell by 40% to 23.7 million in 2020 (with international nights down 66% and domestic nights down just 8.6%). City tourism was particularly hard hit, with overnights plummeting by around 60% in 2020. Switzerland has recorded strong domestic tourism numbers, driven by its Alpine destinations. Total domestic tourist nights hit 34.3 million in 2021, a 16.8% increase compared to pre-pandemic levels.

An inbound tourism recovery to pre-COVID-19 levels is expected in 2023-24.

Tourism governance and funding

The State Secretariat for Economic Affairs (SECO), interacting with numerous political bodies at a national and regional level, is responsible for designing and implementing Switzerland's tourism policy. SECO enforces the Federal Act on the Promotion of Innovation, Cooperation and Knowledge Building in Tourism (Innotour) and supervises two associations tasked with implementing various tourism-related measures: Switzerland Tourism carries out marketing activities relating to Swiss tourism, and the Swiss Society for Hotel Credit supports investment in the accommodation sector.

As tourism is an important economic contributor in many cantons, each has a tourism office with promotion carried out at the cantonal level. The Swiss Tourism Forum facilitates a close exchange between the central government, the cantons and tourism stakeholders. The central government and the cantons promote the mountain region, urban and rural areas and the border regions.

For the years 2020-23, the regular federal contribution to Switzerland Tourism amounts to CHF 230 million. CHF 30 million in regular funds is available over the same period via Innotour to promote innovation. The promotional activities of the Swiss Society for Hotel Credit (SGH) are based on a standing federal loan of CHF 236 million. Within the New Regional Policy framework, CHF 200 million in loans is available for investment and CHF 120 million for contributions to projects with regional economic impact.

Switzerland: Organisational chart of tourism bodies

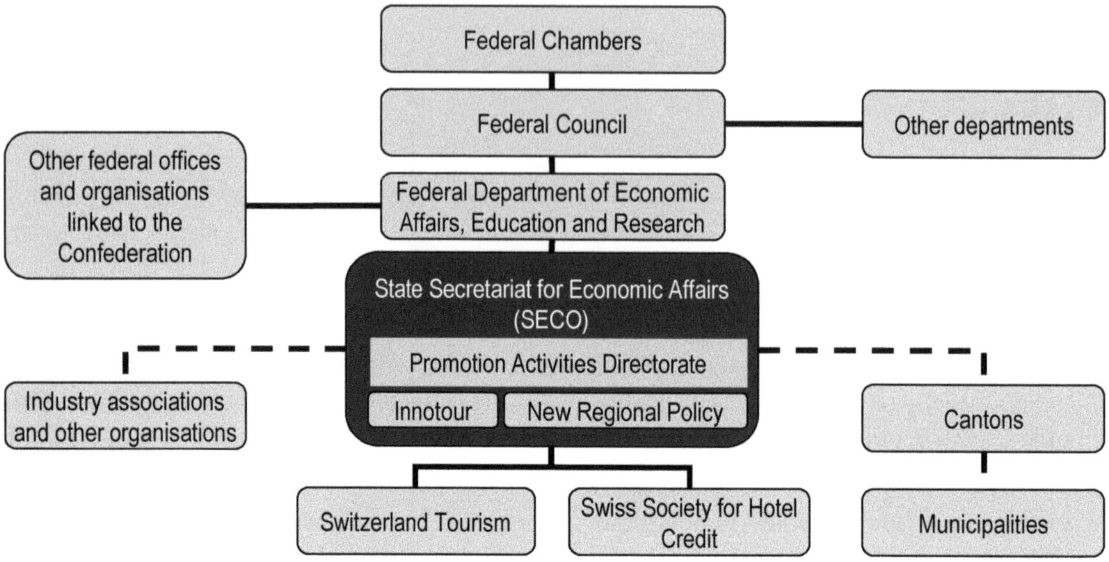

Source: OECD, adapted from the State Secretariat for Economic Affairs, 2022.

Tourism policies and programmes

Switzerland approved the updated and renewed Tourism Strategy in November 2021. This Strategy draws on the previous tourism strategy and retains a number of objectives:

- **Improve framework conditions** focuses on the co-ordination of tourism policy. The Swiss Tourism Forum serves as a dialogue and co-ordination platform contributing to a 'tourism-friendly' regulatory environment, focusing on the interface between tourism and spatial planning.
- **Promote entrepreneurship:** aims to contribute to structural change in tourism. Start-ups are promoted, succession plans are supported, and approaches to strengthen the tourism labour market are developed in co-operation with industry associations.
- **Contribute to sustainable development:** focuses on adapting tourism to tackle climate change, particularly by better understanding the interface between tourism, landscape and development. Under the "Swisstainable" initiative, the importance of sustainable development for tourism is anchored more broadly.
- **Maximise the opportunities of digitalisation:** focuses on data and statistics as well as the monitoring of digitalisation strategy.
- **Strengthen the attractiveness of the offer and market presence:** focuses on the further development of federal investment promotion and the revitalisation of city and business tourism.

An Advisory Group consisting of tourism stakeholders and entrepreneurs, as well as political representatives, tourism associations, the cantons and the academic community, will oversee the implementation of the national Tourism Strategy.

Switzerland Tourism continues implementing a recovery plan in 2020-23 (see box below). The Federal Government is providing CHF 70 million for the programme in total (CHF 40 million for 2020-21 and CHF 30 million for 2022-23). Half of the funding will be used to provide financial relief to tourism partners. Through the New Regional Policy, Switzerland allowed the cantons to defer repayments under the Investment Assistance Act, which made it possible to support the mountain railway sector in the short term.

In addition, funds of CHF 10 million are made available for project promotion via the New Regional Policy for the period 2020-23.

The promotion of innovative projects in tourism through Innotour is also to be extended for the period 2023-26. The Federal Government's contribution to such projects will increase from 50% to a new maximum of 70%, reducing the costs for innovation in tourism to be borne by the project promoters. For this, the contribution of the Federal Government to Innotour will be increased by CHF 20 million.

In the coming years, Switzerland's tourism policy will be increasingly orientated towards the needs of tourism stakeholders, particularly tourism enterprises. Implementation of the strategy will focus on the identified challenges - in particular, the adaptation of tourism to climate change and raising the potential of the interface between tourism, landscape and building culture, and the issue of the tourism labour market. A further focus will be on developing federal investment promotion to modernise and strengthen investment promotion.

Strategic challenges for Swiss tourism in the long term include digitalisation, changing travel behaviour, climate change, below-average productivity and the tourism labour market. Digitalisation can help address the weakness of Swiss tourism (such as the low productivity of many micro-businesses) by increasing efficiency and promoting new forms of co-operation and co-ordination.

Tourism Recovery Programme 2020-23 in Switzerland

Switzerland Tourism implemented a tourism recovery programme in 2020-23. The programme has four key actions:

- Recover international visitor numbers: to present Switzerland as a desirable tourist destination in international markets and to win back international visitors. The focus will be on local markets, individual travel, and small groups. In addition, the increased demand for land-based arrival will be considered, and corresponding offers will be created and promoted.
- Encourage sustainable tourism development: to establish Switzerland as a sustainable travel destination worldwide. Activities include the "Stay Longer" initiative to motivate guests to extend their stay. This can reduce the ecological footprint and, at the same time, increase added value. Another starting point for promoting sustainable development in Swiss tourism was created with the Swisstainable campaign. This is intended to promote sustainability-oriented product development and position Switzerland as the world's most sustainable travel destination.
- Revitalise city and business tourism: to focus on cities, positioning them as "City Nature Resorts". In this way, cities will also be marketed as a starting point for Swiss holidays. The planned activities should help replenish the cities with visitors and help city hotels achieve higher occupancy rates. At the same time, business tourism is to be stimulated to open up new market segments, for example, event concepts that have been reimagined due to the pandemic.
- Provide relief for tourism partners: financially support tourism partners, such as destinations. The lack of international guests led to a reduction in visitor tax revenue for destinations and a lower turnover for service providers. The financial support for tourism partners adds up to 50% of the additional federal government contribution of CHF 15 million. These relief payments enable tourism partners to participate in Switzerland Tourism's marketing campaigns despite reduced budgets.

Statistical Profile

Switzerland: Domestic, inbound and outbound tourism

	2017	2018	2019	2020	2021
TOURISM FLOWS, THOUSAND					
Domestic tourism[1]					
Total domestic trips	76 309	80 020	78 317	62 951 |	..
Overnight visitors (tourists)	8 231	8 201	7 765	8 319 |	..
Same-day visitors (excursionists)	68 078	71 819	70 551	54 632 |	..
Nights in all types of accommodation	27 768	28 573	29 354	28 260	34 291
Hotels and similar establishments	16 920	17 413	17 922	16 389	20 961
Other collective establishments	10 848	11 160	11 432	11 871	13 331
Private accommodation	..	..	..	..	..
Inbound tourism					
Total international arrivals	..	..	..	..	..
Overnight visitors (tourists)	11 133	11 715	11 818	3 690	4 390
Same-day visitors (excursionists)	..	..	..	..	..
Top markets					
Germany	2 072	2 216	2 220	1 219	1 455
France	788	826	831	489	627
Italy	530	529	514	219	282
United States	1 009	1 118	1 219	167	279
United Kingdom	808	820	818	224	140
Nights in all types of accommodation	25 515	26 784	26 880	10 254	11 593
Hotels and similar establishments	20 473	21 394	21 640	7 341	8 598
Other collective establishments	5 042	5 390	5 241	2 913	2 995
Private accommodation	..	..	..	..	..
Outbound tourism					
Total international departures	24 594	26 397	21 360	8 319 |	..
Overnight visitors (tourists)	16 650	16 735	14 622	6 813 |	..
Same-day visitors (excursionists)	7 944	9 662	6 737	1 506 |	..
Top destinations					
Italy	2 868	2 964	2 594	1 487 |	..
Germany	2 766	3 135	2 816	1 474 |	..
France	3 213	2 441	1 885	1 178 |	..
Austria	1 062	1 078	940	629 |	..
..	..	..	..	..	..
TOURISM RECEIPTS AND EXPENDITURE, MILLION CHF					
Inbound tourism					
Total international receipts	20 053	20 820	21 118	9 416	11 054
International travel receipts	16 958	17 592	17 837	8 511 p	10 070
International passenger transport receipts	3 095	3 229	3 280	906	984
Outbound tourism					
Total international expenditure	21 136	20 985	20 963	9 751	11 578
International travel expenditure	18 774	18 650	18 635	8 974 p	10 675
International passenger transport expenditure	2 362	2 334	2 328	776	903

.. Not available; p Provisional data; | Break in series
1. Trips from demand side surveys; Nights from supply side surveys.
Source: OECD Tourism Statistics (Database).

StatLink https://stat.link/3kl7hp

Switzerland: Enterprises and employment in tourism

	Number of establishments	Number of persons employed				
	2021	2017	2018	2019	2020	2021
Total	..	**169 427**	**172 407**	**173 703**	**162 766**	..
Tourism industries	..	**137 449**	**139 894**	**140 793**	**132 243**	..
Accommodation services for visitors	36 755	35 385	36 409	35 747	33 371 p	..
Hotels and similar establishments	4 574	32 079	32 963	32 185	30 044 p	..
Food and beverage serving industry	..	42 967	43 913	44 219	40 016 p	..
Passenger transport	..	26 192	26 842	27 972	27 721	..
Air passenger transport	..	8 170	8 677	9 082	8 981 p	..
Railways passenger transport	..	12 954	13 037	13 414	13 310 p	..
Road passenger transport	..	4 246	4 243	4 460	4 425 p	..
Water passenger transport	..	821	885	1 017	1 005 p	..
Passenger transport supporting services	..	5 926	6 044	6 157	6 100 p	..
Transport equipment rental	..	627	630	570	545 p	..
Travel agencies and other reservation services industry	..	14 121	13 555	13 435	12 837 p	..
Cultural industry	..	3 896	3 950	3 984	3 932 p	..
Sports and recreation industry	..	6 198	6 452	6 597	6 486 p	..
Retail trade of country-specific tourism characteristic goods	..	..	..	..	..	..
Other country-specific tourism industries	..	2 139	2 100	2 112	1 236 p	..
Other industries	..	**31 978**	**32 513**	**32 910**	**30 523**	..

.. Not available; p Provisional data
Source: OECD Tourism Statistics (Database).

StatLink https://stat.link/h1lzjb

Switzerland: Internal tourism consumption

Million CHF

	2017		
	Domestic tourism expenditure	Inbound tourism expenditure	Internal tourism consumption
Total	**24 251**	**17 020**	**46 360**
Consumption products	**19 421**	**14 147**	**38 657**
Tourism characteristic products	16 912	12 123	33 723
Accommodation services for visitors	2 617	2 774	9 417
Food and beverage serving services	3 666	2 752	6 417
Passenger transport services	5 990	4 196	10 478
Air passenger transport services	3 897	2 789	6 686
Railways passenger transport services	1 351	861	2 504
Road passenger transport services	640	507	1 146
Water passenger transport services	102	39	141
Passenger transport supporting services	453	371	824
Transport equipment rental services	218	207	425
Travel agencies and other reservation services industry	1 233	187	1 572
Cultural services	496	177	890
Sports and recreation services	1 701	1 356	3 057
Country-specific tourism characteristic goods	..	..	..
Country-specific tourism characteristic services	540	103	643
Other consumption products	7 339	4 897	12 637
Tourism connected products	2 509	2 024	4 934
Non-tourism related consumption products	4 830	2 872	7 703
Non-consumption products	..	..	..

.. Not available
Source: OECD Tourism Statistics (Database).

StatLink https://stat.link/dzw47i

Türkiye

Tourism in the economy and outlook for recovery

Tourism is an important contributor to the economy of Türkiye. In 2019, tourism receipts reached USD 41.3 billion, representing 5.4% of GDP. Tourism-related employment accounted for 8.1% of the workforce, or 2.3 million people. The share of tourism employment in total employment declined to 6.6% in 2021. Tourism receipts fell 67% in 2020 to USD 13.6 billion, with tourism's contribution to national GDP falling to 1.9%. In 2021, Tourism receipts increased by 110% compared to the previous year and reached USD 28.6 billion, with a contribution to national GDP of 3.5%.

The number of international arrivals to Türkiye reached a record high of 51.2 million in 2019. In 2020, 15.9 million tourists visited Türkiye, a decrease of 69% compared to the previous year. The number of international visitors to Türkiye rebounded to 30 million in 2021, up 88% from 2020. The relative strength of international tourism saw Türkiye enter the top five global destinations in 2021. The top source markets included Russia (15.6% of total inbound tourism), Germany (10.3%), Ukraine (6.8%) and Bulgaria (4.7%).

Signs of recovery were also seen in domestic tourism, which recorded 52.8 million tourists, a ten million increase from 2020, however remaining 32.5% below pre-pandemic levels.

2022 is expected to see continued growth, with an expected 42 million international arrivals, although remaining below pre-pandemic levels. Türkiye expects to hit 60 million international arrivals in 2023 and 70 million in 2024.

Tourism governance and funding

The Ministry of Culture and Tourism is responsible for tourism in Türkiye. Its duties are to investigate, develop, protect, maintain, evaluate, disseminate and promote tourism in order to contribute to the strengthening of national unity and economic growth.

Overseas marketing and promotion are directed and co-ordinated by the Promotion Directorate within the Ministry of Culture and Tourism and delivered by a network of 46 overseas offices in 41 different countries. At the regional level, Türkiye has 81 Provincial Culture and Tourism offices that conserve the historical, cultural and natural heritage, diversify tourism, and promote the region through cultural events, festivals and fairs.

Several professional institutions and private sector associations work closely with the Ministry to plan tourism and address specific issues. These bodies include the Association of Turkish Travel Agencies, Touristic Hotels and Investors Association, Hoteliers Federation, Turkish Tourism Investors Association and the Union of Tourist Guides' Chambers. The investment Office of the Presidency of the Republic of Türkiye also promotes Türkiye's investment opportunities to the global business community and assists investors.

Founded in 2019, the Türkiye Tourism Promotion and Development Agency is dedicated to promoting Türkiye as a brand and a popular destination in both domestic and international tourism markets;

discovering, developing and promoting tangible and intangible natural, cultural and heritage assets; boosting the tourism capacity of Türkiye, increasing the rate of tourism investments in the national economy and raising the quality of service with short, medium and long-term communication and marketing activities.

Operating under the auspices of the Ministry of Culture and Tourism, the Agency is subject to private law provisions. The Agency comprises the Board of Directors, Executive Board, and Advisory Board, with the Board of Directors serving as the decision-making body. The Board of Directors comprises 15 members chaired by the Minister of Culture and Tourism of the Republic of Türkiye.

Türkiye also plans to develop domestic and international tourism in new destinations, using a destination management model to redesign the management structure in the provinces.

Türkiye: Organisational chart of tourism bodies

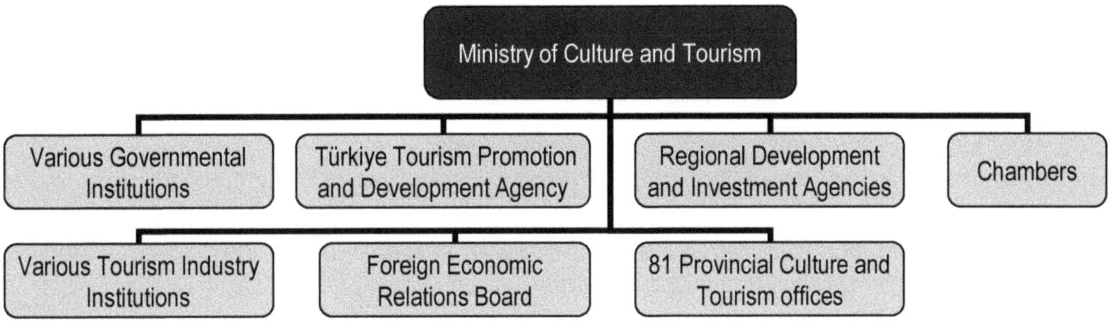

Source: OECD, adapted from the Ministry of Culture and Tourism, 2022.

Tourism policies and programmes

To prepare Türkiye's tourism industry for future shocks, the Ministry is updating the Tourism Masterplan and setting new goals for 2022-24.

Sustainable tourism is a key priority for Türkiye's post-COVID-19 strategy and a main pillar in the updated Masterplan. In order to redesign Türkiye's sustainable tourism policies and efforts, the Ministry of Culture and Tourism co-operates with local, national, and international stakeholders and academia. Türkiye also updated its Tourism Master Plan 2023 to reflect the impacts and challenges of the pandemic on tourism. In accordance, a crisis management strategy outline was added to the Plan.

Türkiye's tourism industry has been growing steadily over the last 40 years, with new investments in infrastructure such as large hotels, holiday villages, luxury boutique hotels, ports, airports, high-speed trains, roads, highways, and metros in almost all big cities. The rate of tourism-related investment has decreased with the impact of the COVID-19 pandemic.

Türkiye introduced a set of policies and practices to keep tourism businesses running during the restrictions associated with the COVID-19 pandemic, including:

- Providing bank loans for advance payments covering preliminary reservations.
- Delaying social security payments by six months.
- Allowing Ministry-approved travel agencies to work online.
- Postponing debt payments from tourism facilities located on public land.
- Providing fast bank loans with repayment holidays to small-scale tourism operations.
- Postponing accommodation tax in hotels and tourism facilities and hotel rents.
- Paying TRY 1 000 to 3 million households financially affected by the crisis.

The slowdown of travel during the pandemic provided time for tourism policymakers to develop new policies and innovative practices. During this period, the Ministry took the opportunity to redesign its five-year tourism policies, prioritising sustainability and competitiveness.

New programmes include the Safe Tourism Certification to assess COVID-19 measures in tourism businesses across the industry (see box below) and Go Türkiye, a new multi-platform tourism portal. Go Türkiye was completed in 2020 and aims to help spread tourism throughout the country. The portal actively involves tourism NGOs, universities, the private sector, and provincial tourism administrations. A survey conducted in all 81 provinces of Türkiye provided data, opinions, and feedback which will be used for developing new destinations and redesigning tourism in the post-COVID-19 era.

To increase the competitiveness of Türkiye's tourism industry, the Ministry enhanced co-operation with international stakeholders such as the UNWTO, Global Sustainable Tourism Council and the World Economic Forum. The Ministry also continues to work closely with national stakeholders such as industry partners, the business association TÜSİAD, and other ministries involved in tourism and sustainability.

Safe Tourism Programme in Türkiye

As an early response to the increasing need for extra hygiene and sanitation, Türkiye introduced the Safe Tourism Certification Programme. The programme, led by the Culture and Tourism Ministry, was developed with contributions from the Ministries of Health, Internal Affairs and Foreign Affairs, and in co-operation with all the stakeholders in the industry

Facilities which have received verification are publicised on the Ministry of Culture and Tourism's website, and the Safe Tourism Certification logo is placed on visible areas of the verified facility. QR codes on all logos allow guests and customers to access the facility's inspection data, making the process transparent. The certification is designed for the tourism sector, including accommodation facilities, food and beverage facilities, tour and transfer vehicles, culture, art and congress facilities, theme parks and ski lifts.

The programme criteria have been updated several times since 2020 due to the changing needs and new regulations. The Safe Tourism Program sets a series of measures with over 600 parameters and is obligatory for many businesses (for example, accommodation establishments with 30 or more rooms) and is recommended for smaller businesses.

Since the programme started, more than 12 000 facilities have been certified.

Statistical Profile

Türkiye: Domestic, inbound and outbound tourism

	2017	2018	2019	2020	2021
TOURISM FLOWS, THOUSAND					
Domestic tourism					
Total domestic trips	120 872	126 446	124 639	67 142	75 883
Overnight visitors (tourists)	77 179	78 523	78 202	42 847	52 774
Same-day visitors (excursionists)	43 693	47 923	46 437	24 295	23 109
Nights in all types of accommodation	665 194	633 721	637 070	469 091	458 872
Hotels and similar establishments	49 786	55 815	51 633	23 569	41 654
Other collective establishments	19 030	19 116	19 087	9 926	16 480
Private accommodation	596 378	558 790	566 350	435 596	400 738
Inbound tourism[1]					
Total international arrivals	37 970	46 113	51 747	15 971	30 039
Overnight visitors (tourists)	37 601	45 768	51 192	15 894	29 925
Same-day visitors (excursionists)	369	345	555	77	114
Top markets					
Russia	4 702	5 954	6 996	2 117	4 684
Germany	3 518	4 464	4 993	1 119	3 083
Ukraine	1 266	1 372	1 515	979	2 049
Bulgaria	1 850	2 383	2 710	1 242	1 402
Netherlands	2 434	2 066	1 989	271	645
Nights in all types of accommodation	80 063	112 245	132 808	40 093	93 124
Hotels and similar establishments	79 960	112 226	132 776	40 083	93 093
Other collective establishments	103	19	32	10	31
Private accommodation	..	..	..	..	..
Outbound tourism					
Total international departures	8 887	8 383	9 651	2 243	2 738
Overnight visitors (tourists)	..	..	..	..	..
Same-day visitors (excursionists)	..	..	..	..	..
Top destinations					
Iraq	581	1 014	1 046	..	453
Europe not specified	1 105	1 229	1 448	..	403
Bulgaria	949	987	1 253	..	403
Georgia	1 016	778	1 015	..	275
Greece	1 058	884	918	..	87
TOURISM RECEIPTS AND EXPENDITURE, MILLION USD					
Inbound tourism					
Total international receipts	29 116	37 175	41 284	13 595	28 611
International travel receipts	20 691	25 243	29 813	10 221	20 909
International passenger transport receipts	8 425	11 932	11 471	3 374	7 701
Outbound tourism					
Total international expenditure	4 620	5 003	5 259	1 410	2 093
International travel expenditure	4 302	4 601	4 108	1 040	1 657
International passenger transport expenditure	318	402	1 151	370	437

.. Not available

1. Arrivals from demand side surveys; Nights from supply side surveys.

Source: OECD Tourism Statistics (Database).

StatLink https://stat.link/pdkbye

Türkiye: Enterprises and employment in tourism

	Number of establishments[1]	Number of persons employed				
	2020	2017	2018	2019	2020	2021
Total	..	..	..	..	..	..
Tourism industries	**501 608**	**2 062 809**	**2 222 378**	**2 284 072**	**1 851 788**	**1 897 069**
Accommodation services for visitors	23 024	294 958	343 928	368 941	297 322	313 745
Hotels and similar establishments	19 091	247 100	286 101	303 333	230 471	246 583
Food and beverage serving industry	271 214	1 189 288	1 253 134	1 305 850	1 045 965	1 059 197
Passenger transport	162 567	391 243	411 351	399 845	344 636	350 232
Air passenger transport	186	..	..	..	..	..
Railways passenger transport	.. c	..	..	..	..	..
Road passenger transport	159 178	..	..	..	..	..
Water passenger transport	3 203	..	..	..	..	..
Passenger transport supporting services	..	..	..	..	..	..
Transport equipment rental	10 424	24 250	27 593	28 855	27 606	24 204
Travel agencies and other reservation services industry	11 195	44 157	50 103	50 929	40 964	56 481
Cultural industry	5 455	56 491	55 111	54 065	41 076	35 686
Sports and recreation industry	17 729	62 422	81 158	75 587	54 220	57 525
Retail trade of country-specific tourism characteristic goods	..	..	..	..	..	..
Other country-specific tourism industries	..	..	..	..	..	..
Other industries	..	..	..	..	..	..

.. Not available; c Confidential data
1. Data refer to number of enterprises.
Source: OECD Tourism Statistics (Database).

StatLink https://stat.link/j6n8oh

United Kingdom

Tourism in the economy and outlook for recovery

Tourism is an important economic sector in the United Kingdom. In 2019, tourism directly contributed GBP 73.6 billion or 3.7% of total GVA. The impacts of the pandemic saw this fall to GBP 34.4 billion or 1.8% of national GVA in 2020. Tourism directly supported 1.7 million jobs in 2019, with 240 944 enterprises involved in tourism activities.

International overnight visitors fell 73% to 11.1 million in 2020. This greatly impacted tourism receipts, which declined 64% to GBP 14.8 billion. There were 6.2 million international visits to the United Kingdom in 2021, with a gradual increase throughout the year as travel restrictions loosened and international travel resumed. The 2021 top source markets were the United States, Ireland, France, Spain and Germany.

The impact on domestic trips is also crucial as domestic tourism typically makes up more than 80% of tourism expenditure in the United Kingdom. Domestic tourism is not expected to recover to 2019 levels until 2023. The latest forecast suggests that international arrivals to the United Kingdom will not return to 2019 levels until 2025.

Tourism governance and funding

The Department for Digital, Culture, Media and Sport (DCMS) is the lead department responsible for tourism policy in the United Kingdom. It co-ordinates tourism policy across the United Kingdom, leads the relationship with the British Tourist Authority (the national tourist board) and has control over a number of distinct policy areas such as tourism marketing, heritage, arts, culture, and business events.

Engagement with other departments is overseen on an ad-hoc basis by the Tourism Minister responsible for policy which affects the overall tourism sector, including the departments for Business, Energy and Industrial Strategy, Transport, and Environment, Food and Rural Affairs, Her Majesty's Treasury, and the Home Office. This was formalised in 2021 with the creation of an inter-Ministerial Group for the Visitor Economy.

The British Tourist Authority has a statutory duty to encourage visits to Britain and improve tourist amenities. VisitBritain markets and promotes Britain abroad through a global office network. VisitEngland undertakes domestic marketing and business support and development activities. The British Tourist Authority also undertakes tourism research, administers bespoke grant schemes and has a number of commercial revenue streams. In 2021/22, the BTA received GBP 34.2 million of funding from DCMS and GBP 18.9 million from GREAT, an international marketing campaign encouraging people to visit, do business, invest and study in the United Kingdom.

Tourism is largely a devolved competence; thus, the Scottish and Welsh Governments, and the Northern Ireland Executive, formulate their own tourism policy and have their own tourist boards. Tourism Ministers from the four nations meet once a quarter.

The Tourism Industry Council, co-chaired by the Minister for Sport and Tourism and a senior representative of Hilton Worldwide, drives engagement with the tourism sector, facilitating a two-way dialogue. Other forums include the 'Tourism Industry Emergency Response' group run by VisitBritain, which has met regularly during COVID-19, and the Events Industry Board, which supports the government in developing its business tourism policy.

Destination Management Organisations (DMOs) are an important part of the United Kingdom tourism landscape. However, they have no formal relationship with the national government outside of ad-hoc relationships on bespoke grant funding programmes. There is no consistent funding model for DMOs, but some are funded by Local Authorities. In 2021, the United Kingdom commissioned a review of the DMO model (see Box 2.10).

United Kingdom: Organisational chart of tourism bodies

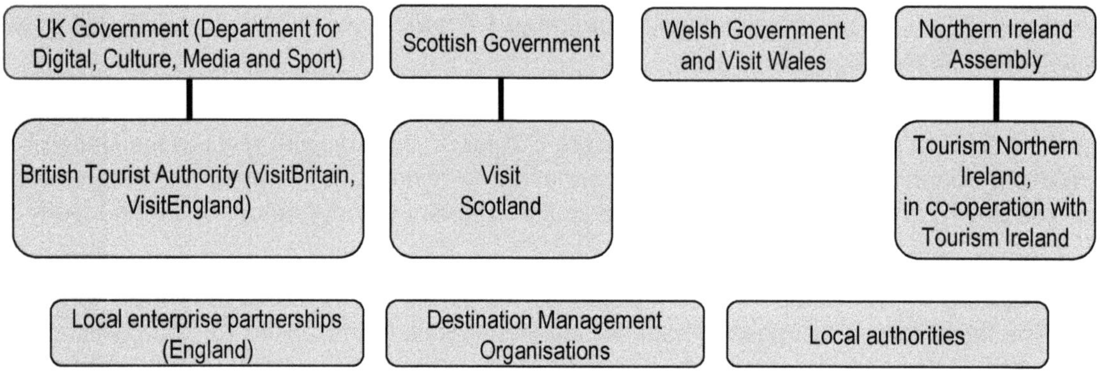

Source: OECD, adapted from the Department for Digital, Culture, Media and Sport, 2022.

Tourism policies and programmes

In June 2021, the United Kingdom published its Tourism Recovery Plan, describing how the government will help the sector recover from the COVID-19 pandemic and 'build back better'. This provides policies to address the challenges caused by the pandemic and sets out high-level aims and objectives for where the United Kingdom would like to be once tourism recovers.

The Tourism Recovery Plan lists a range of policy measures responding to each objective of the Plan. In the short to medium term. Key policy measures include stimulating demand via enhanced domestic and international marketing activities, for example, a GBP 10 million holiday voucher scheme administered by the National Lottery to stimulate domestic tourism in the off-season and introducing a new integrated rail pass for domestic tourists. Other measures include detailed sector guidance on COVID-19 rules, maintenance of the "Good to Go" COVID-19 secure accreditation, consultations on reforming Aviation Tax and Package Travel Regulations, and continued pan-economic support, such as business rates relief, loans and discretionary grant schemes administered by local authorities.

The United Kingdom has spent at least GBP 37 billion in support of the tourism, hospitality and leisure sectors through wage subsidy schemes, tax cuts and reliefs, bespoke COVID-19 loans and other measures.

In the medium to long term, the government has set five high-level objectives:

- The benefits of tourism are spread across every nation and region. This particularly focuses on encouraging inbound visitors to see more of the United Kingdom beyond London.

- A more productive, innovative and resilient sector with better use of digital technologies and data and more employment in year-round, quality jobs.
- A sector that contributes to enhancing and conserving the United Kingdom's cultural, natural and historical heritage and minimises damage to these environments.
- A sector providing an inclusive and accessible offer open to all.
- A leading nation for hosting business events.

Some of these objectives were already being looked at pre-pandemic. For example, the 2019 Tourism Sector Deal included a section on accessibility. Others have emerged during the pandemic or due to a change in government, such as, for example, the focus on spreading visitors and the heightened focus on the green transition.

A range of measures will support these longer-term objectives, such as investment in tourism infrastructure, including attractions and transport (particularly rail and electric vehicles); reform of England's Destination Management Organisations (Box 2.10); exploration of a 'Tourism Data Hub' and consultation on an accommodation registration scheme, relating primarily to regulation of the sharing economy and holiday letting market; commitment to developing a national Sustainable Tourism Plan; and an enhanced Ministerial advocacy programme for business events.

Statistical Profile

United Kingdom: Domestic, inbound and outbound tourism

	2017	2018	2019	2020	2021
TOURISM FLOWS, THOUSAND					
Domestic tourism					
Total domestic trips	1 914 080	1 821 600	1 775 780	..	..
Overnight visitors (tourists)	120 680	118 600	122 780	..	..
Same-day visitors (excursionists)	1 793 400	1 703 000	1 653 000	..	..
Nights in all types of accommodation	..	208 054	220 812	..	..
Hotels and similar establishments	..	144 261	161 881	..	..
Other collective establishments	..	63 793	58 931	..	..
Private accommodation	..	..	..	..	..
Inbound tourism					
Total international arrivals	41 080	40 283	40 857	11 101	6 194
Overnight visitors (tourists)	39 543	38 664	39 418	..	..
Same-day visitors (excursionists)	1 538	1 619	1 439	..	..
Top markets					
United States	..	..	..	..	699
Ireland	..	..	..	..	685
France	..	..	..	..	610
Spain	..	..	..	..	492
Germany	..	..	..	..	388
Nights in all types of accommodation	..	139 759	158 335	..	..
Hotels and similar establishments	..	135 996	155 280	..	..
Other collective establishments	..	3 763	3 055	..	..
Private accommodation	..	..	..	..	..
Outbound tourism					
Total international departures	87 242	90 571	93 086	23 827	19 098
Overnight visitors (tourists)	85 449	88 759	91 516	..	..
Same-day visitors (excursionists)	1 793	1 811	1 570	..	..
Top destinations					
Spain	..	..	..	..	4 232
France	..	..	..	..	1 598
Portugal	..	..	..	..	1 159
Greece	..	..	..	..	1 132
Ireland	..	..	..	..	1 057
TOURISM RECEIPTS AND EXPENDITURE, MILLION GBP					
Inbound tourism					
Total international receipts	38 353	36 742	41 306	14 681	..
International travel receipts	38 353	36 742	41 306	14 681	16 504
International passenger transport receipts	..	..	..	..	..
Outbound tourism					
Total international expenditure	51 330	53 059	55 324	16 849	..
International travel expenditure	51 330	53 059	55 324	16 849	17 657
International passenger transport expenditure	..	..	..	..	..

.. Not available
Source: OECD Tourism Statistics (Database).

StatLink https://stat.link/6p14jh

United Kingdom: Enterprises and employment in tourism

	Number of establishments[1]	Number of persons employed				
	2019	2017	2018	2019	2020	2021
Total	..	**1 585 611 |**	**1 547 496**	**2 165 000**	..	..
Tourism industries	**240 944**	**1 144 441 |**	**1 115 496**	**1 742 000**	..	..
Accommodation services for visitors	18 300	396 000 |	378 000	424 000	..	..
Hotels and similar establishments	..	..	..	..	..	..
Food and beverage serving industry	140 260	411 000 |	404 000	421 000	..	..
Passenger transport	14 352	105 000 |	105 000	120 000	..	..
Air passenger transport	470	32 000 |	31 000	34 000	..	..
Railways passenger transport	73	36 000 |	30 000	30 000	..	..
Road passenger transport	13 085	36 000 |	43 000	55 000	..	..
Water passenger transport	724	1 000 |	1 000	1 000	..	..
Passenger transport supporting services	..	..	..	..	..	..
Transport equipment rental	3 808	5 000 |	4 000	8 000	..	..
Travel agencies and other reservation services industry	8 597	55 000 |	55 000	71 000	..	..
Cultural industry	31 587	61 000 |	82 000	85 000	..	..
Sports and recreation industry	19 734	111 000 |	87 000	119 000	..	..
Retail trade of country-specific tourism characteristic goods	..	..	..	..	..	..
Other country-specific tourism industries	4 306	441 |	496	494 000	..	..
Other industries	..	**441 171 |**	**432 000**	**423 000**	..	..

.. Not available; | Break in series
1. Data refer to number of enterprises.
Source: OECD Tourism Statistics (Database).

StatLink https://stat.link/5hu7d4

United Kingdom: Internal tourism consumption

Million GBP

	2019		
	Domestic tourism expenditure	Inbound tourism expenditure	Internal tourism consumption
Total	..	..	..
Consumption products	**144 149**	**33 295**	**179 220**
Tourism characteristic products	91 772	18 335	110 108
Accommodation services for visitors	11 086	6 705	17 791
Food and beverage serving services	33 968	4 572	38 540
Passenger transport services	23 422	6 040	29 463
Air passenger transport services	15 765	4 651	20 416
Railways passenger transport services	4 478	472	4 950
Road passenger transport services	1 906	624	2 530
Water passenger transport services	1 273	293	1 567
Passenger transport supporting services	..	..	..
Transport equipment rental services	4 163	211	4 375
Travel agencies and other reservation services industry	5 636	131	5 767
Cultural services	6 429	260	6 688
Sports and recreation services	6 584	227	6 811
Country-specific tourism characteristic goods	..	..	..
Country-specific tourism characteristic services	484	189	673
Other consumption products	52 377	14 960	69 112
Tourism connected products	..	..	..
Non-tourism related consumption products	..	..	..
Non-consumption products	..	..	..

.. Not available
Source: OECD Tourism Statistics (Database).

StatLink https://stat.link/t18s65

United States

Tourism in the economy and outlook for recovery

Travel and tourism was a major contributor to the United States economy before COVID-19, directly accounting for 2.9% of total GDP and supporting 3.9% of the nation's workforce in 2019 (this increases to 6.0% of the workforce when including indirect effects). Travel and tourism was the country's third largest export, accounting for 9.4% of U.S. exports of goods and services. The impacts of the COVID-19 pandemic saw travel and tourism's share of the economy fall to 1.7% of total GDP and 2.6% of the workforce in 2020 – a loss of almost 2.2 million direct jobs.

In 2020, inbound tourism to the United States declined by 75.8% to 19.2 million visitors. International visitation increased slightly in 2021 to 22.1 million visitors. However, this remained 72% below pre-COVID-19 levels.

International tourism receipts (travel exports) declined 64.7% to USD 84.3 billion in 2020. In 2021, receipts declined an additional 1.6% to USD 82.9 billion. Mexico overtook Canada as the top source market in the United States for the first time in 2020. Mexico, Colombia, Ecuador, and Peru showed a strong rebound in 2021, with many returning to or surpassing pre-COVID levels.

The United States traditionally has a strong domestic travel market which, in 2019, accounted for 85% of travel demand in the country. Domestic travel demand fell 46% in 2020 to USD 559 billion.

Domestic travel is not expected to reach pre-pandemic levels until 2023, while domestic business travel is not expected to recover until 2025. International arrivals are expected to reach 2019 levels by 2025, according to the U.S. Travel Association.

Tourism governance and funding

Travel and tourism in the United States is highly decentralised. Public authorities manage travel and tourism at the national, regional, state, and local levels. These include the federal government, state governments, and destination marketing organisations.

The National Travel and Tourism Office (NTTO), within the International Trade Administration (ITA) of the United States Department of Commerce, is the central point of contact within the federal government. NTTO is the source of official tourism statistics and works closely with the U.S. Commercial Service at U.S. embassies to promote tourism. Brand USA is a non-profit corporation that promotes travel to the United States, working with the government to provide insights for international visitors.

The Department of Commerce facilitates co-operation between the private sector and other federal agencies for policy co-ordination with respect to travel and tourism issues. Key travel and tourism activities at the Department of Commerce include:

- The Travel and Tourism Advisory Board (TTAB), which includes up to 32 private sector representatives appointed to provide policy advice to the Secretary of Commerce.

- The Tourism Policy Council (TPC), an inter-agency council established to co-ordinate the national policies and programmes of federal agencies that significantly affect international travel and tourism, recreation, and national heritage resources.

NTTO's operational budget for the fiscal year 2021 was approximately USD 7.7 million. The budget is supplemented by the selling of research reports and data and inter-agency agreements. Brand USA is supported by up to USD 100 million per year from the Electronic System for Travel Authorisation (ESTA) fees paid by international travellers from countries participating in the visa waiver programme and matched funds from the private sector. Brand USA funding became a significant challenge during the pandemic due to reduced international visitors from visa-waiver countries. As a result, in March 2022, the Restoring Brand USA Act provided USD 250 million in relief funding to Brand USA for the fiscal year 2022.

United States: Organisational chart of tourism bodies

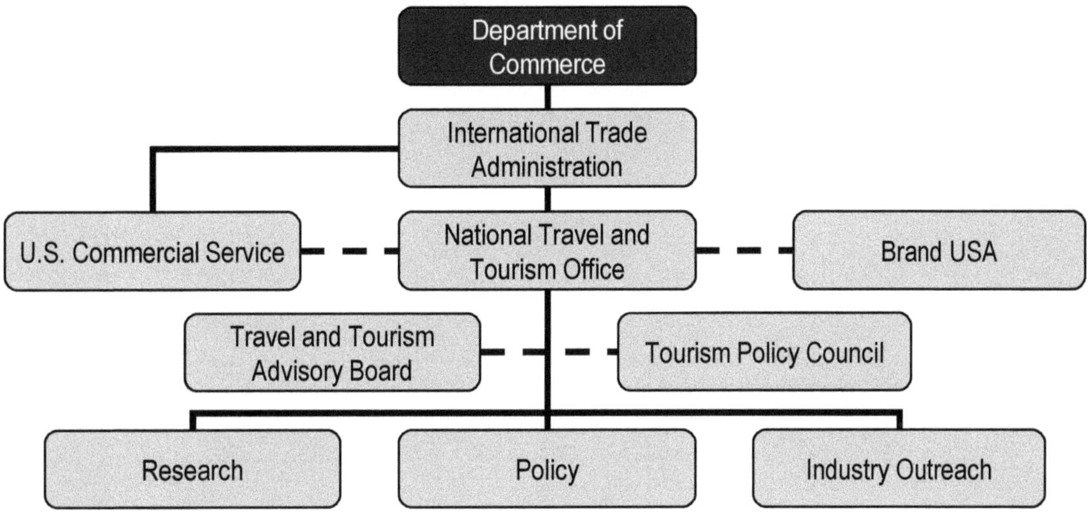

Source: OECD, adapted from the United States Department of Commerce, 2022.

Tourism policies and programmes

The United States developed and launched a new National Travel and Tourism Strategy in 2022 (see Box 1.4). The Tourism Policy Council created the Strategy to focus the United States' efforts in support of the tourism sector, which has been deeply and disproportionally affected by the COVID-19 pandemic. The Strategy follows a four-point approach to reduce the sector's carbon footprint, create safe and secure checkpoints, and bolster tourism in underserved and underrepresented communities across the country

The new Strategy supports the current Administration's priorities of diversity, equity, and inclusion; mitigating the impacts of the climate crisis; job growth and workforce development; and building back a more sustainable and resilient sector. A key recovery priority in the United States has been to "Build Back Better", based on broad-based, equitable, community-led economic development with an emphasis on supporting SMEs and increasing resiliency to future health, environmental and other crises.

The United States passed recovery measures to support small businesses, airlines, airports, and leisure and hospitality businesses. The American Rescue Plan Act of 2021 (ARPA) provided additional relief to address the continued impact of the pandemic on the economy. The USD 1.9 trillion COVID-19 relief package includes federal support for the recovery of the travel and tourism sector.

As part of the ARPA, the Department of Commerce's Economic Development Administration's Travel, Tourism & Outdoor Recreation programme focused on accelerating the recovery of communities that rely on the travel, tourism and outdoor recreation sectors. USD 750 million of EDA's funds were allocated to support the following efforts:

- **State Tourism Grants:** USD 510 million in non-competitive awards to help states quickly invest in marketing, infrastructure, workforce and other projects to rejuvenate safe leisure, business and international travel.
- **Competitive Grants:** USD 240 million to help communities that have been hardest hit by challenges facing the travel, tourism and outdoor recreation sectors to invest in infrastructure, workforce or other projects to support the recovery of the sector and economic resilience of the community in the future.

The funds are being used by states for state-wide or regional marketing campaigns; infrastructure upgrades to existing tourism destinations; outdoor recreation improvement projects; improving accessibility to existing tourism or outdoor recreation sites for individuals who speak other languages or have mobility restrictions; state-wide strategic travel and tourism planning; and creating or building out tourism and hospitality sector workforce development and training programmes. Overall, stimulus packages were effective in reaching the travel and tourism community and helping employees and businesses impacted.

Statistical Profile

United States: Domestic, inbound and outbound tourism

	2017	2018	2019	2020	2021
TOURISM FLOWS, THOUSAND					
Domestic tourism					
Total domestic trips	2 241 000	2 278 000	2 318 000	1 580 000	2 040 000 f
Overnight visitors (tourists)	1 591 916	1 613 987	1 646 614	1 122 368	1 449 134 f
Same-day visitors (excursionists)	649 084	664 013	671 386	457 632	590 866 f
Nights in all types of accommodation	..	..	..	..	..
Hotels and similar establishments	1 257 616	1 286 662	1 306 439	839 532	1 157 503 p
Other collective establishments	..	..	..	..	..
Private accommodation	..	..	..	..	..
Inbound tourism					
Total international arrivals	174 292	169 325	165 477	53 557	46 344 p
Overnight visitors (tourists)	77 187	79 746	79 442	19 212	22 100 p
Same-day visitors (excursionists)	97 105	89 579	86 035	34 345	24 244 p
Top markets					
Mexico	17 788	18 387	18 328	7 042 e	9 700 p
Canada	20 493	21 475	20 720	4 809 e	2 331 p
Colombia	842	943	944	270	1 064 f
United Kingdom	4 483	4 659	4 780	730	461 f
India	1 285	1 378	1 474	336	433 f
Nights in all types of accommodation	404 677	405 682	411 164	95 783 p	95 783
Hotels and similar establishments	208 138	212 207	215 359	38 765 p	38 765
Other collective establishments	17 050	18 546	17 227	3 445 p	3 445
Private accommodation	179 489	174 930	178 578	53 573 p	53 573
Outbound tourism					
Total international departures	148 017	148 083	158 092	61 703 p	..
Overnight visitors (tourists)	87 619	93 137	99 755	33 499	49 097
Same-day visitors (excursionists)	60 398	54 946 |	58 336	28 203	..
Top destinations					
Mexico	35 050	36 923	39 942 p	21 729	28 789
Canada	14 242	14 440	14 994 p	1 929	2 093
Dominican Republic	2 721	2 882	2 957	1 014	..
Jamaica	1 571	1 629	1 927	640	..
United Kingdom	3 756	3 927	3 943	620	..
TOURISM RECEIPTS AND EXPENDITURE, MILLION USD					
Inbound tourism					
Total international receipts	233 759	241 985	239 446	84 206	80 956
International travel receipts	196 469	200 724	198 982	72 481	68 759
International passenger transport receipts	37 290	41 261	40 082	11 393	12 197
Outbound tourism					
Total international expenditure	158 290	176 817	186 080	48 840	74 121
International travel expenditure	117 931	125 717	132 271	34 159	57 940
International passenger transport expenditure	40 359	50 678	52 795	13 032	16 181

.. Not available; e Estimated value; f Forecast value; p Provisional data; | Break in series
Source: OECD Tourism Statistics (Database).

StatLink https://stat.link/eh3ws4

United States: Enterprises and employment in tourism

	Number of establishments	Number of persons employed				
	2021	2017	2018	2019	2020	2021
Total	..	**5 936 000**	**6 103 000**	**6 070 000**	**3 887 000 p**	..
Tourism industries	**912 696 p**	**5 166 000**	**5 316 000**	**5 282 000**	**3 234 000 p**	..
Accommodation services for visitors	67 354 p	1 516 000	1 537 000	1 565 000	1 083 000 p	..
Hotels and similar establishments	59 596 p	..	..	..	..	..
Food and beverage serving industry	666 409 p	1 720 000	1 776 000	1 701 000	878 000 p	..
Passenger transport	24 260 p	772 000	795 000	818 000	611 000 p	..
Air passenger transport	4 344 p	581 000	594 000	618 000	484 000 p	..
Railways passenger transport	..	9 000	9 000	9 000	4 000 p	..
Road passenger transport	16 988 p	141 000	154 000	147 000	95 000 p	..
Water passenger transport	2 928 p	41 000	38 000	44 000	28 000 p	..
Passenger transport supporting services	..	299 000	312 000	319 000	121 000 p	..
Transport equipment rental	15 891 p	103 000	113 000	128 000	103 000 p	..
Travel agencies and other reservation services industry	20 710 p	203 000	204 000	203 000	156 000 p	..
Cultural industry	18 221 p	48 000	48 000	43 000	38 000 p	..
Sports and recreation industry	99 851 p	505 000	531 000	505 000	244 000 p	..
Retail trade of country-specific tourism characteristic goods	..	..	..	..	..	..
Other country-specific tourism industries	..	..	..	..	..	..
Other industries	..	**770 000**	**787 000**	**788 000**	**653 000 p**	..

.. Not available; p Provisional data
Source: OECD Tourism Statistics (Database).

StatLink https://stat.link/sfnorl

United States: Internal tourism consumption

Million USD

	2020		
	Domestic tourism expenditure	Inbound tourism expenditure	Internal tourism consumption
Total	**588 559**	**31 692**	**39 015 145**
Consumption products	**559 246**	**31 692**	**38 985 833**
Tourism characteristic products	473 216	26 767	2 178 332
Accommodation services for visitors	138 810	7 464	146 275
Food and beverage serving services	74 045	4 217	869 580
Passenger transport services	135 875	11 242	202 411
Air passenger transport services	113 545	11 052	124 597
Railways passenger transport services	741	0	741
Road passenger transport services	10 780	85	65 733
Water passenger transport services	10 809	105	11 340
Passenger transport supporting services	28 603	225	607 237
Transport equipment rental services	28 893	357	41 000
Travel agencies and other reservation services industry	23 016	486	23 532
Cultural services	8 826	710	47 168
Sports and recreation services	35 148	2 066	241 129
Country-specific tourism characteristic goods	..	..	..
Country-specific tourism characteristic services	..	..	..
Other consumption products	86 030	4 925	36 807 501
Tourism connected products	86 030	4 925	4 547 773
Non-tourism related consumption products	0	0	32 259 728
Non-consumption products	..	..	..

.. Not available
Source: OECD Tourism Statistics (Database).

StatLink https://stat.link/x32od8

Part II Partner country profiles

Brazil

Tourism in the economy and outlook for recovery

Tourism is an important pillar of Brazil's economy, providing 2.2 million direct jobs, accounting for 2.6% of the country's total employment in 2019.

International tourist arrivals reached 6.4 million in 2019, falling by 66.2% to 2.1 million in 2020. International receipts were USD 6.1 billion in 2019, before declining 49.4% in 2020. The top source market in 2020 remained Argentina, with 888 000 tourists (41.4% of international tourists), despite a decline of 54.6%. The other top markets for Brazil were the United States (8%), Chile (6.1%), Paraguay (5.7%) and Uruguay (5.3%).

Brazil recently began to measure domestic tourism. In 2020, Brazil recorded 9.6 million domestic overnight tourists, and an additional 3.7 million same-day visitors. This fell slightly in 2021, with domestic tourists falling 4.0% to 9.3 million and same-day visitors falling to 3.0 million.

Tourism governance and funding

The Ministry of Tourism has a wide role that includes the cross-governmental co-ordination of tourism, planning and research, marketing and promotional activity, regulation, training and education, as well as the development of new products and related infrastructure.

In 2020, Brazil incorporated the 'culture' portfolio into the Ministry of Tourism, and also strengthened actions related to tourism development, competitiveness, infrastructure, and attracting investment. The new structure of the Ministry of Tourism now allows greater co-ordination between the various decision-making bodies and authorities in states and municipalities. Co-ordination with stakeholders and businesses in the sector happens through shared associations and informal organisations.

The Ministry of Tourism deals directly with authorities at regional, state and municipal levels through its policies, as well as through collegial bodies established within the structure of the Ministry or created by federal entities. The Federal Constitution defines the responsibilities of all the various authorities. The Tourism International Board (EMBRATUR) is a non-profit private organisation supervised by the Federal Government.

The 2021 budget for the Ministry of Tourism is approximately BRL 2.7 billion, down from BRL 3.5 billion in 2020. The decrease is due to the decline in tax revenues and the wider effects of the COVID-19 crisis on various economic sectors, including the need to create support mechanisms for businesses and individuals affected by the pandemic.

Brazil: Organisational chart of tourism bodies

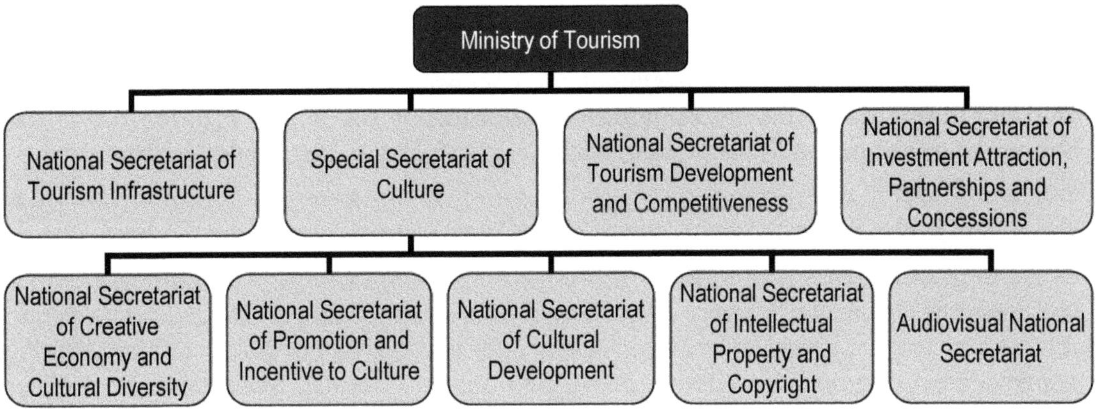

Source: OECD, adapted from the Ministry of Tourism, 2022.

Tourism policies and programmes

The main challenge for the Brazilian government is resuming tourism activities that fell amid the COVID-19 pandemic. The Tourism Recovery Plan aims to establish a national alliance for the recovery of the sector (see box below). Several measures were adopted to provide safe travel. For example, the Responsible Tourism Stamp was granted to institutions which followed the sanitary protocols established by Brazil and the Brazilian Health Regulatory Agency (ANVISA).

During the most critical period of the pandemic, Brazil introduced emergency measures to protect companies and consumers. These actions resulted in three main laws aiming at the maintenance of jobs, the regulation of consumer laws to prevent mass bankruptcy, and a sector credit guarantee, which provided BRL 5 billion for companies to fund infrastructure works and working capital. In addition, over 100 free online training courses were offered to professionals in the sector, which benefited more than 3 000 workers in several segments. Courses included digital marketing, natural resources, and foreign language classes.

The Ministry's actions and policies are based on the National Tourism Plan 2018-22 and the Strategic Plan 2020-23. In consultation with the public and private sectors and civil society, the plan is currently being revised to adapt to the current context and the revised structure of the Ministry.

A lesson of the COVID-19 crisis was the need for reliable data to support managers in decision-making. The Ministry's Directorate of Strategic Management has made a wide range of tourism data available through the General Co-ordination of Data and Information, which was based on official data produced by the Ministry of Tourism, the Ministry of Labour, the Federal Police, and the Brazilian Institute of Geography and Statistics, as well as information provided by tourism private sector associations. Historically, the Ministry of Tourism has produced data on the sector made available to the government and private associations to support the decision-making and policy-designing process.

From this data, new evidence-based priority areas were set. The first was promoting domestic tourism through infrastructure improvements and advertising campaigns promoting domestic destinations. Domestic tourism has been identified as the driving force for tourism recovery and represents a tool for promoting the country to international tourists.

The second priority was to invest in reinforcing biosecurity protocols to increase travellers' sense of security. Brazil also aims to strengthen its understanding of domestic and international tourism demand

and profiles through an agreement with the Brazilian Institute of Geography and Statistics and international tourism surveys.

The Ministry of Tourism has strengthened partnerships with other Ministries to aid the implementation of projects, such as supporting inward investment for concessions for operators in national parks, in collaboration with the Ministry of the Environment. The Ministry has also sought to improve the relationship with the Ministry of Infrastructure to understand and improve tourist transport and mobility.

Tourism Recovery Plan in Brazil

Brazil launched the Tourism Recovery Plan to rebuild visitor confidence to resume the industry's activities. The plan aims to establish a national alliance for the recovery of the sector, bringing together public administration, the private sector, and the third sector. The plan has four axes of action: the implementation of biosafety protocols, promotion and incentive to travel, preservation of companies and jobs in the tourism sector, and improvement of the structure and qualification of tourist destinations.

The process was widely supported by the private sector, with the participation of more than 30 national associations from different touristic sectors.

To achieve its purpose, Brazil adopted four major measures to protect the sector:

- The Emergency Employment and Income Maintenance Program provided an allowance to preserve employment.
- Security for consumers through new legislation that covered both companies and tourists.
- Credit lines for the tourism sector.
- The establishment of biosafety protocols.

Tourism businesses committing to the biosafety protocols in order to protect tourists and workers obtain a Safe Tourism Stamp. Since the protocols were established, more than 30 000 Safe Tourism Stamps have been granted. Citizens can access the Ministry's website to verify the regularity of companies and which ones comply with biosafety protocols.

Finally, the Ministry analysed the trends in tourist behaviour to optimise efforts in the gradual and responsible return of tourist activities, aiming to support and catalyse the process.

Statistical Profile

Brazil: Domestic, inbound and outbound tourism

	2017	2018	2019	2020	2021
TOURISM FLOWS, THOUSAND					
Domestic tourism					
Total domestic trips	..	..	..	13 302	12 247
Overnight visitors (tourists)	..	..	..	9 637	9 256
Same-day visitors (excursionists)	..	..	..	3 665	2 991
Nights in all types of accommodation	..	..	..	..	..
Hotels and similar establishments	..	..	..	..	..
Other collective establishments	..	..	..	..	..
Private accommodation	..	..	..	..	..
Inbound tourism					
Total international arrivals	..	..	..	..	..
Overnight visitors (tourists)	6 589	6 621	6 353	2 146	..
Same-day visitors (excursionists)	..	..	..	..	..
Top markets					
Argentina	2 622	2 498	1 955	888	..
United States	475	539	591	172	..
Chile	342	387	392	131	..
Paraguay	337	357	407	123	..
Uruguay	328	348	365	114	..
Nights in all types of accommodation	..	..	..	..	..
Hotels and similar establishments	..	..	..	..	..
Other collective establishments	..	..	..	..	..
Private accommodation	..	..	..	..	..
Outbound tourism					
Total international departures	..	..	..	..	..
Overnight visitors (tourists)	10 610	10 733	..	..	..
Same-day visitors (excursionists)	..	..	..	..	..
Top destinations					
United States	1 912	2 209	..	..	..
Portugal	981	1 117	..	..	..
Argentina	1 247	947	..	..	..
Chile	545	589	..	..	..
Spain	468	559	..	..	..
TOURISM RECEIPTS AND EXPENDITURE, MILLION USD					
Inbound tourism					
Total international receipts	6 175	6 323	6 127	3 099	..
International travel receipts	5 809	5 921	5 995	3 044	..
International passenger transport receipts	366	403	132	55	..
Outbound tourism					
Total international expenditure	22 991	22 229	21 178	6 490	..
International travel expenditure	19 002	18 266	17 593	5 394	..
International passenger transport expenditure	3 990	3 963	3 585	1 096	..

.. Not available
Source: OECD Tourism Statistics (Database).

StatLink https://stat.link/pd478o

Brazil: Enterprises and employment in tourism

	Number of establishments[1]	Number of persons employed[2]				
	2020	2017	2018	2019	2020	2021
Total	..	..	..	..	..	..
Tourism industries	**260 834**	**2 128 041**	**2 133 822**	**2 192 235**	..	..
Accommodation services for visitors	30 721	312 628	315 481	318 114	..	..
Hotels and similar establishments	..	..	..	..	..	..
Food and beverage serving industry	189 286	1 216 988	1 233 881	1 271 932	..	..
Passenger transport	14 073	469 424	453 943	420 919	..	..
Air passenger transport	649	51 874	50 136	55 057	..	..
Railways passenger transport	..	..	..	..	..	..
Road passenger transport	12 808	363 720	355 246	358 222	..	..
Water passenger transport	616	7 514	7 935	7 640	..	..
Passenger transport supporting services	..	..	..	..	..	..
Transport equipment rental	5 585	46 316	40 626	48 839	..	..
Travel agencies and other reservation services industry	12 437	91 370	90 968	92 865	..	..
Cultural industry	8 732	37 631	39 549	39 566	..	..
Sports and recreation industry	..	..	..	..	..	..
Retail trade of country-specific tourism characteristic goods	..	..	..	..	..	..
Other country-specific tourism industries	..	..	..	..	..	..
Other industries	..	..	..	..	..	..

.. Not available
1. Data refer to number of enterprises.
2. Data refer to number of jobs.
Source: OECD Tourism Statistics (Database).

StatLink https://stat.link/jf3rwh

Bulgaria

Tourism in the economy and outlook for recovery

Tourism in Bulgaria provides an important source of employment and economic earnings. In 2019, tourism-related employment supported approximately 236 300 people. The impacts of the COVID-19 pandemic saw this fall to approximately 194 600 people in 2020, a decline of 41 700 people.

In 2019, international tourism was the driver of the Bulgarian tourism sector. There were 12.6 million international arrivals who accounted for BGN 8.5 billion, or 88.2% of total tourism spend. The impact of the pandemic saw international visitors fall by 60.4% to 4.9 million in 2020 before recovering to 7.2 million in 2021 – 42.7% below pre-pandemic levels.

Domestic tourists reached a record 4.1 million in 2019. Despite a significant decline in 2020, domestic tourists recovered in 2021, with domestic nights in all means of accommodation reaching 9.6 million, 0.5% below 2019 levels.

Bulgaria expects inbound tourism to achieve 2019 levels by 2025 but the total contribution of tourism to GDP is expected to take longer to recover, returning to pre-pandemic levels by 2025-27.

Tourism governance and funding

The Ministry of Tourism is responsible for implementing state policy relating to tourism and co-ordinating the activities of related ministries and other institutions in its implementation. The national tourism policy is formulated by the Council of Ministers.

The Ministry's main activities include developing and implementing the National Strategy for Sustainable Development, developing short-term programmes and plans, regulating the tourism sector; assisting regional management organisations; national marketing and advertising, international relations; and participating in international programmes.

The National Tourism Council is the consultative body which operates under the authority of the Ministry of Tourism. Its members include representatives of tourism-related ministries as well as national, regional and local tourism associations, transport operators and consumer bodies. Regional authorities are in charge of implementing the national tourism policy at the regional level. At the local level, municipal administrations are responsible for tourism development. The municipal council adopts a tourism development programme in line with the priorities of the regional strategy and in accordance with local tourism resources and needs.

Tourism development is co-ordinated and planned horizontally across sectors, including with the digital transformation of SMEs outlined in the Ministry of Economy's programme economic transformation and with reforms targeting energy efficiency, regional development, and the digitalisation of cultural heritage in the National Recovery and Resilience Plan.

In 2020, the budget for tourism totalled BGN 19.6 million. An additional BGN 51.6 million was allocated for schemes supporting tourism businesses during COVID-19. In 2021, the budget for state aid amounted to BGN 59.9 million.

Bulgaria: Organisational chart of tourism bodies

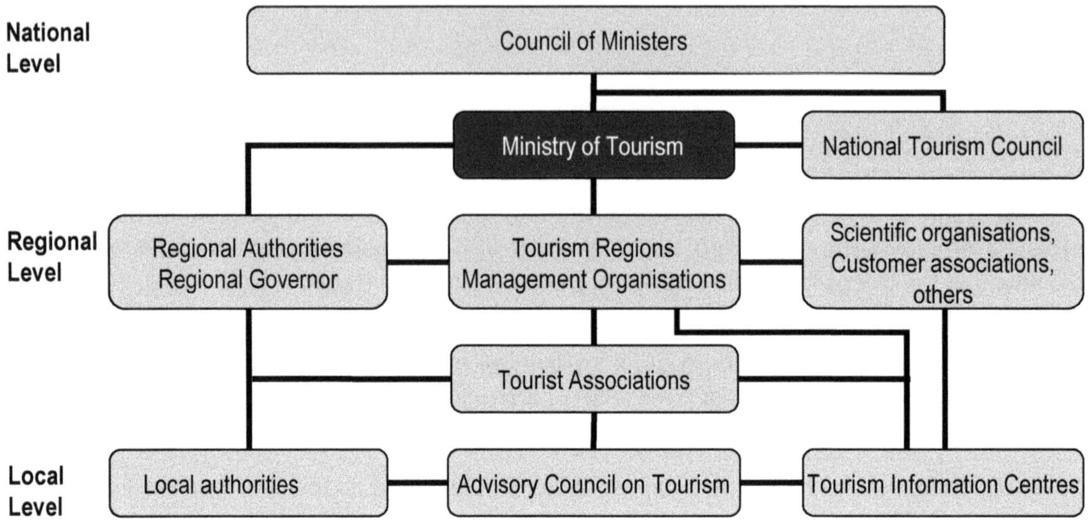

Source: OECD, adapted from the Ministry of Tourism, 2022.

Tourism policies and programmes

In 2022, the Ministry is in the process of updating and adapting the Tourism Sustainable Development Strategy 2030. Upcoming legislative changes will increase the competencies of the Regional Tourism Management Organisations as separate entities (see box below). These provisions should help the DMOs finance their activities and attain financial sustainability in the long run.

As an immediate response to COVID-19, Bulgaria developed a measure for tour operators to stimulate inbound tourism. Those with existing contracts with air carriers were entitled to EUR 35 per passenger taking a flight into Bulgaria through a package tour. Additionally, in response to the suspension of travel, the Ministry of Tourism responded with compensation grants for tour operators and travel agencies to allow them to reimburse customers. There were eight measures in total for supporting tour operators, tour agencies and the tourism sector. Because of the measures, there was no case of tour operators or travel agencies' insolvency in the last two years.

The most important challenges for Bulgarian tourism are sustainable development and digitalisation. These challenges emerged strongly during the COVID-19 crisis and will be key to the rebound and future development of the sector. Increasing tourism sector competitiveness is a priority in the Tourism Sustainable Development Strategy until 2030. The gathering and sharing of tourism data, sustainable management at the regional level, and enhancement of digitalisation in SMEs will help to resolve some of the most pressing problems in tourism and increase competitiveness while contributing to green and digital transitions.

The main policy responses and initiatives aimed at tackling the key high-priority challenges include:

- Enhancing institutional capacity building.

- Encouraging sustainable and effective resource management and measures for climate change adaptation, including using protected natural areas as a resource for the sustainable development of tourism.
- Improving tourists' safety in Bulgaria.
- Upskilling the workforce through higher skills.
- Stimulating tourism investment and securing access to finance.
- Continuing the focus on digitalisation and innovation.
- Controlling air and water quality and achieving sustainable waste and water management.

Regional tourism management organisations in Bulgaria

Destination management is a relatively new dimension in Bulgarian tourism policy. It was outlined in the Concept for Tourism Regions in 2015 and the Tourism Act, after which nine regional tourism organisations were established in 2018-19. The main goal of Regional Tourism Management Organisations is to decrease regional disparities by developing strong regional brands and specialised forms of tourism based on local tourism resources. The aim is to enable the sustainable development of the regions and increase the competitiveness of the tourism sector and the quality of the tourism product based on a partnership between all stakeholders.

In the period from 2019-22, two projects were launched to support the organisations' functioning and capacity building for effective tourism management at the destination level. These are focused on increasing the capacity of SMEs in the tourism sector by providing support for the creation and functioning of Management Organisations in tourist areas and improving the quality of services of SMEs in tourism through the use of ICT and web-based marketing.

In 2021, the nine Regional Tourism Management Organisations developed their marketing strategies, which were approved by their Members and the Ministry.

The strengthening of the Regional Tourism Management Organisations' position as an inevitable factor for tourism management on a regional level will continue in the new programme period 2021-27, in which it is planned that they will also become eligible beneficiaries under the EU-funded operational programmes.

Statistical Profile

Bulgaria: Domestic, inbound and outbound tourism

	2017	2018	2019	2020	2021
TOURISM FLOWS, THOUSAND					
Domestic tourism					
Total domestic trips	..	..	..	..	..
Overnight visitors (tourists)	3 806	3 890	4 120 p	2 848 p	3 755 p
Same-day visitors (excursionists)	..	..	..	..	..
Nights in all types of accommodation	8 949	9 096	9 675 p	7 312 p	9 627 p
Hotels and similar establishments	..	..	..	..	..
Other collective establishments	..	..	..	..	..
Private accommodation	..	..	..	..	..
Inbound tourism[1]					
Total international arrivals	11 596	12 368	12 552	4 973	7 188 p
Overnight visitors (tourists)	..	..	..	..	..
Same-day visitors (excursionists)	..	..	..	..	..
Top markets					
Romania	1 139	1 377	1 287	626	822 p
Greece	1 158	1 116	1 168	271	259 p
Germany	870	850	761	138	288 p
Türkiye	636	625	649	332	401 p
North Macedonia	545	560	554	169	175 p
Nights in all types of accommodation	17 106	17 749	17 480	4 656 p	7 994 p
Hotels and similar establishments	..	..	..	..	..
Other collective establishments	..	..	..	..	..
Private accommodation	..	..	..	..	..
Outbound tourism					
Total international departures	6 228	6 699	7 007	3 973 p	5 182 p
Overnight visitors (tourists)	..	..	..	..	..
Same-day visitors (excursionists)	..	..	..	..	..
Top destinations					
Türkiye	1 311	1 516	1 622	..	..
Greece	1 341	1 403	1 461	..	..
Romania	481	523	554	..	..
Serbia	463	494	515	..	..
Germany	402	422	446	..	..
TOURISM RECEIPTS AND EXPENDITURE, MILLION USD					
Inbound tourism					
Total international receipts	4 598	5 093	4 832	1 779	..
International travel receipts	4 045	4 495	4 287	1 624	..
International passenger transport receipts	553	598	546	155 e	..
Outbound tourism					
Total international expenditure	2 035	2 247	2 196	1 252	..
International travel expenditure	1 684	1 870	1 826	1 039	..
International passenger transport expenditure	351	377	370	214 e	..

.. Not available; e Estimated value; p Provisional data

1. Arrivals from demand side surveys; Nights from supply side surveys.

Source: OECD Tourism Statistics (Database).

StatLink https://stat.link/yxvn6o

Bulgaria: Enterprises and employment in tourism

	Number of establishments[1]	Number of persons employed				
	2020	2017	2018	2019	2020	2021
Total	..	..	..	..	..	..
Tourism industries	..	..	..	..	..	..
Accommodation services for visitors	29 924 p	79 347 p	82 646 p	84 373 p	68 370 p	.. p
Hotels and similar establishments	4 486 p	41 330 p	43 633 p	44 810 p	29 207 p	..
Food and beverage serving industry	20 259 p	94 737 p	93 796 p	94 354 p	77 237 p	.. p
Passenger transport	4 817 p	23 384 p	22 634 p	22 497 p	20 908 p	..
Air passenger transport	55 p	1 691 p	1 865 p	2 042 p	1 744 p	..
Railways passenger transport	.. p	5 954 p	5 831 p	5 853 p	5 705 p	..
Road passenger transport	4 732 p	15 437 p	14 573 p	14 213 p	13 158 p	..
Water passenger transport	.. p	302 p	365 p	389 p	301 p	..
Passenger transport supporting services	..	..	..	..	..	..
Transport equipment rental	2 149 p	2 719 p	2 818 p	3 002 p	2 891 p	..
Travel agencies and other reservation services industry	1 808 p	6 280 p	6 421 p	6 214 p	4 506 p	..
Cultural industry	1 208 p	1 724 p	1 744 p	1 914 p	1 635 p	..
Sports and recreation industry	4 477 p	23 826 p	23 980 p	23 940 p	19 036 p	..
Retail trade of country-specific tourism characteristic goods	..	..	..	..	..	..
Other country-specific tourism industries	..	..	..	..	..	..
Other industries	..	..	..	..	..	..

.. Not available; p Provisional data
1. Data refer to number of enterprises.
Source: OECD Tourism Statistics (Database).

StatLink https://stat.link/yud7s0

Bulgaria: Internal tourism consumption

Million BGN

	2019		
	Domestic tourism expenditure	Inbound tourism expenditure	Internal tourism consumption
Total	..	..	..
Consumption products	**1 129 p**	**8 455 p**	..
Tourism characteristic products	1 084 p	5 528 p	..
Accommodation services for visitors	524 p	2 398 p	..
Food and beverage serving services	297 p	1 980 p	..
Passenger transport services	214 p	641 p	..
Air passenger transport services	..	..	..
Railways passenger transport services	..	..	..
Road passenger transport services	..	..	..
Water passenger transport services	..	..	..
Passenger transport supporting services	..	..	..
Transport equipment rental services	..	..	..
Travel agencies and other reservation services industry	10 p	263 p	..
Cultural services	18 p	98 p	..
Sports and recreation services	22 p	147 p	..
Country-specific tourism characteristic goods	..	..	..
Country-specific tourism characteristic services	..	..	..
Other consumption products	44 p	2 927 p	..
Tourism connected products	..	..	..
Non-tourism related consumption products	..	..	..
Non-consumption products	..	..	..

.. Not available; p Provisional data
Source: OECD Tourism Statistics (Database).

StatLink https://stat.link/4jwgve

Croatia

Tourism in the economy and outlook for recovery

Tourism plays a major role in the Croatian economy. In 2019, the direct contribution of tourism to GDP was estimated to be 11.8%, and tourism provided 91 608 direct jobs or 6.8% of total employment. Direct tourism employment was 11 385 jobs lower in 2021, seeing tourism's share of employment fall to 5.9%.

In 2019, tourism contributed to over 68.5% of Croatia's service exports, which decreased to 48% in 2021. Income from international tourism went from EUR 10.5 billion in 2019 to EUR 9.1 billion in 2021. This was due to a decline in international tourists, who usually contribute to 90% of visits and overnight stays in Croatia and 87% of tourism expenditure. International tourists declined 68% in 2020, and, despite a strong recovery, remained 38.7% below 2019 levels in 2021 (10.6 million tourists).

In 2020, Croatia recorded a 55.3% decline in total tourist overnight stays compared to 2019. Domestic tourism recorded 5.4 million nights in tourism-related accommodation, down 23.7%. In 2021, domestic tourism nights returned to pre-pandemic levels and international nights recovered significantly to remain just 25% below 2019 levels. 2022 preliminary results show a full recovery of the sector.

Tourism governance and funding

Tourism operates under the jurisdiction of the Ministry of Tourism and Sport. The Ministry regularly co-operates with the Chamber of Economy, Chamber of Trades and Crafts and with professional associations in the tourism and hospitality sectors. The Croatian National Tourist Board (CNTB) reports to the Ministry and is in charge of tourism promotion.

At the regional level, 20 county administrative offices, and the city of Zagreb, have tourism departments responsible for accommodation classification and permits associated with services relating to tourism and hospitality. In addition, 280 local tourist offices in towns and municipalities develop tourist products and inform and distribute marketing materials under guidance from regional tourism offices.

The collaboration between the Ministry, other ministries, and state and private organisations in shaping common policies is extensive, including:

- The Ministry of Finance: rights to reimbursement of fixed costs, various fees, and VAT payments.
- The Ministry of Regional Development and EU Funds: loans and benefits for entrepreneurs and the implementation of EU operational programmes.
- The Ministry of Labour and Pension System, Family and Social Policy: job preservation measures.
- The Ministry of Maritime Affairs, Transport and Infrastructure: extending certificates in national navigation, concession fees and charges in ports.
- The Ministry of Physical Planning, Construction and State Assets: renting business premises owned by Croatia.
- Banks: loans rescheduling, liquidity and working capital loans and state guarantees.

- The ACI Club (Croatia's marine tourism company): fee payments in large marinas, including exemptions and instalments.

The budget of the Ministry increased from HRK 224.6 million in 2019 to HRK 399 million in 2020 and HRK 713 million in 2021. Compared to 2019, the total CNTB budget was cut by more than 50% in 2020, to HRK 150 million, and increased in 2021 to HRK 285 million. CNTB is financed through tourist taxes, membership fees and the state budget. The financial plan of the CNTB is linked to the Strategic Marketing and Operational Plan of Croatian Tourism for the period 2022-26.

Through the EU Recovery and Resilience Mechanism, EUR 292 million has been approved for Croatia. Within the sub-component of the National Recovery and Resilience Plan related to tourism, the Ministry of Tourism and Sports listed investments that contribute to the recovery, resilience and green and digital transition of tourism. 60% of the funds will be intended for entrepreneurs for direct investments in the private sector. The remaining part of the funds will be used for investments in public tourism infrastructure and strengthening human resources capacitates for resilient and sustainable tourism.

Croatia: Organisational chart of tourism bodies

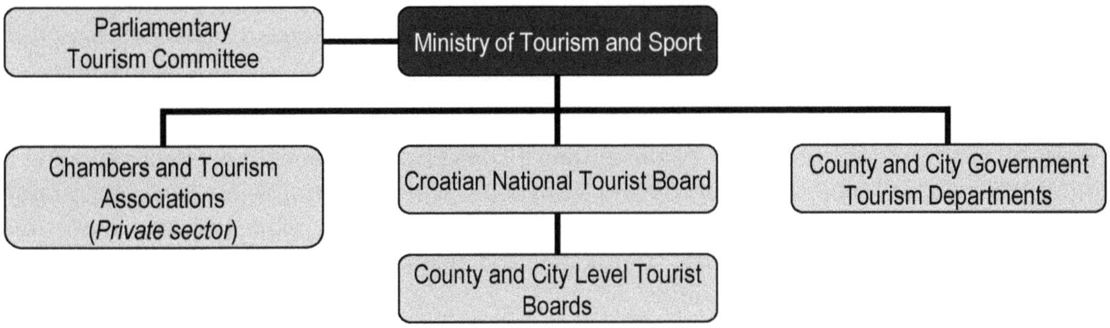

Source: OECD, adapted from the Ministry of Tourism and Sport, 2022.

Tourism policies and programmes

Following the impact of the pandemic, Croatia adopted a series of measures to help vulnerable sectors like tourism maintain liquidity and preserve jobs. The measures included: extending statutory deadlines; reducing and exempting payment of tourist taxes; reducing the rate for tourist board membership fees; postponing and exempting the payment of concession fees; simplifying conditions for accessing certain regulated professions in tourism (e.g. tourist guides and business agency managers); and grants, capital loans, subsidies and additional credit lines.

At the beginning of 2021, Croatia launched the national safety label Safe stay in Croatia for the tourism sector. Security protocols were prepared to meet the guidelines of the Croatian Institute of Public Health and the World Travel and Tourism Council. The website for the programme also offered information on testing points and border crossing conditions.

The pandemic recovery process is mapped out in the National Recovery and Resilience Plan (RRP) 2021-26, with HRK 2.2 billion allocated for tourism recovery.

The Plan aims to transform and modernise the tourism sector while increasing its competitiveness, sustainability and resilience by achieving the following overarching objectives:

- Increase the resilience and sustainability of the tourism sector by supporting the green and digital transitions.

- Contribute to the recovery of the tourism sector from the COVID-19 crisis by improving accommodation capacity and social and territorial cohesion.
- Increase the circular economy in tourism, foster responsible consumption and increase the indirect effects of tourism.

The RRP includes a comprehensive reform of tourism and three related investments. The envisaged reform aims to establish a comprehensive and efficient strategic, regulatory and institutional framework for managing the development of sustainable tourism.

Part of the reform is the new Sustainable Tourism Development Strategy until 2030 (see box below) and National Sustainable Tourism Development Plan until 2027, which are currently under preparation and are expected to be adopted by the end of 2022. Furthermore, a new tourism law to govern sustainable tourism development and the development of a tourism sustainable satellite account is expected by the end of 2023.

Strategy for Sustainable Tourism Development 2030 in Croatia

The Strategy for Sustainable Tourism Development 2030 is the strategic planning act for the development of sustainable tourism in Croatia. It is harmonised with the National Development Strategy of Croatia until 2030 and the relevant documents and policies of the European Union and Croatia, including the National Recovery and Resilience Plan.

The long-term strategic goal is to keep Croatia among the leading European tourist destinations in terms of safety, quality, added value, sustainability and innovation. The Strategy was prepared in co-operation with key stakeholders, including representatives of Croatian tourism, ministries and other relevant institutions. Representatives of the local community and numerous citizens who participated in the survey were also involved in the preparation.

Prior to the Strategy, a Scenario Analysis was prepared and presented the process of strategic assessment of potential alternative futures and their impact on Croatian tourism. It forms the basis for determining development directions, goals and mechanisms. The analysis identified the key challenges associated with the development of sustainable tourism and their impact on sustainability and provided guidelines for the development of sustainable tourism that are the basis for the elaboration of the Strategy.

The Strategy contains a vision of the development of tourism in Croatia in the direction of sustainability, development needs and potentials that need to be realised and brings concrete priority areas for the achievement of strategic goals that are defined in accordance with the key views of stakeholders while respecting global trends. Based on the Strategy, the National Sustainable Tourism Development Plan until 2027 will be prepared and will contain the operationalisation of priority areas through concrete measures.

Statistical Profile

Croatia: Domestic, inbound and outbound tourism

	2017	2018	2019	2020	2021
TOURISM FLOWS, THOUSAND					
Domestic tourism					
Total domestic trips	6 614	8 166	10 445	6 183	6 974
Overnight visitors (tourists)	3 638	3 197	3 708	2 510	3 278
Same-day visitors (excursionists)	2 976	4 969	6 737	3 673	3 696
Nights in all types of accommodation	19 742	17 581	20 712	15 341	19 200
Hotels and similar establishments	1 510	1 524	1 725	1 037	2 844
Other collective establishments	532	583	738	274	974
Private accommodation	17 700	15 474	18 249	14 029	15 381
Inbound tourism					
Total international arrivals	..	..	..	..	..
Overnight visitors (tourists)	15 593	16 645	17 353	5 545	10 641
Same-day visitors (excursionists)	..	..	..	..	..
Top markets					
Germany	2 616	2 784	2 881	1 480	2 737
Austria	1 331	1 370	1 385	355	1 026
Slovenia	1 298	1 364	1 426	769	995
Czech Republic	742	755	742	481	721
Italy	1 110	1 148	1 175	228	417
Nights in all types of accommodation	80 222	83 175	84 148	35 379	62 848
Hotels and similar establishments	28 543	29 319	29 707	7 890	17 423
Other collective establishments	18 277	18 380	18 183	8 228	16 301
Private accommodation	33 402	35 477	36 258	19 261	29 123
Outbound tourism					
Total international departures	2 597	2 980	3 500	678	907
Overnight visitors (tourists)	1 923	2 058	2 255	493	639
Same-day visitors (excursionists)	674	922	1 245	185	268
Top destinations					
Bosnia and Herzegovina	325	390	455	122	214
Germany	211	326	303	86	87
Slovenia	165	171	190	57	63
Italy	210	213	238	27	40
Austria	213	166	197	63	36
TOURISM RECEIPTS AND EXPENDITURE, MILLION USD					
Inbound tourism					
Total international receipts	10 254	11 425	11 994	5 238	10 880
International travel receipts	10 043	11 204	11 773	5 238	10 759
International passenger transport receipts	211	221	221	..	121
Outbound tourism					
Total international expenditure	1 384	1 738	1 808	763	1 098
International travel expenditure	1 354	1 694	1 763	763	1 078
International passenger transport expenditure	30	44	45	..	19

.. Not available
Source: OECD Tourism Statistics (Database).

StatLink https://stat.link/urlisj

Croatia: Enterprises and employment in tourism

	Number of establishments[1]	Number of persons employed[2]				
	2020	2017	2018	2019	2020	2021
Total	..	**79 546**	**86 646**	**91 608**	**78 485**	**80 223**
Tourism industries	**22 531**	**38 778**	**41 826**	**44 326**	**35 071**	**36 204**
Accommodation services for visitors	3 488	..	..	..	..	..
Hotels and similar establishments	1 216	35 120	38 678	41 011	38 198	39 486
Food and beverage serving industry	17 284	..	..	..	..	..
Passenger transport	5 356	..	..	..	..	..
Air passenger transport	13	..	..	..	..	..
Railways passenger transport	1	..	..	..	..	..
Road passenger transport	4 255	..	..	..	..	..
Water passenger transport	1 087	..	..	..	..	..
Passenger transport supporting services	..	..	..	..	..	..
Transport equipment rental	..	5 648	6 142	6 271	5 216	4 533
Travel agencies and other reservation services industry	1 759	..	..	..	..	..
Cultural industry	..	..	..	..	..	..
Sports and recreation industry	..	..	..	..	..	..
Retail trade of country-specific tourism characteristic goods	..	..	..	..	..	..
Other country-specific tourism industries	..	..	..	..	..	..
Other industries	..	**36 430**	**39 756**	**42 368**	**36 445**	**37 543**

.. Not available
1. Data refer to number of enterprises.
2. Data refer to number of employees.
Source: OECD Tourism Statistics (Database).

StatLink https://stat.link/743mq0

Croatia: Internal tourism consumption

Million EUR

	2019		
	Domestic tourism expenditure	Inbound tourism expenditure	Internal tourism consumption
Total	**1 575**	**10 517**	**12 372**
Consumption products	**1 575**	**10 517**	**12 372**
Tourism characteristic products	1 497	9 681	11 458
Accommodation services for visitors	201	3 276	3 757
Food and beverage serving services	284	2 123	2 407
Passenger transport services	459	377	835
Air passenger transport services	99	110	209
Railways passenger transport services	27	12	39
Road passenger transport services	305	75	380
Water passenger transport services	28	180	208
Passenger transport supporting services	..	..	..
Transport equipment rental services	..	..	..
Travel agencies and other reservation services industry	91	370	461
Cultural services	109	726	834
Sports and recreation services	..	..	..
Country-specific tourism characteristic goods	..	..	..
Country-specific tourism characteristic services	353	2 810	3 163
Other consumption products	78	836	914
Tourism connected products	..	..	..
Non-tourism related consumption products	..	..	..
Non-consumption products	..	..	..

.. Not available
Source: OECD Tourism Statistics (Database).

StatLink https://stat.link/8vg5lz

Indonesia

Tourism in the economy and outlook for recovery

The tourism sector is a significant part of Indonesia's economy. In 2019, tourism directly accounted for 5.0% of the country's GDP. The impacts of COVID-19 saw tourism GDP fall by 56% in 2020 to just 2.2% of the total economy.

Prior to 2020, tourism in Indonesia had been steadily growing, fuelled by an influx of international visitors. In 2019, international arrivals (overnight and same-day) reached 16.1 million visitors. In 2020, Indonesia recorded a 74.8% decline in international arrivals, to 4.0 million, with a total loss of IDR 208 trillion in international tourism expenditure. In 2021, international tourist arrivals further decreased to 1.6 million.

Domestic tourism is a driver of the Indonesian tourism economy. In 2019, domestic tourism accounted for 84% of tourism expenditure in Indonesia. Domestic trips (overnight and same-day) decreased by 27.4%, from 722 million trips in 2019 to 524 million trips in 2020. In 2021, domestic trips increased by 15.0% to 603 million. Approximately two-thirds of domestic trips in Indonesia are overnight. Domestic tourists are expected to be the driving force behind the recovery of the tourism sector in Indonesia.

Indonesia expects a recovery of international arrivals to pre-pandemic levels in 2024 at the earliest.

Tourism governance and funding

Tourism is under the responsibility of the Ministry of Tourism and Creative Economy (MoTCE), following the merger in 2019 of the Ministry of Tourism with the Creative Economy Agency.

The merger aims to diversify and support the tourism sector with the creative economy sector. The pandemic has proved that the tourism sector needs diversification as it cannot rely only on physical mobility. Diversification is needed to create a more resilient tourism sector where it will use a variety of tools, including but not limited to digital technology, the internet, and virtual reality.

In formulating policies, the Co-ordinating Ministry for Maritime and Investment has a Deputy of Tourism and Creative Economy who has a duty of co-ordinating and synchronising the formulation, decision-making process, and implementation of the policies of the relevant ministries and agencies related to tourism and creative economy issues, especially with the MoTCE.

The MoTCE regularly co-ordinates with various stakeholders in developing tourism and the creative economy and mitigating the impact of COVID-19. The Ministry is co-ordinating closely with the ministries of Health, Foreign Affairs and Communication and Information. MoTCE also regularly co-ordinates with the Ministry of Public Works and Housing in developing tourism destinations, especially in Indonesia's priority tourism destinations.

The budget for MoTCE in 2022 increased to IDR 3.8 trillion. The budget was IDR 3.6 trillion in 2020 and IDR 3.45 trillion in 2021. The three main funding sources are government revenue, foreign loans, and non-tax state revenue.

Indonesia: Organisational chart of tourism bodies

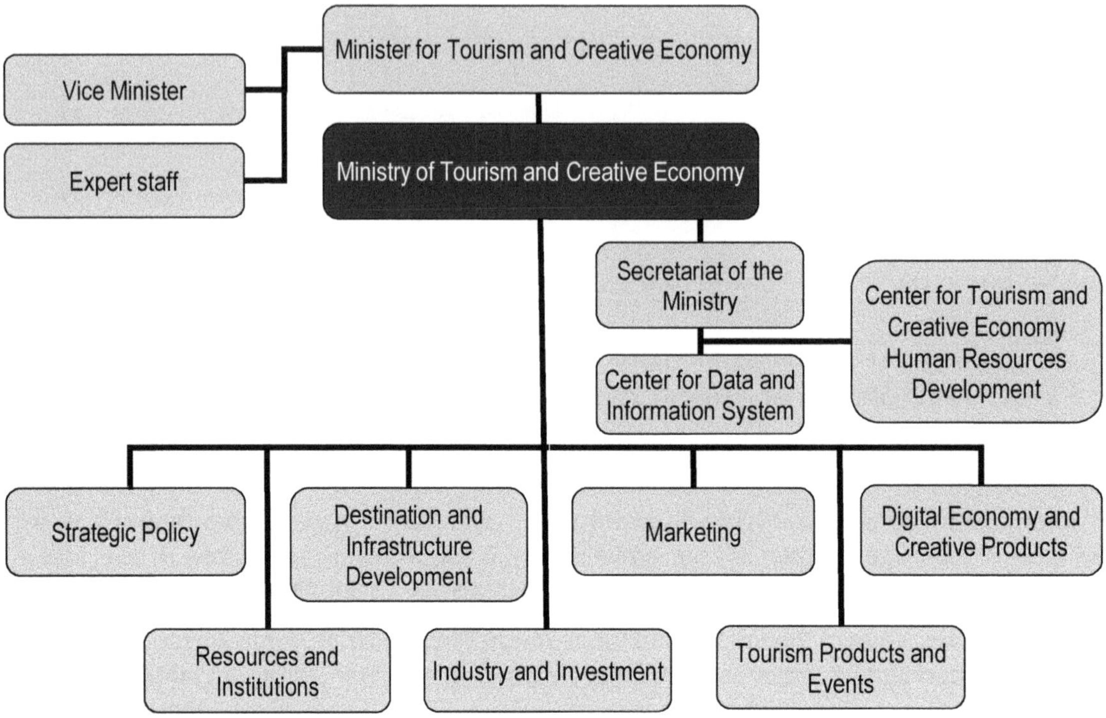

Source: OECD adapted from Ministry of Tourism and Creative Economy, 2022.

Tourism policies and programmes

The Ministry of Tourism and Creative Economy aims to prepare the tourism sector for an adaptive and sustainable future. The core themes in the coming years are recovery policies, which are set in place for 2022-23 to accelerate the recovery and increase productivity. Growth and acceleration are additional priorities in 2024-25.

In 2022, The Ministry of National Development Planning formulated the Institutional Framework for Tourism Policy Development. The formulation is divided into three broad categories: productivity, inclusiveness, and sustainability. In each category, there are several policy guidelines which MoTCE is to implement:

- **Productivity:** involves increasing productivity through improving the supply chain, reskilling and upskilling resources, expanding the tourism market, supporting effective promotion, and accelerating the development of infrastructure, amenities, and attraction in the five priority tourism destinations. There are also plans to increase digital and creative exports and start-ups.
- **Inclusiveness:** involves the improvement of tourism villages, revitalisation of creative economy infrastructure, and expanding the Enhancement National Products Usage Programme.
- **Sustainability:** involves expanding the Health Protocol implementation and service standard in the tourism and creative economy (see box below) and the expansion of sustainable tourism.

Reskilling and upskilling of tourism businesses and stakeholders will be focused on local communities and MSMEs in marketing, destination management, digital literacy, entrepreneur assistance, and related subjects. Revitalising tourism destinations and infrastructure will be especially during the low season.

Indonesia also provides special assistance to Indonesia's Tourism Villages to help develop infrastructure and management.

During the pandemic, health and safety became the top priority. In co-ordination with the Ministry of Health, in 2020, the MoTCE launched the Cleanliness, Health, Safety and Environmental Sustainability (CHSE) protocol, training, and certification to prepare for the reopening of the tourism sector post-pandemic. The protocol developed into several handbooks ranging from hotel safety protocol to specific destination models that can be applied to tourism businesses. The CHSE certificate aims to give assurance to visitors regarding the cleanliness, health, safety and environmental sustainability of destination amenities. Working with local certification institutions, the programme has certified almost 12 000 tourism businesses in 34 provinces or 403 cities. The certification will be renewed annually to ensure the tourism businesses' adherence to the certification.

Statistical Profile

Indonesia: Domestic, inbound and outbound tourism

	2017	2018	2019	2020	2021
TOURISM FLOWS, THOUSAND					
Domestic tourism					
Total domestic trips	..	..	722 159	524 571	603 020
Overnight visitors (tourists)	270 822	303 404	354 353	364 698	399 524
Same-day visitors (excursionists)	..	..	367 805	159 873	203 496
Nights in all types of accommodation	..	..	306 556	378 006	449 310
Hotels and similar establishments	..	..	55 390	117 609	185 971
Other collective establishments	..	..	16 032	36 668	36 664
Private accommodation	..	..	235 135	223 730	226 675
Inbound tourism					
Total international arrivals	14 040	15 810	16 107	4 053	1 558
Overnight visitors (tourists)	12 948	13 396	15 455	3 981	1 546
Same-day visitors (excursionists)	1 092	2 414	652	72	11
Top markets					
Malaysia	2 122	2 503	2 981	980	481
China (People's Republic of)	2 093	2 139	2 072	240	55
Singapore	1 554	1 769	1 934	280	19
India	537	595	657	112	7
Australia	1 257	1 301	1 387	256	3
Nights in all types of accommodation	..	..	..	..	..
Hotels and similar establishments	..	..	..	..	..
Other collective establishments	..	..	..	..	..
Private accommodation	..	..	..	..	..
Outbound tourism					
Total international departures	8 856	9 468	11 689	2 918	1 711
Overnight visitors (tourists)	..	..	..	..	503
Same-day visitors (excursionists)	..	..	..	..	1 208
Top destinations					
	..	..	..	..	..
	..	..	..	..	..
	..	..	..	..	..
	..	..	..	..	..
	..	..	..	..	..
TOURISM RECEIPTS AND EXPENDITURE, MILLION USD					
Inbound tourism					
Total international receipts	14 691	17 915	18 405	3 532	..
International travel receipts	13 139	16 426	16 911	3 312	3 097
International passenger transport receipts	1 552	1 489	1 494	221	..
Outbound tourism					
Total international expenditure	10 945	13 171	14 449	1 980	..
International travel expenditure	8 289	10 314	11 308	1 653	..
International passenger transport expenditure	2 656	2 857	3 141	327	..

.. Not available
Source: OECD Tourism Statistics (Database).

StatLink https://stat.link/e5magc

Indonesia: Enterprises and employment in tourism

	Number of establishments[1]	Number of persons employed[2]				
	2020	2017	2018	2019	2020	2021
Total	..	..	..	..	..	..
Tourism industries	..	..	..	..	..	..
Accommodation services for visitors	..	1 043 448	..	..	..	..
Hotels and similar establishments	30 823	..	408 565	407 292	348 270	..
Food and beverage serving industry	..	8 129 143	..	8 016 863	..	..
Passenger transport	1 985	..	..	21 535	15 428	..
Air passenger transport	..	..	..	..	..	..
Railways passenger transport	3	..	..	57	..	..
Road passenger transport	1 550	..	..	49 120	..	..
Water passenger transport	432	..	..	1 473	..	..
Passenger transport supporting services	..	..	..	..	..	..
Transport equipment rental	..	..	..	..	..	..
Travel agencies and other reservation services industry	10 604	..	..	86 770	65 112	..
Cultural industry	4 174	..	..	117 092	98 539	..
Sports and recreation industry	13 867	..	..	112 669	..	..
Retail trade of country-specific tourism characteristic goods	..	..	..	2 000 499	..	..
Other country-specific tourism industries	3 204	..	..	37 100	..	..
Other industries	..	..	..	..	..	..

.. Not available
1. Data refer to number of enterprises.
2. Data refer to number of employees.
Source: OECD Tourism Statistics (Database).

StatLink https://stat.link/7zysno

Indonesia: Internal tourism consumption

Million IDR

	2020		
	Domestic tourism expenditure	Inbound tourism expenditure	Internal tourism consumption
Total	..	..	..
Consumption products	**674 507 316**	**71 080 512**	**745 587 827**
Tourism characteristic products	653 262 094	62 301 195	715 563 290
Accommodation services for visitors	114 514 144	24 197 504	138 711 648
Food and beverage serving services	207 484 990	16 666 223	224 151 212
Passenger transport services	241 889 120	8 749 838	250 638 958
Air passenger transport services	215 827 566	5 765 994	221 593 560
Railways passenger transport services	732 433	162 310	894 743
Road passenger transport services	16 007 808	1 587 083	17 594 892
Water passenger transport services	9 321 312	1 234 450	10 555 762
Passenger transport supporting services	..	..	..
Transport equipment rental services	22 213 587	461 108	22 674 695
Travel agencies and other reservation services industry	4 630 045	613 839	5 243 884
Cultural services	13 872 288	1 833 053	15 705 341
Sports and recreation services	..	..	..
Country-specific tourism characteristic goods	44 131 761	5 660 575	49 792 336
Country-specific tourism characteristic services	4 526 160	4 119 055	8 645 215
Other consumption products	21 245 221	8 779 316	30 024 538
Tourism connected products	..	..	..
Non-tourism related consumption products	..	..	..
Non-consumption products	..	..	..

.. Not available
Source: OECD Tourism Statistics (Database).

StatLink https://stat.link/60xjud

Malta

Tourism in the economy and outlook for recovery

Tourism is an essential contributor to Malta's economy, providing 40 568 direct tourism jobs or 16.9% of total employment and a total tourism expenditure of EUR 2.2 billion in 2019. Malta estimates that the tourism decline in 2020 contributed to a 7.8% fall in overall GVA. This fall in GVA is likely to have reduced labour income by almost 8% and overall employment by 9.5%.

International tourism is a significant contributor to the Maltese tourism ecosystem, with 2.8 million international tourists in 2019. Inbound tourists declined to 659 000 in 2020, down 76% compared to 2019. In 2020, Malta's top three inbound markets for overnight visitors were the United Kingdom, Italy and Germany.

The pandemic resulted in record domestic overnight stays in Malta, recording 360 500 overnight tourists in 2020, up 51.9% from 2019. However, for a small island state such as Malta, domestic tourism is not a factor that can compensate for inbound tourism.

In 2021, inbound tourists increased to 968 000, but still remained 70.9% below 2019 levels. Total tourism expenditure was estimated to be EUR 870 million, an increase of 91% compared to 2020. Recovery to 2019 levels is not expected until 2024 or 2025.

Tourism governance and funding

Tourism in Malta is the responsibility of the Ministry for Tourism. Its mission is to establish and execute a tourism policy based on the principles of sustainable development. The Ministry strives to improve Malta's competitiveness by working with all stakeholders to ensure that products, services and value reach levels that enable both the island of Malta and Gozo to improve the seasonal spread of tourism and its economic benefits.

The Malta Tourism Authority (MTA) is the destination management organisation under the Ministry's remit. The Malta Tourism Authority is responsible for promoting Malta as a tourist destination, advising the government on tourism operations and issuing licences under the relevant legislation. The Malta Tourism Authority also caters for the needs of the islands Gozo and Comino. MTA liaises with the Ministry for Gozo and the Gozo Tourism Association (GTA), which represents Gozitan tourism stakeholders and the Gozo Regional Development Authority (GRDA).

Throughout the pandemic, the Ministry collaborated with several Ministries, namely:

- Ministry for Health: To discuss the COVID-19 situation and the policy initiatives that the Ministry for Health would propose to address the COVID-19 situation.
- Ministry for Foreign Affairs: To communicate and co-ordinate travel advice (including restrictive measures), the care of COVID-19 patients and repatriation efforts.
- Ministry for Transport and Infrastructure: To collaborate and implement infrastructure projects during the period.

- Ministry for Finance: To discuss and implement assistance measures directed toward the Tourism sector.

The governance and implementation elements of the tourism strategy will be supported by a new Malta Tourism Observatory, which will be charged with the responsibility of monitoring and measuring the delivery of the Tourism Strategy. The Malta Tourism Observatory will have a proactive role and will be empowered to commission studies, undertake KPI measurements and consult stakeholders during implementation.

The budget allocated to tourism in 2020 amounted to EUR 138 million from National Tourism Funds and EUR 4.7 million from EU Direct, Structural and Cohesion Funds.

Malta: Organisational chart of tourism bodies

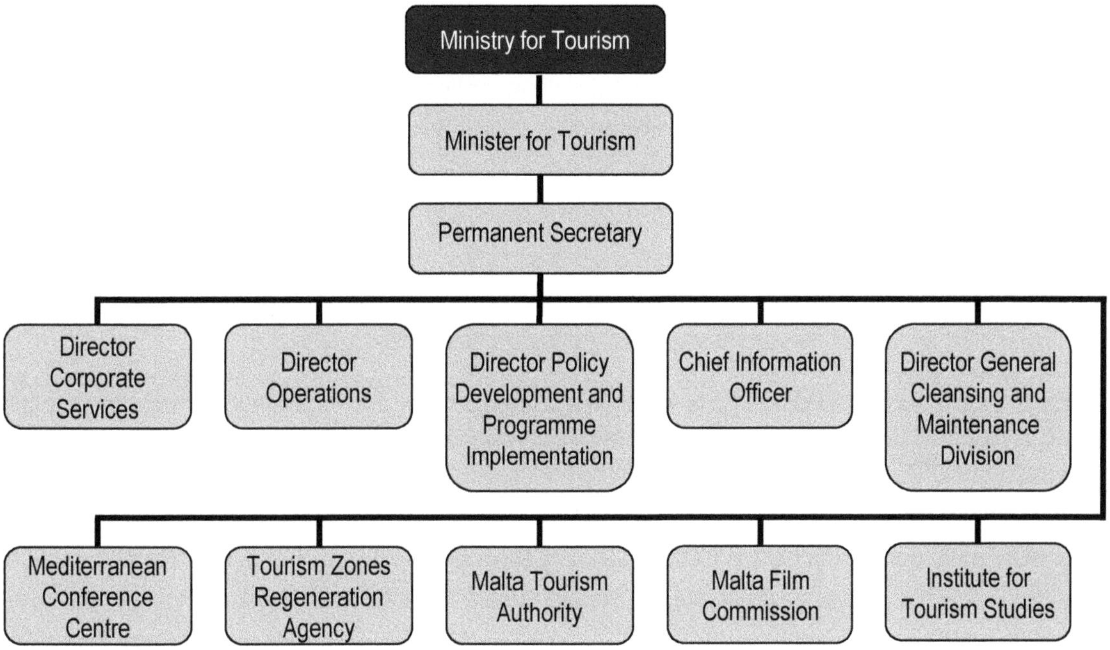

Source: OECD, adapted from the Ministry of Tourism, 2022.

Tourism policies and programmes

Malta launched its new Tourism Strategy for the years 2021-30 called Recover, Rethink, Revitalise, aiming to re-establish the tourism sector on a sounder footing and in line with international ideals and commitments in the fields of sustainable development and climate change. The key priorities of the Strategy are:

- An upskilled tourism workforce.
- Modernised infrastructure.
- Updated tourism legislation.
- Stronger potential for digitalisation.
- Continued development of Malta's airline connectivity.
- An innovative approach towards responding to new travel trends.

The Strategy focuses on developing new services and products and continued marketing efforts to position Malta as a destination of choice in the widest range of geographic and motivational travel segments. It outlines the development of a digitalisation roadmap that seeks to empower public, private and non-profit organisations to invest and ensure that efficiency and market presence are maximised through the use of the latest technologies.

In 2021, Malta looked to kick-start the devastated tourism sector through a direct aid package for local tourism establishments valued at EUR 20 million. The aim was to attract tourism activity to Malta, targeting free and independent travellers (FITs) who plan their own trips and travel alone or in small groups as opposed to mass tourism that relies on large groups and travel packages. There are also initiatives addressing Quality Assured Visitor Attractions, long-stay visitors and sports tourists, including diving enthusiasts. The goal is to get tourism on the road to recovery quickly so Malta can generate the necessary number of tourists to support the investment made by the sector.

In the longer term, there is a need for a two-pronged approach to addressing employment in the Maltese tourism sector. The first is to make the sector a more attractive career for Maltese workers and foreign workers. The second is to ensure that foreign workers are not attracted mainly because of their relatively cheap labour cost but also because of the skills necessary to deliver a higher quality experience to Malta's visitors. In May 2020, Malta launched a EUR 5 million online training programme to develop human resources to improve skills and the tourism product.

Moving forward, Malta will place a greater emphasis on a sustainable approach to tourism development and give less weight to volume growth. The objective is an enhanced offer, improved visitor satisfaction and minimised negative resident impacts.

Institute for Tourism Studies Corporate and Business Strategy in Malta

The Institute of Tourism Studies (ITS) is Malta's leading tourism and hospitality educational institution and a key entity that falls under the Ministry for Tourism portfolio. It offers a broad selection of study programmes and utilises multiple on-campus specialised labs and kitchens to ensure that students receive essential theoretical and practical education.

Students also gain opportunities for further training through the Local Industrial Trade Practice and International Internship, which is included in the student's programme of study.

During the COVID-19 pandemic, the Institute of Tourism Studies launched a corporate and business strategy for 2021-25, which outlined the Institute's ambitions for growth. This includes a EUR 40 million investment to transfer the Institutes facilities to a new site at Smart City, supported through the EU Recovery and Resilience Facility.

The Institute of Tourism Studies recognised that the pandemic brought seismic changes to the higher education industry, and opportunities will arise given these changes. The corporate strategy outlines the updated plans for the Institute in terms of its mission, vision and strategic objectives. The business strategy establishes the activities the Institute will pursue through dedicated business units. Each business unit will have an individual business strategy to guide its operation.

Statistical Profile

Malta: Domestic, inbound and outbound tourism

	2017	2018	2019	2020	2021
TOURISM FLOWS, THOUSAND					
Domestic tourism					
Total domestic trips	..	..	..	..	..
Overnight visitors (tourists)	261	245	237	360	..
Same-day visitors (excursionists)	..	..	..	..	..
Nights in all types of accommodation	708	650	618	1 064	..
Hotels and similar establishments	156	164	145	150	..
Other collective establishments	..	..	..	..	..
Private accommodation	552	486	473	914	..
Inbound tourism					
Total international arrivals	2 840	3 153	3 383	717	984
Overnight visitors (tourists)	2 274	2 599	2 753	659	968
Same-day visitors (excursionists)	566	554	629	59	132
Top markets					
United Kingdom	561	641	650	136	..
Italy	364	391	393	94	..
Germany	193	227	212	72	..
France	176	213	239	71	..
Spain	76	99	116	27	..
Nights in all types of accommodation	16 509	18 570	19 339	5 227	8 390
Hotels and similar establishments	9 418	10 082	10 069	2 362	6 534
Other collective establishments	..	..	..	..	..
Private accommodation	7 092	8 488	9 270	2 865	1 855
Outbound tourism					
Total international departures	632	728	774	218	344
Overnight visitors (tourists)	572	667	707	197	303
Same-day visitors (excursionists)	60	61	67	21	41
Top destinations					
Italy	181	212	214	67	119
United Kingdom	106	119	126	29	26
Spain	28	38	45	10	21
France	22	28	28	8	12
Germany	38	42	38	11	11
TOURISM RECEIPTS AND EXPENDITURE, MILLION USD					
Inbound tourism					
Total international receipts	2 413	1 849	1 897	417	..
International travel receipts	1 726	1 849	1 897	417	..
International passenger transport receipts	687	..	..	..	..
Outbound tourism					
Total international expenditure	468	518	530	128	..
International travel expenditure	468	518	530	128	..
International passenger transport expenditure	..	..	..	..	..

.. Not available

Source: OECD Tourism Statistics (Database).

StatLink https://stat.link/1zyb25

Malta: Enterprises and employment in tourism

	Number of establishments[1]	Number of persons employed				
	2020	2017	2018	2019	2020	2021
Total	**7 785**	..	..	..	..	..
Tourism industries	..	**31 240**	**33 997**	**40 568**	**40 722**	**40 070**
Accommodation services for visitors	744	7 954	7 547	7 723	6 584	6 489
Hotels and similar establishments	..	..	..	..	..	..
Food and beverage serving industry	2 309	6 824	7 215	9 945	9 786	8 163
Passenger transport	1 605	4 462	4 128	4 594	6 051	5 977
Air passenger transport	32	1 461	1 563	1 073 e	1 490	2 250
Railways passenger transport	1	..	..	..	..	..
Road passenger transport	1 472	1 778	1 769	2 927	3 934	2 952
Water passenger transport	100	1 224 e	797	594 e	627 e	776 e
Passenger transport supporting services	454	2 593	2 473	2 983	3 454	4 172
Transport equipment rental	144	125 e	683	1 050	361 e	291 e
Travel agencies and other reservation services industry	490	1 029	1 228	1 349	1 428	1 163 e
Cultural industry	1 445	6 776	8 709	11 052	11 517	12 881
Sports and recreation industry	594	1 477	2 014	1 871	1 542	933 e
Retail trade of country-specific tourism characteristic goods	..	..	..	..	..	..
Other country-specific tourism industries	..	..	..	..	..	..
Other industries	..	..	..	..	..	..

.. Not available; e Estimated value
1. Data refer to number of enterprises.
Source: OECD Tourism Statistics (Database).

StatLink https://stat.link/oudkj6

Malta: Internal tourism consumption

Million EUR

	2010		
	Domestic tourism expenditure	Inbound tourism expenditure	Internal tourism consumption
Total	..	..	..
Consumption products	**112**	**1 033**	**1 150**
Tourism characteristic products	99	859	963
Accommodation services for visitors	7	232	243
Food and beverage serving services	17	258	275
Passenger transport services	31	256	287
Air passenger transport services	29	231	260
Railways passenger transport services	..	..	..
Road passenger transport services	2	25	26
Water passenger transport services	..	..	..
Passenger transport supporting services	..	..	..
Transport equipment rental services	0	19	19
Travel agencies and other reservation services industry	44	36	80
Cultural services	0	13	13
Sports and recreation services	0	23	23
Country-specific tourism characteristic goods	..	..	..
Country-specific tourism characteristic services	..	..	..
Other consumption products	13	174	187
Tourism connected products	4	104	108
Non-tourism related consumption products	9	70	79
Non-consumption products	..	..	..

.. Not available
Source: OECD Tourism Statistics (Database).

StatLink https://stat.link/5i7nwa

Montenegro

Tourism in the economy and outlook for recovery

Tourism is a driving sector for economic growth in Montenegro. The sector directly accounted for 9.5% of total GDP and 9.0% of total employment in 2019. In 2020, international and domestic tourism receipts amounted to about EUR 159 million, 86% lower than in 2019 according to the National Bank of Montenegro.

International tourism is key for tourism in Montenegro, with international tourists accounting for 95.5% of nights in 2019. At this time, international tourists hit a record high, with 2.5 million tourists. This fell by 83.2% to 351 000 tourists in 2020, before recovering to 1.6 million in 2021. The top source markets in 2021 were Serbia (26.7%), Bosnia and Herzegovina (13.8%), Russia (6.9%) and Germany (4.9%). International tourists accounted for 351 000 arrivals (down 86.0%) and 2.2 million overnight stays.

In 2020, domestic tourists fell 31.2% to 93 270 arrivals, which resulted in 360 700 nights. Domestic tourists increased 25.8% to 117 321 tourists in 2021, returning to 86.5% of 2019 levels.

A return of international tourism to pre-pandemic levels is expected in 2023.

Tourism governance and funding

In Montenegro, the Ministry for Economic Development and Tourism, the National Tourism Organisation of Montenegro, and local tourism organisations have a leading role in defining development policies in tourism, destination management and creating a tourism product.

Montenegro is also in the process of establishing a National Tourism Council. The main task of the Council would be to strengthen tourism as a sector, both nationally and internationally. The mission of the Council would consist of proposing and implementing activities of importance for all entities in the country in the field of tourism and complementary branches, as well as raising standards in this sector with the aim of better global positioning of Montenegro as a tourist destination, strengthening the economy through better integration of tourism and other branches of the economy, creating a stable business and investment tourist environment and greater tourist satisfaction.

The Council would have a role in controlling the implementation of the strategy and programme documents. It would include representatives of the private sector, which would further strengthen public-private partnerships and the role of the private sector in making strategic decisions in the field of tourism.

To improve the business and investment environment and create a new destination management model, Montenegro is looking at possibilities to restructure tourism and economic bodies by introducing a destination management model. The synergy of the National Tourism Organisation with local tourism organisations and other tourism actors is necessary through strengthening public-private partnerships, which should be the backbone of the future functioning of the Montenegrin tourism sector.

Montenegro: Organisational chart of tourism bodies

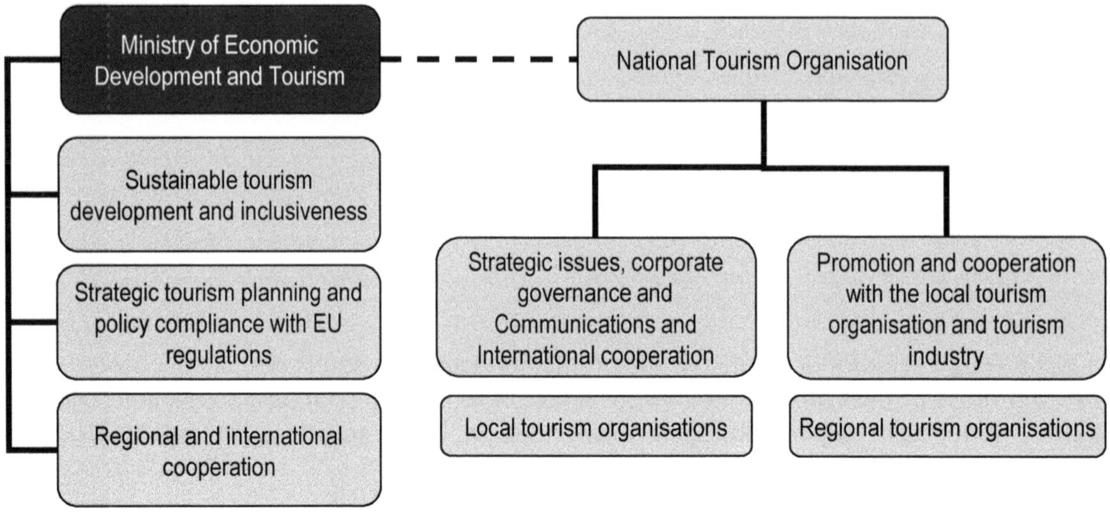

Source: OECD, adapted from the Ministry of Economic Development and Tourism, 2022.

Tourism policies and programmes

Throughout the COVID-19 pandemic, Montenegro worked to support the economy and the tourism sector with the goal of adapting and harmonising the business environment to the new circumstances. The ministries of Health and Tourism created a guide to health and safety protocols for COVID-19, entitled "Montenegro as a safe and responsible tourist destination." The protocols included measures and activities that reduced the risk of infection and covered a range of tourism businesses, including accommodation, food and beverage, transportation, and natural areas. Montenegro also implemented a national health and safety communication strategy.

The Strategy of Tourism Development in Montenegro 2022-25 is aligned with tourism development trends and new circumstances after the pandemic. All the activities and projects are focused on sustainable, inclusive, smart, green and responsible tourism, with the ultimate goal of establishing Montenegro as a globally recognisable tourism destination by 2025.

The road map for achieving the strategic goal is: managing destinations in a sustainable way, creating an innovative, green and inclusive tourism product, influencing the increase in tourism spending, reducing seasonality and regional imbalances, raising the living standards of local populations and increasing tourist satisfaction.

Several key operational goals have been defined in relation to the Strategy, which includes:

- Improving the regulatory framework in tourism with the formalisation of tourism turnover.
- Supporting the development of tourism infrastructure.
- Expanding the quality and quantity of accommodation capacities.
- Diversifying the tourism product while retaining quality.
- Enhanced human resources, knowledge and skills in tourism.
- Developing digital, innovative solutions and new technologies in tourism.

Currently, 95% of tourism overnight stays and income are achieved in coastal regions, and 75% occurs in the summer months. Montenegro is focusing future activities on the quality of coastal tourism products relative to quantity. Another focus is the diversification of the tourism product, especially by encouraging year-round travel and offers based on nature. The development of tourism in the new circumstances is based on the potential of green, smart and inclusive tourism from the aspects of:

- **Improving the quality of accommodation facilities:** developing "green" types of accommodation facilities that meet eco-standards.
- **Upskilling of business:** intensifying the application of new technologies and digitisation in tourism businesses.
- **Raising the quality of the tourism offer:** developing special types of tourist products and activities based on nature and providing a unique experience and healthy lifestyles.

Regarding a green tourism economy, Montenegro is working with the private sector and other stakeholders to assure the commitment to environmentally sensitive tourism development. This is being worked on through areas including carbon-neutral buildings, environmentally appropriate tourism development projects, nature preservation, and building citizen awareness and commitment.

Digitalisation and innovation in tourism are focused on supporting tourism service providers, encouraging the development and promotion of tourism in a sustainable, green, smart and inclusive way, encouraging tourist experiences, quality tourism content with a focus on cultural heritage, and the authenticity of the destination. The Smart Specialisation Strategy 2019-24 and the Health Tourism Development Programme 2021-23 recognise and promote the importance of medical tourism, which has increased due to the COVID-19 pandemic.

Statistical Profile

Montenegro: Domestic, inbound and outbound tourism

	2017	2018	2019	2020	2021
TOURISM FLOWS, THOUSAND					
Domestic tourism					
Total domestic trips	..	..	..	..	..
Overnight visitors (tourists)	..	..	..	..	..
Same-day visitors (excursionists)	..	..	..	..	..
Nights in all types of accommodation	..	..	..	..	..
Hotels and similar establishments	431	445	480	342	376
Other collective establishments	1	1	1	1	0
Private accommodation	52	41	42	18	73
Inbound tourism					
Total international arrivals	..	..	..	..	..
Overnight visitors (tourists)	1 877 |	2 077	2 510	351	1 554
Same-day visitors (excursionists)	..	..	..	..	..
Top markets					
Serbia	405	409	403	58	429
Bosnia and Herzegovina	184	194	204	50	215
Russia	350	338	385	39	108
Germany	58	90	164	18	71
France	61	77	90	10	36
Nights in all types of accommodation	..	..	..	..	..
Hotels and similar establishments	3 435	3 732	4 168	601	2 547
Other collective establishments	24	31	33	1	26
Private accommodation	8 011	8 680	9 733	1 625	6 851
Outbound tourism					
Total international departures	..	..	..	..	..
Overnight visitors (tourists)	..	..	..	..	..
Same-day visitors (excursionists)	..	..	..	..	..
Top destinations					
..	..	..	..	..	..
..	..	..	..	..	..
..	..	..	..	..	..
..	..	..	..	..	..
..	..	..	..	..	..
TOURISM RECEIPTS AND EXPENDITURE, MILLION USD					
Inbound tourism					
Total international receipts	1 109	1 224	1 276	180	..
International travel receipts	1 067	1 171	1 224	166	..
International passenger transport receipts	43	53	52	14	..
Outbound tourism					
Total international expenditure	91	74	72	38	..
International travel expenditure	67	68	58	30	..
International passenger transport expenditure	24	5	14	8	..

.. Not available; | Break in series
Source: OECD Tourism Statistics (Database).

StatLink https://stat.link/vs06ez

Montenegro: Enterprises and employment in tourism

	Number of establishments	Number of persons employed				
		2017	2018	2019	2020	2021
Total	..	..	..	..	..	..
Tourism industries	..	..	..	..	..	..
Accommodation services for visitors	..	6 529	7 102	8 020	5 508	6 469
Hotels and similar establishments	..	5 574	6 094	6 850	4 527	5 335
Food and beverage serving industry	..	8 982	9 444	10 965	8 399	9 416
Passenger transport	..	..	..	..	..	..
Air passenger transport	..	450	442	436	407	97
Railways passenger transport	..	1 354	1 347	1 330	1 232	1 226
Road passenger transport	..	1 791	1 813	2 311	1 960	1 917
Water passenger transport	..	192	208	280	216	219
Passenger transport supporting services	..	..	..	..	..	..
Transport equipment rental	..	509	531	592	515	532
Travel agencies and other reservation services industry	..	1 175	1 458	1 667	1 261	1 279
Cultural industry	..	504	548	551	528	595
Sports and recreation industry	..	3 009	3 192	3 468	3 133	3 124
Retail trade of country-specific tourism characteristic goods	..	..	..	..	..	..
Other country-specific tourism industries	..	..	..	..	..	..
Other industries	..	..	..	..	..	..

.. Not available
Source: OECD Tourism Statistics (Database).

StatLink https://stat.link/28muse

Morocco

Tourism in the economy and outlook for recovery

Tourism is an important sector in the Moroccan economy, directly contributing MAD 82.1 billion or 7.1% of total GDP in 2019 and providing an estimated 565 000 jobs (5.0% of total employment). Tourism is generally a key source of foreign currency, with receipts representing 42% of service exports in 2019, but fell to 28% in 2020.

International tourism plays an important role, with 12.9 million international tourists in 2019. In 2020, international arrivals to Morocco decreased by 78.5% to 2.8 million. Travel receipts from international tourism fell to MAD 36.4 billion in 2020, 53.8% lower than in 2019. The tourism recovery in 2021 remained limited, with 3.7 million international tourists, 71% below 2019.

In 2019, there were 3.5 million domestic overnight visitors (tourists) in classified accommodation establishments. Domestic tourism fell by 55% in 2020, but this relatively smaller decrease compared to international tourism saw the domestic share of total nights in classified accommodation establishments increase to almost 50% in 2020, up from 31% pre-pandemic. Domestic tourism performed stronger in 2021, reaching 2.8 million overnight visitors (tourists) in classified accommodation establishments, 22% below the 2019 level.

Morocco projects a full tourism recovery to pre-pandemic levels by 2023.

Tourism governance and funding

The Department of Tourism sits within the Ministry of Tourism, Handicrafts, and Social and Solidarity Economy and is responsible for developing and implementing government policy on tourism.

Morocco has adopted a framework of 'advanced regionalisation' as a new model of territorial governance. The framework aims to build a strong territorial administration through improved skills and resources. The Department of Tourism carries out missions at the national level. Decentralised services are responsible for overseeing the management of regional public services, implementation of public policies and participation in developing and delivering programmes and projects at the regional level. Decentralised services also ensure the execution of directives and decisions from national government authorities to which they report and carry out programmes and projects at the prefecture or provincial level.

The budget of the Department of Tourism for 2022 was MAD 680 million. It is split between the entities placed under the responsibility of the Department of Tourism:

- Central administration: MAD 125 million.
- Moroccan National Tourist Office: MAD 300 million.
- Moroccan Agency for Tourism Development: MAD 255 million.

Morocco: Organisational chart of tourism bodies

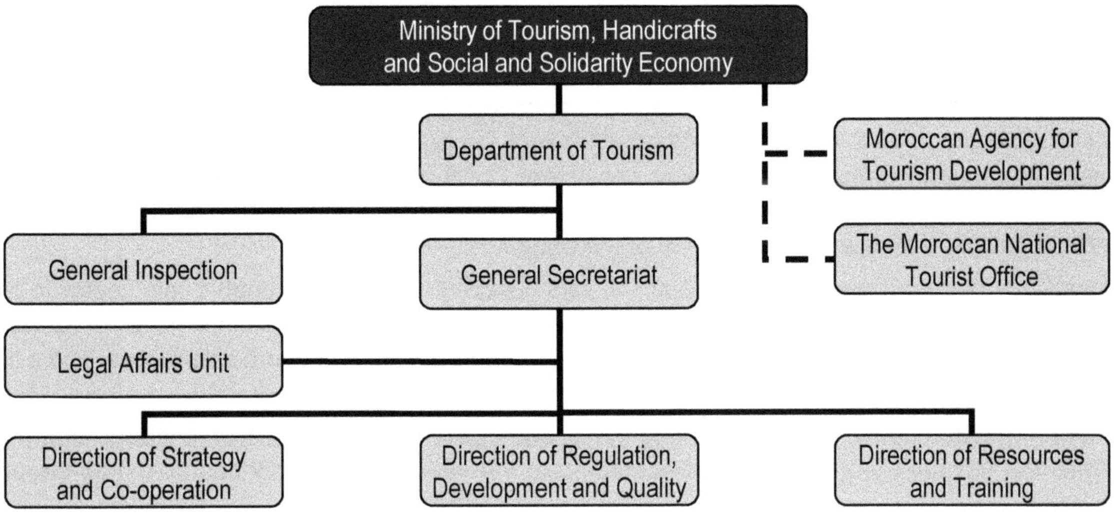

Source: OECD, adapted from the Department of Tourism, 2022.

Tourism policies and programmes

Tourism is a priority sector in Morocco, which benefited from the country's ten-year development strategies - Vision 2010 and Vision 2020 - aimed at supporting and boosting tourist activity while improving its impact on the country. However, the COVID-19 pandemic, which coincided with the expiry of Vision 2020, plunged the sector into crisis and reshaped its development potential.

Public authorities deployed numerous measures allowing specific support for the sector to limit the impact of the crisis, preserve the economy, and accelerate the recovery of the sector. Public and private actors have combined their efforts at national and regional levels by setting up a programme for the revival of the tourism sector over the period 2020-22. The programme aims to give a boost to the sector and breathe new life into its relaunch and transformation through three major objectives: i) preserve the economy and employment, ii) speed up the restart phase, and ii) lay the foundations for a sustainable transformation of the sector.

The programme includes 21 measures intended to position Morocco in the post-COVID-19 era by adapting to new market realities, anticipating changes in the consumption patterns of tourists and taking advantage of new opportunities. The action plan revolves around five strategic areas:

- Preservation of employment.
- Economic and financial support for the recovery.
- Stimulation of investment and transformation.
- Activation and strengthening of tourism demand.
- Cross-cutting measures such as training, governance, legal frameworks and digitisation.

Several actions have been implemented within the framework of the 2020-22 programme. Support was granted to employees of tourist companies and tourist guides through a monthly flat-rate allowance of MAD 2 000. An exemption from tax on additional remuneration of employees was also granted, in addition to establishing social protection for tourist guides. The payment of social security contributions by tourism businesses and the payment deadlines for specific debts were postponed. Three new guarantee mechanisms were put in place for businesses in the sector. A new law was adopted, allowing service providers to substitute reimbursements owed to their clients for credit notes. A partnership agreement was signed to create an "Inmaa Tourism" device to support and accelerate the development of tourism SMEs in the Souss-Massa region (see box below). The "Welcome Safely" label was set up for tourist accommodation establishments to demonstrate compliance with the health and safety measures related to COVID-19.

Considering the persistence of the repercussions of the crisis linked to the COVID-19 pandemic and its uncertain horizon, a new emergency plan was also approved by Morocco in 2022 to release an envelope budget amounting to MAD 2 billion to provide the financial support needed to relaunch the sector. The new emergency plan is part of the continuity and consistency of the programme contract. All the actions are carried out to safeguard companies, avoid the massive destruction of jobs and set up a favourable environment for the revitalisation and revival of the sector.

The emergency plan proposes courses of action and concrete solutions to enable this sector to recover from the crisis through measures such as the extension of lump sum payments for employees in the tourism sector, deferrals of charges due to the Social Security Fund for the same employees, and a subsidy for the hotel sector of MAD 1 billion.

The Department of Tourism is also working on a set of measures as part of a global strategy that guarantees the development of the sector according to the variables and priorities identified through five main pillars:

- Conducting broad promotional campaigns to market tourist assets, particularly through tour operators, platforms and websites.
- Strengthening air transport by securing the greatest number of seats for tourists coming to Morocco, in partnership with Royal Air Maroc and foreign companies.
- Boosting tourism investment by prioritising incentives likely to attract investors and encourage the creation of SMEs in the tourism sector, particularly in the leisure and entertainment fields.
- Rehabilitating the tourist offer through a series of priorities which includes improving the quality of services and the diversification of the offer to promote the tourist experience in the country's different regions and improve the notoriety and competitiveness of Morocco as a destination.
- Emphasising the importance of the qualification of human resources and the creation of new employment opportunities, especially after the labour market crisis caused by COVID-19, which has led to a sharp decline in employment opportunities in the private sector.

Supporting competitiveness and transformation of tourism MSMEs in Morocco

INMAA Tourism is a device dedicated to supporting competitiveness and the transformation of actors. It is a support mechanism for MSMEs aiming to improve their competitiveness and the quality of their services sustainably through general and unified assistance for tourist services and proper support focused on the specific issues of each business. This mechanism targets MSMEs operating in regulated trades (e.g. accommodation, distribution, catering) and trades and activities related to the tourism sector, such as entertainment or digital.

As part of the deployment of this global support mechanism for tourism SMEs, a pilot programme has been initiated in the Souss-Massa Region. A partnership agreement was initiated in 2021 with the Region of Souss-Massa to provide this mechanism with a budget of MAD 100 million shared between the region and the Moroccan Agency for Tourism Development with a target of reaching 150 SMEs. The programme intends to promote entrepreneurship by facilitating access to funding support, advice, and technical expertise.

Statistical Profile

Morocco: Domestic, inbound and outbound tourism

	2017	2018	2019	2020	2021
TOURISM FLOWS, THOUSAND					
Domestic tourism					
Total domestic trips	..	..	..	..	..
Overnight visitors (tourists)	3 121	3 247	3 550	1 442	2 765
Same-day visitors (excursionists)	..	..	..	..	..
Nights in all types of accommodation	..	..	..	..	..
Hotels and similar establishments	7 057	7 166	7 838	3 506	6 378
Other collective establishments	..	..	..	..	..
Private accommodation	..	..	..	..	..
Inbound tourism					
Total international arrivals	..	..	..	..	..
Overnight visitors (tourists)	11 349	12 289	12 932	2 778	3 722
Same-day visitors (excursionists)	..	..	..	..	..
Top markets					
France	1 614	1 844	1 991	412	494
Spain	711	814	881	200	99
Belgium	260	274	272	41	65
United Kingdom	486	511	551	113	56
Germany	331	394	413	79	39
Nights in all types of accommodation	132 585	147 790	..	..	..
Hotels and similar establishments	15 046	16 866	17 406	3 470	2 818
Other collective establishments	26 861	30 953	..	..	..
Private accommodation	90 678	99 971	..	..	..
Outbound tourism					
Total international departures	..	..	..	..	..
Overnight visitors (tourists)	1 849	1 923	2 009	738	643
Same-day visitors (excursionists)	..	..	..	..	..
Top destinations					
..	..	..	..	..	..
..	..	..	..	..	..
..	..	..	..	..	..
..	..	..	..	..	..
..	..	..	..	..	..
TOURISM RECEIPTS AND EXPENDITURE, MILLION USD					
Inbound tourism					
Total international receipts	9 086	9 520	9 949	4 514	..
International travel receipts	7 494	7 774	8 187	3 848	..
International passenger transport receipts	1 592	1 746	1 762	666	..
Outbound tourism					
Total international expenditure	2 829	2 988	3 103	1 509	..
International travel expenditure	1 793	1 976	2 176	1 113	..
International passenger transport expenditure	1 036	1 011	926	396	..

.. Not available
Source: OECD Tourism Statistics (Database).

StatLink https://stat.link/v8pa46

Morocco: Enterprises and employment in tourism

	Number of establishments	Number of persons employed				
	2021	2017	2018	2019	2020	2021
Total	..	**532 000 e**	**550 000 e**	**565 000 e**	..	..
Tourism industries	**6 203**	**412 000 e**	**424 000 e**	**435 800 e**	..	..
Accommodation services for visitors	..	..	..	..	..	..
Hotels and similar establishments	4 549	135 000 e	140 000 e	144 000 e	..	..
Food and beverage serving industry	..	86 000 e	90 000 e	92 500 e	..	..
Passenger transport	..	36 000 e	37 000 e	38 000 e	..	..
Air passenger transport	..	..	..	..	..	..
Railways passenger transport	..	..	..	..	..	..
Road passenger transport	..	..	..	..	..	..
Water passenger transport	..	..	..	..	..	..
Passenger transport supporting services	..	..	..	..	..	..
Transport equipment rental	..	..	..	..	..	..
Travel agencies and other reservation services industry	1 654	23 000 e	24 000 e	24 600 e	..	..
Cultural industry	..	10 000 e	10 000 e	10 300 e	..	..
Sports and recreation industry	..	3 000 e	3 000 e	3 100 e	..	..
Retail trade of country-specific tourism characteristic goods	..	119 000 e	120 000 e	123 300 e	..	..
Other country-specific tourism industries	..	..	..	..	..	..
Other industries	..	**120 000 e**	**126 000 e**	**129 200 e**	..	..

.. Not available; e Estimated value
Source: OECD Tourism Statistics (Database).

StatLink https://stat.link/n96q8r

Morocco: Internal tourism consumption

Million MAD

	2014		
	Domestic tourism expenditure	Inbound tourism expenditure	Internal tourism consumption
Total	..	..	..
Consumption products	**32 000**	**73 508**	**105 508**
Tourism characteristic products	21 648	53 666	75 315
Accommodation services for visitors	6 196	11 962	18 158
Food and beverage serving services	5 318	10 088	15 406
Passenger transport services	4 868	14 212	19 080
Air passenger transport services	..	..	..
Railways passenger transport services	..	..	..
Road passenger transport services	..	..	..
Water passenger transport services	..	..	..
Passenger transport supporting services	..	..	..
Transport equipment rental services	122	..	122
Travel agencies and other reservation services industry	43	1 100	1 143
Cultural services	106	1 017	1 123
Sports and recreation services	2 416	8 032	10 449
Country-specific tourism characteristic goods	2 580	7 256	9 836
Country-specific tourism characteristic services	..	..	..
Other consumption products	10 352	19 841	30 193
Tourism connected products	..	..	..
Non-tourism related consumption products	10 352	19 841	30 193
Non-consumption products	..	..	..

.. Not available
Source: OECD Tourism Statistics (Database).

StatLink https://stat.link/ncmdit

Peru

Tourism in the economy and outlook for recovery

In 2019, the tourism sector contributed 3.9% to GDP and directly generated 725 980 jobs which represented 4.1% of Peru's employed economically active population. The tourism sector's contribution decreased to 1.5% of Peru's GDP, and tourism jobs more than halved to 353 552. Foreign exchange revenues totalled just over PEN 3.5 billion, 79% less than in 2019.

With a total of 897 000 international tourists in 2020, inbound tourism decreased by almost 80% compared to 2019, when there were 4.4 million international tourists. This declined further in 2021, when Peru recorded 444 000 international arrivals, down 50% compared to 2020 and 90% below 2019 levels. Arrivals from the United States rebounded to 177 000, representing 39.8% of total tourists in 2021. Tourists from Chile, historically the top source market, remained low (37 000 tourists compared to 1.2 million in 2019).

Domestic tourism is the driver of tourism in Peru, with 48.6 million domestic tourists in 2019. Domestic tourism was hard hit by the pandemic and remained low in 2021, with 15.6 million tourists, up 8.3% compared to 2020, although still down 70% from pre-pandemic levels.

Given the pace of recovery of tourist trips observed to date, it is unlikely that inbound tourism will reach pre-pandemic levels before 2025 or 2026.

Tourism governance and funding

The Ministry of Foreign Trade and Tourism (MINCETUR) is the tourism sector's lead political and administrative authority. Its role is to define, direct, execute and co-ordinate the country's foreign trade and tourism policy in harmony with the general policy of Peru.

The Vice Ministry for Tourism, part of MINCETUR, oversees the General Directorate of Tourism Development Policy, which is responsible for implementing, evaluating and supervising compliance with tourism policy. The Directorate also formulates and implements actions to improve the quality of tourism services, its environmental management, tourism facilitation, tourist protection, and the promotion of culture. The Vice Ministry for Tourism oversees the General Directorates of Research and Studies on Tourism and Handicrafts, Tourism Strategy, Crafts, and Casino Games and Slot Machines.

MINCETUR has two Specialised Advisory Bodies - the Tourism Advisory Committee and the National Council for Handicraft Development. Two other bodies attached to the Ministry are the Tourism Training Centre (CENFOTUR) and the Exports and Tourism Promotion Board of Peru (PROMPERÚ). Peru's Commercial Offices Abroad are operated by PROMPERÚ.

Regional governments are responsible for formulating, approving and executing policies relating to the development of regional tourist activity, qualification of regional tourist service providers, and co-ordination with local governments on tourism activities. They also maintain and update directories of tourism service providers, tourism resources, and regional events calendars.

The 2021 Ministry of Foreign Trade and Tourism budget was PEN 253 million. The budget for the Tourism Promotion Board was PEN 239.6 million, and the budget for the Tourism Training Centre was PEN 15 million. In 2020, the Ministry of Foreign Trade and Tourism budget was PEN 750 million due to additional financial transfers for the Repatriation Programme implemented by Peru during the COVID-19 pandemic, which provided hotel accommodation to Peruvian citizens repatriated from abroad. The Tourism Promotion Board's budget was PEN 76 million, and the Tourism Training Centre's budget was PEN 7 million.

Peru: Organisational chart of tourism bodies

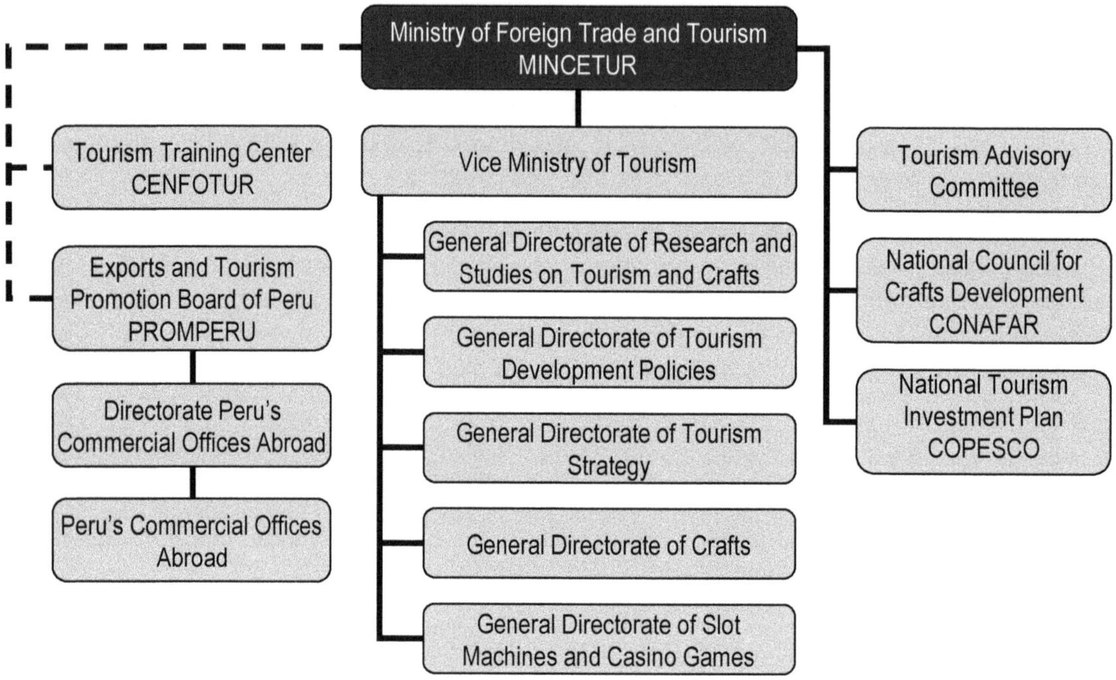

Source: OECD, adapted from the Ministry of Foreign Trade and Tourism, 2022.

Tourism policies and programmes

In response to the pandemic, a Technical Committee for the Reactivation of the Tourism Sector in the Cusco Region (public and private mechanism) has been promoted to provide social solutions in five working subgroups: public investment; planning and management; support to entrepreneurs; facilitation and regulations; and tourism promotion. The Committee's main achievement has been the increase in the capacity for the entry of tourists to the Machu Picchu Archaeological Site.

Peru has developed two management instruments in response to the pandemic: the Tourism Sector Emergency Plan to 2023 and the National Strategy for the Tourism Sector Reactivation 2022-25 (see box below).

Under the Plan, a number of initiatives have taken place, including:

- The Guide of Regional Tourism Marketing Plans, developed by PROMPERÚ in agreement with the Swiss Import Promotion Programme. This is a step-by-step guide for the development of a regional marketing plan. A related training programme was signed with several regional governments.

- The Programme to Stimulate Business Competitiveness, launched in 2020. It was composed of 19 courses designed to strengthen the competitiveness of tourism MSMEs. More than 200 companies participated in the online sessions nationwide.
- The Virtual Classroom, launched in 2021, as an online educational platform that allows entrepreneurs, students and other interested parties access to training and certification on topics related to commercial matters, digital tools, innovation and commercial intelligence. The Virtual Classroom has more than 5 000 users nationwide.
- The Peru Carbon Footprint Scheme, which has registered 27 hotels, demonstrating their commitment to reducing their greenhouse gas emissions and environmental impact.
- The Business Support Fund for SMEs in the tourism sector (FAE-Turismo) was established as a special guarantee fund of PEN 200 million. It was created to promote access to financing for micro and small tourism businesses affected by the adverse international and local context. This fund benefitted 1 969 enterprises across 23 regions in 2020-21.

MINCETUR and CENFOTUR have also been working on the Good Practices Application System, the principal scheme designed for tourism service providers, incorporating content relating to service management, environmental management and health security.

National Strategy for the Reactivation of the Tourism Sector 2022-25 in Peru

The purpose of Peru's National Strategy for the Reactivation of the Tourism Sector 2022-25 is to promote the reactivation of the tourism sector, generating unique and biosecure tourism experiences based on the country's natural wealth and ancestral culture, with inclusion and sustainability. The objective for 2022 is to surpass 1.4 million international tourists and 24 million domestic tourists and exceed 995 000 tourism jobs.

Four strategic objectives have been defined:

- Strengthen tourism planning, organisation, governance and management in destinations: manage resources for the development of the tourism sector and redistribute them in a decentralised manner; improve information systems for tourism and handicrafts; promote the academic complementation of the training offerings in tourism; and generate strategic alliances.
- Improve territorial conditions and tourism facilitation: promote intersectoral co-operation with the regions; improve biosafety conditions in tourism service providers; promote fiscal and labour incentives for tourism service providers; and strengthen tourism safety in the destinations in co-ordination with strategic allies.
- Strengthen and promote the supply of tourism products and experiences: promote the capacity of public spending in tourism to close gaps; encourage private investment in tourism; generate direct support measures for entrepreneurs; promote social tourism actions; and promote handicraft development.
- Improve the promotion and positioning of the tourism offer based on quality, sustainability and biosafety attributes: improve the country's positioning as a destination and strengthen the promotion of domestic and inbound tourism.

Statistical Profile

Peru: Domestic, inbound and outbound tourism

	2017	2018	2019	2020	2021
TOURISM FLOWS, THOUSAND					
Domestic tourism					
Total domestic trips	121 067	128 839	134 995	47 070	64 509
Overnight visitors (tourists)	44 382	46 517	48 575	14 370 p	15 562 e
Same-day visitors (excursionists)	76 684	82 322	86 420	32 700 p	48 947 e
Nights in all types of accommodation	261 000	273 000	291 600	43 109 p	62 250 e
Hotels and similar establishments	..	..	..	..	..
Other collective establishments	..	..	..	..	..
Private accommodation	..	..	..	..	..
Inbound tourism[1]					
Total international arrivals	4 993	5 385	5 275	1 119	444
Overnight visitors (tourists)	4 032	4 419	4 372	897	444
Same-day visitors (excursionists)	960	965	903	222	0
Top markets					
United States	599	641	657	128	177
Colombia	201	219	224	49	41
Chile	1 101	1 159	1 196	288	37
Argentina	205	216	215	45	14
Brazil	174	178	194	34	11
Nights in all types of accommodation	40 323	44 194	43 718	..	..
Hotels and similar establishments	14 676	14 302	14 796	3 415	3 573
Other collective establishments	..	..	..	..	..
Private accommodation	..	..	..	..	..
Outbound tourism					
Total international departures	3 227	3 435	3 634	893	617
Overnight visitors (tourists)	2 875	3 078	3 275	791	617
Same-day visitors (excursionists)	352	357	359	102	0
Top destinations					
United States	292	294	325	89	269
Spain	143	160	184	42	70
Colombia	117	135	177	44	38
Chile	1 359	1 373	1 417	334	36
Argentina	100	109	99	24	7
TOURISM RECEIPTS AND EXPENDITURE, MILLION USD					
Inbound tourism					
Total international receipts	4 573	4 505	4 784	794	1 042
International travel receipts	3 710	3 557	3 819	794 e	688
International passenger transport receipts	863	947	965	..	355
Outbound tourism					
Total international expenditure	2 916	3 352	3 671	744	1 521
International travel expenditure	2 214	2 604	2 818	744 e	1 149
International passenger transport expenditure	702	749	853	..	372

.. Not available; e Estimated value; p Provisional data
1. Arrivals from demand side surveys; Nights from supply side surveys.
Source: OECD Tourism Statistics (Database).

StatLink https://stat.link/mk7ycn

Peru: Enterprises and employment in tourism

	Number of establishments	Number of persons employed				
	2021	2017	2018	2019	2020	2021
Total	..	**674 754**	**700 367**	**725 980 e**	**353 552 e**	..
Tourism industries	..	..	..	..	..	..
Accommodation services for visitors	..	..	..	..	..	..
Hotels and similar establishments	25 323	74 360	80 044	81 964 e	40 741 e	..
Food and beverage serving industry	279 299	242 668	236 632	252 152 e	125 284 e	..
Passenger transport	..	..	..	..	..	..
Air passenger transport	..	4 952	4 799	4 982 e	2 443 e	..
Railways passenger transport	..	..	..	..	..	..
Road passenger transport	..	136 845	139 745	143 582 e	71 127 e	..
Water passenger transport	..	702	711	721 e	362 e	..
Passenger transport supporting services	..	..	..	..	..	..
Transport equipment rental	..	..	..	..	..	..
Travel agencies and other reservation services industry	15 898	27 748	28 047	28 781 e	14 420 e	..
Cultural industry	..	22 244	20 373	20 708 e	10 369 e	..
Sports and recreation industry	..	15 207	15 466	15 843 e	7 872 e	..
Retail trade of country-specific tourism characteristic goods	..	..	..	..	..	..
Other country-specific tourism industries	..	50 811	53 744	55 033	27 355	..
Other industries	..	**99 217**	**120 806**	**122 214 e**	**53 579 e**	..

.. Not available; e Estimated value
Source: OECD Tourism Statistics (Database).

StatLink https://stat.link/xulrgk

Peru: Internal tourism consumption

Million PEN

	2020		
	Domestic tourism expenditure	Inbound tourism expenditure	Internal tourism consumption
Total	..	..	..
Consumption products	**11 700**	**3 500**	**17 300**
Tourism characteristic products	..	..	..
Accommodation services for visitors	..	..	..
Food and beverage serving services	..	..	..
Passenger transport services	..	..	..
Air passenger transport services	..	..	..
Railways passenger transport services	..	..	..
Road passenger transport services	..	..	..
Water passenger transport services	..	..	..
Passenger transport supporting services	..	..	..
Transport equipment rental services	..	..	..
Travel agencies and other reservation services industry	..	..	..
Cultural services	..	..	..
Sports and recreation services	..	..	..
Country-specific tourism characteristic goods	..	..	..
Country-specific tourism characteristic services	..	..	..
Other consumption products	..	..	..
Tourism connected products	..	..	..
Non-tourism related consumption products	..	..	..
Non-consumption products	..	..	..

.. Not available
Source: OECD Tourism Statistics (Database).

StatLink https://stat.link/dyxlq0

Romania

Tourism in the economy and outlook for recovery

Tourism is an important sector of the economy of Romania. In 2019, tourism directly contributed RON 31.6 billion to Romania's economy, equating to 3.0% of total GDP. The sector directly supported 412 649 jobs, representing 6.3 % of total employment in Romania. The impacts of the COVID-19 pandemic saw tourism employment fall to 393 427 jobs in 2020, or 6.1% of the workforce.

International arrivals at the border totalled 5.0 million in 2020, a decrease of 61% when compared to 2019. International nights in registered accommodation declined by 81.1% to 1.0 million in 2020. An initial recovery in 2021 saw international nights return to 1.8 million, an increase of 83.7% compared to 2020. However, this remained 65.4% below the 2019 level. Romania's main source markets in 2020 were Germany, Italy, and France based on arrivals in accommodation units.

In 2021, domestic tourism remained a driver of recovery, totalling 19 million nights and 91.2% of total nights in accommodation establishments. After falling 44.4% in 2020, domestic tourists (in all accommodation types) recorded 8.5 million tourists in 2021, 20.2% below pre-pandemic levels.

Tourism governance and funding

The Ministry of Entrepreneurship and Tourism has responsibility for tourism in Romania. The main tourism-related fields of activity include:

- Developing and implementing national and sectoral tourism strategies.
- Promoting Romania as a tourist destination domestically and internationally.
- Developing destinations and tourist products.
- Developing tourism-related infrastructure.
- Authorising and controlling tourism services.
- Representing Romania in international tourism organisations.

The Consultative Council for Tourism includes representatives of the central and local administration, the private sector, academia, associations for different tourism sectors or destinations in Romania, and cultural institutions of national interest. In 2022, Romania established the National Tourist Brand Council, which includes representatives of the public and private sectors, to co-ordinate tourism promotion activities.

The local administrations collaborate with the ministry in implementing tourism policy. At the local level, tourism associations bring together interested parties to contribute to developing tourism in their area. Additionally, 14 territorial representatives of the ministry work with local partners to help implement the national tourism policy.

There are three main budget lines related to tourism: the Programme for Tourist Products Development, the Programme for Tourist Marketing and Promotion and transfers from the central budget to the local budget for tourism investments (part of the Programme for Tourist Products Development). Additional funds may be allocated to tourism, as was the case with the state aid scheme for the enterprises affected by the COVID-19 pandemic. The total tourism budget increased over the period 2020-22, from RON 11.6 million to RON 117.5 million.

Romania: Organisational chart of tourism bodies

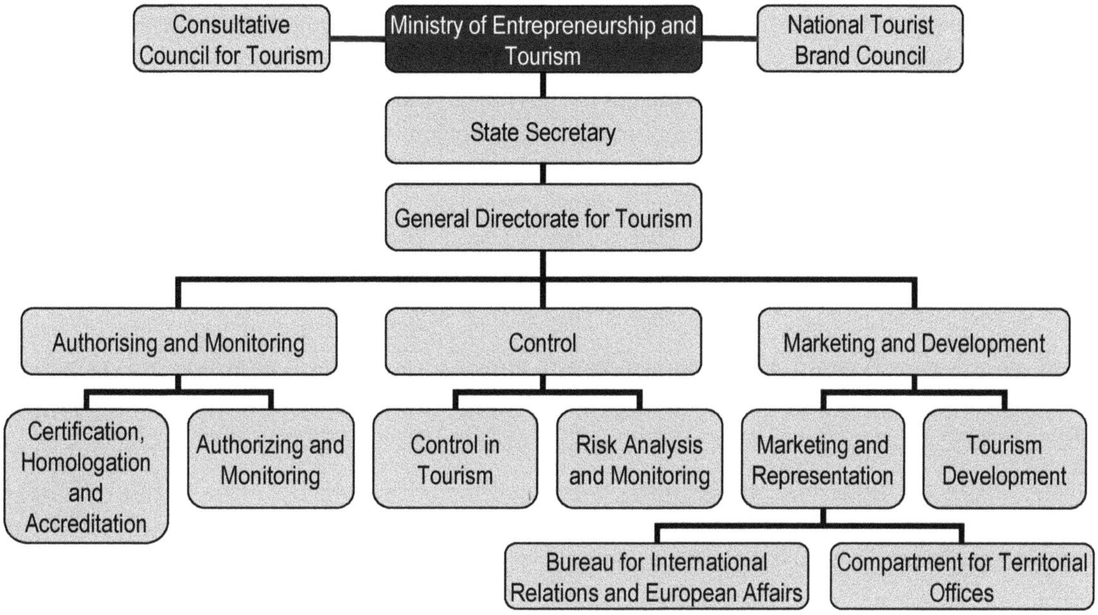

Note: The chart shows only the tourism section of the Ministry of Entrepreneurship and Tourism.
Source: OECD, adapted Ministry of Entrepreneurship and Tourism, 2022.

Tourism policies and programmes

To support tourism enterprises affected by the COVID-19 pandemic, Romania implemented a state aid scheme for accommodation and food services businesses, travel agencies, travel guides and event organisers. The state aid was given in the form of grants of 20% of the turnover difference resulting from the eligible activities in 2019 compared to 2020, limited to RON 4 million (EUR 800 000) at the enterprise level. Romania also extended the validity of travel vouchers issued before or during the pandemic. Both public and private sector employees can benefit from the travel vouchers.

Romania's National Recovery and Resilience Plan (NRRP) includes a chapter related to Tourism and Culture. The tourism chapter refers to developing Destination Management Organisations, creating and promoting 12 cultural-touristic routes, creating and upgrading nine museums and memorials, and developing cycling tourism.

The National Tourism Development Strategy was developed with the support of the World Bank and is built upon previous related documents, such as the National Tourism Development Master Plan for Romania 2007-26, which was developed in collaboration with the UNWTO.

There are also two sectoral strategies:

- The National Strategy for Ecotourism Development 2019-29, which has the general objective of creating the conditions for ecotourism development in natural protected areas. It aims to develop a network of certified ecotourism destinations and create competitive ecotourism products for both national and international markets. Based on the National Strategy for Ecotourism Development, the Ministry, together with other institutions and organisations from Romania, such as the Ministry of Environment, Waters and Forests, the National Institute for Research and Development in Tourism and the Ecotourism Association of Romania, developed a system for evaluating ecotourism destinations in Romania. The system is based on the Global Criteria for Sustainable Tourism (GSTC) and the European Ecotourism Standard (EETLS). So far, five tourism destinations have received this recognition, and two others are under evaluation.

- The Strategy for the Development of Spa Tourism - 2019. The strategy is based on implementing an innovative approach combining public-private partnerships to support the development of a wide variety of health tourism-related products. It aims to provide a new and innovative green and spa tourism product.

The Ministry of Entrepreneurship and Tourism runs a programme for financial support to local public administration authorities to finance investment projects in tourism infrastructure. The programme is carried out based on the Master Plan for Tourism Investments.

Recognising cultural tourism routes in Romania

In 2020, Romania's national tourism administration initiated a programme related to the recognition of cultural-touristic routes in Romania, taking into consideration the experience and knowledge gained as a member of the Enlarged Partial Agreement on Cultural Routes of the Council of Europe.

As of 2022, 116 cultural-touristic routes have been recognised, of which 27 are at the national level, 53 are at the regional level, and 36 are at the local level. Additionally, Romania has eight cultural routes in the Council of Europe network and four transnational routes.

The objectives of this programme are the following:

- Highlight rich cultural assets.
- Increase the capacity for accessing funding for developing and promoting cultural assets.
- Include cultural routes as part of the travel trade's offer.
- Develop tourism and stimulate local economic and social development.
- Increase collaboration between the counties in Romania.
- Promote the sustainable development of localities crossed by the routes.
- Increase tourist flows to and into throughout Romania.
- Promote the tangible and intangible heritage of Romania to international markets.
- Promote destinations by organising events with national and international participation.
- Develop collaboration between enterprises that are part of cultural tourism routes.

Statistical Profile

Romania: Domestic, inbound and outbound tourism

	2017	2018	2019	2020	2021
TOURISM FLOWS, THOUSAND					
Domestic tourism					
Total domestic trips	9 383	10 109	10 691	5 945	8 527
Overnight visitors (tourists)	9 383	10 109	10 691	5 945	8 527
Same-day visitors (excursionists)	..	..	..	..	..
Nights in all types of accommodation	21 801	23 315	24 795	13 582	19 003
Hotels and similar establishments	15 584	16 543	17 446	9 224	13 276
Other collective establishments	6 217	6 772	7 349	4 357	5 727
Private accommodation	..	..	..	..	..
Inbound tourism					
Total international arrivals	2 760	2 797	2 684	453	841
Overnight visitors (tourists)	2 760	2 797	2 684	453	841
Same-day visitors (excursionists)	..	..	..	..	..
Top markets					
Germany	325	327	298	57	106
Italy	242	241	223	40	73
France	168	172	155	30	55
Israel	293	278	235	29	50
United States	157	166	162	22	45
Nights in all types of accommodation	5 291	5 330	5 291	997	1 833
Hotels and similar establishments	4 538	4 560	4 544	888	1 626
Other collective establishments	753	769	747	109	207
Private accommodation	..	..	..	..	..
Outbound tourism					
Total international departures	10 446	10 469	13 651	4 267	8 237
Overnight visitors (tourists)	10 354	10 361	13 515	4 237	8 182
Same-day visitors (excursionists)	92	108	136	30	55
Top destinations					
Bulgaria	139	164	209	106	194
Türkiye	140	197	315	68	193
Egypt	..	..	43	16	148
Greece	163	161	130	46	75
Italy	52	69	44	..	13
TOURISM RECEIPTS AND EXPENDITURE, MILLION USD					
Inbound tourism					
Total international receipts	3 530	3 887	4 246	1 608	..
International travel receipts	3 058	3 396	3 578	1 431	..
International passenger transport receipts	472 e	491 e	668 e	178 e	..
Outbound tourism					
Total international expenditure	4 927	6 121	7 178	3 475	..
International travel expenditure	4 349	5 339	6 001	3 026	..
International passenger transport expenditure	578	782 e	1 177 e	449 e	..

.. Not available; e Estimated value
Source: OECD Tourism Statistics (Database).

StatLink https://stat.link/k3jlm8

Romania: Enterprises and employment in tourism

	Number of establishments[1]	Number of persons employed[2]				
	2019	2017	2018	2019	2020	2021
Total	..	..	..	..	..	..
Tourism industries	**48 747**	**403 532**	**409 881**	**412 649**	**393 427**	..
Accommodation services for visitors	7 976	45 360	43 686	40 910	40 849	..
Hotels and similar establishments	7 976	39 294	36 954	35 511	36 947	..
Food and beverage serving industry	17 012	141 695	156 669	163 335	146 888	..
Passenger transport	11 354	156 002	152 623	146 191	143 973	..
Air passenger transport	68	5 896	6 626	6 884	5 208	..
Railways passenger transport	43	31 594	35 010	30 649	31 185	..
Road passenger transport	11 146	115 397	108 754	104 650	102 069	..
Water passenger transport	97	3 115	2 233	4 008	5 511	..
Passenger transport supporting services	..	..	..	..	..	..
Transport equipment rental	679	402	914	1 078	2 607	..
Travel agencies and other reservation services industry	2 198	15 797	11 993	13 718	12 570	..
Cultural industry	1 222	20 219	18 961	15 714	13 968	..
Sports and recreation industry	5 016	24 057	25 035	31 703	32 572	..
Retail trade of country-specific tourism characteristic goods	3 290	..	..	..	..	..
Other country-specific tourism industries	..	..	..	..	..	..
Other industries	..	..	..	..	..	..

.. Not available
1. Data refer to number of enterprises.
2. Data refer to number of employees.
Source: OECD Tourism Statistics (Database).

StatLink https://stat.link/dxsut4

Romania: Internal tourism consumption

Million RON

	2019		
	Domestic tourism expenditure	Inbound tourism expenditure	Internal tourism consumption
Total	..	..	..
Consumption products	**8 186**	**49 352**	**57 787**
Tourism characteristic products	7 641	42 951	50 809
Accommodation services for visitors	3 381	10 155	13 704
Food and beverage serving services	2 306	15 559	17 915
Passenger transport services	523	9 854	10 377
Air passenger transport services	44	3 706	3 750
Railways passenger transport services	24	531	556
Road passenger transport services	438	5 581	6 020
Water passenger transport services	16	36	52
Passenger transport supporting services	..	..	..
Transport equipment rental services	203	83	286
Travel agencies and other reservation services industry	..	4 946	4 946
Cultural services	310	485	795
Sports and recreation services	297	784	1 081
Country-specific tourism characteristic goods	482	..	482
Country-specific tourism characteristic services	140	1 084	1 224
Other consumption products	544	6 401	6 977
Tourism connected products	..	..	..
Non-tourism related consumption products	..	..	..
Non-consumption products	..	..	..

.. Not available
Source: OECD Tourism Statistics (Database).

StatLink https://stat.link/whkdj0

Saudi Arabia

Tourism in the economy and outlook for recovery

Tourism is one of Saudi Arabia's fastest-growing sectors. It is a significant contributor to the national economy and is a key source of jobs. In 2019, tourism directly contributed to 3.8% of GDP, supported 571 152 jobs (5.1% of total employment) and generated nearly SAR 165 billion in tourism spending. Following the pandemic in 2020, tourism's direct GDP fell 61%, with tourism's direct contribution to GDP falling to 1.7%.

International tourism arrivals in Saudi Arabia plunged by 76.4% to 4.1 million in 2020 and declined an additional 16.0% in 2021 to 3.5 million. International tourism receipts fell by 80.6% to SAR 21.1 billion in 2020 and decreased a further 26.8% in 2021 (85.8% down from 2019).

Domestic tourism showed a gradual and faster recovery, with 42.1 million domestic overnight visitors recorded in 2020 (down 11.9% from 2019). Domestic tourists in 2021 hit a record high of 63.8 million, up 34% compared to 2019. Similarly, domestic tourism receipts recorded a new high of SAR 80.9 billion, exceeding 2019 by 32%. Overall, domestic tourism spending contributed to 84.6% of total tourism receipts.

Saudi Arabia's outlook remains positive in terms of long-term prospects. By 2030, Saudi Arabia targets annually 100 million tourist visits, 10% direct contribution to GDP, and 1 million additional tourism jobs.

Tourism governance and funding

Saudi Arabia's tourism policy is centred around the Ministry of Tourism, which focuses on strategy, regulations, destination development, human capital development, and investment attraction. It is supported by the Saudi Tourism Authority (STA), which is in charge of branding, marketing and promotional efforts with the different travel agencies and tour operators. The Tourism Development Fund is in charge of funding iconic projects and supporting the private sector to develop offerings and accommodations.

The tourism policy ecosystem works closely with all the relevant government entities (Ministry of Foreign Affairs, Ministry of Interior, Ministry of Transport, Ministry of Electricity, Water and Agriculture) through a government body called the Tourism Development Committee, where major cross-governmental initiatives are discussed and monitored. Governance has also been put in place to manage the development of the tourism sector through the Regional Tourism Development Committee, which gathers provincial administration, regional development entities, the different entities in charge of developing sites and destinations, and professional associations.

During COVID-19, efforts and policies have been focused on promoting domestic tourism while continuing to develop the offering, regulations, and policies to welcome inbound tourism after the pandemic. In terms of funding, Saudi Arabia plans to invest more than SAR 3 trillion in the tourism sector over the next ten years. This will take shape through investments in every aspect of tourism.

Saudi Arabia: Organisational chart of tourism bodies

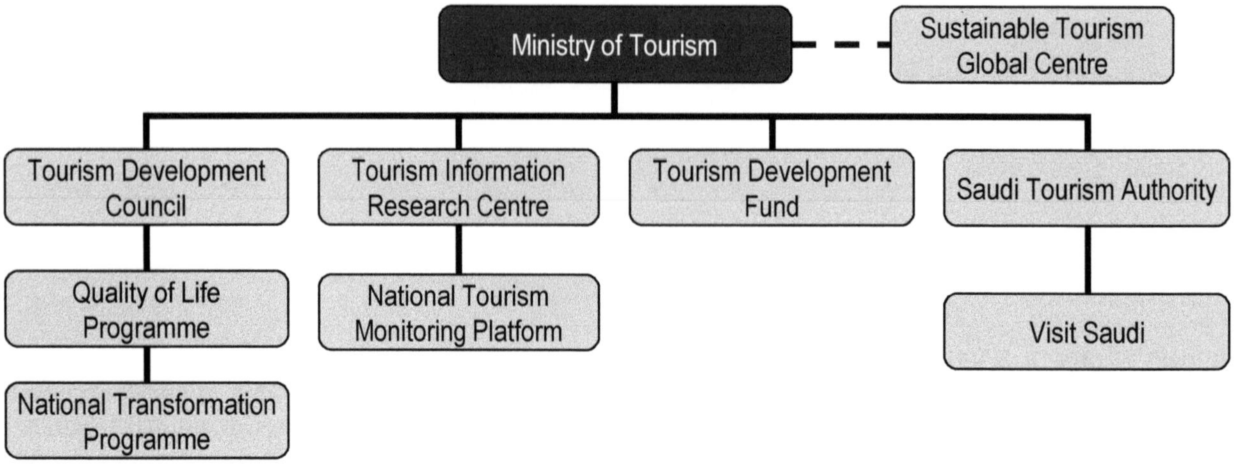

Source: OECD, adapted from Ministry of Tourism, 2022.

Tourism policies and programmes

The National Tourism Strategy aims to leverage the opportunities of Saudi Arabia's Vision 2030, which focuses on creating a vibrant society, thriving economy, and an ambitious nation. Reforms under Vision 2030 have played a key role in helping the national economy navigate the pandemic.

The Ministry of Tourism's main policy priorities include maximising tourism's contribution to GDP, creating jobs, improving tourism infrastructure and competitiveness, transforming tourism to be a more resilient and sustainable sector, and attracting investment to the sector.

In 2021, Saudi Arabia announced the Sustainable Tourism Global Centre, a multi-country, multi-stakeholder coalition established to lead, accelerate, and track the tourism industry's transition to net-zero emissions, as well as driving actions to protect nature, climate, and communities.

Sustainability policies are issued to support sustainability and tackle climate change in the sector. Initiatives on this topic will be led by the Saudi Green Initiative, the new Sustainable Tourism Global Centre, tourism destination management organisations and the Ministry of Environment, Water and Agriculture.

As for the recovery from COVID-19, Saudi Arabia's COVID-19 policy responses were aimed at ensuring the survival of businesses in stage one and a faster recovery to sustainable growth in stage two. The government closely observed and calibrated its response against a set of key indicators and aspects that stimulated and catered to the needs of MSMEs, and the tourism sector (see box below).

In 2020, Saudi Arabia announced the creation of a Tourism Development Fund with an initial capital of approximately SAR 15 billion. Additionally, Saudi Arabia exempted companies operating in the tourism sector from issuance/renewal license fees.

Since the pandemic, Saudi Arabia has launched several initiatives surrounding skills and employment:

- A new human capital development (AHLHA) strategy, launched in 2020, which aims to develop the tourism sector by attracting more Saudi nationals to the sector. Several local efforts have followed to support those ambitions.
- The Tourism Shapers programme, launched in 2021 by STA, is an employment initiative that aims to equip the local private sector with the support needed to navigate and manage the evolving tourism landscape.

- The Ministry of Tourism launched the "Tourism Pioneers" programme, which aims to develop the capabilities of 100 000 young people and provide them with key skills in the field of hospitality, tourism and travel to prepare them to work in the tourism sector. The programme includes investments worth over USD 100 million.

Saudi Arabia has also launched several initiatives around innovation and entrepreneurship:

- The Tourism Entrepreneurs Bootcamp was launched in 2021, with the aim to transform innovative ideas into sustainable businesses via an intensive programme for entrepreneurs. The Bootcamp received over 3 000 applicants across 15 cities, of which 30 were ultimately nominated to take part in the final round to obtain funding.
- The Ministry also launched the Tourism Entrepreneurship Accelerator in 2021 to support select start-ups in the tourism space in scaling up their business and expanding service offerings. The Accelerator programme received over 1 200 tourism start-up applications, of which 15 were selected to enter the six-month programme. Throughout this programme, the Ministry of Tourism provided benefits and services totalling over SAR 1 million, alongside 180 hours of workshops and 1 300 hours of one-to-one mentoring.
- In 2022, the Mustasharik programme (also known as Mix & Mentor programme) was launched following feedback from the Saudi tourism entrepreneurship community, aimed at providing mentorship and workshop sessions for entrepreneurs across the start-up lifecycle from ideation to scale-ups.

Support measures for tourism SMEs in Saudi Arabia

Tourism SMEs, which represent 99.8% of all tourism businesses in Saudi Arabia, were hit the hardest by the COVID-19 pandemic and faced several challenges to their continued development, such as lack of access to finance, market uncertainty, competition from major international players, and low research and development. To address these challenges, Saudi Arabia's policy responses were initially aimed at ensuring the survival of businesses, followed by a focus on fostering a faster recovery to sustainable growth. Policy measures broadly involved:

- Fiscal policies: including a stimulus package, exemption from issuance and renewal license fees for companies operating in the tourism sector, a delay in loan payments, a loan guarantee programme, and supporting employee wages.
- Employment related measures: including providing unemployment insurance, introducing supportive labour market regulations, providing training and supporting job matching.
- Social measures: including launching an indirect lending initiative for SMEs, providing investment for sustainability focused SMEs, starting a venture capital fund initiative for SMEs, refunding fees paid by SMEs, and providing packages for institutional quarantine in hotels for visitors.

Preliminary impact assessments have showed positive results. Employment in tourism SMEs was largely preserved, with only a low number of establishments going out of business.

Saudi Arabia: Domestic, inbound and outbound tourism

	2017	2018	2019	2020	2021
TOURISM FLOWS, THOUSAND					
Domestic tourism					
Total domestic trips	46 910	46 512	53 074	48 399	72 930
Overnight visitors (tourists)	43 821	43 255	47 805	42 107	63 845
Same-day visitors (excursionists)	3 089	3 256	5 269	6 292	9 085
Nights in all types of accommodation	224 212	232 122	268 751	228 538	384 043
Hotels and similar establishments	130 971	140 452	155 540	121 909	204 646
Other collective establishments	11 982	9 034	7 874	4 900	9 359
Private accommodation	81 259	82 637	105 337	101 730	170 039
Inbound tourism					
Total international arrivals	18 607	17 570	20 292	4 882	3 869
Overnight visitors (tourists)	16 109	15 334	17 526	4 138	3 477
Same-day visitors (excursionists)	2 498	2 236	2 767	744	392
Top markets					
Kuwait	..	..	..	..	..
India	..	..	..	..	..
Pakistan	..	..	..	..	..
Qatar	..	..	..	..	..
Egypt	..	..	..	..	..
Nights in all types of accommodation	171 036	173 929	189 036	37 824	31 771
Hotels and similar establishments	146 118	153 005	164 526	30 447	16 081
Other collective establishments	482	5 298	1 011	119	210
Private accommodation	24 435	15 626	23 499	7 258	15 480
Outbound tourism					
Total international departures	28 748	27 425	27 196	6 657	10 678
Overnight visitors (tourists)	21 146	19 751	19 010	4 839	8 415
Same-day visitors (excursionists)	7 602	7 674	8 186	1 819	2 263
Top destinations					
..	..	..	..	..	..
..	..	..	..	..	..
..	..	..	..	..	..
..	..	..	..	..	..
..	..	..	..	..	..
TOURISM RECEIPTS AND EXPENDITURE, MILLION USD					
Inbound tourism					
Total international receipts	15 020	16 975	19 849	5 960	..
International travel receipts	12 056	13 790	16 431	4 036	3 977
International passenger transport receipts	2 964	3 184	3 418	1 924	804
Outbound tourism					
Total international expenditure	19 065	17 940	16 414	9 069	..
International travel expenditure	17 552	16 651	15 140	8 533	14 489
International passenger transport expenditure	1 513	1 288	1 275	536	2 008

.. Not available
Source: OECD Tourism Statistics (Database).

StatLink https://stat.link/ex71tf

Saudi Arabia: Enterprises and employment in tourism

	Number of establishments[1]	Number of persons employed				
	2021	2017	2018	2019	2020	2021
Total	**101 980 p**	**535 941**	**552 556**	**571 152**	**679 539**	**762 957 p**
Tourism industries	**101 980 p**	**535 941**	**552 556**	**571 152**	**679 539**	**762 957 p**
Accommodation services for visitors	10 346 p	114 957	118 941	124 676	93 720	98 492 p
Hotels and similar establishments	10 346 p	114 957	118 941	124 676	93 720	98 492 p
Food and beverage serving industry	74 337 p	289 491	298 487	306 508	451 999	520 643 p
Passenger transport	2 913 p	67 782	69 855	72 441	49 597	45 282 p
Air passenger transport	109 p	27 136	28 232	29 547	20 439	20 106 p
Railways passenger transport	2 p	1 593	1 655	1 716	2 297	282 p
Road passenger transport	2 682 p	38 771	39 669	40 860	26 066	23 823 p
Water passenger transport	120 p	282	299	319	795	1 071 p
Passenger transport supporting services	..	..	..	..	..	..
Transport equipment rental	859 p	20 493	21 084	21 868	12 003	13 447 p
Travel agencies and other reservation services industry	1 565 p	25 140	25 560	26 327	14 471	15 771 p
Cultural industry	337 p	2 192	2 256	2 339	5 114	4 710 p
Sports and recreation industry	1 086 p	12 966	13 359	13 843	8 247	10 046 p
Retail trade of country-specific tourism characteristic goods	9 002 p	..	..	..	..	42 424 p
Other country-specific tourism industries	1 535 p	2 920	3 014	3 150	7 334	12 142 p
Other industries	**0**	**..**	**..**	**..**	**0**	**0**

.. Not available; p Provisional data
1. Data refer to number of enterprises.
Source: OECD Tourism Statistics (Database).

StatLink https://stat.link/8unxar

Saudi Arabia: Internal tourism consumption

Million SAR

	2020		
	Domestic tourism expenditure	Inbound tourism expenditure	Internal tourism consumption
Total	**48 493**	**25 354**	**77 473**
Consumption products	**35 714**	**18 397**	**54 111**
Tourism characteristic products	35 714	18 397	54 111
Accommodation services for visitors	9 846	8 443	18 290
Food and beverage serving services	11 376	3 182	14 558
Passenger transport services	7 942	4 270	12 212
Air passenger transport services	5 653	3 026	8 679
Railways passenger transport services	213	43	257
Road passenger transport services	1 968	1 201	3 169
Water passenger transport services	107	0	107
Passenger transport supporting services	..	..	..
Transport equipment rental services	2 348	173	2 521
Travel agencies and other reservation services industry	357	1 954	2 311
Cultural services	1 538	113	1 650
Sports and recreation services	2 306	263	2 569
Country-specific tourism characteristic goods	..	..	..
Country-specific tourism characteristic services	..	..	..
Other consumption products	12 779	6 957	23 362
Tourism connected products	..	..	..
Non-tourism related consumption products	..	..	..
Non-consumption products	**..**	**..**	**..**

.. Not available
Source: OECD Tourism Statistics (Database).

StatLink https://stat.link/eih3tb

Serbia

Tourism in the economy and outlook for recovery

Tourism is an important source of employment in Serbia. In 2019, tourism provided 4.2% of total employment or 85 092 direct jobs. This remained steady at 4.3% of employment in 2021, with the number of jobs increasing to 99 216 jobs.

In 2021, international arrivals increased 95.5% compared to 2020 and hit 871 000, however, this remained 52.8% below pre-pandemic levels. The top source markets in 2021 were Bosnia and Herzegovina (11.8%), Montenegro (6.7%), Türkiye (5.6%), and Croatia (4.5%).

Domestic tourism has performed stronger. After domestic tourists declined 25.4% in 2020 to 1.4 million, they returned to 1.7 million tourists in 2021, just 6.7% below 2019 levels. Domestic nights in hotels remained just 12% lower than in 2019 at 4.3 million nights.

Serbia is expecting a return of inbound tourism to pre-pandemic levels by 2025.

Tourism governance and funding

The Ministry of Trade, Tourism, and Telecommunications is responsible for tourism affairs, dealing with all aspects of tourism strategy, policy, promotion, and development. The Ministry provides direct and indirect support to regional and local authorities, including incentive programmes for tourism development projects (such as infrastructure, promotion, education, and training) and supporting local government and regional development agencies with jointly funded projects.

The Ministry co-operates closely with other ministries, particularly the Ministry of Culture and Information (on international bilateral co-operation and the development of cultural routes), the Ministry of Agriculture, Forestry and Water Management (on the development of rural tourism and the support instruments in the field of rural development), the Ministry of Environment (on tourist zoning) and the Ministry of Health (on medical tourism development, safe travel protocols and measures against COVID-19). The Ministry works closely with the private sector and is active in regional initiatives and international organisations on related programmes and projects.

The total budget for tourism in Serbia is RSD 8 billion. The share of tourism in the total 2021 national budget is 0.36% - more than double the share of the 2020 budget.

Serbia: Organisational chart of tourism bodies

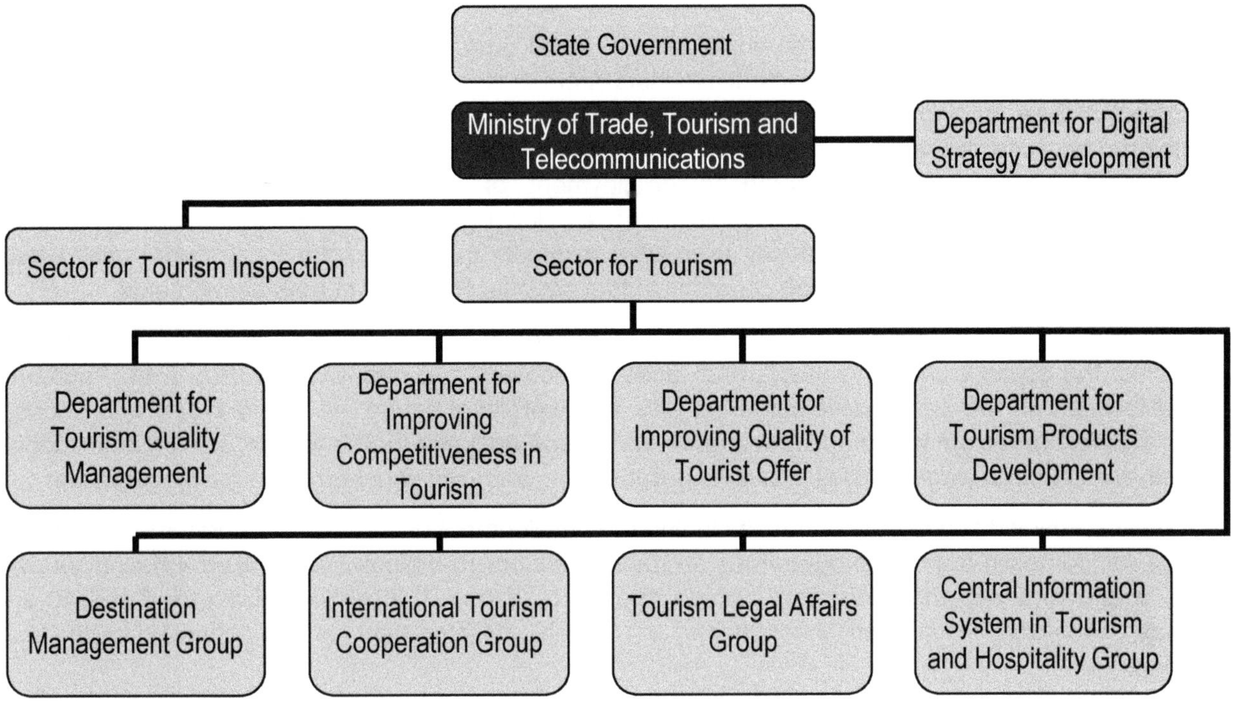

Source: OECD, adapted from Ministry of Trade, Tourism and Telecommunications, 2022.

Tourism policies and programmes

During the pandemic, Serbia put the following support measures in place through a specific programme for the tourism and hospitality sectors, with funding of RSD 5.4 billion:

- Payment of the minimum wage to employees in the fields of hospitality and tourism.
- Subsidies to support the work of tourist guides, tour escorts and the hotel sector.
- Support for night bars and nightclubs as well as travel agencies and tour operators.

Serbia has a Tourism Development Strategy for the period 2016-25. The Strategy is implemented through a mixture of strategic master plans, a Strategic Marketing Plan, a Product Development Programme, and spatial and urban plans. The Tourism Development Strategy also establishes a competitive arena for the business sector in Serbian tourism. The National Tourism Development Strategy is being revised due to the changed situation in the market in the post-COVID-19 era.

Beyond the National Development strategy, Serbia is implementing the following strategies and programmes for tourism:

- A programme for allocating and using subsidies, transfers, and grants for tourism development projects.
- Legislation on approving and using credit funds to encourage a high-quality tourist offer.
- Legislation on allocating funds to encourage the improvement of domestic tourism.
- Continued support for the tourism and hospitality sectors as the COVID-19 pandemic evolves.

A Central Information System (CIS/e-tourist) was recently introduced as a unique and centralised information system that combines data on all accommodation providers and facilities (see box below). The digitalisation of the tourism offer in Serbia was recently started and is expected to be completed in May 2023.

Lessons from the pandemic include the importance of developing tourism in smaller rural areas, not only in large cities. During the pandemic, domestic tourists spent their summer holidays in rural areas engaging in outdoor activities, leading to an increase in tourism-related businesses to accommodate the new visitors, provide food services and rent private rooms, houses, and apartments for people working from home. This had positive impacts, including increased employment of women in rural areas, encouraged entrepreneurship, and boosted tourism employment (e.g. local guides, national park rangers, and food suppliers). It also revealed the necessity to involve residents in creating the local tourist offer where possible. This creates an attractive and competitive tourism offer for different market segments.

Serbia has co-ordinated existing regulations, legal frameworks, standards, and protocols to ensure that they reflect the sector's changing needs and facilitate recovery and post-COVID-19 growth. Pandemic support focused on two areas: developing the safe travel protocol (using the World Travel and Tourism Council's Safe Travels standard) and creating a new support package for the tourism sector. This support was delivered through wage subsidies, business subsidies, domestic vouchers, and business grants.

The ministry provided support measures, including the development of a voucher programme for catering services for domestic tourists; programmes for tour operators to welcome organised inbound tourism groups; improvement of the investment climate through a system of incentives (both for domestic and overseas investors) to support investments in tourism development in co-ordination with local governments.

Serbia also finances projects for promotion, education, and training to support the improvement of tourism facilities, with co-financing of up to 100% for capital projects and 50% for promotion.

Development of a Central Information System for Tourism in Serbia

Serbia has introduced the Central Information System (CIS/e-Tourist), a database that generates the number of tourist arrivals and overnight stays according to accommodation capacities and destinations in Serbia. Through this portal, all accommodation providers are registered when categorising their facilities.

The digitisation of Serbia's tourism offer is in progress and will partly be connected to the e-Tourist platform. Serbia recognises the need to implement the green and digital agendas, including, in co-operation with the Western Balkans, the implementation of e-government, e-procurement, and e-health, the introduction of more affordable, roaming-free mobile charge rates for Western Balkan countries, and increased cybersecurity, trust, and digitalisation across the sector. Through joint projects, Serbia aims for positive employment rates, entrepreneurship growth, and innovative solutions to respond to future challenges.

Statistical Profile

Serbia: Domestic, inbound and outbound tourism

	2017	2018	2019	2020	2021
TOURISM FLOWS, THOUSAND					
Domestic tourism					
Total domestic trips	1 589	1 720	1 843	1 374	1 720
Overnight visitors (tourists)	1 589	1 720	1 843	1 374	1 720
Same-day visitors (excursionists)	..	..	..	..	..
Nights in all types of accommodation	5 150	5 678	6 063	4 937	5 733
Hotels and similar establishments	4 384	4 624	4 916	3 572	4 327
Other collective establishments	31	48	35	18	21
Private accommodation	735	1 006	1 112	1 347	1 385
Inbound tourism					
Total international arrivals	1 497	1 711	1 847	446	871
Overnight visitors (tourists)	1 497	1 711	1 847	446	871
Same-day visitors (excursionists)	..	..	..	..	..
Top markets					
Bosnia and Herzegovina	108	121	136	51	103
Montenegro	79	82	90	26	59
Türkiye	100	97	108	25	49
Croatia	83	94	104	27	39
China (People's Republic of)	52	102	145	18	16
Nights in all types of accommodation	3 175	3 658	4 010	1 265	2 430
Hotels and similar establishments	2 992	3 416	3 761	1 201	2 290
Other collective establishments	20	24	20	1	9
Private accommodation	163	218	229	63	131
Outbound tourism					
Total international departures	..	..	..	..	..
Overnight visitors (tourists)	..	..	..	..	..
Same-day visitors (excursionists)	..	..	..	..	..
Top destinations					
..	..	..	..	..	..
..	..	..	..	..	..
..	..	..	..	..	..
..	..	..	..	..	..
..	..	..	..	..	..
TOURISM RECEIPTS AND EXPENDITURE, MILLION USD					
Inbound tourism					
Total international receipts	1 706	1 941	2 001	1 421	..
International travel receipts	1 345	1 547	1 604	1 245	..
International passenger transport receipts	361	394	396	177	..
Outbound tourism					
Total international expenditure	1 549	1 837	1 999	1 178	..
International travel expenditure	1 381	1 643	1 806	1 115	..
International passenger transport expenditure	168	194	194	64	..

.. Not available
Source: OECD Tourism Statistics (Database).

StatLink https://stat.link/4olbg8

Serbia: Enterprises and employment in tourism

	Number of establishments[1]	Number of persons employed				
	2021	2017	2018	2019	2020	2021
Total	..	..	..	..	..	..
Tourism industries	**31 249**	**74 981**	**81 411**	**85 092**	**87 767**	**99 216 p**
Accommodation services for visitors	2 525	14 194	15 374	16 348	17 151	17 478 p
Hotels and similar establishments	1 269	10 088	11 133	11 743	12 216	12 240 p
Food and beverage serving industry	27 548 e	56 176	61 348	63 961	66 159	69 498 p
Passenger transport	..	..	..	..	..	..
Air passenger transport	..	..	..	..	..	..
Railways passenger transport	..	..	..	..	..	..
Road passenger transport	..	..	..	..	..	..
Water passenger transport	..	..	..	..	..	..
Passenger transport supporting services	..	..	..	..	..	..
Transport equipment rental	..	..	..	..	..	..
Travel agencies and other reservation services industry	1 176	4 611	4 689	4 783	4 457	3 489 p
Cultural industry	..	..	..	..	..	..
Sports and recreation industry	..	..	..	..	..	..
Retail trade of country-specific tourism characteristic goods	..	..	..	..	..	..
Other country-specific tourism industries	..	..	..	..	..	..
Other industries	..	..	..	..	..	..

.. Not available; e Estimated value; p Provisional data
1. Data refer to number of enterprises.
Source: OECD Tourism Statistics (Database).

StatLink https://stat.link/9u74vr

South Africa

Tourism in the economy and outlook for recovery

In 2019, the tourism sector's direct contribution to South Africa's GDP was ZAR 209 billion, representing 3.7% of GDP. A total of 773 532 direct jobs were sustained, representing 4.7% of total employment. The direct contribution of tourism to employment declined to 509 000 employees in 2020, 3.4% of total employment and a decrease of 35% from 2019. The sector's contribution to GDP decreased to 1.1%.

In 2020 the number of international tourists fell to 2.8 million, a decrease of 72.6%. International arrivals declined further in 2021 to 2.3 million, impacted by the discovery of the Omicron variant of COVID-19, which subdued demand. International tourism expenditure amounted to ZAR 20.8 billion in 2021, 74.4% below 2019 revenue. The African continent is South Africa's main source of tourist arrivals, contributing 76% of total international arrivals in 2020. Europe is the main overseas source market.

Domestic tourism in South Africa remained significantly impacted in 2021. Domestic tourists were 47.9% below 2019 levels at 14.8 million, with same-day visitors more heavily impacted, with 68.8 million visitors in 2021, 70.9% below 2019.

South Africa sees a stronger recovery in 2022. A full recovery to pre-pandemic levels is projected for 2024.

Tourism governance and funding

Tourism is a concurrent function in South Africa's Constitution, meaning that all three levels of government (national, provincial and local) have jurisdiction and direct responsibility. The Minister of Tourism oversees both South African Tourism (the national tourism organisation) and the Department of Tourism which is responsible for promoting the inclusive growth of tourism through research, policy, destination development, international relations and sector support services.

The Department of Tourism co-ordinates the activities of public and private sector stakeholders through the implementation of the National Tourism Sector Strategy. A multi-stakeholder sector forum, the National Tourism Stakeholder Forum (NTSF), is regularly convened and chaired by the Director-General among the main co-ordination structures.

Horizontal co-ordination is pursued through bilateral engagement and co-operation with key ministries on areas including visa policy, air connectivity and licensing. Vertical co-ordination is conducted through a model of strategy implementation outlined in the National Tourism Sector Strategy (NTSS). The model identifies local, provincial and national structures for co-ordination, joint planning and reporting involving the private and public sectors. Workstreams to allow vertically co-ordinated action with respect to the Strategy's focus areas continue to operate with the integration of emerging issues from the COVID-19 pandemic and the Tourism Sector Recovery Plan.

South Africa has collaboration arrangements in place with ministries responsible for areas such as immigration and transport. These ministries are participants in implementing the NTSS, with further interaction on a case-by-case basis. For example, the Ministry of Environmental Affairs is a key partner in developing and implementing programmes focusing on responsible and sustainable tourism.

The national budget was ZAR 2.4 billion for the 2021/22 financial year, of which ZAR 1.3 billion was transferred to the national destination marketing authority, South African Tourism. The 2020/21 allocation was revised downwards in the first half of the fiscal year to fund COVID-19 responses and is therefore an anomaly. The national budget for the year 2019/20 was ZAR 2.3 billion.

South Africa: Organisational chart of tourism bodies

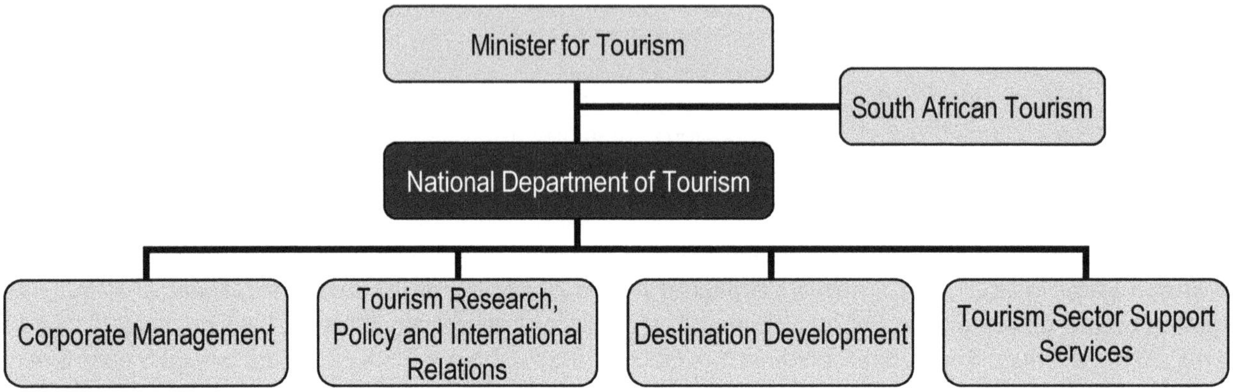

Source: OECD, adapted from the Department of Tourism, 2022.

Tourism policies and programmes

South Africa's policy ecosystem for tourism includes the White Paper on the Development and Promotion of Tourism (1996), currently under redesign (see box below), the Tourism Act (2014), the National Tourism Sector Strategy (NTSS, a ten-year strategy to 2026), and the Tourism Sector Recovery Plan (2020). These constitute a framework guiding tourism development and growth promotion in the country.

South Africa implemented a variety of measures to support the economy during the initial restrictions related to COVID-19, including The Tourism Relief Fund targeting small enterprises through which some 4 000 entities benefited. The Temporary Employee Relief Scheme supported workers by paying wages directly to employees to enable businesses to avoid laying off their workforce.

The country's economic recovery plan prioritises tourism recovery as one of the key inputs into the overall economic recovery. Among others, it is critical to recover tourism jobs to contribute to easing the challenge of unemployment in the country. Priorities include enhanced demand stimulation, the protection of supply and regaining adequate aviation capacity to support demand. Norms and standards were developed and implemented to enable safe operations throughout the tourism value chain and cultivate confidence within the market regarding the health-related safety protocols in place.

South Africa developed a Tourism Sector Recovery Plan to systematically respond to the effects of the pandemic and facilitate joint collaboration with the sector and key actors. The Plan aims to deliver a comprehensive set of actions for the sector and its partners to support and enable recovery. Implementation has a government-wide mandate and is monitored at the Cabinet level.

The Plan identifies three pillars as drivers of recovery:

1. Protecting and rejuvenating supply (including supporting the protection of core tourism infrastructure and assets): interventions include developing and implementing standards for safe

operations across the tourism value chain and increased consumer confidence, and a Tourism Infrastructure Maintenance in National Parks programme.

2. Reigniting demand: this pillar includes launching a global brand campaign to reposition South Africa as a domestic and international tourism destination in the post-COVID era. The campaign comprises leisure, business events, lifestyle and cultural tourism across domestic, regional and international markets and is positioned to drive tourism growth over the next five to ten years.
3. Strengthening enabling capability: interventions included an incubator programme to increase the resilience of SMEs during the pandemic and beyond.

Key factors that have emerged due to the pandemic include the need for accelerated economic digital transformation and promoting enhanced resilience of SMEs. South Africa has initiated a crisis management framework to address these issues and developed training programmes to include resilience. South Africa has also incorporated targeted surveys into their programmes and plans to better understand and cater for the domestic market.

The Green Tourism Incentive Programme, focused on assisting small and micro tourism enterprises to adopt sustainable tourism practices, was reviewed in view of the pandemic to cover the full energy and water audit costs and the grant funding range increased. The resource efficiency grant funds approved water and energy efficiency interventions up to a capped amount of ZAR 1 million (see Box 3.3).

A new global advocacy campaign has been launched to stimulate renewed demand from key source markets and domestically. Moving towards a greener economy aligns with South Africa's long-standing commitment to responsible tourism, as outlined in the 1996 White Paper on the Development and Promotion of Tourism and other country-level commitments such as reducing emissions (see Box below). A review of tourism policy to provide enhanced support for sector growth and development has begun. The exercise will update the White Paper and result in a revised Policy for tourism, taking into account environmental changes.

Review of the White Paper on the Development and Promotion of Tourism in South Africa

Despite successes registered since the country moved to pursue tourism growth in a comprehensive manner in the mid-1990s, South Africa's tourism economy is yet to fully exploit its potential. The need to stimulate tourism growth in line with its unrealised capacity has been recognised in various country-level economic revitalisation assessments and strategies.

With the vast impacts of COVID-19 on the sector as an impetus, the review of the overall policy for tourism was identified in the Tourism Sector Recovery Plan as one of the actions to develop a responsive, updated policy framework to guide the sector to sustainably recover and grow in line with its potential. The process to review the White Paper on the Development and Promotion of Tourism in South Africa (1996) was initiated, guided by a panel of experts in consultation with sector stakeholders and supported by research on trends and a consideration of the current and future context.

Key themes addressed in the review respond to the demand and supply side and include adaptability (incorporating approaches to digitalisation and the platform economy), tourism human resource development and employment creation, destination marketing, and sector transformation. Cross-cutting policy issues, such as transport, immigration and safety, and tourism governance and co-operation, are also included. Amongst the policy objectives is a desire to increase tourism's contribution to the broader economy through geographically spread visitor volumes and revenue. Policy proposals to cement South Africa's commitments to sustainable, responsible tourism are also core to the updated framework.

Statistical Profile

South Africa: Domestic, inbound and outbound tourism

	2017	2018	2019	2020	2021
TOURISM FLOWS, THOUSAND					
Domestic tourism					
Total domestic trips	152 200	133 650	264 980	125 077	83 597
Overnight visitors (tourists)	17 200	17 650	28 456	17 038	14 837
Same-day visitors (excursionists)	135 000	116 000	236 524	108 039	68 760
Nights in all types of accommodation	70 100	69 300	94 144	56 808	51 185
Hotels and similar establishments	..	..	..	..	..
Other collective establishments	..	..	..	..	..
Private accommodation	..	..	..	..	..
Inbound tourism					
Total international arrivals	14 976	15 004	14 797	3 886	2 664
Overnight visitors (tourists)	10 285	10 472	10 228	2 802	2 256
Same-day visitors (excursionists)	4 691	4 532	4 569	1 084	408
Top markets					
Mozambique	1 339	1 361	1 333	423	523
Zimbabwe	2 040	2 209	2 259	685	411
Lesotho	1 747	1 739	1 563	449	355
Eswatini	877	884	918	215	178
Botswana	681	689	668	129	103
Nights in all types of accommodation	..	..	..	..	..
Hotels and similar establishments	..	..	..	..	..
Other collective establishments	..	..	..	..	..
Private accommodation	..	..	..	..	..
Outbound tourism					
Total international departures	5 786	6 015	6 076	1 624	1 624
Overnight visitors (tourists)	..	..	..	..	..
Same-day visitors (excursionists)	..	..	..	..	..
Top destinations					
..	..	..	..	..	..
..	..	..	..	..	..
..	..	..	..	..	..
..	..	..	..	..	..
..	..	..	..	..	..
TOURISM RECEIPTS AND EXPENDITURE, MILLION USD					
Inbound tourism					
Total international receipts	9 706	9 790	9 064	2 717	2 113
International travel receipts	8 817	8 989	8 390	2 607	2 108
International passenger transport receipts	889	800	674	109	5
Outbound tourism					
Total international expenditure	6 068	6 348	5 866	1 594	1 669
International travel expenditure	3 258	3 402	3 141	928	991
International passenger transport expenditure	2 810	2 946	2 725	666	678

.. Not available
Source: OECD Tourism Statistics (Database).

StatLink https://stat.link/mdc9zq

South Africa: Enterprises and employment in tourism

	Number of establishments	Number of persons employed[1]				
	2021	2017	2018	2019	2020	2021
Total	..	..	..	..	..	..
Tourism industries	**49 488**	**575 909**	**611 737**	**773 532**	..	..
Accommodation services for visitors	10 876	127 228	125 819	118 346	..	..
Hotels and similar establishments	3 189	..	..	..	..	..
Food and beverage serving industry	19 732	94 397	96 725	147 833	..	..
Passenger transport	6 922	186 990	201 694	276 393	..	..
Air passenger transport	1 215	28 541	29 050	28 541	..	..
Railways passenger transport	37	5 137	4 779	6 318	..	..
Road passenger transport	5 383	148 769	165 144	241 155	..	..
Water passenger transport	287	4 543	2 721	379	..	..
Passenger transport supporting services	..	..	..	..	..	..
Transport equipment rental	416	8 845	11 402	9 966	..	..
Travel agencies and other reservation services industry	2 164	30 960	31 318	32 536	..	..
Cultural industry	4 944	17 089	18 487	19 564	..	..
Sports and recreation industry	4 434	8 323	9 430	17 269	..	..
Retail trade of country-specific tourism characteristic goods	..	102 077	116 862	151 625	..	..
Other country-specific tourism industries	..	..	..	..	..	..
Other industries	..	..	..	..	..	..

.. Not available
1. Data refer to number of jobs.
Source: OECD Tourism Statistics (Database).

StatLink https://stat.link/d1xsef

South Africa: Internal tourism consumption

Million ZAR

	2019		
	Domestic tourism expenditure	Inbound tourism expenditure	Internal tourism consumption
Total	..	..	..
Consumption products	**329 962**	**121 512**	**451 474**
Tourism characteristic products	217 938	81 678	299 616
Accommodation services for visitors	26 456	21 011	47 467
Food and beverage serving services	44 508	13 778	58 286
Passenger transport services	108 271	25 372	133 643
Air passenger transport services	45 586	9 220	54 806
Railways passenger transport services	475	216	691
Road passenger transport services	47 084	15 269	62 352
Water passenger transport services	1 977	422	2 400
Passenger transport supporting services	..	..	..
Transport equipment rental services	13 148	246	13 394
Travel agencies and other reservation services industry	15 624	6 567	22 191
Cultural services	5 558	4 266	9 824
Sports and recreation services	17 521	10 683	28 204
Country-specific tourism characteristic goods	..	..	..
Country-specific tourism characteristic services	..	..	..
Other consumption products	112 024	39 835	151 758
Tourism connected products	22 732	19 620	42 352
Non-tourism related consumption products	89 292	20 215	109 406
Non-consumption products	..	..	..

.. Not available
Source: OECD Tourism Statistics (Database).

StatLink https://stat.link/c193ru

www.ingramcontent.com/pod-product-compliance
Ingram Content Group UK Ltd.
Pitfield, Milton Keynes, MK11 3LW, UK
UKHW051456290926
15471UKWH00008B/1244

9 789264 377509